BHAVAN'S BOOK UNIVERSITY

Ten Upanishads of Four Vedas

Researched and Edited by

Ram K. Piparaiya

2003

INDUSvista

All Rights reserved

© 2003 by Ram K. Piparaiya

First Edition: 2003

ISBN: 81-7276-298-4

Price Rs.850/-

Printed in India

By Sanjay Jain at Yatisha Creations,

B-55 Akurti Industrial Estate, Akurli Road, Kandivali (E), Mumbai - 400 101.

Published jointly by

S. Ramakrishnan, Executive Secretary and Director General,

Bharatiya Vidya Bhavan, Kulapati K. M. Munshi Marg, Mumbai - 400 007

&

Indusvista Publications (A division of Aridhi Hi-Tech Industries Limited),

C-106, Mittal Court, Nariman Point, Mumbai - 400 021.

In memory of my father

A firm believer in the Vedic pronouncement that all religions lead to One Truth, he studied the Upanishads post-retirement for two decades, and concluded that gradually, even sciences will converge on that Truth.

CONTENTS

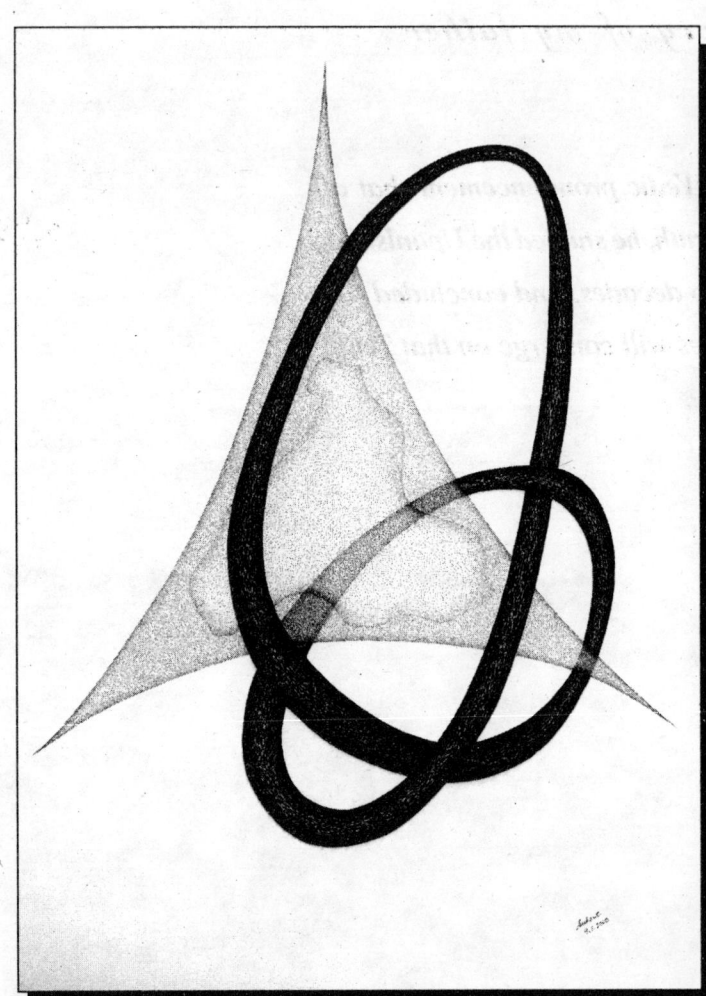

Acknowledgements
Foreword... Dr. Karan Singh
Benediction... Swami Bhoomananda Tirtha
Publisher's Preface... S. Ramakrishnan
Editor's Preface... Ram K. Piparaiya

PART I
THE UPANISHADS:
INTRODUCTION AND HIGHLIGHTS

1. Why study the Upanishads? 3
2. What are the Upanishads? 5
3. Tributes to the Upanishads 12
4. Road Map of the Upanishads ... 17
5. Invocations for Peace 25
6. Imaginative Metaphors and Analogies 29
7. Ten Insightful Parables and Allegories 45
8. Overview of Ten Profound Dialogues 56
9. Maxims on 'God and I' 65

Glossary 587
Index 599
Important Verses 605
Bibliography 609

CONTENTS

PART II
TEN COMPLETE PRINCIPAL UPANISHADS
SYNOPSES, TRANSLATION AND COMMENTARIES

Upanishad of Rg Veda

1. Aitareya Upanishad
   Origin of Man from Consciousness . 75

Upanishads of Yajur Veda

2. Brhadaranyaka Upanishad
   God and I are One 97

3. Isa Upanishad
   Harmony of Opposites 239

4. Katha Upanishad
   Dialogue with Death 259

5. Taittiriya Upanishad
   Five layers of human personality .. 295

Upanishads of Sama Veda

6. Chandogya Upanishad
   That thou art 333

7. Kena Upanishad
   Evolution of Matter-Life-Mind ... 471

Upanishads of Atharva Veda

8. Mandukya Upanishad
   Three states of Consciousness 495

9. Mundaka Upanishad
   One Absolute behind every Relativity .
   519

10. Prasna Upanishad
    The Cosmic Person within us 557

ACKNOWLEDGMENTS

First and foremost, I thank *THAT* which inspired this project and ensured its completion by showering Its bountiful Grace through many individuals and institutions.

I feel a sense of gratitude to:

- Dr. Karan Singh for suggesting the project, providing valuable ideas and writing the Foreword. I have also quoted him from his commentary on Mundaka Upanishad.
- Sri S. Ramakrishnan for his publishing support and for writing the Publisher's Preface.
- Swami Bhoomananda Tirtha for his Benedictions.

I am indebted to undermentioned publishers and authors for their kind permission to reproduce excerpts and ideas from their translations and commentaries on the Upanishads.

- Sri Aurobindo Ashram Trust, Pondichery – 605 002, for quoting Sri Aurobindo.
- The Divine Life Society, Shivanandanagar – 249 192, for quoting Swami Sivananda and Swami Krishnananda.
- Central Chinmaya Mission Trust, Books Division, Mumbai – 400 072, for quoting Swami Chinmayananda.
- Sri Ramakrishna Math, Chennai - 600 004, for quoting Swami Sarvananda, Swami Swahananda and Swami Paramananda.
- Dr. Klaus G. Witz, for selections from his book, *The Supreme Wisdom of the Upanishads*.

I am also indebted to certain commentators or their publishers/successors whom I have been unable to contact for a formal permission. These include Advaita Ashram, Kolkata, Paul Deussen, Dr. S. Radhakrishnan, Rohit Mehta and N. A. Nikam.

It is emphasized that I have abridged, simplified and assigned appropriate titles/subtitles to selections presented in this publication. Extreme care has been exercised to retain the original import; and any shortcomings are unintended.

I am obliged to Mr. Sukant Saran for permission to reproduce some of his captivating Pen Art Works. More details about these appear on the last page.

For the cover page, I thank Millennium World Peace Summit / World Council of Religious Leaders and Mr. Bawa Jain for permission to utilize a part of their logo, which contains symbols of world's major religions. I also thank Mr. Vikas Vinayak Patnekar for his suggestions.

I am grateful to two young ladies, Ms. Clementine Rodrigues and Mrs. Gayatri Panjabi, for transforming a huge handwritten manuscript into 600-plus creatively designed pages, ready for printing. Considering the subject matter of the text processed by them, their hard work, efficiency and commitment are all the more commendable.

A project like this requires peaceful and supportive environment at home, and for this my wife Aparna deserves a very special acknowledgement.

FOREWORD

Dr. Karan Singh
MEMBER OF PARLIAMENT
(RAJYA SABHA)

3, NYAYA MARG
CHANAKYAPURI
NEW DELHI - 110 021

The Upanishads represent a high watermark not only of India but of world philosophy. Unparalleled in their power, and aglow with spiritual vibrations, these immortal dialogues between self-realized Rishis and earnest seekers for the truth deal with the great problems of human existence. From where does this universe arises; what is the goal and purpose of human life; what is the nature of the immortal spark within each of us, and its relationship with the all pervasive divine; what are the modalities through which a union – *yoga* – between these two can be achieved in this very lifetime; these are some of the great conundrums with which philosophers and seekers around the world have grappled from the dawn of civilization.

Hinduism is unique in that it is the only religion not based upon the teachings of a single prophet or revealed book, but upon the collective wisdom and insight of a whole galaxy of Rishis, seers and savants. Ranging in size from 12 verses to many hundreds, there are eleven principal Upanishads. These have been translated extensively over the last two centuries, and many luminous commentaries upon them have been written from the great Adi Shankaracharya all the way down to Sri Aurobindo, Sri Krishna Prem and Shri Eknath Eshwaran in the 20th century. Shri Ram Piparaiya has evidently made a deep study in this area, and has brought together in one volume a useful compendium of original Upanishadic texts and commentaries. I hope this volume will be welcomed by serious students of the Upanishads and of Hindu philosophy in general not only in India but around the world.

Karan Singh

BENEDICTION

Vedic Upanishads are India's most ancient treasure of Knowledge. They reveal the **fundamental values** as well as the **ultimate goal** of human life. By this, have they derived the power to remain eternal and ever-relevant. Though forming part of the Vedic religious dissertations, the Upanishads discuss and reveal only pure wisdom, to be accessed by mind and intelligence. They deal alike with intricacies of human personality and world constitution.

The Upanishads excell in the art of making relentless and dedicated observations, enquiries and findings. Hence, interrogation, examination and conclusion constitute the content and message of the Upanishadic themes.

By all means, such dedicated enquiries can be directed only to (a) the visible world around, together with its conceptual source, and (b) one's Self – the cause as well as terminus of all perceptions, experiences and knowledge. With these, the Vedic Upanishads stand complete both in their enquiry and findings. That is why these ancient texts have remained valid even today, as they were ages ago.

Any object becomes so only in front of a Subject. In our interactions with the complex and infinite world, the interacting individual alone is the sole Subject – constant and changeless. All objects of the world are but changeful in nature. The changeless, ever-surviving character of the Subject, namely the 'I' in every one, the Upanishads declare, is the Supreme Source and Reality. To drive home this supreme truth and message, a variety of discussions, dialogues, analyses and findings are set forth by the Upanishadic authors.

The Upanishads give Knowledge the supreme place in human life – a level and dimension the Western world is yet to understand and assess in full. In the final scrutiny of any 'object perception', the 'perceived' is led to extinction, and the 'perceiving consciousness' alone survives. The object in front, by any standard of judgment, depends upon 'the Subject', but 'the Subject' does not, at any time, depend upon 'the object'. This is evidenced from the Deep Sleep state, in which body, mind, intelligence and ego become extinct; but the Sleeper – his Consciousness – endures and survives unaffectedly.

This inner Deep Sleep state, called *sushupti,* constitutes a full subject of study for the Upanishadic thinker and student. It unravels the entire mystery of existence and creation. Mandukya Upanishad undertakes a thorough discussion of *Turiya,* the Fourth, the supreme sovereign Consciousness. "This indeed is the *Atman,* the Self, peaceful, quiescent, one without a second, to be ascertained, known and realized", are the words in the seventh *mantra* of the text. It is the Self, constantly denoted by the term 'I' by all, about which none can doubt or feel strange.

This 'I' is the first and last factor in all our experiences, perceptions, knowledge and memory. Even when one forgets everything, the forgetting 'I' in him survives. "Only when this shines, do all the others shine", are the matchless, inspiring words of the Upanishads. The 'I' denotes the one centre on which subsist all the smaller and bigger circles in the entire universe. Everything in the endless universe constitutes a speck, line, curve or segmental part of the huge circle, which is but the expanse of this one supreme Centre, the 'I', the Self in one.

To a man of religion, the Vedic Upanishads clearly indicate where does his God abide. To a skeptic mind, the Upanishadic exhortation is to realize that mind's own depth and essence constitute the Supreme Reality. Yes, pure and unconditioned mind is itself the key to rip open the whole mystery of existence. To the philosophically inclined, the Upanishads have the most rational and scientific statements to inspire, guide and determine where indeed reign the source of Knowledge, and the Supreme Reality. To the spiritually inclined, needless to say, the Upanishads explain the magnificence, infinitude and comprehensive nature of the Self.

The whole quest and finding are thus, according to Vedic Upanishads, **within man**, accessible to his mind and intelligence, at zero distance. The inescapability and compulsion of the Upanishadic declarations and exhortations are instantaneous and final. And what is the result? The mortal human ascends to immortality. The agitated mind becomes unshakeable and poised. The aggrieved transcends grief and actualizes unstinted bliss. What more can one ever aspire any time?

Mr. Ram Piparaiya, entering into the spirituo-religious field of study from his managerial background, is evidently gripped by the structure, spirit and purpose of Vedic Upanishads. Allured and inspired by their content and message, he has been impelled to beckon many others to this arena of Spiritual Knowledge. Even a small measure of this, when gained, will insulate one from all kinds of fear, doubt, oscillation and discontent. The Upanishads bestow inestimable confidence, clarity and contentment, besides the assurance of immortality.

I compliment his effort at propagation of this eternal classic. It is a persuasion to himself as well as the readers, to go into the subject with spirit of tenacity and dedication.

May this great Knowledge – and the culture and gifts it bestows – be available to more and more people in the world. My hearty good wishes to all. May Mr. Piparaiya's effort be helpful to many, who admit the role of Knowledge in bringing forth excellence. Pronouncing benedictions, I wish him all effectiveness and felicity.

Narayanashrama Tapovanam
Thrissur, Kerala - 680 575

Swami Bhoomananda Tirtha

PUBLISHER'S PREFACE

"Sanskrit is like the river Ganga for our languages. I always feel that if it were to dry up, the regional languages would lose their vitality and power. It seems to me that an elementary knowledge of Sanskrit is essential".

- Mahatma Gandhi

Sanskrit is the classical language of India. It is the language of the culture of our country. Sanskrit is rightly revered as the Mother of all languages. Like Sanskrit, the oldest scriptures of India are the Vedas. The Rig Veda, the first of the Vedas, is probably the earliest book that humanity possesses. In it we can find the outpourings of the human mind, the glow of poetry, the rapture at nature's loveliness and mystery.

The term Vedas not only names a large body of texts composed in times indefinitely remote and handed down by generation after generation to our own generation, it stands for nothing less than Divine Truth itself, the inexpressible truth of which the Vedic texts are of necessity but a pale reflection. Regarded in this aspect, the Vedas are infinite and eternal. They are that perfect knowledge which is God.

When we look at the great landscape of Indian culture, we find that, like the mighty Himalayas themselves from whence our culture originated, stands the mighty structure of the Vedas. If you look upon the Vedas as the Himalayas of our cultural traditions, the Upanishads can well be described as those great peaks which are so prominent when you view the Himalayas from the air. The peaks are only a part of the entire mountain range, and yet it is they with eternal snow upon them that draw our minds and our admiration.

The Vedas constitute the scripture and reveal the Godhead that is common to us. They also teach us how to lead our life and they do us the ultimate good by showing us in the end the way to become that very Godhead ourselves. The Vedas are the source not only of the various divisions of Hinduism but all the religions of the world may be traced back to them. It is our bounden duty to preserve them for all time to come with their glory undiminished.

The Upanishads are the Vedanta, meaning the end of the Vedas, because they came at the end of the Vedic hymns. The Upanishads are also the noblest upshot, the highest watermark of the Vedic civilization and genius. The word *Upanishad* means sit nearby. In the Indian tradition, the Guru would be seated under a tree, near a river or a lake and the disciples would cluster around him to learn the wisdom.

The Upanishads deal with the supra-rational knowledge. It does not negate rationality; it transcends rationality, because while the mind is a brilliant and multifaceted instrument, it is nonetheless limited by its very structure. There are ranges of knowledge and experience, which do not come within the ambit of so-called rational thinking. At some point in our consciousness the mind has to be transcended and the Upanishads deal with the higher knowledge, the supra-rational realization which comes not by intellectual gymnastics but by spiritual realization. This is the basis of the Upanishadic teachings, that the ultimate goal of all knowledge is spiritual realization.

Whatever power there is in the world, whatever intellectual brilliance, whatever skills and talents, all must be present in God in a rudimentary form. The Vedas and Upanishads proclaim: "All this has not sprung without a root cause. The power that is in the root or the seed is the same as the power that pervades the entire universe. Where is that seed or root? The self that keeps seeing all from within, what we call '*idam*', is the root.

Out of the past is born the present and out of the present is born the future. Change is the unchanging law of life. There can be no doubt that our youth should acquire the best of modern knowledge and specialize in different subjects so that they fare well in life and at the same time society gets the best out of them. To be able to achieve this twin objective they cannot afford to forget the past, the cultural values that had flowed from the past.

In this volume of more than 600 pages Shri Ram K. Piparaiya makes a sincere effort to trace the contemporary relevance of the Vedas and Upanishads. It is a monumental effort reflecting enormous, dedicated and unremitting labor over a long period of time. The Bhavan is beholden to Shri Piparaiya.

Bhavan's Book University,
Bharatiya Vidya Bhavan,
Mumbai - 400 007.

S. Ramakrishnan
General Editor

EDITOR'S PREFACE

We, the people of India, are privileged inheritors of Wisdom whose importance has not yet been fully realized by the world, or even by us. Some glimpses are:

- ➢ 'Truth is One' and 'That thou art'.
- ➢ 'The Lord pervades everything' and therefore, 'The whole world is one family'.
- ➢ 'Do not covet the wealth of others' because eventually, 'Truth alone triumphs'.

Vedas, Upanishads and Bhagavad Gita are the prime sources of India's spiritual heritage. The Upanishads are a link between the Vedas and the Bhagavad Gita. As the concluding parts of the Vedas, the Upanishads are synonymous with the philosophy called Vedanta. The Bhagavad Gita contains the essence of the Upanishads, like flowers in a bouquet. If the Vedas are like a tradition-bound grandmother, the Upanishads symbolize a wise mother and the Bhagavad Gita is comparable to a pragmatic daughter of modern times.

Study of the Upanishads has been generally confined to philosophers and preachers. This publication is one of the exceptions. It is an inspired work by a businessman. I hope it leads to greater awareness of the Wisdom contained in the Upanishads.

The Upanishads and I?

In order to bring out the wide appeal, context, editor's perspective and contemporary relevance of the Upanishads, I wish to share with you my own profile.

I was born in a middle class family. My father was a school teacher and my primary education was at home. After secondary schooling at elitist Mayo College in Ajmer, I graduated in science from University of Allahabad; and in engineering from Indian Institute of Science, Bangalore. Good academic record enabled me to pursue post-graduate studies at School of Engineering, Columbia University and Stern School of Business, New York University. Next two decades were spent *enjoying* the climb up the corporate ladder in MNCs, first in USA and then in India. Thereafter, my wife and I decided to *experiment* being entrepreneurs. We were also able to educate our two sons at Universities in USA, like Rochester, Cornell and California (Berkeley). With their education nearing completion, it was time to PAUSE… and INTROSPECT… WHAT NEXT?

'*Explore* India's spiritual heritage', said the Inner Voice. This was in 1997. I started with the Bhagavad Gita. Simultaneously, I started reading scriptures of other Faiths.

In August 2000, at the United Nations Millennium Peace Summit in New York, I had the opportunity to listen to speeches by dozens of world's topmost religious and spiritual leaders. Despite their diversity, two common themes stood out in all the speeches. First, they all referred to One Creator. Second, they all emphasized that there cannot be peace in the world unless there is peace in our mind. Around the same time, I interacted with a very respected philosopher-politician, Dr. Karan Singh. He explained that all scriptures teach the same Truth in different words. For deeper insights, he recommended the Upanishads. Thanks to Dr. Karan Singh, the call of the Upanishads became irresistible. Also, by God's Grace, I was able to have two years' sabbatical for researching the Upanishads.

What did I learn from the Upanishads?

I started my study in alphabetical order, with Aitareya Upanishad. Its main theme is that 'Consciousness is *Brahman*' and that everything – Matter, Life and Mind – has originated from Consciousness. Around the same time, I also happened to read *Sri Aurobindo or the Adventures of Consciousness* by Satprem (Translated from French by Michel Danino). Besides, a few years earlier, I had attended a lecture on Consciousness by an internationally famous mathematician, Roger Penrose. Now I pulled out his book, titled, *Shadows of the Mind* and sub-titled, *The Missing Science of Consciousness*. Then I again studied Aitareya Upanishad a second time, and a third time. My reaction was that if Roger Penrose had read Aitareya Upanishad, perhaps he would have titled his book, 'Light behind the Mind' and sub-titled it, 'The Missing Consciousness in Science.'

Next, I skipped alphabets and selected Mandukya Upanishad for my study because of its brevity – just 12 verses. Its main theme is that the primordial sound *Aum* is an excellent symbol of both Absolute Consciousness and Its relative manifestations; or what the Upanishads call *Brahman*. Simultaneously, I happened to read *The Elegant Universe* by Brian Greene. It explains that physicists now regard vibrating strings as the ultimate building block of Matter, and that the String Theory may turn out to be the link between Quantum Mechanics and Relativistic Physics. Around the same time, the Strings-2001 Conference held in Mumbai and attended by luminaries like Stephen Hawings was making news. I started wondering if there could be any connection between a primordial sound like *Aum* and a vibrating string?

Though I did not know the answer, I felt encouraged to continue my study of the Upanishads. Isa Upanishad was next on my list – again because of its brevity, just 18 verses. I think its revelations about harmony of opposites – material possessions and inner renunciation, dynamic activity and meditational peace, empirical learning and spiritual wisdom – are very relevant for modern times.

I found Taittiriya Upanishad relevant because it deals with knowledge about Self – a subject which is being given increasing importance even in management education. Simultaneously, I re-read my earlier favorite, *Emotional Intelligence* by Daniel Goleman. While Goleman advocates a formal course in 'Self Science', in Taittiriya Upanishad, Bhrigu discovers Self by his own efforts, with just two short hints from his father.

By now I was deeply immersed in the Upanishads and genuinely enjoying their study. I found that commentaries on the Upanishads are indispensable for their understanding. The commentators covered by me represent a wide spectrum of profiles – spiritual masters with the prefix 'Swami' before their names, philosopher-thinkers, worldly persons with spiritual inclinations and scholars with Western background. There are many overlaps in their commentaries, but there are also significant differences. I have tried to avoid duplication in my selections. Taken together, the commentaries add up to a beautiful mosaic. Metaphorically, if the Upanishads are compared to gold, the commentaries shape them into fascinating ornaments.

Continuing my study of the Upanishads, I found many similarities between Katha Upanishad and the Bhagavad Gita; both have the Immortal Self or *Atman* as their major theme. Kena Upanishad, like Aitareya, deals with evolution of Matter-Life-Mind from Consciousness. Prasna Upanishad is almost like a summary of all the ten Upanishads, presented in an interesting Questions-Answers format. Mundaka Upanishad emphasizes the oneness and the inseparability of the Creator and His creation, the Absolute behind every Relativity. It makes one wonder if inclusion of 'One Absolute' in Einstein's Theory of Relativity could lead to a Unified Field Theory.

Brhadaranyaka and Chandogya Upanishads were the last on my study list, mainly because of their length. In retrospect, however, except for some sections, they are very interesting to read, as their presentation is mostly in the form of dialogues. I found these so captivating that I have rewritten some of these as easy-to-read renditions.

What to look for in this publication?

This publication is in two parts. Part I begins with an answer to the basic question that every busy person will like to ask: 'Why study the Upanishads?' Next, it introduces the reader to some important metaphors, parables, dialogues and maxims from the Upanishads. Part-II contains synopses, translated texts and commentaries. The publication also contains a glossary of Sanskrit words that appear frequently in the text, and an index of major themes and important verses.

Ten Upanishads. Nineteen commentators. Complete and comprehensive coverage. Contents suitable for both beginners and advanced readers. Understandably, the treatise runs into more than 600 pages. These, however, can be read selectively. So do not let the size discourage you. Even a random perusal of its pages could slowly lead to an inner awakening.

The Bhagavad Gita inspires us with the philosophy of selfless Work in the outer world; the Upanishads empower us with Wisdom about our inner life. Happiness requires harmony between Work and Wisdom. We experience fulfillment when there is both purpose and peace in life.

The Sanskrit word for peace is *Shanti*. It also happens to be my mother's name and her life's guiding principle. Every Upanishad begins with an invocation for Peace and ends with the word *Shanti* recited three times. I also conclude with the closing words of every Upanishad.

Om Shanti, Shanti, Shanti
Let there be Peace. Let there be Peace. Let there be Peace.

Mumbai - 400 021
January 8, 2003

Ram K. Piparaiya

Part I

The Upanishads

Introduction and Highlights

1. **Why study the Upanishads?** 3

2. **What are the Upanishads?** 5
   VEDAS AND UPANISHADS, HOW ANCIENT ARE THE UPANISHADS, ETERNAL TRUTHS AND SITUATIONAL WISDOM, HOW MANY UPANISHADS, WHAT MAKES THE UPANISHADS DIFFERENT, AND OBSCURE TEXTS, WAITING TO BE DISCOVERED.

3. **Tributes to the Upanishads** 12
   HIMALAYAS OF THE SOUL, UNIVERSAL VALUE, MEANS FOR PERFECTION, THE HIGHEST WISDOM, A RECOMMENDATION, STRONGEST SUPPORT, SPIRIT OF INQUIRY, GREAT SOURCE OF STRENGTH AND FREEDOM, CONSTRUCTIVE DOUBT, SOURCE OF INDIA'S HERITAGE, THOUGHTS... LIKE PACES OF A TITAN, AGE OF ENLIGHTENMENT, GLOBAL INFLUENCE, HIMALAYAN PEAKS, NEED TO DIVE DEEP, AND ROOTS OF BUDDHISM.

4. **Road Map of the Upanishads** 17
   METHOD OF STUDY, UPANISHADS, METHODS OF PRESENTATION, UPANISHADS COVERED, COMPLETE TRANSLATED TEXT, AND SYNOPSES; COMMENTARIES AND RENDITIONS.

5 Invocations for Peace 25

PRAYER FOR TRUTH, PRAYER ABOUT CREATION, PRAYER FOR AWARENESS OF SUPREME, PRAYER FOR MUTUAL UNDERSTANDING, PRAYER FOR HEALTH AND HAPPINESS, AND PRAYER FOR DIVINE PROTECTION.

6 Imaginative Metaphors and Analogies 29

SUN AND MOON, CITY OF GOD, CHARIOT AND JOURNEY OF LIFE, RIVERS, OCEAN AND CONSCIOUSNESS, WATER, SALT AND SELF, FIRE, SPARKS, SPIDER AND UNIVERSE, TREE, PLANTS AND TRASMIGRATION, WHEEL, HUB AND LIFE PRINCIPLE, BOW AND ARROW, MEDITATION, SPIDER, HERBS, HAIR AND UNIVERSE, MUSICAL INSTRUMENTS AND SELF, BIRDS AND MIND, AND MISCELLANEOUS METAPHORS.

7 Ten Insightful Parables and Allegories 45

ALLEGORY OF CREATION, EVERY PERSON IS INHERENTLY GOOD, QUALITIES OF A GOOD LEADER, FIVE COSMIC FIRES, PATHS OF LIBERATION AND REBIRTH, LEARNING AND REFLECTION, POWER BEHIND MATTER, LIFE AND MIND, FRIENDSHIP WITH GOD, DIALOGUE WITH DEATH, AND SELF-STUDY OF SELF.

8 Overview of Ten Profound Dialogues 56

GARGYA, MAITREYI, YAGYAVALKYA, JANAKA, RAIKVA, SATYAKAMA, UPAKOSALA, SHVETAKETU, SANATKUMAR, AND MEDITATION ON INNER SELF.

9 Maxims on 'God and I' 65

WHAT IS GOD, ONE GOD, MANY NAMES AND FORMS, WHO AM I, YOU AND I ARE GOD, GOD IS HIDDEN FIVE LAYERS DEEP, AND COSMIC PERSON AND INNER SELF.

1 Why study the Upanishads?

Two biggest problems of modern times: Tension at personal level and Terrorism at universal level.

Root Causes: Neglect of inner life at personal level and intolerance of contradictory viewpoints at universal level.

Possible solutions:

> - AT PERSONAL LEVEL: Know that God, who is in Heaven, is also in your heart. More you know Him, happier you feel.
> - AT UNIVERSAL LEVEL: Know that your God and my God are One and the same. It is just that we call Him by different names and perceive Him in different forms. Also, know that it is God-created diversity which makes the universe beautiful. More you know Him, more love and understanding you will radiate, even when faced with absolutely unacceptable situations.

To know Him and to know your inner Self more correctly, you need to reflect more deeply on scriptures of your own Faith, as also become more familiar with scriptures of other Faiths. Interfaith appreciation of universal Truths and multi-faith world-view are the two greatest needs of modern times

Problems of modern times are deep rooted in history – family history at personal level and history of nations at universal level. Therefore, it makes sense to turn to ancient wisdom for deeper insights, leading to innovative solutions.

The Upanishads are India's most ancient high-wisdom texts. Their objective is not to preach, but to create an awakening.

The Upanishads demystify God. They also remind us about our inherent divinity. They emphasize that peace in our inner life is as important as success in the outer world; and that happiness means harmony between the two.

Modern times are characterized by turbulence in society and advancements in technology. As a result, we are losing balance. Our lives are governed more by external developments than our inner aspirations. We need to re-evaluate what we want from life and how to get it in the midst of all the uncertainties. For this, we need to know basic truths about God, about us, about the world; and how the three are interconnected. This, precisely, is the main theme of the Upanishads.

The Upanishads qualify our attention for two more reasons:

> They are Religion-neutral.

   The Upanishads represent a search for universal truths – principles and values which are valid at all times, in all places and in all situations. Therefore, it is not surprising that there are remarkable similarities between the wisdom of the Upanishads and the teachings of Prophets or the thinking of philosophers from different epochs and parts of the world.

> They are ahead of their times, even today.

   Some of the thoughts contained in the Upanishads point to convergence of Philosophy and Psychology for study of human mind. They also suggest new perspectives in Physics for study of Consciousness.

The Upanishads raise our mind to a higher plane of Consciousness, which makes our lives not only more peaceful, but also more purposeful.

The Upanishads reveal that everything that exists in the Cosmos – Space-Time, Matter-Energy, Life-Mind – has originated from Consciousness and is sustained by Consciousness. What we call God is nothing but Consciousness, Pure and Absolute. When we become aware of God's presence in us, we also become aware of our immense strengths and potentialities. We experience self-mastery and self-enlargement. We rise above self-interest and strive for universal good.

Another important revelation made in the Upanishads is that life is eternal. Birth and death are only stages in the evolutionary journey of life. Hardships of life are only passing phases in our evolution towards perfection.

A study of the Upanishads will empower us with Wisdom to live a more healthy and more happy life; as also to make the world a more healthy and more happy place to live.

② What are the Upanishads?

The Upanishads are the earliest record of mankind's attempt to define God, discover Self and enquire into meaning of life. These philosophical texts of Wisdom constitute the concluding parts of the most ancient scriptures of India – the Vedas.

VEDAS AND UPANISHADS

Veda means wisdom. Vedas are a vast collection of spiritual hymns and rituals, as also the principles which underlie them. Like the scriptures of other religions, Vedas are believed to be direct revelations from the Divine. There are, however, two noteworthy differences. First, the Vedas preceded other holy scriptures by many centuries – even millenniums. Second, the enlightened sages to which the Vedas were revealed have remained anonymous.

The Vedas are four in number: Rg Veda, Sama Veda, Yajur Veda and Atharva Veda. They were taught in Vedic schools called *Shakhas* (literally, branches of a tree). These differed widely in their teaching of even common subjects; and therefore, they produced distinctly different works. More than 5,000 years ago, a sage named Krishna Dvaipayana compiled the works of as many as 1,131 *Shakhas*. However, most of his compilations were destroyed during repeated foreign invasions. At present, works of only about a dozen *Shakhas* are available.

For the purpose of study, each Veda is generally divided into two parts:

> Karma Kanda: This deals with prayers and rituals.
> Gyana Kanda: This deals with the rationale and the philosophy underlying prayers and rituals.

In a second system of classification, each Veda is said to contain four books:

> Samhita: These are a collection of hymns or mantras.
> Brahmana: These explain the use of mantras and the procedure for performance of various rituals.
> Aranyaka: These explain the implied symbolism or the inner significance of various mantras and rituals. They are also called Forest Books, as they were conceived and taught in the solitude of forests.

> UPANISHADS: These are either independent books or continuation of any of the previous books. They deal with philosophical questions, which could be understood only by those who wanted to go deep into the rationale for hymns and significance of rituals. Therefore, as a rule, they were always appended at the end of a Veda, and taught only to advanced students nearer the completion of their study.

The word *Upanishad* literally means *knowledge* received sitting close to the teacher, not just physically, but also mentally. (*Up* means *near*, *ni* means *down*, *shad* means *sit*). As a subject becomes more deep and subtle, it becomes difficult to explain it in words. Sitting close to the teacher helps in grasping the subject through his facial expressions and body language.

Another meaning given to the word *Upanishad* is that, which *shatters ignorance.*

Whatever the etymological meaning, in due course the Upanishads came to signify secret or esoteric knowledge. This knowledge was imparted only to those students who had undergone a long preparation and shown a strong aptitude for it. It involved spending many years in austerities and meditation under the feet of a *guru*. A very important reason for their secrecy was that they questioned the popular beliefs and practices, which the traditional society of those times followed very obediently.

HOW ANCIENT ARE THE UPANISHADS?

The Upanishads are of very ancient origin. It is difficult to be exact about their date. However, all historians agree that they belong to pre-Buddha, pre-Socrates era. Generally, the Upanishads are said to have been revealed during 1000 BC to 300 BC. According to Dr. S. Radhakrishnan, 'These are the earliest literature of what has been called the Axial Era of the world (800-300 BC), when – for the first time, simultaneously and independently – thinking men in India, China and Greece questioned the traditional pattern of life.'

ETERNAL TRUTHS AND SITUATIONAL WISDOM

Vedic literature is of two types: *Shruti* and *Smriti*. A text dealing with eternal and universal truths is called *Shruti*. A *Shruti* does not glorify any historical or mythological person. In contrast, a *Smriti* always glorifies some mythological or historical person.

Also, it deals with rules of conduct which may need to be revised according to the dictates of time and place. A *Smriti* is based on a *Shruti* and is like its corollary literature.

A *Shruti* is considered to be timeless because the principles enunciated in it will remain valid for all times – irrespective of the place or situation.

The Upanishads are *Shruti* texts, and therefore, they are considered timeless. In comparison, the Bhagavad Gita – the most widely revered scripture of India – is an example of a *Smriti* text.

HOW MANY UPANISHADS?

In ancient times, the title Upanishad was used generically to signify authenticity and wide acceptance of an advanced text on philosophy. It is therefore impractical to assign a precise number to extant Upanishads. One of the Upanishads, Muktika gives a list of 108 Upanishads. Depending upon their subject matter, these have been classified into five groups: Vedanta, Yoga, Sanyas, Vishnu and Shiva.

Etymologically, *Vedanta* means *the ultimate in knowledge*. Vedanta Upanishads discuss fundamental issues of creation and life: What caused the cosmos? Who am I? What is the purpose of life? What do birth and death signify? Yoga and Sanyas (asceticism) Upanishads deal with the philosophy of these two important spiritual disciplines. Vishnu and Shiva symbolize preservation and dissolution; these are the main themes of Upanishads in the last two groups.

Vedanta Upanishads were conceived over a span of a few centuries before Jesus Christ. Sri Sankara, one of the greatest spiritual masters of India, selected ten (eleven, according to some) Vedanta Upanishads and wrote masterly commentaries on them. They came to be known as Principal, Classical or Major Upanishad. Of these, one belongs to Rg Veda, four to Yajur Veda, two to Sama Veda and three to Atharva Veda. Ten of the Principal Upanishads along with corresponding year of their origin are presented in Table-1 on the next page.

Table-1

	TEN PRINCIPAL UPANISHADS		
Sr. No.	Name of Upanishad	Name of corresponding Veda	Year of Origin
1.	Aitareya	Rg Veda	800 BC
2.	Brhadaranyaka	Yajur Veda	800 BC
3.	Chandogya	Sama Veda	800 BC
4.	Isa	Yajur Veda	Uncertain
5.	Katha	Yajur Veda	Uncertain
6.	Kena	Sama Veda	Uncertain
7.	Mandukya	Atharva Veda	200 BC
8.	Mundaka	Atharva Veda	600 BC
9.	Prasna	Atharva Veda	200 BC
10.	Taittiriya	Yajur Veda	800 BC

WHAT MAKES THE UPANISHADS DIFFERENT?

The Upanishads are different from other scriptures in many respects.

➢ Upanishads are texts of spiritual wisdom, not religion.

Religion and Spirituality are two different things, though we often confuse one for the other. A religious person is not necessarily a spiritual person, and vice versa.

The religion of a person can be identified by the rituals practiced by him, and the beliefs expressed by him. In other words, religion relates to external behavior, generally in a group. Spirituality, however, is entirely internal and personal. A spiritual person does not feel bound by doctrines or injunctions of any one religion. He formulates his own philosophy of life.

A spiritual person has two very important characteristics. First, he respects all religions. Second, he is always aware that all religions lead to only one Truth, though the paths may be different.

The Upanishads are not religious texts. They do not advocate any dogma, creed or ritual. Their emphasis is clearly and unmistakably on a spiritual perspective of life. Most important, they encourage freedom in formulating a personal philosophy of life.

- Upanishads encourage enquiry and dialogue.

The main purpose of the Upanishads is to know the Ultimate Reality, the Eternal Truth of everything that exists. This is done by method of enquiry and dialogue.

In the Upanishads, the students ask very fundamental questions: What caused the creation of the cosmos? And of human beings? What drives the mind and the senses? Is there anything that exists after death? If so, what is it? What is God? Why can't It be perceived by the senses? Of what use is It? How to attain It? And so on. These questions are invariably followed by long discussions. The participants in the discussions represent diverse profiles: father and son, husband and wife, teacher and students, king and priest, senior sage and young warrior, one scholar against many others, and the like. There are even discussions between the chiefs of gods and demons and the Creator Himself, between a young boy and the Lord of Death, between another young student and representatives of Nature, and between still another young aspirant and Fire. On some occasions, a learned teacher begins to instruct a king on what is God, but ends up becoming his student!

The spirit of enquiry in the Upanishads is evident from even the names of two of the ten Upanishads: *Prasna* means 'Question' and *Kena* is translated, 'By What?'

The main finding of Upanishadic enquiry – that One Absolute Consciousness is the Ultimate Cause and the Substratum of both man and universe – is also in sharp contrast to faith in worship of Vedic deities, as prescribed in *Karma Kanda* of the Vedas.

- Upanishads generally avoid rituals and sermons.

Religion is a result of man's sense of wonder and awe in the face of mighty forces of Nature and unpredictable events of life. By and large, the whole mankind believes in God as a supernatural Power. Religion prescribes prayers and rituals to please that Power. It will be recalled that the first part of the Vedas, called *Karma Kanda,* is also devoted to performance of rituals. The

Upanishads pay very little attention to rituals. As the Upanishads are a continuation of the books of rituals (*Brahmanas* and *Aranyakas*), there are inevitably some passages which refer to certain rituals. However, the Upanishads emphasize the futility of rituals performed without knowledge of their significance or inner meaning. A few passages seem to reflect even mockery and contempt. Some renowned commentators have, however, emphasized that rituals have hidden meanings. They also have tremendous value as preparatory steps for purifying the mind, a prerequisite for gaining spiritual wisdom.

In ancient times, religion laid down Do's and Don'ts for our actions. These were enforced through expectations of reward and fear of punishment. However, there are very few sermonizing passages in the Upanishad; and even these touch upon the fundamental methods of harmony between a man's inner life and outer world. Also, they have universal value and validity.

> Upanishads have influenced great thinkers, but remained anonymous.

The Upanishads are not the thoughts of a single philosopher, or a school of philosophy committed to some specific belief. They are a collection of the thoughts of many thinkers interested in different aspects of life. Also, as the Upanishadic teachers followed a tradition of remaining anonymous, their teachings are free from all prejudices. In fact, the teachers proclaimed that the knowledge communicated by them was not what they discovered – it was revealed to them by intuition, without any effort. As a result the Upanishads have been a rich treasure-chest of some very original teachings, covering a wide spectrum of philosophy. These have influenced great thinkers and religious leaders of not just Hinduism, but also of other faiths – like Buddhism, Jainism and Sikhism. Upanishadic doctrines like *Karma* and Rebirth are common to all these religions. Thus, the Upanishads have shaped the philosophy of life of millions of people for nearly three millenniums. Their impact in India has been direct. Outside India, their impact has been through the media of Buddhism.

OBSCURE TEXTS, WAITING TO BE DISCOVERED

The Upanishads are high-wisdom texts, which are not easy to comprehend. Therefore, unlike other scriptures, they are not widely known. Even in India – the country of their origin – they were considered a threat to the tradition of ritualism, and therefore classified as 'secret teachings' for nearly 2000 years. They came out of their obscurity only in 9th century when Sri Sankara (788-820 AD) wrote scholarly commentaries on the Principal Upanishads and made them accessible to a wider audience.

Unlike the Bhagavad Gita, which has attracted hundreds of commentaries, there are less than two dozens good commentaries on the Upanishads. Commentaries on the two large Upanishads – Brhadaranyaka and Chandogya, which account for two-thirds of Upanishadic texts – are fewer still, and not easy to understand. As a result, despite their vast wealth of wisdom, the Upanishads are not known widely, even in India.

The West was first exposed to the Upanishads 2500 years after their conception and 700 years after Sri Sankara's commentary on them.

The original Upanishads as well as the commentary by Sri Sankara are in Sanskrit. The first translation of the Upanishads was from Sanskrit to Persian. This was done in 1657 under the supervision of a most unlikely person – Prince Dara Shikoh, son of Mughal Emperor Shah Jehan who built the famous Taj Mahal. Nearly 150 years later, in 1801, the Persian translation was used by a French scholar, A. H. Antequil Duperron, to produce a Latin translation of 60 Upanishads. This was called *Oupnek'hat*. Famous German philosophers like K.C.F. Krause (1781-1832) and A. Schopenhauer (1814-1870) were immensely inspired by *Oupnek'hat*. They drew heavily from it in formulating their own philosophical works.

The first English translation of the principal Upanishads appeared in 1879 as Volume 1 of F. Max Muller's *Sacred Books of the East*. Paul Deussen (1845-1919) was another famous thinker who contributed significantly to making Western philosophers aware of the Upanishads. His translation of 60 Upanishads and his book, *The Philosophy of the Upanishads* – first in German, but now also translated in English – are considered valuable references.

Western philosophy is concerned mainly with life in the world around us. The Upanishads deal exclusively with our inner life. As a result, the Upanishads have not yet caught the fancy of the West.

At present relativity obscure, the Upanishads are waiting to be discovered by the world.

3. Tributes to the Upanishads

The Upanishads represent the loftiest heights of Indian thought. As a treatise on spiritual wisdom, they are without a parallel in the world. They have earned rich tributes from scholars – both in India and abroad. Here are a few examples.

1. HIMALAYAS OF THE SOUL

    'The Upanishads are the Himalayas of the soul'.

    – Juvan Mascaro, Spanish Writer

2. UNIVERSAL VALUE

    'In the long history of man's endeavour to grasp the fundamental Truth of being, the metaphysical treatise known as the Upanishads hold an honored place. They reflect sublime conceptions and intuitions of universal value'.

    And again,

    'The earnestness for the search of Truth is one of the delightful and commendable features of the Upanishads'.

    – R. E. Hume, Author, 'The Thirteen Principal Upanishads'

3. MEANS FOR PERFECTION

    'If I were asked under what sky the human mind has most deeply pondered over the greatest problems of life, …… I should point to India.

    And, if I were to ask myself from what literature we here in Europe…. may draw the corrective which is most wanted to make our inner life more perfect, more comprehensive, more universal… again, I should point to the Upanishads'.

    And again,

SO SIMPLE, SO TRUE

'(The Upanishads are) like the light of the morning, like the pure air of the mountains – so simple, so true, if once understood'.

– Max Muller, German Philosopher

4. THE HIGHEST WISDOM

'In the whole world, there is no study.... so beneficial and so elevating as that of the Upanishads...... they are products of the highest wisdom...... they are destined sooner or later to become the faith of the people of the world'.

And again,

SOLACE OF MY LIFE..... AND DEATH

'The study of the Upanishads has been the solace of my life, it will be the solace of my death'.

– A. Schopenhauer, German Philosopher

5. A RECOMMENDATION

'It is to the Upanishads that the western student must turn for illumination, who wishes to form a true idea of the general trend of Indian thought, but has neither time nor inclination to make a close study of its various systems'.

– Edmond Holmes, in 'Introduction to the Philosophy of the Upanishads'

6. STRONGEST SUPPORT

'(The philosophy of the Upanishads is) the strongest support of pure morality, the greatest consolation in the sufferings of life and death'.

And again,

'(The Upanishads are)*.... one of the most remarkable and prolific creations of thought that the world possesses'.

And again,

COMPARISON WITH BIBLE

'The Upanishads are for the Vedas what the New Testament is for the Bible'.

– Paul Deussen, German Philosopher

7. SPIRIT OF INQUIRY

'The Upanishads are instinct with a spirit of inquiry, a mental adventure, a passion for finding out the truth about things. The search for truth is, of course, not by the objective methods of modern science; yet there is an element of the scientific method in the approach. No dogma is allowed to come in the way'.

– Jawaharlal Nehru, in Discovery of India

8. GREAT SOURCE OF STRENGTH AND FREEDOM

'Strength, strength is what the Upanishads speak to me from every page. This is the one great thing to remember. The Upanishads are the great mine of strength. They will call with trumpet voice upon all races, all creeds, all sects to stand on their feet and be free. Freedom – physical freedom, mental freedom and spiritual freedom – is the watchword of the Upanishad'.

– Swami Vivekananda

9. CONSTRUCTIVE DOUBT

'In the Upanishads, we have scriptures that, among all the holy scriptures of the world, display the most scientific spirit in connection with spiritual enquiry. The sages, whose thoughts and teachings are contained in the Upanishads, seem to be as much inspired by constructive doubt as the most modern men of science'.

– C. Rajagopalachari, First Governor General of India

10. SOURCE OF INDIA'S HERITAGE

'The spiritual heritage of India is both vast and rich. But there is nothing sectarian or regional about it. It is so universal in its appeal and so catholic in its approach that it belongs to the whole world. The source of this heritage lies in the Upanishads'.

– Rohit Mehta, Author, 'The Call of the Upanishads'

11. THOUGHTS… LIKE PACES OF A TITAN

'In the Upanishads there are separate phrases, single couplets and brief passages. Each of these contains the substance of a vast philosophy, and yet each is thrown out as an aspect or a portion of infinite self-knowledge. Each follows the one that precedes, with a certain interval full of an unexpressed thought – which the mind is left to work out. And these intervals of pregnant silence are large. The steps of the seers' thoughts are like the paces of a Titan, striding from rock to distant rock, across infinite waters. There is a perfect totality, a comprehensive connection of harmonious parts, in the structure of each Upanishad'.

– Adopted from Sri Aurobindo's 'Foundations of Indian Culture'

12. AGE OF ENLIGHTENMENT

'The Upanishads are not based on theological reasoning, but on experience of spiritual life. Moreover, the Upanishads do not present the experience of any one great individual, but of a great age of enlightenment'.

– Nobel Laureate Poet, Rabindranath Tagore

13. GLOBAL INFLUENCE

'The Upanishads represent a great chapter in the history of human spirit. They have dominated Indian philosophy, religion and life for three thousand years. Every subsequent religious movement has had to show itself to be in accord with their philosophical statements. Even doubting and denying spirits found in them anticipations of their hesitancies, misgivings, and negations. They have survived many changes – religious and secular – and helped many generations of men

to formulate their views on the chief problems of life and existence....
Their thought – by itself, and through Buddhism – influenced the
cultural life of even other nations far beyond the boundaries of India'.

– Dr. S. Radhakrishnan, Author, 'The Philosophy of the Upanishads'

14. HIMALAYAN PEAKS

'The Upanishads have been rightly described as the supreme expression of Hindu mind'.

– Dr. Karan Singh

15. NEED TO DIVE DEEP

'The contents of the Upanishads are the esoteric spiritual knowledge recorded for the purpose of reflection and contemplation. Therefore, the deeper a man dives into the significance of the passages, the greater shall he discover their hidden meaning'.

– Swami Chinmayananda

16. ROOTS OF BUDDHISM

'There is no important form of Hindu thought, heterodox Buddhism included, which is not rooted in the Upanishads'.

– Bloomfield in 'The Religion of the Vedas'

4 Road Map of the Upanishads

METHOD OF STUDY

A study of the Upanishads means an exploration of the 'City of God' within us, and our oneness with the world around us. The Upanishads contain very profound, very brilliant and very original thoughts about life, happiness and meaning of the word 'God'. However, they also present some difficulties in their study.

> The Upanishads are not the work of a single author. They are records of spiritual visions of many seers over a period of around 1000 years. One should therefore not expect a systematic flow of thought in the Upanishads.

> The utterances of the seers are direct and sincere, but at times they are also incoherent and repetitive. Traditionally, the Upanishads have been vehicles more of spiritual illumination than systematic study.

> Some parts of the Upanishads appear to us to be trivial, tedious and meaningless. However, they should have had significance at the time they were composed – around 3000 years ago. We must not judge ancient writings from our standards. It is our task to distil from them whatever is relevant to us.

> The Upanishads were never intended to be popular texts of philosophy. Also, as they were transmitted orally from teacher to students, the language was very condensed – like notes of lectures intended to assist students' memory in subsequent recollection. Isolated from a teacher and without any personal spiritual experience, these notes-like compositions may confuse us. Under such circumstances, it useful to refer to available commentaries.

> The Upanishads deal with concepts and principles which are not easy to understand. Words and phrases like Self, Absolute, Totality, Eternal Truth, Ultimate Reality or Supreme Being are instantly impressive. However, they become enlightening only when we are able to comprehend their underlying meaning.

It is to be noted that the method of studying the Upanishads is different from studying science or reading a novel. It requires some adjustment in our reading habit. The

Upanishadic seers are in quest of Truth. There is a repeated emphasis in the Upanishads that Truth can be realized only by intuitive experience, and not by intellectual reasoning. If we wish to grasp the thoughts expressed in the Upanishads, we must study them with Faith, Patience and Concentration.

The ten important Upanishads presented here need not be studied in any particular sequence. You can start your study from any Upanishad, or from any page, and continue your study in any manner. The only requirement is that your mind should be suitably conditioned for not just study, but also reflection. Also, do not impose any time-limits for your daily study, or targets for completion of the study. In short, select whatever section makes you feel elated; and continue your study only for as long as you feel absorbed in the study.

UPANISHADS' METHODS OF PRESENTATION

The beauty of the Upanishads is that they make use of multiple methodologies – with remarkable imagination – to explain difficult subjects from different perspectives. These make their study interesting even for beginners.

Here is a brief description of the beautiful landscape of the Upanishads. A more detailed overview appears on pages 25-72.

INVOCATIONS FOR PEACE

Every Upanishad starts and ends with an Invocation for Peace. The six invocatory prayers contained in the ten Upanishads are summarized on pages 25-28. It is suggested that you select a favorite for starting your daily study.

METAPHORS AND ANALOGIES

The Upanishads make extensive use of metaphors and analogies to explain difficult concepts. Some of these are summarized on pages 29-44. Their study is a good starting point for beginners.

PARABLES AND ALLEGORIES

The Upanishads also contain some very interesting parables and allegories which have deep hidden meanings. Some of these are summarized on pages 45-55.

ENQUIRY AND DIALOGUES

The Upanishads are full of penetrating questions, followed by prolonged dialogues.

A question implies that the person asking the question has become aware of his ignorance. In the absence of such awareness, there cannot be an enquiry. Thus, a question is a symbol of awakened ignorance, an inquiring spirit.

A good question is a prerequisite for a good dialogue. In Katha Upanishad, the teacher compliments the student by saying, "May we find a questioner like you".

The ten most famous dialogues and discussions of the Upanishads are summarized on pages 56-64. These appear mainly in Brhadaranyaka Upanishad and Chandogya Upanishad, two largest of the ten Upanishads.

MAXIMS ON 'GOD AND I'

The Upanishads contain some very profound maxims which are quoted frequently by spiritual masters in their discourses. Famous maxims on God, man and the relationship between the two are discussed and summarized on pages 65-72.

UPANISHADS COVERED

This publication covers ten complete Upanishads, also called Principal or Classical Upanishads. These are enumerated in Table 2.

Table - 2

TEN UPANISHAD: NAMES AND STRUCTURE

Sr. No.	Name of Upanishads	Abbreviation	No. of Chapters	No. of Sections	No. of Verses
1.	Aitareya Upanishad	AU	3	5	33
2.	Brhadaranyaka Upanishad	BU	6	47	438
3.	Chandogya Upanishad	CU	8	152	600
4.	Isa Upanishad	Isa	-	-	18
5.	Katha Upanishad	Katha	2	6	119
6.	Kena Upanishad	Kena	-	4	35
7.	Mandukya Upanishad	Man	-	-	12
8.	Mundaka Upanishad	MU	3	6	65
9.	Prasna Upanishad	PU	-	6	65
10.	Taittiriya Upanishad	TU	3	31	52

Some scholars regard Svetasvatara Upanishad also as a Principal Upanishad. However, despite its importance, it could not be included in this publication.

As the Upanishadic texts were composed around three millenniums ago, some portions in them may not be of much relevance in modern times. Nonetheless, the publication in your hands contains the complete text. This avoids the risk of giving only that which is easy to read, or which agrees with the editor's views. It also gives the readers freedom to concentrate on what interests them.

The length of the Upanishads varies considerably. Some of the Upanishads are very short with less than two dozen verses; while others are very long with six hundred verses.

The original text of the Upanishads is divided in chapters and each chapter is subdivided in sections. The shorter Upanishads, however, may be without any chapter, section, or both. The original organization has been retained in the translated text.

The names of the Upanishads are not easy to recall or pronounce accurately, atleast in the initial stages of study. Beginners may therefore use the abbreviations as tabulated in Table-2.

Numbering System

In this publication each of the 1400 + verses of the ten Upanishads is identifiable by an alpha-numeric code, based on the following system:

- Alpha Code: denotes the Upanishad
- Digits before comma (,): denote Chapter and / or Section.
- Digits after comma(,): denote verse numbers.
- Digits with a hyphen (-) between them: denote the first and the last verse of the series.

Illustrations

- AU 1.1, 3 refers to chapter 1, section 1, verse-3 of Aitareya Upanishad.
  AU 1.1, 3-5 refers to verses 3 to 5 of the above.
  The same applies to BU, CU, Katha, MU and TU
- PU 6, 1 refers to question 6, verse-1 of Prasna Upanishad.
  Kena 1, 2-4 refers section 1, verses 2-4 of Kena Upanishad.
- Isa 1 refers to verse 1 of Isa Upanishad.
  Man 3-4 refers to verses 3 to 4 of Mandukya Upanishad.

COMPLETE TRANSLATED TEXT

Every translator of philosophical texts has two conflicting desires – to be faithful to the original and to produce a readable translation. Different languages have different idioms and different modes of expression. Accuracy in translation, if pressed to the limit, will result in incomprehensible English. Excessive concern for readability will distort the spirit of the original. One therefore tries to strike a balance between accuracy and readability. In the process, in any translation there is always some loss of 'originality' and some addition of a 'bias'.

The translation presented here is not the work of any single translator, but an amalgamation of many translations. Contemporary relevance and ease of comprehension were the two main factors that guided the production of a synthetic translation. Understandably, it lacks the richness of melody and the power to uplift, which the Sanskrit text contains. Also, translation of certain passages is open to debate, as some Sanskrit words can be interpreted differently, depending upon the perspective of the translator. Such differences have been pointed out in a few places as illustrative examples.

Readers are requested to bear these limitations in mind when reading the translated text.

Titles, Headings and Sub-headings

The original text of the Upanishads is in a conversational style, with long narrations without any titles or subtitles. This makes it difficult for the reader to know in advance the main theme of a particular Upanishad or its various chapters, sections or blocks of verses. The Editor has tried to overcome this constraint by assigning titles to each Upanishad and headings/sub-headings within an Upanishad. It is emphasized that these do not appear in the originals, and that they represent editor's viewpoint.

SYNOPSES, COMMENTARIES AND RENDITIONS

The truths enunciated in the Upanishads are based not on logical reasoning, but on intuitive revelations. Accordingly, the Upanishadic texts are not always very structured in their presentation. Quite often, they lead the reader step-by-step from gross to subtle, from relative to Absolute, from external world to inner Self. However, there are also many instances when the seers switch from one thought to another, leaving the readers confused. At times, even an important principle is expressed very briefly in just a few words, which are beyond the comprehension of an average reader. There are also occasions when the same thought is repeated again and again with minor variations, thereby distracting the reader from the main theme. In view of all these limitations, the Upanishads as stand-alone texts are not easy to understand, at least during the first few readings. Readers are therefore advised to refer to synopses and commentaries as often as they consider it necessary. With regular study, however, the readers will discover that deeper they reflect on the original passages, more enlightened they become.

Synopses

Synopses cover individual chapters in any Upanishad and are presented in the beginning of related chapter. At times, a synopsis may cover a block of consecutive sections or verses.

A synopsis is always followed by translated text and then commentaries. Its objective is to help the reader decide whether what follows is of interest to him, and also to prepare him for more detailed study.

All synopses are written by the Editor.

Commentaries, Focussed and General

Commentaries by knowledgeable scholars and thinkers are extremely useful aids in study of the Upanishads. Unfortunately, there are not too many commentaries available in English, particularly in respect of the two largest Upanishads – Brhadaranyaka and Chandogya.

The earliest commentary on the ten Upanishads was by Sri Sankara (788-820 AD), in Sanskrit. Translations of his commentary by Swami Gambhirananda, Swami Madhavananda and Swami Nikhilananda have been covered here selectively. Commentary by another famous spiritual master, Sri Madhava, as edited by Nagesh D. Sonde, has also been quoted in some places.

In recent decades, many spiritual teachers have written insightful commentaries on the ten Upanishads. Commentaries covered in this publication include Swami Sarvananda, Swami Swahananda and Swami Paramananda of Ramakrishna Math, Swami Sivananda and Swami Krishnananda of Divine Life Society, Swami Chinmayananda of Chinmaya Mission, and Swami Madhavananda of Advaita Ashram, Kolkatta. There is also a reference to Swami Vivekananda's commentary on Mundaka Upanishad.

Among philosopher-thinkers of India, Dr. S. Radhakrishnan is perhaps the most well known commentator on the Upanishads. His commentaries have been quoted very frequently in this publication. Extracts have also been included from Dr. Karan Singh's commentary on Mundaka Upanishad, which is regarded highly for its contemporary relevance. Besides, there are references to general writings on Upanishads by N. A. Nikam and Rohit Mehta.

Sri Aurobindo's commentaries on Isa and Kena Upanishads reflect very original and futuristic thinking, though his style of presentation creates some difficulty in its comprehension. Simplified versions of his commentaries have been reproduced extensively.

Paul Deussen is perhaps the most respected Western commentator and writer on the Upanishads. His original works were in German but now they have also been translated in English. Klaus G. Witz is another well-known German–born US-settled author of 'The Supreme Wisdom of the Upanishads'. Both Deussen and Witz have been quoted in this publication at appropriate places.

In all, the publication contains extracts and adaptations from the writings of as many as 19 authors, both Indian and of other nationalities, from 9th century till date. Their names and the Upanishads commented upon by them are listed in Table-3 on next page.

Most commentators have commented sequentially upon specific verses or blocks of consecutive verses. Extracts from their writings have been presented under 'Focused Commentaries.' In some instances, however, the commentaries are on some important themes of particular Upanishads. These are presented under 'General Commentaries'. The names of individual commentators have been identified in all cases.

It is emphasized that there are very few instances where commentaries have been quoted verbatim. In most cases, only extracts considered to have contemporary and contextual relevance have been presented. Also, in many cases, the text has been simplified or abbreviated.

Renditions

As stated earlier, the Upanishads contain some very insightful and interesting dialogues. However, to grasp their full meaning, one must refer to various commentaries. Back and forth movement between text and commentary interrupts the flow of thought. More important of these dialogues have therefore been presented as Renditions by the editor. These are a synthesis of the originals and the commentaries.

Complete translated texts, Synopses, Commentaries and Renditions constitute Part-II of this publication.

COMMENTARIES ON UPANISHADS COVERED IN THIS PUBLICATION

Table-3

Sr. No.	Commentators	AITAREYA	BRHAD.	CHANDOGYA	ISA	KATHA	KENA	MANDUKYA	MUNDAKA	PRASNA	TAIT.
1.	Sri Aurobindo		*		*	*	*				*
2.	Swami Chinmayananda	*			*	*	*	*	*	*	
3.	Paul Deussen	**	*	*		*	*			*	*
4.	Swami Gambhirananda (Translation of Commentary by Sri Sankara)	*		**				*	*		*
5.	Dr. Karan Singh								*		
6.	Swami Krishnananda		*						**		
7.	Sri Madhava (Translated by Nagesh D. Sonde)								**		
8.	Swami Madhavananda (Translation of Commentary by Sri Sankara)		*								
9.	Rohit Mehta	*			*	*	*	**	*	*	
10.	N. A. Nikam	*					*	**	*		*
11.	Swami Nikhilananda (Translation of Commentary by Sri Sankara and Gaudapada)							**			
12.	Swami Paramananda Sri Ramakrishna Math				*	*					
13.	Dr. S. Radhakrishnan	*	*	*	*	*	*	**	*	*	*
14.	Swami Sarvananda Sri Ramakrishna Math	*				*	*		*		*
15.	Swami Sivananda Divine Life Society	*	*		*	*	*	**	*	*	
16.	Swami Swahananda Sri Ramakrishna Math			*							
17.	Swami Vivekananda					*			*		
18.	Klaus G. Witz	**		*		*					*
19.	Renditions by Editor			R							

*   Focussed Commentaries
** General Commentaries
R   Renditions

5 Invocations for Peace

The Upanishads represent an exploration into our inner life. Study of inner life requires a peaceful environment and a concentrated mind.

Every Upanishad begins with a Peace Invocation, *Shanti Path*, to create a proper atmosphere of serenity and purity. The teacher and his disciples pray with a loving heart to the Supreme for His grace and protection.

The Invocation ends with the word *Shanti* repeated three times. *Shanti* means Peace. Three repetitions are intended to ward-off three types of obstacles:

> - ADHYATMIC: These originate from self, e.g. physical or mental sickness.
> - ADHIBHAUTIC: These originate from external environment, e.g. accidents or thefts.
> - ADHIDAIVIC: These are providential in nature, e.g. calamities like earthquakes.

The invocatory prayer is also repeated at the end of a Upanishad, as a thanksgiving reverence to the cosmic powers who have helped in grasping the knowledge contained in that Upanishad.

There are six peace invocations in the ten Upanishads. Some invocations are common to more than one Upanishad.

PRAYER FOR TRUTH

> *Om*
>
>> *May my Speech be rooted in my Mind.*
>> *May my Mind be rooted in my Speech.*
>> *O Brahman, Reveal Thyself to me.*
>> *O Mind and Speech, enable me to grasp*
>>   *the Truth which the scriptures teach.*
>> *Let me not forget what I have learnt.*
>> *Let me study day and night.*
>> *May I think Truth. May I speak Truth.*
>> *May Truth protect me. May Truth protect the Teacher.*
>>
>> *Om Shanti, Shanti, Shanti.*
>> *Let there be Peace. Let there be Peace. Let there be Peace.*

The Peace Invocation is addressed to the Supreme. It prays that the Supreme reveal Itself to the aspirant. It then prays to Mind and Speech that they be consistent with each other. This is followed by an earnest desire for Truth - a desire to study Truth, understand Truth, reflect on Truth, memorize Truth and practice Truth in daily life. The aspirant then seeks protection of Truth, both for himself and his teacher.

The invocation ends with traditional chant: *Shanti, Shanti, Shanti*. It appears in Aitareya Upanishad, both in the beginning and at the end.

PRAYER ABOUT CREATION

> *Om*
>
> *That is Whole; this is whole.*
> *From That Whole comes forth this whole.*
> *Taking whole from Whole,*
> *Whole remains unchanged.*
>
> *Om Shanti, Shanti, Shanti.*
> *Let there be Peace. Let there be Peace. Let there be Peace.*

This peace invocation looks very confusing in first reading. However, it has compressed the profound wisdom of all the Upanishads in just three key words, used very imaginatively in a short passage of 28 words.

> THAT: It denotes Eternal Truth, Ultimate Reality, Absolute Consciousness, or *Brahman* of the Upanishads.
> THIS: It denotes the world of relative objects and phenomena.
> WHOLE: It denotes infinity. Both 'This' and 'That' are infinite. 'Whole', when spelt with a capital 'W' refers to 'That'; when spelt with a small 'w', it refers to 'This'.

The passage says that both relative universe and Absolute Consciousness are Infinite. Absolute is the cause; relative is the effect. The nature of Absolute Consciousness is such that It remains unchanged even after projecting out of It the world of relativity.

A repeated chant of this prayer makes one's mind attuned to the Absolute, which is same as one's Self.

INVOCATIONS FOR PEACE

This peace invocation appears both in the beginning and end of two Upanishads – Brhadaranyaka and Isa. It appears again in Brhadaranyaka Upanishad as verse 5.1,1.

PRAYER FOR AWARENESS OF SUPREME

Om

> *May my limbs, speech, eyes, ears, life-breath*
> *and senses grow in strength.*
> *All existences are Brahman of the Upanishads.*
> *May I never be unaware of Brahman.*
> *May Brahman never spurn me.*
> *May there be no ignorance of Brahman.*
> *May the Truths stated in the Upanishads repose in me.*
> *Delighting in Atman, may they repose in me.*
>
> *Om Shanti, Shanti, Shanti.*
> *Let there be Peace. Let there be Peace. Let there be Peace.*

This invocation appears in both Kena and Chandogya Upanishads. It prays that let there be no ignorance of *Brahman* Consciousness.

PRAYER FOR MUTUAL UNDERSTANDING

Om

> *May He (Brahman) protect us both.*
> *May He cause us both to enjoy His Bliss.*
> *May we work together to understand*
> *the true meaning of scriptures.*
> *May our studies be fruitful.*
> *May we never misunderstand each other.*
>
> *Om Shanti, Shanti, Shanti.*
> *Let there be Peace. Let there be Peace. Let there be Peace.*

This invocation appears in Katha and Taittiriya Upanishads, as also in some editions of Kena Upanishad. It is particularly relevant in modern times of strife and conflict. In the invocation, the word 'both' refers to teacher and student. However, it could apply to any two persons or groups. It could also be replaced by the word 'all'.

PRAYER FOR HEALTH AND HAPPINESS

Om

O gods, may we hear auspicious words with our ears.
O worshipful One, may be see auspicious things with our eyes.
May we live our allotted life cheerfully and in good health,
  offering our praises unto Thee.
May Indra, the ancient and famous, bless us.
May Pusan, the all-knowing, bless us.
May Vayu, the Lord of swift motion, who protects us
  from all harms, bless us.
May Brhaspati, the Lord of wisdom, bless us.

Om Shanti, Shanti, Shanti.
Let there be Peace. Let there be Peace. Let there be Peace.

This invocation appears in three Upanishads – Prasna, Mandukya and Mundaka. It seeks harmony with forces of Nature – symbolized by various deities – for a healthy, virtuous and peaceful living.

PRAYER FOR DIVINE PROTECTION

Om

May Mitra, Varuna, Aryaman, Indra, Brhaspati and
  Vishnu of wide strides be favorable to us.
I bow to Brahman.
O Vayu, I bow to Thee. Indeed, you are the visible Brahman.
I shall call you Righteousness.
I shall call you Truth.
May that Brahman known as Vayu protect me.
May that Brahman protect my teacher.

Om Shanti, Shanti, Shanti.
Let there be Peace. Let there be Peace. Let there be Peace.

This invocation appears in Taittiriya Upanishad. Again, it seeks harmony with forces of Nature and praises them as manifestations of the Absolute.

6 Imaginative Metaphors and Analogies

The Upanishads use various objects of Nature as metaphors and analogies to help us understand our inner life. Some of these are recapitulated here.

1. SUN AND MOON

   Mankind from times immemorial has venerated Sun and Moon. The Upanishads regard them as symbols of important spiritual truths.

   Sun symbolizes spiritual wisdom. A rising sun vanquishes darkness, allowing us to see and act. Likewise, with the dawn of spiritual wisdom, our confusion disappears. We experience an inner transformation and our attitude towards life becomes more positive.

   In addition to giving light, sun also emits heat. Just as the intense heat of sun scorches everything, spiritual wisdom has the power to burn our evil desires, baseless fears and harmful attachments.

   The Upanishads use Sun as a metaphor for Self, *Atman*. Our experiences of joy and sorrow do not have any effect on our Self, which is changeless; just as Sun remains unaffected by the objects on which its rays fall. Katha Upanishad says:

   > *'Just as Sun – the eye of the whole world – is not contaminated by external impurities seen by the eye; so also Atman – the innermost essence of all beings – is not contaminated by external sorrows of the world. It is beyond them.'*
   >   – Katha 2.2, 11

   Isa Upanishad and Brhadaranyaka Upanishad use a beautiful analogy of a golden lid for the world of ignorance, which covers the Truth. We are so enamored by the golden lid that we are hesitant to remove it. A prayer invokes Sun – also called *Pusan* – to remove ignorance and reveal the Truth.

   > *'The face of Truth (Satya, Brahman) is covered with a golden lid. Unveil it, O Pusan, so that I, who have been worshipping Truth, may see it.'*
   >   – Isa 16 and Brhadaranyaka 5.15, 1

According to the Upanishads, all our sense-powers have cosmic counterparts, which are called deities. Sun is the deity of sight – we cannot see in the absence of light. The other deities are: Fire of speech, Space of hearing, Air of smell, Earth of taste and Water of touch.

An important theme of the Upanishads is that everything in the universe is interdependent. This theme is discussed in Brhadaranyaka Upanishad and Chandogya Upanishad under *Madhu Vidya*. *Madhu* means honey – a delicious and nourishing blend of the essence of many flowers. The Upanishads use the metaphor of Sun to illustrate the principle of interdependence of everything, and the dependence of everything on Self, or *Brahman*.

> *'The Sun is (like) honey for all beings, and all beings are (like) honey for this Sun. This shining, immortal Person who is in the Sun and this shining, Immortal Person who is in the eye – indeed these four are all just this Self. This is Immortal. This is Brahman. This is all.'*
> – Brhadaranyaka 2.5, 5

The verse emphasizes the Oneness of the Sun as an astronomical object, all living beings, the Power which illumines the Sun, and the Power behind the human eyes. All four are rooted in One *Brahman*, Cosmic Consciousness.

Chandogya Upanishad starts its description of *Madhu Vidya* with following passage:

> *'The yonder Sun, indeed, is the honey of the gods. Of this honey, heaven is the cross beam, sky is the honeycomb and Sun's rays are the eggs.'*
> – Chandogya 3.1, 1

And it concludes...

> *'Verily, the sun neither rises nor sets for one who knows this secret teaching of the Vedas; for him there is perpetual daylight.'*
> – Chandogya 3.11, 3

The famous *Gayatri Mantra* is also a prayer to Sun as a symbol of the Supreme (Brhadaranyaka 5.14 and Chandogya 3.12).

Chandogya Upanishad suggests meditation on Sun as *Brahman* (Chandogya 3.19).

In another very profound metaphor, sun's rays are compared to a highway connecting two places – Self in man and Cosmic Person in Sun (Chandogya 8.6, 2).

Moon symbolizes the mind. It has no light of its own; it shines only because of the reflected light of Sun. Likewise, mind has no Consciousness of its own, it functions only because of the reflected Consciousness of Self, *Atman*.

How was the universe born? According to the Upanishads, it all started with Consciousness – One Absolute, without a second. Prasna Upanishad uses the word *Prajapati* for It and says that the duality of Matter and Life was the first to emerge. It denotes Matter with Moon and Life with Sun.

> *'Prajapati, the Creator, desired the joy of creation. He remained in meditation and then came, a pair of Matter (Rayi) and Life (Prana). ....The Sun, verily, is Life and the Moon is Matter.'*
> – Prasna 1, 4-5

In the metaphorical language of the Upanishads, the Soul (*Jivatman*) travels either to the realm of Light (Wisdom) or to the realm of Darkness (Ignorance). These are denoted by Sun and Moon respectively (Brhadaranyaka 6.2 and Chandogya 5.10).

Everything in the universe has two aspects – Absolute and relative. The Absolute is changeless, while the relative is always undergoing change. Brhadaranyaka Upanishad explains it with the analogy of Moon. In a lunar fortnight, moon appears to be of different size everyday; though in reality, it is always the same. Metaphorically, the Creator is said to have 'sixteen parts' – fifteen of these are variable, and the sixteenth is constant. The constant part is the Cause of the universe and the fifteen variable parts correspond to its effects, the universe. In the words of the Upanishad:

> *'Entering into all these living beings through his constant part on the new moon night, he is born therefrom next morning'.*
> – Brhadaranyaka 1.5, 14

2. CITY OF GOD

The Upanishads have great respect for human body and they refer to it as 'City of God'.

Chandogya Upanishad describes the heart as a small lotus-shaped mansion. Though Self or Consciousness pervades the whole body, metaphorically, it is said to reside in a small space in the heart. As Self is the essence of the whole universe, the Upanishad makes a dramatic declaration. This infinitesimally small space contains the entire infinitely large universe.

> *'Whatever there is in this world and whatever is not, all that is contained within it (space in the heart).'*
>
> – Chandogya 8.1, 3

Katha Upanishad describes the 'City of God' as having eleven gates. These refer to the eleven openings in human body, including the crown in the head. The Self which resides in the human body is also the Self which resides in everything outside – as brightness in sun, as air in space, etc. It pervades all living beings, physical objects and natural phenomena. This Self is the power behind life-breath and the senses. Without this Self, body ceases to function and disintegrates. The Upanishad declares:

> *'A man who meditates on It grieves no more.'*
>
> – Katha 2.2, 1-6

Mundaka Upanishad describes human body as a luminous city of Absolute *Brahman* and gives it the name *Brahmapuri*. It says:

> *'He has become the mind and He is seated in the heart. He lives in the whole body, and guides the body as well as the life in it. By their perfect knowledge, the wise realize Him as a state of blissful immortality.'*
>
> – Mundaka 2.2, 7

3. CHARIOT AND JOURNEY OF LIFE

Life is an evolutionary journey of individual Consciousness (conditioned Self, *Jivatman*) from one birth to another, until it attains God-like perfection. It then becomes one with pure and universal Consciousness, or *Brahman* of the Upanishads.

Self uses human body as a vehicle for its journey. Katha Upanishad compares man to a chariot on the move. Here are the similes:

Chariot	=	Human body
Horses	=	Sense organs
Reins	=	Mind
Roads	=	Sense objects
Driver	=	Intellect (*Buddhi*)
Master	=	Self (*Atman*)

The chariot with its horses represents the psychophysical vehicle in which Self rides. Mind holds the reins. It may either control or be dragged by the senses. In order to reach its destination, the driver must be able to discriminate between the paths of righteousness and pleasures – *Shreya* and *Preya*. He must also be able to discipline his mind and senses and keep them moving in perfect harmony, on the chosen track. To quote from the Upanishad:

> *'The man who has a discriminating intellect as his driver,*
> *and a disciplined mind as the reins,*
> *he reaches the end of the journey,*
> *the Supreme abode of the All-pervading.'*
>
> – Katha 1.3, 9

Chandogya Upanishad also elaborates on the destination of Self's journey in the chariot of human life. Yagyavalkya tells King Janaka that when a person wishes to go on a long journey, he acquires a chariot. He also congratulates Janaka for being well equipped for the journey of life. 'But what is your destination?', he asks.

King Janaka is already endowed with immense wealth, wisdom and fame. So he admits that he does not know what else he wants from life; and therefore, where to he is headed? Yagyavalkya then tells Janaka that the ultimate goal of human life is to be free from every fear, fear of even death. Also, he again congratulates King Janaka that he has already attained such a state of fearlessness. King Janaka expresses his gratitude by offering his good wishes and even his wealth. He says:

> *'Venerable Sir, may fearlessness come to you, as you have educated us on (the state of) fearlessness. Salutations to you. Here are the people of Videha, here am I (at your service).'*
>
> – Chandogya 4.2, 4

4. RIVERS, OCEAN AND CONSCIOUSNESS

A river symbolizes the journey of man through diverse experiences of life. It originates in places hidden from human eyes. It flows through hills, valleys, forests and plains. Eventually, it merges into the ocean. Likewise, man has his origin in Cosmic Consciousness, which is imperceptible to the senses. His life flows along – sometimes through joy, sometimes through suffering, sometimes smoothly, sometimes with difficulty – until it eventually merges into Cosmic Consciousness.

Ocean symbolizes Cosmic Consciousness. Like Consciousness, it is infinite. Waves are constantly rising and disappearing in the ocean. Likewise, everything of this universe appears and disappears in Consciousness. Just as the ocean is the source and the support of waves, Consciousness is the cause and the substratum of all existences.

From a different perspective, rivers originate from ocean through the process of evaporation, cloud formation and rains. Rain water forms rivers, and these merge in ocean. Likewise, our lives originate from Cosmic Consciousness and merge into Cosmic Consciousness.

The analogy of rivers and ocean, to explain the eventual merger of individual Consciousness into universal Consciousness, is a recurrent theme in the Upanishads. For example:

'As flowing rivers disappear into the ocean, losing their separate names and forms; so also the wise, freed from all identification of name and form, becomes one with the Highest of the high, the Supreme Divinity.'

– Mundaka 3.2, 8

'These eastern rivers, dear son, flow along to the east and western ones to the west. They rise from the ocean and merge in the ocean, and become that ocean itself. And there, these rivers do not know themselves as, "I am this river, I am that river"; even so, all these creatures, having come from Being, do not know, "We have come from Being."...'

– Chandogya 6.10, 1-2

'Just as rivers flowing towards the sea disappear upon reaching it; their names and forms perish in the ocean and everything is spoken of as the ocean; likewise, the sixteen parts of a seeker who has Purusha (Cosmic Person) as his goal, disappear

> *on reaching Purusha. His name and form get merged with Purusha and thereafter he is called simply as Purusha, Formless and Immortal.'*
>
> – Prasna 6.5

5. SALT WATER AND SELF

Water is a widely used metaphor in the Upanishads. Some examples are: water running down mountain-tops, salt dissolved in water, and a fish swimming back-and-forth between two banks of a pond of water.

Katha Upanishad says that a person who fails to see the Oneness of all existences is like rain water falling on a mountain top and running down the rocks. It flows here and there, in all conceivable directions. In contrast, a person who sees Oneness of divine presence in every being is like pure water being poured into pure water.

> *'Rain water falling on top of a mountain runs down the rocks on all sides. Similarly, he who views things as different (overlooking their underlying unity), runs after them in all directions.*
>
> *O Gautama (Nachiketa), as pure water poured into pure water becomes one, so also the Self of an illumined knower (becomes One with the Supreme).'*
>
> – Katha 2.1, 14-15

In the celebrated husband-wife dialogue of Brhadaranyaka Upanishad, Yagyavalkya explains to his wife Maitreyi that the Ultimate Reality of every existence in the universe is Pure Consciousness. It is imperceptible, infinite and limitless. It cannot be separated from that in which It pervades – like a lump of salt dissolved in water.

> *'As a lump of salt dissolves when put in water and there is none of it to seize forth as it were, but wherever one may taste, it is salty indeed; so, verily, this great, infinite, limitless Reality consists of nothing but Pure Consciousness.'*
>
> – Brhadaranyaka 2.4, 12

In another famous father-son dialogue of Chandogya Upanishad, the great aphorism 'That thou art' is repeated nine times, and each repetition is accompanied by an illustration. One illustration is that of salt and water. Uddalaka Aruni first tells his son Shvetaketu to dissolve some salt in water, and then he asks him to take it out. Understandably, Shvetaketu is unable to separate the dissolved salt from the salty solution. However, by tasting it, he is able to confirm its presence. Uddalaka concludes:

> 'Dear son, likewise, you cannot perceive That Being, though It surely exists in this body.'
>
> – Chandogya 6.13, 1-2

In another dialogue of Brhadaranyaka Upanishad, Yagyavalkya explains to King Janaka that the Ultimate Light in man is Self, Pure Consciousness. The Upanishadic seers found support for this revelation from their observation of man in states of wakefulness and sleep (including dreams). Self moves from one state to another, like an unattached witness. It is unaffected by the actions or desires of the mind and the sense organs. It is like a fish moving between the two banks of a river, unaffected by the intervening currents of water.

> 'Just as a large fish moves between the two banks of a river, here and there, so also this Person moves along both these states – the state of dream (or sleep) and the state of waking.'
>
> – Brhadaranyaka 4.3, 18

In Prasna Upanishad, spiritual wisdom is compared to a ferry for crossing over the sea of ignorance. At the end of an enlightening Question-Answer session, the six disciples thank their teacher Pippalada in following words:

> 'You are indeed our father. You have ferried us to the shore across the sea of ignorance. We salute all the great Rishis. We salute all the great Rishis.'
>
> – Prasna 6, 8

6. FIRE, SPARKS, SPIDER AND UNIVERSE

Self (*Atman* or Consciousness) is formless. However, it assumes different forms according to what It enters – like fire assumes the form of what it burns.

> 'Just as fire, after it has entered the world, though one, assumes different forms according to what it burns; so also Atman, though one within all living beings, takes different forms according to what It enters. It also exists outside them.'
>
> – Katha 2.2, 9

Self or Consciousness is imperceptible to the senses, like fire hidden in firewood.

> *'It (Self) entered into these bodies up to the tip of the nails – as a razor is (hidden) in razor-case, or as fire in firewood. People do not see It, or they see It only partially.'*
>
> – Brhadaranyaka 1.4, 7

Self or Consciousness is the ultimate source of everything that exists in the world – animate or inanimate. Everything has emerged from Self, like small sparks from a fire.

> *'As a spider moves about in its web, as small sparks come forth from the fire, even so from this Self come forth all senses, all worlds, all gods, and all beings.'*
>
> – Brhadaranyaka 2.1, 20

7. TREE, PLANTS AND TRANSMIGRATION

Like chariot and river, tree is another metaphor for man. In Brhadaranyaka Upanishad, Yagyavalkya compares a man to a tree as follows:

Hair	=	Leaves
Skin	=	Outer bark
Blood	=	Sap
Flesh	=	Inner bark
Bones	=	Woods
Marrow	=	Pith

Yagyavalkya then asks: 'What is the root of man? If a tree is pulled up with the roots, it will not grow again. From what roots is man born again, after he is cut-off by death?' He then answers his question as follows:

> *'It is Brahman. It is Knowledge and Bliss.'*
>
> – Brhadaranyaka 3.9, 28

In Katha Upanishad, the whole universe is compared to an inverted *Pipal* or *Ashwattha* tree. This tree is extensive in growth, sturdy in build and long in its duration of life. Etymologically, *Ashwattha* means that which will not be tomorrow. Thus, it represents the world of perishable objects. The symbolism of its being inverted suggests that the world is rooted in *Brahman*, Absolute Consciousness.

> 'This ancient Ashwattha tree has its roots above, and branches below. That (root)
> is, verily, Pure. That is Brahman. That alone is called the Immortal. All the worlds
> rest in That. None can transcend That. This, verily, is That.'
>
> – Katha 2.3, 1

It is difficult to comprehend that this vast universe of diverse forms has emerged from an imperceptible mass of formless Consciousness. Again, Chandogya Upanishad uses the analogy of the emergence of a large banyan tree from the subtle essence of its small seed. While explaining the great aphorism, 'That thou art', Uddalaka tells his son Shvetaketu:

> 'This subtle essence which you do not perceive, growing from this subtle essence,
> the large banyan tree thus stands.'
>
> – Chandogya 6.12, 2

In the aforesaid father-son dialogue, Uddalaka also explains that Consciousness pervades everything – even plants and trees.

> 'As that tree is pervaded by living Self,
> it stands firm, drinking constantly and rejoicing.'
>
> – Chandogya 6.11, 1

Katha Upanishad says that birth, growth, old age and death of mortal beings are analogous to that of plants.

> 'Mortal beings decay and die like corn,
> and they are born again like corn.'
>
> – Katha 1.1, 6

8. WHEEL, HUB AND LIFE PRINCIPLE

The wheel – with its hub, spokes and rim – is a frequently used metaphor in the Upanishads. Prasna Upanishad compares the hub of a wheel to Life Principle – both in man and in cosmos.

> 'As spokes on the hub of a wheel,
> everything is established in Prana, Life Principle –
> the mantras of Rg, Yajur and Sama Vedas,
> all dynamic activities, and all spiritual endeavors.'
>
> – Prasna 2.6

> *'The sixteen 'parts' are established in Purusha, Cosmic Person,*
> *like spokes in the hub of a wheel.'*
>
> – Prasna 6.6

Chandogya Upanishad also compares *Prana* or Life Principle to the hub of a wheel and then glorifies it as father, mother and *Brahman*.

> *'Prana, Life-breath surely is greater than aspiration. Just as the spokes of a wheel are fastened to its hub, so also all this is fastened to this Prana. Prana moves by Prana, gives Prana to Prana. Prana is the father, Prana is the mother, Prana is the brother, Prana is the sister, Prana is the preceptor, Prana is Brahman.'*
>
> – Chandogya 7.15,1

Mundaka Upanishad says that Self or *Atman* is the hub of our life. Hub is that part in a wheel which is in contact with every point on its circumference – through the spokes. It equalizes all the tensions working in the entire wheel. Similarly, our Self is in contact with all our thoughts, words and deeds. Figuratively, it is stated that all the nerves meet in the heart and Self moves within the heart. The nerves are not physical arteries, but rays of psychic forces. They radiate from Self – as subtle channels of Consciousness – to every conceivable part of the body, controlling and directing it.

However fast the wheel may rotate and wherever it may travel, its center remains the hub. Without the hub – the Self – the whole structure of the wheel would collapse into a jumble of twisted metal, like lifeless body.

> *'Where all the nerves meet – like spokes of a chariot wheel meet at the hub – He moves there, within the heart, and becomes manifold. Meditate on that Atman as Aum. Blessings to you in crossing over to the other shore, beyond darkness.'*
>
> – Mundaka 2.2, 6

In Brhadaranyaka Upanishad, the periphery of the wheel is equated with wealth, and hub with life. Like any point on the periphery, wealth has its ups and downs. Even if a man loses wealth, he can make up the loss if he continues to live.

> *'Wealth alone increases and diminishes. That which is life is like the hub of a wheel, wealth a periphery. Therefore even if one loses everything but he himself lives, people say that he has lost only his peripheral possessions (which can be acquired again).'*
>
> – Brhadaranyaka 1.5, 15

In another passage, Brhadaranyaka Upanishad gives a cosmic dimension to the analogy of wheel. It says:

'This Self, verily, is the Lord of all beings, the king of all beings. Just as all the spokes are held together in the hub and rim of a wheel; so also in this Self, all beings, all gods, all worlds, all breathing creatures, all these selves are held together.'
– Brhadaranyaka 2.5, 15

The metaphor of wheel conveys a very important message. Our life-style must be centered on what we are, our inner Self. If our life is governed pre-dominantly by the dictates of external circumstances, it loses alignment with our inner center. Under such a situation, the faster the wheel of life turns, the more violently it vibrates. We must then bring the center of our external life close to our inner Self. This is accomplished by turning our attention inward, for example, in meditation.

9. BOW AND ARROW, MEDITATION

Self-realization means to become aware of the divinity within and without – *Atman* and *Brahman*. This requires two things: Wisdom and Meditation. Mundaka Upanishad explains it with a beautiful metaphor of a bow and arrow. It says:

'The knowledge contained in the Upanishads is like a great weapon, the bow. Fix in it the arrow, sharpened by meditation. Draw it with the mind fixed on Brahman. Then, O handsome youth! reach that target – the Immoral Brahman.'

'The Pranav (Aum) is the bow. Atman is the arrow, and Brahman is said to be the target. It should be aimed at with full concentration. Your Self should become one with Brahman, like an arrow becomes one with the target.'
- Mundaka 2.2, 3-4

In the analogy:

Bow   =   Knowledge contained in Upanishads, symbolized by *Aum*.
Arrow   =   Self, *Atman*.
Target   =   Universal Consciousness, *Brahman*.

Oneness of *Atman* and *Brahman* can be experienced only in deep meditation. If our mind is divided and scattered, we cannot meditate; and without the power of meditation, we cannot gain direct experience of *Atman-Brahman*.

10. SPIDER, HERBS, HAIR AND UNIVERSE

The three analogies of spider, herbs and hair illustrate beautifully the creation of the universe from Consciousness, *Brahman*.

The moment we think of *Brahman* as the Creator, we imagine Him as a pot-maker, creating the world out of some material. This image is denied here.

Brahman is both the material and the maker. Just as a spider creates a web out of itself, Consciousness creates the world out of Itself. It is both the material cause and the efficient cause of the universe. Stated differently, God is universe and universe is God.

Creation is an effortless projection from Consciousness, without any motivation or self-interest on part of *Brahman*, like growth of herbs on earth.

Creation is not a mechanical, lifeless process. It is a sign of vitality – like growth of hair on a living body.

In the words of Mundaka Upanishad:

> *'As a spider spreads out and withdraws (its thread), as herbs sprout upon earth, as hair grow on the head and body of a living man; so from the Imperishable comes out the universe.'*
>
> – Mundaka 1.1, 7

The analogy of spider also appears in Brhadaranyaka Upanishad alongside the analogy of sparks from fire, described earlier on page 36.

11. MUSICAL INSTRUMENTS AND SELF

The root cause and the inmost essence of man – as also of the world – is Consciousness, or *Atman-Brahman* of the Upanishads. Everything around us is an effect of this First Cause, also called Self.

When our actions are based on our perception of only an effect – without an understanding its root cause – it is like trying to catch the sound of a musical instrument with bare hands. We get nowhere if we act merely on the basis of what our senses are transmitting to our mind. But when we act with knowledge of Self

– the First Cause of everything – it is like taking control of the musical instrument, or the source from which the sound originates. By grasping the cause of the sound, our understanding of the sound also improves. Likewise, wisdom about Self makes us more effective in our dealings with the world.

This principle is illustrated in Brhadaranyaka Upanishad with the analogy of a musical instrument. Giving essentially the same analogy in three forms emphasizes the importance of the principle.

> *'As when a drum is beaten, one is not able to grasp its sound; but by grasping the drum, or the beater of the drum, the sound is grasped.*
>
> *As when a conch is blown, one is not able to grasp its sound; but by grasping the conch, or the blower of the conch, the sound is grasped.*
>
> *As when a veena (lute) is played, one is not able to grasp its sound; but by grasping the veena, or the player of the veena, the sound is grasped.'*
>
> – Brhadaranyaka 2.4, 7-9

12. BIRDS AND MIND

Human beings have a 24-hours cycle of waking, dream and sleep. Three thousand years ago, the Upanishadic seers observed the phenomena of dream and sleep as closely as that of waking; and they made a remarkable revelation: All the three states have Pure Consciousness as their substratum. During wakefulness, Consciousness uses the Mind and sense organs as its instruments for interacting with the external world, as presented to it. During the state of dreams, Consciousness uses the Mind alone as its instrument, and it creates a world of its own. During the state of sleep, even the Mind goes to rest and Consciousness alone keeps awake. Without dreams and sleep, it will be impossible for man to be mentally alert and physically active during the waking state.

The Upanishads illustrate the importance of sleep with the metaphor of a bird coming down to rest.

> *'Just as a falcon or any other swift bird flying in the sky becomes tired, folds its wings and comes down to its nest, so also this Person hastens to that state (of sleep) where he has no desires and he sees no dream.'*
>
> – Brhadaranyaka 4.3, 19

'A bird tied to a string, after flying in various directions and finding no resting-place elsewhere, takes refuge at the very place whereto it is tied. Even so, dear son, that mind, after flying in various directions and finding no resting place elsewhere, takes refuge in Prana alone; for the mind, dear son, is tied to Prana.'

– Chandogya 6.8, 2

'When the mind is overpowered by its own radiance, then it sees no dreams. At that time it enjoys the bliss of deep sleep in the body.'

'Just as birds retire to a tree which provides rest, so indeed all these (man's faculties) rest in Supreme Atman.'

– Prasna 4, 6-7

13. MISCELLANEOUS METAPHORS

Some other metaphors used very imaginatively in the Upanishads are summarized hereunder.

- The process of creation is analogous to morphogenesis. Just as an undifferentiated embryo develops in a highly differentiated structure of a baby, a homogenous mass of Consciousness turns into a heterogeneous Matter-Energy system. (Aitareya Upanishad 1.1).
- Worldly desires are like citadels, preventing the Soul (*Jivatman*) from making itself free. Vamadeva, a Self-realized soul, burst out of the citadel like a hawk (Aitareya Upanishad 2, 5).
- In ancient times, *Ashvamedha Yagya* or ritual of horse-sacrifice was performed to denote conquest of the world. In the Upanishads, it is considered a symbol of self-mastery and sacrifice of self-interest. (Brhadaranyaka Upanishad 1.1-1.2).
- A Self-realized person does not perceive any duality; just 'as a man in the embrace of his beloved knows nothing without or within'. (Brhadaranyaka Upanishad 4.3, 21).
- When the body becomes old and weak, Self departs from it – like a ripe fruit falling from a tree – to start a new life. (Brhadaranyaka Upanishad 4.3, 36).
- Just as a caterpillar moves from one blade of grass to another, Self moves from one body to another (Brhadaranyaka Upanishad 4.4, 3).
- Just as a goldsmith makes new and more beautiful ornaments out of gold, Self creates for Itself new forms of embodiment, suited to new experiences (*Karma*) and tendencies (*Sanskara*). (Brhadaranyaka Upanishad 4.4, 4).

- Persons who regard performance of rituals alone as goal of life are 'fools wandering aimlessly, like blind led by the blind', (Mundaka Upanishad 1.2, 8).
- 'Knots of the heart' is a frequently used analogy in the Upanishads. These refer to ignorance, desires for selfish (illegitimate) gains and work motivated by such desires (e.g. Mundaka Upanishad 2.2, 8).
- Our desires are said to have two layers. The inner layer represents our true desires; they arise from our inner Self. The external layer is 'untruth' imposed by the outside world. Normally we are so preoccupied with the fulfillment of our 'external' desires, that we remain unaware of our 'true desires' – like a person walking on a treasure of gold hidden underground. (Chandogya Upanishad 8.2, 2).

7 Ten Insightful Parables and Allegories

The Upanishads use some very insightful parables and allegories to explain abstract principles. At times, the narration may look frivolous, but invariably it hides important truths.

1. ALLEGORY OF CREATION

According to the Big Bang model of Creation in physics, creation began with Space-Time and Matter. Though physicists have still not been able to establish the ultimate building block of Matter, Conscious has no place in their postulations.

The Upanishads regard Consciousness as the First Cause of creation. Their allegorical account of creation is based on following postulates.

- All Matter and Forces of Nature have originated from Consciousness alone.
- Man is a mini-cosmos. Cosmic Forces exist in man as sense-powers.
- One and the same Consciousness, which created the universe out of Itself, is also present in man as his inmost Self, *Atman*.
- Waking, dream and deep sleep are the three states of Consciousness in human beings.
- Desires wanting fulfillment is a universal urge.

Aitareya Upanishad says that in the beginning there was nothing but self-created Consciousness. It willed: 'Let me create the worlds.' First It created four fields – Space, Water, Earth and Heaven. Then It raised a lump of Matter from primordial Water, and gave it the shape of a Cosmic Person, *Purusha*. Thereafter, various Cosmic Powers emerged from the symbolic 'body-parts' of the Cosmic Person.

'Body-parts' of Cosmic Person	Emergent Cosmic Powers
Mouth	Speech and Fire
Nostrils	Smell and Air
Eyes	Sight and Sun
Ears	Hearing and Space
Skin	Touch and Vegetation
Heart	Mind and Moon
Navel	Out-breath and Death
Genitals	Procreative fluid and Water

The implication is that all Matter and all Forces of Nature have originated from Consciousness.

Next, the Cosmic Powers fell into vast ocean-like world. Then Consciousness (*Atman*) inflicted them with Hunger and Thirst. These symbolize desires. So the Cosmic Powers felt hungry and thirsty. They asked for a place to live, where they could satisfy their hunger and thirst. *Atman* first offered them a cow and then a horse for their residence; but these were unacceptable to Cosmic Powers. Finally, *Atman* offered them a human being. The Cosmic Powers were delighted at the sight of a human being and exclaimed in joy: 'Excellent. It is a masterpiece. We will live in its body'. All the Cosmic Powers then entered the body of man. Thus, Fire became speech and entered through the mouth; Air became power of smell and entered through the nostrils; and so on. What it means is that sense-powers have their origin in Cosmic Powers. The Upanishads refer to sense-powers as gods, deities or *Deva*.

When Hunger and Thirst saw Cosmic Powers enter man as sense-powers, they also asked *Atman* for an abode. But *Atman* did not assign them an independent place to live. Instead, It asked them to share the abode of sense-powers. This explains why all our sense powers are afflicted with desires.

Cosmic Powers had become sense-powers and settled down in man. Presence of Hunger and Thirst in their midst made them ask for Food. So *Atman* produced Food. As soon as sense-powers saw Food, they ran for it; but food tried to run away, like a mouse running away from cats. It was good that none of the sense-powers could catch Food. For example, if speech had caught Food, one would have been satisfied merely by talking about Food, and so on. Finally, Food was caught by out-breath (*Apana*). It regulates the digestive system.

The incidence of sense-powers running after Food made Consciousness think of the need for a unifying force in the body. Consciousness, *Atman* Itself became that unifying force. It entered human body through the topmost portion in the head. It resides in the eye when a person is awake, in the mind when a person is dreaming and in the heart when a person is asleep.

After descending in man, Consciousness peeped out to see if there was any other primary entity different from It. However, It saw that every thing and every being was pervaded by Itself alone.

The aforesaid allegory of creation constitutes chapter 1 of Aitareya Upanishad.

Brhadaranyaka Upanishad contains a somewhat similar narration of creation. It says that in the beginning everything was covered by Death. Death refers to Consciousness at the time of dissolution. The implication is that Creation-Dissolution is a cyclical process, without a beginning and without an end. Consciousness first created primordial Water out of Itself. Next, It crated Matter, Life and Mind. The whole universe is said to be Cosmic Body of Consciousness, *Atman*. (Brhadaranyaka Upanishad 1.2)

2. EVERY PERSON IS INHERENTLY GOOD

There has always been a conflict between Good and Evil. These are symbolized by *Devas* and *Asuras*, or gods and demons. Once gods decided to defeat demons by making use of *Udgitha*. *Udgitha* is a sacred song, which begins with *Aum*. It appears in the second chapter of Sama Veda.

The gods first asked speech to sing *Udgitha*. When speech was singing *Udgitha*, the demons rushed towards it and pierced it with evil. Therefore man speaks both good words as well as evil words.

Next, gods asked sight, hearing and mind to sing (concentrate on) *Udgitha*. They all did so one-by-one. However, every time the demons struck the sense-power and the mind with evil. This is why evil coexists with good in the mind and in sense-powers.

Finally, the gods asked Life Force to 'sing' *Udgitha*. The demons again tried to inflict Life Force with evil. This time, however, the demons were destroyed, like a clod of earth striking against a rock. This is why Life Force is not tainted by evil. Self of a saint and a sinner is one and the same. Only their minds differ. Inherently, every person is divine.

The parable brings out that the innate nature of man is to be good. It is the mind and the sense organs, which drive man towards evil deeds. (Brhadaranyaka Upanishad 1.3).

3. QUALITIES OF A GOOD LEADER

There is a parable in the Upanishads about the supremacy of Life Force over Mind and sense powers. It seems to suggest that a good leader never asserts: 'I am the boss'. His leadership is recognized from the support he provides to those who are dependent upon him. If there is a rebellion against his leadership, he does not fight back. Confident of his indispensability, he simply walks out.

Once the Mind and the sense-powers – Speech, Sight, Hearing and Procreation – started arguing about their superiority. Each claimed itself to be the leader. Unable to arrive at a consensus, they all went to *Brahma*, their Creator, for an answer. *Brahma* did not give a direct reply. Instead, he suggested a practical test. Whosoever is the most indispensable is also the most important. To find out who was the most indispensable, each of the sense powers and the Mind departed from the body one-by-one, and came back after one year. During the absence of each, the body managed to survive, though with some difficulty. Then Life Force prepared to depart – like a powerful horse shaking off the pegs to which its feet are tied. Immediately, the sense powers and the Mind realized that they could not function without the presence of Life Force in the body. So they accepted the superiority of Life Force.

The parable is repeated four times in the Upanishads, with some minor variations. (Brhadaranyaka Upanishad 1.5 and 6.1, Chandogya Upanishad 5.1-5.2 and Prasna Upanishad 2).

4. FIVE COSMIC FIRES

The allegory of five cosmic fires uses the illustration of childbirth to emphasize that every event is a consequence of a multitude of interrelated occurrences.

Yagya or *Agnihotra* is an important fire-ritual prescribed in the Vedas. It involves making a sacred Fire with special wood, and offering oblations of melted butter etc. into it. The ritual generates smoke, flame, sparks and embers. It also leads to some favorable outcome for the performer.

A fire-ritual signifies that every thing in the universe is interrelated. Nothing can exist as an isolated entity. Every action creates many side effects – besides the main effect – just as an oblation creates side effects like fire, fuel, smoke, flame, sparks and embers. Moreover, the effect of one action becomes the cause for another action, and so the chain-reaction continues.

Consider childbirth, for example. Figuratively, It may appear to be the outcome of a simple father-mother union. In reality, however, the whole universe participates in some way in the birth of a child. Allegorically, child-birth is said to be an outcome of actions offered as oblations in five Cosmic Fires. These are: Heaven, Rain, Earth, Man and Woman. They are discussed under the title *Panchagni Vidya*.

Every action of man accumulates to form a subtle body, which rises to heaven at the time of death. This is like an oblation in the first Cosmic Fire, Heaven. Its outcome – the mythological nectar called King Soma – becomes an oblation for the second Cosmic Fire, Rain. Its outcome, rain water, pours in the third Cosmic Fire (Earth) and produces Food. Food is consumed by man, the fourth Cosmic Fire, and transformed into procreative fluid. When this is offered as an oblation in woman as the fifth Cosmic Fire, the outcome is child-birth. The child grows and lives as long as he is destined to live. Then he dies, and the cycle is repeated again. His subtle body ascends to heaven as nectarial body, which descends back to earth as rain, rain is transformed into food; food is transformed into procreative fluid in man's body. When cast into woman's body, it may lead to birth of next generation child.

The whole creation is like a great ritual of innumerable Cosmic Fires.

This allegory is described in Brhadaranyaka as well as Chandogya Upanishad in the form of a dialogue with a king, Pravahana Jaivali.

> *'If the soul of a dead person goes to heaven, with so many people dying, why is there no overcrowding in heaven?'*

This is one of the five questions, king Jaivali asks young Shvetaketu. The young boy goes to his father Uddalaka Aruni and complains why he has not been instructed fully? Pleading ignorance, Uddalaka comes to Jaivali and requests an answer. Jaivali then enunciates the doctrine of transmigration, and explains it with the remarkable imagery of five Cosmic Fires. (Brhadaranyaka Upanishad 6.2 and Chandogya Upanishad 5.3-5.9).

5. PATHS OF LIBERATION AND REBIRTH

What happens to man after death? Depending upon his deeds, his Soul or *Jivatman* is said to follow one of the two paths – *Devayana* or *Pitrayana*. Devayana is the path of light. It leads to Sun, and thence to *Brahma Loka* or state of eternal Bliss. *Pitrayana* is the path of darkness. It leads to Moon and thence to rebirth on earth. Light and Sun signify wisdom about Oneness of man, world and God. Darkness signifies lack of wisdom.

The two paths are presented as extensions of *Panchagni Vidya*, both in Brhadaranyaka Upanishad (6.2) and Chandogya Upanishad (5.10).

6. LEARNING AND REFLECTION

Learning without reflection can lead to erroneous inferences.

Once, Indra and Virochana – chief of gods and chief of demons – went to their father Prajapati to learn about Self, *Atman*. Prajapati asked them to live like students for 32 years. Thereafter, they were asked to look at their reflections in water and report back what they saw. The two described that they saw the images of their bodies, well dressed and well groomed. Prajapati then told them that what they saw is *Atman*. He also added with a purpose: 'It is Immortal and Fearless'.

Prajapati imparted the same teaching to both Indra and Virochana. Virochana accepted it without reflecting upon it. He concluded that the body – whose reflection he saw in water – is *Atman*, Self.

Indra reflected upon the teaching and noticed a flaw. Human body is mortal and subject to fear, whereas Prajapati had said that Self is immortal and fearless. So body cannot be Self. He went back to Prajapati for clarification and spent another 32 years living like a student. Thereafter, Prajapati gave an additional description of *Atman*: 'It moves about adored in dreams'. Again, Indra reflected upon it and noticed another flaw. Dreams are creations of the mind. However, mind cannot be *Atman* because some dreams are full of fear, while *Atman* is fearless. He again went to Prajapati and after another 32 years of studentship, he was told: '*Atman* is fully composed in deep sleep'.

Once again, Indra reflected on the latest update, but he was not convinced. Sleep is like annihilation of oneself, while Prajapati said that *Atman* is immortal. He again went to Prajapati and spent another five years as a student. Thereafter, Prajapati provided a more detailed explanation of *Atman*. He said that *Atman* or Self is Pure Consciousness. Body and mind are only its instruments. *Atman* is mistaken as body and mind during waking state, and as mind alone during dream state. In deep sleep, mind is unconscious of *Atman*. In reality, *Atman* or Self is the substratum of all the three states. It is also the driving force behind the mind and the sense powers. It is the Highest Light, the Highest Person.

This parable appears in Chandogya Upanishad (Chandogya Upanishad 8.7-8.12).

7. POWER BEHIND MATTER, LIFE AND MIND

In the Upanishads, Matter-Energy is symbolized by *Agni* (Fire), Life by *Vayu* (Air) and Mind by *Indra* (chief Vedic deity). Once, these three were proudly discussing their successes and taking credit for their achievements. Suddenly, an unknown entity called *Yaksha* appeared before them. All three were curious to know who it was.

First, *Agni* (Matter-Energy) was sent to find out about the unknown. When *Agni* went near *Yaksha*, it asked him: 'Who are you?' 'I am Fire. I have the power to burn any thing', said *Agni*. 'Then burn this', said *Yaksha*, pointing to a small blade of grass. *Agni* tried hard to burn it, but could not do so. It returned back, disappointed.

Next, *Vayu* (Life Principle) was sent to find out about the unknown *Yaksha*. Again, *Yaksha* asked: 'Who are you?' 'I am Air, I have the power to move anything', said *Vayu*. 'Then move this', said *Yaksha*, again pointing to small blade of grass. *Vayu* tried hard to move it, but could not do so. It also returned back, disappointed.

Finally, *Indra* (Mind) was sent to enquire who the unknown was. But as soon as *Indra* approached the unknown *Yaksha*, it disappeared from his view. However, *Indra* did not return back, he stood there contemplating who the unknown could be? At that very spot, there appeared a beautiful lady, *Uma*, a symbol of Nature. She told *Indra* that the unknown was *Brahman*, or Consciousness.

The parable appears in Kena Upanishad (3.1-4.3). It suggests some significant truths.

- Matter-Energy, Life and Mind derive their power and glory from Consciousness.
- Consciousness cannot be perceived by the senses.
- When Mind tries to reason about Consciousness, the very concept of Consciousness disappears from its view.
- Everything in Nature is a manifestation of Consciousness. This realization comes to Mind as an intuitive experience – like a flash of lightening – when it is in a state of meditation.

8. FRIENDSHIP WITH GOD

In times of tension or fear, look upon God as your best friend. All your anxieties and sorrows will disappear. This, in essence, is the message of an allegory of two birds that lived on the same tree. They symbolize man and God. Stated differently, they symbolize ego and Self, while the tree symbolizes human body. Man's inmost substratum, Self, is God Itself.

The birds were bound to each other in close friendship. However, their life-styles were different. The tree on which they lived was unique. It had a wide variety of fruits on it – some sweet and some bitter. The bird called 'ego' was always busy eating the fruits. It was filled with pleasure when the fruit it ate turned out to be sweet. However, when the fruit happened to be bitter, it felt very helpless and sad. The bird called Self never ate any fruit. It just watched its friend experiencing the fruits of life.

Occasionally, when under great stress or sorrow, the bird called 'ego' looked at its friend, Self. This refers to ritualistic worship, prayer or meditation. To its surprise, 'ego' discovered that all its tensions or tears disappeared at the mere sight of its friend. Friendship with God empowers man to go through difficult periods in life with greater fortitude.

This parable appears in Mundaka Upanishad (3.1, 1-2).

9. DIALOGUE WITH DEATH

Katha Upanishad contains a very unusual story of a young boy. He learns about the mystery of death from none other than the Lord of Death. His name was Nachiketa. Once he watched his father performing a sacrificial rite and gifting cows to priests. What surprised him was that the cows, which his father was giving away, were old and weak. To him, charity meant giving away what you hold dear, and not what is surplus to you. So he asked his father politely: "Father, to whom will you give me away?" The father realized what Nachiketa was hinting at. Therefore, he avoided giving an answer. But Nachiketa was concerned about his father's mistaken notion of charity. Hence he repeated his question a second time, and a third time. This infuriated his father, and he said in an angry voice: "I shall give you to Death."

Nachiketa took his father's words literally. He knew that his father loved him. So he thought that his father's angry outburst must have some divine purpose behind it. His father was filled with repentance, but Nachiketa consoled him and proceeded to meet the Lord of Death, Yama.

When Nachiketa reached the abode of Death, Lord of Death was not at home. Nachiketa could have come back to his father; but he did not. Instead, he waited patiently at the doorsteps of Death. Lord of Death returned home after three days and found Nachiketa waiting for him. He apologized for the neglect of his guest and to make up for it, he offered him three boons.

Nachiketa loved his father very much. So the first boon he asked was that his father should not feel sad about whatever has happened. Yama granted his wish and assured him that his father will be happy to see him released from the mouth of Death.

The second boon Nachiketa asked was some knowledge about the path of rituals. In contemporary context, rituals should be taken to mean work. Yama readily granted even the second boon.

The third boon which Nachiketa asked, posed a problem for Yama. Nachiketa wanted the Lord of Death to reveal what Death really meant? So he asked: "Is there anything of man that exists even after he dies?"

Lord of Death was hesitant to reveal the secrets of death. So he tried to persuade Nachiketa to ask for another boon. In addition, he offered him a long life with all the wealth and pleasures of the material world. But Nachiketa remained firm in his determination to acquire wisdom about death. Finally, Yama agreed to teach Nachiketa what is meant by death.

The essence of Yama's teaching is that the word 'death' applies to human body alone. The inmost essence of man – called *Atman*, Self or Consciousness – is immortal. Also, Self in man is one and the same as universal Self.

The entire Katha Upanishad is in the form of a dialogue between young Nachiketa and Lord of Death.

10. SELF-STUDY OF SELF

A good teacher does not spoon-feed his student with knowledge; he merely guides him step-by-step to discover the truth by his own efforts. This fact is illustrated beautifully through a case study of Self. Self is the inmost essence of man.

Bhrigu – a young boy who later became famous as a learned sage – once approached his father Varuna with a request: 'Please teach me about Self'. The Upanishad uses the word *Brahman* for Self. *Atman*, *Purusha* and Consciousness are other names for It.

Varuna did not give a long discourse on Self. Instead, he provided two hints.

- Food, Life-breath and Mind are aids in knowledge of Self.
- Try to reflect on 'That' from which all living beings are born, by which they remain alive and into which they eventually merge.

Bhrigu reflected on what his father had said. His first inference was that Food must be Self. Man is born from Food – in the sense that in human body, food is transformed into procreative fluid, which causes birth of a child. Man is obviously sustained by food. Also, after death human body disintegrates and merge into primal elements, which are 'food' (inputs) for other objects of creation.

It is to be noted that 'Food' in the Upanishads also refers to physical layer of human personality.

When Bhrigu went to his father for confirmation of his inference, all that his father said was: 'Seek to know Self through meditation. Meditation is Self.'

Bhrigu reflected more on the subject. Stated differently, he practiced meditation. Slowly he realized that physical body is only a part of Self, and that Life-breath must be Self. He again went, to his father and was again asked to reflect more on the subject.

After further practice of meditation, Bhrigu arrived at the conclusion that mind must be Self. For the third time, his father repeated his earlier advice for more reflection. Continuing his self-study, Bhrigu's next inference was that the spiritual layer of human personality – *Vigyana* – must be Self. *Vigyana* is also translated as intellect.

For the fourth time, his father sent him back with advice for further reflection.

Next, Bhrigu suddenly realized that Self is nothing but Bliss or *Ananda*. After this realization, he did not go back to his father for confirmation. Correct realization of Self makes one free from all doubts.

This parable constitutes chapter 3 of Taittiriya Upanishad.

8. Overview of Ten Profound Dialogues

In the study of spiritual wisdom, a question must be followed by a dialogue, or a discussion. Wisdom is not just information or definitions; it is intuition and experience. A question seeking some information or definition will never turn into a dialogue. A dialogue arises not because a question is asked and answered, but because the question is used as an opportunity to share wisdom.

Dialogue, said Plato, 'is giving and taking of reason'. In the Upanishads, dialogue is 'giving and taking of spiritual experience'.

This chapter provides an overview of ten very profound dialogues contained in the Upanishads. However, their deep wisdom can be appreciated only by studying the originals.

1. GARGYA: A PROUD TEACHER WHO BECAME A HUMBLE STUDENT

Gargya was proud of his knowledge of God, and impatient to exhibit his knowledge. So he went to the court of a king, Ajatashatru, and offered to teach the king about God. The king welcomed the opportunity, but soon discovered that Gargya's description of God was incomplete. Gargya realized his shallow learning and requested Ajatashatru to teach him what is God? A learned teacher becoming a student of a king was quite unusual. The method Ajatashatru used to teach Gargya about God was still more unusual. He took Gargya to a sleeping person, woke up that person and asked Gargya: 'Where was the Consciousness of this person when he was asleep?' Ajatashatru then analyzed the three states of human experience – waking, dream and deep sleep – and explained God as that Consciousness, which keeps awake in all the three states. He concluded:

'Its secret meaning is the Truth of truths. Life-breaths are truths, and It is their Truth.'

– Brhadaranyaka 2.1, 20

This dialogue appears in Brhadaranyaka Upanishad (2.1).

2. MAITREYI: WIFE WHO PREFERRED WISDOM TO WEALTH

Maitreyi considered herself a very lucky person. Her husband, Yagyavalkya was endowed with rare combination of wealth and wisdom. He was a very famous teacher of philosophy, and he had also been able to accumulate immense wealth by legitimate means. He had two wives, but Maitreyi was the one he loved more. One day, Yagyavalkya shocked Maitreyi by declaring that he planned to renounce everything and retire into the solitude of forests. Maitreyi loved her husband so much that she thought she would not be happy without him. So when her husband offered half his wealth to her, she asked him if that would make her happy? 'No', said Yagyavalkya, 'It will only enable you to live a comfortable life, like any rich person'. This was not acceptable to Maitreyi. She wanted to know how she could live happily even in the absence of her loving husband. 'For that you need wisdom and not wealth', said Yagyavalkya. What followed was a profound dialogue between Maitreyi and Yagyavalkya on what sustains genuine love in human relationships.

Two persons love each other not because they are related to each other, but because they regard each other as one. In the famous words of Yagyavalkya:

> *'Verily, not for the sake of husband is husband dear, but husband is dear for the sake of Self,*
> *..... and so also for wife, son or any other relationship.'*
>
> – Brhadaranyaka 2.4, 5

3. YAGYAVALKYA: A WISE MAN WHO ALSO LOVED WEALTH

Yagyavalkya did not see any contradiction between simultaneous pursuit of wealth and wisdom. He was a contemporary of King Janaka, who is famous for ruling his kingdom like a true *Karma Yogi* – with great zeal but without any self-interest. Once Janaka felt curious to know who in his kingdom was the wisest of all spiritual masters? So he held what may be called a contest of wisdom and invited all great thinkers of his times. He also set aside a very attractive prize for the winner – a thousand cows, each having ten gold coins tied to its horns. Janaka then declared: "Learned ladies and gentlemen, whoever among you is the wisest, that person can drive home these cows!"

There followed complete silence. No one dared to declare himself the wisest. Finally, Yagyavalkya stood up and directed his disciple to drive home the cows.

Suddenly, everyone was in an uproar. Everyone cried out; 'How can he declare himself to be the wisest without having said even one word of wisdom? He must prove himself.' It was then agreed that they question him one-by-one.

Yagyavalkya is questioned by eight scholars on a wide range of subjects:

- Asvala, on the modalities and benefits of sacrificial rituals.
- Artabhaga, on death. Death swallows everything, what swallows death? Also, what remains of a person after his death?
- Bhujyu on what happens after death to those who have lived a life of rituals?
- Usasta, on God. Where can God be perceived or experienced directly?
- Kahola repeats Usasta's question. Yagyavalkya answers from a different perspective.
- Gargi, a renowned lady philosopher of her times, questions Yagyavalkya twice. She says that cause pervades it effect and then asks a series of questions, to arrive at the Ultimate Cause which pervades everything.
- Uddalaka on what holds the world together and what rules it from within?
- Sakalya, on how many gods are there? Yagyavalkya says 3306 and progressively reduces the number to one. Then follows a discussion on what is that One God?

Finally Yagyavalkya asks a question: From what is man born? None is able to answer it. So Yagyavalkya gives the answer and walks away with the big prize.

The dialogues with Yagyavalkya contain some very profound statements. An illustrative example from each dialogue is reproduced hereunder.

One becomes good by good actions, bad by bad actions.
– Brhadaranyaka 3.2, 13

'You cannot see the seer of seeing,
You cannot hear the hearer of hearing,
You cannot think of the thinker of thinking
You cannot know the knower of knowledge.
He is your Self, which is in all things.
Everything else is perishable.'
– Brhadaranyaka 3.4, 2

'A knower of Brahman lives like a child, but with strength that comes from wisdom.'
– Brhadaranyaka 3.5, 1

'He is your Self, the Inner Controller, the Immortal. Everything else is perishable.'

— Brhadaranyaka 3.7, 23

'By this Imperishable, O Gargi, is space woven like warp and woof.'

— Brhadaranyaka 3.8, 11

'Sakalya: Which is the One God?
Yagyavalkya: The Cosmic Life Principle, Prana. He is Brahman. They call Him 'That' (tyat).'

— Brhadaranyaka 3.9, 9

'This Self is That which has been described as 'neti, neti; Not this, Not this'. It is imperceptible because It is never perceived. It is indestructible because It is never destroyed. It is unattached because It does not attach Itself. It is unfettered. It does not suffer. It is not injured.'

— Brhadaranyaka 3.9, 26

4. JANAKA: A KING OF GREAT VALOR AND WISDOM

Janaka was an ideal king. He was famous for his valor as well as wisdom. His subjects loved him. He also managed to find time for learned discussions with spiritual masters. Once he was having discussions with Yagyavalkya on what is God and what happens after death? The discussion then turned to that Light which illumines man from within – in all the three states of waking, dream and deep sleep – and which transmigrates to another body after death. Yagyavalkya explained that the Ultimate Light of man is Consciousness. Its nature is bliss. In state of deep sleep, It is beyond any perception of duality.

'Verily, when there is duality, then one might see the other, one might smell the other, one might hear the other, one might think of the other, one might touch the other, one might know the other.

In deep sleep, the non-dual Consciousness becomes one homogeneous mass, like water. This is the state of Brahman. This is his highest goal. This is his highest treasure, this is his highest world, this is his greatest bliss. Other creatures subsist just on a fraction of this bliss.'

— Brhadaranyaka 4.3, 31-32

And at the time of death, It departs as subtle *Jivatman*, which includes man's deeds and mind.

> *'Then the top of his heart becomes lighted up and by that light the Self departs either through the eye, or through the head, or through other apertures of the body. And when He thus departs, life departs after Him. And when life thus departs, all the senses depart after Him. He becomes one with Consciousness. Whatever has intelligence departs with Him. Dying man's knowledge and his work depart with Him, as also his past experience.'*
>
> – Brhadaranyaka 4.4, 2

5. RAIKVA: A CART-DRIVER WHO TAUGHT MEDITATION TO A KING

This conversation is between Janashruti and Raikva, a king and a cart-driver. It illustrates a technique of meditation on an object, with qualities of higher order superimposed on it. Here, Absolute *Brahman* is visualized as *Vayu* or Air at the cosmic level and as *Prana* or Life Force at the individual level.

To make the conversation interesting, it is preceded by an anecdote of two swans. They are talking about the wisdom of Raikva being so intense that its heat could scorch anything. Overhearing the conversation, Janashruti is anxious to know what sort of wisdom this cart-driver has? He locates him with difficulty, but Raikva is reluctant to part with his wisdom. Eventually, the king offers his daughter's hand in marriage. Raikva then teaches the technique of meditation, known as *Samvarga Vidya*.

> *'These, indeed are the two absorbers: Air at the macro level, and Life Force at the level of sense organs.'*
>
> – Chandogya 4.3, 4

There is another anecdote at the end of conversation. Two learned priests refuse to give food to a poor beggar-boy when they are enjoying a feast. The boy says that they have 'withheld food from Him for whom it is meant'. The dialogue then describes a different technique of meditation in which the object of meditation is raised by stages from the ordinary plane to the cosmic plane. Also, everything is seen to merge in its cause, which is called the 'eater of food'. The final eater is none other than *Purusha*, the Cosmic Person (Chandogya Upanishad 4.3, 7).

The story of Raikva also contains some important implied messages:

- A wise man can also be worldly man. Wisdom is not a monopoly of ascetics.
- We need both Wealth and Wisdom, as exemplified by both Raikva and Janashruti.
- Do not underestimate the wisdom of poor and/or young persons. Appearances can be deceptive.

6. SATYAKAMA: YOUNG BOY WHO DID NOT TRADE-OFF TRUTH FOR AMBITION

Satyakama was a young boy with a great ambition. He wanted to study spirituality under a renowned teacher, just as young boys and girls these days want to study at a top-ranked university. But there was a problem. Satyakama was an illegitimate and fatherless son of a serving girl; and prospective students were required to declare their family names before the teacher. So he asked his mother for his father's name. Without feeling least embarrassed, she said, 'I do not know who your father was. However, your name is Satyakama and my name is Jabala, so you may call yourself Satyakama Jabala'.

Thereafter, Satyakama approached Haridrumata Gautama for being accepted as his student. When asked about his family name, he could have simply said 'Satyakama Jabala', as advised by his mother. That would have been disguised truth. But Satyakama was not willing to compromise on his principles in pursuit of his ambitions. So he narrated verbatim what his mother had replied: 'I do not know who your father was. However, your name is Satyakama and my name is Jabala. So you may call yourself Satyakama Jabala.' The teacher, Gautama, was impressed by his truthfulness and also convinced that only one of noble birth could be so truthful. So he accepted him as his student.

One hurdle over, Satyakama was confronted with another surprise. After the initiation ceremony, his teacher selected 400 cows and asked Satyakama to look after them. He was to return back only after their number had increased to a thousand. But they were so old and weak that they were more likely to perish, than to multiply. Anyone else would have seen unfair motives behind such an assignment. Satyakama, however, had full faith in his teacher. He accepted the challenge.

While looking after the cows in the forest, Satyakama also marveled at the wonders of Nature. His truthfulness, devotion and hard work were duly rewarded. On four different days, he had four supernatural revelations about the 'four feet' of Absolute Consciousness, *Brahman*. The four feet are equivalents of Space, Matter, Energy and

Life Principle. Each of the four feet is again said to have 'four parts'. For example, in case of Life Principle:

'Prana is one part, the eye is one part, the ear is one part, and the mind is one part. This indeed, dear boy, is one foot of Brahman, consisting of four parts, named the Support.'
— Chandogya 4.8, 3

The number 'four' is used only as basis for a dialogue. The main theme of the dialogue is that everything that exists in the universe is a manifestation of One Absolute Consciousness, which the Upanishads call *Brahman*.

Gautama did not want to spoon-feed his student with knowledge about *Brahman*; he wanted Satyakama to acquire the same from Nature. So he sent him to the forest with 400 cows. When Satyakama returned to his teacher's hermitage, after the cows had multiplied to a thousand, the teacher noticed that his face was shining with a very distinct radiance. This was indicative of knowledge of the Absolute. The teacher had succeeded in his plan.

7. UPAKOSALA LEARNS THE TRUTH FROM FIRES

In due course, Satyakama himself became a renowned teacher. He had a student named Upakosala. Just as Satyakama learned about Truth from Nature, Upakosala's revelations came from three Fires. They told him,

'Life is Brahman, Happiness is Brahman, Space is Brahman'
— Chandogya 4.10, 4

In other words, God means a life of happiness.

Satyakama supplemented Upakosala's knowledge of *Brahman* in following words:

'He is the Self, Atman, He is Immortal and Fearless......... All things that are sought after proceed from Him....... He bestows all merits.......... He shines in all regions.'
— Chandogya 4.15, 1-4

8. SHVETAKETU LEARNS FROM HIS FATHER WHAT HIS TEACHERS DID NOT TEACH

Shvetaketu had studied scriptures for 12 long years at a *gurukul* – a boarding school of ancient times. When he returned back home, his father Uddalaka Aruni noticed certain arrogance in his behavior. This, he thought, was sign of shallow learning and not deep knowledge. So one day he engaged him in a conversation and asked: 'Do you know that by knowing which everything gets known?' 'What sort of knowledge is that? If there was anything like that, surely my teachers would have taught me', said Shvetaketu. Thereupon, Uddalaka explained to his son the knowledge of 'That' which is the ultimate cause of everything in the universe. He then made the startling revelation: 'That thou art'.

The significance of this eternal Truth is made comprehensible through as many as nine very appropriate metaphors, all drawn from Nature: a bird tied to a string, bees extracting honey from flowers, rivers merging in ocean, a tree exuding sap, a seed growing into a tree, salt dissolved in water, a blindfolded man left in an unknown place, a person on his deathbed, and a person on trial by ordeal. During the discourse, Shvetaketu is even made to fast for fifteen days.

The father-son dialogue in Chandogya Upanishad is the most famous of all Upanishadic dialogues. Its essence is contained in the under-mentioned passage, which the father repeats to his son as many as nine times.

> 'That Being which is the subtle essence of all,
> this world has That for its Self.
> That is the Truth. That is Atman.
> That Thou art, O Shvetaketu.'

– Chandogya 6.8–6.16

9. SĀNATKUMAR: A warlord who taught a sage, what is happiness?

This dialogue in Chandogya Upanishad between a young warlord and a senior sage-Sanatkumar and Narada – contains an excellent account of what makes a person feel happy? Interestingly, the young Sanatkumar is the teacher in this case. He says that there is no happiness in anything which is small, or finite. As soon as a person achieves a finite object of happiness, his mind realizes that there is something even greater than what has been achieved. So he starts his search for another object of happiness. As a result, every experience of happiness from finite objects is only momentary. There is true happiness in the Infinite alone. In the words of Sanatkumar:

> 'There is no happiness in anything finite.
> Infinite alone is happiness.'

– Chandogya 7.23, 1

Sanatkumar then describes what is that Infinite?

> *'That Infinite alone is below*
> *That is above. That is behind.*
> *That is in front. That is in the south.*
> *That is to the north. That alone is all this.'*
>
> – Chandogya 7.25, 1

The knowledge imparted by Sanatkumar is called *Bhuma Vidya*. A study of the text as well as the commentaries is strongly recommended for understanding the correct meaning of happiness.

10. MEDITATION ON INNER SELF

Meditation on inner Self is an important technique of meditation. It is described in chapter 8 of Chandogya Upanishad under *Dahara Vidya*, in the form of a dialogue between a seeker and a preceptor. The seeker is asked to imagine that the infinitely large universe is present in an infinitesimally small space within his heart; and that Self, *Atman* is seated in this space. It is this Self which should be meditated upon. Also, this Self is to be visualized as: *'free from evil, free from old age, free from death, free from sorrow, free from hunger, free from thirst. Its desire is Truth, Its resolve is Truth'* (Chandogya Upanishad 8.1, 5).

Rendition and commentaries on this section deal with meanings of the words 'true desires' and 'true resolve' – *Satyakama* and *Satya sankalpa'* – and how they are always fulfilled.

The more we go deeper and inward into our Self, the greater is the purity of our desires, as also the strength of our Will-power.

In our lives, there is often a conflict between external compulsions and inner voice. External compulsions are like commanders – the more dependent we make ourselves on them, the less is our freedom of action. However, the more we understand our inner Self, the more we are in harmony with the external world as well. In the words of Chandogya Upanishad:

> *'This Atman is in the heart. He who meditates thus, indeed, goes daily into the heavenly world ... For him, there is freedom to act as he wishes, in all the worlds.'*
>
> – Chandogya 8.3, 3 and 8.4, 3

9 Maxims on 'God and I'

WHAT IS GOD?

Over the ages, religious prophets and masters have pronounced many concepts of God. These occupy a wide spectrum of thought: mysterious forces of Nature; a far-away Almighty Power which must be worshipped and feared; a loving Father who sent his Son to earth to spread the message of love; a personal Deity; a Formless Creator, the Beneficent and the Merciful; the Unborn, Unformed and Uncreated who can be described only by a Noble Silence; and so on.

In modern times, our concept of God has two layers: an inner core which we inherit from the religious background of our families; and an outer covering which we acquire from our own interactions and observations. Also, in our daily life, we express our love of God and faith in God in many ways, which differ vastly from person to person. Broadly, these cover one or more of the following:

> WORK: We serve God by working hard and honestly in our profession, doing our duties sincerely, and contributing something to our society – be it wealth, skills or time.
>
> WORSHIP: We connect with God through regular or occasional participation in rituals, prayers or meditation.
>
> WISDOM: We come closer to God by knowing more about It through study of scriptures or listening to discourses of spiritual masters.

Clearly, the question 'What is God?' evokes innumerable answers. According to the Upanishads, all possible descriptions of God are correct, as each represents some aspect of It. However, no conceivable description of God can be considered complete, as God is Limitless. Describing It in words is like confining the Limitless to certain limits. In the language of mythology, even if the Goddess of Learning, Saraswati, used the water of all oceans as writing ink and all the trees on planet earth as writing instruments, she would be unable to write a complete description of God.

In the language of Vedas,

'Truth is One, but learned persons speak of It in different words'.

ONE GOD, MANY NAMES AND FORMS

The Upanishads recognize that God is beyond conceptualization by the mind and beyond description in words. Nonetheless, they make It the main theme of their enquiry. The question, 'What is God?' is raised in the Upanishads many times by persons of diverse profiles; and then discussed from different perspectives, leading to many descriptions of God. Some of these are summarized in Table-4 on pages 71-72.

God has been called by different names in different cultures and belief systems. The two Sanskrit words used most frequently in the Upanishads are *Brahman* and *Atman*. God and Soul are popular translations of *Brahman* and *Atman*. A more secular translation of these words is universal Self and individual Self. An important and recurring theme in the Upanishads is that universal Self and individual Self are One and same. Accordingly, the Upanishads use the words *Brahman* and *Atman* as synonymous; and both are translated here as Self.

WHO AM I?

We all live in two worlds: outer and inner

If you were to self-introduce yourself, what would you say? You will first state your name and then probably describe your work, your family, and those of your worldly achievements which you consider relevant to the occasion. All these establish your identity in the world outside you.

When you are alone in a relaxed and reflective mood, ask yourself the question: Who am I? Perhaps you will find yourself struggling with various possible answers.

Great teachers of mankind have always urged the need to 'Know yourself', which was first articulated in the West by a Greek Philosopher, Thales (625-545 BC). This was commendable, as the Greeks paid very little attention to inner life. They lived entirely in the world outside them. They loved beauty of Nature and of human form; and they glorified their gods more for their pleasure than for their spiritual satisfaction. Under the influence of Greek philosophy, Western societies were generally more concerned with achievements in the outer world than an understanding of Inner life. In an age of globalization, this Western trait has now spread almost all over the world.

Three thousand years ago, the Upanishadic seers foresaw that the mystery of the outer world would only deepen, and not diminish – in spite of advancing knowledge – if the mystery of the inner world of man is not resolved. There is need to have data from both the fields of experience – outer and inner.

The Upanishadic seers first realized that God is Consciousness:

'Consciousness is Brahman.'

- Aitareya Upanishad 3, 1

Their next realization was that this whole universe is a manifestation of God Itself. This is stated in maxims like:

'Verily, all this universe is Brahman.'

- Chandogya Upanishad 3.14, 1

'Verily, Lord pervades every thing.'

- Isa Upanishad 1

'All this is verily, Brahman.'

- Mandukya Upanishad 2.1, 2

'This, verily, is That.'

- Katha Upanishad 2.1, 5-15

Finally, the Upanishadic seers realized that the power which drives man from within is also God. Stately differently, One God drives both the outer and inner world of man. In the words of Mandukya Upanishad:

'This Atman is Brahman.'

- Mandukya Upanishad 2.1, 2

YOU AND I ARE GOD!

In a very famous dialogue in Chandogya Upanishad, a young man is very conceited about his study of scriptures. However, he is not able to answer a question to the effect: 'What is God?' After some explanations, his father makes a startling revelation:

'That thou art.'

- Chandogya Upanishad 6.8-6.16

The Upanishads frequently use the word 'That' for God.

The core or innermost essence of human personality is God Itself. This is one of the most fundamental propositions of the Upanishads. It is expressed repeatedly in aphorisms like:

'That I am.'

– Isa 16

'I am Brahman.'

– Brhadaranyaka Upanishad 1.4, 10

A few centuries later, this principle about the inherent potentialities of man was reaffirmed in Buddhism. Though Buddhist do not believe or disbelieve in God, they regard every person as an embryo of the Buddha, *tathagata garbha*. Every human being has a potential to become the Buddha.

The Upanishadic revelation about inherent divinity of man was stated again in a different era and place when Jesus Christ declared:

'The Kingdom of God is within you.' (Luke 17:21)

GOD IS HIDDEN FIVE LAYERS DEEP

New Age literature identifies Body-Mind-Soul as three elements of human personality. The ancient Upanishads declared that what a person calls 'I' is a composite of five 'Is'. In the language of Upanishads, a man has five selves, with one Self as their driver. Self with capital 'S' is used here synonymously with God. That Self is covered by five selves.

The five selves are: physical, vital, mental, spiritual and blissful.

Physical pleasures and material successes originate from the interaction of the first three layers with the outside world. A feeling of self-fulfillment and happiness flows from the last two layers of our inner life – spiritual and blissful. These are nourished by wisdom, and by practice of meditation. To some extent, mind overlaps between both the outer and the inner worlds.

Disharmony between the five selves of a person causes stress and anxiety. Inability to see oneness of Self in all beings causes tension and terror. However, when a person becomes aware of the oneness of his five selves and oneness of Self in all living beings, his understanding of the world undergoes a transformation. He discovers a different world. It is not the world which undergoes change, but his personality changes. He feels happy in whatever he does, and he radiates happiness to whosoever comes in contact with him.

COSMIC PERSON AND INNER SELF

According to the Upanishads, this universe of infinite forms has been created out of Formless Consciousness. Creator and His creation – Absolute Consciousness and relative universe – are inseparable.

Another important theme of the Upanishads is that just as the universe is an embodied form of Consciousness at macro level, man is Its embodied form at micro level. This point is emphasized by denoting Supreme Being by the word *Purusha*, translated as Cosmic Person; and by stating that It resides in an infinitesimally small space in man's heart.

Aitareya Upanishad describes the emergence of Cosmic Powers from Cosmic Person, and their descent in man. As a result, man is a mini-cosmos. Our sense-powers and mind have their cosmic counterparts. (Aitareya Upanishad 1.1-1.3).

Brhadaranyaka Upanishad states that Cosmic Person first produced Male-Female Principle, and this duality gave rise to multiplicity. It emphasizes the Oneness of man and Cosmic Person in a great aphorism : *'I am Brahman'*. (Brhadaranyaka Upanishad 1.4). Later, it elaborates upon the parallel existence of Life Principle – both at individual and cosmic levels (Brhadaranyaka Upanishad 1.5, 21-23).

Chandogya Upanishad uses the word *Vaisvanara* for Cosmic Person and discusses meditation on *Brahman* as Totality, under *Vaisvanara Vidya*. Six learned teachers approached a king, Ashvapati, for knowledge about *Atman-Brahman*. The king asked them one-by-one, what did they concentrate upon during meditation? Each gave a different answer: Heavens, Sun, Air, Space, Water, and Earth. The king pointed out that they were making a mistake. Whatever they were meditating upon was only a part of the whole Reality, and not the Reality in its totality. The objects of their meditation are like various limbs of the Cosmic Person. In meditation, one has to bring the parts together, and meditate on *Brahman* as Totality. (Chandogya Upanishad 5.11-5.18).

Similar mistakes are pointed out in Brhadaranyaka Upanishad by King Ajatashatru to Balaki Gargya (Brhadaranyaka Upanishad 2.1) and by Yagyavalkya to Sakalya (Brhadaranyaka Upanishad 3.9, 10-18).

Katha Upanishad describes Cosmic Person figuratively as, 'of the size of a thumb, residing in the body as the Lord of the past and the future, like a flame without smoke.' (Katha Upanishad 2.1, 12-13).

Mundaka Upanishad states that the universe is like the body of the Cosmic Person.

> *'Fire is His head; Sun and Moon His eyes, Space His ears; revealed Vedas His speech; Air His breath and the universe His heart. From His feet, Earth has originated. He is the inner Self of all.'*
>
> – Mundaka 2.1, 4

And again.

> *'That Supreme Being (Purusha) alone is all this – universe, work and willpower. O handsome youth, he who knows this Immortal Being as hidden in the secret caverns of the heart cuts asunder the knots of ignorance, even during this life on earth.'*
>
> – Mundaka 2.1, 10

The Cosmic Person is without any forms or attributes. However, He manifests Himself in many forms. Prasna Upanishad enumerates sixteen of these.

1	Life
2	Faith
3-7	Five primal elements, of which this beautiful universe is constituted – Space, Air, Light/Fire, Water and Earth.
8	Sense organs
9	Mind
10	Food
11	Sex
12	Self-discipline
13	Worship (*Mantra*)
14	Work
15	Wisdom (*Loka* or levels of Consciousness)
16	Name (a distinct identity).

In the Upanishad, the disciple asks the teacher, Pippalada: 'Where is that *Purusha* located?' Pippalada replies:

> *'My beloved son, That Being, Purusha, in whom originate these 16 parts, is right here, within the body.'*
>
> – Prasna 6, 2

Table-4

GOD: SOME ILLUSTRATIVE DESCRIPTIONS FROM THE UPANISHADS

Light of lights	Unattached	Truth	Happiness
Life of lives	Unfettered	Knowledge	Love
Mind of minds		Infinitude	
Truth of truths			Radiance
	Beyond suffering		
	Beyond injury	Existence	Effulgence
Beyond space		Consciousness	Foundation
Beyond time	Formless	Bliss	
Beyond causality	Eternal		Self-existent
	Omnipresent	Ultimate Reality	Self-created
Unborn	Omniscient	Totality	Self-effulgent
Unchanging	Omnipotent	One	
Undifferentiated			Absolute
Imperceptible	Immortal	Pure	Immanent
Incomprehensible	Fearless	Non-dual	Transcendent
Indestructible			True Desires
Imperishable			True Resolve

➢ That which has projected all this universe out of Itself, which sustain the universe, and into which the universe will eventually dissolve.
➢ That which keeps awake in man during states of waking, dream and deep sleep.
➢ The inmost essence of man – beyond the five layers of physical, vital, mental, spiritual and blissful self.
➢ Metaphorically, said to have four feet – external, internal, universal, and transcendental.
➢ Neither subject nor object. Beyond all dualities. That in which subject and object merge into one.
➢ Without any relative attributes or qualities like hunger, thirst, old age etc. This is expressed in the famous aphorism: '*Neti, Neti*, not this, not this.'
➢ Regulates all objects and phenomena in endless Space-Time, but is beyond Space and Time.
➢ Regulates Law of Cause and Effect, but is beyond all Causality.
➢ Not an object of sense perception, but is Itself the basis of all sense perception.
➢ Unmanifested, but cause of the manifested world.
➢ Cosmic string which holds the worlds together.
➢ Inner Controller. Regulates everything from within.
➢ He dwells in the mind, yet He is different from the mind and He controls the mind from within. So also for matter-energy, and life; in fact for all cosmic objects and phenomena.
➢ Seer who cannot be seen, Hearer who cannot be heard, Knower who cannot be known.
➢ Cosmic Person, Cosmic Consciousness, Cosmic Mind.

- State of Eternal and Infinite Bliss.
- Self in you, Self in me, Self in all existences – animate and inanimate.
- Eternal Truth, Ultimate Reality, Truth of truths.
- Pure and Absolute Consciousness. Ultimate constituent and support of Matter-Energy, Life and Mind; but different from Matter-Energy, Life and Mind.
- That in which contradictions co-exist. This is described in a language of paradox: It moves, It moves not; It is far and It is near; etc.
- Truth-Knowledge-Infinitude. This description of Supreme Being was later modified to Existence-Consciousness-Bliss, which is used very frequently in Vedanta literature.
- 'That'. Use of the word 'That' with a capital of 'T' for Absolute Supreme signifies that It cannot be confined to any name or description.
- It exists in the cavity of the heart and in the farthest space.
- *Brahman* is both with form and formless, mortal and immortal, limited and unlimited, perceptible and imperceptible.
- Everything that exists – the mind and the senses, cosmic powers, living beings or material objects – has Absolute Consciousness as its fundamental support as well as its impelling power. This Absolute Consciousness is the Ultimate Reality, the Transcendental Power, the Eternal Truth, the Supreme God.
- The five primal elements that constitute the inorganic world – Space, Air, Fire, Water, and Earth – have emanated from Absolute Consciousness. The organic world of vegetation and food evolved from the inorganic world. This was followed by emergence of Life, and then Mind. Man is the highest form of life, with a most developed mind.
- All living beings emerge from Absolute Consciousness and eventually dissolve into Absolute Consciousness – like sparks leaping from a blazing fire and leaping back into it. Each one of us embodies in some mysterious fashion a divine spark of Absolute Consciousness.
- Absolute Consciousness is both the instrumental cause and the material cause of the universe. Stated differently, It is both the First Cause and the First Principle of the universe. The Absolute has become relative. Cause has become effect. God has become universe.
- This universe of innumerable relative manifestations has emerged from the one unmanifested Absolute Consciousness. Rightly, the universe is called self-created and well-made.
- The whole universe is like footprints, which ultimately lead to Absolute Consciousness.
- The universe owes its elegance to all this diversity, which is only a manifestation of Absolute Consciousness.
- The Upanishads take our mind beyond the body-senses and beyond the cosmos to a state which cannot be described in words. So, the Upanishads describe it in negatives:

    'There the sun does not shine, nor the moon, nor the stars.... All these, shine in the reflected glory of the Absolute, so how can the relative illumine the Absolute?'

Part II

Ten Complete Principal Upanishads

Synopses, Translation and Commentaries

Upanishad of Rg Veda

    1. Aitareya Upanishad... *Origin of Man from Consciousness* 75

Upanishads of Yajur Veda

    2. Brhadaranyaka Upanishad... *God and I are One* 97

    3. Isa Upanishad... *Harmony of Opposites* 239

    4. Katha Upanishad... *Dialogue with Death* 259

    5. Taittiriya Upanishad... *Five layers of human personality* 295

Upanishads of Sama Veda

    6. Chandogya Upanishad... *That thou art* 333

    7. Kena Upanishad... *Evolution of Matter-Life-Mind* 471

Upanishads of Atharva Veda

    8. Mandukya Upanishad... *Three states of Consciousness* 495

    9. Mundaka Upanishad... *One Absolute behind every Relativity* 518

   10. Prasna Upanishad... *The Cosmic Person within us* 557

Aitareya Upanishad

Origin of Man from Consciousness

OVERVIEW

Aitareya Upanishad points to Oneness of philosophy and physics. It contains a great aphorism, a forethought of a 'Unified Field Theory' or a 'Theory of Everything', which modern physicists are trying to discover. It declares: 'Consciousness is Brahman'. It also provides an allegorical description of the creation of the universe – as also of man – from Consciousness.

It is to be noted that the Upanishads use the word Brahman for universal Consciousness and Atman for individual Consciousness. These two words embrace all possible concepts about 'God' and all known names of 'God' – without any contradiction whatsoever.

COMMENTARIES

The translated text has been supplemented with extracts adapted from commentaries by Sri Sankara (translated by Swami Gambhirananda), Swami Chinmayananda, Swami Sivananda, Swami Sarvananda, Dr. S. Radhakrishnan, N. A. Nikam and Rohit Mehta. These are followed by two general commentaries by Klaus G. Witz and Paul Deussen.

AITAREYA UPANISHAD
Origin of Man from Consciousness

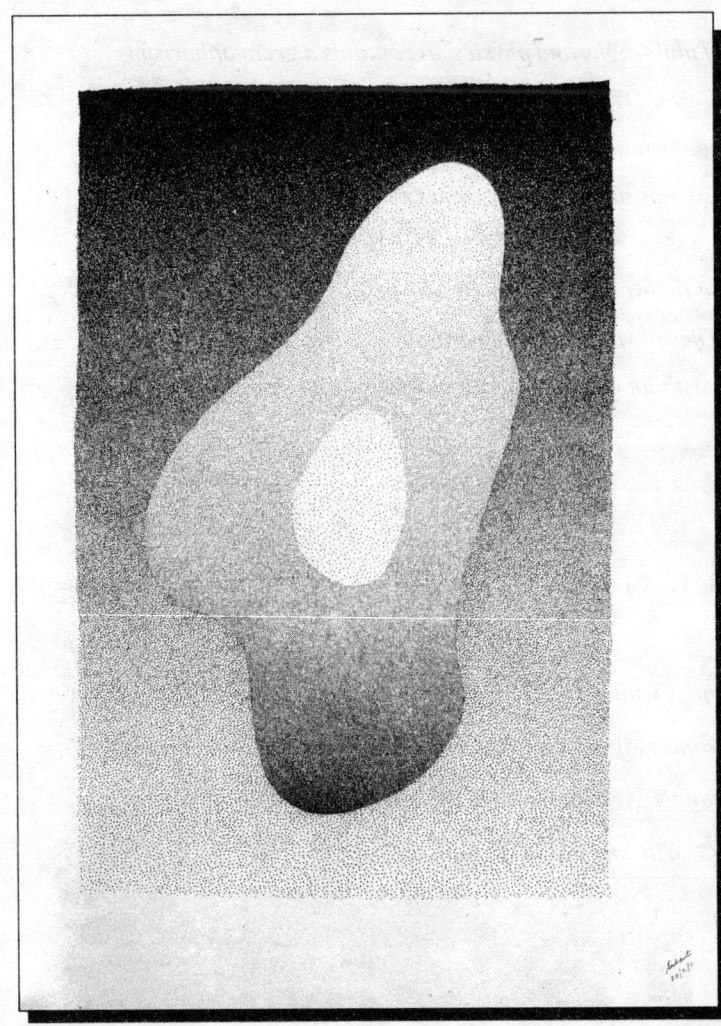

Peace Invocation

CHAPTER 1
Man is created from Consciousness
.... **77**

1.1	Creation of Cosmic Person and Cosmic Powers
1.2	Descent of Cosmic Powers in sense organs
1.3, 1-12	Descent of Consciousness in man
1.3, 13-14	An Enlightened Vision

CHAPTER 2
Continuity of Creation **88**

2.1, 1-4	Birth, son's birth and rebirth
2.1, 5-6	Prenatal knowledge of Self

CHAPTER 3
Consciousness is Absolute, *Brahman*
.... **92**

1 Man is Created from Consciousness

SIMPLIFIED SYNOPSES

As of today, Science does not recognize Consciousness as a factor in creation of the universe. However, Aitareya Upanishad identities Consciousness as the First Cause of creation – It created the universe and then entered into it. In fact, the Upanishad goes a step further and states that Consciousness continues to dwell in everything – animate or inanimate, gross or subtle, object or phenomenon, microcosm or macrocosm – as its guide and support.

1.1 Creation of Cosmic Person and Cosmic Powers

The story of creation in Aitareya Upanishad starts when there was nothing other than Consciousness, also called *Atman*. This One and Absolute Consciousness *willed* to create a world of multiplicity and relativity. Creation is a consequence of that Will Power (*tapas*).

First, there emerged four fields for the functioning of the universe. These have been identified here as the ocean beyond the heavens, the region of light, death in the form of earth, and primeval waters supporting the earth (1.1, 1-2).

'In the beginning, there was Absolute Consciousness (Atman) alone.'

Next, the Formless Consciousness created a universe of forms – metaphorically called *Purusha* or Cosmic Person in the Upanishads. It gradually evolved into various Cosmic Powers, called *devata* or deities. The Upanishad says: 'From mouth came out speech; from speech, fire; and likewise seven other deities.' The process of creation described here is analogous to the development of embryo in egg, or foetus in womb. The microcosm of man and macrocosm of cosmos follow an identical pattern.

The Cosmic Powers then fell into the world of plurality and change. (One commentator identifies this fall with force of gravity.) They were also inflicted with hunger and thirst. The deities then asked for an abode where they could live and grow. The allegory signifies a basic fact of life – desires want fulfillment. This applies to the whole of Creation.

1.2 Descent of Cosmic Powers in sense organs

The allegory continues. The Creator offered the Cosmic Powers a cow, a horse and finally a man as an abode for them. The Cosmic Powers accepted man as a masterpiece and entered into him through his various sense organs. The Upanishad says that Fire becoming speech entered the mouth, etc. It will be observed that the process of entry of any Cosmic Power into man is reverse of the process of its origin in the Cosmic Person.

'Man alone is a Masterpiece.'

The Upanishad gives eight illustrative examples of Cosmic Powers, which reside in man and empower his various organs of perception and action. These are tabulated hereunder:

Organ	Function	Presiding Deity
Mouth	Speech	Fire
Nostrils	Smell	Air
Eyes	Sight	Sun
Ears	Hearing	Space
Skin	Hair (Touch)	Plants
Heart	Mind	Moon
Navel	Out-breath	Death
Generative organ	Seed (Procreation)	Water

Seeing various deities occupy their allotted places in man, hunger and thirst also demanded an abode for themselves. Instead of assigning them an independent abode, the Creator asked them to share the abode with all the other deities. This signifies that desires afflict all the senses. Some commentators interpret this as a rationale for offerings in sacrificial rituals (1.2, 1-5).

After creating the fields for functioning of the universe and human beings – both empowered by cosmic forces – the third step in the creative process is said to be creation of food. Here the allegory of creation takes an interesting turn. Different senses urged by hunger and thirst run after food to catch it, like a cat running after a mouse. It is good that none of them was successful – that would have led to competition among the senses for fulfillment of their desires. Finally, food was caught by out-breath (called *Apana*), which is one of the five forms of life-breath. It regulates the digestive system (1.3, 1-10).

1.3, 1-12
Descent of Consciousness in man

'Then It (Atman) opened the suture of the skull and entered by that door.'

The incident of senses running after food made Consciousness think of the need for a unifying force in the body. So Consciousness or *Atman* Itself entered the body. Its entry from the suture in the skull points to Its being unmanifest and imperceptible. Its point of entry, *Vidriti* is considered to be the door of Bliss. The soul passing through it at death attains progressive liberation, *kramamukti*.

Consciousness pervades the whole body. However, by way of illustration, it is stated that It has three abodes and three states of existence. One interpretation is that It resides in the eyes during waking state, in the mind during dream state and in the heart during deep sleep (1.3, 11-12).

1.3, 13-14
An Enlightened Vision

'Self-realization is Self seeing Self.'

The allegorical narration now changes gears to a philosophical realization. Having descended in man, Consciousness (*Atman*) looked around to see if there was any other Principle different from Itself. And what did it see? It saw the same *Atman*, Self in all beings! It realized that this *Atman*, manifested as the Cosmic Person (*Purusha*), was in fact the all-pervading *Brahman*. The Self in man is nothing but Cosmic Consciousness. It is called Idandra – or Indra as a mark of respect. This denotes an object beyond the range of vision. The narration signifies realization by individual Self that the same *Brahman*, Cosmic Consciousness pervades in all beings.

Verses 1.3, 13-14 are the climax of the creation account in Chapter 1 of Aitareya Upanishad.

'Self in man is nothing but Cosmic Consciousness.'

TRANSLATED TEXT

Peace Invocation
Om.
May my speech be rooted in my mind.
May my mind be rooted in my speech.
O *Brahman*, reveal Thyself to me.
O Mind and Speech, enable me to grasp
 the Truth which the scriptures teach.
Let me not forget what I have learned.
Let me study day and night.
May I think Truth.
May I speak Truth.
May Truth protect me.
May Truth protect the teacher.
Protect me; protect the teacher, protect the teacher.

Om. Shanti. Shanti. Shanti.
Let there be Peace, Let there be Peace, Let there be Peace.

CHAPTER 1

Section 1

In the beginning, all this was Absolute Self (*Atman*) alone. There was nothing else whatsoever that winked. He (*Atman*) willed. "Let me create the worlds." **1**

He (*Atman*) created all these worlds (*loka*): Ambhah, Marichi, Maram and Apah. Ambhah is above the heavens, heaven is its support. Marichi is the sky. Maram is the earth. Apah is waters below the earth. **2**

He then reflected: "Here are the worlds. Let me now create guardians of the worlds." He then raised a Cosmic Person (*Purusha*) from the waters, and shaped It. **3**

Then He meditated (*tapas*) upon that lump. There burst forth in it a hole in the shape of a mouth, just as if it were an egg. From mouth came out speech; and from speech, Fire.

Then nostrils came forth; from nostrils, power of smell; and from power of smell, Air.

(Next) eyes were separated out; from eyes, sight emerged; and from sight, *Aditya,* the Sun.

(Next) ears burst forth; from ears, hearing; and from hearing, Space.

Then skin was separated out. From skin grew hair; and from hair, herbs and trees.

Then heart sprang up; from heart, the mind; and from mind, the Moon.

The navel came next; from navel, out-breath, *Apana*; and from *Apana*, Death.

"In the beginning, all this was Absolute Self (Atman) alone."

Finally, the generative organ burst forth; from it the seed; and from the seed, the Waters. **4**

Section 2

These gods (*Devatas*), so created, fell into the vast ocean-like world (*samsara*). Then He (*Atman*) induced hunger and thirst in them. They said to Him: "Find for us a place in which we may live and eat food." **1**

He (*Atman*) brought a cow to them. They said "Indeed, this is not good enough for us". He brought a horse to them. They said: "This is not good enough for us." **2**

Then He brought a man to them. They said: "Oh! Well done, indeed. Man alone is a masterpiece." He said to them: "Enter into your respective abodes." **3**

Fire becoming speech, entered the mouth. Air becoming smell, entered the nostrils. Sun becoming sight, entered the eyes. Space becoming hearing, entered the ears. Herbs and trees becoming hair, entered the skin. Moon becoming mind, entered the heart. Death becoming out-breath, entered the navel. Water becoming semen, entered the generative organ. **4**

Then hunger and thirst said to Him: "Find an abode for both of us as well." He replied: "I assign to both of you a place along with these gods and make you both share it with them." Therefore, when an offering is made to whatever god (senses), hunger and thirst become partakers of it. **5**

Section 3

He thought: Now, here are the worlds and their guardians. Let me now create food for them. **1**

He brooded over the waters; and from the waters so brooded over, sprang an organic form. Verily, the form so produced is food. **2**

The food so created tried to run away. He wished to catch it by speech, but He could not catch it by speech. If He had caught it by speech, then one would be satisfied by merely talking of food. **3**

He wished to catch it by in-breath (*Prana*, smell) but He could not catch it by smell. If He had caught it by smell, then one would be satisfied by merely smelling food. **4**

He wished to catch it by the eye, but He could not catch it by the eye. If He had caught it by the eye, then one would be satisfied by merely seeing food. **5**

He wished to catch it by the ears, but He could not catch it by the ears. If He had caught it by the ears, then one would be satisfied by merely hearing of food. **6**

He wished to catch it by the skin (touch), but He could not catch it by the skin. If He had caught it by the skin, one would be satisfied by merely touching food. **7**

"Fire becoming speech, entered the mouth."

He wished to catch it by the mind, but He could not catch it by the mind. If He had caught it by the mind, one would be satisfied by merely thinking of food. **8**

He wished to catch it by the generative organ, but He could not catch if by the generative organ. If He had caught it by the generative organ one would be satisfied merely by sex. **9**

Then He tried to catch it by out-breath (*Apana*), and He caught it. Therefore, *Apana* alone is that which digests food. Indeed, *Apana* is the main factor in support of life by food. **10**

He (Self, *Atman*) then thought: How can this frame (body and senses) exist apart from Me? So He pondered: By which of the two ways shall I enter it? He again thought: Speaking is done by speech, smelling by nose, seeing by eyes, hearing by ears, touching by skin, thinking by mind, eating by out-breath and sex by generative organ; where should I be? **11**

Then He opened the suture of the skull and entered by that door. This door is called *Vidriti*, cleft. It is, verily, the place of bliss. He (*Atman*) has three abodes and three conditions: waking, dream and sleep. This (eye) is one abode. This (mind) is another abode. This (heart) is the third abode. **12**

Thus born, He looked around upon other living beings. He wondered if He knew anyone else? But He saw the same *Purusha*, pervading in all as *Brahman*. "Oh, I have seen this", He said. **13**

Therefore, He is called Idandra. Idandra is verily His name. Though He is Idandra, they cryptically call Him Indra. The gods are fond of being called by indirect names. **14**

"How can this frame (body and senses) exist apart from Me?"

FOCUSSED COMMENTARIES

Peace Invocation

The disciples and the teacher chant a Peace Invocation before they commence study of any Upanishad. The invocation here is addressed to Truth and it invokes the grace of the Supreme. Also, it prays for perfect consistency between thought and expression, mind and speech.

Repetition of 'protect the teacher' at the end of the passage is to indicate the conclusion of the invocation.

After the prayer, both the teacher and the students chant in chorus 'Shanti, Shanti, Shanti' (three times) – to ward-off all possible obstacles.

CHAPTER 1

1.1 Creation of Cosmic Person and Cosmic Powers

Charles Darwin (1802-82) put forward his theory of evolution in the second half of 19th century. Even today science is discovering newer and newer facets about evolution.

All great religions of the world – like Hinduism, Buddhism and Christianity - have also had some theory of evolution – but in a form almost unintelligible to the common man. Moreover, it should not be forgotten that these have preceded Charles Darwin by many centuries. Also, Darwin's theory has no place for Consciousness. According to the Upanishads, Consciousness is both the material cause and the efficient cause of creation.

Aitareya Upanishad describes creation in a symbolic language. It says that in the beginning, there was nothing but Consciousness (*Atman*, Self), which Itself is self-created, *svayambhu* (1.1, 1). The self-creation of the spirit is a mystery – the greatest mystery in the whole universe. It is only when the inquirer is merged in the spirit, that he can know the secret of this great mystery. The mind of a man can know only that which has a beginning and that which has an end. *Atman* is eternal, without a beginning and without an end.

The Upanishad says that *Atman* first created a field into which it could project Itself. In fact, It created four fields – Ambhah, Marichi, Maram and Apah (1.1, 2). The first three symbolize the mental, the astral and the physical fields. The third field – the physical world – was filled with water, *Apah*. This allowed the seething mass of fire – which earth was at that time – to cool down.

Thus, the story of creation has three phases – creation of the field, preparation of the field and inhabiting of the field. The process of inhabiting the field began in water (1.1, 3). This is in accord with scientific discoveries made three millenniums later – that life appeared first in water.

Verse 1.1, 3 says that the spirit drew forth a Person (*Purusha*) from the primeval waters and then gave It a form. Here, the Person is not to be understood as a human being. *Purusha*, translated as the Cosmic Person, denotes life impulse. Here the Upanishad lays down a fundamental principle of creation, that *life precedes form*. First came the stirring of life; and then a form was created.

That the Person was not a human being is made clear in the next verse which refers to the egg-born (1.1, 4). In evolution, we see different methods of reproduction. The first is exemplified by the amoeba – a part of the body extends, separates and begins to live its own life. Then came the sweat-born, followed by the egg-born, and finally the womb-born.

Verse 1.1, 4 gives a very detailed description of how the various organs of the body appeared. The bursting forth of the egg took place because it was heated up. The spirit, by brooding over the form (*tapas*), gave it warmth, which caused it to burst.

Verse 1.2, 1 says that hunger and thirst were induced into these forms or senses, called gods in the Upanishads. They asked for a resting place where they could quench their hunger and thirst. In verse 1.2, 2, the cow and the horse provide a clear reference to the arrival of mammals on the evolutionary scene. It is a movement from egg-born to womb-born. Verse 1.2, 3 refers to the arrival of man, the *homo sapien*.

'Consciousness is both the material cause and the efficient cause of creation.'

The verse also says that the senses were asked to occupy appropriate places in the bodily organism of man. Scientific discoveries have now proved that evolutionary growth moves from the unicellular to multicellular, from homogeneous to heterogeneous, from simple to complex. In this movement, there takes place, a remarkable differentiation and specialization of functions. The Upanishad is speaking of this functional specialization when it speaks of *Agni* becoming speech and entering the mouth, *Vayu* becoming smell and entering nostrils, etc.

Then hunger and thirst cried out, saying: 'What about us? Where do we go?' The spirit asked them to occupy their places within the functional elements themselves – they were not to be separate from any of the functions. Hunger and thirst represent the urges that impel the functioning organism to act (1.2, 5).

Next, the spirit created food to feed the senses (1.3, 1-2), but an interesting situation arose. The different senses, urged by hunger and thirst, desired to grasp food by their own powers. If they had succeeded, then the sight of food, the hearing of the word 'food', touching of food, smelling of food, uttering the word 'food', or thinking about food would have been the means to satisfy hunger (1.3, 3-9). This would have satisfied the hunger of only those senses, which succeeded in catching the food. Man would have remained hungry even if he would have seen or smelled or touched food. At last, food was grasped by *Apana*; the vital breath operating in the lower regions of the body (1.3, 10). It is the function of *Apana* to process food, convert it into energy through the digestive system, and distribute it appropriately to various parts of the body. Thus, verses 1.3, 1-10 touch upon the differentiation and the specialization of bodily functions. Over the last three thousand years we have obviously gathered much more scientific information on this subject.

Differentiation and specialization require co-ordination. Without co-ordination each functional agency would do as it pleases, and no one would think of the entire body. The Spirit entered the body to provide this co-ordination (1.3, 11-12). The presence of the Spirit in the body is a unifying force, giving the bodily organism, a harmony, a synthesis. But it has a deeper meaning too. Verse 1.3, 12 says that the Spirit has three abodes, and three states. The three abodes are the eyes, the throat and the heart – these symbolize the visible, the invisible and the Intangible aspects of the Spirit respectively. The three states are: waking, dream and sleep.

The entry of the Spirit from the suture in the skull points to the fact that the Spirit is unmanifest and as such can only be felt by him who has the sensitivity to commune with the Unmanifest.

With the entry of the Spirit, which is another name here for *Brahman* and *Atman,* man becomes aware of *Brahman* in Its manifested forms (1.3, 13). A person of such awareness is called *Idandra* or *Indra*, says the Upanishad (1.3, 14).

— Rohit Mehta

The abrupt opening suggests a question about creation: How did creation begin? The seer starts his answer by stating that before the manifested creation came into existence, Self alone existed. It was all Consciousness alone... all-pervading and eternal. There was no other active principle or living entity at that time.

According to the Upanishadic philosophy, creation is without a beginning, *anadi*. This needs some explanation.

Time, as we know it, is an interval between two successive experiences. As long as we are in one homogeneous experience, mind does not think of time. For example, when we are asleep, we have no concept of time. Or, when we are absorbed deeply in any activity – like watching a movie or even meditation – we forget time. Therefore, time can express itself only in that mind which is engaged in multiple experiences, multiple fields of objects, multiple relationships.... or, a world of multiplicity, the creation itself. Thus, time also is a part of creation, a created factor.

If we state that the world was created on a certain day, say January 1, it will imply that there was no creation on the previous day, Dec. 31. This leads to the conclusion that on Dec. 31, 'time' was in existence, but not the 'created world'. This conclusion is certainly erroneous, because as explained earlier, time itself is a created factor.

'Presence of Spirit in the body is a unifying force, giving the bodily organism a harmony, a synthesis.'

One could say that creation was started in zero-year, on zero-date, at zero-hour, zero-minute, zero-second. In the language of the Upanishads, creation is declared to be without a beginning, *anadi*.

According to Vedic philosophy, creation and dissolution are continuous processes. Creation, *shrishti* is followed by dissolution, *pralaya*, which in turn is followed again by creation. The cycle goes on.

On dissolution of the cosmos, a bundle of unfulfilled desires (*vasana*) alone exist. In due course, these mature and express themselves as the next creation.

A child cannot be kept within the womb when pregnancy has matured to its full. When this happens, on its own the child quits the mother's womb and forces its way out. Similarly, mature *vasanas* push themselves out from the quiet infinitude of Consciousness and project themselves as a finite, created world of multiplicity. In the words of the Upanishad, Self (Cosmic Consciousness) thought: "Let me now create the worlds."

Cosmic Consciousness, working through the mass of *vasanas* – in which state the world was at the time of *pralaya*, dissolution – became a personality that is capable of willing and doing. It created conducive worlds, wherein all *vasanas* can find an efficient field to fulfil themselves.

The Sanskrit word for world is *loka*. However, *loka* has a wider connotation. It means a field for experiencing.

Ambhah means the area above the atmosphere; Marichi means atmosphere; Marah means the world of mortals, or Earth; and Apah implies the five elements below the earth, of which the most abundant is water.

Purusha, the created form, is not the first man, or the equivalent of Adam. It represents the totality of all gross forms, called *Virat* in Sanskrit.

The process of creation described here is analogous to the development of embryo in the egg, or foetus in the womb. What happens in the case of microcosm of man is supposed to take place in the macrocosm of *Virat Purusha*. *Virat Purusha* too has evolved out of waters, like foetus, which develops in the fluid in mother's womb. The various organs, senses and presiding deities of the senses develop in the same order as that of the child in a womb. In the evolution of foetus, the organs are the first to appear; then gradually the power of utilizing the organ (during what is called the 'quickening' stage); and finally the expression of the principle of Consciousness through all these senses and organs. The sequence in the evolution of *Virat Purusha* at the macro-cosmic level seems to be identical.

— *Swami Chinmayananda*

Atman is the first principle, the first cause. It is the absolute reality. It is derived from a root which means 'to obtain', 'to eat', 'to enjoy', and 'to pervade all'. It is eternal, pure, and free. It is birthless, ageless and immortal. It is all-powerful, all-knowing, all-pervading. It is without a second.

Before creation, the universe was one with *Atman*. It had no manifestations of name and form. It was denoted by the word *Atman* alone. Now it is denoted by many words, and also by the one word '*Atman*'. As an example, foams, bubbles and waves, which originate in an ocean, have different names and forms, but one substance - water. The idea of foam, bubble etc. remains merged in water before these become manifest from water, and are given names and forms. Foam, waves etc. are equivalent of the created world; water corresponds to *Atman*, Consciousness.

— *Swami Sivananda*

The worlds mentioned in the verse seem to reflect the popular beliefs of the ancient times.

— *Swami Sarvananda*

1.2 Descent of Cosmic Powers in sense organs

The word *devata* or *deva* is translated as 'deity'. In the Upanishads, however, this word is used frequently as per its etymological meaning, 'to illumine'. The illuminating power is generally referred to as *deva*, *devata or* the presiding deities of the senses.

Various deities like Fire, Air, Death etc. – enumerated in verse 1.1, 4 and described as presiding over the functions of various organs of the body – were created

---

'Foam and waves in ocean are equivalent of the created world; water corresponds to Atman, Consciousness.'

from Cosmic Person, *Virat Purusha*. Thereafter, they were thrown into the world of plurality and constant change, *samsara*. They were also subjected to hunger and thirst. Thus whipped up by these two impulses, they, as it were, approached the Creator and demanded separate havens for themselves.

Sense objects cannot give that texture of happiness to animals, as they give to man. An animal can instinctively repeat activities like eating, sheltering and breeding. However, a man alone can add aesthetic value to these activities and get from them a joy more subtle than mere satisfaction of the senses. For example, to an animal the Taj Mahal is only a shaded building to roam about or to rest; to a man like Tagore, it was 'a tear drop on the face of Eternity'.

Verses 1.1, 3-4 describe the creation of Cosmic Person (*Virat Purusha*), the totality of all gross forms conceived together as one structure. The concept of *Virat* is the concept of Totality. As long as there was the concept of Totality alone, sense organs did not need to find any sense objects other than *Virat*. However, as soon as the phenomenon of hunger and thirst was introduced, a pluralistic world became justified. (A man cannot satisfy his hunger by eating parts of his own body).

In verse 1.1, 4 we have a description of the elemental forces emerging from sense organs. In verse 1.2, 4 we have a description of these forces identifying themselves with sense organs, with a desire to enjoy. The main idea of the Rishi is to emphasize that man is nothing but *Virat Purusha*; microcosm and macrocosm are identical. A small piece of gold removed from a large block has the same qualities as the large block. Totality of the universe, *Virat*, is represented intrinsically in the individual. Man has the qualities and the power of the Cosmos.

— Swami Chinmayananda

The *devatas* prayed for separate bodies for their residence, as they were not satisfied in the body of *Virat Purusha*. "To eat food" means to perceive the objects which correspond to the senses.

Hunger and thirst are limitations of life. *Atman* has neither hunger nor thirst.

— Swami Sivananda

Samsara is often compared to an ocean. According to Sri Sankara, water in the ocean is like sorrow resulting from unfulfilled desires. Huge crocodiles in the ocean correspond to various types of suffering in the world. Like the ocean, it is difficult to cross over the mortal world to the realm of immortality. Yet, the ocean has in it the ship of wisdom, which can help us cross over the round of births and deaths.

The gods or cosmic deities – Fire, Air, Sun etc. – function in man as the impelling power behind the senses. They are both macro-cosmic and microcosmic. Originating from the all-inclusive Cosmic Person, *Virat Purusha*, the aggregate of everything, they prayed for separate existences. Thus, multiplicity was born from unity.

The reference to the form of cow and horse points to creation of animal life. These are devoid of higher intelligence and discrimination, and therefore inferior to human beings. The Upanishad says that having been created in the image of God, man is the masterpiece of creation.

The deities entered their respective body-organs. This means that organs of body function because of the indwelling cosmic powers; like eye and sight function because of the light of Sun. The relationship between the cosmic power and the senses is that of coexistence, not of cause and effect.

Hunger and thirst are possible only when they are associated with the gross body of a living being. By stating that hunger and thirst coexist with gods and not in *Virat Purusha*, it is suggested that the nature of *Purusha* as *Atman* is beyond the attributes of *samsara*, like hunger and thirst.

— Swami Sarvananda

1.3, 1-12 Descent of Consciousness in man

Critics and commentators consider this section as most confusing and the allegories in it most childish. However, it has a very deep meaning.

The various sense objects can function only when they are fed with nutrition that is drawn from digested food.

'Organs of body function because of the indwelling cosmic powers;
like eyes and sight function because of the light of Sun.'

Earlier, Self had brooded and produced the Cosmic Person (1.1, 3). He brooded (performed *tapas*, Willed) again, and produced food in the form of organic matter. Here, the term water is again representative of the five elements. Water is an important input or ingredient for all foods.

When food was created by the Lord, it was infected by desire for self-preservation. So it tried to runaway, like a beast of prey, from the reach of its devourers. The various faculties in man pursued it, but could not catch it. Verses 1.3, 1-9 are repeated only to emphasize that each sense organ and sense is a limited faculty, and each can enjoy only its corresponding objects – we cannot hear with eyes. According to the Upanishad, food was finally caught and consumed by out-breath through the cavity of mouth. Thus, Air is the supporter of life through the media of food.

Self, *Atman*, when performing vigorous activities as Life-Energy, is called *Prana*. In that sense, *Prana* is not different from *Atman*, but is an expression of the same Supreme.

The seer of the Upanishad wants the students to understand that the grosser power of action, *kriya shakti* entered by a lower gateway; while the power of knowledge, *gyana shakti* made its entry by the highest gateway.

The term 'entry' here should not be construed in its literal sense. We can enter a place only when we are not already there. We cannot enter a room in which we are now sitting. The Upanishad is only giving us the sequence of the development of a biological being: organs of senses, senses and their powers (gods), life force and Consciousness.

— *Swami Chinmayananda*

It is not possible to swallow food without the help of out-breath, *Apana*. *Apana* is the vital energy that works throughout the digestive organs. Hence, it is the seizer of food.

The point of entrance (crown of the head) can be easily felt in newborn babies. Also, one experiences a cooling sensation when it is anointed with oil.

— *Swami Sivananda*

The significance of these verses is that the body with all its senses would be meaningless and incapable of functioning without the intelligence principle, the Soul, to guide it from within.

A house built with different materials is meant for someone other than its constituent materials. Likewise, the body built with different organs must be for someone different from its constituent organs. This is one of the arguments adopted by the Sankhya school to prove the existence of *Purusha*, the principle of pure Consciousness. The body is composed of different modifications of *Prakriti*, or Matter. *Purusha* dwells in the body, but is quite different from the body.

Elsewhere, in Aitareyaranyaka (of which the Upanishad is an extension), it was stated that Life Principle (*Prana*) entered the body through the tip of the feet. Life Principle is a lower expression of *Atman*. The place from where *Prana* entered the body is not fit for entry by *Atman*, the Overlord. Therefore, *Atman* entered the body through the crown of the head. This is called *Brahmarandhra*, or *Gyana shakti*, or Knowledge Principle. This doorway by which a ray of the Supreme Being (*Paramatma*) entered the body and became *Jivatman*, is also called *Vidriti*. It is the door of Bliss. The soul passing through it at death attains progressive liberation, *kramamukti*.

Paramatma, which has entered the body as *Jivatman*, has three places of residence, and three states of Consciousness. According to Sri Sankara, in the waking state, It resides in the right eye; in the state of dream, It resides in the mind (throat according to some commentators); in the state of deep sleep, It resides in the heart.

Another interpretation is that the three abodes of *Atman* are the father's body, the mother's body and one's own body.

— *Swami Sarvananda*

The top-centre of the head is the highest centre of spiritual Consciousness. It is called *sahashra*, the thousand-petalled lotus.

— *S. Radhakrishnan*

'The top-centre of the head is the highest centre of spiritual Consciousness.'

1.3, 13-14 An Enlightened Vision

Verse 1.3, 13 if translated literally, appears very broken, with many emotional pauses. However, these seem to be deliberate. They are suggestive of the breathless ecstasy when one realizes the Self. When a state of Self-realization is described, the language is broken, stammering and halting.

The verse tries to describe the experience of Self when, having entered the physical body, It looked out upon the pluralistic world through the various sense organs, mind and intellect. All that It could perceive was Its own essential nature everywhere! So It cried out in ecstasy: "Oh! I have seen this!"

In the Upanishads, *Atman* or Self is indicated both by 'That' and 'this'. The term 'That' is used to indicate distance, to refer to something which is farther from us. The term 'this' describes something nearer to us.

Each of us is a prototype of the Cosmic Person that was created by Self and into which Self entered. If we look out into the world outside us – free from false identification with body, mind and intellect – we shall detect the same Consciousness, which is within us. We shall then sing the same song of wondrous ecstasy: "Oh, I have seen this, *idam-adarsam-iti.3*."

The figure '3' appearing after *iti* indicates prolongation of the sound of '*i*' to indicate deep deliberation.

In Self-realization, it is the Self seeing the Self.

— *Swami Chinmayananda*

Jivatman desired to see what other principle besides his own Self could be there in the world outside. He saw only the all-pervading *Atman-Brahman*, and expressed great wonder: "I have seen this!"

The substratum of this world is *Brahman*. The world is superimposed on *Brahman* due to ignorance. When ignorance is removed, one realizes that *Brahman* is the only Reality. *Brahman* is the all-pervading Consciousness.

Idandra literally means 'It-seeing'. Self saw the all-pervading *Brahman* directly as *Idam*. This *Brahman*, therefore, is *Idandra*. In the Vedic tradition, a senior person is not addressed directly by his personal name; he is addressed indirectly as *Pitaji* (father), *Mataji* (mother), *Swamiji* (holy person), etc. Therefore, *Brahman*, who is *Idandra*, is called by an indirect name, *Indra*, in prayer and worship.

— *Swami Sivananda*

Self (*Atman*), individualizing Itself as *Jiva*, enters the body as a king enters his own city. But *Jiva* forgets its original nature. When it awakens to the truth that it is essentially *Atman*, it perceives the essence of everything as identical to its own Self. The verse thus describe the state of Self-illumination.

When ignorance clouds the mind, dual cognition of subject and object based on relative consciousness appears to be the only truth. However, when the mind begins to scrutinize the nature of objects and the true meaning of their plurality, it realizes *Brahman* as the First Principle. This transformation of individual Consciousness into Cosmic Consciousness is called Self-realization. It is expressed by the phrase, "I have seen this!"

Sri Sankara points out that gods love to be referred to indirectly, to be behind the veil. There is also a custom in cultured societies not to call the father or the teacher by his personal name, but by some respectful title.

— *Swami Sarvananda*

Idandra means 'perceiver of this'. *Indra* is a word denoting an object beyond the range of vision.

— *S. Radhakrishnan*

'The substratum of this world is Brahman. Brahman is all-pervading Consciousness.'

② Continuity of Creation

SIMPLIFIED SYNOPSES

2.1, 1-4
Birth, son's birth and rebirth

'Child is father's own Self...'

Creation continues through procreation. A man is born, he gives birth to a son and he takes rebirth after death. This signifies that a person really has three births. The procreative fluid of a father is said to be the essence of his Self. The mother looks after it during pregnancy as her own Self. After birth, the parents nourish the child so that he can be their substitute for performance of pious deeds. Verses 2.1, 1-4 also bring out the importance of natal care and emphasize the oneness of father and son.

2.1, 5-6
Pre-natal knowledge of Self

'A hundred iron citadels held me down; yet, I burst out of it with the swiftness of a hawk...'

The central theme of creation account in Chapter 1 was the presence of Self in all of us. However we remain ignorant of Its presence due to our preoccupation with desires of the senses. Verses 2.1, 5-6 cite the example of a sage, Vamadeva who realized Self even while he was in the womb, and thereby became immortal after the death of his body. The verses compare worldly desires to iron citadels preventing the soul from making itself free. Only a Self-realized person like Vamadeva can burst out of the citadel, like a hawk.

Translated Text

(Pregnant women please leave for some time)

In man, this (*Jiva*) first becomes what is called semen. It contains the strength extracted from all the limbs. Man holds this essence of his Self in his own body. When he casts this in a woman, he procreates himself. This is one's first birth. **1**

This (semen) becomes one with the woman, like a limb of her own. Therefore, it (foetus) does not produce any suffering for her. She nourishes man's Self which has come into her. **2**

As she becomes the nourisher of his Self within her, she should also be nourished. The mother bears the foetus in her womb. The father nourishes the child before and after its birth. While doing so, he is nourishing his own Self for the continuation of these worlds. Thus, these worlds are perpetuated by progeny. This is one's second birth. **3**

That child, who is the father's own Self, is made his substitute for performing pious deeds. Then Self of the father departs after having accomplished its work and having reached ripe age. After departing from here, verily, he is born again. That is one's third birth. **4**

This fact has been stated by a Rishi:

"While I was in the womb, I knew all the births of the gods. A hundred iron citadels held me down; yet, I burst out of it with the swiftness of a hawk." Vamadeva spoke this verse even when he was in the womb. **5**

Knowing Self, he (Vamadeva) ascended upwards after the dissolution of the body. He fulfilled all his desires in the heavenly world and became immortal. Yes, immortal. **6**

(Pregnant women, please take back your seats).

"A person has three births - his or her own birth, birth of a child and rebirth after death."..... (Adapted)

Focussed Commentaries

CHAPTER 2

2.1, 1-4 Birth, son's birth and rebirth

This section puts forward a view that through the process of procreation, a father becomes his own son. Pre-natal, natal and postnatal conditions of a transmigrating *Jiva* are also described in this section.

The section starts with an instruction: "Pregnant women please vacate". This suggests that in ancient times women enjoyed equal privilege with man in study of scriptures. In this particular case, only pregnant women - and not all women – are being asked to retire for a short duration and avoid listening to certain verses, which explain the various stages of a child's birth from conception to delivery. The Rishi thought that these verses may arouse sexual thoughts and thereby have an adverse effect on the mind of the child in the womb.

Procreative fluid is nothing but a miniature of oneself. When it is poured into the womb of a woman, there emerges an infant out of oneself. In this sense we may say that conception is the first birth of an individual.

The mother nourishes the child, not only physically but also mentally. Since the child in the womb is nothing other than its father's essence, the father must feel a great debt of gratitude to the mother for nourishing his Self in her womb and give birth to it as his child. This is the sacred basis upon which the sanctity of marriage is to be recognized. In Vedic scriptures, marriage is not a civil contract, but a sacred sacramental tie.

After conception of the child, its birth is the second stage in the metamorphosis of the father. The father expresses and re-lives himself in the son.

After death, the departed *Jiva* again seeks birth in another suitable form. This rebirth is the third birth.

— *Swami Chinmayananda*

Self (*Jiva*) first becomes semen in man. The first birth of *Jiva* is in man, in the body of the father. Explaining the process of conception, the scriptures declare: This *Atman* (man) offers that *Atman* (semen) to that *Atman* (woman). When *Jiva* leaves the mother's womb as son, he takes his second birth. Rebirth of the father after his death is the son's third birth. This is difficult to accept, because the identity between the son and the father has already been spoken of. It is intended to mean that the son and the father are one and the same.

— *Swami Sivananda*

Identification of father's soul with son and vice-versa is not to be taken as a philosophical truth. It is based on rather a lose conception of life which continues through procreation.

— *Swami Sarvananda*

For the transmigrating soul, the first birth is in the form of semen from the father. The second birth is in relation to the delivery from mother's womb. Rebirth of the dead father is enumerated as the third birth of the son. The intention here is to emphasize the oneness of the father and the son. In due course, the son also departs, assigning responsibility to his own son.

— *Swami Gambhirananda*

The three births refer to the three states of waking, dream and deep sleep.

— *Rohit Mehta*

The Upanishad says that "birth" of a son to a father is "rebirth" of father in the son. It is the continuity of father in the son. Creation is continuity. While the father is born in the son, the world is born in God.

— *N. A. Nikam*

2.1, 5-6 Pre-natal knowledge of Self

Through the effect of self-purification and meditation in previous lives, sage Vamadeva was suddenly illumined while he was still in the womb. He realized that even gods like *Surya* (Sun) and *Agni* (Fire)

'In Vedic scriptures, marriage is not a civil contract, but a sacred sacramental tie.'

undergo several births (as described earlier in Chapter 1 of this Upanishad); and *Atman* alone is beyond the cycle of birth and death. He broke through his citadel - like body through the power of Self-knowledge, and attained immortality.

— *Swami Sarvananda*

In Vedic mythology, there are many examples of a child acquiring specialized knowledge while still in mother's womb. In Mahabharata, Arjuna once narrated to his pregnant wife the secret art of penetrating certain war-formation, *Chakravyuh*. In the process, the child in her womb (later named Abhimanyu) gained this knowledge. Unfortunately, the mother fell asleep midway during the narration, so Abhimanyu's knowledge remained incomplete. Later, as a young hero, he used the knowledge acquired in the womb to successfully penetrate his opponent's war-formation. But as his knowledge was incomplete, he could not come out of the formation and was killed, fighting bravely.

If such mythological accounts have some truth in them, they suggest the possibility of pre-natal education.

— *Editor*

Here, at the end of this section, we again have the instruction requesting pregnant women to reassemble to listen to the next section.

— *Swami Chinmayananda*

'Atman alone is beyond the cycle of birth and death.'

[3] Consciousness is Supreme Oneness

SIMPLIFIED SYNOPSES

3.1
Consciousness is Absolute, *Brahman*

It all started with Consciousness, *Atman*. *Atman* projected the universe out of It and then entered into it. It looked around and found that everything is pervaded by It. Earlier, it has been stated that this *Atman* is nothing but Consciousness. But *Atman* and *Brahman* are one and the same. It follows that Consciousness is *Brahman*. This great saying is contained in verse 3.1,3 of Aitareya Upanishad.

'Consciousness is Brahman.'

Start of the Chapter suggests some participants in a discussion, raising doubts as to which of the 'two' should be meditated upon as *Atman*? It is not clear what this 'two' refers to? The reference could be to Life-breath and Self, or to the manifested self and the unmanifested Self, or the individual Self and the universal Self. The text that follows implies that such doubts are of no consequence. Everything that exists – mind, senses, Cosmic Powers, living beings or material objects – has Consciousness as its fundamental basis, as well as its inner power. Verses 3.1, 2-3 contain many illustrative examples. The text concludes that the whole universe is guided by Consciousness and supported by Consciousness. So Consciousness must be the Ultimate Reality, the Transcendental Power, the Absolute Truth, the Supreme God. In the words of Aitareya Upanishad, Consciousness is *Brahman*, the Absolute.

Translated Text

CHAPTER 3

Section 1

Who is He upon whom we meditate as *Atman* (Self)? Which of the two is He? Is He that by which one sees forms, hears sound, smells odor, articulates speech, and discriminates between what is tasteful and what is not? **1**

He is this heart (intellect) and mind that were mentioned earlier. Sentience, power, perception, direction, understanding, knowledge, retentive power, vision, firmness, power of reflection, freedom of thinking, mental depression, memory, recollection, determination, vitality, desire, love, and the like – all these are but names of Consciousness (*Pragyan*). **2**

This very Consciousness is *Brahma*, *Indra*, *Prajapati*, all the gods, the five primeval elements viz. Earth, Water, Air, Fire and Space. All living creatures, viz. the egg-born, womb-born, sweat-born, and earth-born (plants, trees); horses, cattle, elephants, men, and whatever living beings are there, including those that walk and those that fly and objects that do not move. All these are impelled by Consciousness and rooted in Consciousness. The universe is guided by Consciousness and supported by Consciousness. **Consciousness (*Pragyan*) is Brahman**. **3**

He who has realized this *Atman* as Consciousness, ascends upwards after dissolution of the body. He fulfils all his desires in the heavenly world and becomes immortal. Yes, immortal. **4**

"The universe is guided by Consciousness and supported by Consciousness."

Focussed Commentaries

CHAPTER 3

3-1, 1-4 Consciousness

The Upanishad has provided us with an understanding of how the Cosmic Person (*Virat Purusha*) arose from *Brahman-Atman*; and how due to hunger and thirst in the senses, there arose multiplicity of beings from one Cosmic Person. In this section, the Upanishad provides us with an understanding of what is *Brahman-Atman*?

Atman working through its conditioning is called conditioned *Atman*, or *Jiva*. Absolute Truth is the unconditioned *Atman*. The light in the bulb is the equivalent of conditioned *Atman*; the energy which we call electricity, corresponds to Absolute Truth, unconditioned *Atman*. Self with a capital 'S' is the English word used to denote *Atman*.

Which of the two is He? This indicates a choice between the Universal Self (*Brahman*) and the individual Self (*Atman*). Both are one and the same. *Brahman* = *Atman*.

Pure Consciousness is another name for *Atman*. It is Pure Consciousness, which illuminates the activities of the sense organs, as enumerated in verse-1. Verse-2 enumerates some of the many mental states and emotions which arise when Pure Consciousness plays on the mind. Thought, impulse, memory etc. are nothing but Consciousness; like different types of ornaments are nothing but gold.

Consciousness is the fundamental basis of not just internal faculties – the senses and the mind – but It is also the basis of various objects that constitute the world outside. Verse-3 contains a long list of many illustrative examples covering a wide spectrum – from the highest gods to inanimate objects.

When water is poured in ten bottles of different shapes and colors, it assumes corresponding shapes and colors. However, irrespective of the size and the shape of the bottles, water in all of them is one and the same. Consciousness also remains the same in all the existences of the universe.

Verse-3 contains one of the four great sentences, *Mahavakyas*, of Upanishadic philosophy: Consciousness is *Brahman*, *Pragyanam Brahma*.

— *Swami Chinmayananda*

Brahman is called by different names depending upon the context. It becomes *Hiranyagarbha* when it is identified as cosmic mind, which is the seed of all the manifested world. It is called *Virat*, and also *Prajapati*, when It comes forth from the cosmic egg with a cosmic body. It becomes a *Devata* – Sun, Air, Fire etc. – when It illumines any of the senses in human beings. From *Hiranyagarbha* down to the smallest worm, *Brahman* acquires several names, depending upon its limiting conditions.

Aitareya Upanishad begins with the text 'In the beginning all this was verily *Atman* (Self) alone. It concludes with the text 'Consciousness is *Brahman*.'

— *Swami Sivananda*

Some of us think that our soul, *Atman* is nothing but the aggregate of the senses and the mind. This is not correct. *Atman* must be permanent and unchanging. Therefore, It cannot have a variable element as an integral part of Its being. The mind and the senses are changeable, hence they can never be a part of immutable *Atman*. *Atman*, however, illumines the mind and the senses and stands behind them.

Verse-3 describes beautifully the relationship between the universe and the Supreme Reality called *Brahman*, or the Principle of Consciousness. It says, 'Consciousness is *Brahman*'.

— *Swami Sarvananda*

'The light in the bulb is the equivalent of conditioned Atman; the energy which we call electricity, corresponds to Absolute Truth, unconditioned Atman.'

General Commentaries By Klaus G. Witz And Paul Deussen

CREATION ACCOUNT

Aitareya Upanishad has three chapters. Chapter 1 is a creation account. Chapter 2 teaches that a man has three births – one in his mother's womb, one in his son and one in his next life. Chapter 3 is a high-level text culminating in the great saying 'Consciousness is Brahman'.

The main theme of the Upanishad is that there was a Self, *Purusha*, before any creation.

What is called *Purusha* in verse 1.1, 3 is really an undifferentiated mass of Consciousness out of which arose all aspects of the universe. *Atman* shaped *Purusha* or Cosmic Person – Its limbs and organs – and then willed that cosmic powers (called deities) develop from It and be associate with It. Finally, in verse 1.2, 1-4 an individual man – a new principle which is well-made – is motivated and introduced. The universal deities enter into this man, thus demonstrating graphically their concrete participation in the individual, and in their own individualization.

The fact, that hunger and thirst afflicted the *Purusha* and the deities that arose from It, shows a basic fact of life – desires want fulfillment. It applies to the whole of creation.

HIGH-LEVEL REALIZATION

Atman, having been born in an individual person, looks at all beings and sees all as Himself. "What else would one desire to speak?", He says; in view of the fact that He, *Atman*, is all beings. Alternatively, the exclamation may be translated: "What other Self would one desire to proclaim?", since He has entered all beings. "I have seen this," He goes on. He also gives Himself a name, which signifies the individual Self. Verse 1.3,13 plays a double role: It is the climax of the creation account and it signifies a state of high-level realization. All that *Atman* sees is One Self in all beings. There is nothing else to see, nor any other entity to proclaim. Seeing only Oneself in all beings, and seeing all as *Brahman* is high-level realization.

Finally, having entered a person, *Atman* has three dwelling places corresponding to three states of Consciousness. Sri Sankara suggests that these are: the right eye corresponding to waking state, the mind corresponding to dream, and the space within the heart corresponding to deep sleep.

ATMAN IS THE ONLY REALITY

It appears Chapter 1 aims to teach knowledge of Reality and uses the form of creation account largely as an outward garb. In effect the text is saying: "Look, here is the Divine world framework, here is the principle of individualization, here are the basic facts of life, and this is the paradigm for becoming aware of the whole construction. You, having entered in this construction of yours, see this now as it really is". The fact that at every stage *Atman* creates and directs everything means that all these creations and processes are of a lower order compared to *Atman* Itself. They are mere effects, forms; the basic reality is *Atman*. By constantly repeating "*Atman* created such and such," "*Atman* did or supervised such and such", "*Atman* caused such and such to happen" – the text points to a single Transcendental Power. This Power, *Atman*, is the only Reality. It is what one really is. All other ingredients of the world are effects of It.

— *Klaus G. Witz*

WORLD AND MAN ARE CREATIONS OF *ATMAN*

In the beginning *Atman* alone exists. It resolves to create the world. First it creates four spheres: flood of heavenly ocean, the light-atom of aerial space, earth as 'death' and primeval water serving as base for the whole structure below the earth.

Next, *Atman* creates eight world guardians. They fall back in the fluctuating waves of primeval waters. The Creator exposes them to two evil powers – hunger and thirst. Afflicted by these, the world guardians ask for an abode. The Creator offers them a cow, then a horse and finally a man. The world guardians enter into man through his various sense organs. Here they can receive nutrition only because they allowed hunger and thirst to share their abode. Therefore, hunger and

---

'Seeing only Oneself in all beings, and seeing all as Brahman is high-level realization.'

thirst have their share in every sacrifice offered to gods (senses).

Next, *Atman* creates a third entity – food. This food seeks to run away from the senses – as a mouse from the cat – until it is finally caught by out-breath, which regulates the digestive system.

Finally, *Atman* enters into man through the cleft. It has three places of residence in man (senses, mind and heart) and three states (waking, dream and deep sleep). It looks around at all beings and finds that among them there is no one whom It could designate as 'other' or different from Itself. All men are *Brahman*.

This presentation is closely connected with the *Purusha* hymn of *Rg Veda* (10.90).

— *Paul Deussen*

---

*'Atman has three places of residence in man (senses, mind and heart)
and three states (waking, dream and deep sleep).'*

Brhadaranyaka Upanishad

God and I are One

OVERVIEW

Brhadaranyaka Upanishad contains a great aphorism which asserts the inherent divinity of man. It declares: 'I am Brahman'.

The Upanishad is divided in six long chapters. These cover many important subjects, memorable maxims and famous dialogues. For example:

- The prayer, 'Lead me from Untruth to Truth'.
- Definitions of Brahman as 'Truth of truths', 'Light of lights', 'Inner Controller', 'Not this, not this, neti, neti'.
- A husband-wife dialogue on what creates and sustains love?
- At death, what dies and what does not die?
- Doctrine of Transmigration.
- Oneness of God and universe, as also of God and man.
- Meditation on the famous Gayatri Mantra.

COMMENTARIES

Commentaries on Brhadaranyaka Upanishad are very few and not easily comprehensible. The main commentators quoted here are Swami Sivananda, Dr. S. Radhakrishnan and Paul Deussen. There are also a few references to commentary by Sri Sankara, as translated by Swami Madhavananda.

BRHADARANYAKA UPANISHAD
God and I are One

Peace Invocation

CHAPTER 1
Who am I? 97

1.1-1.2	Self-mastery and self-sacrifice
1.3	Lead me from untruth to Truth
1.4	I am *Brahman*, all this Totality
1.5, 1-13	Seven kinds of food
1.5, 14-15	Two aspects of Creation: Variable and Constant
1.5, 16-20	Son's role in spiritual life
1.5, 21-23	Superiority of Life Principle: Cosmic and Individual
1.6	World is a triad: Name, Form and Work

CHAPTER 2
What is Love? 121

2.1	Incomplete definitions of *Brahman*
2.2	Meditation on *Prana*
2.3	Two profound descriptions of *Brahman*
2.4	Love means to see one Self in two bodies
2.5	*Madhu Vidya* or Honey doctrine
2.6	Lineage of teachers

CHAPTER 3	WHAT IS *BRAHMAN*? 143
3.1	Benefits of sacrificial rituals
3.2	Name and deeds survive death
3.3	Where do good deeds lead to?
3.4	*Brahman* is that which breathes in you
3.5	*Brahman* is beyond relative attributes
3.6	*Brahman* is woven like warp and woof
3.7	*Brahman*, the inner controller
3.8	Imperishable *Brahman*
3.9, 1-9	Many gods but one *Brahman*
3.9, 10-18	Incomplete definitions of *Brahman*
3.9, 19-20	Space, Mind and Self
3.9, 27-28	Man compared to a tree

CHAPTER 4	TRANSMIGRATION AND SELF-REALIZATION 175
4.1	Incomplete definitions of *Brahman*
4.2	Journey beyond death
4.3,	Ultimate Light and Its three states
4.4, 1-9	Transmigration of the Soul
4.4, 10-15	Self-realization
4.4, 16-25	What is *Brahman*?
4.5	Love means to see one Self in two bodies
4.6	Lineage of teachers

CHAPTER 5	OBJECTS OF MEDITATION 204
5.1	That, this and *Aum*
5.2	Three principal virtues: *da, da, da*
5.3-5.9	Meditation on *Brahman*
5.10	Journey after death
5.11	Illness and death are austerities
5.12	Food and Life-breath
5.13	Meditation on life-breath
5.14	The sacred *Gayatri Mantra*
5.15	The last prayer

CHAPTER 6	BIRTH FOLLOWS DEATH 218
6.1	*Prana*: Parable on its superiority
6.2	Five cosmic fires, two paths
6.3	*Mantha* rite for prosperity and harmony
6.4	Procreation ceremonies
6.5	Lineage of teachers

1 Who am I?

SIMPLIFIED SYNOPSES

1.1-1.2
Self-mastery and self-sacrifice

In ancient times, performance of *Ashvamedha Yagya* – sacrifice of a horse – signified sovereignty over the world. Here, the ritual is considered to be symbolic of a very profound thought – conquest of self (ego), followed by sacrifice of self-interest.

In section 1, different objects and phenomena of the universe are compared to various limbs and actions of a horse.

'The universe is like the cosmic body of Self.'

Section 2 contains a description of creation of the universe. Before creation, there was nothing except Death, the unmanifested aspect of Life Principle. Mind was the first to emerge. Water was the next, and from Water came forth Earth. This was followed by manifestation of Life Principle. Both Death and Life Principle then divided themselves threefold into Sun, Fire and Air. Then followed creation of speech, union of speech with mind and creation of time. The universe that emerged thereafter is like the cosmic body of Self (*Atman*). An important fact explained graphically in Section 2 is that everything in the universe is mortal – a food for Death (1.2, 5).

The section concludes with an analogy between *Ashvamedha* ritual and self-sacrifice. The Creator created a cosmic body out of Himself through austerities and meditation (*tapas*). Thereafter, He offered it as an oblation to Himself. A horse is a symbol of that cosmic body. The implied message is that one should gain self-mastery by developing a spirit of sacrificing self-interest.

1.3
Lead me from untruth to Truth

This section describes the perennial struggle between good and evil – represented by *deva* and *asura*, or gods and demons. *Deva* (lit. shining ones) wanted to surpass *asura* in sacrifice. For this they made use of *Udgitha* – a sacred song beginning with Om and appearing in the second chapter of Sama Veda.

'Evil coexists with good.'

The gods asked the sense organs – speech, smell, eye, ear and mind – to 'sing' (concentrate on) *Udgitha*; and they all did so one-by-one. However, every time the demons struck the sense organ with sin. This is why evil coexists with good.

Finally, the gods asked *Prana*, life force to sing *Udgitha*. The demons again tried to inflict life force with evil. This time, however, the demons were destroyed like a clod of earth striking against a rock. Thus, life force – the power behind the senses – is untainted by evil. Life force or *Prana* alone could restore divinity to sense organs, and keep them active – away from death. In fact, *Prana* took the sense organs to a higher cosmic level, and beyond. Thus, speech corresponds to Fire, smell to Air, sight to Sun, hearing to Space, and mind to Moon.

> 'A leader protects and nourishes those who are dependent on him.'

The text also states that life force secured nourishment for itself - and through it for all the sense organs - by singing *Udgitha*.

Verse 1.3,18 suggests that we should imbibe leadership qualities like those of life force – protecting and nourishing those who are dependent on us.

Verses 1.3, 19-20 are in praise of *Prana*, life force. Singing of *Udgitha* requires speech, and speech is dependent on *Prana*. So *Prana* is *Udgitha*. He who can sing *Udgitha* well and correctly is duly rewarded.

The concluding verse 1.3,28 contains the famous hymn called *Pavamana mantra*:

Asato ma sad gamaya
Tamso ma jyotir gamaya
Mrityorma amratam gamaya.

"Lead me from untruth to Truth,
 from darkness to Light,
 from death to Immortality".

1.4 I am *Brahman*, all this Totality

In the beginning there was only Self. It was alone, undifferentiated and unmanifested. It is called *Purusha*, the Cosmic Person. The word 'I' was born when *Purusha* became conscious of Himself.

Purusha was not happy being alone. So He projected out of Himself a pair – the male principle and the female principle. This was the beginning of the universe of living beings. Urge to reproduce is a cosmic urge.

> 'That Self which is the Totality of the whole universe is also the Self in me.'

The entire creation is Self, the Cosmic Person Himself. The food that we eat and the energy that is derived from it is also He alone. He made the universe differentiated by name and form. He entered all these differentiated entities of the universe – up to the tips of their nails – like a razor in a razor case, like fire in a source of fire. He is the Person that breathes, sees, speaks, hears and thinks. He is the Self that should be meditated upon as Totality. Everything becomes One in Him. This whole universe is like footprints which ultimately lead to Him alone (1.4, 1-7).

That Self which is the whole universe is also the Self in me. Therefore I am all this Totality, Brahman, *Aham Brahmasmiti*. This is one of the four great sayings, *Mahavakya* of the Upanishads (1.4, 10).

The universe owes its elegance to its diversity. This diversity was also created by Him (Cosmic Person). For example, He created the four vocational orders in society – *Brahmins* (teachers and priests), *Kshatriyas* (rulers), *Vaisyas* (farmers and businessmen) and *Sudras* (service-providers). He also created law and justice, *Dharma*.

He is the Self in all of us. We must meditate on this Self and know It in our lifetime. If we do so, all our craving will disappear, as all our desires would have been fulfilled.

'This whole universe is like footprints which ultimately lead to Him alone.'

Self is the support of all beings – gods, sages, ancestors, men and animals. Thus, everything in the universe is interdependent and everything is dependent on Him. When we realize and practice this Truth, all living beings will wish well for us, just as we pray for our well being (1.4, 11-16).

A man is complete only when he has a mind of his own, a loving wife, lovable children, adequate wealth and a life-style of performing good deeds. Metaphorically, these five are like his Self, speech, breath, eyes and ears respectively.

The number five occupies an important place in many objects and phenomena of the universe (1.4, 17).

1.5, 1-13
Seven kinds of food

The word 'food' in the Upanishads has much wider connotation than what we normally understand by it. Here it stands for inputs required to sustain life – both at individual and at cosmic level.

The Upanishad talks of seven kinds of 'foods': eatables (solid food), milk (liquid food), sacrifice, symbolic offerings to gods, mind, speech and life-breath. The first four 'gross foods' sustain our physical life. The last three 'subtle foods' are significant for our metaphysical life – both at the individual and the cosmic level. Their significance is brought out by many metaphors: three worlds; three Vedas; spirit of gods, ancestors and men; father, mother and children in a family; as also, what is known, what is to be known and what is unknown. Finally, the Upanishad enumerates the cosmic equivalents of speech, mind and life-breath. Speech has earth as its body and fire as its luminous nature. Mind has heaven as its body and sun as its luminous nature. Life-breath is born from a union of heaven and sun. In other words, life originates from cosmic mind, as has been propounded elsewhere in greater detail. It is said to have water as its body (support) and moon as its luminous nature.

1.5, 14-15
Two aspects of Creation:
Variable and Constant

'The Creator is both changeless and ever changing.'

The Creator, *Prajapati* is both changeless and ever changing. This is illustrated by the analogy of a lunar fortnight. The moon appears to be of different size everyday, even though it is always the same. Likewise, the Creator appears to have 15 variable parts – which constitute the world of multiplicity – and a constant part, *Brahman*. Accordingly, the Creator is also called a Cosmic Person, *Purusha* of sixteen parts. Like Him, man also has a constant spiritual Self and a variable physical self.

The analogy of a waxing and waning moon is extended to wealth – it increases and decreases so often. In a second analogy, wealth is compared to the rim of a wheel, while life is like its hub.

1.5, 16-20
Son's role in spiritual life

There are three worlds, each requiring performance of a specific task for its attainment by man. The material world requires continuity of family name; the world of ancestors requires performance of sacrifice and certain rituals; and the world of cosmic powers (called gods) is attained by spiritual knowledge.

Verse 1.5, 17 describes a ritual for handing over one's responsibilities to a son. Thereafter, according to verses 1.5, 18-20, the divine speech, mind and

---

'A man is complete only when he has a mind of his own, a loving wife, lovable children, adequate wealth and a life-style of performing good deeds.'

life of the departing person enter his son, while he becomes one with Cosmic Speech, Cosmic Mind and Cosmic Life. Thereby, the son acquires tremendous powers.

1.5, 21-23
Superiority of Life Principle: Cosmic and individual

'Life Principle is eternal, changeless and always the same.'

Our organs of perception and action – five *gyana indriyas* and five *karma indriyas* – are dependent on Life Principle (*Prana*) for their functioning. Life Principle is supreme, not just at the individual level but also at the cosmic level. It is said to be *a priori* to other principles like Energy and Mind. The Upanishad regards Air, Fire and Sun as symbols of Principles of Life, Energy and Knowledge (light) respectively.

Life Principle is eternal, changeless and always the same. It has no individuality. It supports all body functions. Using Sun as a simile, the text says that everything rises from *Prana* and also sets therein.

1.6
World is a triad: Name, Form and Work

This vast complex world can be reduced to a triad of name, form and work, *nama*, *rupa* and *karma*. Speech is the cause, the support, the common factor in all names; sight in all forms and body in all works. The essence of all the three is *Prana*. This Immortal Principle is veiled by the empirical world.

'The Upanishad regards Air, Fire and Sun as symbols of Life, Energy and Knowledge (light).'

Translated Text

Peace Invocation

That is Whole; this is whole.
From That Whole comes forth this whole.
From That Whole when this whole is subtracted,
  what remains again is the Whole.

Om. Shanti. Shanti. Shanti.
Let there be Peace, Let there be Peace, Let there be Peace.

CHAPTER 1

Section 1

Aum,
Dawn, verily, is head of the sacrificial horse, sun is eye.
Wind is breath, *Vaisvanara* fire is open mouth.
Year is body of the sacrificial horse, sky is the back.
Atmosphere is belly, earth is hoof.
Quarters are sides, intermediate quarters are ribs.
Seasons are limbs, months and half-months are joints.
Days and nights are feet, stars are bones.
Clouds are flesh, sand is food in stomach.
Rivers are blood vessels, mountains are liver and lungs.
Herbs and trees are hair.
Rising (sun) is fore part, setting (sun) is hind part.
His yawn is like lightening; when he shakes himself, it is like thunder.
When he urinates, it is like rain. Sound indeed is his voice.   **1**

Day, verily, arose for the horse as the vessel called *mahiman* appeared in front
  (of the horse). Its source is in eastern sea.
Night, verily, arose for the horse as the vessel called *mahiman* appeared
  behind (the horse). Its source is in western sea.
These two vessels, verily, arose on two sides of the horse as two sacrificial
  vessels.
Becoming a steed he carried gods; as a stallion he carried Gandharvas.
As a runner he carried the demons; as a horse he carried men.
The sea, indeed, is his relative. The sea is his source.   **2**

Section 2

There was nothing whatsoever here in the beginning. By death indeed was this covered; or by hunger, for hunger is death. He created the mind, thinking: 'Let Me have a Self (mind).' Then he moved about, worshipping himself. From him, thus worshipping, water was produced. He thought: 'While I was worshipping, water appeared.' Therefore water is called *arka* (fire). Water (happiness) surely comes to one who thus knows why water is called *arka* (fire).   **1**

Water, verily, is *arka*. That which was froth of water became solidified; that became

---

"There was nothing whatsoever here in the beginning.
By death indeed was this covered; or by hunger, for hunger is death."

earth. Being tired and distressed, He rested on it. Then Life Principle came forth (as) fire. **2**

He (Death) divided himself threefold: (fire is one-third), sun is one-third and air is one-third. This life-breath (*Prana*) also divided itself threefold. Eastern direction is his head. His arms are that and that – northeast and southeast. (Likewise) western direction is his hind part, and his two hipbones are that and that (northwest and southwest). Southern and Northern directions are his sides. Sky is back side, atmosphere is belly. This (earth) is chest. It (*Prana*) stands firm on water. He who knows thus stands firm wherever he goes. **3**

He (Hunger or Death) desired: 'Let a second self (body or form) be born of me.' He then brought about union of Word and Mind. The seed that was there became year. Previous to that there was no year. He reared him for as long as a year and after that time he sent him forth. When he was born, Death opened its mouth (to devour him). He (the babe) cried, *bhan*. That, indeed, became speech. **4**

He thought: 'If I kill him (new born babe), it shall make very little food.' Thus, by reflection on Word and Mind he brought forth all this, whatsoever exists here – *Rg Veda*, *Yajur Veda* and *Sama Veda*, meters, sacrifices, men and cattle. Whatever he brought forth, he resolved to eat that. Verily, because he (Death) eats everything, therefore Aditi (Death) is so called. He who knows thus – how *Aditi* came to have this name – becomes an eater of everything, and everything becomes food for him. **5**

He desired: 'Let me make a sacrifice again, a greater sacrifice.' He rested himself, he practiced austerity (*tapas*). While he was thus rested and heated (with power of *tapas*), fame and vigor came forth. Vital breaths, verily, are fame and vigor. So when his vital breaths departed, his body began to swell, but his mind was set on the body. **6**

He desired: 'Let this (body) of mine be fit for sacrifice and let me be embodied through this'. Thereupon, it became a horse. 'Because it has swelled, it has become fit for sacrifice' (he thought). Therefore horse-sacrifice came to be known as *Ashvamedha*. He who knows it thus, verily, knows *Ashvamedha*.

Letting it free, he reflected upon it. At the end of a year he offered it to himself (sacrificed himself for himself). He assigned the other animals to gods. Therefore (men, priests) offer to *Prajapati* the sanctified (horse) dedicated to all gods.

Verily, that (sun) which gives forth heat is horse-sacrifice. His body is year. This fire is *arka* (universal fire) and these worlds are his limbs. So these two – fire and sun – are the sacrificial fire (*arka*) and the horse-sacrifice *Ashvamedha*. Yet again, both are the same god, Death.

He (who knows this) overcomes repeated death. Death cannot get hold of him; death becomes his body, and he becomes one with these divinities. **7**

Section 3

There were two classes of descendants of *Prajapati*, gods and demons. Of these,

---

"He desired: 'Let a second self (body or form) be born of me.'..."

gods were younger and demons elder. They were fighting with each other for (the mastery of) these worlds. The gods said: 'Come, let us defeat the demons at a sacrifice through Udgitha.' **1**

They said to speech, 'Chant (Udgitha) for us'. 'So be it,' said speech and chanted Udgitha for them. Whatever enjoyment there is in speech, it secured that for the gods by chanting; while the quality of speaking it kept for itself. The demons knew that by this chanter the gods will overcome them. They rushed upon it and pierced it with evil. Speaking what is improper is that evil. **2**

Then they said to in-breath, 'Chant (Udgitha) for us'. 'So be it,' said in-breath and chanted for them. Whatever enjoyment there is in in-breath, it secured that for the gods by chanting; while the quality of smell it kept for itself. The demons knew that by this chanter the gods will overcome them. They rushed upon it and pierced it with evil. Smelling what is improper is that evil. **3**

Then they said to the eye, 'Chant (Udgitha) for us'. 'So be it,' said the eye and chanted for them. Whatever enjoyment there is in the eye it secured that for the gods by chanting; while the quality of seeing it kept for itself. The demons knew that by this chanter the gods will overcome them. They rushed upon it and pierced it with evil. Seeing what is improper is that evil. **4**

Then they said to the ear, 'Chant (Udgitha) for us'. 'So be it,' said the ear and chanted for them. Whatever enjoyment there is in the ear, it secured that for the gods by chanting; while the quality of hearing it kept for itself. The demons knew that by this chanter, the gods will overcome them. They rushed upon it and pierced it with evil. Hearing what is improper is that evil. **5**

Then they said to the mind, 'Chant (Udgitha) for us'. 'So be it,' said the mind and chanted for them. Whatever enjoyment there is in the mind, it secured that for the gods by chanting; while the quality of thinking it kept for itself. The demons knew that by this chanter, the gods will overcome them. They rushed upon it and pierced it with evil. Thinking what is improper is that evil. Likewise they also pierced other divinities (senses) with evil. **6**

Then they said to life-breath in the mouth, 'Chant (Udgitha) for us'. 'So be it,' said life-breath and chanted for them. They (the demons) knew that by this chanter, the gods will overcome them. They rushed upon it and desired to pierce him with evil. But just as a clod of earth is scattered by striking it against a rock, likewise they were scattered in all directions and they perished. Therefore the gods became stronger but the demons were crushed. He who knows this becomes his true Self, and any enemy who hates him is crushed. **7**

Then they said, 'where is he who restored our divinity to us?' Here he is within the mouth. He (life-breath) is called Ayasya Angirasa for he is the essence of all the limbs (*anga*, members of the body). **8**

This deity is Dur by name, because death is far from it. Death is far from one who knows thus. **9**

This deity took away death, the evil of these gods, and carried it to where the

---

"Thinking what is improper is evil."

quarters end. There it left the evil. Therefore one should, not go to people (of that region), nor go to the end (of the quarters), lest he meets there that evil, death. **10**

This deity after taking away death, the evil of these gods, next carried them (gods) beyond death. **11**

Verily, it carried across speech first. When that (speech) was freed from death it became fire. This fire, when it crosses beyond death, shines forth. **12**

Then it carried across (the organ of) smell. When that was freed from death, it became air. This air, when it crosses beyond death, blows. **13**

Then it carried across the eye. When that was freed from death, it became the sun. This sun, when it crosses beyond death, glows. **14**

Then it carried across the ear. When that was freed from death, it became the quarters. These quarters have crossed beyond death. **15**

Then it carried across the mind. When that was freed from death, it became the moon. That moon, when it crosses beyond death, shines. He who knows thus is carried beyond death, by this deity. **16**

Then it (life-breath) chanted food for itself (obtained food by chanting). Therefore, whatever food is eaten, it is life-breath that eats it and nourishes itself. **17**

The gods said, 'Verily, whatever food there is, you have obtained that for yourself by chanting. Now let us have a share in this food.' It (life-breath) said, 'Then sit around, facing me (or enter into me)'. 'So be it,' they said and sat around (entered into) it on all sides. Therefore, whatever food one eats by this breath, the gods (senses) are nourished by it. Relatives come to him who knows thus. He becomes their support, their chief, their foremost leader, and a good eater of food. Whoever among his people desires to rival him who has this knowledge, he becomes powerless to support even his own dependents. But whoever follows him is able to support his dependents. **18**

This (life-breath) is called Ayasya Angirasa for it is the essence of all limbs. Yes, life-breath is the essence of all limbs. Therefore, from whatever limb life-breath departs, that dries up. Verily, life-breath is the essence of all limbs. **19**

And this is also Brhaspati (Master of Rk). Brhati is speech and life-breath is its lord. Therefore this (life-breath) is Brhaspati. **20**

And this is also Brahmanaspati (Master of Yajus). Brahmana is speech and life-breath is its lord. Therefore, it is Brahmanaspati. **21**

And this is also Saman. Speech is *sa* (chant) and life-breath is *ama*. That is why Saman is called Saman. Or because it is equal to a white ant, equal to a mosquito, equal to an elephant, equal to these three worlds, nay, equal to this universe, therefore it is Saman. He who knows this Saman to be such, attains union with it. He lives with it in the same world. **22**

"Whatever food is eaten, it is life-breath that eats it and nourishes itself."

And this is also Udgitha. Indeed, the Life-breath is *ut* because everything is upheld by Life-breath, and speech is *githa* or song. This is Udgitha, *ut* and *githa*.   **23**

Regarding this there is a story. Brahmadatta Caikitaneya, while drinking *Soma*, said: Let *Soma* strike off my head if I say that Ayasya Angirasa chanted the Udgitha by means other than this (Life-breath and speech). Indeed, he chanted the Udgitha with speech and Life-breath alone.   **24**

He who knows the wealth of Saman attains wealth. Saman's wealth, indeed, is its tone. Therefore, one who is going to perform the duties of a priest should have a rich tone in his voice. Only when possessed of such a voice, he should perform the duties of a Rtvij priest. Therefore, people desire to see at a sacrifice a priest with a good voice, just as (they like to see) one who has wealth. He who knows the wealth of Saman to be such, attains wealth.   **25**

He who knows the gold (correct sound) of Saman obtains gold. The tone, verily, is its gold. He who knows thus obtains gold.   **26**

He who knows the support of this Saman is, indeed, supported. Speech, verily, is its support. Life-breath is supported on speech. But some say it is (supported) on food (body).   **27**

Now the repetition only of the purification hymns.

The Prastotr priest recites the Saman, and while he recites it, let the sacrificer recite these (three Yajus verses):

> **From unreal lead me to the real.**
> **From darkness lead me to light.**
> **From death lead me to immortality.**

When he says 'from the unreal lead me to real,' unreal is death, real is immortality. 'From darkness lead me to light'; darkness is death, light is immortality. 'From death lead me to immortality', make me immortal, that is what he says. There is nothing here that is hidden (or obscure, and so requires no explanation).

Now whatever other verses (there are) in the hymns of praise, by chanting them one secures food. Therefore, while they are being chanted, one should ask for a boon – whatever he desires. That Udgatr priest who knows this, whatever he desires – either for himself or for the sacrificer – he obtains that by chanting.

This (meditation) certainly wins the world. He who knows the Saman, for him there is no fear of his being without a world.   **28**

Section 4

In the beginning this (world) was only Self, *Viraj*, in the form of a Cosmic Person. Looking around he saw nothing else except Self. He first said, 'I am *Aham*.' Thus arose the word of 'I'. Therefore, even to this day when one is addressed, he says first, 'It is I' and then speaks whatever other name he may have. Because before

"From darkness lead me to light."

all this, He had destroyed all evils, therefore He is called *Purusha*, a Person. He, who knows thus, verily, destroys him who wishes to rival him and become (*Viraj*) before him. **1**

He was afraid. Therefore, people are afraid to be alone. He then thought: 'Since there is nothing else than myself, of what am I afraid?' From that alone His fear was gone, for what was there to fear? Surely, it is from a second entity that fear arises. **2**

He was not happy (being alone). Therefore, people are not happy when alone. He desired a second. He became as large as a woman and a man in close embrace. He caused that Self to fall into two parts. From that arose husband and wife. Therefore, as Yagyavalkya used to say, this (body) is only one half of oneself, like one of the two halves of a split pea. One's wife is the other half. He became united with her. From them, human beings were produced. **3**

She thought, 'How can he unite with me after having produced me from himself?' Well, let me hide myself. She became a cow, the other became a bull and was united with her, and from that cows were born. The one became a mare, the other a stallion. The one became a she-ass, the other a he-ass and was united with her; and from that one-hoofed animals were born. The one became a she-goat, the other a he-goat. The one became a ewe, the other became a ram and was united with her; from that goat and sheep were born. Thus, indeed, he produced everything, whatever exists in pairs, down to ants. **4**

Then He (*Viraj*) realized, 'I am indeed this creation, for I have produced all this'. Therefore He was called Creation. He who knows this becomes (a creator) in this creation of *Viraj*. **5**

Then he patted his mouth with his hand thus (teacher demonstrates), and produced fire from its source, mouth and hands. Both these are without hair at the inside.

When they (the people) say 'sacrifice to him,' 'sacrifice to the other one,' (they are wrong) since all this is His projection indeed, and He Himself is all the gods.

And now whatever is moist, that he produced from semen, and that is Soma. This whole (world) is just food and eater of food. Soma is food and fire is eater of food. This creation here is the highest creation of *Brahman*, because he created the gods who are even superior to him. Although himself mortal, he created the immortals. Therefore it is the highest creation. Verily, he who knows this becomes (a creator) in this highest creation. **6**

At that time, this (universe) was undifferentiated. It became differentiated by name and form; (so it is said) he has such a name and such a form. Therefore to this day, name and form differentiate this (universe); (so it is said) he has such a name, and such a form.

It (Self) entered into these bodies up to the tip of the nails – as a razor is (hidden) in the razor-case, or as fire in the fire-wood. People do not see It, or they see It only partially.

"It (Self) entered into these bodies up to the tip of the nails, as fire in fire-wood. People do not see It, or they see It only partially."

When breathing, It is called the Life force; when speaking the speaker, when seeing the seer, when hearing the hearer, when thinking the thinker. These are merely the names of Its acts. He who meditates on one or another of these (aspects), he does not know; for being qualified by any of these aspects, It is incomplete.

Self is to be meditated upon in Its totality because all these become One in It. This Self alone should be realized, because through It one knows all these; just as one can find an animal by its footprints. He who knows this obtains fame and liberation. **7**

Self is dearer than a son, is dearer than wealth, is dearer than everything else, because it is innermost. If one were to say to a person who speaks of anything else than Self as dear, 'You will lose what you hold dear', it will come true. One should meditate on Self alone as dear. One who meditates on Self alone as dear, he does not become attached to perishable objects. **8**

They say: 'Men think that by knowledge of *Brahman* they become all'. What was it that *Brahman* knew by which It became all? **9**

Brahman, indeed, was all this in the beginning. It knew itself only as 'I am *Brahman.*' Therefore it became all. Whoever among the gods realized this, he became just the same. It is same in case of seers, same in case of men. Realizing this, indeed, the seer Vamadeva exclaimed, 'I was Manu and also Sun.'

Even now, whoever knows thus, **'I am Brahman**,' becomes all this universe. Even gods (senses) cannot prevent his becoming thus, for he becomes their Self. So whoever worships another divinity (than his Self) thinking that he is one and (*Brahman*) another, he knows not. He is like an animal to gods (senses). As many animals serve a man, so does such men serve gods. Even if one animal is taken away, it causes displeasure, what to speak of many. Therefore it is not pleasing to those gods (senses) that men should know (Self). **10**

Verily, in the beginning this (world) was *Brahman*, one only. Being one, it did not become unfolded (manifold). He created a superior form, rulers. Rulers among the gods are: Indra, Varuna, *Soma* (Moon), Rudra, Parjanya, Yama, Mrtyu (Death), and Isana. There is nothing higher than a ruler. Therefore at the Rajasuya sacrifice *Brahmin* sits below *Kshatriya*. A ruler alone is given this honor. But *Brahmin* is nevertheless the source of the ruler (*Kshatriya*). Therefore, even when a king attains supremacy, at the end of the sacrifice, he reveres *Brahmin* as his source. He who slights a *Brahmin* strikes at his own source. He becomes wicked, as he injures one who is superior. **11**

Yet He did not become fully unfolded. He created middle-class (*Vaisya*). These gods are designated in groups; Vasus, Rudras, Adityas, Vishvedevas and Maruts. **12**

Still He did not become fully unfolded. He created *Sudra* order, as *Pusan*. Verily, this (earth) is *Pusan* (the nourisher), for she nourishes everything that lives. **13**

"Verily, in the beginning this (world) was Brahman, one only."

Yet He did not become fully unfolded. He created another superior form, justice (*Dharma*). This is the power of *Kshatriya* class, viz. justice. Therefore there is nothing higher than justice. So a weak man hopes to defeat a strong man by means of justice, as one does through a king. Verily, that which is justice is truth. Therefore they say of a man who speaks the truth, that he speaks justice, or of a man who speaks justice that he speaks the truth. Verily, both these are the same. **14**

So these (four orders were created): the *Brahmin*, the *Kshatriya*, the *Vaisya* and the *Sudra*. Among the gods He became *Brahmin* as Fire, and among men He became *Brahmin*. He became a (human) *Kshatriya* by means of (divine) *Kshatriya*, a *Vaisya* by means of (divine) *Vaisya*, and a *Sudra* by means of (divine) *Sudra*. Therefore people desire a place among the gods through fire only, and among the men as *Brahmin*; for *Brahman* became manifested (mainly) by these two forms.

If anyone departs from this world without knowing his own world (Self), Self (being unknown) does not protect him; just as unrecited Vedas or unaccomplished deeds do not (protect him).

Even if one performs a great and holy work, but without knowing this (Self), his work is exhausted in the end. One should meditate only on Self as his (true) world. The work of him who meditates on Self alone as his world is not exhausted, because out of that very Self he creates whatsoever he desires. **15**

Now this Self, verily, is the world (support) for all beings. Whatever he offers (in fire), whatever he sacrifices, by that he becomes the support of gods. Whatever he learns of the Vedas, by that he becomes the support of the seers. Whatever libation he offers to ancestors and desires offspring, by that he becomes the support of ancestors. Whatever shelter and food he gives to men, by that he becomes the support of men. Whatever grass and water he gives to the animals, by that he becomes the support of animals. Whatever beasts, birds and ants find a living in his houses, by that he becomes their support. Verily, as one wishes security for oneself, so all beings wish security for him who has this knowledge. This, indeed, has been known and discussed. **16**

Verily, in the beginning this (world) was just Self, One only. He desired, 'Let me have a wife, so that I may have offspring. And let me have wealth, so that I can perform *karmas* (deeds).' This much indeed is the (range of) desire. Even if one wishes, one cannot wish more than this.

Therefore, to this day, a man who is single desires to have a wife, then offspring, then wealth, then performance of *karmas*. So long as he does not obtain each of these, he considers himself incomplete. Now his completeness (is described thus): mind is his Self; speech his wife; breath is his offspring; eye is his human wealth, for he sees it with the eye; ear his divine wealth, for he hears it with his ear. The body, indeed, is his work, for with his body he performs work.

So this sacrifice is fivefold; fivefold is the animal; fivefold is the person; fivefold is all this world, whatever there is. He who knows this as such obtains all this. **17**

"One should meditate only on Self as his (true) world."

Section 5

The Father (of creation) produced by his knowledge and austerity seven kinds of food. One of these foods was common to all beings, two he assigned to gods, three he made for himself, and one he gave to animals. Everything subsists on these foods – whatever breathes and whatever does not.

Why the supply of food does not get exhausted when it is being eaten all the time? He who knows the cause of food's permanence, he eats food with his mouth. He attains the gods; he lives on nectar. These are the verses.   **1**

'The Father produced by his knowledge and austerity seven kinds of food' means that the Father produced them by knowledge and austerity.

'One of these foods was common to all beings' means that the food that is eaten is that which is common to all. He who monopolizes that (common food) is not freed from evil, because that (food) is for everyone.

'Two he assigned to the gods' means making oblations in fire sacrifice and offerings to gods. Therefore one should perform both these. But they also say that the words mean the new moon and the full moon sacrifices. Therefore one should not be engrossed in sacrifice for material ends.

'One he gave to the animals' is milk. At birth, men and animals live on milk alone. Therefore they make a newborn babe first lick clarified butter or suckle (mother's) breast; likewise they speak of a newborn calf as one that does not eat grass.

'Everything subsists on that food – whatsoever breathes and whatever does not' means that everything lives upon milk. It is said that by offerings of milk (in sacrificial fire) for a year, one conquers further death. One should not think so. One conquers further death the very day he makes the offering, for he offers all his food to the gods.

'Why the supply of food does not get exhausted when it is being eaten all the time,' means that as man is very persevering, he produces food again and again.

'He who knows the cause of food's permanence' means that man himself is the cause of food's permanence, for he produces food by his work and by his thought. Should he not do so his food would get exhausted.

'He eats food with his mouth' means pre-eminence of mouth, the principal organ. He attains the gods; he lives on nectar; this is an eulogy.   **2**

'Three he made for himself.' Mind, Speech and Breath – he made these for himself.

'(They say) my mind was elsewhere, I did not see it, my mind was elsewhere, I did not hear it.' It is with the mind, truly, that one sees. It is with the mind that one hears. Desire, determination, doubt, faith, lack of faith, steadfastness, lack of steadfastness, shame, intelligence, fear, all these are truly in the mind. Therefore even if one is touched on his back, he discerns it with the mind.

"Desire, determination, doubt, faith, lack of faith, steadfastness, lack of steadfastness, shame, intelligence, fear, all these are truly in the mind."

Whatever sound there is, it is just speech. Verily, it serves to reveal an object, but is not itself revealed.

The in-breath, the out-breath, the diffused-breath, the up-breath, the equalizing-breath, all these are life-breaths, *Prana* only. Verily, the body consists of Speech, Mind and Breath. **3**

These are also the three worlds. Speech, verily, is this world (the earth), Mind is the atmospheric world (the sky). Breath is that world (heaven). **4**

These are also three Vedas. Speech, verily, is *Rg Veda*. Mind is *Yajur Veda*. Breath is *Sama Veda*. **5**

These are also gods, ancestors and men. Speech, verily, is gods. Mind is ancestors. Breaths are men. **6**

These are also father, mother and offspring. Mind, verily, is father. Speech is mother. Breath is offspring. **7**

These are also what is known, what is to be known and what is unknown. Whatever is known is a form of speech, for speech is the knower. Speech by becoming that (which is known) protects him (the knower). **8**

Whatever is to be known is a form of mind, for mind is what is to be known. Mind by becoming that (what is known) protects him (the knower). **9**

Whatever is unknown is a form of breath, for breath is what is unknown. Breath by becoming that protects him. **10**

This earth is the body of speech. This fire is its luminous nature. Therefore, as far as the speech extends, so far extends this earth, (and) so far (extends) this fire. **11**

Now of this mind, heaven is its body and its luminous nature is sun. As far as the mind extends, so far extends heaven, so far (extends) sun. These two (heaven and sun) became united, and from that union was born life-breath (*Prana*). He (*Prana*) is *Indra* (the supreme lord). He is without a rival. Verily, a second entity is a rival. He who knows this has no rival. **12**

Next, of this breath, water is its body and it luminous nature is moon. As far as the breath extends so far extends water and so far (extends) moon. These are all alike, all endless. Verily, he who meditates on them as finite, wins a finite world. But he who meditates on them as infinite wins an infinite world. **13**

That *Prajapati* (who is also) the year, has sixteen parts (*kalas*). His nights, indeed, have fifteen (variable) parts; his sixteenth part is fixed. He waxes and wanes by nights. Entering into all these living beings through his constant part on the new moon night, he is born therefrom next morning. Therefore, in honor of this deity, on that night let no one cut off the breath of any living being, not even of a lizard. **14**

"The in-breath, the out-breath, the diffused-breath, the up-breath, the equalizing-breath, all these are life-breaths, Prana only."

Verily, the person who knows this is himself that *Prajapati,* who is also the year, and who is possessed of sixteen parts. Wealth is his fifteen parts, the sixteenth part is life. Wealth alone increases and diminishes. That which is life is like the hub of a wheel, wealth a periphery. Therefore even if one loses everything but he himself lives, people say that he has lost only his peripheral possessions (which can be acquired again). **15**

Now, there are, verily, three worlds – the world of men, the world of ancestors, and the world of gods. This world of men is to be obtained through a son alone, not by any other work. The world of ancestors is to be obtained by works (rites); the world of gods by knowledge. The world of gods is, verily, the best of worlds. Therefore they praise knowledge. **16**

Now, therefore, the transmission. When a man thinks that he is about to depart, he says to his son: 'You are *Brahman*, you are the sacrifice and you are the world'.

The son repeats; 'I am *Brahman*, I am the sacrifice, I am the world.'

Then the father instructs the son again: 'Verily, whatever has been learned, all that is unified in the word *Brahman*. Verily, whatever words there are, all these are unified in the word 'world'; whatever sacrifices have been made, all these are unified in the word 'sacrifice'. All this is indeed, just this much. Being this, let him (the son) protect me from (the ties of) this world'.

Therefore a son who is well-instructed is said to be useful in attaining this world. Hence, a father instructs his son. When one who knows thus departs from this world, he enters into his son together with his speech, mind and life-breath. Whatever wrong has been done by him, his son frees him from all that. Therefore he is called a son. Through his son a father continues to exist in this world. His divine immortal speech, mind and life-breath enter into his son. **17**

From earth and from fire the divine speech enters into him (departing father). Verily, that is the divine speech by which whatever one says, all that happens. **18**

From heaven and from sun the divine mind enters into him. Verily, that is the divine mind by which one becomes joyful, and never feels sad. **19**

From water and from moon the divine breath enters into him. Verily, that is the divine breath. Whether moving or not moving, it does not feel pain or injury. He who knows this becomes the Self of all beings. As is this divinity, so is he. As all beings worship this deity, so do all beings respect him who knows this. Whatever suffering creatures may undergo, these remain with them. But only merit goes to him. No evil ever goes to the gods. **20**

Next, a consideration of deities. *Prajapati* produced the organs of action. They rivaled with one another. Speech said, 'I will go on speaking.' Eye said, 'I will go on seeing.' Ear said, 'I will go on hearing.' And thus spoke other organs also, each according to its function. But death captured them in the form of fatigue. Having taken possession of them, death held them back from their work. Therefore speech becomes weary (gets tired), eye becomes weary, ear becomes weary. But death

---

"That which is life is like the hub of a wheel, wealth a periphery."

did not take possession of Life-breath. They (the senses) sought to know him (Life-breath) and said, 'This is, verily, the greatest among us, since it is not perturbed or injured – whether moving or not moving. Let us all acquire its nature.' (Thinking thus) all of them acquired its nature. Therefore they are all called *Prana* or life-breath. In whatever family there is a man who knows this, they name that family after him. And whoever competes with one who knows this withers away and finally perishes. This is with reference to the body. **21**

Now with reference to the gods. Fire resolved 'I will go on burning.' Sun resolved, 'I will go on giving heat.' Moon resolved, 'I will go on shining'. So said the other gods, each according to its divine functions. As life-breath holds central position among sense organs, so does Air (*Vayu*) among these gods. Other gods have their ups and downs, but not Air. Air is the deity that never sets (never goes to rest). **22**

On this there is this verse:

'From whom does the sun rise and in whom does it set? In truth, it rises from *Prana* and it sets in *Prana*. The gods made this law. It is so today, it will be so tomorrow. What the gods fixed in the past, they observe till date.

Therefore, let a man observe one vow only. He should breathe-in and breathe-out, wishing, 'Let not the evil of death get me.' And when he follows this vow, let him try to complete it. Thereby, he wins complete union with that deity and he lives in the same world as that deity (*Prana*). **23**

Section 6

Verily, this (world) is a triad of name, form and work. As regards names, speech is their source, because from it all names arise. It is their common feature, because it is common to all names. It is their *Brahman,* for it sustains all names. **1**

As regards forms, eye is their source, because from it all forms arise. It is their common feature, because it is common to all forms. It is their *Brahman*, for it sustains all forms. **2**

As regards work, body is their source, because from it all works arise. It is their common feature, because it is common to all works. It is their *Brahman*, for it sustains all works.

These three together are one – this body. The body, though one, is these three.

The immortal is veiled by the real. Life Principle, *Prana*, is immortal; names and forms are real. Life Principle is veiled by names and forms. **3**

"Life Principle, Prana, is immortal; names and forms are real. Life Principle is veiled by names and forms."

Focussed Commentaries

CHAPTER 1

1.1-1.2 Self-mastery and self-sacrifice

In the first section, the world is compared to a sacrificial horse. Twenty-five different parts of the universe are compared to various limbs and actions of the horse. In ancient times, *Ashvamedha* was a very well-known and popular sacrifice. The performer of the sacrifice aimed at achieving victory over the kingdoms of the earth. However, the wise seer of the Upanishad penetrates deep into its spiritual significance. To him the sacrificial horse symbolizes the universe. The passages suggest sacrifice of self-interest.

Before creation of the universe, everything was in an unmanifested state. There was neither cause nor effect. Death here refers to the unmanifested aspect of life-principle. Hunger is an epithet of death. Mind corresponds to the power to will, *ichha shakti*. The act of worship symbolizes creative power, *kriya shakti*. These lead to an awareness of the activity of the mind and of the feeling of happiness arising from such activity. They have been called fire and water, respectively. They are collectively called *arka*; *arc* means worship and *ka* means happiness (1.2, 1).

Water is the main principle on which life subsists in this creation. Out of primordial water sprang forth the embryonic state of the universe, which solidified into earth. Thereafter, *Prajapati* became tired and distressed – because he had separated from the Supreme Self, His Abode, the stable of the sacrificial horse. Then came forth the life-principle, as fire.

After creation, both death and life-principle became divided threefold into sun, fire and air. The whole universe – the entire space with all its directions – is the cosmic body of Self, *Atman*.

Soon after the creation of cosmic organism, there followed creation of speech, union of speech and mind, and creation of time. This is how the newborn babe in the form of universe sprang out of death. Every kind of life presupposes death as its cause. Death causes life to manifest. The whole creation owes its origin to death.

Death now wanted to swallow the new born babe. Why did it want to eat its own offspring? This is a graphical statement of the fact that everything in the universe is fleeting every second towards death. The babe cried in terror, as each of us would do when faced with death. It produced the sound *bhan,* which was the first manifestation of speech (1.2, 3-4).

Having manifested Himself as time and space, He created the universe – Vedas, hymns, rituals, men and animals – by a combination of speech (knowledge), and mind (will power). Thus, the fact of creation is a sort of His Self-expression.

Again, whatever He projected, He was intent on eating it. This again is graphical statement of the fact that everything is subject to death. This death has been called *Aditi* because it consumes all.

He who knows that there is one all-pervading Consciousness in the entire cosmos, he becomes free from the clutches of birth and death. The text puts this fact metaphorically by saying that he becomes the eater of all this – names and forms (1.2, 5).

The performer of *Ashvamedha Yagya* purifies the horse by means of specific rituals and then lets it free for one year. In the same way, a man should resolve to make a greater sacrifice. For this, he has to first purify his entire being – senses, mind and his gross nature. The sacrificial horse denotes the individual soul. *Ashvamedha* sacrifice is a symbol of purifying one's mind from the instinctive animal nature and making it fit for higher, divine attainments. In short, one should perform the horse-sacrifice to conquer oneself, rather than to conquer others. Horse-sacrifice is a symbolic representation of conquest and sacrifice of self-interest. Such a sacrifice is like the Sun, which shines and gives light to all throughout the year.

The seer of the Upanishad has tried to express a big volume of philosophical truth in a metaphorical style.

– Swami Sivananda

The world is created by *Prajapati*. He is both life and death. In order to be devoured as an oblation in a sacrifice – performed by none other than Himself

---

'Death causes life to manifest. The whole creation owes its origin to death.'

– *Prajapati* transforms Himself into a horse. This is offered to Him in horse-sacrifice and along with Him to the rest of the gods.

In the imagination of the Upanishadic seer, the horse is the universe created by *Prajapati*. *Prana*, life force is the preserver of vital organs – both in psychical and cosmic sense. Mind, speech and *Prana* are the three products *Prajapati* has created out of Himself for His food. *Atman*, Self, appears threefold as name, form and work.

– Paul Deussen

The horse sacrifice is given here a cosmic interpretation. The idea of sacrifice as a means to account for creation goes back to the *Purusha Sukta* of *Rg Veda*; where from each of the members of the Primeval Person, *Purusha,* some part of the world is made.

At the horse sacrifice, two vessels are placed in front and behind the horse. These are made of gold and silver and are meant to hold the sacrificial libations. They are interpreted here cosmically as the eastern sea (Bay of Bengal) and the western sea (the Arabian Sea). Also, the gold vessel is compared to day and night. The sea is taken as the Supreme Self.

– S. Radhakrishnan

1.3 Lead me from untruth to Truth

Commentaries have been summarized under 'Simplified Synopses' on pages 100-101.

– Editor

1.4 I am *Brahman*, all this Totality

In the beginning, all this was Self (*Atman*) in the form of a Cosmic Person, *Purusha*. He said to Himself: "I am". That is how the word 'I' originated (1.4, 1). He then divided Himself into two – Male and Female principles. Human beings – as also other creatures – were born from a union of these two principles (1.4, 3-4). Thus, creation is nothing but Cosmic Person (1.4, 5).

He produced Fire from His mouth. He is Himself all the gods. All sacrifices must therefore be addressed to Him and not this god, or that god. Also, Water is like the regenerative fluid of the Cosmic Person. Water nourishes the crop; and Fire as Life-energy consumes it. Therefore, it is said that Water is food and Fire is eater of food. These – Water and Fire – are like super-creation. Out of awe and respect, they are said to be superior even to the Creator.

The undifferentiated, unmanifested *Purusha* became manifested through the cosmic mind. Individual mind is a miniature of the cosmic mind, the senses are its powers. So the Cosmic Being, *Purusha*, is *Prana* when He performs the function of breathing; speech when speaking; eyes when seeing, and so on. However, each of these is merely one of His aspects. In Him, all these unite and become One. He should therefore be worshipped as the all-inclusive Self, Self of All (1.4, 7).

Self is dearer and nearer than anything else. When we meditate upon Self as the dearest of all, we do not become attached to perishable objects. We should also meditate upon Self as the all-inclusive Supreme, *Brahman*. When we do so, we also become All. (1.4, 8-9).

And what did *Brahman* know by which He became All? He only knew Himself as: "I am *Brahman*". Whosoever realizes 'I am *Brahman*' becomes *Brahman*, as did Rishi Vamadeva (1.4, 10).

The *Mahavakya*, "I am *Brahman*" is followed by a strong indictment of worship of senses, generally referred to as gods. Verse 1.4, 10 says that the worshiper of a god is like an animal serving the god. No god would like to lose a servant, so the gods (senses) do not like that we should know *Brahman*.

Verses 1.4, 11-15 describe the creation of various social classes – the priests, the rulers, the traders and the service class – and also of *Dharma,* or Righteousness, which holds the society together.

Atman is the support of all living beings in the world. Likewise, a householder becomes support of all when he performs fivefold sacrifice (*panchamahayagya*) – in favor of gods, sages, ancestors, the needy and the animals (1.4, 16).

Family and wealth are the two basic desires of a man; without these a man considers himself incomplete.

'Individual mind is a miniature of the cosmic mind, the senses are its powers.'

Once again, emphasizing the importance of number five, verse 1.4, 17 says that a man is complete when besides himself he has a wife, children, wealth and spiritual wisdom. Symbolically, these are like the mind, speech, life, eyes and ears. They all are the support of the body, which is needed for doing work, *karmas*. All these five facilities should be integrated through meditation (1.4, 17).

– *Miscellaneous sources*

1.5, 1-13 Seven kinds of food

The Creator, the Father – by means of knowledge and contemplation, *medha* and *tapas* – produced seven kinds of foods. By food is meant any input required for sustenance. The foods were: (1) what we generally call as 'food', for consumption by all; (2-3) sacrifice and offerings for the gods, (4) 'milk' for newborns, both men and animals, (5-7) mind, speech and life-breath. The supply of these seven 'foods' is never exhausted. Like *Prajapati* Himself, man continues to produce them through *karma*, work.

Verse 1.5,2 says that all existences – animate and inanimate – exist on 'milk' alone. The word 'milk' is not to be taken literally, it should be understood as 'nourishment' of any kind. The verse also says that sacrifice should not be done for material ends.

The three 'foods' which *Prajapati* created – speech, mind and life force – are also the essence of human body, as well as the cosmos. Speech is earth, mind is sky and life force is 'other world'. These are also like the three Vedas (*Rg, Yajur, Sama*); the three spirits (of gods, ancestors, and men); and like father, mother and children (1.5, 3-7).

Speech, mind and life are also identifiable with what is known, what is to be known, and what is unknown (1.5, 8-10). These three have earth, heaven and water as their bodies. They have fire, sun and moon as their illumination. Each of these is infinite. He who meditates upon speech, mind, and life as infinite, conquers the finite world and attains the infinite world of the Cosmic Person (called *Hiranyagarbha*) (1.5, 11-13).

– *Miscellaneous sources*

In verses 1.5, 1-13, the term 'food' stands for objects of senses. The whole universe is food of *Prana*, the Cosmic Life force. The object may be said to be the food for the subject, because the former is 'eaten' or experienced by the latter. The experiencer is the eater, and that which is experienced is the food. In this sense, *Prakriti*, Nature is to be considered as food of *Purusha*, the Cosmic Person.

This section also enjoins meditation an speech, mind and life, and their external symbols – the three worlds, the three Vedas, the three spirits, the three aspects of knowledge, and the family – consisting of father, mother and children. Thus, there is nothing left to stand outside one's speech, mind and vital force. These meditations help one to absorb the whole of objectivity into one's Self, which is pure subject itself. By absorbing the whole of the universe in all its aspects into one's Self, the individual 'I' becomes the cosmic 'I'.

– *Swami Sivananda*

1.5, 14-15 Two aspects of Creation: Variable and Constant

These verses draw an analogy between the Creator and lunar fortnight to bring out the following:

(i) Time is a created aspect. It is not eternal, unborn.

(ii) The creator has two aspects – the changeless Unmanifest, and the ever-changing Manifest. The moon in the sky – like the world of multiplicity – appears of a different size everyday of the fortnight. In reality, however, the moon – like the Unmanifest *Brahman* – is always the same. It never changes.

(iii) The fourteen phases of moon in a fortnight, the visible full moon and the invisible moon add up to sixteen. Hence the creator is also known as a Cosmic Person of sixteen aspects, *kala*.

(iv) *Prajapati*, the Creator, symbolically 'enters' all the living beings with all his sixteen aspects on the new moon night, and is 'born' the next day as crescent moon. The verse advocates a vow of non-violence, at least once a fortnight.

(v) In this creation, the fifteen parts of *Prajapati* undergo fluctuations, – they increase and decrease; but the sixteenth part remains constant. It permeates the entire universe, and at the same time it is transcendent. The universe is projected again and again at the beginning of every cycle, through this constant and eternal aspect, just like the beginning of a lunar fortnight.

Elaborating further on the changeless and the changing

'The Creator has two aspects – the changeless Unmanifest, and the ever-changing Manifest.'

aspects of the Creator, verse 1.5, 15 says that wealth – like the waxing and the waning of moon – comes and goes. However, life is eternal. The verse also repeats the analogy of a wheel. Wealth is like the rim of a wheel, while life is like its hub.

Even if a man is deprived of material wealth, he will make good the loss if he is alive.

– Swami Sivananda

A man of knowledge finds herein a consolation that though he loses all that he has, he is still alive. He knows that the essential thing (*Prana*) – the sixteenth part of *Prajapati* – is preserved. Out of it, all the rest can originate again.

– Paul Deussen

1.5, 16-20 Son's role in Spiritual Life

The three worlds represent three levels of Consciousness. As one rises to the higher realms of Consciousness – symbolized by these worlds – one approaches nearer and nearer to one's Self.

A father, when he feels that he is about to die, calls his son and entrusts him with the task of continuity and completing his responsibilities towards the three worlds – the worlds of sages, forefathers and gods – in the form of study, sacrifice and meditation. The son fulfills the unaccomplished tasks and liberates his father from these obligations. Thus, a properly instructed son becomes a means to attain all the three worlds. Thereafter, the man's speech, mind and life become identical with Cosmic Speech, Cosmic Mind and Cosmic Life, respectively; just as a river merges in an ocean. The individual 'I' becomes the cosmic 'I' by absorbing into it the whole of the universe in all its aspects – without allowing anything to remain outside. In this meditation, the individual identifies himself with the universe.

Having enjoined meditation on the *adhibhautic* manifestations of Speech, Mind and Life, the Upanishad describes meditation on the *adhidaivic* side.

- Earth and Fire are to be meditated as divine Speech.
- Sky and Sun are to be meditated as divine Mind.
- Water and Moon are to be meditated as divine Life.

When Speech is based on Truth, it becomes all-powerful. Mind gets immense power when it attaches itself to One Universal Consciousness. *Prana* also becomes invincible when it identifies itself with Truth. These three lose their powers and become weak only when they are attached to and limited by the individual's body. If one meditates upon these as finite, one attains finite results; while if one meditates upon them as infinite, the result that accrues will also be infinite.

– Swami Sivananda

Without any visible connection with the foregoing, possibly in order to provide an introduction to the ceremony of bequest, here appears the doctrine of three worlds. These are; the world of men, which is gained through a son; the world of ancestors which is gained through rituals; and the world of gods which is gained through knowledge. The passage appears to contain the first germ of the doctrine of *Pitrayana* and *Devayana*.

Here follows the ceremony of bequest – *sampratti*. It describes how the divine *Vac* (Speech), *Manas* (Mind) and *Prana* (Life) – contained in earth, sky and water – enter into the father after he has bequeathed his power of life to his son. On account of it – provided he has this knowledge – he becomes the Self of all beings and participates in all good things; whereas the evil of beings does not touch him.

– Paul Deussen

1.5, 21-23 Superiority of Life Principle: Cosmic and Individual

Prajapati created the organs of perception. They vied with each other, each wanting to establish its superiority over the others. The eye boasted that the function of seeing was most important; the ear boasted that the function of hearing was most important, and so on. The sense organs and their respective gods took a vow to confine themselves to their respective functions only. Now, death in the form of fatigue possessed them. Death harmonizes and restores equilibrium wherever it is disturbed. Thus affected by death, the organs stopped functioning. But *Prana* has no individuality and separateness like the organs. It is the universal force behind every activity – both in an individual and in the universe. Death could not possess *Prana* and it went on functioning without stopping. Therefore the organs identified themselves with *Prana*.

'Mind gets immense power when it attaches itself to One Universal Consciousness.'

Through this story, the Upanishad instructs that one should meditate thus:

"All the organs in all beings, as well as their presiding deities, are really a part and parcel of me. I am *Prana*, the Self of all, the source of their movement". The result of this meditation – if done perfectly – is identification with Cosmic *Prana*.

– Swami Sivananda

Air and life – *Vayu* and *Prana* – are never exhausted, they are imperishable. Other psychic powers like speech, sight and hearing – and cosmic powers like fire, sun and moon – are exposed to exhaustion and death; but *Prana* is an imperishable cosmic principle. Here we recognize the first germ of *Pranayama* (regulation of breath) practiced in later Yoga.

– Paul Deussen

1.6 World is a triad: Name, Form and Work

This world is constituted of name, form and work. These have sound, eye and body as their cause (Uktha), equalizing force (*Saman*) and support (*Brahman*). The cosmos, which is only one, appears as three – name (matter), form (mind) and work. The subtle in the cosmos is hidden by the gross. All names, all forms, and all actions are contained in the universal Cosmic Being. The general is veiled by the particular. The Supreme is covered by the world. Therefore one sees the name and the form, and not the Being. It is like one seeing the waves, foam and bubbles on the surface of the ocean, and missing the vision of the great majestic ocean that lies beneath the surface.

– Swami Sivananda

The objective world factors – name, form and work – have their origin in *Atman*, Consciousness. *Atman* is their Uktha (*Rg Veda*), their *Saman* (*Sama Veda*), their *Brahman* (*Atharva Veda*). It is the principle out of which they originate, just as Veda (Knowledge, Consciousness) is the principle out of which the world has originated. Thus the triad is traced back to speech, eyes and body; and through them to the *Atman* or *Prana*. *Atman* is the immortal principle (*amratam*); the triad is the empirical reality (*satyam*).

The immortal principle is veiled by empirical reality, *amrtam satyena channam*.

– Paul Deussen

'The objective world factors – name (matter), form (mind) and work – have their origin in Atman, Consciousness.'

② What is Love?

SIMPLIFIED SYNOPSES

2.1
Incomplete definitions of *Brahman*

'The universe – including our body with all its senses – has emanated from Consciousness, like sparks from a fire.'

This section contains a dialogue between a learned priest Balaki Gargya and a wise king Ajatashatru on what is *Brahman*? Gargya says that the great objects and phenomena of Nature personify *Brahman*. One-by-one, Gargya enumerates a dozen 'limited adjuncts' or 'conditioned forms' of *Brahman* – Sun, Moon, Lightening, Sky, Air, Fire, Water, Reflection, Sound, Directions, Shadow and Mind - and says that he meditates upon them as *Brahman*. However, in every instant, Ajatashatru stops Balaki Gargya from further elaboration, implying that his concept of *Brahman* is incomplete.

While rejecting these definitions of *Brahman*, Ajatashatru acknowledges their greatness and the benefits of meditating upon them. He also suggests that Balaki Gargya is making a mistake in limiting the Limitless. (2.1, 1-13)

Balaki had put forth his definitions of 'conditioned' *Brahman* progressively from gross to subtle. Ajatashatru bluntly states that whatever Balaki had said was already known to him, and that this was not sufficient to comprehend *Brahman*. Admitting his ignorance, Balaki wants to become a disciple of Ajatashatru. Ajatashatru takes him to a sleeping person and wakes him up. He then explains the Ultimate Reality, *Brahman*, through an analysis of the states of dream and deep sleep.

The ultimate reality in man is Self, *Atman*. It is same as *Brahman*. It is also called *Purusha* or Cosmic Person, which is nothing but Consciousness. During dream state this Consciousness withdraws the senses into Itself and moves around in a world of Its own – like a great king, or a learned person or an ordinary man – as It pleases. In deep sleep, this individual Consciousness is said to rest in the heart – like a youth or a great king who has reached the summit of bliss. The journey to the heart is said to be through 72,000 subtle channels, called *hita*. Ajatashatru concludes his explanation with two analogies – a spider and sparks from a fire. A spider makes its own web out of itself, and then moves about in it. Likewise we weave our life and then move along in it. This is true of the whole creation. The universe – including our body with all its senses – has emanated from Consciousness, like sparks from a fire.

Then follows a famous saying that *Brahman* is Truth of truths, *Satyas satyam*. Life-breaths are truth and their Truth is Self. (2.1,14-20).

2.2 Meditation on Prana

This section describes meditation on *Prana*. It compares *Prana* to a young calf. Human body is like calf's stable; head is the roof of the stable; breath is the post to which *Prana* is tied; and energy produced from food is the rope, which ties *Prana* firmly to the post. He who understands this analogy is said to conquer even hostile relatives. The seven orifices in the head through which perception takes place are said to be hostile because they divert ones vision away from Self, and attach it to sense objects. Seven divinities – Rudra, Parjanya, Aditya, Agni, Indra, Earth and Heavens – dwell in the eyes and keep a watch over *Prana*.

While *Prana* resides in the whole body, the head – the portion over the neck – is its special resort. This is compared to an upside-down drinking bowl with seven seers – two eyes, two ears, two nostrils and the tongue – sitting around it. The eighth seer is speech. The tongue being the organ of taste as well as speech is counted as two. Pointing out to each of the eight organs one-by-one, the seer also gives them the names of great sages. For example, the tongue is given the name Atri – derived from the word Atti, which means to eat.

2.3 Two profound descriptions of Brahman

This section attempts a definition of *Brahman*. It says that *Brahman* has two aspects – Relative and Absolute. Relative is gross, mortal, limited and perceptible. Absolute is subtle, immortal, unlimited and imperceptible. Stated differently, Relative is 'becoming', Absolute is 'being'.

Also, *Brahman* is to be comprehended at two levels – cosmic and individual. Relative and Absolute aspects of *Brahman* apply to both these levels.

The Upanishad places the five elements also on a continuous scale, from the relative to the absolute. As an approximation, earth, water and fire are considered 'relative'; as they are relatively more gross, perishable, limited and perceptible than air and space, which are considered 'absolute.'

The physical sun is said to be the essence of the relative aspect of *Brahman* at the cosmic level, and the eyes at the individual level. The Cosmic Person, *Purusha* – which is both in the sun and the eye – is said to be the essence of Absolute *Brahman* at the cosmic as well as the individual level.

Verse 2.3,6 provides a synthesis of the seemingly contradictory aspects of *Brahman*, Relative and Absolute. It enumerates certain colors – these are to be considered merely as examples of the infinite forms and impressions of the Cosmic Person. It also says that *Brahman* is realized as a flash of lightening. The verse concludes by defining *Brahman* as *neti*, *neti*, not this, not this; and as *satyas satyam*, Truth of truths, Reality of realities.

'Brahman is neti, neti; not this, not this. He is Satyasa satyam, Truth of truths.'

2.4 Love means to see one Self in two bodies

This section is considered a crest jewel in the crown of Upanishadic literature. It explains with many analogies and metaphors the concept of Self, *Atman*, as the Ultimate Reality.

Yagyavalkya, a very learned spiritual aspirant, wanted to relinquish his household duties. He therefore proposed to divide his wealth between his two

---

'Brahman is to be comprehended at two levels – cosmic and individual. Relative and Absolute aspects of Brahman apply to both these levels.'

> *'Individual Consciousness loses its individuality when it merges in the totality of its source, the Absolute.'*

wives. The first wife, Maitreyi enquired if wealth would make her happy? No, said the husband. So Maitreyi declined the offer of wealth. Instead, she asked for that knowledge which would make her happy.

Yagyavalkya starts his discourse with a very profound statement: We love our husband, wife or children not because they are our husband, wife or children, but because we see their Self and our Self as one. When a couple regards each other as one, it is happy; and not when husband and wife think of themselves as two separate entities. The same applies to wealth, social status, or anything you can think of. When you harmonize other persons or objects with your inner Self, there is happiness; when you chase other persons or objects as something external, which you must possess, there is tension. Yes, there is Self (Consciousness) even in wealth and other things or concepts. So Yagyavalkya suggests to Maitreyi that she should reflect on Self. (2.4, 5).

The love for a person or an object is really the love for that which is eternal in the person or object; and that is Self. We wrongly think that love is for the temporal name and form. (2.4, 6).

Yagyavalkya then explains the relationship between Self and the empirical world with a metaphor of three musical instruments – a drum, a conch and a *veena*. Self is like a musical instrument, and the empirical world is like the sounds emanating from it. One can regulate the sounds only by grasping the instrument. (2.4, 7-9).

Next, the origin of Vedas and other branches of knowledge from Self is compared to emergence of smoke from a fire (2.4, 10).

Yagyavalkya then says that mind, intellect, five sense organs of perception and five of action – each is the 'one goal' of their respective objects or functions. Also, just as ocean is the one goal of all rivers, Self is the one goal of all phenomena and objects of the world. (2.4, 11).

Next, Yagyavalkya uses the analogy of salt dissolved in water to explains how individual Consciousness loses its individuality when it merges in the totality of its source, the Absolute. In the concluding verse, Yagyavalkya asserts that in Self, there is no distinction between the subject and the object, the observer and the observed, the experiencer and the experienced. All dualities merge into One Self.

2.5
Madhu Vidya, or Honey doctrine

What is the relationship between living beings and various objects or phenomena of the universe? They support each other and nourish each other, each being like honey for the other. This relationship of mutual support arises because of the One Self which is common to all. As an example, the same Self pervades the earth, the living beings, the consciousness in earth and the consciousness in living beings. This applies to all gross elements or abstract principles. The examples considered here are: five primeval elements (Earth, Water, Fire, Air, Space), five cosmic phenomena (Sun, Moon, Directions, Lightening, Clouds), Law (*Dharma*), Truth, Mankind and Mind.

'When a couple regards each other as one, it is happy; and not when husband and wife think of themselves as two separate entities.'

> *Everything in the universe is interconnected - vitally and organically - through Consciousness.*

According to one commentator, Kant's doctrines of 'affinity of phenomena' and 'synthetic unity of apperception' are very similar to the 'Honey doctrine'.

Self is the Ultimate Cause of all beings. It is the support of everything, like a hub in a wheel (2.5, 15).

Everything in the universe is interconnected – vitally and organically –through Consciousness. There is nothing that exists as an isolated entity. Also, everything in the universe is an effect of the Ultimate Cause, variously called Self, *Atman* or *Brahman*. Every effect tends to gravitate towards its Ultimate Causeless Cause, and eventually merge into It.

Verses 16-17 allude to a mythological story associated with the teaching of this honey doctrine. The story conveys an important message: keeping one's solemn promise is more important than life.

Verse 18 declares that Self dwells in all beings. There is nothing that is not pervaded by It. The text says that everything – including the ten organs of perception and action – are yoked to Self. Self is without cause or effect, without interior or exterior. Self, the Absolute, reveals Itself through the relative universe. To say that the world veils Self is ignorance. To recognize that the world reveals Self is knowledge.

There is a repeated emphasis that Self is Immortal. It is *Brahman*. It is All.

2.6 Lineage of Teachers

In ancient times, important texts were passed on from one generation to the next through a unique tradition. A teacher taught the text to his students. They memorized it and in turn passed it on to their own students. Thus, knowledge was passed on from one generation to the next through the media of human memory. This section enumerates a long lineage of teachers.

'To say that the world veils Self is ignorance. To recognize that the world reveals Self is knowledge.'

TRANSLATED TEXT

CHAPTER 2

Section 1

Once, there lived Drpta Balaki of Gargya clan. He was an eloquent speaker. He said to Ajatashatru of Kashi, 'I will tell you about *Brahman*.'

Ajatashatru said, 'I will give you a thousand (cows) for this. Indeed people rush to Janaka (with such proposals, so why not to me?)'. **1**

Gargya : The person who is yonder in the sun, on him, indeed, do I mediate as *Brahman*.

Ajatashatru : Please, do not talk to me about him. I meditate on him, verily, as the all-surpassing; as the head and king of all beings. He who meditates on him as such becomes all-surpassing, the head and king of all beings. **2**

Gargya : The person who is yonder in the moon, on him, indeed, do I meditate as *Brahman*.

Ajatashatru : Please, do not talk to me about him. I meditate on him, verily, as the great white-robed king *Soma*. He who meditates on him as such, for him *soma* is poured out (in principal sacrifices) and poured forth (in subsidiary sacrifices) every day. His food does not get exhausted. **3**

Gargya : The person who is yonder in lightning, on him, indeed, do I meditate as *Brahman*.

Ajatashatru : Please, do not talk to me about him. I meditate on him, verily, as the radiant. He who meditates on him as such becomes radiant, and his offsprings also become radiant. **4**

Gargya : The person who is here in space, on him, indeed, do I meditate as *Brahman*.

Ajatashatru : Please, do not talk to me about him. I meditate on him, verily, as the full and the unmoving. He who meditates on him as such is filled with offspring and cattle, and his progeny does not become extinct from this world. **5**

Gargya : The person who is here in air, on him, indeed, do I meditate as *Brahman*.

Ajatashatru : Please, do not talk to me about him, I meditate on him, verily, as Indra, lord of an irresistible and unconquerable army. He who meditates on him as such becomes victorious, unconquerable, and conqueror of enemies. **6**

Ajatashatru's implied message is: 'Objects of Nature are merely conditioned forms of Brahman, Absolute Consciousness.' ......Editor

Gargya	: The person who is here in fire, on him, indeed, do I meditate as *Brahman*.
Ajatashatru	: Please, do not talk to me about him. I meditate on him, verily, as forbearing. He who meditates on him as such becomes forbearing and his offspring, too, becomes forbearing. **7**
Gargya	: The person who is here in water, on him, indeed, do I meditate as *Brahman*.
Ajatashatru	: Please, do not talk to me about him. I meditate on him, verily, as agreeable. He who meditates on him as such, to him comes what is agreeable, and never what is not agreeable. Also from him are born children who are agreeable. **8**
Gargya	: The person who is here in a mirror, on him, indeed, do I meditate as *Brahman*.
Ajatashatru	: Please, do not talk to me about him. I meditate on him, verily, as the shining one. He who meditates on him as such becomes shining indeed. His offspring, too, becomes shining. He also outshines all those with whom he comes in contact. **9**
Gargya	: The sound here which one follows as one walks, on that, indeed, do I meditate as *Brahman*.
Ajatashatru	: Please, do not talk to me about that. I meditate on him, verily, as life. He who meditates on him as such attains a full term of life in this world. Breath does not depart from him before (the completion of) his time. **10**
Gargya	: The person who is here in the quarters (of space) on him, indeed, do I meditate as *Brahman*.
Ajatashatru	: Please, do not talk to me about him. I meditate on him, verily, as the second (like twins) who never leaves us. He who meditates on him as such gets companions. His companions never depart from him. **11**
Gargya	: The person here who consists of shadow, on him, indeed, do I meditate as *Brahman*.
Ajatashatru	: Please, do not talk to me about him. I meditate on him, verily, as death. He who meditates on him as such attains a full term of life in this world. Death does not come to him before (the completion of) his time. **12**
Gargya	: The person who is here in the mind, on him, indeed, do I meditate as *Brahman*.
Ajatashatru	: Please, do not talk to me about him. I meditate on him, verily, as

---

Ajatashatru's implied message is: 'Consciousness is Infinite. It is a mistake to equate it with any finite form.'
....Editor

the embodied one. He who meditates on him as such he becomes embodied. His offspring becomes embodied.

Gargya then became silent. **13**

Ajatashatru : Is that all?

Gargya : That is all.

Ajatashatru : With that much, *Brahman* is not known.

Gargya : Let me come to you (for more knowledge) as a pupil. **14**

Ajatashatru : Verily, it is contrary to usual practice that a *Brahmin* should approach a *Kshatriya*, thinking that he will teach me about *Brahman*. However, I shall instruct you about Him.

Taking him by the hand he rose. The two together came to a person who was asleep. They addressed him with these names: Great, White-robed, Radiant *Soma*. The man did not get up. Ajatashatru than woke him by shaking him by his hand. The man then got up. **15**

Ajatashatru : (To Gargya) When this man was in deep sleep, where was the Person who consists of Consciousness (*Vigyana*)? From where did it come back?

And this Gargya did not know. **16**

Ajatashatru : When this man was asleep, then the Person (*Purusha*) who is Consciousness itself withdrew the consciousness of these sense organs into Itself and was resting in the space within the heart. When the Person withdraws the senses, the man is said to be asleep. (In sleep) the senses are withdrawn – the speech is withdrawn, the eye is withdrawn, the ear is withdrawn, the mind is withdrawn. **17**

When the Person moves about in dream state, the dreams are his worlds. Then he becomes, as it were, a great king or a learned man. He attains high and low states. Just as a great king moves about in his country with his retinue as he pleases; so also this one, having withdrawn his senses, moves about in his body as he pleases. **18**

Again, when one is in sound sleep, one knows nothing whatsoever. Having come through the seventy two thousands channels called *hita* – which extend from the heart to the whole body – the Person rests in the body. As a youth or a great king or a great *Brahmin* might rest when he has reached the summit of bliss, so does He rest. **19**

"When this man was asleep, then the Person (Purusha) who is Consciousness itself withdrew the consciousness of these sense organs into Itself."

As a spider moves about in its web, as small sparks come forth from the fire, even so from this Self come forth all senses, all worlds, all gods, and all beings. Its secret meaning is the Truth of truths. Life-breaths are the truths, and It is their Truth. **20**

Section 2

Verily, he who knows a newborn calf – as also its dwelling place, shed, post and rope – keeps off his seven hostile kinsmen. Verily, life-breath in the body is like the calf. It dwelling place is this (body). Its shed is this (head). Its post is the breath. Its rope is food. **1**

These seven imperishable ones stand near it (*Prana*, Life-breath). Thus, there are these red streaks in the eye and by them *Rudra* is united with it. Then there is water in the eye, by it *Parjanya* (is united with it). There is the pupil of the eye, by it *Aditya* (Sun is united with it). By the black (of the eye), Fire (is united with it); by the white (of the eye), *Indra* (is united with it); by the lower eyelash Earth (is united with it); by the upper eyelash, Heaven (is united with it). He who knows this, his food does not diminish. **2**

On this there is the following verse:

'There is a bowl with its mouth below and bottom up. In it is placed knowledge of manifold forms. Around it sit seven seers. The eighth, speech, communicates knowledge.'

The upside-down bowl is symbolic of the head. 'In it is placed the knowledge of manifold forms' refers to the sense organs. 'Seven seers' refer to the seven deities of the senses in the head. **3**

These two (ears) here are Gotama and Bharadvaja. This is Gotama, and this is Bharadvaja (the teacher explains by gesture of hands). These two (eyes) here are Visvamitra and Jamadagni. This is Visvamitra, this is Jamadagni. These two (nostrils) here are Vasistha and Kasyapa. This is Vasistha, this is Kasyapa. The tongue is Atri, for by the tongue food is eaten. Verily, eating is the same which is called Atri. He who knows this becomes the eater of everything; everything becomes his food. **4**

Section 3

Verily, there are two forms of *Brahman* – formed and formless, mortal and immortal, limited and unlimited, perceptible and imperceptible. **1**

Whatever is different from air and space (i.e. earth, water and fire) is the formed (gross). It is mortal. It is limited. It is perceptible. The essence of it is the yonder sun. That which shines is the essence of the perceptible. **2**

Now the formless is air and space. It is immortal, it is unlimited, and it is imperceptible. The essence of this unformed, this immortal, this unlimited, this imperceptible is the *Purusha* (Cosmic Person). He is in the region of the sun. He is the essence of the imperceptible. This is with reference to the divinities. **3**

"There are two forms of Brahman - formed and formless, mortal and immortal, limited and unlimited, perceptible and imperceptible."

Now with reference to the individual, the gross is that which is different from the life-breath and the space within the body. It is mortal, limited and perceptible. The essence of this gross, this mortal, this limited, this perceptible is the eye. The eye is the essence of the perceptible. **4**

Now the formless is *Prana* (life-breath) and the space within the body. It is immortal, unlimited and imperceptible. The essence of this unformed, immortal, unlimited, imperceptible is this *Purusha* (Cosmic Person) who is in the right eye. He is the essence of the imperceptible. **5**

The form of this *Purusha* (Cosmic Person) is like a saffron-colored robe, like white wool, like the insect Indragopa, like a flame of fire, like a white lotus, like a sudden flash of lightning. He who knows It thus attains splendor like a sudden flash of lightning. **6**

Now, therefore, there is this definition (of *Brahman*): He is not this, Not this, *Neti, Neti*. There is no higher definition than this, that He is *neti, neti*, 'not this, not this'. He is the Truth of truths, *Satyasa Satyam*. Verily, *Prana* (life-breath) is truth and He is the Truth of that. **7**

Section 4

Yagyavalkya : Maitreyi. Verily, I am about to renounce from this state (of householder). Look, let me make a final settlement between you and Katyayani. **1**

Maitreyi : If, indeed, venerable Sir, this whole earth filled with wealth were mine, would I become immortal through that?

Yagyavalkya : No. Like the life of the rich, so would your life be. Of immortality, however, there is no hope through wealth. **2**

Maitreyi : What should I do with that by which I do not become immortal? Tell me that, indeed, venerable Sir, what you know (of the way to immortality). **3**

Yagyavalkya : Ah, dear, you have been dear (even before), and you (now) speak dear words. Come, sit down. I will explain to you. Even as I am explaining, reflect (on what I say). **4**

Verily, not for the sake of husband is husband dear, but husband is dear for the sake of Self.
Verily, not for the sake of wife is wife dear, but wife is dear for the sake of Self.
Verily, not for the sake of sons are sons dear, but sons are dear for the sake of Self.
Verily, not for the sake of wealth is wealth dear, but wealth is dear for the sake of Self.
Verily, not for the sake of *Brahmin* is *Brahmin* dear, but *Brahmin* is dear for the sake of Self.

"Verily, not for the sake of husband is husband dear, but husband is dear for the sake of Self."

Verily, not for the sake of *Kshatriya* is *Kshatriya* dear, but *Kshatriya* is dear for the sake of Self.
Verily, not for the sake of worlds are worlds dear, but worlds are dear for the sake of Self.
Verily, not for the sake of gods are gods dear, but gods are dear for the sake of Self.
Verily, not for the sake of beings are beings dear, but beings are dear for the sake of Self.
Verily, not for the sake of all are all dear, but all are dear for the sake of Self.
Verily, O Maitreyi, it is Self that should be seen, heard of, reflected on and meditated upon.
Verily, by seeing, hearing, thinking and understanding of Self, all this is known. **5**

The *Brahmin* ignores one who knows him as different from Self.
The *Kshatriya* ignores one who knows him as different from Self.
The worlds ignore one who knows them as different from Self.
The gods ignore one who knows them as different from Self.
The beings ignore one who knows them as different from Self.
All ignore one who knows all as different from Self.
This *Brahmin*, this *Kshatriya*, these worlds, these gods, these beings and this all are this Self. **6**

As when a drum is beaten, one is not able to grasp its sound; but by grasping the drum, or the beater of the drum, the sound is grasped. **7**

As when a conch is blown, one is not able to grasp its sound; but by grasping the conch, or the blower of the conch, the sound is grasped. **8**

As when a *veena* (lute) is played, one is not able to grasp its sound; but by grasping the *veena*, or the player of the *veena*, the sound is grasped. **9**

As from a lighted fire laid with damp fuel, various (clouds of) smoke issue forth; even so, my dear, *Rg Veda, Yajur Veda, Sama Veda, Atharva Veda*, history, ancient lore, sciences, Upanishads, verses, aphorisms, explanations and commentaries – all these are breathed forth from this (Self), indeed. **10**

As the ocean is the one goal (uniting place) of all rivers,
as the skin is the one goal of all kinds of touch,
as the nostrils are the one goal of all smells,
as the tongue is the one goal of all tastes,
as the eye is the one goal of all forms,
as the ear is the one goal of all sounds,
as the mind is the one goal of all determinations,
as the heart is the one goal of all forms of knowledge,
as the hands are the one goal of all acts,
as the organ of generation is the one goal of all kinds of enjoyment,

---

"The gods ignore one who knows them as different from Self."

as the excretory organ is the one goal of all excretions,
as the feet are the one goal of all movements,
as speech is the one goal of all Vedas. **11**

As a lump of salt put in water becomes dissolved and there would not be any of it to seize forth as it were, but wherever one may taste, it is salty indeed; so, verily, this great, infinite, limitless Reality consists of nothing but Pure Consciousness. Arising out of these elements It vanishes into them. When It has departed (after death) there is no more Consciousness. This is what I say, my dear. **12**

Maitreyi : Venerable Sir, you have indeed, bewildered me by saying: "When It has departed there is no more Consciousness."

Yagyavalkya : Certainly I am not saying anything bewildering. Let me explain. **13**

Where there is duality as it were, there one smells another, there one sees another, there one hears another, there one speaks to another, there one thinks of another, there one understands another. Where everything has become Self, then by what and whom should one smell? Then by what and whom should one see? Then by what and whom should one hear? Then by what and to whom should one speak? Then by what and about whom should one think? Then by what and whom should one understand? By what should one know that by which all this is known? By what, my dear, should one know the Knower?' **14**

Section 5

This earth is (like) honey for all beings, and all beings are (like) honey for this earth. This shining, immortal Person who is in this earth and this shining, immortal Person who is in the body – indeed, these four are just this Self. This is immortal, this is *Brahman*, this is all. **1**

This water is (like) honey for all beings, and all beings are (like) honey for this water. This shining, immortal Person who is in this water and this shining, immortal Person who exists as procreative fluid (in the body) – indeed these four are just this Self. This is immortal, this is *Brahman*, this is all. **2**

This fire is (like) honey for all beings, and all beings are (like) honey for this fire. This shining, immortal Person who is in this fire and this shining, immortal Person who is in speech – indeed these four are just this Self. This is immortal, this is *Brahman*, this is all. **3**

This air is (like) honey for all beings, and all beings are (like) honey for this air. This shining, immortal Person who is in this air and this shining, immortal Person who is in this breath (in the body) – indeed these are four just this Self. This is immortal, this is *Brahman,* this is all. **4**

This sun is (like) honey for all beings and all beings are (like) honey for this sun. This shining, immortal Person who is in this sun and this shining, immortal Person

---

"This (Self) is Immortal. This is Brahman, this is all (everything)."

who is in the eye – indeed these four are just this Self. This is immortal, this is *Brahman*, this is all. **5**

These quarters are (like) honey for all beings, and all beings are (like) honey for these quarters. This shining, immortal Person who is in these quarters and this shining, immortal Person who is in this hearing – indeed, these four are just this Self. This is immortal, this is *Brahman*, this is all. **6**

This moon is (like) honey for all beings, and all beings are (like) honey for this moon. This shining, immortal Person who is in this moon and this shining, immortal Person who is in the mind – indeed, these four are just this Self. This is immortal, this is *Brahman*, this is all. **7**

This lightning is (like) honey for all beings, and all beings are (like) honey for this lightning. This shining, immortal Person who is in this lightning and, this shining, immortal Person who is in the light – indeed, these four are just this Self. This is immortal, this is *Brahman*, this is all. **8**

This cloud is (like) honey for all beings, and all beings are (like) honey for this cloud. This shining, immortal Person who is in this cloud and this shining, immortal Person who is in the sound and in tone – indeed, these four are just this Self. This is immortal, this is *Brahman*, this is all. **9**

This space is (like) honey for all beings and all beings are (like) honey for this space. This shining, immortal Person who is in this space and this shining, immortal Person who is in the space in the heart – indeed, these four are just this Self. This is immortal, this is *Brahman*, this is all. **10**

This law, *Dharma* is (like) honey for all beings and all beings are (like) honey for this law. This shining, immortal Person who is in this law and this shining, immortal Person who exists as compliance with law – indeed, these four are just this Self. This is immortal, this is *Brahman*, this is all. **11**

This truth is (like) honey for all beings, and all beings are (like) honey for this truth. This shining, immortal Person who is in this truth and this shining, immortal Person who exists as truthfulness – indeed, these four are just this Self. This is immortal, this is *Brahman*, this is all. **12**

This mankind is (like) honey for all beings, and all beings are like honey for this mankind. This shining, immortal Person who is in this mankind and this shining, immortal Person who exists as a human being – indeed, these four are just this Self. This is immortal, this is *Brahman*, this is all. **13**

This Self is (like) honey for all beings and all beings are (like) honey for this Self (cosmic body). This shining, immortal Person who is in this cosmic Self and the shining, immortal Person who is in this (individual) Self – indeed, these four are just this Self. This is immortal, this is *Brahman*, this is all. **14**

This Self, verily, is the lord of all beings, the king of all beings. Just as all the spokes are held together in the hub and rim of a wheel; so also in this Self, all beings, all gods, all worlds, all breathing creatures, all these selves are held together. **15**

"In this Self, all beings, all gods, all worlds, all breathing creatures, are held together."

Indeed, this is that honey doctrine which Dadhyacha Atharvana declared to the two Asvins. Seeing them the seer said: 'O Asvins in human form, I will proclaim that terrible deed of yours which you did out of greed, just as thunder (proclaims) the coming rain – how you learned the honey doctrine from the head of a horse (deceptively transplanted) on me. **16**

This, verily, is the honey doctrine which, Dadhyacha Atharvana declared to the two Asvins. Seeing them, the seer said, 'O Asvins, you substituted a horse's head on Dadhyacha Atharvana, O terrible ones, he taught you the honey doctrine to keep his word.' This doctrine should be kept a secret. **17**

This, verily, is the honey doctrine which, Dadhyacha Atharvana declared to the two Asvins. Seeing them, the seer said: 'He (Supreme Being) made bodies with two feet and bodies with four feet. He first entered the bodies as a bird (the subtle body). On account of His dwelling in all bodies, He is called a Person, *Purusha*.' There is nothing that is not covered by Him, nothing that is not pervaded by Him. **18**

This, verily, is the honey doctrine which, Dadhyacha Atharvana declared to the two Asvins. Seeing them the seer said, 'He (Self, *Brahman*, *Atman*) transformed Himself in many forms. His forms were meant for making Him known. The Lord is perceived as manifold on account of *Maya* (notions superimposed by ignorance). To Him are yoked ten organs – nay, hundreds of them. He is indeed these sense-organs, ten thousands, many and innumerable. This *Brahman* is without cause or effect, interior or exterior. This *Brahman* is Self, the all-perceiving. This is the teaching.' **19**

Section 6

Now the line of teachers:
Pautimasya (received the teaching) from Gaupavana,
Gaupavana from (another) Pautimasya.
(This) Pautimasya from (another) Gaupavana.
(This) Gaupavana from Kausika, Kausika from Kaundinya,
Kaundinya from Sandilya,
Sandilya from Kausika and Gautama. Gautama from Agnivesya.
Agnivesya from Sandilya and Anabhimlata,
Anabhimlata from (another) Anabhimlata.
Anabhimlata from (still another) Anabhimlata.
(This) Anabhimlata from Gautama.
Gautama from Saitava and Pracinayogya,
Saitava and Pracinayogya from Parasarya.
Parasarya from Bharadvaja and Gautama,
Gautama from (another) Bharadvaja, Bharadvaja from (another) Parasarya,
Parasarya from Baijavapayana, Baijavapayana from Kausikayani,
Kausikayani from Ghrtakausika, Ghrtakausika from Parasaryayana.
Parasaryayana from Parasarya, Parasarya from Jatukarnya.
Jatukarnya from Asurayana and Yaska.
Asurayana from Traivani. Traivani from Anupajandhani.
Anupajandhani from Asuri. Asuri from Bharadvaja.
Bharadvaja from Atreya. Atreya from Manti.

"This Brahman is without cause or effect, interior or exterior.
This Brahman is Self, the all-perceiving. This is the teaching."

Manti from Gautama. Gautama from Vatsya.
Vatsya from Sandilya. Sandilya from Kaisorya Kapya.
Kaisorya Kapya from Kumaraharita. Kumaraharita from Galava.
Galava from Vidarbhikaundinya.
Vidarbhikaundinya from Vatasanapat Babhrava.
Vatasanapat Babhrava from Pathah Saubharat.
Pathah Saubharat from Ayasya Angirasa.
Ayasya Angirasa from Abhuti Tvastra.
Abhuti Tvastra from Visvarupa Tvastra.
Visvarupa Tvastra from the two Asvins.
The two Asvins from Dadhyacha Atharvana.
Dadhyacha Atharvana from Atharvan Daiva.
Atharvan Daiva from Mrtyu Pradhvamsana.
Mrtyu Pradhvamsana from Pradhvamsana.
Pradhvamsana from Ekarsi. Ekarsi from Vipracitti.
Vipracitti from Vyasti. Vyasti from Sanaru.
Sanaru from Sanatana, Sanatana from Sanaga.
Sanaga from Paramesthin. Paramesthin from Brahma.
Brahma is self-born. Salutations to Brahma.

1-3

Focussed Commentaries

Chapter 2

2.1 Incomplete definitions of *Brahman*

All results of meditation are shown to be transient when meditation is on a conditioned and limited object, be it the greatest.

It is not obligatory for an spiritual aspirant to confine himself to one of the twelve objects (enumerated by Gargya), he can choose any other object of his liking. However, meditation should not be limited to the object; it should be on that Principle which underlies the object, which gives the object its very existence.

Balaki Gargya was not an ignorant person. He had practiced meditation on several progressive phases of *Brahman*, up to *Hiranyagarbha*, the Cosmic Mind. But he had not known the Absolute, which transcends all – the manifested and the unmanifested. However, king Ajatashatru had realized that Absolute *Brahman*. Therefore, he could not accept all these lower forms of meditation suggested by Balaki – he had practiced all of them and transcended them. Balaki now realized his ignorance about the Supreme, *Brahman*. He offered himself to be a disciple of the king and prayed for instruction about that aspect of *Brahman* of which he was unaware. Though it was against the then – prevailing custom – that a *Kshatriya* teacher should impart knowledge to a *Brahmin* disciple – Ajatashatru agreed to instruct Balaki on the Supreme, unconditioned *Brahman* (2.1, 1-14).

Then Ajatashatru took Balaki to a man who was fast asleep, and woke him up. He then put two questions to Balaki:

(i) Where was the Consciousness of this man while he was asleep?
(ii) From where did this Consciousness come back when he woke up?

As Balaki could not answer these questions, the king himself gave the answers.

When the man was asleep, the Consciousness in him, together with all the sense-organs, was resting in that place which is referred to as the space in the heart. That Consciousness is *Brahman*. Moreover, this Consciousness in an individual is really cosmic and infinite by nature. Although sometimes it is said that individual Consciousness is a counterpart of Cosmic Consciousness, both are one and the same. This space within the heart is the same as the all-pervading space. When this Consciousness withdraws the senses into Itself, then the person falls asleep. The sense-consciousness is then unified with Self-consciousness; and there is a mass of bliss which individual Consciousness may be said to experience. So the answer to the first question is that during deep sleep, individual Consciousness of the sleeping man was unified with its source – Cosmic Consciousness.

The answer to the second question is that individual Consciousness came back from Cosmic Consciousness (2.1, 15-17).

During dream state, Consciousness moves, as it were, wherever it pleases and projects out of Itself whatever it desires – a great king, or a learned parent, or something else. Just as a king collects all his citizens and moves about in his city, so also this Self (Consciousness) in the individual withdraws the sense-organs from the objects experienced in waking state, and moves about with the vital force inside this body.

When a person goes to deep sleep, there is no longer any gulf between subject and object. Normal Consciousness of the subject as 'I' and the object as 'the world' is superseded by the unitary Consciousness of Self, which creeps in through the 72,000 nerves named *hita*, proceeding from the heart to every part of the body.

Just as a man in rapturous embrace of his beloved does not have any consciousness of the outer world, or his inner world of thoughts; even so, embraced by Self, he has no particular consciousness of the outer universe or the inner mental world. The individual Self remains in a state of bliss in deep sleep. It is a state in which Self experiences Self – there is no triad of the experiencer, the experienced and the experience.

Thus, Ajatashatru enumerated to Gargya the different states of Consciousness – gross sense consciousness in waking state, subtle mental-consciousness in dream-

---

'In deep sleep, there is no duality of subject and object – 'I' and 'World' – just as two lovers in embrace are unaware of their outer world or even inner thoughts.'

state, and absolute Self-consciousness in dreamless sleep state (2.1, 18-19).

ANALOGIES OF SPIDER AND FIRE

The analogy of spider and its web illustrates that the material of this world comes out of God, and therefore the world is non-different and identical with God. The next analogy of fire and sparks proves that the created world is fundamentally of the nature of God, just as sparks and fire are of same nature. Everything in the universe is therefore non-different in essence from the Supreme. The empirical reality of this waking world and the illusionary reality of the dream world have the same Absolute Reality at their bottom – without it they could not have any existence.

While commenting on this *mantra*, Sri Sankara has cited a very interesting and instructive parable to establish the identity of individual Self and Supreme Self. He also states that no change or modification takes place in Supreme Self when individual Self appears to come out of It, or when the world phenomenon is projected from It.

A certain prince got lost when he was a child. A hunter brought him up in a forest. Later, in his adulthood, someone informed him that he was really the prince of the country. The boy immediately left his false notion of being a hunter and assumed his original royalty. Did any change take place in the prince before he was lost, when he was living as a hunter, or after he returned to royalty? The prince was a prince all along. Likewise, this individual Self, nay the whole world, is really the Absolute, Supreme Self; but this knowledge somehow appears to be forgotten (2.1, 20).

– *Swami Sivananda*

Around the heart, there are 72,000 subtle veins. It is said that the sun and the heart are connected with each other through these veins and the rays of the sun. There is another suggestion that only one vein out of 101 veins leads to the sun. It is called *Brahmarandhra* (Aitareya Upanishad 1.3, 12). *Brahman* is said to enter the body as *Atman* through this vein. The two versions of 72,000 and 101 veins are mixed up in later accounts.

– *S. Radhakrishnan*

It is said: 'Having created the creation, the Creator entered into it.' This is true of us as well. We create our world and then enter into that world. We live in the world that we create. Like a spider, a person weaves his life and then he moves along in it. When his heart is pure, he creates a beautiful, enlightened life.

Moreover, the world is like the sparks. It is a part of *Brahman*, just as sparks are a part of fire. The sun, the moon, the lightening – all are parts of *Brahman*, like the sparks in a fire. *Brahman* is totality. *Brahman* is wholeness. And *Brahman* is known by knowing the Self. *Prana*, life-principle, is the Truth, *Brahman* is the truth of *Prana*. It is the Truth of truths, *Satyas satyam*.

– *Miscellaneous sources*

2.2 Meditation on *Prana*

The whole creation is a manifestation of Cosmic Life Principle (*Prana*) in varying degrees – least in inert objects, greater in vegetable and animal kingdom, still greater in human beings, and in super-humans like ancestors and celestials.

The seven divinities – Rudra, Parjanya etc. – preside over things connected with the eye, like red streaks, watering portion, pupil etc. One should meditate on these divinities as present in one's own eyes. Such a meditator realizes that the divine *Prana* is the unifying factor, the support of all his organs and their actions.

The seven orifices in the head are contemplated as the abode of seven sages. The entire manifested creation is to be meditated upon as located in the head. Similar meditations are given elsewhere also. For instance, Chandogya Upanishad instructs *inter alia* meditation on one's heart as if it contains the whole universe. The scriptures are stating a great truth in a graphical manner: The microcosm, verily, contains the macrocosm.

– *Swami Sivananda*

The two halves of this section appear to have originated out of different views. In the first half, the body is the chief topic; in the second, the head. In the first half, seven gods dwell in the eyes; in the second the two eyes are given the names of two Rishis.

– *Paul Deussen*

'Like a spider, a person weaves his life and then he moves along in it.'

2.3 Two profound descriptions of *Brahman*

Reality seems to possess two different and seemingly contradictory attributes. This is on account of the limiting adjuncts superimposed upon It through ignorance. The two attributes are: (i) grossness, perishability, finite limit or perceptibility on one side; and (ii) subtlety, imperishability, infinity, or imperceptibility on the other. It is difficult to comprehend how one and the same thing can have two contradictory natures at the same time? Just as formless light assumes the form of the object on which it falls, so also *Brahman* appears as possessed of the qualities of the limiting adjuncts, which are superimposed on It.

The entire creation is the result of five fundamental elements, designated as truth, *satyam* in this section. These elements – together with their effects, the human body and the senses – form the phenomenal existence, or the empirical reality from a relative point of view. To us, this relative existence seems to be the truth. *Brahman* is the basis of this relative existence, the Truth of truths.

After having established the absolute reality of *Brahman* as the basis for empirical reality, the Upanishad negates all attributes, all limiting adjuncts, which are superimposed on *Brahman* due to ignorance. The Ultimate Reality cannot be described in any positive and determinate terms. Every determination is a limitation. To define *Brahman* is to deny Him.

While eliminating the limiting adjuncts, the Upanishad reveals the real nature of *Brahman* in a breathtaking aphoristic expression: 'Not this, Not this, *neti, neti.*'

It may be asked how *Brahman* is described by these negations? The answer is that *Brahman* is indicated by the exclusion of all definitions which may be made with regard to the nature of *Brahman*. This, however, does not negate *Brahman*, the Absolute, as He is recognized to be the basis of all relative existences and phenomena. It means that *Brahman* is transcendent, and hence different from all this manifested world; He is beyond all possible assumptions that can be made about Him by the mind and the intellect. After asserting the negation *neti neti*, the text describes the Ultimate Reality as the substratum of everything, as the 'Truth of truths, *satyas satyam*. Thus, these two expressions deny the limitations of *Brahman* and at the same time assert that *Brahman* is the Ultimate Reality.

– *Swami Sivananda*

In *Republic*, God is an impersonal form of the good. In Timaeus, God is a self-moving spirit. This section of the Upanishad suggests that the two cannot be left unreconciled, but are to be treated as two forms of one Reality.

The fourth Gospel insists that God 'works' in the world, but he works through the Logos. Logos is God, not Godhead. Plotinus believes that while there is a realm which consists in the duality of subject and object, there is also an absolute unity from which all dualities proceed, which itself is above duality. Hooker calls Him the Most High and says: "Our soundest knowledge is to know that we know Him not, as indeed He is…. Our safest eloquence concerning Him is our silence." Many systems of thought distinguish between the absolute transcendent Godhead who 'dwells in the light which no man can approach unto' and the Creator God.

In this famous passage, the Upanishad speaks to us of the Absolute, transcendent, non-empirical Godhead. This is Sri Sankara's view.

– *S. Radhakrishnan*

In verse 2.3,6 the Upanishad finally takes to the formula *neti, neti* in order to express the complete distinction of *Brahman* from all knowable phenomena.

– *Paul Deussen*

2.4 Love means to see one Self in two bodies

Even as I am explaining, reflect…(Verse 2.4,4)

Those who recite the Vedas without understanding their meaning are like lifeless pillars, which bear the weight of a roof. Also, just as a donkey bearing the weight of sandalwood knows its weight but not its fragrance, so also is a *Brahmin* who knows the text of the Vedas and the scriptures, but not their significance. Further, it is said that some people are clever only at expounding doctrines, while others have the ability to practice what they learn. The hand carries the food to the mouth, but only the tongue knows the flavor.

'Just as formless light of sun assumes the form of the object on which it falls, so also Brahman appears as possessed of the qualities of the limiting adjuncts, which are superimposed on It.'

Verily, by seeing, hearing, thinking and understanding of Self, all this is known (Verse 2.4,5).

All objects of the world, earthly possessions and romantic delights provide opportunities for realization of Self. Contemplation is not mere philosophical thought. It is a higher stage of spiritual consciousness. It secures direct conviction of Reality. While a teacher can help, personal effort alone can take us to the goal of realization.

The Jain and the Buddhist systems also recognize three stages of religious development. The three jewels of Jainism are: right belief, right knowledge and right conduct.

You have bewildered me... (Verse 2.4,13)

The confusion is due to the seeming contradiction that Self is pure Consciousness, and that when It has departed from the body, there is no more Consciousness (2.4,12). The same fire cannot be both hot and cold. Sri Sankara points out that *Brahman*, pure intelligence, remains unchanged. It does not pass out with the destruction of the elements. However, individual existence caused by *avidya*, ignorance, is overcome.

– S. Radhakrishnan

Verses 2.4, 1-4 contain an introduction to the important passage that follows. All earthly goods are perishable and therefore worthless. More desirable than all these is knowledge.

Everything that exists – husband, wife, children, property, social status (represented by priestly and warrior classes), worlds, gods, Vedas, living beings and the universe – all these are dear to us not for their own sake, but for the sake of *Atman*. This indicates that we can know, possess or love a thing in this world only so far as we carry it as an idea in our Consciousness. He who has not raised himself to this level of knowledge – who thinks of husband, wife etc. as outside himself – he feels as an individual isolated from them. He feels like a foreign thing, 'abandoned', as it were.

To know *Atman* is to know the reality of everything.

An exquisite elucidation of the aforesaid thoughts is provided through the simile of three musical instruments. *Atman* is like a musical instrument, the world is like the sounds arising from it. The sounds are dependent on the musical instrument and graspable through it alone. Likewise, the world is dependent on *Atman* and graspable through It alone (2.4, 7-9).

Just as smoke arises out of fire, so also all Vedas and branches of knowledge have been 'breathed out' by *Atman*. Corresponding to our inspiration, the Indians have a kind of 'expiration'. *Brahman* breathes out the Vedas, whereupon these are experienced by the Rishis (2.4, 10).

Atman is the focal point – point of unity – of all the senses of knowledge and action, as also the mind and the heart. In fact, *Atman* is the focal point of all the states and conditions of the external world (2.4, 11).

Atman is merged or dissolved in the five elements – which have originated out of it – like a lump of salt in water. It raises Itself out of them as Consciousness in the body; and It is dissolved into them again with the death of body (2.4, 12-14).

– Paul Deussen

Immortality is total cessation of all types of desires. It is a state of 'perfect satisfaction' under all conditions. Wealth coexists with feverishness, begets cravings, leads to dissatisfaction, and finally destroys the mental and spiritual peace of the individual. While wealth helps one to lead a so-called 'affluent' life in this world, it cannot help one attain immortality.

Noticing that Maitreyi is greatly interested to know about the means of attaining immortality, and seeing in her a qualified pupil endowed with the spirit of renunciation, Yagyavalkya begins to instruct her about the Supreme Self, whose nature is immortality (2.4, 1-4).

Verse-5 states that Self is dearer than a son, husband or wife; dearer than wealth, dearer than all objects. It means that our love for Self is the basis for our love of all other objects. Generally, we love others because we think that they give us pleasure and joy; or remove some kind of dissatisfaction. Our actions are either motivated by an urge for subjective happiness – the happiness of our own selves – or impelled by selflessness, which seeks objective happiness through the happiness of others. But there is a superior kind of love, which knows no subject-object distinction. This

---

'Atman is like a musical instrument, the world is like the sounds arising from it.
The world is dependent on Atman and graspable through It alone.'

love is due to the underlying and all-encompassing soul, which is non-different from and inextricably identical with everything here. Husband, wife, son, wealth – things enumerated or not enumerated in this verse – are the objects of love for the subject, for the mere fact of their mutual oneness and identity. In such love, subject-object distinction falls flat, and the essential unity of Self is comprehended. This, as declared previously, is the dearest of all.

To those who consider Self as something different from the object, who involve themselves in the duality of a knowing subject and a knowable object, Yagyavalkya sounds a note of warning. Those who postulate that the world or God or anything else is different from Self, they will find themselves rejected by the world, God or anything else. Reject duality and realize Unity – this is what the mantra says (2.4, 6).

Why is so much emphasis laid on knowledge of *Atman*? Verses 7-9 answer this question of the materialist, raised against the doctrine of oneness and the non-dual nature of Self.

One standing at a distance is not able to grasp or stop the external sounds of a drum, or a conch or a lute. For this, one has to go to the musical instrument and stop it by hand. Here, in this analogy, musical instruments stand for Self. Different universes emanate from Him like different notes from musical instruments.

The underlying idea of these metaphors – drum, conch and lute – is that knowledge of the phenomenal universe cannot confer full and complete knowledge upon us. It is only by grasping the Reality, through direct realization, that we can know all about the universe. Know thy Self, and you will know everything – this is the import of these mantras (2.4, 7-9).

The entire universe is not something distinguishable from its cause. The apparent gulf between the phenomenal reality of the universe and ultimate Reality of the Absolute is bridged by the declaration in this mantra about the relationship between fire and smoke, cause and effect. Even as breaths come out of man naturally and without any thought or effort on his part, so do these eternally existing forms of knowledge issue spontaneously out of Supreme Self. It is like the smoke, embers and flames spontaneously issuing forth from fire (2.4, 10).

Prior to its manifestation the universe was *Brahman* only. Even after its origination – when it is differentiated, as it were, by name, form and action – the universe is not distinct from its original substance, viz. *Brahman*. Verse-11 says that at the time of dissolution, it again becomes one with *Brahman*. This is illustrated through many examples. Self is pictured as the abode of the mind, the intellect and the sense organs – five senses of perception and five organs of action. The ocean is the only abode of all rivers. The above-mentioned twelve body-parts are the only abode of their respective objects. Likewise, Self is the only abode of all phenomena (2.4, 11).

This identity is further explained through the analogy of salt and water. When a lump of salt has dissolved in water, one is not able to separate it from water. But from whichever part one might take a few drops and sip, they will taste saline. When individual Consciousness is merged in the totality of its source, the Absolute Self, It loses its individuality and separateness, like the lump of salt dissolved in water. Self is a homogeneous mass of Consciousness in which empirical reality is merged, like salt is merged in water.

Human body has sprung forth from primeval elements. The Absolute appears in it as an individualized entity. But as soon as these elements are annihilated, through the knowledge of Self, individual existence is also destroyed (2.4, 12).

In the previous verse, Yagyavalkya had said that the great Being is a mass of Consciousness (Sanskrit word *Vigyana* is also translated as Knowledge). He had also said that when the individual soul realizes its identity and frees itself from the fetters of body and senses, 'there is no more Consciousness'. Maitreyi requested reconciliation of these two apparently contradictory statements.

When Yagyavalkya said that having departed from here, there is no Consciousness, he meant that after death, there is no Consciousness of individuality. Freed of all objectivity and subjectivity, It merges in the great Reality of universal Consciousness (2.4, 13).

In order to see another, hear another, smell another and so forth, duality has necessarily to be presupposed. In this context, when Yagyavalkya says that there is duality, 'as it were', it is very clear that he is not prepared to accept duality at any cost and under any

---

'Those who postulate that the world or God or anything else is different from Self, they will find themselves rejected by the world, God or anything else. Reject duality and realize Unity.'

condition, even at the present state of our consciousness. Our senses are relevant in the realm of plurality. They fail in the realm of non-dual Supreme Self. In that realm, there is complete cessation of the triad of seer, seeing and sight; knower, knowing and knowledge, and so on (2.4, 14).

– Swami Sivananda

This section, Yagyavalkya-Maitreyi dialogue, is the crest jewel in the crown of Upanishadic literature. A wife who considers her husband as her own Self enjoys all happiness, and not one who treats him as different from herself.

The source of all joy is *Atman*, and not the objects outside, as wrongly conceived by a non-discriminative mind.

In this section, knowledge of *Brahman* as a means to immortality has been imparted to Maitreyi. Also, wealth has been deprecated, and by implication rites have been shunned. Besides, there is a rejection of caste system as we see in the text: '*Brahmin* ignores one, *Kshatriya* ignores one... (2.4,6). For a man who does not identify his Self as a *Brahmin* or a *Kshatriya*, the benefits of rites and their accessories are automatically dropped.

– Sri Sankara, translated by Swami Madhavananda

2.5 *Madhu Vidya* or Honey doctrine

The earth and all its living beings are mutually dependent, just like bees and honey. Bees make the honey and honey supports the bees. *Brahman* is the Self, both in earth and in living beings.

This law: Though law is not directly perceived, it is described by the word 'this', as though it was directly perceived; because the effects produced by it are directly perceived. Self and *Dharma* or righteousness are regarded as equivalent (2.5, 11).

Cosmic Self and individual Self are referred to, in verse 2.5, 14.

The two *Asvins* desired instruction from Dadhyan but he was unwilling to impart it, as Indra had threatened Dadhyan that he would cut-off his head if he taught this *Madhu Vidya*, honey doctrine, to any one else. So the *Asvins* cut off Dadhyan's head and substituted for it a horse's head. Dadhyan taught the honey doctrine to the two *Asvins* with the substituted horse's head. Indra carried out his threat, and the two *Asvins* restored to Dadhyan his own head. This story illustrates the extreme difficulty, which even the gods had to face, to acquire the knowledge of honey doctrine. It also contains an important teaching: keeping one's solemn promise is more important than life.

– S. Radhakrishnan

According to Vedanta, all organic beings (e.g. plants, animals, men, and gods) are wandering souls, and are as such *Brahman*. Inorganic nature (earth, water, fire, air and space) forms only the scene or the field on which organic beings obtain the fruits of their action. This inorganic field also originated out of *Brahman*. We see this thought germinating in this section. It establishes the mutual dependence of the inorganic and the organic (called *bhutani*). It says that in both the organic and the inorganic, there is one powerful immortal spirit, *Purusha*, who makes mutual dependence possible.

In the statement of this basic thought, fourteen phenomena of the external world are enumerated. These are: five elements (Earth, Water, Fire, Air, and Space), five cosmic phenomena (Sun, Moon, Directions, Lightening, and Clouds) and four potencies of nature (Righteousness, Truth, Mankind and Self). All these are honey for human beings and the beings are honey for them, i.e. they nourish one another. The beings are nourished by earth, earth by beings, etc. How is this possible? Because within the beings, there exist the following potencies: (1) Body, (2) Semen (3) Speech (4) Life-breath (5) Eyes (6) Ears (7) Mind (8) Light (9) Word (10) Space in the heart (11) Law, *Dharma*. (12) Truth, *Satyam* (13) Human beings and (14) Self, *Atman*.

In both the psychic and the cosmic potencies enumerated above, there dwells a shining immortal Person; *tejomaya amrtamaya Purusha*. He is identical in all the 28 manifestations. He is also the *Atman* in us.

These thoughts about *Atman* are comparable to Kant's doctrine of 'the affinity of phenomena' and the 'synthetic unity of apperception'.

– Paul Deussen

---

*'The earth and all its living beings are mutually dependent, just like bees and honey.
Bees make the honey and honey supports the bees.'*

There is mutual helpfulness among the parts of the universe, including the earth. Also, it is common experience that those things, which are mutually helpful, spring from the same cause and dissolve into the same thing. Therefore, this universe must also be like that. This is the meaning expressed in this section.

This earth is the honey or effect of all beings. Likewise, all beings are the honey or effect of this earth. Together, with the shining immortal Person is who is in the earth and the shining immortal Being who is in the body, these four are the composite effects, the universe. Hence the universe has originated from the same cause. That one cause alone, from which it has sprung, is real – It is *Brahman*. Everything else is an effect, a modification, a mere name. This is the essence of this section dealing with a series of mutually helpful things.

– Sri Sankara, translation by Swami Madhavananda

Everything is dependent on everything else. The infinite number of objects and phenomena of this universe are inextricably connected with one another, like threads in a network. All this is, verily, nothing but Supreme Reality, *Brahman-Atman*. This, in short, is the essence of this section on *Madhu Vidya*. Everything from the creator to man to matter is organically and vitally connected. When one touches an object, one touches the whole cosmos. When one sees something, it is not an isolated object one sees, but it is the whole universe. Everything here and everywhere is honey, *Atman*. One's own Self is the Self of all.

The conscious principle in the earth is the same as present in all beings. These four – the earth, the beings, Consciousness in earth and Consciousness in beings – are nothing but *Atman* (2.5, 1). One can substitute in place of earth any other element or heavenly body or abstract principle (2.5, 2-14). The same Consciousness is immanent in the microcosm as well as the macrocosm.

The term honey or *madhu* in this section is used to convey the sense of correlation, mutual co-operation, or interdependence existing among earth, other primeval elements and all creatures – in their gross and subtle, individual and cosmic forms. Bees collect honey from various kinds of flowers and honey serves them as nourishment. Likewise, all beings are nourished by the elements (earth, water, air, fire, and space); and all beings nourish the elements.

Every object in the universe is an effect of the Supreme Cause.

Seed is the cause of a tree, and tree is the cause of a seed. Thus, both cause and effect are blended in each other. From this we postulate that all objects – which are the effects of some causes, and which in turn are the causes of some effects – are essentially the effects of the ultimate Causeless Cause. The analogy of honey brings home to us that all objects – despite their mutual cause and effect relationship – are nothing but the composite effects of the Supreme Cause. Creatures, earth, Consciousness in creatures and Consciousness in earth – these fourfold effects are blended in one cause, and their relationship is denoted by honey. They are inter-blended, interrelated, and interdependent. A relationship is ascribed to them due to ignorance of the fact that they have one cause; and this cause is Self.

Verses (2.5, 1-14) contain a repetition of four statements: '….indeed, these four are just this Self. This is immortal, this is *Brahman*, this is all'. They remind us that this universe is in essence Self, which is *Brahman*, the immortal, the All. The terms 'Self', '*Brahman*', 'Immortal' and 'All' are identical and they refer to the same non-dual Reality. Earth, beings, Consciousness in earth, and Consciousness in beings – all four are Self, and Self alone (2.5, 1-14).

In verse-15 the interconnection and interdependence of every thing in this universe is likened to that existing between the spokes of a wheel, the rim and the hub.

Verses 16-19 refer in aphoristic language to the well know story connected with this secret knowledge, *madhu vidya* or honey doctrine.

Verse-16 is eulogistic, even though it may seem to condemn the actions of *Asvins*. It reveals the glory of Self-knowledge, and the difficulty of attaining it.

Verse-17 is connected with a rite called *pravargya* for restoring the head of a person identified with the sacrificial rite.

'The terms 'Self', 'Brahman', 'Immortal' and 'All' are identical and they refer to the same non-dual Reality.'

Verse-18 declares the unity of Self. The Supreme Lord created human beings with two feet and animals with four feet. Having thus created different bodies comparable to citadels, the Lord entered into them as the subtle principle. 'Bird' in this verse represents the subtle body, and 'bodies' stand for gross bodies. On account of His dwelling in all bodies, He is designated as *Purva*. He pervades all - from inside, as well as from outside. He is identical with *Brahman*.

Verse-19 states the conclusion. It is the Supreme Being who appears through His power of *maya* as innumerable beings, objects and concepts. This is the secret truth. To say that the world veils Him is ignorance and to realize that the world reveals Him is knowledge. Existence is He, creation is He and destruction is He. The creator is He and the created is He alone. He does not change by His creation. He is non-different from His creation. His creation is not external to Him.

Due to ignorance, we hold Self as something different from the organs. We wrongly believe that there are as many souls as there are individual bodies and organs. In reality, there is only one *Brahman*. With a view to avoid any misunderstanding of the teachings of this section and to reconcile all apparent contradictions, the concluding verse says that *Brahman* is without cause and effect, without interior and exterior, and thus transcends all duality.

This is the great mystery of God and His Creation. Meditation on 'Honey' reveals this mystery, reconciles all apparent contradictions, resolves all problems, and brings about supreme peace and bliss.

– *Swami Sivananda*

3. What is *Brahman*?

SIMPLIFIED SYNOPSES

Janaka, king of Videha organized a contest of wisdom. The event saw a great discussion between learned scholars of spirituality. These discussions form the contents of the present chapter. In the discussions, Yagyavalkya maintains his superiority over nine interlocutors – Asvala, Artabhaga, Bhujyu, Usasta, Kahola, Gargi, Uddalaka, Gargi (once again) and Sakalya - one after another.

3.1 Benefits of sacrificial rituals

Asvala's questions relate to modalities and benefits of sacrificial rituals. According to this section, performance of sacrifice is a means of communion with the all-pervading Self. The four priests of a sacrifice are equated here with speech, sight, life-breath and mind; as also their cosmic counterparts – Fire, Sun, Air and Moon.

3.2 Name and deeds survive death

In this section, Artabhaga puts five questions to Yagyavalkya.

The first question is about sense organs and their objects. These are called *graha* and *atigraha*, literally translated as 'perceivers' and 'over-perceivers'. Yagyavalkya enumerates eight of them, but not in any structured sequence: five organs of knowledge, two of action, and the mind. The implied message here is that objects of senses stimulate the senses and are therefore stronger than the senses (3.2, 1-9).

'Objects of senses stimulate the senses and are therefore stronger than the senses.'

It is noted that Yagyavalkya's answer omits three organs of action - procreation, excretion and movement.

The second question is a tricky one. Death swallows everything, but is there something that swallows death? Yagyavalkya answers this question with the analogy of fire and water. Fire destroys every thing, but is itself destroyed by water. Likewise, death is swallowed by Absolute *Brahman*; like pickle or sauce, says another Upanishad.

The third question: When a liberated person dies, what happens to his senses? Answer: These merge in his Self. His physical body swells and disintegrates, but not his Self or *Atman*, which is immortal. In the case of an ordinary person, the senses merge with the primal elements.

The fourth question: What remains of a liberated person when he dies? Answer: His name. His Self becomes one with Universal Self.

The fifth question: What is left of an ordinary person (not liberated), when he dies? Answer: His works, *karmas*. These produce rebirth.

3.3 Where do good deeds lead to?

In this section Bhujyu wants to know what happened to the descendents of Parikshit, who are known to have performed many sacrificial rituals? The answer given by Yagyavalkya is open to interpretation. According to one commentator, the soul of a person who performs good deeds merges with the Cosmic Mind, *Hiranyagarbha,* which pervades both microcosm and macrocosm. Metaphorically, Indra, the chief Vedic deity, assumes the form of a bird and carries the subtle body of a performer of sacrifices to the Cosmic Mind through an ultramicroscopic opening on the circumference between the two halves of the Cosmic Egg. The word used for the Cosmic Mind here is Air, *Vayu*.

3.4 *Brahman* is that which breathes in you

Usasta : What is *Brahman*?
Yagyavalkya : *Brahman* is the Self in you. It is also the Self in all things. *Brahman* is that which breathes in you. It cannot be perceived. You cannot see the seer, hear the hearer, think of the thinker, or know the knower.

3.5 *Brahman* is beyond relative attributes

Kahola's question is identical to that of Usasta in the previous section: 'What is *Brahman*?'

Earlier, Yagyavalkya described *Brahman* as that which breaths in man. This time, he describes *Brahman* from a different perspective. He says *Brahman* is that which is beyond all relative attributes like hunger, thirst, old age etc. He also describes certain requirements for realizing *Brahman* – discipline desires, study scriptures, practice meditation in silence and live like a child, without any ego or deception.

3.6 *Brahman* is woven like warp and woof

'Every effect is pervaded by its cause.'

In this section, Yagyavalkya is questioned by Gargi, a leading lady philosopher of ancient times. She starts on the presumption that every effect is pervaded by its cause – like threads woven in cloth lengthwise and crosswise ('warp and woof' in the text). For example, primeval water as the cause pervades its effect – earth – like warp and woof. 'What is the cause which pervades water?' 'Air', answers Yagyavalkya. 'And what is the cause which pervades air?' asks Gargi. The series of questions and answers lead from one element to another – earth, water, air and space. The elements are so arranged that each preceding element is held together by the succeeding element, which is its cause and is more subtle as well as more pervasive. Fire is not included because it cannot manifest itself independently without help from other elements.

What is the cause of space? After exhausting the primeval elements. Yagyavalkya identifies the worlds of *gandharvas*, sun, moon, stars, gods, *Indra*, and *Prajapati* and *Brahma* (not to be confused with *Brahman*) in increasing order of subtlety (or decreasing order of relativity). The worlds enumerated here represent various states of Consciousness.

When Gargi wants to know what pervades the world of *Brahma*, the Creator, or what is the cause of *Brahma*, Yagyavalkya cautions her that she should not cross the limit beyond which logical enquiry becomes irrelevant. Mind can reason only about relative objects and phenomena. Reasoning is irrelevant in the realm of the Absolute.

'Mind can reason only about relative objects and phenomena. Reasoning is irrelevant in the realm of the Absolute.'

3.7 Brahman, the inner controller

In this section, Yagyavalkya declares that *Brahman* is the cosmic string, which holds the worlds together. *Brahman* is also the Inner Ruler. He dwells in anything you can think of. For example: "He dwells in the mind, yet is other than the mind, whom mind does not know, whose body the mind is, who controls the mind from within. He is your Self, the Inner Controller, the Immortal". This profound statement is repeated 21 times with different example.

There are 13 examples relating to the cosmos and 8 relating to man. These are: Five elements (Earth, Water, Fire, Sky, Air), seven cosmic objects and phenomena (Heavens, Sun, Directions, Moon and Stars, Space, Darkness, Light), beings, life-breath, mind, understanding, procreative fluid, and selected sense organs of perception and action (speech, eye, ear, skin).

Yagyavalkya concludes with the statement: '*Brahman* is the seer who cannot be seen, hearer who cannot be heard, the knower who cannot be known. He is your Self, the Inner Controller, the Immortal. Everything else is perishable.'

3.8 Imperishable *Brahman*

'The Unmanifested is the cause of the manifested world.'

It will be recalled that in section 3.6, Yagyavalkya had avoided answering Gargi's question: What is the ultimate cause of the manifested world, (denoted by *Brahma*)? In this section, she seeks permission to question Yagyavalkya again, and repeats her question. This time, Yagyavalkya gives an answer: 'The Unmanifested (denoted by *Akash*, Space) is the cause of the manifested world'. But what is the cause of the unmanifested? persists Gargi. What follows in 3.8, 8-11 is a very profound description of the indescribable *Brahman*, the Ultimate Cause of all, manifested as well as unmanifested.

- It is Imperishable, Absolute, *Akshara* (8)
- It is different from Matter (8)
- It is without any relative attributes or qualities (8)
- It is neither the subject, nor the object (8)
- It regulates all objects and phenomena in the endless space (9)
- It regulates Time in all its measurements, from year to nanosecond (9)
- It regulates causality - the law of cause and effect (10)
- It is not an object of sense perception, but It is Itself the basis of all perceptions (11)

3.9, 1-9 Many gods but one *Brahman*

Question: How many gods are there?

Answer: Infinite, so to say; but in reality, only One. That is, *Prana*, Life Principle. *Prana* is *Brahman*. It is also called That.

This is the essence of section 9. It starts with Sakalya asking: How many gods are there?

Yagyavalkya puts the number at 3306. This is on the authority of *nivid*, a set of hymns, which are eulogistic invocations to gods. Yagyavalkya then explains that these 3306 'gods' are in fact only different aspects of gods which according to Vedic scriptures are only 33 in number. These 33 gods, also known as Vedic gods, are:

'Brahman is the seer who cannot be seen, hearer who cannot be heard, the knower who cannot be known.'

Vasus	: Fire, Earth, Air, Space, Sun, Heaven, Moon and Stars	8
Rudras	: Five sense organs of knowledge, five of action, and the mind	11
Adityas	: Twelve months of the year	12
Indra	: Symbol of vigor and strength, personified by thunder	1
Prajapati	: Symbol of sacrificial rituals	1
		33

> *'The infinite gods are reducible to just one god - Prana, or Life Principle.'*

Yagyavalkya further explains that these 33 gods are in fact included in just six gods; and the six gods are further reducible to three; and the three to two. These are Matter and Life Principle, *Prana* (3.9,8)

Interestingly, Yagyavalkya then says, that the two gods can be reduced to one-and-a-half, Air. Why a fraction? Because we all live only on Air, so Air is more than itself.

Apparently, Upanishadic view of god, *deva*, the 'shining one' is deeper than what we normally refer to as God.

In a broad sense, the cause of a thing is the god of that thing. As there are infinite things in the universe, there are infinite gods. *Prana* is the cosmic vital-force that vibrates in every thing – from subatomic particles to vast galaxies. In the ultimate analysis, therefore, the infinite gods are reducible to just one god – *Prana*, or Life Principle. It is the sum total of all gods. Hence it is *Brahman*. It is also called That.

3.9, 10-18
Incomplete definitions of *Brahman*

This section is like an earlier section 2.1, in which Balaki Gargya provided twelve definitions of *Brahman*, but these were considered incomplete by Ajatashatru; as each of these represented just one of the infinite aspects of Totality. Here Sakalya describes *Brahman* as that Cosmic Person, *Purusha* who has many abodes, and he enumerates eight of them. According to Sakalya, this *Purusha* is illumined by the mind. He perceives through Heart, Eyes or Ears – these are said to be His worlds – and He is the ultimate support of every soul. Yagyavalkya identifies the presiding deities of each abode as follows:

> *'Brahman is that Cosmic Person, Purusha, who has many abodes.'*

	Abode of Cosmic Person	Instrument of Perception	Presiding deity	Verse
1.	Earth	Fire	Immortality	(3.9,10)
2.	Desire	Heart	Woman	(3.9,11)
3.	Forms	Eyes	Truth	(3.9,12)
4.	Space	Ear	Quarters	(3.9,13)
5.	Darkness	Heart	Death	(3.9,14)
6.	Colors	Eyes	Life	(3.9,15)
7.	Water	Heart	Varuna	(3.9,16)
8.	Procreative fluid	Heart	Prajapati	(3.9,17)

'The cause of a thing is the god of that thing. As there are infinite things in the universe, there are infinite gods.'

[3.9] WHAT IS BRAHMAN?

Yagyavalkya then becomes impatient with questions of repetitive nature and alleges that Sakalya was being used as a front by the learned *Brahmins* assembled there, as they did not have the courage to question him directly.

3.9, 19-26
Space, Mind and Self

Sakalya expresses his displeasure at the contemptuous remark of Yagyavalkya. Thereafter, in response to a series of questions by Sakalya, Yagyavalkya describes the presiding deities of the five quarters of Space together with their supports, as follows:

Quarter	Presiding	Deity Support	Verse
East	Sun	Eyes, forms, heart	3.9, 20
South	Yama	Sacrifice, offerings to priests faith, heart	3.9, 21
West	Varuna	Water, semen, heart	3.9, 22
North	Soma	Initiatory rites, truth, heart	3.9, 23
Zenith (up)	Agni (Fire)	Speech, heart	3.9, 24

'Self is imperceptible, indestructible, unattached and unfettered; It is beyond suffering and injury.'

It will be observed that the ultimate support of all that exists in all the five directions of Śpace is the Mind (referred to as the heart in the Upanishads). Feeling disappointed, Sakalya asks: On what is the heart supported? Yagyavalkya's satirical reply is that obviously the heart is supported by the body (Verse 25).

'On what is the body supported?' asks Sakalya. 'On life-breath and its five forms: in-breath, out-breath, diffused-breath, equalizing-breath and ascending-breath. This life-breath, *Prana* is identical with Self.'

Yagyavalkya then describes Self. It is imperceptible, indestructible, unattached and unfettered. It is beyond suffering and injury. It is described as '*neti, neti*, not this, not this'. Whatever Sakalya talked about in verses 3.9, 10-17 are only abodes, worlds, gods and beings of the Self, the Cosmic Person, *Purusha*.

Next, Yagyavalkya turns the tables and asks a question to Sakalya: 'Who is that Cosmic Person, *Purusha*?' He also announces a curse if Sakalya is unable to answer, and Sakalya becomes its victim.

3.9, 27-28
Man compared to a tree

In this section, Yagyavalkya compares man metaphorically to a tree. He then asks: 'Just as a tree arises from a seed, from what is a man reborn after his death?' He cautions that procreative fluid cannot be the answer as that is produced from a living being. He then answers his own question: 'It is from *Brahman* that a man is reborn. *Brahman* is both Knowledge and Bliss. *Brahman* is the final goal of everyone – whether one follows the path of righteous work or of spiritual wisdom.'

'It is from Brahman that a man is reborn. Brahman is both Knowledge and Bliss.'

Translated Text

CHAPTER 3

Section 1

Janaka (King) of Videha performed a sacrifice at which many presents were offered to *Brahmins* of Kurus and Panchala gathered there. In Janaka of Videha arose a desire to know which of these *Brahmins* was the most learned in scripture. He set apart a thousand cows. To the horns (of each cow) were fastened ten coins (of gold). He then addressed the *Brahmins*: **1**

'Venerable *Brahmins*, let the wisest among you take away these cows'.

Those *Brahmins* did not dare (to take the cows). Then Yagyavalkya said to his pupil, Samasravas:

'My dear, drive them away.'

Samasravas stood up to drive them away. The *Brahmins* were enraged (and said): 'How can he declare himself to be the wisest among us?'

Now, there was Asvala, the Hotr priest of Janaka of Videha. He asked him,

'Yagyavalkya, are you, indeed, the wisest *Brahmin* among us?'

He replied, 'I bow to the wisest *Brahmin* but I also wish to have these cows'.

Therefore, Asvala, the Hotr priest, decided to question him. **2**

Asvala : Since everything here is pervaded by death, since everything is overcome by death, by what means does the sacrificer free himself from the reach of death?

Yagyavalkya : By the Hotr priest, by fire, by speech. Verily, speech is the Hotr of sacrifice. That which is this speech is this fire. This (fire) is Hotr. This is freedom. This is complete freedom. **3**

Asvala : Since everything here is pervaded by day and night, since everything is overcome by day and night, by what means does the sacrificer free himself from the reach of day and night?

Yagyavalkya : By the Adhavaryu priest, by the eye, by the sun. Verily, the eye is the Adhavaryu of the sacrifice. That which is his eye is the yonder sun. This is Adhavaryu. This is freedom. This is complete freedom. **4**

Asvala : Since everything here is overtaken by bright and dark fortnights, since everything is overcome by bright and dark fortnights, by what means does the sacrificer free himself from the reach of bright and dark fortnights?

"Venerable Brahmins, let the wisest among you take away these cows."

Yagyavalkya	:	By the Udgatr priest, by air, by breath. Verily, breath is the Udgatr priest of the sacrifice. That which is this breath is air. This is Udgatr priest. This is freedom. This is complete freedom. **5**
Asvala	:	Since the sky appears to be without a support, by what means of ascent does a sacrificer reach the heavenly world?
Yagyavalkya	:	By the Brahma priest, by the mind, by the moon. Verily, mind is the Brahma of the sacrifice. That which is the mind is the yonder moon. This is Brahma. This is freedom. This is complete freedom.
		This is concerning freedom; and now the achievements. **6**
Asvala	:	How many (kinds of) Rk verses will the Hotr priest use today in this sacrifice?
Yagyavalkya	:	Three.
Asvala	:	Which are these three?
Yagyavalkya	:	The introductory verse, the verse accompanying the sacrifice and the benedictory verse as the third.
Asvala	:	What does one win by these?
Yagyavalkya	:	Whatever that is here and has breath. **7**
Asvala	:	How many (kinds of) oblations will the Adhavaryu priest offer today in this sacrifice?
Yagyavalkya	:	Three.
Asvala	:	Which are these three.
Yagyavalkya	:	Those which blaze upward, those which make a great noise and those which, when offered, sink downward.
Asvala	:	What does one win by these?
Yagyavalkya	:	By those which blaze upward one wins the world of gods, for the world of gods burns bright, as it were. By those which make a great noise one wins the world of ancestors, for the world of ancestors is excessively (noisy). By those which sink downwards one wins the world of men, for the world of men is down below, as it were. **8**
Asvala	:	With how many divinities does the *Brahma* priest on the right protect the sacrifice today?
Yagyavalkya	:	With one.
Asvala	:	Which is that one?

"Question: By what means of ascent does a sacrificer reach the heavenly world?
Answer: By the mind."

Yagyavalkya :	The mind alone. Verily, the mind is infinite; the *Visvedevas* are infinite. He thereby, wins an infinite world **9**
Asvala :	How many hymns of praise will the Udgatr priest chant today in the sacrifice?
Yagyavalkya :	Three.
Asvala :	Which are these three?
Yagyavalkya :	The introductory hymn, the hymn accompanying the sacrifice and the benedictory hymn as the third.
Asvala :	Which are these three with reference to Self?
Yagyavalkya :	The introductory hymn is the in-breath, the hymn accompanying the sacrifice is the out-breath. The benedictory hymn is the diffused-breath.
Asvala :	What does one win by these?
Yagyavalkya :	By the introductory hymn one wins the world of earth; by the accompanying hymn, the world between earth and heaven; by the benedictory hymn one wins the world of heaven.
	Thereupon the Hotr priest Asvala kept silent. **10**

Section 2

Then Jaratkarava Artabhaga questioned him.

Artabhaga :	How many organs of perception (*graha*) are there? How many objects of perception (*atigraha*) are there?
Yagyavalkya :	There are eight organs of perception, and eight objects of perception.
Artabhaga :	Those eight organs of perception and eight objects of perception, which are they? **1**
Yagyavalkya :	Nose is an organ of perception. It is seized (controlled) by odor as its object. One smells odor by in-breath. **2**
	Speech is an organ of perception. It is seized by name as its object. One utters names by speech. **3**
	Tongue is an organ of perception. It is seized by taste as its object. One knows tastes by the tongue. **4**
	Eye is an organ of perception. It is seized by form as its object. One sees forms by the eye. **5**

"Verily, the mind is infinite."

	Ear is an organ of perception. It is seized by sound as its object. One hears sounds by the ear. **6**
	Mind is an organ of perception. It is seized by desire as its object. One desires through the mind. **7**
	Hands are organs of perception. They are seized by action as their object. One performs actions by the hands. **8**
	Skin is an organ of perception, It is seized by touch as its object. One feels through the touch of skin.
	These are the eight organs of perception, and eight objects of perception. **9**
Artabhaga	: Since everything here is food for death, what, pray, is that divinity for whom death is food?
Yagyavalkya	: Fire, verily, is death. It is food for water. He (who knows this) overcomes further death. **10**
Artabhaga	: When a liberated sage dies, do his senses go up from him or do they not?
Yagyavalkya	: No, they merge in him. (The body) swells up, gets inflated and in that state lies dead. **11**
Artabhaga	: When such a person dies, what is it that does not leave him?
Yagyavalkya	: His name. His Name is infinite and infinite are the *Visvedevas*. He (who knows this) wins an infinite world. **12**
Artabhaga	: When speech (voice) of a dead person enters into fire, breath into air, eye into sun, mind into moon, hearing into quarters, Self into space, hairs of the body into herbs, hairs on the head into trees and blood and semen are deposited in water, what then is left of this person?
Yagyavalkya	: Artabhaga, my dear, take my hand. We two alone shall know of this; this is not for us (to speak of) in public.
	The two went away and deliberated. What they said was *karma* and what they praised was *karma*. Verily, one becomes good by good actions, bad by bad actions. Thereafter, Artabhaga kept silent. **13**

Section 3

Then Bhujyu Lahyayani asked Yagyavalkya:

'Once we were travelling around as wanderers among the Madra tribe and came to the house of Patanchala Kapya. He had a daughter who was possessed by a

"Verily, one becomes good by good actions, bad by bad actions."

gandharva. We asked him, 'Who are you?' He said, 'I am Sudhanvan, a descendant of Angirasa.' Then, talking to him about the limits of the world, we asked him, 'What has become of the descendents of Parikshit? What has become of the descendents of Parikshit?' And I ask you, Yagyavalkya: 'What has become of the descendents of Parikshit?' 1

Yagyavalkya replied:

'He (the *gandharva*) evidently told (you) that they went where those who perform horse sacrifice go.'

'And where do the performers of horse sacrifice go?' (asked Bhujyu).

'Thirty two times the space covered by the sun's chariot in a day makes this world. Around it covering twice the area is the earth. Around it covering twice the area is the ocean. In between there is a space as fine as the edge of a razor, or the wing of a mosquito. *Indra*, having become a bird, delivered the descends of Parikshit to Air (Cosmic Mind). Air, placing them in itself led them to the place where the performers of horse sacrifice were. Thus he (the *gandharva*) would have extolled Air. Therefore, Air is microcosm as well as macrocosm. He, who knows it as such, conquers further death.'

After that Bhujyu Lahyayani kept silent. 2

Section 4

Then Usasta Chakrayan asked him:

Usasta : Explain to me the *Brahman* that is immediately present and directly perceived as Self in all things.

Yagyavalkya : That is your Self. That is within all things.

Usasta : Which is within all things, Yagyavalkya?'

Yagyavalkya : He who breathes in with your in-breathing is the Self of yours. He is in all things. He who breathes out with your out-breathing is the Self of yours, which is in all things. He who breathes about with your diffused-breathing is the Self of yours, which is in all things. He who breathes up with your up-breathing is the Self of yours, which is in all things.' 1

Usasta : This has been explained as one might say 'This is a cow.' 'This is a horse.' Explain to me the *Brahman* that is immediately present and directly perceived as Self in all things.

Yagyavalkya : This is your Self that is within all things.

Usasta : Which is within all things, Yagyavalkya?

"He who breathes-in with your in-breathing is the Self of yours. He is in all things."

Yagyavalkya : You cannot see the seer of seeing, you cannot hear the hearer of hearing, you cannot think of the thinker of thinking, you cannot know the knower of knowledge. He is your Self that is in all things. Everything else is perishable.

Thereupon Usasta Chakrayan kept silent. **2**

Section 5

Now Kahola Kausitakeya questioned Yagyavalkya:

Kahola : Explain to me the *Brahman* that is immediately present and directly perceived, that is the Self in all things.

Yagyavalkya : That is your Self, which is in all things.

Kahola : Which is within all things, Yagyavalkya?

Yagyavalkya : It is that which transcends hunger and thirst, sorrow and delusion, old age and death. Knower of *Brahman*, having known that Self, having overcome desire for sons, desire for wealth, desire for worlds, lives the life of a mendicant. That which is desire for sons is desire for wealth, that which is desire for wealth is desire for worlds, for both these are but desires. Therefore, a seeker of *Brahman*, after gaining knowledge, should live like a child, but with strength that comes from knowledge. Then he becomes a silent meditator. Having known (both) the non-meditative and the meditative states, he becomes a knower of *Brahman*.

Kahola : How does a knower of *Brahman* behave?

Yagyavalkya : Howsoever he may behave, he is what he is. Everything else is perishable.

Thereupon Kahola Kausitakeya kept silent. **1**

Section 6

Then Gargi Vachaknavi asked him:

Gargi : Yagyavalkya, all this here is woven in water, like warp and woof. On what is water woven, like warp and woof?

Yagyavalkya : On air, O Gargi.

Gargi : On what then is air woven, like warp and woof?

Yagyavalkya : On the worlds of the sky, O Gargi.

Gargi : On what then, pray, are the worlds of the sky woven, like warp and woof?

"A seeker of Brahman, after gaining knowledge, should live like a child, but with strength that comes from knowledge."

Yagyavalkya	: On the worlds of the *gandharvas*, O Gargi.
Gargi	: On what then, pray, are the worlds of the *gandharvas* woven, like warp and woof?
Yagyavalkya	: On the worlds of the sun, O Gargi.
Gargi	: On what then, pray, are the worlds of the sun woven, like warp and woof?
Yagyavalkya	: On the worlds of the moon, O Gargi.
Gargi	: On what then, pray, are the worlds of the moon woven, like warp and woof?
Yagyavalkya	: On the worlds of the stars O Gargi.
Gargi	: On what then, pray, are the worlds of the stars woven, like warp and woof?
Yagyavalkya	: On the worlds of the gods, O Gargi.
Gargi	: On what then, pray, are the worlds of the gods woven, like wrap and woof?
Yagyavalkya	: On the worlds of Indra, O Gargi.'
Gargi	: On what then, pray, are the worlds of Indra woven, like warp and woof?
Yagyavalkya	: On the worlds of *Prajapati*, O Gargi.
Gargi	: On what, then, pray, are the worlds of *Prajapati* woven, like warp and woof?
Yagyavalkya	: On the worlds of *Brahma*, O Gargi.
Gargi	: On what then, pray, are the worlds of *Brahma* woven, like warp and woof?
Yagyavalkya	: Gargi, do not question too much lest your head fall off. Verily, you are questioning too much about Divinity; this you should not do. Do not, O Gargi, question too much.

Thereupon Gargi Vachaknavi kept silent.   **1**

Section 7

Then Uddalaka Aruni spoke:

Uddalaka	: Yagyavalkya, we lived in the house of Patanchala Kapya in Madra, studying scriptures on sacrifice. Kapya had a wife who was

"Verily, you are questioning too much about Divinity; this you should not do."

possessed by a *gandharva*. He asked the *gandharva*, 'Who are you?' Then the following conversation followed:

Gandharva : I am Kabandha Atharvana. Do you know, O Kapya, that thread by which this world, the other world and all beings are held together?

Kapya : I do not know it, venerable Sir.

Gandharva : Do you know, Kapya, that inner controller from within who controls this world and the next, and all things.

Kapya : I do not know it, venerable Sir.

Gandharva : He, who knows that thread, O Kapya, and that inner controller, indeed knows *Brahman*. He knows the worlds, the gods, the Vedas, the beings and the Self. He knows everything.

Thus he explained to those assembled there. I know it. If you, Yagyavalkya, do not know that thread and that inner controller, and you still take away the cows that belong only to a knower of *Brahman*, your head will fall off.

Yagyavalkya : I know, O Uddalaka, that thread and that inner controller.

Uddalaka : Anyone might say so.

Yagyavalkya : I know, I know.

Uddalaka : Tell us what you know?   **1**

Yagyavalkya : Air (Life Principle), verily, O Gautama, is that thread. By air, as by a thread, this world, the other worlds and all beings are held together. Therefore, they say of a person who dies that his limbs have been loosened, for they are held together by air, as by a thread.

Uddalaka : Quite so, Yagyavalkya.

Now describe the inner controller.   **2**

Yagyavalkya : He who dwells in earth, yet is other than earth, whom earth does not know, whose body earth is, who controls earth from within, he is your Self, the inner controller, the immortal.   **3**

He who dwells in water, yet is other than water, whom water does not know, whose body water is, who controls water from within, he is your Self, the inner controller, the immortal.   **4**

He who dwells in fire, yet is other than fire, whom fire does not know, whose body fire is, who controls fire from within, he is your Self, the inner controller, the immortal.   **5**

"He who dwells in everything and controls everything from within,
He is your Self, the inner controller, the immortal." ..... (Adapted)

He who dwells in sky, yet is other than sky, whom sky does not know, whose body sky is, who controls sky from within, he is your Self, the inner controller, the immortal. **6**

He who dwells in air, yet is other than air, whom air does not know, whose body air is, who controls air from within, he is your Self, the inner controller, the immortal. **7**

He who dwells in heaven, yet is other than heaven, whom heaven does not know, whose body heaven is, who controls heaven from within, he is your Self, the inner controller, the immortal. **8**

He who dwells in sun, yet is other than sun, whom sun does not know, whose body sun is, who controls sun from within, he is your Self, the inner controller, the immortal. **9**

He who dwells in quarters (of space), yet is other than quarters, whom quarters do not know, whose body quarters are, who controls quarters from within, he is your Self, the inner controller, the immortal. **10**

He who dwells in moon and stars, yet is other than moon and stars, whom moon and stars do not know, whose body moon and stars are, who controls moon and stars from within, he is your Self, the inner controller, the immortal. **11**

He who dwells in ether, yet is other than ether, whom ether does not know, whose body ether is, who controls ether from within, he is your Self, the inner controller, the immortal. **12**

He who dwells in darkness, yet is other than darkness, whom darkness does not know, whose body darkness is, who controls darkness from within, he is your Self, the inner controller, the immortal. **13**

He who dwells in light, yet is other than light, whom light does not know, whose body light is, who controls light from within, he is your Self, the inner controller, the immortal. **14**

He who dwells in beings, yet is other than beings, whom beings do not know, whose body beings are, who controls beings from within, he is your Self, the inner controller, the immortal.

This is with reference to cosmos. Now with reference to man. **15**

He who dwells in breath, yet is other than breath, whom breath does not know, whose body breath is, who controls breath from within, he is your Self, the inner controller, the immortal. **16**

He who dwells in (the organ of) speech, yet is other than speech, whom speech does not know, whose body speech is, who controls

---

"He who dwells in beings, yet is other than beings, whom beings do not know, whose body beings are, He is your Self."

speech from within, he is your Self, the inner controller, the immortal. **17**

He who dwells in the eye, yet is other than the eye, whom the eye does not know, whose body the eye is, who controls the eye from within, he is your Self, the inner controller, the immortal. **18**

He who dwells in the ear, yet is other than the ear, whom the ear does not know, whose body the ear is, who controls the ear from within, he is your Self, the inner controller, the immortal. **19**

He who dwells in the mind, yet is other than the mind, whom the mind does not know, whose body the mind is, who controls the mind from within, he is your Self, the inner controller, the immortal. **20**

He who dwells in the skin, yet is other than the skin, whom the skin does not know, whose body the skin is, who controls the skin from within, he is your Self, the inner controller, the immortal. **21**

He who dwells in understanding, yet is other than understanding, whom understanding does not know, whose body understanding is, who controls understanding from within, he is your Self, the inner controller, the immortal. **22**

He who dwells in procreative fluid, yet is other than procreative fluid, whom procreative fluid does not know, whose body procreative fluid is, who controls procreative fluid from within, that is your Self, the inner controller, the immortal.

He is never seen but is the seer, he is never heard but is the hearer. He is never known, but is the knower. He can never be thought of, but is the thinker. There is no other seer but He, there is no other hearer but He, there is no other knower but He, there is no other thinker but He.

He is your Self, the inner controller, the immortal. Everything else is perishable.

After that Uddalaka Aruni kept silent. **23**

Section 8

Then Vachaknavi Gargi said:

Venerable *Brahmins*, I shall ask him two questions. If he answers, none of you can defeat him in arguments about *Brahman*.

Yagyavalkya : Ask Gargi. **1**

"He is never known, but is the knower. There is no other knower but He.
He is Immortal. Everything else is perishable."

Gargi	:	Just as a mighty prince of Kashi or Videha might rise against an enemy, having strung his unstrung bow and having taken in his hand two pointed foe-piercing arrows; like that, O Yagyavalkya, I face you with two questions. Answer these for me.
Yagyavalkya	:	Ask Gargi. **2**
Gargi	:	That, O Yagyavalkya, of which they say, it is above the heaven, it is beneath the earth, it is between these two – heaven and earth; that which people call the past, the present and the future; across what is that woven, like warp and woof? **3**
Yagyavalkya	:	That which is above the heaven, that which is beneath the earth, that which is between these two – heaven and earth; that which people call the past, the present and the future; across space (*Akash*) is that woven, like warp and woof. **4**
Gargi	:	Adoration to you, Yagyavalkya, you have answered this question for me. Prepare yourself for the other.
Yagyavalkya	:	Ask Gargi. **5**
Gargi	:	That, O Yagyavalkya, of which they say, it is above the heaven, it is beneath the earth, that which is between these two – heaven and earth; that which people call the past, the present and the future; across what is that woven, like warp and woof? **6**
Yagyavalkya	:	That which is above the heaven, that which is beneath the earth, that which is between these two – heaven and earth; that which people call the past, the present and the future; across space is that woven like warp and woof.
Gargi	:	Across what is space woven, like warp and woof? **7**
Yagyavalkya	:	That, O Gargi, the knowers of *Brahman* call the 'Imperishable'. It is neither gross nor subtle, neither short nor long, neither glowing red (like fire) nor viscous (like honey). (It is) neither shadow nor darkness, neither air nor space. It is unattached, without taste, without smell, without eyes, without ears, without voice, without mind, without radiance, without breath, without a mouth, without form. It has no within and no without. It eats nothing and no one eats it. **8**
		Verily, at the command of that Imperishable, O Gargi, sun and moon stand in their respective positions. At the command of that Imperishable, O Gargi, heaven and earth stand in their respective positions. At the command of that Imperishable, O Gargi, what are called moments, hours, days and nights, half-months, months, seasons and years, they stand in their respective positions. At the command of that Imperishable, O Gargi, some rivers flow to the east from the white (snowy) mountains, others to the west,

---

"Verily, at the command of that Imperishable, O Gargi, sun and moon stand in their respective positions."

and still others in whatever direction they flow. By the command of that Imperishable, O Gargi, men praise those who give, gods depend on sacrifice and manes go after libations to the dead. **9**

In this world, O Gargi, without knowing this Imperishable, whosoever performs sacrifices, worships or practices austerities even for a thousand years, his work will have an end. Whosoever, O Gargi, departs from this world without knowing this Imperishable, is pitiable. But, O Gargi, he who knowing the Imperishable departs from this world, is a knower of *Brahman*. **10**

Verily, this Imperishable, O Gargi, is unseen but is the seer, is unheard but is the hearer, is unthought but is the thinker, is unknown but is the knower. There is no other seer but This, there is no other hearer but This, there is no other thinker but This, there is no other knower but This. By this Imperishable, O Gargi, is space woven like warp and woof. **11**

Gargi : Venerable *Brahmins*, you may think it a great thing if you get off from him by bowing to him. Not one of you will defeat him in knowledge of *Brahman*.

Thereupon (Gargi) Vachaknavi kept silent. **12**

Section 9

Then Vidagdha Sakalya asked Yagyavalkya:

How many gods are there, Yagyavalkya?

Yagyavalkya : I rely on the authority of *nivid* (invocation to gods). There are as many gods as are mentioned in the *nivid*, the hymns of praise to the *Visvedevas*, namely, three hundreds and three, and three thousands and three.

Sakalya : Yes. But how many gods are there, Yagyavalkya?

Yagyavalkya : Thirty three.

Sakalya : Yes. But how many gods are there, Yagyavalkya?

Yagyavalkya : Six.

Sakalya : Yes. But how many gods are there, Yagyavalkya?

Yagyavalkya : Three.

Sakalya : Yes. But how many gods are there, Yagyavalkya?

Yagyavalkya : Two.

Sakalya : Yes. But how many gods are there, Yagyavalkya?

"Innumerable gods are but manifestations of One God." ..... (Adapted)

Yagyavalkya : One and a half.

Sakalya : Yes. But how many gods are there, Yagyavalkya?

Yagyavalkya : One.

Sakalya : Yes. But then which are those three hundreds and three and three thousands and three? **1**

Yagyavalkya : They are His manifestations, they are thirty three gods.

Sakalya : Which are these thirty three?

Yagyavalkya : The eight *Vasus*, the eleven *Rudras*, and the twelve *Adityas*, these are thirty one, *Indra* and *Prajapati* (make up) thirty three. **2**

Sakalya : Which are the *Vasus*?

Yagyavalkya : Fire, earth, air, sky, sun, heaven, moon and stars; these are the *Vasus*. All these are placed in them, therefore they are called *Vasus*. **3**

Sakalya : Which are the *Rudras*?

Yagyavalkya : These ten breaths in a person with mind as the eleventh. When they depart from this mortal body, they make us (our relatives) weep. Because they make us weep, they are called *Rudras*. **4**

Sakalya : Which are the *Adityas*?

Yagyavalkya : Verily, the twelve months of the year, these are the *Adityas*, for they move carrying along all this. Since they move carrying along all this, therefore they are called *Adityas*. **5**

Sakalya : Which is *Indra*? Which is *Prajapati*?

Yagyavalkya : *Indra* is thunder, *Prajapati* is sacrifice.

Sakalya : Which is the thunder?

Yagyavalkya : The thunderbolt.

Sakalya : Which is the sacrifice?

Yagyavalkya : The (sacrificial) animals. **6**

Sakalya : Which are the six gods?

Yagyavalkya : Fire, earth, air, sky, sun and heaven; these are the six. These six are all this. **7**

"Sakalya : Yes. But how many gods are there, Yagyavalkya?
Yagyavalkya : One."

Sakalya	: Which are the three gods?
Yagyavalkya	: They are, verily, the three worlds, for in them all these gods exist.
Sakalya	: Which are the two gods?
Yagyavalkya	: Matter and Life Principle.
Sakalya	: Which is the one-and-a-half god?
Yagyavalkya	: This one here, that blows (Air, as symbol of Life Principle). Regarding this, some ask: 'Since he who blows is one, how is he one-and-a-half?' (The answer is) because in him (when he blows), all this grew up. **8**
Sakalya	: Which is the one God?
Yagyavalkya	: The Cosmic Life Principle, *Prana*. He is *Brahman*. They call him *tyat*, That. **9**
Sakalya	: Verily, he who knows that Person whose abode is earth, whose world is fire, whose light is mind, who is the ultimate support of every soul, he would be a knower, O Yagyavalkya.
Yagyavalkya	: Verily, I know that Person, who is the ultimate support of every soul, of whom you speak. This very Person who is in the body is He. Go on, Sakalya.
Sakalya	: Who is his god?
Yagyavalkya	: Immortality. **10**
Sakalya	: Verily, he who knows that Person whose abode is desire, whose world is heart, whose light is mind, who is the ultimate support of every soul, he would be a knower, O Yagyavalkya.
Yagyavalkya	: Verily, I know that Person who is the ultimate support of every soul, of whom you speak. This very Person who is made of desire is He. Go on, Sakalya.
Sakalya	: Who is his god?
Yagyavalkya	: Woman. **11**
Sakalya	: Verily, he who knows that Person whose abode is forms, whose world is eye, whose light is mind, who is the ultimate support of every soul, he would be a knower. O Yagyavalkya.
Yagyavalkya	: Verily, I know that Person who is the ultimate support of every soul, of whom you speak. This very Person who is in the sun is He. Go on, Sakalya.

"Cosmic Life Principle is Brahman. They call him tyat, That."

Sakalya	: Who is his god?	
Yagyavalkya	: Truth.	**12**
Sakalya	: Verily, he who knows that Person, whose abode is space, whose world is the ear, whose light is mind, who is the ultimate support of every soul, he would be a knower. O Yagyavalkya.	
Yagyavalkya	: Verily, I know that Person who is the ultimate support of every soul, of whom you speak. This very Person who is in hearing and who is in echo is He. Go on, Sakalya.	
Sakalya	: Who is his god?	
Yagyavalkya	: Directions.	**13**
Sakalya	: Verily, he who knows that Person whose abode is darkness, whose world is heart, whose light is mind, who is the ultimate support of every soul, he would be a knower. O Yagyavalkya.	
Yagyavalkya	: Verily, I know that Person who is the ultimate support of every soul, of whom you speak. This very Person who is made of shadow is He. Go on, Sakalya.	
Sakalya	: Who is his god?	
Yagyavalkya	: Death.	**14**
Sakalya	: Verily, he who knows that Person whose abode is colors, whose world is eye, whose light is mind, who is the ultimate support of every soul, he would be a knower, O Yagyavalkya.	
Yagyavalkya	: Verily, I know that Person who is the ultimate support of every soul, of whom you speak. This very Person who is in the mirror is He. Go on, Sakalya.	
Sakalya	: Who is his god?	
Yagyavalkya	: Life.	**15**
Sakalya	: Verily, he who knows that Person whose abode is water, whose world is heart, whose light is mind, who is the ultimate support of every soul, he would be a knower, O Yagyavalkya.	
Yagyavalkya	: Verily, I know that Person who is the ultimate support of every soul, of whom you speak. This very Person who is in water is He. Go on, Sakalya.	
Sakalya	: Who is his god?	
Yagyavalkya	: *Varuna*.	**16**

"Verily, he who knows that Person, he would be a knower."

Sakalya	:	Verily, he who knows that Person whose abode is procreative fluid, whose world is heart, whose light is mind, who is the ultimate support of every soul, he would be a knower, O Yagyavalkya.
Yagyavalkya	:	Verily, I know that Person who is the ultimate support of every soul, of whom you speak. This very Person who is in a son is He. Go on, Sakalya.
Sakalya	:	Who is his god?
Yagyavalkya	:	*Prajapati*. **17**
		O Sakalya, have these *Brahmins* chosen you to be their tong for extinguishing burning coals? **18**
Sakalya	:	Yagyavalkya, what is the *Brahman* you know that you have talked with contempt about the *Brahmins* of Kurus Panchala?
Yagyavalkya	:	I know the quarters of space with their deities and supports.
Sakalya	:	If you know the quarters with their deities and supports, what deity is there in the eastern quarter? **19**
Yagyavalkya	:	The deity Sun.
Sakalya	:	That Sun, on what is it supported?
Yagyavalkya	:	On the eye.
Sakalya	:	On what is the eye supported?
Yagyavalkya	:	On forms, for one sees forms with the eye.
Sakalya	:	On what are forms supported?
Yagyavalkya	:	On the heart, for one knows forms through the heart; on the heart only are forms supported. **20**
Sakalya	:	What deity is there in the southern quarter?
Yagyavalkya	:	The deity Yama.
Sakalya	:	That Yama, on what is he supported?
Yagyavalkya	:	On sacrifice.
Sakalya	:	On what is sacrifice supported?
Yagyavalkya	:	On offerings to priests.
Sakalya	:	And on what are offerings to priests supported?

"O Sakalya, have these Brahmins chosen you to be their tong for extinguishing burning coals?"

Yagyavalkya	:	On faith, for when one has faith, one gives offerings to priests.
Sakalya	:	On what is faith supported?
Yagyavalkya	:	On the heart, for through the heart one knows faith. Verily, on the heart alone is faith supported. **21**
Sakalya	:	What deity is there in the western quarter?
Yagyavalkya	:	The deity Varuna.
Sakalya	:	That Varuna, on what is he supported?
Yagyavalkya:		On water.
Sakalya:		On what is water supported?
Yagyavalkya:		On procreative fluid.
Sakalya	:	On what is procreative fluid supported?
Yagyavalkya	:	On the heart. Therefore they say of a newborn child that he resembles (his father), as if he came forth from his heart, or that he is made out of his heart. On the heart alone is procreative fluid supported. **22**
Sakalya	:	What deity is there in northern quarter?
Yagyavalkya	:	The deity Soma.
Sakalya	:	That Soma, on what is he supported?
Yagyavalkya	:	On initiatory rite.
Sakalya	:	On what is initiation supported?
Yagyavalkya	:	On truth. Therefore, they say to one who is initiated; 'Speak the truth'. On truth alone is initiation supported.
Sakalya	:	On what is truth supported?
Yagyavalkya	:	On the heart, for through the heart one knows truth. Therefore it is on the heart that truth is supported. **23**
Sakalya	:	What deity is there in the fixed quarter (zenith)?
Yagyavalkya	:	The deity *Agni* (Fire).
Sakalya	:	On what is Fire supported?
Yagyavalkya	:	On speech.

"When one has faith, one gives."

Sakalya	:	On what is speech supported?
Yagyavalkya	:	On the heart.
Sakalya	:	On what is the heart supported?
Yagyavalkya	:	You ghost! Do you think that the heart could be elsewhere other than in the body? If it were anywhere else than in the body, the dogs might eat it or the birds tear it to pieces.
Sakalya	:	On what is the body supported?
Yagyavalkya	:	On, *Prana* (in-breath).
Sakalya	:	On what is *Prana* supported?
Yagyavalkya	:	On *Apana* (out-breath).
Sakalya	:	On what is *Apana* supported?
Yagyavalkya	:	On *Vyana* (diffused-breath).
Sakalya	:	And on what is *Vyana* supported?
Yagyavalkya	:	On *Udana* (ascending-breath)
Sakalya	:	On what is *Udana* supported?
Yagyavalkya	:	On *Samana* (equalizing-breath).

24

25

> This Self is That which has been described as '*neti, neti*, not this, not this'. It is imperceptible because it is never perceived. It is indestructible because it is never destroyed. It is unattached because it does not attach itself. It is unfettered. It does not suffer. It is not injured. (What you talked about, Sakalya are Its) eight abodes, eight worlds, eight gods. After projecting them and withdrawing into them, It passes beyond them. It is the Cosmic Person (*Purusha*), taught in the Upanishads, about whom I ask you. If you do not explain It to me, your head will fall off.

Sakalya did not know him, and his head fell off. Indeed robbers took away his bones, thinking they were something else. **26**

Then he (Yagyavalkya) said:

> Venerable *Brahmins*, whosoever among you wishes to do so, he may question me, or you may all question me, or I will question him who wishes (to be questioned), or I will question all of you.

27

"You ghost! Do you think that the heart could be elsewhere other than in the body?"

Those *Brahmins*, however, did not dare (to say anything). Then Yagyavalkya questioned them with the following verses:

> As is a mighty tree so, indeed, is a man. His hairs are like leaves and his skin like the outer bark of a tree.
> From his skin blood flows forth, like sap from the skin (of a tree). Therefore, when a man is wounded, blood flows like sap from a tree that is struck.
> His flesh is its inner bark, his nerves are tough like inner fibers. His bones are the woods within, and marrow resembles the pith.
> A tree when it is felled, springs up from its root in a newer form. From what root does man spring forth when he is cut-off by death?
>
> Do not say 'from procreative fluid', since that is produced only from a living man.
> A tree springs also from the seed, after it is felled. But if a tree is pulled up with the root, it will not spring again.
> From what root does a mortal spring forth when he is cut-off by death?
>
> If you say 'he is never born', (I say): No. He is born again (after death).
> Who creates him again?
>
> It is *Brahman*. He is Knowledge and Bliss. He is the final goal of him who offers charities, as well as of him who stands firm and knows (*Brahman*). **28**

"As is a mighty tree so, indeed, is a man. From what root does he spring forth when he is cut-off by death?"

FOCUSSED COMMENTARIES

CHAPTER 3

3.1 Benefits of sacrificial rituals

In the first section, the questions of Hotr Asvala (a priest in sacrificial rites) are concerning two things:

(i) Through what would the performer of a sacrifice release himself from the vicissitudes of earthly existence?
(ii) What would be the gains to the performer of a sacrifice?

The four priests – Hotr, Adhavaryu, Udgatr and Brahma – are in reality Speech, Sight, Life-breath and Mind; and the corresponding divinities, Fire, Sun, Air and Moon. So the gains from a sacrifice do not consist of any individual rewards, but having communion with *Atman* which pervades the universe.

— *Paul Deussen*

Performance of sacrifice as an aid to meditation is conducive to spiritual evolution of man. By realizing the correct import of sacrifice, one learns that one is not a separate entity or an isolated creature, but is identical with the deity who is worshipped in the sacrifice. That deity, in turn, is a manifestation of the Supreme.

Sacrifices have got an inner meaning. Symbolically, a sacrifice stands for annihilation of ego, lust, greed, and other demonical qualities.

Despite some imperfections, defects and difficulties, the system of ritualistic sacrifices opens before us the door to the discovery of spiritual principle in every object in this entire creation.

— *Swami Sivananda*

3.2 Name and deeds survive death

The two terms used to signify the senses and the objects of senses – *graha* and *atigraha* – are very significant. They grasp each other. The senses grasp the objects and the objects grasp the senses. The Upanishad says that the objects are stronger than the senses, because they stimulate the senses. Objects in their turn become more attractive or repulsive when they are contacted by the senses (3.2, 1-9).

Through the illustration of fire and water, it is shown that there exists death for 'death' also. This great Being, *Atman-Brahman*, swallows death. Katha Upanishad says that for this great Being, Death of death, death is like a pickle or a sauce.

Verse 3.2,10 also furnishes us with the idea that until death in the form of desires and attachment is eliminated, there can be no chance of release from its bondage. Death of death is nothing but extinction of desires and attachment. This state is attained when individual consciousness shifts its center from the sensual to the spiritual, from the object to the subject. By knowing this, the aspirant averts death and becomes liberated.

After the death of a man who is liberated, his subtle body – the senses, and their objects in the form of impressions – gets dissolved and united in Self. What remains is the physical gross body, which undergoes the so-called process of death. It swells up, gets inflated and lies motionless. This answer removes the commonly misunderstood notion of ascent of spirit from one lower plane to another higher plane. Transcendence, according to Yagyavalkya, is freedom from fetters of bondage, and never a departure from one particular center to another (3.2, 11).

Karmas or works remain dormant in a dead person's causal body and subtle body in the form of *samskaras*. When all *karmas* are completely exhausted the *jiva* becomes unfettered and freed from individualization (3.2, 12-13).

— *Swami Sivananda*

It is the name which does not perish at death. Compare this with the Buddhist doctrine that the element which is reborn is *nama-rupa*, name and form (3.2, 12).

The results of *karma* produce rebirth. This view finds a parallel in the Buddhist doctrine – that at death different parts of the individual are scattered to their different sources, but *karma* remains and causes a new existence (3.2, 13).

— *S. Radhakrishnan*

'Symbolically, a sacrifice stands for annihilation of ego, lust, greed, and other demonical qualities.'

On the death of a man, everything goes back into elements but *karma* remains as the seed of next birth. Possibly, this view is the first germ of the Buddhist theory, which rejects *Atman* and allows only *karma* to continue.

– Paul Deussen

3.3 Where do good deeds lead to?

The first chapter of this Upanishad gives horse sacrifice, *Ashvamedha Yagya* as a symbol for meditation on the Cosmic Being. The result of this meditation is the attainment of identity with *Hiranyagarbha*, also known as Cosmic Mind. Bhujyu, instead of asking a direct question, relates an incident from his own life and enquires about the whereabouts of the descendents of Parikshit, the performers of many horse sacrifices.

The four questions raised in Section 3.3 and their answers are as follows:

Question 1 : What is the maximum limit to which performers of noble deeds can rise?
Answer : Up to the limits of the manifested worlds.

Question 2 : What is the path they follow?
Answer : There is a very fine opening – like the edge of a razor or the wing of a mosquito – at the junction of the two halves of the cosmic shell. The souls of performers of good deeds pass through this very subtle, ultramicroscopic opening.

Question 3 : What is their fate?
Answer : Their astral body is taken out of its physical limitations. Then their good deeds, referred to here as *Indra*, carry them and make them identical with Cosmic Mind, which is designated here as *Vayu*, Air. Thus, these *jivas* become identical with Cosmic Mind.

Question 4 : What is the extent of space covered by Cosmic Mind?
Answer : Cosmic Mind covers the entire space from the microcosm to the macrocosm. It fills the entire universe as a whole, and also the microcosm in each individual.

He who knows this becomes identified with Cosmic Mind and does not take further birth.

– Swami Sivananda

The questioner believes in the phenomenon of 'possession' by spirits. Patanchala's daughter was possessed by a *gandharva,* an aerial spirit, and so served as a medium. Modern psychology is investigating the phenomena of possession and medium-ship, as these cannot be explained by principles of psychology.

– S. Radhakrishnan

The question of Bhujyu gives Yagyavalkya an occasion to show his knowledge of cosmography.

– Paul Deussen

3.4 *Brahman* is that which breathes in you

Usasta questioned Yagyavalkya about the immediate and direct *Brahman*, which means the unmanifested Absolute. Yagyavalkya's precise reply was that the Self in Usasta is the immanent Self in all. Usasta could not follow, and so sought further elaboration. Yagyavalkya replied: 'That which makes the life-breath function in all its five aspects – in-breath, out-breath, equalizing-breath, diffused-breath and ascending- breath – is *Brahman*.' Usasta was still not satisfied. He said that Yagyavalkya's reply was like saying 'This is a cow', when asked, 'What is a cow?' He wanted a more precise and definite description of *Brahman*.

Being thus pressed by his ignorant opponent, Yagyavalkya said that one cannot define Self in the way Usasta wanted. Such a definition would contradict the very nature of *Brahman*. Self is the witness of sight itself. All channels of perception – such as seeing, hearing and the like - are united and founded in Self.

Self is beyond the duality of subject and object. Therefore, It cannot be cognized, or known, or experienced by means of objective apprehension.

– Swami Sivananda

'On the death of a man, everything goes back into elements, but karma remains as the seed of next birth.'

3.5 *Brahman* is beyond relative attributes

Like Usasta, Kahola also questioned Yagyavalkya about the immediate and direct *Brahman*, the Absolute. Earlier, Yagyavalkya had said that *Brahman* is that which makes life-breath function in all its five aspects. This time, Yagyavalkya describes *Brahman* from a different perspective. He says *Brahman* is that which is beyond all relative attributes like hunger, thirst, sorrow, delusion, old age and death. What is required to realize *Brahman*, the Self in us and in all things? Overcome all desires, like desire for wealth, children and the material world. Learn the scriptures. Live the life of a child – without any ego, sensual passion or deception. And practice meditation.

How does a knower of *Brahman* behave in this world? Yagyavalkya says that he may not adopt any specific mode of conduct, but being beyond desires, he is eternally satisfied. Anything related to desires is perishable.

Hearing this most erudite exposition of *Brahman*, Kahola withdrew from the debate.

– *Swami Sivananda*

To become a child involves sacrifice of intellectual conceit. It requires returning to the roots. To become like little children is not easy. It takes much effort to acquire the grace and meekness of a child; to measure our smallness against the greatness of the Supreme. "Except ye become like little children, ye shall not see the kingdom of God."

Silence or *mauna* is abstinence from speech. It is regarded as helpful for meditation. To become aware of the Reality, which transcends Time and Space, we must turn away from the world of noise into inward stillness, 'The word of God cannot be heard in the noise of the world. And if it is spoken loudly so that it can be heard even in the midst of all other noise, then it is no longer the word of God. Therefore, create silence …' (Kierkegaar).

– *S. Radhakrishnan*

Sections 4 and 5 belong together. Section 4 teaches that *Brahman* is theoretically unknowable. Because it is the knowing subject of all knowledge, it can never be the object of knowledge for us. Section 5 rejects the mind as a means of comprehending *Brahman* in a practical way. *Brahman* is comprehended when one transforms from being a scholar to a child, then to the state of *Muni* (recluse observing silence); and from that to the state of a *Sanyasi* (renouncer).

– *Paul Deussen*

3.6 *Brahman* is woven like warp and woof

Gargi started by saying that this earth is founded in, or pervaded by water; as an effect is by a cause. Thus, earth is the effect of water, its cause. As the cause pervades the effect, like warp and woof in cloth, water pervades the earth. Water is the support for earth. What is the support for water?

Yagyavalkya replied that water is pervaded by air, which is subtler and finer than water and which is its cause. Gargi pushed further and asked for the cause of air. Through a series of questions that followed, they passed on from gross to subtle, and then to more subtle manifestations – intermediate worlds, sun, moon, stars, gods, Indra and *Prajapati*. They finally arrived at the world of *Brahma*, or *Hiranyagarbha*, the first born, the supreme person, the cosmic mind. He is the first manifest cause of the universe.

Gargi did not stop. She questioned Yagyavalkya on the cause of *Brahma*. But Yagyavalkya warned her not to pursue this method of logical enquiry for knowing the ultimate cause. The cause of *Brahma* is *Ishvara*, the personal God; and the cause of *Ishvara* is *Brahman*, the Absolute. *Ishvara* and *Brahman* are beyond the reach of mind and speech. Logical arguments, which depend upon these two instruments, cannot function beyond the realm of *Hiranyagarbha*. One who attempts to know the Absolute through the intellect will only meet with utter failure, which is figuratively referred to as 'falling of the head'.

– *Swami Sivananda*

Gargi concurs with the oft-recurring view that the world is interwoven lengthwise and crosswise (*ota and prota*) in the primeval waters. She asks about that in which waters are interwoven lengthwise and crosswise. The answer of Yagyavalkya leads to a description of cosmography, which does not conform with the one given earlier in Section-3. There, the abode of Parikshit's descendents is supposed to be the end of worlds. Here, the world interwoven into

---

'To become a child involves sacrifice of intellectual conceit.'

3.7 *Brahman*, the inner controller

The seventh interrogator, Uddalaka Aruni – father and teacher of Shvetaketu in Chandogya Upanishad – begins his narration almost with the same words as Bhujyu in 3.3. The only difference is that in that section the clairvoyant is the daughter while in the present section the clairvoyant is the wife of Patanchala Kapya.

The questions put to Yagyavalkya refer to:
(i) the thread, *sutra* by which all the worlds and beings are held together.
(ii) the inner controller, *antaryami,* who controls from within the whole external world.

The thread is Air. As life-breath or *Prana* in an individual, its holds together the parts of the body. As cosmic *Prana* or Life Principle, it holds together the whole universe.

The inner controller is *Atman*. Residing in us as the immortal one, It dwells in all objects and phenomena of Nature. Twelve of these have been enumerated here, but without any order (3.7, 3-14). It also dwells in all living beings (3.7, 15) and in organs of senses. Eight of these have been enumerated here, again not in any order (3.7, 15-23). All these phenomena of nature, beings and organs of senses form the body of *Atman*. They are different from It, they do not know It, but still they are controlled by It. Air or *Vayu*, as the psychical and cosmic *Prana*, is only a symbol of *Atman*. *Atman* is the *antaryami*, the inner controller. Thus, *Prana* and *Atman*, Life Principle and Self, are basically identical. The unitary idea of the whole section is that *Atman*, the knowing subject in us, regulates all things from inside, as also from outside. It also holds together the whole world.

– Paul Deussen

Uddalaka, the son of Aruni questions Yagyavalkya on the Cosmic String, the *sutra* holding all the worlds together. It is also *antaryami*, the Inner Ruler. Yagyavalkya declares that the Cosmic String is Air, or *Vayu*, which is symbolic of Life Principle, or *Prana*. In the absence of this Cosmic String, the worlds would have been scattered; like pearls in a necklace or flowers in a garland without a string. When the cosmic principle leaves the individual body, the person is said to be dead and his limbs get loosened (3.7, 1-2).

Then Yagyavalkya explains the Inner Ruler. This explanation extends up to the end of this section. One-by-one, he considers many examples: the five elements (earth, water, fire, space, air), heaven, sun, quarters, moon, stars, sky, darkness, light, all beings, vital force, the senses (speech, eye, ear, skin), mind, intellect and procreative fluid. In a set of beautiful passages he narrates their common and immanent Reality. For example, He dwells in the earth, as the cause pervades the effect. Still, He is different from the earth, as the cause is different from the effect. He is within the earth as its very Self, the Inner Controller, the Immortal. He pervades the earth without being tainted by its names and forms. He controls the earth from within and directs it to perform its definite functions.

The mantras identify the entire creation – gross and subtle – with Self, which is shown to pervade them in their entirety, as a homogeneous mass of Consciousness (3.7, 3-22).

Self is the unseen seer. He sees everything, but none can see Him. He hears everything, but none can hear Him. He is the thinker of thoughts, but none can think accurately about Him. He is the knower of everything, but none can know Him completely. To remove all presumptions of anything different from Him, the text says that other than Him there is no seer, no hearer, no thinker, no knower. This cuts at the very root of all possibility of presuming a second entity other than Him (3.7, 23).

– Swami Sivananda

3.8 Imperishable *Brahman*

In Sec. 3.6, Gargi had pursued her questions regarding the interwoven character of the world, up to the point that there should not be any questioning. She was warned by Yagyavalkya not to press her questions further. It could not be the intention of the author to allow the same lady-questioner to appear on the scene

---

*'Atman, the knowing subject in us, regulates all things from inside,
as also from outside. It also holds together the whole world.'*

once again with the same question. It therefore appears that the narration of Gargi was current in two versions (3.6 and 3.8). The second version is more valuable and significant.

Yagyavalkya teaches Gargi that the whole world – past, present and future – is interwoven lengthwise and crosswise in *Akash* (space, ether). Space is conceived here as an all-encompassing material element, including Time. *Akash* is again interwoven in *Akshara*, the 'Imperishable'. This *Akshara* cannot be known or characterized. On It depends the spatial and the temporal order of nature, as also the eternal basic laws that are obeyed by everything in the universe. This *Akshara*, according to Yagyavalkya, is *Atman*, the knowing but unknowable subject in each of us.

Thus, *Atman* is the subject which remains ever unknowable, in which the laws are grounded (founded), which everything in nature obeys, and into which the whole space, and along with it everything that it contains, is inter-woven.

All this is, in the Indian manner of expression, Kantian philosophy.

– Paul Deussen

Gargi asked the assembled *Brahmins* for permission to interrogate Yagyavalkya once more, with two questions. Earlier, she had already been warned by Yagyavalkya against a logical enquiry into the cause of *Hiranyagarbha*, the ultimate cause of the universe. She started from where she left, this time not on logical grounds, but on spiritual basis.

Gargi compared her two questions to two piercing arrows in the hands of a mighty warrior. She asked: 'What is the cause of *Hiranyagarbha* who pervades the whole universe that exists in space and time – heaven above, earth below and intermediate region in between; as also the past, the present and the future?' '*Akash* or Space, the Unmanifested', replied Yagyavalkya (3.8, 1-7).

Gargi accepted the answer. She then repeated her question, verbatim, in order to lay emphasis on truth, and also for confirmation of his answer by Yagyavalkya. '*Akash* or Space, the Unmanifested', replied Yagyavalkya again.

'Across what is Space woven, like warp and woof?' was the second question put by Gargi. 'On *Akshara*', replied Yagyavalkya.

Thereafter, Yagyavalkya gave one of the most magnificent, awe-inspiring and sublime description of the Absolute, *Akshara*.

Akshara is neither gross nor subtle, neither short nor long. By negating these four characteristics, the Upanishad negates the characteristics of a substance. *Akshara* is therefore not a substance.

Akshara is neither red like fire, nor viscous like honey. So, It is devoid of qualities, or attributes.

Akshara is neither shadow nor darkness, it is without organs of senses - like eye, ear, mind etc. It is without an interior or exterior. It is neither an eater, nor is it eaten. In short, *Akshara* is neither the subject nor the object.

By this negative description of the Absolute, one should not jump to the conclusion that *Brahman* is a complete blank, or a non-being. It only means that *Brahman* cannot be subjected to empirical definitions, which are valid only in the relative world of space, time and causation.

Quite contradictory statements are made about *Brahman* in the same breath. All this is to denote that these attributes – which are based on our relative ideas within the time-space complex – are unable to express the Absolute. For instance, if He is indicated as 'not gross', one may infer that He is 'subtle'. So we say that 'He is neither gross nor subtle'. It means that He is not conditioned to any kind of logical definition, which would make Him an object of human perception by the senses or the mind. (3.8, 8).

The previous mantra has negated all relative attributes in the Absolute Reality, which is given the name *Akshara*, the Imperishable. This does not mean that the Absolute is a non-entity. In order to remove such a misunderstanding, the present *mantra* gives inferential evidence in favor of the existence of the Absolute. It is due to the supreme command of the Imperishable that the sun and the moon move in their fixed orbits with unmistakable accuracy. Inference is a process of logical reasoning by which we come to

---

'We infer the existence of the Absolute by observing the well-regulated functioning of the endless cosmos.'

know some unknown thing through the medium of a known thing. Thus, we infer the existence of the Absolute by observing the well-regulated functioning of the sun, the moon, and other harmonious phenomena in the endless cosmos.

In the government of that Imperishable, all divisions of Time – past, present and future, moments, hours and years, etc. – are carefully created and controlled by Him. Similarly, phenomena of Nature – like flow of rivers – are also regulated by Him. Also, in His government, men praise the givers of charity. Why? Because there is someone who connects the givers with the results of their giving (3.8, 9).

Whoever does any work without knowing the Self, fruits of his actions – however great and magnificent they may be – get exhausted some day or the other. The life of a man who departs from this world without knowing the Imperishable, is pitiable. But one who drops his mortal coil after knowing the Imperishable as his Self and Self of all beings, he is a knower of *Brahman*; he does not transmigrate any more (3.8, 10).

Imperishable *Brahman* is not an object of sense perception, but Itself the basis of all perceptions. There is no knowing subject other than this Imperishable. This is the conclusive view expressed by the great sage, Yagyavalkya (3.8, 11).

– Swami Sivananda

This passage brings out that the Imperishable is neither a substance nor a possessor of attributes. *Akshara* is not an alphabet, as commonly translated, but the Supreme Self. It is the changeless Reality (3.8, 8).

Verse 3.8, 9 gives inferential evidence from the orderliness of the world. Maintenance of the respective positions of heaven and earth is not possible without the guidance of an intelligent transcendent ruler.

Sri Sankara says that the same *Brahman* is called differently on account of differences in limiting adjuncts. The unconditioned Self, being beyond speech and mind, undifferentiated and one, is defined as 'not this', 'not this'. When it has the limiting adjuncts of the body and the organs – the products of ignorance, desire and work – it is called individual ego. When Self has the limiting adjuncts of eternal knowledge and power, it is called the Inner Controller, the Supreme Lord. The same Self – Absolute, alone, and pure – is called Imperishable Supreme Self. Self is thus assuming different forms everywhere. For Sri Sankara, the differences are traceable to limiting adjuncts, and to nothing else (3.8, 12).

– S. Radhakrishnan

3.9, 1-9 Many gods but one *Brahman*

By first enumerating variety in the number of gods, and then by reducing them to a single deity, this section tries to explain how the many are but manifestations of One. Thus, the apparent multiplicity and the real unity are not contradictory.

In a broad sense, we may say that the cause of a thing is the deity of that thing. God is the power that works from within. In this sense, every object has got a deity and the number of deities is infinite. All these infinite deities are not really different among themselves. They are manifestations or expressions of only one deity. That deity is designated here as *Prana*, Life Principle.

Prana is the cosmic vital force, which vibrates and fills the entire being of every atom in this universe. All the infinite gods are reducible to this comic vital force. It is identified with *Brahman* because like *Brahman*, it is One, but it expands to pervade everything. The word *Brahman* is derived from the root *brh*, which means 'to grow' to 'expand'. Thus, one vital force expands into any number of gods with different functions and characteristics.

Since *Prana* is not perceived directly by sense organs, it is denoted by the word *tyat*, meaning That (3.9, 9).

– Swami Sivananda

Vasus transform themselves into bodies and organs of all beings. These serve as the support for their work and its fruition, as also their dwelling-places. They help other beings to live and they themselves live. Because they help others to live, they are called *Vasu* (3.9, 3).

Earth and fire make one god, the sky and air another, sun and heaven, a third (3.9, 8).

'The word Brahman is derived from the root 'brh', which means 'to grow', 'to expand'...'

The one God has different names, representing its innumerable forms, activities, attributes and powers.

- Sri Sankara, quoted by S. Radhakrishnan

The basic thought of this section is that *Brahman* (*Atman*, the Upanishadic *Purusha*) is the ultimate unity to which the Vedic gods (1-9), the vital power in man (10-18, 26), the guardian deities in man (19-26), and man himself (27-28), are traced back.

- Paul Deussen

3.9, 10-18 Incomplete definitions of *Brahman*

In these *mantras* Sakalya describes eight manifestations and instruments of perception of the cosmic Life Principle, and says that these are the ultimate resorts of the body and the senses. Yagyavalkya corrects him. He says that the eight manifestations are only the basis for divine unity. It is therefore necessary for us to transcend the idea of manifestations, attributes etc. by recognizing the essential identity of the Absolute with one's own Self.

It is to be noted that here *Brahman* is revealed as manifest in a person's psychical activities. It has its seat in earth, desire, forms, space, darkness, colors, water, semen etc. It has three means of effecting perceptions viz. heart, eyes and ears. All these are but attributes of Self.

Sakalya says that one who boasts himself as the best scholar should know that God whose body is the earth, whose eyes is the fire, who cogitates through the mind, and who is identified with the body and organs. Yagyavalkya says he knows this and much more. He knew that what Sakalya thought as *Purusha* was only a medium of His manifestation, and not the actual Him. In verse 3.9,18, Yagyavalkya says that *Brahmins* were making use of Sakalya as an instrument to oppose him – like a pair of tongs used to pick burning coal – and thereby avoid facing the consequences.

- Swami Sivananda

3.9, 19-26 Space, Mind and Self

The Life Principle is unified in the mind (heart, according to the Upanishad). It is through the mind that one projects one's Consciousness everywhere in space, which is reducible to five quarters. When Self identifies itself with all the five directions, these together with their deities and their counterparts in the body are unified in the mind.

But in what is the mind or the heart unified? This question irritates Yagyavalkya, who calls Sakalya a ghost. If heart were elsewhere and not in the body, the body would be dead. It means that the heart and the body rest on each other.

It has been said that the heart is dependent on Life Principle, and Life Principle on *Brahman*, indicated by the word That or *tyat*. Verse 3.9,26 enumerates the five components of Life Principle – *Prana, Apana Vyana Samana* and *Udana* – each being the support of the previous one.

Yagyavalkya now says that Self is indicated by '*neti, neti*, not this, not this'. It is to inform Sakalya to stop further questioning, for the description of *Brahman* is endless. Everything, every being, every phenomenon, the infinite objects of the world, can all be defined in relation to Self, because Self is their essential reality, their essence. If Sakalya went on questioning, it would take him nowhere (26).

Yagyavalkya states some more facts about Self. It is:
- Imperceptible
- Indestructible
- Unattached
- Unfettered
- It does not suffer
- It does not perish.

Now Yagyavalkya put one question to Sakalya and pronounces a curse, if he is unable to answer it: "There are eight abodes, eight means of perception, eight gods and eight beings, as already set forth (3.9, 10-17). Now I ask you about the Supreme Person who first projects them and then withdraws into them, passing beyond all conditioning factors. If you do not answer me properly, your head will fall off."

Sakalya could not answer Yagyavalkya, so his head fell off. It is said that even the bones did not reach home – some robbers snatched them away! (obviously, all this is an exaggeration).

- Swami Sivananda

'It is through the mind that one projects one's Consciousness everywhere in space.'

Whatever form we meditate upon, we become identified with that.

Hridaya means heart. It refers to the intellect and the mind taken together (3.9, 20).

Semen is said to be an effect of the heart, as desire for sex is a modification of the heart, and semen issues when the heart of a man is under the influence of such desire (3.9, 22).

Brahman is incomprehensible because It goes beyond the attributes of effects (3.9, 26).

– Sri Sankara, quoted by S. Radhakrishnan

3.9, 27-28 Man compared to a tree

Then Yagyavalkya challenged the assembly to question him, or be questioned by him, either individually or jointly. None dared, fearing they also might meet the fate of Sakalya! Thereafter, Yagyavalkya compared man to a tree. Man is similar to a tree in many respects. His hair correspond to leaves, skin to outer bark, blood to sap, flesh to inner bark, nerves to fiber, bones to wood and marrow to pitch. Then Yagyavalkya posed a question:

"When a tree falls, it springs up again from its roots in a newer form. From what root is a man reborn after his death?"

Yagyavalkya himself ruled out that the cause of rebirth inheres in semen. Semen is produced only in a living man and the question relates to rebirth after death.

If one would uproot the tree together with its roots and seeds, it would die, never to be born again. But a man is reborn after death, even though his body is completely destroyed. So, who causes this rebirth?

If rebirth is not accepted, there could be no logical explanation for the variety of experiences of beings – some painful, some pleasurable. We would have to resort to illogical conclusion that one could go scot-free from all that he does in this life, and that one experiences results for which he is not at all responsible.

The learned people in the assembly could not answer the question about rebirth posed by Yagyavalkya. So he himself gave the answer. It is *Brahman*, who is the cause of rebirth of man, just as He is the cause of this vast creation. *Brahman* is Knowledge, Bliss, and Absolute. He is the supreme goal of all – those who lead a life of selfless work as well as those who are in quest of spiritual wisdom.

– Swami Sivananda

A man struck down by death does not come to life from seed; because human seed comes from living being only, while trees springing from grain are seen to come to life after the tree is dead.

Philo Judaeus says: 'Are not the parents, as it were, concomitant causes only, while Nature is the highest, elder and true cause of begetting of children?'

St. Thomas Aquinas: 'The power of the soul which is in the semen through the spirit enclosed therein fashions the body.'

Ramanuja: '*Brahman* is the principle or the root of a new life – both for those who practice works and those who stand firm in knowledge.'

– S. Radhakrishnan

'Non-acceptance of rebirth would imply that one could go scot-free from evil deeds, and that one experiences results for which one is not responsible.'

4. Transmigration and Self-realization

SIMPLIFIED SYNOPSES

4.1
Incomplete definitions of *Brahman*

In this section, Yagyavalkya asks king Janaka what he has learned about *Brahman* from other teachers. Janaka narrates the opinions of six teachers. They told him one-by-one that *Brahman* is Speech, Life-breath, Sight, Hearing, Mind and Heart. Yagyavalkya says that *Brahman* as described by any of these principles reflects only one-fourth of Him. Janaka asks, 'What are the remaining three-fourths?' Yagyavalkya says that the abode, the support and the object of meditation are the remaining three feet of *Brahman* (metaphorically). He then enumerates these as follows:

> *'No object or concept is an isolated entity, everything in the universe is interconnected.'*

Principle	Abode	Support	Object of meditation
Speech	Speech	Space	Consciousness
Life-breath	Life-breath	Space	Love
Sight	Eyes	Space	Truth
Hearing	Ears	Space	Infinitude
Mind	Mind	Space	Bliss
Heart	Heart	Space	Stability

It is to be noted that Space is the support of all the six principles. In each of the six instances, Yagyavalkya explains the essence or the nature of the object of meditation and the benefits of such meditation. Meditation on any one of the aforesaid phenomenal forms of *Brahman* is good, but incomplete. A common mistake in meditation is to meditate on a chosen object as an isolated entity. This mistake is rectified by bringing in the left-out parts and making the 'whole' an object of meditation. No object or concept is an isolated entity; everything in the universe is interconnected. In meditation, all the four aspects of the object of meditation – external, internal, universal and transcendental – should be meditated upon as One Totality, *Brahman*.

Pleased with Yagyavalkya's teaching, Janaka promises to reward him suitably. However, Yagyavalkya shows restraint and says that as per the views of his father, one should not accept wealth from a disciple without instructing him fully.

Yagyavalkya's instructions to Janaka continue in subsequent sections.

4.2
Journey beyond death

In this section Yagyavalkya compares Janaka – a rich and respected king – to a long-distance traveller, and his knowledge of scriptures to a chariot. He asks Janaka: 'Where will you go after you are separated from this body?' As Janaka says he does not know, Yagyavalkya proceeds to instruct him.

'The Cosmic Person and the Cosmos are like husband and wife.'

Speaking allegorically, Yagyavalkya says that the Cosmic Person and the Cosmos – *Indra* and *Viraj* – are like husband and wife. It is as if they reside in the right eye and the left eye respectively. Their place of union is the heart. Their food – subtle essence of gross food consumed by the body – moves along very fine nerves. The net-like structure in the heart is their wrap.

A Self-realized person identifies himself with life-breath of everything that exists in various directions of space. His Self is That which has been described as '*neti, neti,* not this, not this'. As stated in earlier sections, It is imperceptible, indestructible, unattached and unfettered. It is beyond suffering and injury.

Yagyavalkya then tells Janaka: 'You have already reached that state of fearlessness.' This is in fulfillment of his earlier promise in verse 4.2,1: 'I shall tell you where you will go (after death)'.

In conclusion, the Upanishad equates *Brahman* with fearlessness. Janaka expresses his gratitude by wishing that as Yagyavalkya has educated him on *Brahman* (state of fearlessness), may he also attain fearlessness (*Brahman*). As a gracious gesture, he also places his kingdom and himself in service of Yagyavalkya.

Commentators interpret this section as an exposition on the three states of waking, dream and deep sleep.

4.3 Ultimate Light and Its three states

This section contains an excellent description of Self – the Ultimate Light of man – in the three states of waking, dream and deep sleep. It also describes how Self departs from the body at the time of death.

The section starts with a profound question by Janaka: 'What is that which serves as light for man?' Yagyavalkya first points to relative objects and phenomena of light - sun, moon, fire and speech – and then says that Self is the Ultimate Light of man (1-6). Janaka wants to know more about that Self.

'Self is the Ultimate Light of man.'

Yagyavalkya says that Self is the Cosmic Being, *Purusha,* which is identified with Consciousness. It enters the body upon birth and leaves it at death. During its sojourn in the body, Self alternates between two states – waking and deep sleep – each representing a very different world. There is also an intermediate dream state in which Self sees both the worlds of waking and deep sleep. Then follows a very elaborate description of dream state (9-18) and deep sleep state (19-34). In the Upanishads, these states have deep spiritual significance that has been overlooked in western studies on philosophy.

Yagyavalkya's discourse in this section contains some beautiful metaphors and profound statements. For example:

In dream state:

- There are no chariots or roads, but Self (Consciousness) creates them out of impressions of the waking world (9-10).
- He puts the senses to sleep, but Himself remains awake, like a golden person (self-effulgent), like a lonely swan (11).

'The Upanishad equates Brahman with fearlessness.'

- Dream world is like a sport projected by Self out of Itself. Everyone sees His sport, but none sees Him (14).
- Whatever He sees in dream state, He is not affected by it (15).
- Just as a large fish moves between two banks of a river, so also this Person (Self, Consciousness, *Purusha*) moves between these states – waking and dream or deep sleep (18).

In deep sleep state:

- Just as a falcon comes down to its nest after it becomes tired, so also this Person (Self) hastens to that state of sleep where He has no desires and He sees no dreams (19).
- This, indeed, is His highest state, His true nature.
- As a man in embrace of his beloved, He knows nothing without or within (20-21). The analogy shows that deep sleep is not a state of unconsciousness.
- He is not affected by good or evil. He is beyond all sorrows of the heart (22).
- He does not see, smell, taste, speak, hear, think, touch or know in the normal sense. In reality, however, He does all these. There is no cessation of any of these activities. He is both the subject and the object. There is no second to Him whom He could see, smell, taste, speak to, hear, think about, touch or know (23-30).
- In deep sleep, the non-dual Consciousness (Self) is a homogeneous mass, like an ocean. This is a state of *Brahman* (Cosmic Consciousness). This is a state of greatest bliss. Living beings subsist just on a fraction of this bliss (32).
- The bliss of deep sleep is a billion times the happiness of a person who is healthy, wealthy, powerful and provided with all possible material enjoyments. This is the highest bliss. This is the world of *Brahman*. The hierarchy of bliss described here is a repetition from Taittiriya Upanishad, 2.8 (34).

At the time of death

- Self moves like a heavily loaded cart making creaking noises (35).
- Self releases itself from the body like a ripe fruit releases itself from a tree (36).
- The elements await the arrival of Self in a new body like courtiers welcoming their king (37).
- The senses gather around Self, just as courtiers gather around their king leaving on a tour (38).

The subtle body moves between birth and death just as gross body moves between waking and deep sleep states. Birth is association of Self with the body, death is dissociation.

4.4, 1-11
Transmigration of the Soul

Continuing the discourse of previous section, Yagyavalkya says that at the time of death, Self withdraws the resplendent energy of the senses into Itself and descends into the heart (mind). At this stage powers of sense organs become one with the subtle body. When a person dies, Self – along with life-

'The bliss of deep sleep is the highest bliss. This is the world of Brahman.'

breath and the subtle body consisting of past deeds and impressions – departs from the body through one of its apertures (Verses 1-2). Its rebirth is explained by analogies of a caterpillar and a goldsmith.

Just as caterpillar takes hold of another blade of grass before it leaves the one on which it is resting, the soul has a vision of its next birth before it leaves its present body. Also, a goldsmith makes new ornaments of progressively better designs out of same block of gold. Likewise, the soul acquires new bodies suited to experiences of varied kinds, depending upon past deeds, *karmas* (Verses 3-4).

Self is nothing but *Brahman*, Cosmic Consciousness. It is identified with everything that exists or does not exist – the elements, life principle, senses, mind and intellect, presence or absence of emotions, righteousness, etc. It is called 'This' when It is identified with things that can be perceived and 'That' when It is identified with things that cannot be perceived, but only inferred (Verse 5).

The deeds and impressions of this life determine the embodiment of Self in next life. Rebirth is an opportunity to fulfill all those desires which have hitherto remained unfulfilled. When a person has no desires, he is not born again. His Self becomes one with *Brahman*, Cosmic Consciousness. This state can be achieved even when a person is alive (Verses 6-7).

The body without the Self is like the discarded skin of a snake (Verse 7).

Verses 4.4, 12-25 contain many significant statements on Self-realization, and on *Brahman*.

4.4, 12-15 Self-realization

- Those who practice rituals without understanding their spiritual significance enter into blind darkness, but those who are absorbed only in study of scriptures enter into even greater darkness (10).
- When a person knows, 'I am this *Atman*, Self', he becomes free from all desires. The world belongs to him. In fact, he is the world (12-13).
- Great is the loss if we remain ignorant of *Brahman* in this life (14).

4.4, 16-25 What is *Brahman*?

- *Brahman*, Self is Light of lights, Life of life, Mind of mind (16-18).
- Self is pure, beyond space, unborn, infinite, unchanging, undifferentiated, non-dual, One (19-20).
- Self – which has been described as '*neti, neti,* not this, not this' – is incomprehensible, indestructible, unattached and unfettered. It is beyond suffering and injury (22).
- Self, which lies in the space within the heart, is the Controller of all, the Lord of all, the Ruler of all (22).
- He who knows Self as such becomes calm, self-controlled, and indifferent to pleasures. Evil does not affect him. He sees all as one Self (23).
- Fearlessness, indeed, is *Brahman* (25).

4.5 Love means to see one Self in two bodies

This is a repetition of Chapter 2, Section 4, except for verse-1 and the second half of verse-15.

'Rebirth is an opportunity to fulfill all those desires which have hitherto remained unfulfilled.'

'Brahman is Light of lights, Life of life, Mind of mind.'

TRANSLATED TEXT

CHAPTER 4

Section 1

Janaka (King) of Videha was seated (to give audience). Then Yagyavalkya came up. He (Janaka) said to him:

Yagyavalkya for what purpose have you come, wishing for cattle (wealth), or for answering philosophical questions?'

Yagyavalkya : For both, Your Majesty. **1**
Let me hear what any one (of your teachers) may have told you (about *Brahman*).

Janaka : Jitvan Sailini told me that speech, verily, is *Brahman*.

Yagyavalkya : As one who has a mother, a father and a teacher should say, so did that Sailini say that speech is *Brahman*, for what can one have who cannot speak? But did he tell you the abode and the support (of *Brahman*)?

Janaka : He did not tell me.

Yagyavalkya : This *Brahman* is only one-footed, Your Majesty.

Janaka : Yagyavalkya, please tell us more.

Yagyavalkya : Its abode is just speech, its support space. One should worship it as consciousness.

Janaka : What is the nature of that consciousness, Yagyavalkya?

Yagyavalkya : Just speech, Your Majesty. Verily, by speech, a friend is recognized. By speech alone, Your Majesty, are *Rg Veda, Yajur Veda, Sama Veda, Atharva Veda,* history, ancient lore, arts, the Upanishads, verses, aphorisms, explanations, commentaries, (the effects of) sacrifices, oblations, food and drink, this world, other world and all beings are known. Speech, in truth, Your Majesty, is the highest *Brahman*. Speech does not desert him, who knowing thus, worships it as such. All beings approach him. Having become a god he attains the nature of gods.

Janaka : I shall give you a thousand cows with a bull as large as an elephant.

Yagyavalkya : My father thought that one should not accept gifts without having instructed. **2**
Let me hear what any one (of your teachers) may have told you!

"My father thought that one should not accept gifts without having instructed."

Janaka	: Udanka Saulbayana told me that life-breath, verily, is *Brahman*.
Yagyavalkya	: As one who has a mother, a father and a teacher should say, so did that Saulbayana say that Life-breath is *Brahman,* for what can one have who cannot breathe? But did he tell you the abode and the support?
Janaka	: He did not tell me.
Yagyavalkya	: This *Brahman* is only one-footed, Your Majesty.
Janaka	: Yagyavalkya, please tell us more.
Yagyavalkya	: Life-breath, verily, is its abode and space is its support. Verily, one should worship it as love.
Janaka	: What is the nature of that love, Yagyavalkya?
Yagyavalkya	: Life-breath itself, Your Majesty. Verily, out of love for life-breath, a man offers sacrifices to one for whom one should not offer sacrifices; he accepts gifts from one from whom they should not be accepted. Out of love for life-breath, one runs the risk of life in whatever direction one goes. Life-breath is, in truth, Your Majesty, the highest *Brahman*. Life-breath does not desert him, who knowing thus, worships it as such. All beings approach him. Having become a god he attains the nature gods.
Janaka	: I shall give you a thousand cows with a bull as large as an elephant.
Yagyavalkya	: My father thought that one should not accept (gifts) without having instructed. **3** Let me hear what any one (of your teachers) may have told you.
Janaka	: Barku Varsna told me that sight, verily, is *Brahman*.
Yagyavalkya	: As one who has a mother, a father and teacher should say, so did that Varsna say that the sight, verily, is *Brahman,* for what can one have who cannot see? But did he tell you the abode and the support?
Janaka	: He did not tell me.
Yagyavalkya	: This *Brahman* is only one-footed, Your Majesty.
Janaka	: Yagyavalkya, please tell us more.
Yagyavalkya	: The eyes are its abode and space its support. Verily one should worship it as truth.
Janaka	: What is the nature of truth, Yagyavalkya?

"Life-breath is Brahman" ..... *"This Brahman is only one-footed, Your Majesty"*

Yagyavalkya	: Sight itself, Your Majesty. Verily, Your Majesty, when they say to a man who sees with his eyes, "have you seen?" and he answers, "I have seen," that is the truth. Sight, in truth, Your Majesty, is the highest *Brahman*. Sight does not desert him, who knowing thus, worships it as such. All beings approach him. Having become a god he attains the nature of gods.
Janaka	: I shall give you a thousand cows with a bull as large as an elephant.
Yagyavalkya	: My father thought that one should not accept (gifts) without having instructed. **4** Let me hear what any one (of your teachers) may have told you.
Janaka	: Gardhabhivipita Bharadvaja told me that hearing, verily, is *Brahman*.
Yagyavalkya	: As one who has a mother, a father and teacher should say, so did that Bharadvaja say that hearing, verily, is *Brahman* for what can one have who cannot hear? But did he tell you the abode and the support?
Janaka	: He did not tell me.
Yagyavalkya	: This *Brahman* is only one-footed, Your Majesty.
Janaka	: Yagyavalkya, please tell us more.
Yagyavalkya	: The ears are its abode and space its support. Verily one should worship it as infinitude.
Janaka	: What is the nature of infinitude, Yagyavalkya?
Yagyavalkya	: The quarters themselves, Your Majesty. Therefore, to whatever quarter one goes, he does not come to the end of it, for quarters are endless. Verily, quarters are hearing. Hearing, in truth, Your Majesty, is the highest *Brahman*. Hearing does not desert him, who knowing this worships it as such. All beings approach him. Having become a god he attains the nature of gods.
Janaka	: I shall give you a thousand cows with a bull as large as an elephant.
Yagyavalkya	: My father thought that one should not accept (gifts) without having instructed. **5** Let me hear what any one (of your teachers) may have told you.
Janaka	: Satyakama Jabala told me that mind, verily, is *Brahman*.
Yagyavalkya	: As one who has a mother, a father and a teacher should say, so did that Jabala say that mind, verily, is *Brahman* for what can one have who is without a mind?' But did he tell you the abode and the support?

"Mind is Brahman"..... "This Brahman is only one-footed, Your Majesty"

Janaka	: He did not tell me.
Yagyavalkya	: This *Brahman* is only one-footed, Your Majesty.
Janaka	: Yagyavalkya, please tell us more.
Yagyavalkya	: Mind is its abode and space its support. Verily one should worship it as bliss.
Janaka	: What is the nature of bliss, Yagyavalkya?
Yagyavalkya	: Just the mind, Your Majesty. By the mind one takes to a woman. A son resembling him is born of her. He is (the source of) bliss. Mind, in truth, Your Majesty, is the highest *Brahman*. Mind never deserts him who knowing thus worships it as such. All beings approach him. Having become a god he attains the nature of gods.
Janaka	: I shall give you a thousand cows with a bull as large as an elephant.
Yagyavalkya	: My father thought that one should not accept (gifts) without having instructed. **6** Let me hear what any one (of your teachers) may have told you.
Janaka	: Vidagdha Sakalya told me that the heart, verily, is *Brahman*.
Yagyavalkya	: As one who has a mother, father, teacher should say, so did that Sakalya say that the heart, verily, is *Brahman* for what can one have who is without a heart? But did he tell you the abode and the support?
Janaka	: He did not tell me.
Yagyavalkya	: This *Brahman* is only one-footed, Your Majesty.
Janaka	: Yagyavalkya, please tell us more.
Yagyavalkya	: Heart is its abode and space is its support. One should worship it as stability.
Janaka	: What is the nature of stability, Yagyavalkya?
Yagyavalkya	: Just the heart, Your Majesty. Heart is the abode and the support of beings. Heart, in truth, Your Majesty, is the highest *Brahman*. Heart never deserts him, who knowing thus, worships it as such. All beings approach him. Having become a god he attains the nature of gods.
Janaka	: I shall give you a thousand cows with a bull as large as an elephant.
Yagyavalkya	: My father thought that one should not accept (gifts) without having instructed. **7**

"Janaka : What is the nature of bliss, Yagyavalkya?
Yagyavalkya : Just the mind, Your Majesty."

Section 2

Janaka (King) of Videha, descending from his lounge and approaching Yagyavalkya said:

Salutations to you, Yagyavalkya, please instruct me.

Yagyavalkya : Your Majesty, he who wishes to go on a long journey, procures a chariot or a ship. Likewise, you have well equipped your mind with the teachings of the Upanishads. You are also rich and respected. You have studied the Vedas and the Upanishads. Where will you go when you are separated (from this body)?

Janaka : Venerable Sir, I do not know where I shall go.

Yagyavalkya : Then truly, I shall tell you where you will go.

Janaka : Tell me, Venerable Sir. **1**

Yagyavalkya : This Person who is in the right eye is called Indha. Though he is Indha people call him Indra, because gods are fond of indirect names. They dislike to be addressed by direct names. **2**

Now that which is in the form of a Cosmic Person in the left eye is his wife *Viraj* (Matter). Their place of union is the space within the heart. Their food is the red lump (of blood) in the heart. Their covering is the net-like structure in the heart. Their path for moving is that channel which goes upward from the heart. Like a hair divided a thousandfold, so are the (subtle) channels called *hita*, which are established within the heart. Through these flows the essence of food as it moves on. Therefore, that Self (composed of Indha and *Viraj*) is, as it were, an eater of finer food than the gross body. **3**

The eastern direction is the eastern breaths. The southern direction is the southern breaths. The western direction is the western breaths. The northern direction is the northern breaths. The upper direction is the upper breaths. The lower direction is the lower breaths. All quarters are different breaths.

Self is described as *'neti, neti* not this, not this'. It is imperceptible, for It is never perceived. It is indestructible, for It cannot be destroyed. It is unattached, for It does not attach Itself. It is without fetters, It does not suffer, It is not injured. Verily, Janaka, you have reached (that state of) fearlessness.

Janaka : Venerable Sir, may fearlessness come to you, as you have educated us on (the state of) fearlessness. Salutations to you. Here are the people of Videha, here am I (at your service). **4**

"Where will you go when you are separated (from this body)?"

Section 3

Yagyavalkya went to Janaka (King) of Videha. He thought (to himself): 'This time I will not speak anything.' Now (once) Janaka (King) of Videha and Yagyavalkya had a discussion about *agnihotra* ceremony. Yagyavalkya had then granted a boon to Janaka that he could ask any question he wished. So this time it was the king who questioned him first. **1**

Janaka : What light does a person here have? (What serves as light for a man?)

Yagyavalkya : The sun indeed is his light, Your Majesty. With sun as the light, one sits, moves about, does one's work, and returns.

Janaka : Just so, Yagyavalkya. **2**
When the sun has set, Yagyavalkya, what light does a person here have?

Yagyavalkya : The moon, indeed is his light. With moon as the light, one sits, moves about, does one's work, and returns.

Janaka : Just so, Yagyavalkya. **3**
When the sun has set, Yagyavalkya, and the moon has set, what light does a person here have?

Yagyavalkya : The fire, indeed, is his light. With fire as the light, one sits, moves about, does one's work, and returns.

Janaka : Just so, Yagyavalkya. **4**
When the sun has set, Yagyavalkya, and the moon has set and the fire has gone out, what light does a person here have?

Yagyavalkya : Speech, indeed, is his light. With speech as the light, one sits, moves about, does ones work and returns. Therefore, Your Majesty, even when one's own hand is not visible, when speech is uttered one goes towards it.

Janaka : Just so, Yagyavalkya. **5**
When the sun has set, Yagyavalkya, and the moon has set, and the fire has gone out and speech has stopped, what light does a person here have?

Yagyavalkya : Self, indeed, is his light. With Self as the light, one sits, moves about, does one's work and returns. **6**

Janaka : What is Self?

Yagyavalkya : Self is the Person who consists of knowledge and resides among the senses. He is also the light within the heart. Being identical to Intelligence, He wanders along the two worlds, seeming to think, seeming to act. On being identified with sleep, He transcends this world of mortal forms of death. **7**

"With Self as the light, one sits, moves about, does one's work."

Verily, when this Person is born, He obtains a body which, becomes connected with evils. When He departs, on dying He leaves all evils behind. **8**

Verily, there are two states of this person – this world (waking) and the other world (deep sleep). There is an intermediate third state, that of dream. By standing in this intermediate state he sees both these states, of being in this world and of being in the other world.

Now whatever outfit he may have for the next world, having obtained that, he sees both the evils (of this world) and the joys (of the other world). When he dreams, he takes along the impressions of the waking state, tears them apart, and builds them up into a dream. He dreams by his own brightness, by his own light. In that state he becomes self-illuminated. **9**

There are no chariots there, nor animals to be yoked to them, nor any roads; but he creates (projects from himself) chariots, animals to be yoked to them and roads. There are no joys there, no pleasures, no delights; but he creates joys, pleasures and delights. There are no tanks there, no lotus pools, no rivers; but he creates tanks, lotus-pools and rivers. He, indeed, is the agent (maker or creator). **10**

On this there are the following verses.

Having put aside the body in dream, and himself remaining awake, he looks down on the sleeping (senses). Having taken the shining functions of the senses with him, he again comes back to the waking state. He is the golden Person, the lonely swan. **11**

Guarding the inferior nest (body) with the vital breath, the Immortal moves outside the nest. That, Immortal and Radiant Being, who roams alone, attains whatever he wants. **12**

In the state of dream, going up and down, he makes many forms for himself, as it were – enjoying himself in the company of women, or laughing, or even beholding fearful sights. **13**

Everyone sees his sport but none sees him. Therefore they say that one should not wake him (the sleeping person) suddenly; for it is difficult to cure if he does not get back (rightly to his body). Others, however, say that (the state of dream) is just his waking state, for whatever objects he sees when awake, he sees those also when he dreams. This is wrong. In dream state the person is self-illuminated.

Janaka : I give you a thousand (cows), Venerable Sir. Please instruct me further. **14**

"There are no joys there, no pleasures, no delights; but he creates joys, pleasures and delights (in dream state)."

Yagyavalkya :	After having rejoiced, roamed about and seen good and evil in dream state, he stays in a state of deep sleep and then comes back to dream state. Whatever he sees in dream state, he is not affected by it, for this person is not attached (to anything).
Janaka :	Just so, Yagyavalkya, I give you a thousand (cows), Venerable Sir. Please instruct me further. **15**
Yagyavalkya :	After having rejoiced, roamed about and seen good and evil in dream state, he comes back to the state of waking. Whatever he sees in dream state, he is not affected by it, for this person is not attached (to anything).
Janaka :	Just so, Yagyavalkya, I give you a thousand (cows) Venerable Sir. Please instruct me further. **16**

Yagyavalkya :

After having rejoiced, roamed about and seen good and evil in waking state, he comes back to the state of dream (or deep sleep). **17**

Just as a large fish moves between the two banks of a river, here and there, so also this person moves along both these states – the state of dream (or sleep) and the state of waking. **18**

Just a falcon or any other (swift) bird flying in the sky becomes tired, folds its wings and comes down to its nest, so also this person hastens to that state (of sleep) where he has no desires and he sees no dream. **19**

In him, verily, are those channels called *hita*, which are as fine as a hair split a thousandfold. They are filled with (subtle) white, blue, yellow, green and red (fluids in which impressions are stored).

Now when (he feels) as if he were being killed, or overpowered, or pursued by an elephant, or falling into a well, these are the fears he has experienced in the waking state.

But when he thinks as if he is a god, or a king, or 'all this', that is his highest state. **20**

This, verily, is his true nature. It is free from craving, free from evils, free from fear. As a man in the embrace of his beloved knows nothing without or within, so also the person when in the embrace of his intelligent Self knows nothing without or within. That, verily, is his nature in which all his desires are fulfilled, in which the Self is without desire, free from any sorrow. **21**

There (in that state), a father is not a father, a mother is not a mother, the worlds are not the worlds, the gods are not the gods, the Vedas are not the Vedas. There, a thief is not a thief, a murderer is not a murderer, a *chandala* is not a *chandala*, a *paulkasa* is not a *paulkasa*, a mendicant is not a mendicant, an ascetic is not an ascetic. (In this state) he is not affected by good or evil, he is beyond all the sorrows of the heart. **22**

"As a man in the embrace of his beloved knows nothing without or within, so also the person when in the embrace of his intelligent Self, knows nothing without or within, (in the state of deep sleep)."

Verily, when there (in the state of deep sleep), he does not see. Even though he is really seeing, he does not see in the normal sense. There is no cessation of the seeing of a seer, because of the imperishability (of the seer). There is no second to him; there is nothing separate from him that he could see. **23**

Verily, when there (in the state of deep sleep), he does not smell. Even though he really smells, he does not smell in the normal sense. There is no cessation of the smelling of a smeller, because of the imperishability (of the smeller). There is no second to him, there is nothing separate from him that he could smell. **24**

Verily, when there (in the state of deep sleep), he does not taste. Even though he really tastes, he does not taste in the normal sense. There is no cessation of the tasting of a taster, because of the imperishability (of the taster). There is no second to him; there is nothing separate from him that he could taste. **25**

Verily, when there (in the state of deep sleep), he does not speak. Even though he is really speaking, he does not speak in the normal sense. There is no cessation of the speaking of a speaker, because of the imperishability (of the speaker). There is no second to him, there is nothing separate from him that he could speak. **26**

Verily, when there (in the state of deep sleep), he does not hear. Even though he is really hearing, he does not hear in the normal sense. There is no cessation of the hearing of a hearer, because of the imperishability (of the hearer). There is no second to him, there is nothing separate from him that he could hear. **27**

Verily, when there (in the state of deep sleep), he does not think. Even though he is really thinking, he does not think in the normal sense. There is no cessation of the thinking of a thinker, because of the imperishability (of the thinker). There is no second to him, there is nothing separate from him that he could think. **28**

Verily, when there (in the state of deep sleep), he does not touch. Even though he is really touching, he does not touch in the normal sense. There is no cessation of the touching of a toucher, because of the imperishability (of the toucher). There is no second to him, there is nothing separate from him that he could touch. **29**

Verily, when there (in the state of deep sleep), he does not know. Even though he really knows, he does not know in the normal sense. There is no cessation of the knowing of a knower, because of the imperishability (of the knower). There is no second to him (Self), there is nothing separate from him that he could know. **30**

Verily, when there is duality, then one might see the other, one might smell the other, one might taste the other, one might speak to the other, one might hear the other, one might think of the other, one might touch the other, one might know the other. **31**

In deep sleep, the non-dual Consciousness becomes one homogeneous mass, like water (ocean). This (state of homogeneous Consciousness) is the state of *Brahman*. This is his highest goal, this is his highest treasure, this is his highest world, and this is his greatest bliss. Other creatures subsist just on a fraction of this bliss. **32**

"There is no second to him (Self), there is nothing separate from him that he could know."

When one is healthy in body, wealthy, lord over others, lavishly provided with all human enjoyments, that is the highest bliss of a man.

This human bliss multiplied a hundred times makes one unit of the bliss of ancestors who have won their world.

The bliss of these ancestors who have won their world multiplied a hundred times makes one unit of the bliss of *gandharva* world.

The bliss of *gandharva* world multiplied a hundred times makes one unit of the bliss of gods-by-action, those who attain divine status by (meritorious) deeds.

The bliss of gods-by-action multiplied a hundred times makes one unit of the bliss of gods-by-birth as well as of one who is versed in Vedas, who is without sin and who is not overcome by desire.

The bliss of gods-by-birth multiplied a hundred times makes one unit of the bliss in the world of *Prajapati,* as well as of one who is versed in Vedas, who is without sin and is not overcome by desire.

The bliss in the world of *Prajapati* multiplied a hundred times makes one unit of the bliss in the world of *Hiranyagarbha*, as well as of one who is versed in Vedas, who is without sin and who is not overcome by desire.

Janaka : I will give you, Venerable Sir, a thousand (cows). Please instruct me further on liberation.

At this point Yagyavalkya was afraid that this intelligent king would constrain him to impart all his knowledge about *Brahman*. (But he continued his instructions).

Yagyavalkya : This is the highest bliss. This is the world of *Brahman*, Your Majesty.
33

After having enjoyed this state of dream (or sleep), after having roamed about and seen good and evil, he returns again as he came to the place from which he started, to the state of waking.
34

When breathing becomes difficult, when one is about to die, just as a heavily loaded cart moves on, making creaking noise, even so, Self in the body – directed by Cosmic Consciousness – moves on making creaking noise.
35

When either through old age or disease, this body becomes weak, this Person frees himself from these limbs, just as a mango or a fig or a fruit of a pipal tree releases itself from its stalk. He returns back through the same route from which He came, to start a (new) life.
36

Just as policemen, officials and leaders of a village wait for a visiting king with food, drink and lodging, saying, "here he comes, here he comes," even so all the elements wait for the transmigrating soul, saying, "here comes *Brahman*, here He comes."
37

"All the elements wait for the transmigrating soul, saying, "here comes Brahman, here He comes"..."

Just as policemen, officials and leaders of a village gather round a king who is leaving on a tour, even so do all the breaths (senses) gather round the Self when one is breathing with difficulty (when one is about to die). **38**

Section 4

When (at the time of death) the body becomes weak and unconscious, then the senses gather round the Self. He takes into himself these particles of light, the resplendent energies of sense organs, and descends into the heart. When the Person (*Purusha*) in the eye turns away, then man becomes unconscious of forms. **1**

He (the eye) is becoming one (with the subtle body, therefore) he does not see, they say;
He (the nose) is becoming one, he does not smell, they say;
He (the tongue) is becoming one, he does not taste, they say;
He (the speech organ) is becoming one, he does not speak, they say;
He (the ear) is becoming one, he does not hear, they say;
He (the mind) is becoming one, he does not think, they say;
He (the skin) is becoming one, he does not feel touch, they say;
He (the intellect) is becoming one, he does not know, they say.
Then the top of his heart becomes lighted up and by that light the Self departs either through the eye, or through the head, or through other apertures of the body. And when He thus departs, life departs after Him. And when life thus departs, all the senses depart after Him. He becomes one with Consciousness. Whatever has intelligence departs with Him. Dying man's knowledge and his work depart with him, as also his past experience. **2**

Just as a caterpillar reaching the end of a blade of grass, catches hold of another blade, and draws itself towards it, so also this Self – after having thrown away this body and dispelled ignorance – draws Itself on another body (support). **3**

As a goldsmith turns a piece of gold into another newer and more beautiful shape, so also Self – after having thrown away this body and dispelled its ignorance – makes for Itself another, newer and more beautiful shape, like that of the fore-fathers or of the *gandharvas*, or of the gods, or of *Prajapati*, or of *Brahma*, or of other beings. **4**

That Self is, indeed, *Brahman*. It is identified with intellect, mind, life, sight, hearing, earth, water, air, ether, light and no-light, desire and absence of desire, anger and absence of anger, righteousness, in fact, with everything which can be perceived (this) or inferred (that). As one acts and as one behaves, so does one become. The doer of good becomes good, the doer of evil becomes evil. One becomes virtuous by virtuous action, bad by bad action. Some say that a person consists of desires. As is his desire so is his will; as is his will, so is the deed he does, whatever deed he does; that he attains. **5**

On this there is the following verse:

"The subtle Self together with Its deeds (*Karma*) goes to that alone to which the mind is attached. Exhausting the results of whatever works it did in this world, It

---

"Dying man's knowledge and his work depart with him, as also his past experience."

returns from that to this world for (fresh) work."

This (is for) the man who has desires. But the man who does not have desires, who is without desire, who is free from desire, whose desire is satisfied, whose desire is Self, his breaths do not depart. Being *Brahman* he goes to *Brahman*. **6**

On this there is also the following verse:

"When all the desires that dwell in the heart are cast away, then the mortal becomes immortal; then he attains *Brahman* here (in this very body)."

Just as the slough of a snake lies dead and discarded on an anthill, even so lies this body. But this disembodied, immortal Life (*Prana*) is *Brahman* only, it is the Light (of consciousness) indeed, Your Majesty.

Janaka : I give you, Venerable Sir, a thousand cows. **7**

Yagyavalkya : On this there are the following verses:

The subtle, far-reaching, ancient path has been touched (found) by me, has been realized by me. By this path, the wise, the knowers of *Brahman* go to the heavenly world beyond, after the fall of this body here. **8**

Some speak of that path as white, others as blue, yellow, green or red. That path is found by a knower of *Brahman*. The knower of *Brahman*, the doer of right, the shining one, goes by that path. **9**

Into blind darkness enter those who worship *avidya* or ignorance (rites). Into greater darkness than that, as if, enter those who delight in *vidya*, knowledge alone. **10**

Miserable are those worlds which are covered with blind darkness. To them after death go those people who are ignorant and unwise. **11**

If a person knows Self as 'I am this *Atman*,' then for what desire and for whose sake would he suffer (the pains of) the body? **12**

Whoever has understood and realized the Self that has entered into this perilous and inaccessible place (the body), he is the creator of all. His is the world; indeed, he is the world itself. **13**

Verily, we have to know That *(Brahman)* while we are in this body. Great is the loss if we remain ignorant of It. Those who know It become immortal, while others are subject to pain. **14**

One who clearly realizes Self as the Lord of what has been and what will be, he does not hide himself from Him. **15**

The gods worship that Light of lights – under the order of which the year with its days rolls on – as life immortal. **16**

"Verily, we have to know That (Brahman) while we are in this body.
Great is the loss if we remain ignorant of It."

That in which the five groups of five and space are established, that alone I regard as Self. Knowing that immortal *Brahman*, I am immortal. **17**

They who know the Life of life (*Prana*), the Eye of eye, the Ear of ear and the Mind of mind, they have realized the ancient primordial *Brahman*. **18**

That (*Brahman*) should be realized by the mind alone. There is no diversity in It. He who sees diversity in It goes from death to death, as it were. **19**

That unknowable and eternal Self should be realized as One only. The Self is pure, beyond space, unborn, infinite and unchanging. **20**

A wise person should practice (the means to) wisdom only after knowing Him. Let him not reflect on many words that are tiring to the organ of speech. **21**

Verily, He is the great, unborn Self consisting of knowledge among the senses.

He lies in the space within the heart as the controller of all, the lord of all, the ruler of all.
He does not become greater by good works, or smaller by evil works.
He is the bridge that serves as the link to keep the different worlds connected.
Him the *Brahmins* seek to know by study of Vedas, by sacrifices, by gifts, by penance, by fasting.
On knowing Him, in truth, one becomes an ascetic. Desiring Him only as their world, monks wander forth.
Verily, because they knew this, the ancient (sages) did not wish for offspring. They said, 'What shall we do with offspring as we have attained this Self, this world.'

They, having risen above desire for sons, desire for wealth, desire for worlds, led the life of a mendicant.

Desire for sons is desire for wealth and desire for wealth is desire for worlds; both these are, indeed, desires only.

This Self is (that which has been described as) '*neti, neti*, not this, not this'.

He is incomprehensible, for He is never comprehended. He is indestructible, for He cannot be destroyed. He is unattached, for He does not attach Himself. He is unfettered, He does not suffer, He is not injured.

He who knows thus is not overcome by these two thoughts: 'I have done an evil deed' or 'I have done a good deed'. He overcomes both. He is not troubled by what he does or what he does not do. **22**

This doctrine has been expressed in a hymn.

The eternal glory of the knower of *Brahman* is not increased or diminished by work. One should know the nature of That alone. Having found That, one is not tainted by evil action.

"Having found 'That', one is not tainted by evil action."

Therefore he who knows That as such, becomes calm, self-controlled, indifferent to pleasures, enduring and absorbed in meditation.

He sees Self in his own self (body). He sees all as the Self. Evil does not overcome him, he overcomes all evil.

Evil does not burn (affect) him, he burns (consumes) all evil.

Free from evil, free from taint, free from doubt, he becomes a knower of *Brahman*.

This is the world of *Brahman*, Your Majesty. You have attained it.

Janaka : Venerable Sir, I give you the (empire of) Videha and myself also to serve you. **23**

Yagyavalkya : This is that great, unborn Self, who is the eater of food and the giver of wealth. He who knows thus obtains wealth. **24**

This is that great Self who is unborn, undecaying, undying, immortal, fearless, *Brahman*. Fearlessness indeed is *Brahman*. He who knows this becomes fearless, *Brahman*. **25**

Section 5

Now (it is said that) Yagyavalkya had two wives - Maitreyi and Katyayani. While Maitreyi was learned in speaking about *Brahman*, Katyayani possessed only such knowledge as women normally have. Yagyavalkya wished to get ready for another mode of life. (One day, he said to Maitreyi): **1**

Yagyavalkya : Maitreyi, I am going to renounce this materialistic life. Let me make a final settlement (of my property) with you and with Katyayani. **2**

Maitreyi : My Lord, if this whole earth filled with wealth becomes mine, will I become immortal by it?

Yagyavalkya : No. Your life will be like that of people who have plenty of wealth, but there is no hope of immortality through wealth. **3**

Maitreyi : What shall I do with that by which I do not become immortal? What you know (about immortality), venerable Sir, please explain that to me. **4**

Yagyavalkya : You have always been truly dear to me. Now, you have made yourself even dearer. Therefore, I shall explain to you whatever you wish to know. Please reflect on whatever I explain. **5**

Yagyavalkya : Verily, not for the sake of husband is husband dear, but for the sake of Self is husband dear.
Verily, not for the sake of wife is wife dear, but for the sake of Self is wife dear.

"This is that great Self who is unborn, undecaying, undying, immortal, fearless, Brahman. Fearlessness indeed is Brahman."

Verily, not for the sake of sons are sons dear, but for the sake of Self are sons dear.
Verily, not for the sake of wealth is wealth dear, but for the sake of Self is wealth dear.
Verily, not for the sake of cattle are cattle dear, but for the sake of Self are the cattle dear.
Verily, not for the sake of *Brahmin* is *Brahmin* dear, but for the sake of Self is *Brahmin* dear.
Verily, not for the sake of *Kshatriya* is *Kshatriya* dear, but for the sake of Self is *Kshatriya* dear.
Verily, not for the sake of worlds are worlds dear, but for the sake of Self are worlds dear.
Verily, not for the sake of gods are gods dear, but for the sake of Self are gods dear.
Verily, not for the sake of the Vedas are Vedas dear, but for the sake of Self are Vedas dear.
Verily not for the sake of beings are beings dear, but for the sake of Self are beings dear.
Verily, not for the sake of all is all dear, but for the sake of Self is all dear.
Verily, Self is to be seen (realized), to be heard, to be reflected on, to be meditated upon. When Self is seen, heard, reflected on and known, then all this is known. **6**

Brahmin deserts him who knows him as different from Self.
Kshatriya deserts him who knows him as different from Self.
The worlds desert him who knows the worlds as different from Self.
The gods desert him who knows the gods as different from Self.
The Vedas desert him who knows the Vedas as different from Self.
The beings desert him who knows the beings as different from Self.
Everyone deserts him who knows everyone as different from Self.
This *Brahmin,* this *Kshatriya*, these worlds, these gods, these Vedas, these beings, everything is this Self. **7**

When a drum is beaten, one cannot grasp its several different notes, but they are grasped when the drum or the beater of the drum is grasped. **8**

When a conch is blown one cannot grasp its different notes, but they are grasped when the conch or the blower of the conch is grasped. **9**

When a *Veena* (or lute) is played one cannot grasp its different notes, but they are grasped when the *veena,* or the player of the *veena* is grasped. **10**

When a fire is kindled with damp fuel, various kinds of smoke issue forth from it. Similarly, from this great Being have been breathed forth *Rg Veda, Yajur Veda, Sama Veda*, hymns of *Atharva Veda*, legend, ancient lore, sciences, sacred teachings, verses, aphorisms,

---

"Self is to be seen (realized), to be heard, to be reflected on, to be meditated upon."

explanations, commentaries, sacrifice, oblation, food, drink, this world and the other world, and all beings. From it, indeed, has everything been breathed forth. **11**

As the ocean is the one goal (meeting-place) of all waters,
as the skin is the one goal of all kinds of touch,
as the nose is the one goal of all smells,
as the tongue is the one goal of all tastes,
as the eye is the one goal of all forms,
as the ear is the one goal of all sounds,
as the mind is the one goal of all deliberations,
as the heart (intellect) is the one goal of all knowledge,
as the hands are the one goal of all kinds of work,
as the generative organ is the one goal of all forms of delight,
as the anus is the one goal of all excretions,
as the feet are the one goal of all movements,
as the (organ of) speech is the one goal of all *Vedas*. **12**

As a mass of salt is saline in taste at every spot – without an inside or outside – likewise this Self is a homogeneous mass of Pure Consciousness only, without an inside or outside.
Having arisen out of these elements, (Self) vanishes again into them.
And when Self has departed (from the body) there is no more (a distinctly identifiable, individual) Consciousness. This is what I say, dear. **13**

Maitreyi : Venerable Sir, you have put me in bewilderment. I do not at all understand this (Self).

Yagyavalkya : I have not said anything bewildering. This Self, indeed, is imperishable and of indestructible nature. **14**

Where there is duality, as it were, there one sees the other, one smells the other, one tastes the other, one speaks to the other, one touches the other, one knows the other. But where everything has become just one's own Self, by what and whom should one see, by what and whom should one smell, by what and whom should one taste, by what and whom should one speak? By what and whom should one hear, by what and about whom should one think, by what and whom should one touch, by what and whom should one know?

By what should one know him by whom all this is known? That Self is described as '*neti, neti,* not this, not this'. It is incomprehensible, for It cannot be comprehended. It is indestructible, for It cannot be destroyed. It is unattached, for It does not attach himself. It is unfettered, It does not suffer. It is not injured. Indeed, by what would one know the knower? O Maitreyi, This is what I can tell you about immortality, life eternal.

Having said this, Yagyavalkya went away (into the forest). **15**

"When Self has departed (from the body) there is no more (a distinctly identifiable, individual) Consciousness."

Section 6

Now the line age of teachers.
Pautimasya (received the teaching) from Gaupavana,
Gaupavana from Pautimasya, Pautimasya from Gaupavana,
Gaupavana from Kausika, Kausika from Kaundinya,
Kaundinya from Sandilya, Sandilya from Kausika and Gautama,
Gautama from Agnivesya, Agnivesya from Gargya,
Gargya from Gargya, Gargya from Gautama,
Gautama from Saitava, Saitava from Parasaryayana,
Parasaryayana from Gargyayana, Gargyayana from Uddalakayana,
Uddalakayana from Jabalayana, Jabalayana from Madhyandinayana,
Madhyandinayana from Saukarayana, Saukarayana from Kasayana,
Kasayana from Sayakayana, Sayakayana from Kausikayani,
Kausikayani from Ghrtakausika, Ghrtakausika from Parasaryayana,
Parasaryayana from Parasarya, Parasarya from Jatukarnya,
Jatukarnya from Asurayana and Yaska, Asurayana from Traivani,
Traivani from Anupajandhani, Anupajandhani from Asuri,
Asuri from Bharadvaja, Bharadvaja from Atreya,
Atreya from Manti, Manti from Gautama,
Gautama from Gautama, Gautama, from Vatsya,
Vatsya from Sandilya, Sandilya from Kaisorya Kapya,
Kaisorya Kapya from Kumaraharita, Kumaraharita from Galava,
Galava from Vidarbhikaundinya,
Vidarbhikaundinya from Vatsanapat Babhrava,
Vatsanapat Babhrava from Pathin Saubhara,
Pathin Saubhara from Ayasya Angirasa,
Ayasya Angirasa from Abhuti Tvastra from the two Asvins,
the two Asvins from Dadhyach Atharvan,
Dadhyach Atharvan from Mrtyu Pradhvamasana,
Pradhvamasana from Ekarsi, Ekarsi from Vipracitti,
Vipracitti from Vyasti, Vyasti from Sanaru,
Sanaru from Sanatana, Sanatana from Sanaga,
Sanaga from Paramesthin, Paramesthin from Brahma;
Brahma is self-existent. Salutation to Brahma. 3

"Brahma is Self-existent. Salutation to Brahma."

Focussed Commentaries

CHAPTER 4

4.1 Incomplete definitions of *Brahman*

In this section, King Janaka presents before Yagyavalkya the doctrinal opinions of six other teachers about *Brahman*; that *Brahman* is Speech, Life-breath, Sight, Hearing, Mind and Heart. Yagyavalkya calls these definitions as one-sided, as they omit their abode (*ayatanam*), support (*pratistha*) and essence. Yagyavalkya then describes, one-by-one, the essence of the six phenomenal forms of *Brahman*.

Phenomenon	Essence
Speech	Consciousness, *Pragyan*
Life Breath	Love, *Priyam*
Sight	Truth, *Satyam*
Hearing	Endless *Ananta*
Mind	Bliss *Ananda*
Heart	Stability, *Sthiti*

Yagyavalkya adds that one should adore (*upasate*) these as *Brahman*, but this expression signifies that with these, the proper essence of *Brahman* is still not grasped.

– *Paul Deussen*

Meditation on speech as *Brahman* is good as far as it goes, and is productive of beneficial results. However, it is incomplete and not comprehensive; it is one-footed, or one-sided.

As one who has a mother, a father and a teacher: An instructor of *Brahma Vidya*, knowledge of *Brahman*, should be one who has been properly instructed by his mother in childhood, by his father later on, and by a teacher after proper initiation. Absence of any one or more of these will seriously affect one's spiritual progress.

This section points out the mistake generally committed by aspirants in meditation on a chosen subject – considering it as an individual, limited entity. This mistake is rectified by bringing into the scope of meditation the left-out parts, and thus making the 'whole' the object of meditation.

The following six meditations are given in this section:
- Speech identified with Fire and Consciousness
- Life, *(Prana)*, identified with Air, *(Vayu)* and Love
- Sight, identified with Sun and Truth
- Hearing, identified with Directions and Infinity
- Mind, identified with Moon and Bliss
- Heart, identified with Creator *(Prajapati)* and Stability.

The instructions given in regard to the six objects apply equally to all objects and concepts. When any object or concept is meditated upon alone, it is incomplete contemplation. For, any object or concept is not really an isolated entity, but is invisibly and essentially connected with the rest of the universe. Its all four aspects – external, internal, universal and transcendental – should be taken into consideration in meditation. This, in short, is the instruction of Yagyavalkya to Janaka.

– *Swami Sivananda*

4.2 Journey beyond death

In contrast to the first section, Yagyavalkya pursues a subjective approach in the second section. He starts with the question: Where does the soul go after death?

In reply to the aforesaid question, he first describes the subject of knowledge. This according to him dwells as *Indra* and *Viraj* – as husband and wife – in both the eyes. Their point of union is the ether of the heart. Here a clot of blood forms its food, a plexus of arteries its garment, another ascending artery is the way leading above, and still other arteries named as *hitah* carry their choicest food to the soul. But suddenly Yagyavalkya drops that esoteric idea of the soul as an individual soul and explains space as its vital breath. He also describes the soul – unknowable, free, invulnerable, eternal, subject of knowledge – by his famous formula, *neti, neti*. The supplement 'you have reached the state of fearlessness' signifies that for a man like Janaka, who has such knowledge, the question as to where the soul goes after death has no significance.

– *Paul Deussen*

'Any object is invisibly and essentially connected with the rest of the universe.'

Viraj or Matter is the wife of *Indra* or Self, also called *Vaisvanara*. They are united in dreams. *Visva* (or *Vaisvanara*), *Taijasa* and *Pragyan* are the names of Self, as identified with gross, subtle and causal body, respectively, in the states of wakefulness, dream and dreamless sleep. The verses contain the idea that *Taijasa* is nourished by finer food than *Vaisvanara* (4.2, 2-3).

— Sri Sankara, translated
by Swami Madhavananda

This section is an exposition on the condition of Consciousness in the three states of waking, dream and deep sleep. The right eye is said to be the seat of Self in waking state, as it is thought to be more powerful than the left eye.

The analogy of husband and wife for relationship between the right eye and the left eye – the twin instruments of perception – is to show that perception in waking state takes place on account of contact of the subject (perceiver, Self) with the object (Matter, *Viraj*). Hence, in waking state there is what is known as subject – object distinction. In dream state – when both these are united – the distinction between subject and object vanishes. In this state, mind alone is both the subject and the object.

Self, when identified with the gross body in waking state, is called *Vaisvanara*. It is called *Taijasa* when It is identified with the subtle body in dream state. In deep sleep, Self is identified with Life-breath, *Prana*. In this state, Self is identified with everything in the universe, which is comprised of *Prana* alone. Verse 4.2, 4 expresses this fact by the statement, 'eastern direction is the eastern breath', etc.

— Swami Sivananda

4.3 Ultimate Light and Its three states

This dialogue between Janaka and Yagyavalkya is regarding *Atman* – the soul together with God – in the states of wakefulness, dream, deep sleep and death. It stands out unique in its richness and warmth of presentation – indeed, the only one in Indian literature, and perhaps in the literature of all peoples.

Janaka confronts Yagyavalkya with a profound question: 'What is that which serves men as light?' He attempts to elude the real answer by saying one-by-one that it is the sun, the moon, the fire and the speech; but the king draws him back again to his question (4.3, 1-6).

At last Yagyavalkya answers that it is the Light of all lights, *Atman*, the subject of knowledge, *Vigyanamaya antar jyotir Purusha*. Upon being asked by the king to explain it in greater detail, Yagyavalkya dwells long on the states of waking, dream, deep sleep and death.

Interestingly, in the narration of this section, there is no mention of *devayana* and *pitrayana* – the path of gods and the path of ancestors – one of which the soul is believed to follow after death, as stated elsewhere in the Upanishads.

According to verses 4.3, 9-10, *Atman* constructs for Itself in dream state a second world out of the material of wakeful state. According to verses 4.3, 11-14 however, the soul leaves the body in dream state in order to roam about in the world according to its pleasure.

Thus, during a man's lifetime, the soul roams between the states of wakefulness and dream, just as a fish in a river or a pond glides now to this side of the bank, now to that side of the bank.

Deep sleep is a state of serene bliss, it is a temporary communion with *Brahman*; It is ascent to the world of *Brahman*.

First, there is an excellent description of the state of dreamless sleep (4.3, 19-22).

Then follows a description of the objectless subject of knowledge. Verses 4.3, 31-34 contains a description of Bliss. Verse 4.3, 33 is identical with verse 2.8 in Taittiriya Upanishad.

The soul of an ordinary dying man (not a man of Self-realization) lets the limbs fall away – just as ripe fruits fall down from a tree – and enter into Life-force, *Prana* (4.3, 36). In this state, all the vital organs (eyes, ears etc.) assemble around it, just as the retinue of a king assembles around the king when he wishes to set out on a journey.

Verse 4.3, 37 does not belong here, it has come into the text through external similarity.

— Paul Deussen

'In waking state there is what is known as subject–object distinction. In dream state, mind alone is both the subject and the object. Deep sleep is a state of serene bliss, of temporary communion with Brahman.'

Self is present in all the three states of waking, dream, and sleep. It is the light different from one's body and organs. It illumines them, though It is Itself not illumined by anything else (Sri Sankara).

Seeming to think: Self does not really think, but only witnesses the act of thinking.

Seeming to act: Thought and action do not belong to the real nature of Self. Universal Self appears limited on account of Its conjunction with *buddhi* or understanding, with desire and aversion, pleasure and pain. In state of liberation this connection with understanding terminates (Sri Sankara).

According to Sri Sankara, the agency attributed to Self is only figurative. The light of Self, which is pure intelligence, illumines the body and organs; and they perform their functions, being illumined by It.

While one is in a state of dream, Self makes the body sleep, but Itself remains awake and notices the impressions of the deeds that have been left upon the mind. However, in waking state, It associates Itself with sense organs and causes the body to be awake (4.3, 6-10).

the golden person: *hiranmayah Purusha*, the light that is pure intelligence.

the lonely swan: *eka hamsah*, he moves alone in waking and dream states, in this world and in the next. These are symbols of the spirit of the universe (4.3, 11).

Sleep is an indispensable condition of physical health and mental sanity. In sound sleep there is a respite from cravings and aversions, fears and anxieties. In that state the individual is obscurely one with the divine ground of all beings.

None sees him: everyone is aware of the experiences but none sees the experiencer. Regret is expressed that Self is so near to us, yet It is not perceived by us.

One should not wake the sleeping person suddenly: this has reference to the popular belief that Self leaves the body in dream state (4.3, 14).

Self is different from the body and its sense organs. In waking state it appears, through ignorance, as connected with attachments and death; in dream state as connected with desires but free from death; in state of deep sleep It is perfectly serene and unattached. The sense of this passage is that Self is by nature, eternal, free, enlightened and pure (Sri Sankara). Even as a large fish moves from one bank of a river to another, so does Self move between dreaming and waking (4.3, 18).

hita: The subtle body is said to be in these channels (4.3, 20).

In deep sleep, self-consciousness disappears, as also the distinction between the inner and the outer world. The highest reality, the all-consciousness – free from fear and grief – is reached in this state.

Dream states are traced to impressions of waking experiences. Ignorance, *avidya* is not natural to Self. If it was so, ignorance could not be removed just as heat and light cannot be removed from the sun (Sri Sankara).

The analogy of a man and his beloved wife is given to show that it (state of deep sleep) is not a state of unconsciousness.

In sex we have an act of pure delight. It is not mere physical satisfaction, but a psycho-spiritual communion. We get on earth the kingdom of heaven. The rich deep fulfillment of love between a man and a woman is a condition of earthly beatitude. It is so simple, so natural and so real that it is the happiest of all earthly conditions. Many mystics employ this as a symbol of divine communion. The mystic union of the finite and the divine is compared in this passage to the self-oblivion of earthly lovers where each is the other. It is a fuller identity than mere sympathetic understanding of two individuals.

In Vaishnav literature, the soul pinning for union with God is said to be the bride; and the divine love – which sanctifies, purifies and elevates the soul to itself – is said to be the bridegroom.

For some Sufis, God is Eternal Feminine. Muslim poet Wali of Delhi composed love poems in which the lover is God and the loved one sought is the human soul invited to unite with God (4.3, 21).

'Sex is not mere physical satisfaction, but a psycho-spiritual communion.'

The state (of deep sleep) is beyond empirical distinctions. It exceeds the limitations of caste and stages of life. Self is untouched either by good or by evil. Sorrows of the heart cease to be sorrows and are turned into joys (4.3, 22).

Even in state of deep sleep when the eye and other senses are at rest, Self is the seer, though it does not see with the physical eyes. The seer can never lose the character of seeing, just as fire cannot lose the character of burning so long as it is fire. Self sees by Its own light, like the sun. Even when there is no second, no object but Self that could be seen, the seer is (4.3, 23).

Those who live within the bonds of ignorance experience but a small portion of the infinite bliss (4.3, 33).

Self in the body: The subtle body moves between this and the next world as between waking and dream-states, through birth and death. Birth is association of Self with the body and its organs, death is dissociation.

Breathing with difficulty: grasping for breath. The body groans as a cart with a heavy load groans under its burden (4.3, 35).

Self of a dying man separates from his gross body, even as a fruit separates itself from its stalk. It goes back to Its new abode the same way It came; and then It assumes another body to begin a new life (4.3, 36).

— *S. Radhakrishnan*

This section is known as *Jyotir Brahmana*. It deals with *jyotir*, or light – not the ordinary light but the Light of all lights. The name is very significant. The first six mantras, through a progressive enquiry, come to the conclusion that the ultimate light which illumines the universe is Self, *Atman-Brahman*. It gives the power of revelation to the great illuminants of the universe – such as sun, moon and fire at the cosmic level, as also speech and other organs at the individual level.

This section describes in detail the three states of waking, dream and deep sleep. Fatigued by search for happiness in waking state, man goes to another world in dream state, where there seems to be more freedom of action and enjoyment. Then he goes to deep sleep. All the three states have deep spiritual significance, but man generally fails to discover the truth behind them.

The great secret is that all the three states are different scenes of a drama by Him, the Supreme. One sees His play but not Him, who has put up these scenes and characters of the drama.

These three states are the conditions of the mind alone. Consciousness remains, as it were, hidden behind its expressions in the form of the mind and its modifications. Through two analogies, this section explains how Consciousness remains unaffected by the experiences of the three states. One is of a great fish in a river, always swimming from one bank to the other bank, unaffected by the currents of the water. The other example is of a falcon, which flies during the day here and there in search of prey and mate; and in the evening it returns to its nest for rest. Even so, it is said that Consciousness experiences the fruits of past *karmas* in two states of waking and dream, and then merges in Self, *Atman*, in deep sleep.

Scriptures say that there is similarity between the state of deep sleep and liberation, *susupti* and *Turiya*. There is no experience of any object in both. However, the two are like opposite poles – there is ignorance in deep sleep, but knowledge in liberation. In liberation one is aware of the absence of duality; in deep sleep one is unaware of the presence of duality.

No one can deny the existence of Self, Pure Consciousness, in any of the three states – waking, dream and deep sleep. Self is the eternal, non-dual substratum of the three states. However, non-discrimination has resulted in confusion, which forms a veil in all the three states. This veil of confusion may be said to be gross in waking state, subtle in dream state and causal in the state of deep sleep.

Self is different from and independent of the body. Taking another body after death is similar to entering into dream state from waking state (4.3, 8).

The three states are referred to as the three worlds. The world of dreams is a link between waking and sleep worlds. Impressions and experiences of waking state form material for dream-state (4.3, 9).

'There is ignorance is state of sleep, but knowledge in state of liberation. In sleep one is unaware of the presence of duality, in liberation, one is aware of the absence of duality.' ..... (Adapted)

The dream world is expressed metaphorically as the sport projected by Self. Dream impressions are His manifestations. Everyone sees His manifestations, but not Him (4.3, 14).

Self moves from one state to another like an unattached witness. It is unaffected by the actions or desires of the body and the organs. It is like a fish moving between the two banks of a river, unaffected by the intervening current of water (4.3, 18).

When a man is tired of his actions in waking state and of his experiences in dream state, he enters into deep sleep. In this state, he withdraws into himself all experiences pertaining to the two states of waking and dreaming, and rests in his own Self – the one non-dual, homogeneous, absolute Consciousness. In other words, individual Self, freeing Itself from all relative attributes and limitations, is united with the Supreme Self. But this union is temporary. By the force of latent desires, Self again comes back to the waking world or to the dream world (4.3, 19).

The fact of non-duality as experienced in deep sleep is explained through seemingly contradictory statements. The Upanishad says: he does not see, though he is seeing; so also with functions of other organs. Here the word seeing, hearing etc. have peculiar spiritual connotation. In deep sleep, the mind does not see anything, but Self sees everything, as it does in all the states. But anything 'seen' by Him is a part of Him, the Seer. In that sense, there is no 'seen' separate from the 'seer'. In other words, Self, the seer, cannot be oblivious of Itself. So, the Upanishad says: He is 'seeing' but his 'seeing' is not a verb with separate subject and object. He is always the seer, the seen and the seeing, merged into One, Non-dual.

As regards His 'not seeing', to Him there is nothing other than He; and therefore, He does not see. The subject cannot see the subject.

The eternal power of sight or hearing or knowledge is as natural to Self as heat and light are natural to the sun. There is no contradiction in Self between its eternal nature of 'seeing' in waking state, and 'not-seeing' in the state of deep sleep (4.3, 23-30).

Jiva, in state of deep sleep, is freed of all its limiting adjuncts and becomes infinite and homogeneous, like the ocean. It attains its natural state of non-dual consciousness by losing its individuality, born of ignorance. This is the state of *Brahman*. This is Supreme Attainment. This is Supreme Bliss (4.3, 32).

Happiness, which is enjoyed through the contact of senses with their objects, is merely an infinitesimal fraction of the Bliss of *Brahman*. There is no higher or lower degree in the Supreme Bliss of *Brahman*, as it is in sensual pleasures (4.3, 33). A similar passage also appears in section 2.8 of Taittiriya Upanishad.

Verse 34 is a repetition of first part of Verse16.

Transmigration of Self is said to be full of pain. It is compared to a heavily loaded cart making creaky noises. The gasping for breath is indicative of other innumerable miseries. The comparison is intended to induce dispassion for relative existence and attraction for liberation, avoidance of rebirth (4.3, 35).

The separation of life or subtle body from gross body is compared to a fruit freeing itself from its stalk when it ripens or withers. The subtle, astral body comes to life again through the same route, which it followed in the present and previous births. Transmigration is not new to it (4.3, 36).

How does *Jiva* attain another body? This is explained figuratively. It attains a new body according to its work, knowledge and subtle impressions. In that new body, it is welcomed by all the five elements with their presiding deities - like a visiting king. The individual soul is in reality *Brahman*, the Absolute. Therefore, it is addressed as *Brahman* (4.3, 37).

As the officers of a king gather around a king when he goes on a tour, so also all the sense organs gather around Self at the time of death (4.3, 38).

– *Swami Sivananda*

4.4, 1-11 Transmigration of the Soul

When a person dies, the corporeal eyes get separated and fall away, as the function of seeing returns back to sun from which it had originated. But the psychical organ of sight – the power of seeing – gathers itself with other organs and *Prana,* in the heart, around *Atman*. The apex of the heart then becomes

---

'Happiness, which is enjoyed through the contact of senses with their objects, is merely an infinitesimal fraction of the Bliss of Brahman.'

illuminating. Then the soul, together with the psychical organs, pulls out through any part of the body, as per its pleasure (4.4, 1-2).

(Compare Chandogya 8.6,6 and Katha 2.3,16.)

Purvapragya: Consciousness of what has been previously experienced, impressions of past actions and sufferings. Organs are predisposed through the impressions of earlier experiences. This explains certain skills inherent in many persons from birth, without any practice, e.g. skill in painting (Sri Sankara).

"I teach that as wax can easily be impressed with new fingers and does not remain as it had been nor retains the same form, and yet itself remains the same; thus the soul remains the same, yet assumes various shapes. (Pythogoras)"

Transmigration of the soul extends through all the worlds from the world of *Brahma* down to the world of plants. After exit from the body, the soul enters into a new body corresponding exactly to its intellectual and moral constitution. This has been explained with similes of a caterpillar and making of new ornaments from gold. Interestingly, these verses do not suggest any retribution in the yonder world. It is not clear if the soul, *jiva* suffers a double retribution – first in the yonder world, and then through a new earthly life (4.4, 3-4).

The soul of a Self-realized person, or as it is called here, one who has no desires (*kamayamana*), does not pull out; being *Brahma*n, it enters in *Brahma*n. This is the main passage for the esoteric doctrine of deliverance (4.4, 6).

— *Paul Deussen*

Self is figuratively said to be devoid of strength and in a seemingly unconscious state. In reality, it is the body, which becomes weak and unconscious at the time of death. Self takes to Itself the particles of light, i.e. the resplendent energies of sense-organs and then enters the heart. When the Being in the eye, *Purusha*, the presiding deity of the eye, withdraws Itself, man becomes unconscious of forms (4.4, 1).

On withdrawal of the presiding deities from the organs of senses (e.g. the sun from the eye) at the time of death, every sense organ gets united with the subtle body. At this time people sitting around a dying person say that he does not see, he does not hear, and so on.

The nerves of the heart at the orifice, through which *jiva* makes its exit, become luminous due to the light of Self. *Jiva*, it is said, departs through different parts of the body in different persons, according to the nature of their actions and impressions awaiting fructification. It departs through the eye, for example, for obtaining the world of Sun and through the head for attaining liberation. Along with Self, life-force (*Prana*) and sense organs also depart from the physical body.

Self becomes conscious of the next body as determined by past *karmas*, and departs in the light of that consciousness. Knowledge, work and past experiences also depart at the same time (4.4, 2).

A caterpillar takes hold of another blade of grass, or a straw, before it leaves the one on which it is resting. Even so, the soul has a vision of the future body before it leaves the present one (4.4, 3).

Like a goldsmith, so to say, the Soul again and again crushes the five gross elements of which the body is constituted, and shapes them into new bodies suited to the experience of different worlds, according to past *karmas*. This new body may be in any of the different worlds – from the highest world of *Hiranyagarbha*, down to the lowest of moths and insects, or even the so-called inanimate world of stones and rocks (4.4, 4).

Self or *jiva* is in reality *Brahman*. It attains its real nature by shaking-off identifications with 'this' or 'that' – intellect, mind, vital force, five sense organs, five elements, and innumerable modifications of the mind. Some of these are perceptible, like the body; and some are imperceptible, like anger and desire. However, according to some commentators, Self is identified with desires alone.

One becomes meritorious through meritorious actions, and sinful through vicious actions (4.4, 5).

A Self-realized person does not have any desires because *Brahman* is all full, eternal bliss, everlasting peace, and supreme satisfaction. Such a person is freed from rebirth. His organs do not depart because he is identified with one and all; they merge in their universal counterparts. A Self-realized person is not

---

'A Self-realized person is not just a knower of the Absolute, but the Absolute Itself.'

just a knower of the Absolute, but the Absolute Itself (4.4, 6).

With the cessation of all desires, egoism in the form of 'I' ceases to lay its hold upon the body. A snake, which has caste off its slough, does not identify itself with it, as it did before. Even so, Self, though in the body, no longer identifies Itself with the body. It is then said to be disembodied (4.4, 7).

The Upanishad quotes a few verses to emphasize that liberation is attained only by those who are desirous of it and who know *Brahman*.

The path of knowledge leading to liberation is very difficult. It is far-reaching and extensive, because it is related to Infinite *Brahman*. A first-person assertion: 'It has been realized by me' requires no other extraneous proof to bear testimony (4.4, 8).

Those who attain gradual liberation experience the colors of different nerves while passing through different routes, according to their different degrees of evolution (4.4, 9).

– *Swami Sivananda*

Every organ becomes united with the subtle body, *lingatman* (Sri Sankara). The impressions of the past, under the control of knowledge and work, stretch out like a leech from the body, and build another body in accordance with past work (Ramanuja) (4.4, 2).

Compare Plato: 'Such as are the trend of our desires and the nature of our souls, just such each of us becomes'.

Desire is the root of empirical existence. He who has desires continues to be subjected to rebirth. A man free from desires realizes *Brahman* even here. What the blind needs is sight? Sight is not change of place or transportation into another world. For liberation one need not wait for the death of body. Liberation is the cessation of ignorance. He in whom desire is stilled suffers no rebirth (Sri Sankara) (4.4, 5).

Verse 9 seems to suggest a blend of knowledge and work.

– *S. Radhakrishnan*

4.4, 12-15 Self-realization

A Self-realized person has the firm conviction that he is all, and nothing is outside him. This unshakable conviction frees him from all desires and selfish actions. In the scriptures, such a knower of *Brahman* is referred to as: *maha karta*, *maha bhokta* and *maha tyagi*, a great doer, a great enjoyer and a great renouncer – all at the same time. These statements appear to contradict each other, but really they do not. The thoughts, words and deeds of a Self-realized person are quite unlike others. An ignorant person considers his small and single body as his own. To a knower of *Brahman*, the universe is his body, and he himself is *Brahman*. Therefore, his thoughts, words and deeds loose their individual nature and acquire universality.

Verse-12 throws a flood of light on the conduct of a Self-realized person.

Verse-13 shows that a Self-realized person attains complete identity with one and all.

Great is the loss of the ignorant, as ignorance is the root cause of all suffering. An ignorant person is caught in the rounds of birth and death. A knower attains immortality (4.4, 14).

– *Swami Sivananda*

He does not hide himself from Him: A knower of *Brahman* is not afraid. He does not hide himself from the Supreme (4.4, 15).

The Eternal may be realized even while we live in the ephemeral body. To fail to realize Him is to live in ignorance, to be subject to birth and death. The knowers of *Brahman* are immortal; others continue in the region of sorrow.

– *S. Radhakrishnan*

4.4, 16-25 What is *Brahman*?

Brahman is the light of both microcosm and macrocosm. He alone is the illuminator of luminaries like the sun and the moon; hence He is called the Light of lights. Also, He is eternity with respect to what we call 'Time'. He is Life Immortal (4.4,16).

'A Self-realized person is a great doer, a great enjoyer and a great renouncer – all at the same time.'

The immortal *Atman* is described here as *pancha-panchajanah*, meaning five times five, as also Space (*Akash*). Followers of Sankhya interpret it as 25 principles referred to in their philosophy. Another interpretation is 'all five of a group of five.' The group of five could be: Vital Force of vital force, Eye of eye, Ear of ear, Food of food and Mind of mind. The five could also be gods, ancestors, celestials, minstrels and demons (4.4, 17).

Akash means the unmanifested Space upon which everything is woven, like thread in a cloth.

Brahman is beyond the field of operation of the mind and the senses. Yet, it is by mind alone that *Brahman* can be realized – a mind purified by knowledge (4.4, 18).

In *Brahman* there is no internal or external diversity of any sort (4.4, 19).

Brahman is pure, unborn, great, unchanging, and beyond space. It is unknowable by ordinary means of objective knowledge. It should be realized as One homogeneous mass of Consciousness (4.4, 20).

Brahman cannot be known by vain and idle arguments (4.4, 21).

The glory of Supreme *Brahman* as narrated in verses 4.4, 16-25 is summarized here. *Brahman* is:

- Great, unborn Self.
- Controller of all, residing in the cavity of the heart.
- Beyond good or evil works.
- Principle of interdependence between various objects and phenomena of the world.
- Ultimate goal of monks and ascetics, who are above all desires.
- Incomprehensible, indestructible, unattached, unfettered, imperishable, beyond suffering, beyond injury.
- *Neti, neti*, not this, not this.
- Knowing that *Brahman*, who is one's own *Atman*, one frees oneself completely of all commissions and omissions. A knower of *Brahman* does not attach himself to the results of any action - good or bad.
- Knower of *Brahman* is calm, controlled, indifferent to enjoyments, enduring, devoid of sins, absorbed in concentration. He beholds all as Self.
- Eater of food. He dwells in all beings and eats all food, which they eat. Another interpretation is that the whole manifested universe merges into him.
- Giver of wealth. He is the giver of fruits of action. He enables all beings to obtain the results of their actions.
- He is fearless. He, who knows Brahman, becomes fearless.

– Editor

4.5   This is a repetition of 2.4; except for two additional verses – verse-1 and second half of verse-15.

For synopsis and commentaries please refer to section 2.4

'Brahman is beyond the field of operation of the mind and the senses.
Yet, it is by mind alone that Brahman can be realized – a mind purified by knowledge.'

5 Objects of Meditation

SIMPLIFIED SYNOPSES

5.1
That, this and *Aum*

Section 5.1 contains only one verse.

The first half of this verse is a repetition of Peace Invocation. It contains a very profound thought: That Absolute Reality is infinite, and this relative universe is also infinite. The relative emanates from the Absolute, but the Absolute remains unchanged. Thus, *Brahman*, which is Pure Consciousness, is one and the same in its two aspects of unity and plurality.

The second part of the verse reaffirms what has been stated many times in other Upanishads: *Aum* is the best symbol and name for meditation on both unmanifested and manifested *Brahman*.

5.2
Three principal virtues: *da*, *da*, *da*

This section uses a short parable to prescribe three spiritual practices: self-discipline, charity and compassion. The Sanskrit equivalents of all the three start with the letter *da*, prompting an allegorical reference to the heavenly voice of thunder.

There are no gods or demons other than men. When a man lacks self-discipline but is otherwise virtuous, he comes in the category of gods. Cruelty is a demonic vice. Greed is typical of men. All the instructions – *damyata*, *datta* and *dayadharma*, or self-discipline, charity and compassion – are therefore meant for mankind alone.

5.3-5.9
Meditation on *Brahman*

Brahman is That which lives in the heart (5.3). *Brahman* is Truth (5.4 - 5.5). *Brahman* is Mind (5.6), Lightening (5.7), Speech (5.8), Universal Fire (5.9). These definitions of *Brahman* are intended to serve as aids in meditation. Some passages in these sections contain etymological interpretations of the original Sanskrit words, like *hridaya* (heart) and *satya* (Truth). Truth is imagined as the Cosmic Person in the Sun, as also in the right eye. The three worlds – *Bhur, Bhuvah and Suvaha* – are metaphorically said to be His head, arms and feet, respectively.

5.10
Journey after death

In this section, the soul is said to ascend in stages to air, sun, moon and then a world which is free from suffering of all kinds. The seer uses the metaphors of a hole in a chariot wheel, a musical instrument and a drum to describe the ascent of the soul.

5.11
Illness and death are austerities

It is suggested that one should think of illness as an austerity, because both entail suffering. One should not feel dejected during sickness. Also, the journey of a dead body to the forest for last rites is compared to the journey of an ascetic to a place of solitude, for performance of austerities.

5.12 Food and Life-breath

The words *Anna* and *Prana* as used here signify Matter and Energy at cosmic level, as also body and life force at individual level, respectively. Both are interdependent. Also, both are expressions of One Reality, *Brahman*; though neither of them is independently *Brahman*, the Absolute. Can a union of the two be *Brahman*, or lead to *Brahman*? No, says the text. The concluding sentence, however, seems to lack relevance. It says that a person is pleased only when he has both a body and strength (life force).

5.13 Meditation on Life-breath

The text here identifies life-breath with the verses of three Vedas (*Rg*, *Yajur*, *Sama*), and also praises it as a savior. Concentrating the mind on our breathing while contemplating on its cosmic significance is an important technique of meditation.

5.14 The sacred *Gayatri mantra*

Gayatri mantra is the most sacred *mantra* of Vedas. It has three lines. The first line represents all existences, symbolized by the three worlds – earth, heavens and intervening space. The second line represents all knowledge, symbolized by the three Vedas – *Rg*, *Yajur* and *Sama*. The third line represents all life-breaths, symbolized by *Prana, Vyana* and *Apana*.

Besides the aforesaid three lines, *Gayatri mantra* has a fourth invisible line, which represents the Absolute, *Brahman*. The Upanishad glorifies Sun as Its manifested symbol.

The fourth foot of *Gayatri* rests on Truth, Truth rests on Sight, and Sight rests on Life force. Chanting of *Gayatri mantra* protects sense organs from committing evil acts.

Meditation on even a single part of *Gayatri mantra* yields immense results. Nonetheless, the Upanishad emphasizes that one should meditate on *Gayatri mantra* in its totality.

5.15 The last prayer

'The prayer is for lifting the veil which covers the Truth.'

This section also appears in Isa Upanishad, verses 15-18 (Pages 242, 244, 254). It is a prayer to Sun as a symbol of *Brahman*. Just as *Atman* is covered by body, *Brahman* is covered by the world, as it were. The text uses the simile of a golden lid for the covering – the body at the micro level and the world at the macro level. The lid is so attractive that the Mind is disinterested in going beyond it to realize the Truth. The prayer is for lifting the veil which covers the Truth. When this happens, a man realizes that he is identical with the Cosmic Person, *Purusha*. (1-2).

In verses 3-4, the man who is praying – presumably in his last moments – takes a retrospective look at his life and prays for forgiveness for any sins that he may have committed. One commentator advises that such contemplation should be done every night before going to sleep.

Verse-3 refers to the widely held belief about what happens after death – the body is reduced to ashes which merge in the primeval element, and the eternal divine principle merges in Cosmic Consciousness.

'Just as Atman is covered by body, Brahman is covered by the world.'

Translated Text

CHAPTER 5

Section 1

That (*Brahman*) is full, this (Cosmos) is full. Fullness emanates from fullness. If we take away fullness from fullness, even then fullness remains. **1(a)**

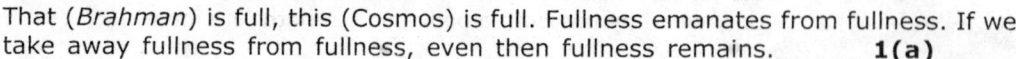

(The syllable) Aum is the ether *Brahman*, the eternal ether, the ether containing Air (Life-Principle). Thus, verily, the son of Kauravyayani used to say. This is the Knowledge, which the knowers of *Brahman* know; through it one knows what is to be known. **1(b)**

Section 2

The threefold offspring of *Prajapati* – gods, men and demons – lived with their father, *Prajapati*, as students of sacred knowledge. Having completed their studies, gods said to him, 'Please tell (instruct) us, Sir.' To them he uttered the syllable *da* (and asked), 'Have you understood?' They (said), 'We have understood. You said to us *damyata*, control yourselves.' He said, 'Yes, you have understood.' **1**

Then men said to him, 'Please tell (instruct) us, Sir.' To them he uttered the same syllable *da* (and asked), 'Have you understood?' They (said), 'We have understood. You said to us *datta*, give.' He said, 'Yes, you have understood.' **2**

Then demons said to him, 'Please tell (instruct) us, Sir.' To them he uttered the same syllable *da* (and asked), 'Have you understood?' They (said), 'We have understood, you said to us *dayadhvam*, be compassionate'. He said, 'Yes, you have understood.'

This very thing, the heavenly voice of thunder repeats *da, da, da*. It says: Discipline yourselves, give, be compassionate. One should practice this triad: self-control, giving and compassion. **3**

Section 3

This is *Prajapati,* (the same as) in this heart (intellect). It is *Brahman*. It is all. It has three syllables, *hr, da, yam*. *Hr* is one syllable. His own people and others bring (presents) to him who knows this. *Da* is one syllable. His own people and others give to him who knows this. *Yam* is one syllable. He who knows this goes to the heavenly world. **1**

Section 4

This, verily, is That. This indeed was That, the Truth. He who knows That wonderful Being, the first born, the *Satya Brahman,* conquers these worlds. He who knows that wonderful Being, the first born as Satya *Brahman,* his enemy is defeated and made a nonentity; for *Satya* is Brahman. **1**

"The heavenly voice of thunder repeats da, da, da. It says: Discipline yourselves, give, be compassionate."

Section 5

In the beginning this universe was just water. That water produced *Satya*, the Truth (or the Real). *Brahman* is the Truth. *Brahman* (produced) *Prajapati* and *Prajapati* (produced) the gods. Those gods meditated on the Real. *Satya* consists of three syllables, *sa, ti, yam*: *sa* is one syllable, *ti* is one syllable, and *yam* is one syllable. The first and the last syllables are the Truth; in the middle is untruth. This untruth is enclosed on both sides by Truth; it partakes of the nature of Truth itself. He who knows this is not injured by untruth. **1**

Truth is that yonder Sun. That being, who is there in that orb and This being who is here in the right eye, these two rest on each other. Through his rays, That rests on This; through the phenomenon of sight, This rests on That. When one is about to depart, he sees that orb clearly. These rays no more come to him. **2**

Of the Cosmic Person in that orb, the syllable *bhur* is the head; for head is one and this syllable is one. *Bhuvah* is the arms. There are two arms and these are two syllables. *Suvaha* is the feet. There are two feet and these are two syllables. His secret name is day. He who knows this, destroys and shuns evil. **3**

Of the Person who is in the right eye, the syllable *bhur* is the head. The head is one and the syllable is one. *Bhuvah* is the arms. There are two arms and these are two syllables. *Suvaha* is the feet. There are two feet and these are two syllables. His secret name is 'I'. He who knows this, destroys and shuns evil. **4**

Section 6

This *Purusha* (Cosmic Person) who is reflected in the mind, is of the nature of light. It resides in the heart, like a grain of rice or of barley. It is the Ruler of all, the Lord of all. It governs all this, whatever there is.

Section 7

Lightning is *Brahman*, they say. It is called lightning because it scatters (darkness). He who knows that lightning is *Brahman*, scatters evils; for lightning is, indeed, *Brahman*.

Section 8

One should meditate on speech as a milch cow. She has four udders, which are the sounds, *svaha, vasat, hanta* and *svadha*. The gods live on two of her udders, the sounds *svaha* and *vasat*; men on the sound *hanta*; and forefathers on the sound *svadha*. Life breath is her bull and mind is her calf.

Section 9

This fire which is here within a person is Universal Fire (*Vaisvanara*) by means of which food that is eaten is cooked (digested). It is the sound thereof that one hears by covering the ears thus (teacher demonstrates). When one is about to depart (from this life) one does not hear this sound.

"This Purusha (Cosmic Person) who is reflected in the mind, is of the nature of light."

Section 10

Verily, when a person departs from this world, he goes to Air. It makes an opening for him like the hole of a chariot wheel. Through that he goes upwards. He goes to the sun. It makes an opening for him like the hole of a musical instrument, a drum. Through that he goes upwards. He reaches the moon. It makes an opening for him like the hole of a tabor. Through that he goes upwards. He goes to the world free from mental and physical suffering, free from cold. There he dwells for eternal years.

Section 11

Verily, this is an excellent austerity which a man laid up with illness suffers. He who knows this wins the supreme world. Verily, this is the supreme austerity when they carry a dead person into the forest. He who knows this wins the supreme world. Verily, this is the supreme austerity when they lay a dead person on fire. He who knows this wins the supreme world.

Section 12

'Food is *Brahman*' say some. This is not so, for food decomposes without life. 'Life is *Brahman*' say some. This is not so, for life dries up without food. But when these two deities become united, they attain their highest state. So Pratrda said to his father: 'What good, indeed, can I do to one who knows this, or what evil, indeed, can I do to him.' The father said to him with (a gesture of) his hand, 'Oh no, Pratrda, who would attain the highest state (merely) by entering into unity with these two?' Then he said to him thus, 'This is *vi*. Food is *vi*, for all these beings rest in food. This is *ram*. Life-breath is *ram*, for all these beings delight in life. Verily, indeed, all beings enter into him, all beings delight in him who knows this.'

Section 13

Uktha : Life-breath, verily, is Uktha, (a hymn of praise) for it is life-breath that raises this universe. From him who knows Uktha rises a son. He who knows this wins union with and abode in the same world as Uktha. **1**

Yajus : Life-breath, verily is Yajus for in life-breath are all beings united. All beings are united for (securing) his eminence. He who knows this wins union with and abode in the same world as Yajus. **2**

Saman: Life-breath, verily, is Saman for in life-breath are all these beings united. All beings are united for securing his eminence. He who knows this wins union with and abode in the same world as Saman. **3**

Ksatra: Life-breath, verily, is a savior Ksatra, for verily, life-breath is Ksatra. Life-breath protects one from being hurt. He attains a Ksatra that needs no protection. He who knows this wins union with and abode in the same world as Ksatra. **4**

"Verily, this is an excellent austerity which a man laid up with illness suffers."

Section 14

(The earth) *Bhumi*, (the sky) *Antariksha* and (the heaven) *Dyaus* – these add up to eight syllables. Verily, one foot (line) of *Gayatri* is also of eight syllables. This, (one foot) is That. He who knows this foot of *Gayatri* to be such wins all that there is in the three worlds. **1**

Richah (Rk verses), *Yajumshi* (sacrificial formulae), and *Samani* (chants) – these add up to eight syllables. Verily, one foot of *Gayatri* is also of eight syllables. This, (one foot) is That. He who knows this foot of *Gayatri* to be such wins as much knowledge as the three *Vedas* confer. **2**

Prana (in-breath), *Apana* (out-breath), and *Vyana* (diffused breath) – these add up to eight syllables. Verily, one foot of *Gayatri* is also of eight syllables. This, (one foot) is That. He who knows this foot of *Gayatri* to be such wins all the living beings that are in the universe. **3(a)**

Of this (*Gayatri*), that which glows yonder (the sun) is the fourth, apparently visible foot above the dark skies. This fourth is the same as *Turiya*. It is called apparently visible because it is seen, as it were. It is called above the dark skies, because it glows yonder, far higher and higher than everything dark. He who knows that foot of *Gayatri* to be such, he glows with prosperity and fame. **3(b)**

This *Gayatri* rests on that fourth, the apparently visible foot above the dark skies. That again rests on truth. Verily, truth is sight; for, verily, truth is sight. Therefore, if two persons come disputing, one saying, 'I saw,' and the other 'I heard,' we should trust the one who says, 'I saw.'

Verily, that truth rests on strength. Life-breath, verily, is strength. Truth rests on life-breath. Therefore they say that strength is more powerful than truth.

Thus *Gayatri* rests on life-breath. *Gayatri* protects the *gayas*; the *gayas* are life-breaths and it protects life-breaths. Now because it protects life-breaths, therefore it is called *Gayatri*. That *Savitri* verse which (the teacher) teaches, it is just this. And whomsoever he teaches, it protects his life-breaths. **4**

Some teach (to the pupil) this Savitri verse as an *anustubh* meter (saying) that speech is *anustubh* and that we impart (teach) that speech to him. One should not do like this. One should teach *Savitri*, which is *Gayatri*. Even if one who knows thus receives plenty (of gifts), these will not equal even a single foot of *Gayatri*. **5**

If one accepts the three worlds full (of wealth), he would receive (the fruits of knowing) the first foot of *Gayatri*. If one accepts the threefold knowledge (of Vedas), he would receive (the fruits of knowing) the second foot. If one accepts the threefold life-breath, he would receive the (fruits of knowing) the third foot. But that fourth, the apparently visible foot above the dark skies, which glows yonder is not attainable by anyone whatsoever. How could anyone accept so much as gift? **6**

"The sacred Gayatri Mantra burns all evil." ..... (Adaptation from next page)

Its salutation: O *Gayatri*, you are one-footed, two-footed, three-footed, four-footed. You are footless, for you do not go about. Salutation to you, the fourth, the apparently visible foot, above the dark skies. May he not attain this (may the enemy never attain his object). (Should the knower of the *Gayatri*) bear hatred towards anyone (he should say), 'May his wish not prosper.' or 'May I attain that (cherished wish) of his.' **7**

On this point, verily, Janaka (King) of Videha said to Budila Asvatarasvi: 'Well, how is it that you, who spoke of yourself as the knower of *Gayatri*, have come to be an elephant and are carrying (load)?' 'Because, Your Majesty, I did not know its mouth,' said he. Fire is, indeed, its mouth. Verily, even if they lay a large quantity of fuel on fire it burns it all. Similarly, even if one who knows this commits much evil, it (*Gayatri*) burns it all, and he becomes clean and pure, ageless and immortal. **8**

Section 15

The face of Truth (*Satya*, *Brahman*) is covered with a golden lid. Unveil it, O *Pusan*, so that I, who have been worshipping Truth, may see it. **1**

O *Pusan,* the sole Seer, O Controller, O Sun, Offspring of *Prajapati*, spread forth your rays and gather your radiant light, so that I may behold your loveliest form. Whosoever is that Person (yonder), that I am. **2**

May this life enter into the immortal breath; then may this body end in ashes. O Intelligence, remember, remember, what has been done. Remember, O Intelligence, what has been done. Remember. **3**

O *Agni* (Fire), lead us along the auspicious path to prosperity, O Lord, you know all our deeds. Take away from us our deceitful sin. We shall offer many prayers unto thee. **4**

"The face of Truth is covered with a golden lid. Unveil it, O Pusan, so that I may see it."

Focussed Commentaries

CHAPTER 5

5.1 That, this and *Aum*

That is full: the reference is to the Absolute.
This is full: the reference is to the manifested world, presided over by the personal Lord, *Ishta Devata*.

While this world is infinite, it has its roots in the Absolute. The manifestation of this world does not take away from the fullness or integrity of the Absolute.

– S. Radhakrishnan

This mantra establishes the Oneness of *Brahman*, man and the world, *Brahman* is Infinite, and the relative world is not different from *Brahman*, the Absolute. It has come out of *Brahman* and it too is infinite. Infinite *Brahman* is partless and indivisible. So, there is no possibility of a part emanating from the Infinite. Thus, whatever is said to emanate from Infinite must also be infinite, Therefore, the universe is essentially the same as *Brahman*.

The individual is also the same as *Brahman*. It is said that both microcosm and macrocosm are infinite. In other words, the entire universe is reflected in an atom, just as the entire personality of a man is contained in every cell of his. So much so, by knowing one cell, one can know the whole man.

The snake, which is superimposed on the rope due to ignorance, is essentially rope itself. When the snake is taken out of the rope, as it were, with the aid of light, the rope remains unaffected. The relationship between *Brahman* and the world is something like that existing between the rope and the snake in the above analogy.

This mantra is a *vidya*, a meditation by itself. It is a very superior meditation wherein the meditator, the act of meditation, and the object of meditation viz. the Absolute – all three are fused into one non-dual, pure Consciousness [5.1(a)].

Next, the Upanishad describes another *vidya* – meditation on lower *Brahman* – for those who cannot practice the first one. *Om kham Brahma*: This is meditation on *Om* as a symbol and name of both conditioned and unconditioned *Brahman*. *Kham* is ether or space. This *Kham* is different from *Akash*, even though both have the same translation in English. Thus, through meditation on *Om* and *Kham*, one attains both the higher and lower *Brahman*. That which a man worship and meditates intensely, that he becomes [5.1, 1(b)].

– Swami Sivananda

'That' and 'This': *Brahman*, which is the main theme of all the Upanishads, is described once more in this mantra.

'That' is a pronoun denoting something remote; it means the Supreme *Brahman*. It is complete, all-pervading like ether, continuous, and unconditioned.

'This' is the conditioned *Brahman,* manifesting through name and form and coming within the scope of relativity (the universe).

This differentiated *Brahman*, the effect, proceeds or emanates from That undifferentiated *Brahman*, the cause. Although the universe emanates as an effect, it does not give up its nature of infinitude. Also, even after the emanation of this infinite, conditioned *Brahman*, That unconditioned *Brahman* does not change. What remains is *Brahman,* the infinite, homogeneous mass of Pure Consciousness.

There is another interpretation. From the infinite cause, the infinite effect is manifested at the time of creation. Again, at the time of dissolution, taking the infinite effect into itself, the infinite cause alone remains. Thus in all the three states of origin, continuance and dissolution, the cause and the effect are infinite. It is just one infinity, spoken of as divided into cause and effect. Thus, *Brahman*, Pure Consciousness, in Its two aspects of unity and plurality is one and the same.

'*Aum* is ether-*Brahman*, *Aum kham Brahma*', is a *mantra* for meditation. The symbol *Aum* is used as a means to meditate on *Brahman*. As other Upanishads say:
- *Aum* is the best and the highest support (for the realization of *Brahman*) (Katha 1.2, 17).
- *Aum* is *Atman* (Self) that should be realized (meditated upon). (Verses 7 and 12 Mandukya).

'Brahman, Pure Consciousness, in Its two aspects of unity and plurality is one and the same.'

- One should meditate upon the Supreme Being through the syllable *Aum*' (Prasna 5.5)
- Meditate upon Self with the help of the syllable *Aum* (Mundaka 2.2.6).

Thus, on the authority of *shruti*, we know that *Aum* is the most intimate appellation of *Brahman*.

The text says that *Aum* is ether-*Brahman*. The text also says that *Aum* is both eternal ether – meaning unconditioned *Brahman* – and ether containing the Life Principle, symbolized by Air and meaning conditioned *Brahman*. In either case, the symbol *Aum* is a means of realizing *Brahman*. Thus, *Aum* is both a name and a symbol of unconditioned *Brahman* as well as conditioned *Brahman*.

– *Sri Sankara, translated by Swami Madhavananda*

Brahman suffers no loss or change through the creation of the world, but It continues to endure in Its undiminished integrity. Also, on the one hand *Brahman* is the unending expanse filled with vital breath, and on the other hand it is the equally unending knowledge (*Veda*) which encompasses everything.

– *Paul Deussen*

5.2 Three principal virtues: *da*, *da*, *da*

The gods are said to be naturally unruly, and so are asked to practice self-control. Men are naturally avaricious, and so they should practice charity to the best of their ability. The demons are cruel, given to inflicting injury on others; they should have compassion and be kind to all (Sri Sankara).

It is suggested that there are no gods or demons, other than men. If they are lacking in self-control while endowed with other two qualities, they are gods; if they are particularly greedy, they are men; if they are cruel, they are demons.

The three injunctions require us to go about doing charity even though we find ourselves in the world of evil. Self-control is necessary, for we must not be elated by success or deterred by failure. Compassion is more than sympathy. It is love in action, fellowship in suffering. Practice of these three virtues will preserve, promote and enhance the values of life.

– *S. Radhakrishnan*

Three main vices, which prevent perception of Truth, are *kama*, *lobha* and *krodha* – desire, avarice and anger. The three means to overcome them are *damyata*, *datta*, and *dayadhvam* – restraint, charity and compassion. The advice given by the Creator to his children is very short and enigmatic. It would seem that he has given the same advice to all the three – gods, demons and men. All that he said was '*da*'. It is a thundering proclamation, which vibrates everywhere like the thunderclap. It is the eternal message of God to mankind.

There are three *gunas* (qualities) in all of us – *sattva*, *rajas* and *tamas*. According to predominance of a particular *guna* in men, they are divided into gods, men and demons. Gods have a predominance of *sattva*, but they lack self-control. Therefore they are instructed to practice restraint. Men are dominated by *rajas* and are greedy by nature. They are instructed to practice charity. People dominated by *tamas* are called demons – they are very cruel in nature. They should practice compassion.

Thus, through a short parable, this section prescribes three profound disciplines – self-control, charity and compassion.

– *Swami Sivananda*

There are no gods or demons (*asuras*) other than men. Those among men who are wanting in self-control, but are otherwise endowed with many good qualities, are gods. Those who are particularly greedy are men. Those who are cruel and given to injuring others are demons. Hence, it is men who should practice all the three instructions. *Prajapati* meant his advice for them alone.

– *Sri Sankara, translated by Swami Madhavananda*

'*Aum is both a name and a symbol of unconditioned Brahman as well as conditioned Brahman.*'

5.3-5.9 Meditation on *Brahman*

5.3 *BRAHMAN* IS IN THE HEART

Shopenhauer, and after him Goeth (1827), recognized that "the core of human nature is in the heart". The Upanishads go still further. They teach that the whole nature, the essence of all things, abides in the heart, as *Atman*. To him who knows this is offered whatever all things offer, and after death he attains communion with *Brahman*. This is explained by playing on the etymology of the word *hridaya*, heart.

– Paul Deussen

This section is an eulogy of intellect or heart. Heart is one thing for the physician and quite a different thing for the Upanishadic seer. To the latter, it is the spiritual essence in every being.

The Sanskrit word for heart is *hridaya*, which consists of three syllables – *hr da* and *ya*. Etymologically, *hr* means to bring, to attract; *da* means to give; and *ya* means to go. As in other meditations, one has to superimpose the characteristics of universality on the chosen object of meditation, which here is one's own heart. The result of this meditation is that everything in the cosmos would gravitate towards the meditator (*hr*). One who succeeds in this meditation creates a super-physical force, which makes everyone to give his powers (*da*). One, who meditates intensely on the heart, goes to heavenly world (*ya*).

– Swami Sivananda

5.4 *BRAHMAN* IS TRUTH

He who knows Reality (*satyam*) as *Brahman* wins these worlds. This idea is developed, relying on the formula, 'This, verily, is That, *etad vai tad*', which is repeated eleven times.

– Paul Deussen

This, verily, is That: This universe is That *Brahman*, the Truth, the Reality.

This section introduces meditation on *Brahman* as Truth, Reality, *Satya- Brahman*. This *Brahman* consists of *sat* and *tyat*, gross and subtle. This *Satya-Brahman* is born before all other relative manifestations. Hence, He is first born. He who meditates on *Satya-Brahman* wins these worlds, and his enemy is vanquished. He also realizes *Satya-Brahman* as his own Self, and becomes That.

– Swami Sivananda

5.5 TRUTH EXPLAINED

This somewhat obscure section considers *Brahman* as *satyam*, the Reality, with play on the syllables, *sa, ty, yam* (compare Chandogya 8.3,5). *Brahman* as *satyam* is identical with Sun, and the Cosmic Person, *Purusha* in it. *Purusha* in Sun (cosmic-*Brahman*) is the same as *Purusha* in the eye (psychic-*Brahman*). Both are the universe, the three worlds, *bhur, bhuvah,* and *suvaha*. He, who knows this, overcomes evil. This is explained again etymologically, by the two secret names of *Purusha* - *ahar* (day) and *aham* (I).

– Paul Deussen

Water is the seed of the universe (5.5, 1). In commenting on Thales' choice of Water as the first principle, Aristotle suggests that 'he got the notion perhaps from seeing that the nutriment of all things is moist, and that heat itself is generated by evaporation of moisture and kept alive by it.... and that the seed of all creatures has a moist nature, and water is the origin of moistness.'

– S. Radhakrishnan

This section deals with meditation on *Hiranyagarbha*, the first-born Cosmic Being, *Purusha*. He was born out of the unmanifest, which is symbolically represented as primordial water. The text suggests meditation on the three syllables constituting the word *satya*. The first and the last syllables represent (unmanifested Absolute) Truth; while the middle syllable represents untruth (the manifested world).

Satya-Brahman is identical with the Being in the sun and the Being in the right eye of the meditator. The same Consciousness resides in the sun and in the eyes. Mantras 5.5, 3-4 state that *Purusha* in the sun is to be meditated as having *bhur bhuvah* and *suvah* as His head, two arms and two feet; and *ahar* as His secret name. *Bhur, bhuvah* and *suvah* represent the earth, the intermediate region and the heaven, respectively; *ahar* means day. Similarly, *Purusha* in the right eye has these three – *bhur, bhuvah* and *suvah* – as the head, the arms and the feet; and *aham* or 'I' as His secret name. When, through meditation as prescribed herein, one identifies *aham* with *ahar* – 'I' with day, or

---

'This, verily, is That. This universe is That Brahman, the Truth, the Reality.'

subject with object – and Self with Cosmic Being, one is not hurt by anything. Such a meditator destroys evil.

5.6 BRAHMAN IS MIND

This is a short description of the all-powerful *Purusha*, Cosmic Person, dwelling the heart (mind) like a grain of rice or barley. *Brahman* is both infinitely large and infinitesimally small. The example of a grain of rice is only symbolic.

5.7 BRAHMAN IS LIGHTENING

Here we are asked to contemplate on flash of lightening as *Brahman*. Scriptures say that aspirants sometimes get visions like a lightening flash.

5.8 BRAHMAN IS SPEECH

Here speech is to be meditated upon as *Brahman*. Speech is symbolized with a cow. The four sounds, which are uttered during sacrificial rituals, are considered like the udders of a milch-cow. Bull is compared to vital breath.

This contemplation is intended for those who cannot take to higher forms of meditation. One can meditate on one's own cow in one's house. A symbol helps meditation. A road is not a destination, yet it is necessary to reach the destination. Likewise, a symbol is not the end, still it is a necessary step to reach the ultimate goal.

5.9 BRAHMAN IS UNIVERSAL FIRE

In this section, Universal Fire, *(Vaisvanara Agni)* is identified with digestive fire in man. It is said to produce a peculiar psychical sound which can be 'heard' when the ears are plugged and there is concentration of mind. This should not be confused with the sound heard when the digestive system is in disorder.

5.10 Journey after death

This section describes the ascent of the soul after death. A more detailed description is provided later in 6.2, and in Chandogya Upanishad 5.10.

The Upanishad says that after death, the soul goes to air, sun, moon, and finally reaches a world where there is no mental or physical suffering, *asokam* or *ahimam*. There it lives for everlasting years.

– Swami Sivananda

5.11 Illness and death are austerities

The Upanishad says that sorrows of life and even death are higher austerities (*tapas*) than self-imposed physical hardships. The idea is a forerunner of Buddhist views.

– Paul Deussen

5.12 Food and Life-breath

This section brings out the interdependence of food and Life force – one cannot survive without the other. The word 'food' denotes body at the level of an individual and matter at the cosmic level.

The whole universe is constituted of matter and Life force, *Anna* and *Prana*. (*Anna* is translated literally as food). Some say that matter alone is *Brahman*; some say that life alone is *Brahman*. Both are wrong. Pratrda thought that a synthesis of the two-matter and life – is essential for reaching the Supreme. His father corrected him. Matter is with form, and life is without form. Both are expressions of one Reality, the Absolute *Brahman*. All beings are rooted in food (*vishtani*) and all beings delight in *Prana* (*ramante*). Therefore, this section enjoins meditation on the first syllables of these two words – *vi* and *ram* – as the two constituents of the whole world.

– Swami Sivananda

Neither food alone nor vital force alone can be understood to be *Brahman*. This is because food (body) decomposes without vital force, and vital force dries up without food; while *Brahman* is imperishable. However, when these two deities – food and vital force – unite, they attain the highest, *Brahman*.

Food provides nourishment to all creatures, and vital force gives delight to all. A person is pleased only when he has both longevity and good health.

– Sri Sankara, translated by Swami Madhavananda

'Sorrows of life and even death are higher austerities (tapas) than self-imposed physical hardships.'

5.13 Meditation on Life-breath

Concentrating the mind on our breathing during meditation is an important technique of meditation. Life-breath is identified here figuratively with three Vedic hymns of praise called Uktha, Yajus and Saman. It is also equated with *Ksatra*, a savior.

Four basic principles of Vedas are equated to Life-breath, or *Prana*. These are:

(i) Uktha : A hymn of praise, the principal feature of the *mahavratha* sacrifice or *soma yagya*.
(ii) Yajus : Prose mantras chanted in sacrificial rituals. Also, one of the four Vedas.
(iii) Saman : A particular portion of *Sama Veda*.
(iv) Ksatra : A savior or protector from sorrow and misery.

The Upanishad advises meditation on *Prana* and its identification with the aforesaid Vedic principles. These are purely Vedic meditations. They help the mind to move away from blind rituals and contemplate on higher principles underlying them.

– Swami Sivananda

The Uktha is another meditation. What is Uktha? Vital force is Uktha among hymns of praise. The result of meditation on vital force as Uktha is twofold. The visible result is the birth of a son who is a knower of vital force. The invisible result is union with and abode in the same world as Uktha.

– Sri Sankara, translated by Swami Madhavananda

5.14 The sacred *Gayatri mantra*

One of the most sacred verses of *Rg Veda* is *Savitri*, a prayer to the Sun. (*Rg Veda* 3.62,10). More popularly called *Gayatri mantra*, it reads as follows:

tat savitur varenyam	(first foot)
bhargo devasya dhimahi	(second foot)
dhiyo yo nah prachodayat	(third foot)

"We meditate on the adorable glory of the radiant Sun. May he inspire our intelligence."

There is a meter called *Gayatri*, which has three feet of eight syllables each. *Gayatri mantra* is in this meter.

- *Bhumi, antariksha* and *dyaus*, meaning earth, sky and heaven – these three words in Sanskrit together consist of eight syllables, and are identical with the first foot of *Gayatri mantra*. He who meditates thus attains mastery over the three world (5.14, 1).

- *Richah, yajumshi* and *samani* also consist of eight syllables. These words are the plural forms of the words signifying the three Vedas, *Rg, Yajur* and *Sama*, respectively. Here the three Vedas, the treasure house of all knowledge, are identified with the second foot of *Gayatri mantra*.

The meditator on this identity attains all knowledge (5.14, 2).

- *Prana, Apana* and *Vyana* – these also have eight syllables. They represent three types of life-breath, and these are identified with the third foot of *Gayatri mantra*.

He who meditates thus becomes the master of all living beings (5.14, 3a).

Generally, people who practice *Gayatri japa* know only the three feet of *Gayatri*, which they chant daily. But there is also a fourth foot, which is the Sun. It is said to be invisible; what we see as Sun is not 'the Solar Being', but only His manifestation.

While the three feet of *Gayatri* comprehend within them all that is within space and time, the fourth foot is supra-spatial and supra-temporal. It stands for the Absolute, which is beyond all space and time, beyond all names and forms. The Upanishad refers to it as *Turiya*, like the fourth, beyond the states of waking, dream and deep sleep. This fourth foot transcends all worlds, all knowledge and all life-breaths, which are identified with the three feet. The epithet 'Sun' represents the invisible Being within the sun which illumines the sun itself, as also the whole universe. He is the object of such meditation, to be identified with the fourth foot of *Gayatri*. The result of meditation is the attainment of all glory, effulgence, fame, and splendor, like the Sun. [5.14, 3(b)].

The fourth foot of *Gayatri* rests on Truth. And Truth, which is the Sun, is also the eye; because the Sun

---

'We meditate on the adorable glory of the radiant Sun. May he inspire our intelligence.'

rests on the eye (see verse 3.9, 20). Eye is the best means of confirmation of an empirical truth, and therefore, metaphorically, it is said to be the supreme Truth. *Gayatri*, with all her four feet, therefore, rests on the eye.

Again, the eye rests on strength, which is life-breath. Strength is said to be mightier than truth, because strength increases as one approaches truth through meditation. Life-breath in its cosmic form encompasses the whole universe (see verse 3.7, 2). Therefore, the whole universe rests on *Gayatri*.

Gayatri is derived from the word *gayas*, which primarily means speech; but here all the sense organs are meant by the word. Chanting of the *Gayatri mantra* saves sense organs from committing evil acts.

Savitri, or hymn to Sun-god, conditioned by the limiting adjuncts of Sun, is none other than this *Gayatri mantra* (5.14, 4).

Some followers of certain recensions of the Vedas impart to their pupils a different version of *Gayatri mantra* – *Savitri mantra* in *anustubh* meter, which consists of four lines. Verse-5 says that one should not do so.

A person who understands and meditates on *Gayatri mantra* in its totality is identified with the universe. There is no limit to his receiving wealth (5.14, 5).

Verse-6 eulogizes the knowledge of *Gayatri*. The knowledge of the fourth foot, which is nothing but Supreme Self, can never be equated with any amount of wealth. Hence, *Gayatri* should be meditated upon in its complete form – the three feet, and the fourth which transcends the three.

Verse-7 is a prayer. *Brahman* is indivisible and partless, but concepts like one-footed, two-footed and the like are given to help meditation. *Gayatri mantra* offers obeisance to the Supreme, both in its manifested and unmanifested forms. By this prayer, one gets fulfillment of all desires, and one can also prevent anything undesirable from taking place.

Verse-8 narrates an eulogistic story to emphasize that one must understand *Gayatri mantra* fully before taking up its meditation.

Budila was a great meditator of *Gayatri*, but his knowledge of it was incomplete. So he was reborn as an elephant. When queried by Janaka, he said that he did not know one part of *Gayatri* – mouth. Then Janaka instructed him that Fire is the mouth of *Gayatri*. Fire is the presiding deity of the organ of speech – the mouth. Fire has come out of the mouth of the Cosmic Person, *Virat Purusha*, or *Hiranyagarbha*.

The wise are of the view that *Gayatri mantra* should not be chanted, worshipped or meditated upon in its parts, although great results are promised for meditation on each foot.

– Swami Sivananda

Gayatri is repeatedly employed as a symbol *Brahman*. Three phenomenal forms of *Brahman* – (i) spatially extended world (ii) world of knowledge and (iii) world of living beings – are equated with three visible verse-feet of *Gayatri*. A fourth invisible verse foot is identified with the sun. The sun is traced back to the eye, eye equated with truth, truth with power, and power with *Prana*, which is comprehended as *Brahman*. Etymological play on the word, promises, and polemically oblique references are joined with one another, and the inestimable benefit of instruction is properly emphasized. At the conclusion there follows a formula regarding the way one should adore *Gayatri*. There is appended a legend in which Agni (Fire) is explained as the mouth of *Gayatri*. This could possibly mean that the sacrificial cult is an entrance door to higher knowledge.

– Paul Deussen

5.15 The last prayer

This section is a repetition of Isa 15-18. According to some commentators, it is a prayer at the time of death, but it may not necessarily be so. The dying man requests *Pusan*, the Sun-god to disperse its rays which veil the Truth (5.15, 2). He then sees in the Sun – a symbol of *Brahman* – the Cosmic Person, and realizes that he is identical with Him. With a significant retrospective look at his works, he departs from this world; while perhaps those standing around him recite the concluding verses borrowed from *Rg Veda* (1.189.1).

– Paul Deussen

covered : 'No one whose mind is not concentrated can see the truth. Verily,

---

'Strength is said to be mightier than truth, because strength increases as one approaches truth.'

face	: essential nature
Pusan	: Sun, the god of light. He is the protector of the world. His nature is protection of those who seek refuse in him.
Unveil	: Remove the cause of obstruction to the vision. Reality likes to hide. Being remains essentially concealed and hidden. It is a primary mystery. Reality is uncovered only when we break down the surface of appearances.
	Multiplicity, if it is divorced from the One, becomes the obscuring veil of the One. We must look upon the One as the manifold One, which itself is an expression of the Absolute One (5.15, 1).
the sole seer	: One who travels alone. The sun moves alone.
Soham asmi	: That am I. It refers to a form of worship in which the worshipper contemplates the immanent God as one with himself. He who dwells in the Sun is also the light in one's deepest nature. In this verse, the seeker wishes to have God-realization, a direct perception of Reality (5.15, 2).

thou art a god that hidest thyself'. Isaiah.

'Now that I am dying, may my life principle, abandoning its bodily adjunct, enter the immortal breath' (5.15, 3).

According to his physician, the last words of Plotinus, which he heard, were: 'I was waiting for you before the divine principle in me departs to unite itself with the divine in the universe.'

At the hour of death, we have to remember our past, and also meditate on the Supreme.

You know all our deeds: It is an expression of humility born from the awareness that we are always in God's presence; all our thoughts, words and deeds are open to His sight. He is at all times present with us.

Take away from us our deceitful sin: It is an imploring or supplication concerning sins. God is a searcher not of words, but of hearts (5.15, 4).

– S. Radhakrishnan

This is a prayer to sun for a free passage beyond the realm of sun to the realm of *Hiranyagarbha*. The disc of the midday sun is invisible to the naked eye due to its effulgence. The Being inside the sun is made invisible by a covering of the visible orb. Likewise, *Atman* is covered by this body and *Brahman* is covered by the world, as it were. Both the body and the world are like golden vessels. They are so attractive that the senses and the mind get attached to them, and refuse to go into the real Truth, piercing the outer name and form. The prayer is therefore to lift the veil of worldly objects. The veil prevents the seeing of Reality, on which the world is superimposed.

'Seeing' in verse-1 is not like ordinary seeing; it is transcendence, which is meant by 'seeing'. And transcendence can be had only after complete communion. Hence, the *jiva* who prays at the time of death identifies itself with Sun-god and prays for transcendence.

The next prayer in verse-3 is addressed to one's own mind: 'Remember, Remember, what has been done so far'. This may be repentance at the last moment. Repentance washes off all sins and evils when it comes from the depths of one's heart. This is a contemplation, which should be done every night before one goes to sleep, as sleep is similar to death in many respects. All that has been done during the day may be brought before the mind with a feeling of repentance for all omissions and commissions. This will bring peace and calmness. Such daily practice will result in the last thought at the time of death also being of the same nature. The secret is that if one does this kind of self-investigation every night, he will not have cause for repentance at the time of dropping the body.

– Swami Sivananda

More commentaries appear on pages 254-257.

– Editor

'Repentance washes off all sins and evils when it comes from the depths of one's heart.'

6 Birth follows death

SIMPLIFIED SYNOPSES

6.1
Prana: Parable on its superiority

'The attributes of sense-organs are rooted in life-breath, Prana.'

Speech, sight, hearing, mind and procreation – all these are important functions of the body; but which of these is the most important? The Upanishad relates a parable in which each of these thought that it alone was the most important. Unable to arrive at a consensus, they all went to *Brahma*, their creator, for an answer. *Brahma* did not give a direct reply, but suggested a practical test: 'Whosoever is most indispensable is also most important.' To find out who was most indispensable, each of them departed from the body one-by-one and came back after one year. During the absence of each, the body survived, but with some handicap. But when life-breath was about to depart – like a powerful horse shaking off the pegs to which its feet are tied – the sense organs realized that they could not function without its presence in the body. So they accepted the superiority of life-breath. The story says that life-breath demanded a tribute from the organs, to which the organs readily agreed. (6.1,1-13)

The next verse (6.1,14) says that the organs offered their own attributes to life-breath as a tribute to it. In reality also, all the attributes of sense-organs are rooted in life-breath, *Prana*.

The verse also says that the food eaten by any being is like food of *Prana*. Obviously, no life can exist without nourishment from food.

Likewise, water is like a garment of life-breath. Interestingly, the verse suggests a sip of water before and after meals.

6.2
Five cosmic fires, two paths

'The whole creation is like a great sacrificial rite.'

The section starts with King Jaivali asking young Shvetaketu five questions about soul's journey after death and its rebirth in a new body. Neither Shvetaketu nor his father know the answers. Jaivali accepts Shvetaketu's father, Gautama Aruni, as a student. He then provides answers to his questions by using the simile of a ritualistic fire-sacrifice.

Sacrificial rites symbolize profound spiritual truths. Typically, the performance of a ritualistic sacrifice requires a fire, a fuel for lightening it, and an oblation, which is offered into the fire. Smoke, flame, embers and sparks are the phenomena observed during the performance of a sacrifice. Different types of sacrifices yield different end-results.

The section describes five types of sacrifices, and hence the title *Panchagni Vidya*, meaning knowledge relating to five fires. The section is full of very imaginative and interconnected similes. These, when taken together, describe beautifully the inter-connectedness of human birth and the cosmos.

BIRTH FOLLOWS DEATH [6.2]

The essence of this section is that the whole creation is like a great sacrificial rite. Every action is like an oblation. It produces a subtle vibration, which in due course assumes a gross form, like the outcome of a sacrifice. Besides, everything in the universe is interrelated; just as in a sacrifice, fire, fuel, smoke, etc. are all interrelated. Also, the outcome of one sacrifice is an oblation for another sacrifice. For example, cosmic phenomena are like oblations in the first fire. They produce a subtle body called *King Soma* in allegorical terms. This acts as an oblation in the second fire, whose outcome is rain. This is offered as an oblation in the third fire, and the outcome is food. The fourth fire is symbolic of man himself. He receives food as an oblation and the outcome is procreative fluid in man. This is poured as an oblation in a woman – symbolic of the fifth fire – and the outcome is a newborn child. This is how a man's subtle body – comprising of his deeds and impressions – travels through the 'five fires' and eventually acquires the gross body of a newborn child.

It is to be noted that even a sexual act acquires spiritual significance if it is performed as a sacrifice for obtaining progeny.

The five fires (*Panchagni*) are: Heaven, Rain, Earth, Man and Woman. Fire is symbolic of sacrifice performed through contemplation. For each fire, the Upanishad provides imaginative similes for fuel, smoke, flame, embers, spark, oblation and end-results. These are summarized hereunder (Verses 6.2, 1-13).

'A sexual act acquires spiritual significance if it is performed for obtaining progeny.'

Fire	Fuel	Smoke	Flame	Embers	Sparks	Oblations	Outcome
1. Heaven	Sun	Rays	Day	Directions	Intermediate quarters	Faith	King Soma
2. Rain	Year	Clouds	Lightening	Thunderbolt	Rumbling sounds of clouds	Soma (Moon)	Rain
3. Earth	Earth	Fire	Night	Moon	Stars	Rain	Food
4. Man	Mouth	Life-breaths	Speech	Eyes	Ears	Food	Semen
5. Woman	Sexual organ	Hair	Womb	Sexual act	Pleasurable feelings	Semen	Newborn child

When a man dies, offering of the dead body to the cremation fire is the final sacrifice (6.2, 14).

Depending upon his deeds in this world, the subtle body of a person follows one of the two paths after death – *devayana* or *pitrayana*. *Devayana* is the path of light, leading to the Sun, and then to the world of *Brahma*. This is symbolic of knowledge leading to the state of liberation. *Pitrayana* is the path of smoke and darkness. It symbolizes ignorance. One who is obliged to travel on this path goes only as far as the moon, and then he returns back, to be born again on earth. (6.2, 15-16)

'After death, the subtle body follows one of the two paths (planes of Consciousness) – Path of Light or Path of Darkness.' ..... (Adapted)

6.3 Mantha rite for prosperity and harmony

This section describes a ritual performed in ancient times for attaining greatness and material wealth. It required fasting for 12 days, offering of a specially prepared paste as an oblation in fire and recitation of certain invocatory hymns. The ritual is called *mantha* or *srimantha*. If translated literally, it means paste for prosperity (1-13).

Mantha is a paste prepared by mixing the powder of ten specific varieties of grains (enumerated in verse-13) with curd, honey and *ghee* (a variety of butter). The utensils used for preparing the paste – ladle, bowl, two mixing rods – and even the fuel are to be made of a special wood called *udumbara*. The rite is performed on an auspicious day. The performer should live on milk during the preceding twelve days and then offer oblations to all the specified deities. Next, the Supreme Being is eulogized. The paste left over from oblations is then eaten by the performer in four installments, with recitation of *Gayatri mantra*. He then washes his hands and lies behind the fire, with his head to the east. In the morning he should salute the Sun god and repeat the lineage of teachers of this ritual.

The *mantha* rite has also been covered in Chandogya Upanishad (5.2, 4-8). Generally, however, the Upanishads are indifferent to rituals.

6.4 Procreation ceremonies

In this section, sexual union is transformed from a pleasure-seeking act to a spiritual act of procreation. The section is surprisingly explicit about sexual act, so much so that many puritan commentators have skipped translating some of its verses. However, its inclusion by the Upanishadic seers in their teachings is indicative of an important message. The spiritual masters of ancient times did not shy away from imparting sex education to their students of *Brahma Vidya* (knowledge of Supreme Being). This is perhaps because they believed that a healthy attitude towards sex is the first step in self-discipline, a prerequisite for *Brahma Vidya*. Nonetheless, some of the passages in this section are clearly controversial.

The translation provided here is by Dr. S. Radhakrishnan.

'The spiritual masters of ancient times did not shy away from imparting sex education to their students.'

TRANSLATED TEXT

CHAPTER 6

Section 1

Verily, he who knows the eldest and the greatest becomes the eldest and the greatest of his people. Life-breath is, indeed, the eldest and the greatest. He who knows this becomes the eldest and the greatest of his own people as well as of those whom he wishes to become his own. **1**

Verily, he who knows the most excellent becomes the most excellent of his people. Speech is, indeed, the most excellent. He who knows this becomes the most excellent of his own people as well as of those whom he wishes to become his own. **2**

Verily, he who knows steadiness lives steadily in difficult as well as smooth places and times. Eye, indeed, has the nature of steadiness. He who knows this, lives steadily in difficult as well as smooth places and times. **3**

Verily, he who knows prosperity attains whatever he desires. The ear, indeed, is prosperity, for through the ear is the knowledge of Vedas attained. He who knows this, attains whatever he desires. **4**

Verily, he who knows the abode becomes the abode of his own people as well as of (other) people. The mind, indeed, is the abode. He who knows this becomes the abode of his own people as well as of (other) people. **5**

Verily, he who knows procreation procreates himself with offspring and is enriched with cattle. Semen, verily, is procreation. He who knows this, procreates himself with progeny and is enriched with cattle. **6**

These vital powers, disputing among themselves about their superiority went to *Brahma* and asked, 'Which of us is the most excellent?' He replied, 'He is the most excellent after whose departure this body is thought to be worse off.' **7**

(The organ of) speech departed and having remained absent for a year came back and said, 'How have you been able to live without me?' They said, 'As the dumb; not speaking with speech but breathing with the breath, seeing with the eye, hearing with the ear, knowing with the mind, procreating with the semen. Thus have we lived.' Then speech entered in. **8**

The eye departed and having remained absent for a year came back and said, 'How have you been able to live without me?' They said, 'As the blind; not seeing with the eye, but breathing with the breath, speaking with the speech, hearing with the ear, knowing with the mind, procreating with the semen. Thus have we lived.' Then the eye entered in. **9**

The ear departed and having remained absent for a year came back and said, 'How have you been able to live without me?' They said, 'As the deaf; not hearing

---

"He is most excellent after whose departure this body is thought to be worse off."

with the ear, but breathing with the breath, speaking with the speech, seeing with the eye, knowing with the mind, procreating with the semen. Thus have we lived.' Then the ear entered in. **10**

The mind departed and having remained absent for a year came back and said, 'How have you been able to live without me?' They said, 'As the stupid; not knowing with the mind, but breathing with the breath, speaking with the speech, seeing with the eye, hearing with the ear, procreating with the semen. Thus have we lived'. Then the mind entered in. **11**

The semen departed and having remained absent for a year came back and said: 'How have you been able to live without me?' They said, 'As the impotent; not procreating with the semen, but breathing with the breath, speaking with the speech, seeing with the eye, hearing with the ear, knowing with the mind. Thus have we lived.' Then the semen entered in. **12**

Then as the life-breath was about to depart, it uprooted the sense organs, just as a great fine horse of Sindhu land might pull out the pegs to which his feet are tied. They said: 'Venerable Sir, do not go out, verily, we shall not be able to live without you.' 'Then give me tributes, said life-breath.' 'So be it,' said the senses. **13**

Speech said:	Verily, the attribute of excellence, which I have, is yours.
Eye said:	Verily, the attribute of steadiness, which I have, is yours.
Ear said:	Verily, the attribute of prosperity, which I have, is yours.
Mind said:	Verily, the attribute of abode, which I have, is yours.
Semen said:	Verily, the attribute of procreation, which I have, is yours.
Then *Prana* said:	'If such I am, what is my food, and what is my garment?'
Sense organs said:	'Whatever is known as food – including dogs, worms, insects and birds – that is your food; water is your garment'. He who knows the food of breath as such, he never eats anything that is not food, he never accepts anything that is not food.

Therefore, wise men versed in Vedas sip a little water before and after a meal. They regard this as equivalent to putting a dress on life-breath. **14**

Section 2

Shvetaketu Aruneya went to an assembly of Panchala. He went to Pravahana Jaivali who was being attended by his courtiers.

Seeing him, the king addressed him: Young man
Shvetaketu	:	Yes Sir.
Jaivali	:	Has your father taught you well?
Shvetaketu	:	Yes Sir.
Jaivali	:	Do you know how people on departing (from this life) separate in different directions?

1

"Wise men sip a little water before and after a meal."

Shvetaketu	:	No Sir.
Jaivali	:	Do you know how they come back again into this world?
Shvetaketu	:	No Sir.
Jaivali	:	Do you know why the yonder world is not filled up, with so many people going there again and again?
Shvetaketu	:	No Sir.
Jaivali	:	Do you know in which oblation water becomes the voice of a person, it rises up and speaks?
Shvetaketu	:	No Sir.
Jaivali	:	Do you know the means of access to the path leading to gods, or the one leading to ancestors? That is, by doing what do people go to the path of gods or the path of ancestors? Have you heard ever the saying of the seer: 'I know of two paths for men, the one that leads to ancestors and the one that leads to gods. By these two all that lives moves on, whatever there is between father (heaven) and mother (earth).'
Shvetaketu	:	Not a single one of them do I know, Sir. **2**

Then he (the King) gave him an invitation to stay (back for learning). Disregarding the invitation to stay, the young man ran off. He went to his father and spoke to him thus:

Shvetaketu	:	Father, did you not tell me earlier that I was well instructed?
Father	:	What happened, wise one?
Shvetaketu	:	Five questions, that fellow of princely class asked me. Not a single one of them did I know.
Father	:	What are these (questions)?
Shvetaketu	:	These are the questions. (He repeated the questions). **3**
Father	:	My child, you should understand that whatsoever I myself know, all that I have told you. But come, let us go (to the king) and live there as (his) students, to know the answers.
Shvetaketu	:	You may go alone, Sir (I am not coming).

Then Gautama went to Pravahana Jaivali. (The King) offered him a seat and had water brought for him. He gave him a respectful welcome. Then (the following dialogue followed):

Jaivali	:	A boon we offer to the revered Gautama. **4**
Gautama	:	You have promised me this boon. Please tell me the answers to what you asked the young man (my son). **5**
Jaivali	:	Gautama, it is asking for a divine boon. Please ask for some human boon. **6**
Gautama	:	It is well known that I have enough of gold, cows and horses, maidservants, retinue and apparel. Be not ungenerous towards me, Sir, in regard to knowledge of That (*Brahman*) which is plentiful, infinite, unlimited.

"Be not ungenerous towards me, Sir, in regard to knowledge of That (Brahman) which is plentiful, infinite, unlimited."

Jaivali	: Then, verily O Gautama, you should seek it in the usual form.
Gautama	: I come to you, Sir, as a pupil.

With this declaration disciples used to approach a teacher. So with this mere declaration, he (Gautama) became a disciple of the King.   **7**

Jaivali	: Please do not be offended with us, just as your paternal grandfathers were not (offended). This knowledge has never hitherto been given to any *Brahmin* whatsoever. But I shall teach it to you, for who can refuse you when you speak like this? **8**

Yonder world, Gautama, is (sacrificial) fire. Sun itself is its fuel, rays are its smoke, day is the flame, quarters are the coals, and intermediate quarters are the sparks. In this fire the gods offer faith. Out of that offering King *Soma* arises.   **9**

Parjanya (god of rain), Gautama, is fire. Year itself is its fuel, clouds are its smoke, lightning is the flame, thunderbolt is the coal, rumbling sounds of clouds are the sparks. In this fire the gods make an offering of *Soma*. Out of that offering rain arises.   **10**

This world, verily, Gautama, is fire. Earth itself is its fuel, fire is the smoke, night is the flame, moon is the coal, stars are the sparks. In this fire the gods offer rain. Out of that offering food arises.   **11**

Man, verily, Gautama, is fire. The open mouth itself is its fuel, vital breaths are the smokes, speech is the flame, eyes are the coals, ears are the sparks. In this fire the gods offer food. Out of that offering semen arises.   **12**

Woman, verily, Gautama, is fire. Sexual organ itself is its fuel; hair is the smoke, womb is the flame, sexual act is the coal; pleasurable feelings are the sparks; In this fire the gods offer semen. Out of this offering a person is born. He lives as long as he is destined to live. Then he dies.   **13**

They carry him to (be offered in) fire. The fire becomes his fire; the fuel his fuel; the smoke his smoke; the flame his flame; the coals his coals; the sparks his sparks. In this fire the gods offer the dead person. Out of this offering arises another shining person (in next birth).   **14**

Those who know this as such and those who meditate in the forest on Truth with faith, reach this flame. From this flame they reach into day, from day into half-month of waxing moon, from half-month of waxing moon into six months during which sun travels northward. From these months they reach into the world of gods, from the world of gods into sun, from sun into lightning (fire). Then a Person born of Mind leads them to the worlds of *Brahma*. In

---

"Out of this offering (of a dead person in cremation fire), arises another shining person (in next birth)."

those worlds of *Brahma* they live for long periods. For them there is no return. **15**

But those who – by sacrificial offerings, charity and austerity – conquer the worlds; they pass into the smoke (of the cremation fire). From this smoke into night, from night into half-month of waning moon, from half month of waning moon into six months during which sun travels southward, from these months into the world of ancestors, from the world of ancestors into moon. Reaching moon they become food for gods. There gods feed upon them like priests drinking the shining Soma Juice (saying, as it were), 'Do flourish, do dwindle'. When that (results of past *karmas*) is exhausted, they pass forth into space, from space into air, from air into rain, from rain into the earth. Reaching the earth they become food. Again, they are offered in the fire of man. Thence they are born in the fire of woman. (Then they again perform work, *karma*) with a view to going to other worlds. Thus do the souls rotate. But those who do not know these two ways, become insects, moths and whatever that bites. **16**

Section 3

Whoever wishes to attain greatness, he should perform *Srimantha* ritual on a day in the northern course of the sun, or on an auspicious day in the half-month of the waxing moon. The ritual is as follows: perform *upasad* ceremony (live on milk) for twelve days; collect certain herbs in a wooden dish; sweep and wash the floor; prepare the fire; purify melted butter in the prescribed manner; prepare the pastes (*mantha*) with specified ingredients and make an offering, saying:

'O fire (all-knower), to all those gods under you who spitefully slay the desires of a person, I offer them a share. Let them, being satisfied, satisfy me with all desires. Hail (*Svaha*).

To that deity who becomes spiteful under your protection, thinking that she is the support all, I offer this stream of melted butter. Hail (*Svaha*). **1**

To the oldest, hail; to the greatest, hail.
To the vital breath, hail; to the richest, hail.
To speech, hail; to steadfastness, hail.
To the eye, hail; to prosperity, hail.
To the ear, hail; to the abode, hail.
To the mind, hail; to procreation, hail.
To the semen, hail. **2**

To the fire, hail.
To the moon, hail.
To the earth, hail.
To the atmosphere, hail.
To the sky (heaven), hail.
To the earth, hail.
To the *Brahmin*, hail.

"Thus do the souls rotate (from birth to death to rebirth)."

To the Ksatra, hail.
To the past, hail.
To the future, hail.
To the universe, hail.
To all (things) hails.
To *Prajapati*, hail.'   **3**

Note: Recitation of each of the above lines (verses 2-3) is accompanied by an offering in the fire; and pouring the remnant sticking to the ladle into the paste.

Then he touches it (the mixed potion) saying:

'You are movement (as breath).
You are burning (as fire).
You are infinite (as *Brahman*).
You are steadfast (as the sky).
You are the one resort (as the earth).
You are the sound *hin* (uttered by Prastotr).
You are the chant (chanted by Udgatr).
You are recited forth (by Adhavaryu).
You are recited back (by Agnidhra).
You are the glow in moist (clouds).
You are the all-pervading.
You are the ruler.
You are food.
You are light.
You are death.
You are that, in which all things merge.'   **4**

Then he raises the vessel containing the paste, (saying):

'You know all. We too are aware of your greatness. You are, indeed, the King, the Ruler, and the Highest Lord. Make me the king, the ruler and the highest lord.'   **5**

Then he sips it (saying):

'The radiant sun is adorable. The wind blows sweetly for the righteous, the rivers pour honey. May the herbs be sweet to us. To earth, hail.

Let us meditate on the divine glory. May the night and the day be sweet. May the dust of earth be sweet. May heaven, our father, be sweet to us. To atmosphere, hail.

May he inspire (illumine) our understanding. May the trees be sweet to us. May the sun be sweet, may the cows be filled with sweetness for us. To heaven, hail.'

Then he repeats the whole *Gayatri Mantra* and the hymns about honey (called Madhumati) (saying):

'May I indeed be all this, hail to earth, atmosphere and heaven'.

"You are That, in which all things merge."

Having thus sipped, having washed his hands, he lies down behind the fire with his head towards the east. In the morning he worships Sun (saying):

'You are the one lotus flower of all the quarters. May I become the one lotus flower among men.'

Then he goes back the same way (by which he came), sits behind the fire (on the altar) and recites the lineage (of teachers). **6**

Uddalaka Aruni told this to his pupil Vajasaneya Yagyavalkya and said, 'If one should sprinkle this even on a dry stump, branches would grow and leaves spring forth.' **7**

Then Vajasaneya Yagyavalkya told this to his pupil Madhuka Paingi and said: 'If one should sprinkle this even on a dry stump, branches would grow and leaves spring forth.' **8**

Then Madhuka Paingi told this to his pupil Chula Bhagavitti and said: 'If one should sprinkle this even on a dry stump, branches would grow and leaves spring forth.' **9**

Then Chula Bhagavitti told this to his pupil Janaki Ayasthuna and said: 'If one should sprinkle this even on a dry stump, branches would grow and leaves spring forth.' **10**

Then Janaki Ayasthuna told this to his pupil Satyakama Jabala and said: 'If one should sprinkle this even on a dry stump, branches would grow and leaves spring forth.' **11**

Then Satyakama Jabala told this to his pupils and said, 'If one should sprinkle this even on a dry stump, branches would grow and leaves spring forth. One should not tell this to one who is not a son, or to one who is not a pupil' **12**

Four things are made from the wood of sacred fig tree – spoon bowl, fuel and the two churning rods.

There are ten cultivated grains (used to make the paste), viz. rice barley, sesame, beans, millet, *Anu*, wheat, lentils, pulse and vetch. They should be ground and soaked in curd, honey and clarified butter, before being offered as an oblation. **13**

Section 4

Earth, verily, is the essence of all these beings; (the essence) of earth is water; of water plants; of plants, flowers; of flowers fruits; of fruits, man; of man semen. **1**

Prajapati thought: 'Well, let me make an abode for it'. So he created woman. Having created her, he revered her below. So one should revere woman. He stretched out for himself that which projects. With that he impregnated her. **2**

"One should revere woman."

Her lower part is the (sacrificial) altar, (her) hairs the (sacrificial) grass, her skin the *soma*-press. The two labia of the vulva are the fire in the middle. Verily, as great as is the world of him who performs the Vajapeya sacrifice (so great is the world of him) who, knowing this, practices sexual intercourse; he turns the good deeds of the woman to himself. But he, who without knowing this, practices sexual intercourse, his good deeds, woman turns to herself.   **3**

This, verily, is what Uddalaka Aruni knew and said; this, verily, is what Naka Maudgalya knew and said; this, verily, is what Kumaraharita knew and said. Many mortal men, *Brahmins* by descent, go forth from this world, impotent and devoid of merit, if they practice sexual intercourse without knowing this. If even this much semen is spilled of one asleep, or of one awake.   **4**

Then he should touch it and recite: "Whatever semen of mine has spilt on earth, whatever has flowed to plants, whatever to water, I reclaim this very semen, let vigor come to me again, let luster (come to me) again; let glow (come to me) again. Let the fire and the altars be found again in their usual place". (Having said this) he should take it with his ring finger and thumb and rub it on his chest or between his eyebrows.   **5**

Now if one sees himself (his reflection) in water he should recite (the following) hymn, "May there be in me the seed capable of producing a progeny having luster, vigor, fame, wealth and merit." Among women, she (his wife) is certainly the goddess of beauty. Therefore when she has removed her soiled clothes and is lovely, he should approach and speak to her.   **6**

If she does not grant him his desire, he should persuade her (with presents). If she still does not grant him his desire he should beat her with a stick or his hand and overcome her (saying) with (manly) power and glory, 'I take away your glory.' Thus she becomes devoid of glory.   **7**

If she grants (his desire), he says, 'I transmit glory into you.' Thus the two become glorious.   **8**

If a man desires a woman (with the thought) that she may enjoy making love with him, after making love with her, he should recite, 'You that have come from every limb, you have sprung from the heart, you are the essence of the limbs. Distract this woman here in me, as if pierced by a poisoned arrow.'   **9**

Now the woman whom one desires (with the thought) 'may she not conceive,' after inserting the member in her, joining mouth to mouth, he should first inhale and then exhale and say, 'with power, I reclaim the semen from you.' Thus she does not conceive.   **10**

Now the woman whom one desires (with the thought) 'may she conceive'; after inserting the member in her, joining mouth to mouth he should first exhale and then inhale and say 'with power, I deposit semen in you.' Thus she becomes pregnant.   **11**

If a man's wife has a lover and he hates him, let him put fire in an unbaked earthen vessel. Let him spread out a layer of reed arrows in an inverse order, and

---

"May there be in me the seed capable of producing a progeny having luster, vigor, fame, wealth and merit."

let him offer (in sacrifice) in inverse order these reed arrows soaked in clarified butter, (saying) 'You have sacrificed in my fire, I take away your in-breath and out-breath, you so and so. You have sacrificed in my fire, I take away your sons and cattle, you so and so. You have sacrificed in my fire. I take away your sacrifices and meritorious deeds, you so and so. You have sacrificed in my fire. I take away your hope and expectation, you so and so'. Verily, he departs from this world impotent and devoid of merits whom a *Brahmin* gives curses. Therefore one should not wish to play with the wife of one, who is learned in the Vedas, who knows this, for such a knower becomes an enemy. **12**

Now, when monthly sickness comes upon one's wife, for three days she should not drink from a bronze cup nor put on fresh clothes. A low-caste man or woman should not touch her. At the end of three nights after bathing she should be made to pound rice. **13**

If a couple wishes that their son should be born of a fair complexion, that he should study all the Veda, that he should attain a full term of life, then they should have rice cooked with milk and eat it with clarified butter. Then they would be able to beget (such a son). **14**

Now if a couple wishes that their son should be born of a tawny or brown complexion, that he should study the two Vedas, that he should attain a full term of life, then they should have rice cooked in curd and eat it with clarified butter. Then they would be able to beget (such a son). **15**

Now if a couple wishes that their son should be born of a dark complexion with red eyes, that he should study the three Vedas, that he should attain a full term of life, then they should have rice cooked in water and eat it with clarified butter. Then they would be able to beget (such a son). **16**

Now if a couple wishes that a daughter should be born, who is learned, that she should attain a full term of life; then they should have rice cooked with sesame and eat it with clarified butter. Then they would be able to beget (such a daughter). **17**

Now if a couple wishes a son who is learned, famous, fond of discussions, a good speaker, expert in study of the Vedas, and that he should attain a full term of life, then they should have rice cooked with meat of a healthy bull, and eat it with clarified butter. Then they would be able to beget (such a son). **18**

Now, toward morning, after having prepared clarified butter according to the mode of the *sthali-paka* (a kind of sacrifice) he makes *sthali-paka* offerings (saying): 'To fire, hail; to Anumati, hail; to the radiant sun, the creator of truth, hail. After having made the offering, he takes up (the remnants of the cooked food) and eats. Having eaten, he offers (the rest) to the other (his wife). After having washed his hands and filled the water vessel, he sprinkles her thrice with it (water), (saying), 'Get up from here, Visvavasu; seek another young woman, a wife with her husband.' **19**

Then he embraces her, (saying), 'I am the vital breath and you are speech; you are speech and I am the vital breath. I am the Saman and you are the *Rg*. I am

---

*"Now if a couples wishes that a daughter should be born,
the two should eat rice cooked with sesame and clarified butter."*

the heaven and you are the earth. Come, let us strive together, let us join together to have a male child.' **20**

Then, he spreads apart her thighs, (saying), 'Spread yourselves apart, Heaven and Earth. After having inserted the member in her, after having joined mouth to mouth, he strokes her three times as the hair lies, (saying), 'Let Vishnu make the womb prepared. Let Tvastr shape the (various) forms. Let *Prajapati* pour in. Let Dhatr place the germ (the seed) for you. O Sinivali, give the seed; give the seed, O broad-tressed dame. Let the two *Asvins* crowned with lotus wreaths, place the seed.' **21**

'Golden are the two fuel sticks which *Asvins* use for churning out the sun. We implore for our success in bringing forth the fruit (the sun) in the tenth month. As the earth contains the germ of fire and as the heavens as wife is impregnated by Indra, the god of lightening, as the air is the germ of quarters, even so I place a germ in you, so and so'. **22**

When she is about to deliver he sprinkles her with water (saying): 'Even as the wind gently moves a lotus pond on every side, even so let your foetus stir and come out along with its chorion. This Indra's fold has been made with a covering enclosed around. O Indra, cause it to come forth along with babe.' **23**

After a child's birth, he should take the child in his lap and offer oblation of curd and butter in the fire with following words: 'Growing in this house as my child, may you make a thousand people happy. May fortune never depart with offspring and cattle. Hail. I offer to you mentally the vital forces that are in me. In my sacrificial work, if I have done too much or too little, let *Agni* the all-knowing, the beneficent, make it prosperous for us. Hail.' **24**

Then putting his mouth near the child's right ear, he says thrice, 'speech.' Then mixing curds, honey and clarified butter he feeds him out of a spoon of gold, which is not placed within (the mouth) saying, 'I place in you the earth, I place in you the atmosphere, I place in you the heaven. I place in you everything, earth, atmosphere and heaven.' **25**

Then he gives the child a name (saying), 'You are Veda.' So this becomes the child's secret name. **26**

Then he presents the child to the mother for breast feeding, saying: 'Your breast which is unfailing and refreshing, wealthy, abundant, generous, with which you nourish all worthy beings, Saraswati, give it here (to my wife for my baby) to suck from.' **27**

Then he addresses the mother (of the baby): 'You are Ila, descended from Mitra and Varuna. Being a heroine, you have brought forth a hero. You who have given us a hero, be you the mother of (many) heroes.' Of such a child they say, 'You have gone beyond your father; you have gone beyond your grandfather. You have reached the highest point in prosperity, fame and radiance of *Brahman*.' **28**

"Growing in this house as my child, may you make a thousand people happy."

Section 5

Now the line of teachers:
The son of Pautimasi (received this teaching) from the son of Katyayani;
the son of Katyayani from the son of Gautami,
the son of Gautami from the son of Bharadvaji,
the son of Bharadvaji from the son of Parasari,
the son of Parasari from the son of Aupasvasti,
the son of Aupasvasti from the son of Parasari,
the son of Parasari from the son of Katyayani,
the son of Katyayani from he son of Kausiki,
the son of Kausiki from the son of Alambi and the son of Vaiyaghrapadi,
the son of Vaiyaghrapadi from the son of Kanvi and the son of Kapi,
the son of Kapi from the son of Atreyi,
the son of Atreyi from the son of Gautami,
the son of Gautami from the son of Bharadvaji,
the son of Bharadvaji from the son of Parasari,
the son of Parasari from the son of Vatsi,
the son of Vatsi from the son of (another) Parasari
the son of Parasari from the son of Varkaruni,
the son of Varkaruni from the son of (another) Varkaruni,
the son of Varkaruni from the son of Artabhagi,
the son of Artabhagi from the son of Saungi,
the son of Saungi from the son of Sankrti,
the son of Sankrti from the son of Alambayani,
the son of Alambayani from the son of Alambi,
the son of Alambi from the son of Jayanti,

the son of Sankrti from the son of Alambayani,
the son of Artabhagi from the son of Saungi,
the son of Alambayani, the son of Alambayani and from the son of Alambi from the son of Jayanti, the son of Jayanti from the son of Alambi the son of Jayanti,

the son of Jayanti from the son of Mandukayani,
the son of Mandukayani from the son of Manduki,
the son of Manduki from the son of Sandili
the son of Sandili from the son of Rathitari
the son of Rathitari from the son of Bhaluki
the son of Bhaluki from the two sons of Krauciki,
the two sons of Kraunciki from the son of Vaidabhrti,
the son of Vaidabhrti from the son of Karsakeyi,
the son of Karsakeyi from the son of Pracinayogi,
the son of Pracinayogi from the son of Sanjivi,
the son of Sanjivi from Asurivasin, the son of Prasni,
the son of Prasni from Asurayana.
Asurayana from Asuri, Asuri from Yagyavalkya,
Yagyavalkya from Uddalaka, Uddalaka, from Aruna,
Aruna from Upavesi, Upavesi from Kusri,
Kusri from Vajasravas, Vajasravas from Jihvavant Badhyoga,
Jihvavant Badhyoga from Asita Varsagana,
Asita Varsagana from Harita Kasyapa,

Harita Kasyapa from Silpa Kasyapa,
Silpa Kasyapa from Kasyapa Naidhruvi,
Kasyapa Naidhruvi from Vac (speech),
Vac from Ambhini, Ambhini from Aditya (the sun).

These white sacrificial formulae received from the sun are explained by Yagyavalkya of the Vajasaneyi school. **1-3**

It is the same up to the son of Sanjivi,
the son of Sanjivi from Mandukayani,
Mandukayani from Mandavya,
Mandavya from Kautsa, Kautsa from Mahitthi,
Mahitthi from Vamakaksayana,
Vamakaksayana from Sandilya,
Sandilya from Vatsya, Vatsya from Kusri,
Kusri from Yajnavacas Rajastambayana,
Yajnavacas Rajastambayana from Tura Kavaseya,
Tura Kavaseya from Prajapati, Prajapati from Brahma.
Brahma is the self-existent. Adoration to Brahma. **4**

Peace Invocation

That is Whole; this is whole.
From That Whole comes forth this whole.
From That Whole when this whole is subtracted,
    what remains is again the Whole.

Om. Shanti. Shanti. Shanti.
Let there be Peace, Let there be Peace, Let there be Peace.

"From That Whole, when this whole is subtracted, what remains is again the Whole."

Focussed Commentaries

CHAPTER 6

6.1 *Prana*: Parable on its superiority

Leaving off the imaginary story, this section prescribes meditation on *Prana*, Life-breath in the body along with its cosmic counterpart. The sense organs have their roots in Life-breath. Sense organs are the effects, Life-breath is the cause. The cause is always superior to the effect. Also, the effect is a manifestation of the cause, and non-different from the cause. The organs are therefore not different from life-breath. Thus, one should meditate and merge the organs in Life-breath.

This Life-breath – for which everything here forms food – is the cosmic Life Principle as well. Thus, individual Life-breath should be meditated upon as identical with cosmic Life Principle.

– *Swami Sivananda*

The superiority of *Prana* over other vital organs is illustrated by a parable of rivalry between the organs. This is a favorite theme of the Upanishads. In order to test which of them is most important, the sense organs leave the body one after another, which nevertheless continues to exist. When *Prana* proposes to depart, they become conscious that none of them can exist without it. This narrative is also found in Chandogya Upanishad (5.1-5.2) and Prasna Upanishad (2, 1-4). The most original form is unquestionably in Chandogya Upanishad. Brhadaranyaka Upanishad relates the story in almost the same words but with the substitution of *Brahman* for *Prajapati* and the addition of one more sense organ. Prashna Upanishad uses the illustration of a queen-bee for that of a steed.

– *Paul Deussen*

When a person is in womb, *Prana* or vital force, which makes the foetus grow, starts functioning before all other sense organs. Thus, vital force becomes the eldest in age.

Life continues in spite of the absence of any sense organs, but not in the absence of vital force, *Prana*.

Everything is food for vital force. Whatever food a man eats is really eaten by the vital force.

The root *ana* means 'to act'. When *ana* is preceded by such prefix as *pra*, it comes to mean a special kind of activity. For example, *Prana*, *Apana*, *Samana*, *Udana* and *Vyana* stand for particular kinds of activities of the vital force.

Verse 6.1, 14 refers to the custom of sipping water before and after a meal.

In Chandogya Upanishad, verse 5.2, 3 glorifies the doctrine of meditation on *Prana*. If its narration can cause branches to grow even on a dry stump, what needs be said of the result if it were narrated to a living person?

– *Sri Sankara, translation by Swami Gambhirananda*

Life breath is the eldest because it functions prior to sense activities, even when the child is in the womb (6.1, 1).

The word *Prana* consists of *pra* and *ana*. *Ana* is breath, and *pra* indicates the direction of motion.

Verse 6.1, 14 refers to the usual Indian practice of rinsing the mouth both before and after a meal.

– *S. Radhakrishnan*

6.2 Five cosmic fires, two paths

This section teaches meditation on five fires, *Panchagni vidya*. The teaching is in the form of a dialogue king Pravahana Jaivali had first with Shvetaketu, and then with Shvetaketu's father, Gautama Aruni.

Shvetaketu, a young boy, was proud of his learning of the scriptures. He went to the court of king Pravahana to exhibit his knowledge. The king wanted him to realize his pride, so he posed five questions relating to transmigration of the soul.

1. How, after death, people separate in different directions?
2. How, the dead are reborn on earth?
3. How, with so many people dying, there is no overcrowding in the other world?

'Whatever food a man eats is really eaten by the vital force, Prana.'

4. After how many oblations in sacrificial fire, the watery portion rises and assumes the form of a human?
5. What is the means of access to the path of gods, and the path of ancestors, *devayana* and *pitrayana*? (6.2, 1-2)

Shvetaketu was unable to answer any of these questions. Feeling humiliated, he immediately went to his father Gautama Aruni and asked why he has not been taught all this knowledge? The father replied that he could not teach what he himself did not know. He then asked the son to accompany him to the king to find answers to his questions. Shvetaketu declined, so Gautama Aruni alone went to king Pravahana Jaivali. Initially, the king hesitated as he belonged to the warrior class, while Gautama Aruni belonged to the priestly class. Later, the king accepted Gautama Aruni as his student and began his teachings (6.2, 3-8).

The king first took up the fourth question about human birth. Both the question and the answer are couched in the language of sacrificial rites. Vedas tell us that the whole creation is a great sacrifice. The various factors involved in a ritualistic sacrifice – like the performer, his wife, the priest, the fire, the oblations, the hymns, etc. – are interconnected. Likewise, in the universal sacrifice of creation, several constituent factors are inextricably interrelated with one another. No event in this vast creation, no matter how insignificant, can be isolated from the rest of the events. As an illustration, consider the birth of a child. This may appear to be the outcome of a simple blending of sperms from the father with ovum from the mother under certain conditions. In reality, however, not just the father and the mother, but the whole universe is involved in some way or the other in this apparently simple and common incident. This is the main theme of *Panchagni Vidya*, meditation on the five fires.

The five symbolic fires are: Heaven, Rain, Earth, Man and Woman.

In the fire of heaven, gods like Indra, Agni and Varuna – which are cosmic counterparts of the sense organs in human body – offer 'faith' as an oblation. Out of this arises King Soma, or moon god. The word 'faith' should not be interpreted literally, as it is not capable of being taken out and offered as an oblation. Scriptures equate water with faith.

Going deeper into the subject, one's actions are like oblations in the cosmic sacrifice – they influence world events. Every action produces subtle vibrations, which in due course assume gross forms. The totality of one's actions rises up to heaven at the time of death of this body. Out of this sacrifice arises a new type of subtle body, called King *Soma* in symbolic language. The word *Soma* also means nectar. So what happens is that after leaving the physical body, the *jiva* in man assumes a subtle body and rises up to the heavenly worlds, enjoys the results of its *karmas*, and is reborn when these results are exhausted.

The god of rain is grosser than the heavenly world corresponding to the first fire. In the second fire, the fire of rain, gods offer as oblation the outcome of the first fire viz. King *Soma*. The outcome of the second fire is Rain; this is offered as oblation to the third fire, Earth. The outcome of the third fire is Food; this is offered as oblation to the fourth fire, Man. The outcome of the fourth fire is procreative fluid; this is offered as oblation to the fifth fire, Woman. The outcome of the fifth fire is a newborn child.

Depositing of procreative fluid by man in a woman is to be contemplated as a sacrifice. It then loses its animal aspect and acquires divinity. Sexual act then becomes a divine act, a part of cosmic creation by the creator.

So, how is a child born? According to the Upanishad, *jiva* first ascends to heaven as a nectar-like body, *soma*. It then descends to earth as rain. From rain it becomes food. This food is consumed by man, and *jiva* becomes procreative fluid. Depositing this procreative fluid in a woman results in the birth of a child. This child grows up, lives as long as he or she is destined to live, and then dies; and the cycle is repeated again (6.2, 9-13).

When a man dies, offering of the dead body to cremation fire is the final sacrifice. Out of this sacrifice, the *jiva* in man arises and proceeds to heaven to be reborn, as described above (6.2, 14).

Verses 6.2, 15-16 contain answers to the remaining questions. They also describe the two paths – *devayana*

'No event in this vast creation, no matter how insignificant, can be isolated from the rest of the events.'

and *pitrayana*. Depending upon its *karma*, Jiva travels on one of the two paths. In *devayana*, throughout the path there is illumination, as symbolized by bright objects such as flame, day, bright fortnight, sun and lightening. These represent different planes through which Consciousness rises. This path is also called the northern path or the path of light. It is attained by those who 'know', as also those who 'meditate'. 'Knowing' here does not mean book-learning; it means 'living' in accordance with the truth revealed in the scriptures - either as a householder or as an ascetic in the solitude of a forest. The path leads to what is called *Brahma loka* – that plane of Consciousness from which *jiva* need not return back to earth.

Those who do virtuous *karmas* but are ignorant of the Truth, *Brahman-Atman*, they go by the southern path, *pitrayana*. There is no illumination anywhere in this path. This signifies absence of knowledge. As masters enjoy the services of servants, so gods are said to enjoy the *jivas* who reach them through this path. Food is the source of enjoyment for all beings. So, metaphorically, *jivas* are said to be the food for the gods. When the results of their *karmas* are exhausted, they undertake a return journey – through space, water, food, man and woman - to be born again as human beings (6.2, 15-16).

Those who do neither meditation nor virtuous deeds are born in the world of insects or animals, says the Upanishad.

Recall the remaining questions of verse-2. Their answers are not stated directly; they are implied in verses 6.2, 9-16. Because of the in-out movement of *jivas*, the 'yonder' worlds do not get filled up. The means of attaining *devayana* are knowledge and meditation; their absence leads to *pitrayana*. How people separate in different directions after death? Those who are fortunate to follow the path of light take to the flame, and others take to smoke.

– Miscellaneous sources

Meditation can influence the binding effects produced by natural phenomena. Laws of nature can be overcome – or their effect counteracted – by the techniques of meditation. *Panchagni Vidya* is one particular type of meditation.

Vidya means a specific type of knowledge – different from ordinary knowledge of sciences or arts. It also means meditation.

Our knowledge is finite; it is not all-inclusive. No matter how learned we are, there is always something about which we are ignorant. Wherever there is ignorance, there is also bondage in respect of the subject of ignorance. The more ignorant we are about a thing, the more subservient we are to its laws. For examples, the law of gravitation limited our movement as long as we did not know much about it. Aircraft and spacecraft were invented after we acquired a good understanding of the law of gravitation.

The process of birth and death is a subject about which we are generally ignorant. There is some law, which compels us to follow the course known as transmigration. As we have no knowledge of this law, we have no control over our birth and death.

Vidya as described in the Upanishads aims to provide a comprehensive insight into the nature of reality behind any phenomenon. One such phenomenon is the descent of the soul from other regions to this world, and its ascent from this world to higher regions. How does the soul descend? How does it ascend? This is the subject matter of *Panchagni Vidya*, the doctrine of five fires.

The five fires, *Panchagni*, are not actually fires in the physical sense. They are techniques of meditation. A fire is symbolic of a sacrifice (*yagya*) which one performs through contemplation.

How is a sacrifice performed? There is a sacrificial ground. There is an altar in which oblations are offered through the medium of fire. The *mantras* chanted during the ritual convey the intention of the performer. The oblations are offered to certain deities. Invocation of some deity is the intention behind the performance of a sacrifice. Now, the Upanishad tells us that the whole universal activity may be conceived as a sacrifice – *Yagya*. In a sacrifice, every item or ritual is connected to every other item; and all items are connected to the deity invoked. Likewise, the various activities of the universe are interconnected. Births, deaths and other phenomenal experiences are not isolated events – they are all connected to an ultimate cause. If we can contemplate these interconnections, we can be free from the clutches of laws that govern them.

'The five fires, Panchagni, are not actually fires in the physical sense. They are techniques of meditation.'

Consider the birth of a child. It is not a simple delivery from a mother's womb. It is a tremendous process that takes place throughout the cosmos. The whole universe vibrates with action even when a single baby is to be born somewhere. A child is not just the product of a father and a mother, it has come from every cell of the universe. That is why we say, *Brahmanda* is in *Pindanda*, macrocosm is in microcosm. The Upanishads repeatedly emphasize this secret of cosmic inter-connectedness.

The Upanishads say that things are not just what they seem. There is a deeper significance behind every visible process or activity in nature. The cause of a particular event that is ordinarily regarded as normal, has a transcendental secret behind it. There is some activity, taking place in a subtle form in the cosmos prior to the appearance of a visible effect. This is the great point made out in *Panchagni Vidya*. There are higher powers operating behind and transcendent to the world perceptible to our senses.

Panchagni Vidya is a meditation, it is not an outward ritualistic sacrifice. It says that the ultimate cause of even the smallest thing in this world is that 'yonder world', which is imperceptible to the senses and unthinkable to the mind.

The inter-connectedness of the universe is explained through analogies. The fuel, which ignites the fire and causes the flames to rise, is the sun. The ember, which remains after the flame is extinguished, is comparable to the moon. The sparks, which are ejected from the flame, are the stars.

An important point made in the Upanishad is that our thoughts and methods of living cause vibrations, which emanate like an aura from us. The intensity of these thoughts, or the force of these vibrations, determines their impact on natural phenomena. Thus, strong vibrations – caused collectively by human beings through certain thoughts, sounds or activity – can influence even a natural phenomenon like rainfall.

Human thinking and activity has an influence on the working of Nature.

The Upanishad says that our actions are like oblations offered in a sacrifice. They are vibrations, which produce an invisible effect in the environment. This is called *Apurva*. It activates the higher realms and later becomes the cause of our descent in the next birth.

In *Panchagni Vidya*, the symbolic fire which is the object of meditation has five important aspects – the three worlds (heaven, earth and intermediate space), man and woman. Birth takes place through an interaction of these five levels of manifestations. By birth is meant every event in the universe – animate or inanimate. Every birth is a point of universal pressure. When you meditate in this manner regularly, you will acquire a universal perspective of everything. When you look at any particular object, you will see the whole world in it, and not merely that object.

Panchagni Vidya is highly esoteric and difficult to explain. The Upanishads have used many analogies to explain a difficult subject. A word of caution is in order. The analogies should not be taken literally, or word by word in their meaning.

The whole world – sentient and insentient – is here thought of as a group of factors in a cosmic sacrifice. The sacrifice involves five Cosmic Fires, knit together through a spirit of self-sacrifice, so that a new creation may emerge, a life may come into existence. Thus, faith is poured as an oblation in heaven, which is the highest fire. The result is lunar world which is poured as an oblation in the second fire, rain-god. The result is rain. It pours on earth, the third fire. From this sacrifice grows food. This is offered to man, the fourth fire. From him comes seed. The fifth fire is the woman, and the result is emergence of new life as childbirth. In the spiritual vision of the seers, father, mother and the gods who presided over their organs were all participants in a sacrifice to bring new life into existence.

What happens to the spirit in man, *jiva*, after it departs from the physical body at the time of death? According to the Upanishads, it is led on one of two possible paths.

DEVAYANA

This path is also called the northern path, or the path of gods, or the path of light. It is the path of liberation of the spirit (*jiva*), from the bondage of the cycle of birth and death (*samsara*). A soul, which follows this path after death on the strength of its spiritual life of meditation, does not have to return back to this world.

'Things are not just what they seem. There is deeper significance behind every visible process or activity in nature.'

In this path, on departing from this world, the soul is taken to a higher realm by the Deity of fire. From there, it is taken to a still higher realm by the Deity of day; then by the Deity of the bright half of the lunar month; then by the Deity of the six-months during which the sun moves to the north; then by the Deity of the year, until the soul reaches the Sun. This is said to be a very important halting place in the passage of the soul to liberation. Then the soul goes higher up into the more subtle regions of experience and enjoyment of a divine nature, comparable to cool lunar radiance. Then comes the realm, which the Upanishad calls the 'flash of lightening'. This is not the lightening that we see in the sky, but the lightening of knowledge of Reality. We are on the borderland of the Creator, as it were. A superhuman force begins to work there, and a superhuman Being, *amanava-purusha* appears. It recognizes the soul with joy, and leads it by the hand along the path of light – higher and higher – until it is taken to the realm of the Creator Himself, *Brahma-loka*. This is the path of light, liberation and freedom.

PITRAYANA

This is also called the southern path, or the path of ancestors, or the path of smoke.

Certain persons are unable to live a spiritual life of meditation; but they accumulate merits on account of good deeds – like sacrifices and charities, called by the generic names *Ishta* and *Purta*. After death their souls follow the southern path, and later return back to this world. They are carried by the Deity of smoke (not fire) to the higher realm of the Deity of night; then to the Deity of dark half of the lunar month; then to the Deity of six months during which the sun travels to the south. From here, the soul does not go to the Deity of year and Sun, as in the case of *Devayana*; instead it is said to go to the realm of space or *Akash*; and from there to the moon, *chandra-loka*. Here it enjoys the privileges of the gods, but it is subservient to them. Metaphorically, it is said that the soul is like food to gods, as it is subject to their wishes and orders. When the meritorious deeds of the soul are exhausted, it comes back to this world through the same path it went up.

There is another path, which is not connected with either *Devayana or Pitrayana*. It represents the birth of small creatures like insects, which have a very short life.

– Swami Sivananda

The analogy of the heavenly region to the sacrificial fire is worked out in verse 5.4, 1. The sun is the fuel; as the world shines only when it is lighted up by the sun. The rays are the smokes; they rise from the sun just as smoke rises from the fuel. The day is the flame because it is bright and is the effect of the sun. The moon is the coal or the embers, because moon becomes visible only when the day has ended, just as embers become visible when the flame is put out. The stars are the sparks (Sri Sankara).

Water is offered as a symbol of faith. This passage answers the question raised earlier (5.3, 3): Why at the fifth oblation, water comes to be designated as a person? The performer of a sacrifice eventually ascends to heaven through his offerings, and there he attains a nature like Soma. According to Sri Sankara, water is an important element in the development of a foetus, so water comes to be called man in the fifth oblation (Verse 5.4, 2).

The earliest conception of the path of gods is found in Rg Veda, where Agni serves as intermediary for carrying offerings from men to gods. The path on which oblations were taken to the heavenly world also became the path by which the performer of a sacrifice himself ascended to the world of the gods.

The stations of the two paths need not be taken literally. In *Devayana*, they represent stages of progressive knowledge and light, while in *Pitrayana*, of progressive ignorance and darkness.

The distinction between *Devayana* and *Pitrayana* is one of two different systems of culture – the way of works and the way of knowledge – resulting in two different spiritual conditions. If we pursue wisdom, we travel by the path of gods. If we perform good deeds we travel by the path of ancestors. If we do neither, we will continually revolve like little creatures.

– S. Radhakrishnan

'The distinction between Devayana and Pitrayana is one of two different systems of culture – the way of works and the way of knowledge.'

6.3 Mantha rite for prosperity and harmony

The mantha ceremony is aimed at attaining worldly greatness. It requires preparation of a drink of curd, honey and herbs of all kinds. This is offered along with clarified butter as an oblation for the vital organs – mind, speech, eyes etc. The portion remaining after the ceremony is consumed with recitation of *Savitri* verses. The significance of the ceremony is that a man sets his own vital organs in tune with their cosmic potency, and thereby participates in their greatness.

Chandogya Upanishad (5.2, 4-8) also deals with the same theme.

— Paul Deussen

6.4 Procreation ceremonies

This section describes the methods and ceremonies for giving birth to progeny of the right quality. Similar passages appear in *Rg Veda* and *Atharva Veda* also.

These passages describe methods to incite a woman to yield her love; and techniques to prevent conception or bring it about when desired. The sexual act is explained as a kind of ritual performance, the elements of which are identified with various parts of a woman's body. We are told that if a man practices sex with knowledge of this, he gains a world as great as that obtained by the performance of *Vajapeya* rites (6.4, 1-3).

Apparently, birth control is not a modern device (6.4, 10).

Spells and incantations were familiar practices in the age when the Upanishad was composed (6.4, 12).

The Upanishad seems to grant the privilege of learning and scholarship to women (6.4, 17).

Evidently, meat was permitted on certain occasions. Also, prenatal conditioning of child's character is advised (6.4, 18).

Sthali-paka	: literary, a pot of cooked food.
Anumati	: the feminine personification of divine favor.
Visvavasu	: God of love.
Svaha	: Hail (6.4, 19).
Ila	: Adorable (6.4, 28).

In Buddhist canonical literature, three things are said to be necessary for conception: union of father and mother, mother's periods and presence of *gandharva*. Divine nature, which corresponds to *gandharva*, is the primary cause of procreation; parents are only concomitant cause (6.4, 21).

According to Vedic literature, when a father emits the seed in a womb, it is really the Sun that emits. According to Aristotle, 'Man and Sun generate man'.

Rumi says: 'When the time comes for the embryo to receive the vital spirit, at that time Sun becomes its helper. This embryo is brought into movement by Sun, for Sun is quickly endowing it with spirit.' In a very real sense this commandment is significant, 'Call no man your father on earth; for one is your father, which is in heaven.' John VI.6.3.

— S. Radhakrishnan

In this section, sexual union is transformed from its pleasure seeking nature into a religious ritual combined with meditation and chanting of holy *mantras*. The birth of a child is the fifth oblation in *Panchagni Vidya* – the offering of seed in the sacrificial fire of woman. Mother is the 'cause' and child is the 'effect'. Those, who know this truth that all beings are manifestations of an Ultimate Cause – which is one, non-dual Consciousness – are not bound by their actions and the results thereof.

— Swami Sivananda

Only a person who knows meditation on the vital force and has performed *Srimantha* ceremony for prosperity (6.3) is entitled to the ceremony described in this section, leading to the birth of a son of good qualities.

— Swami Madhavananda

The begetting of a son – for continuance of sacrificial duties of the father – is considered important in Indian religion. It is therefore not surprising that the teacher imparts sex education to his pupils before sending them out into family life. No offence should be taken in respect of the religious earnestness or fervor with which this explanation for rearing of a family is actuated.

— Paul Deussen

'No offence should be taken in respect of the religious earnestness or fervor with which this explanation for rearing of a family is actuated.'

Isa Upanishad

Harmony of Opposites

OVERVIEW

Isa Upanishad emphasizes the Oneness of the universe and God. It declares: 'The Lord pervades everything.'

This Upanishad has a very short but very profound text of just 18 verses. Some of its verses are of immense practical value. The main themes covered in this Upanishad are as follows:

- The universe is characterized by ceaseless movement and change. However, the Lord, who creates it and sustains it, neither moves nor changes.
- Everything belongs to the Lord. We must therefore be happy with whatever the Lord assigns to us. We must not covet the wealth of others.
- We must enjoy the external world, but with a spirit of inner renunciation.
- The Lord and the universe are One. When we become aware of this Oneness, our perspective of life widens from self-interest to universal-good.
- In life, both work and wisdom are important. Work leads to restless activity, wisdom comes from meditation. Avoid extremes of either activity or meditation.
- There is no contradiction between a Formless God and a Deity with a form. They are merely two aspects of One Truth.

The Upanishad ends with a touching prayer for revelation of Truth, forgiveness for sins committed in this life, and a virtuous path in next life.

COMMENTARIES

The eighteen brief verses of Isa Upanishad have been commented upon at length by many learned scholars and spiritual masters. The commentators quoted here are: Sri Aurobindo, Dr. S. Radhakrishnan, Swami Chinmayananda, Swami Paramananda, Swami Sarvananda, Swami Sivananda, Rohit Mehta and Mahatma Gandhi (Verse 1 only).

ISA UPANISHAD
Harmony of Opposites

Peace Invocation

1-3	Fundamentals of spiritual life	245
4-5	It moves and It moves not	248
6-8	Signs of Self-realization	250
9-11	Ignorance and Knowledge	252
12-14	Manifest and Unmanifest	253
15-18	The Last Prayer	254

Verses 1-18 — Harmony of Opposites

SIMPLIFIED SYNOPSES

1-3
Fundamentals of spiritual life

Verse-1 lays down a conceptual foundation. The material world is characterized by constant movement. However, one stable, non-moving Consciousness inhabits and governs the whole world of movement and change.

The verse then gives two rules for spiritual life:

(i) Enjoy the external material world, but with an attitude of inner renunciation.
(ii) Accept whatever you earn legitimately. Do not covet the wealth of others. In modern context, the verse says: 'Do not resort to corrupt practices.'

'Do not covet the wealth of others.'

Verse 2 glorifies work and asks us to pray for a long and productive life. Implying a reference to the previous verse, it also cautions that work must be done in a spirit of inner renunciation; only then we will be able to experience the freedom of our inner soul. According to Sri Aurobindo, manifestation of the Lord in life and in work is the law of our being. We should therefore accept and enjoy life and work in its fullness. At the same time, we should always remain conscious of the unity in the Lord; unity within ourselves and unity with all existences.

Verse 3 warns those who ignore the Divinity within and do not follow the laws of spiritual life. They are doomed to dark worlds after death. Sri Aurobindo interprets this as "involution in states of blind obscurity".

4-5
It moves and It moves not

Like these two verses, there are many instances in the Upanishads where the *Atman-Brahman* Reality is explained through the use of apparent paradox and contradictions.

Verse 4 describes two seemingly contradictory natures of *Atman* – eternal changelessness and unceasing change, stillness and movement. Immovable by Itself, *Atman* is the source of all movements. Unity and multiplicity are its two aspects, like two sides of a coin. Unity is Its Truth, and multiplicity is Its manifestation.

Verse 5 is quoted very often to describe *Atman*, despite the limitations of human thought and language. Thought is symbolic and so cannot conceive of the Absolute, except through negations. But the Absolute is not a void. It is all that is in space and time; and yet, It is beyond space and time.

6-8
Signs of Self-realization

A Self-realized person sees himself in all beings and all beings in himself. He is free from hatred, sorrow and delusion. He sees unity in a world of multiplicity. Such a person is said to have perfect Wisdom.

9-11
Ignorance and Knowledge

Ignorance or *Avidya* is the empirical understanding of plurality. *Vidya* or Knowledge is realization of Oneness in all. These verses denounce the extremes of both. They advocate a harmonious blend of empirical learning and spiritual wisdom.

It is to be noted that in the Upanishads the word *Vidya*, translated as Knowledge, refers to what we generally understand as spiritual wisdom. The word *Avidya*, translated as 'Ignorance', refers to empirical learnings. Knowledge is associated with meditation, Ignorance with work.

12-14
Manifest and Unmanifest

These verses again advocate a balanced viewpoint in life. The manifest and the unmanifest, the Personal God of form and the Impersonal formless God, birth and death, are but two complementary aspects of One Reality.

15-18
The Last prayer

The Reality of Cosmic Consciousness, says the Upanishad in verse 15, is as if It is covered from human Consciousness by a golden lid, which we are hesitant to remove. Sun and Fire represent the divine Light and Force of Consciousness, respectively. The aspirant invokes these powers in verses 15 and 16 so that he may see the Reality, the Truth. The Upanishad states this Truth in a profound aphorism: *Soham*, That I am.

Many commentators regard these verses as the last prayer of a dying person who faces death as happily as he faced life. He prays that let his physical body merge with ashes, and his life-breath merge with the cosmic Life Principle. Let his mind remember all its past deeds. Let him be free from all sins and delusions; and let his soul attain liberation.

These verses also appear in Brhadaranyaka Upanishad (5.15, 1-4). Refer pages (205, 210, 216).

'Vidya or Knowledge is realization of Oneness in all.'

Translated Text

Peace Invocation

That is Whole; this is whole.
From That Whole comes forth this whole.
From That Whole when this whole is subtracted,
  what remains again is the Whole.

Om. Shanti. Shanti. Shanti.
Let there be Peace, Let there be Peace, Let there be Peace.

Om. The Lord pervades every thing – whatever exists in this universe of ceaseless movement. Enjoy the external world with an attitude of (inner) renunciation. Do not covet the wealth of others. **1**

Always doing selfless work, man should wish to live a full hundred years in this world. By this method alone, and not otherwise, action will not cling to man. **2**

Those who slay (neglect) their souls, after death they go to demonic/sunless worlds of utter darkness. **3**

It (*Atman*) is One; motionless, yet more swift than the mind. The gods (senses) cannot reach It, as it is always ahead of them. Standing still, It goes faster than those who run after It. Rooted in It, Air (Sanskrit, *Matarisva*) supports the activity (Sanskrit, *Apah*, lit. water) of all living beings. **4**

It moves and It moves not. It is far and It is near. It is within all this and It is outside all this. **5**

He who constantly sees everywhere all existences in Self, and Self in all existences, does not feel hatred for anything. **6**

He who has perfect knowledge, for whom all existences are one with his own Self (*Atman*), how can he feel deluded? What grief can there be to him who sees Oneness everywhere? **7**

It (*Atman*) is all pervading, bright, bodiless, without scars of imperfection, without sinews, pure, unpierced by evil. As the seer, the thinker, the omniscient, the self-existent, It has ordered objects perfectly according to their nature, for years eternal. **8**

Into deep darkness enter those who worship ignorance. Those who delight in knowledge enter into still greater darkness. **9**

Distinct, indeed, they say, is the result of knowledge; and distinct they say, is the result of ignorance. Thus we have heard from the wise, who have explained this to us. **10**

"Always doing selfless work, man should wish to live a full hundred years."

He who understands both knowledge and ignorance at the same time, he crosses death through ignorance (work) and attains immortality through knowledge (wisdom/meditation). **11**

Into blinding darkness enter these who worship the unmanifest alone; and into still greater darkness, as it were, those who delight in the manifest alone. **12**

Distinct, indeed, they say, is what results from the manifest; and distinct they say, is what results from the unmanifest. Thus we have heard from the wise, who have explained this to us. **13**

He, who understands the manifest and the unmanifest at the same time, crosses death through the unmanifest and attains immortality through the manifest. **14**

The face of Truth is covered by a golden lid. O Sun, remove it for me, the practitioner of Truth, so that I may behold It. **15**

O *Pusan*, the Sun, the Nourisher, the Sole Seer, O Controller of All, *Surya*, son of *Prajapati*! Spread forth your rays and gather your radiant light; so that I may see your radiant form. Whosoever is That Being (*Purusha*), I am also That. **16**

May this life merge with the all-pervading Life Principle; may this body be burnt into ashes. O Mind, remember, remember your deeds; remember, remember your deeds. **17**

O *Agni* (Fire)! Lead us to wealth by a virtuous path. O God, you know all our deeds. Remove all sins and delusions from us. We offer our best salutations to you. **18**

Peace Invocation

That is Whole; this is whole.
From That Whole comes forth this whole.
From That Whole when this whole is subtracted,
  what remains again is the Whole.

Om. Shanti. Shanti. Shanti.
Let there be Peace, Let there be Peace, Let there be Peace.

"The face of Truth is covered by a golden lid."

Focussed Commentaries

Peace Invocation

Adah, That: Supreme Reality, Ultimate Truth, Absolute Being, Universal Consciousness, Unconditioned *Brahman*.

Idam, this: Universe of names and forms, material world, conditioned *Brahman*.

Purna, whole: Complete, full, infinite, everything that exists or does not exist or transcends existence.

The unconditioned *Brahman*, frequently referred to as 'That' in the Upanishads, is Infinite, Whole, Totality. The manifest universe, which comes forth from the unmanifest *Brahman*, is also infinite.

Another interpretation is that the manifest universe is permeated by the Infinite *Brahman*.

When something arises out of another, invariably the source undergoes a change. For example, when a lump of gold is transformed into an ornament, the lump ceases to exist. When a tree grows from a seed, the seed sprouts and then exhausts itself. This is not so in case of *Brahman*. Even after the universe comes forth from It, *Brahman* Itself remains eternally unchanged.

Mathematically:
Brahman − Universe = *Brahman*.

1-3 Fundamentals of spiritual life

VERSE 1

Isa vasyam idagm sarvam:

The opening phrase of this Upanishad, 'The Lord pervades everything', is a profound statement. It is the essence of all the Upanishads. The material world is like a veil, it hides the Divinity from our vision. Therefore, we are unable to perceive Divine Presence everywhere. Whatever names and forms are there in the universe, they all are expressions of Universal Consciousness; just as waves are expressions of the strength and the vastness of the ocean.

yat kinca jagatyam jagat:

The universe around us is characterized by movement. Movement signifies a state of change. Even though the universe is ever-changing, the Lord who pervades it is changeless.

tena tyaktena bhunjitha:

To identify ourselves with the all-pervading Truth is to realize the Self within. There are many methods for doing so. According to Sri Sankara and other ancient commentators, this verse suggests the path of renunciation. It says: 'Renounce the false and enjoy the Real.' Another interpretation of this phrase by a great thinker, Sri Madhava, is: 'Whatever has been given to us by the Lord, enjoy it as His gift, *prasad*.'

— Miscellaneous sources

ma gradhah kasya svid dhanam:

This is translated as: 'Do not covet the wealth of others.' *Gradhah* refers to a bird of prey, a vulture. We are asked to refrain from vulture-like tendency of hankering for others' wealth. We should feel satisfied with whatever is allotted to us by the Lord.

Verse 1 also suggests the idea of trusteeship. The wealth of the world belongs to the Lord. We can enjoy it only as a trustee, without any sense of attachment or ownership. The verse says: 'Enjoy all things by renouncing the idea of a personal proprietary relationship with them.' When a person is not conscious of the unity behind multiplicity, he is not in harmony with the universe, and thus fails to enjoy. Self-denial is at the root of spiritual life.

When we realize that we are all creations of the same Creator, the objects of His care, we feel within ourselves that everyone has a right to his own place in the same universe.

— S. Radhakrishnan

This verse is the most profound of all the verses in all the Upanishads. The seer to whom this verse was revealed was not satisfied with the very frequent statement that God was to be found everywhere. He

---

'Whatever has been given to us by the Lord, enjoy it as His gift, prasad.'

therefore went further and said: 'Since God pervades everything, nothing belongs to you, not even your body.' The verse contains many messages:

- The message of universal brotherhood – not just brotherhood of all human beings, but all living beings.
- The message of unshakable faith in the Lord that He will supply all that I need.
- The doctrine of equality of all creatures, since He pervades every fiber of my being, and all beings.

This mantra says that I cannot hold as mine anything that belongs to God; and that my life – as also the life of all who believe in this mantra – has to be a life of perfect dedication, a life of continual service of fellow beings.

– Mahatma Gandhi

This verse is in itself a miniature philosophical textbook; complete with philosophical enunciation of Truth, explanation of the technique of realizing that Truth, and vivid exposition of the values of life that a perfect man should entertain.

– Swami Chinmayananda

The whole world is a movement of the Spirit in Itself. Every separate object in the universe is, in truth, itself the whole universe. The microcosm is one with the macrocosm. Movement has been created in order to provide a habitation for the Spirit. The Spirit is one, yet It dwells multitudinously in the multiplicity of Its mansions. It is the same Lord who dwells in the totality and in its parts; in the cosmos as a whole and in all beings, forces and objects in the cosmos. Since It is one and indivisible, the Spirit in all is one and the same. Multiplicity is a play of Cosmic Consciousness. Therefore, each human being is in essence one with all others.

Enjoyment of the universe is the object of worldly existence, but renunciation of desires is the condition for free enjoyment of the universe.

The renunciation demanded here is not self-denial or physical rejection, but liberation of the spirit from greed.

The terms of this liberation are freedom from ego, and consequently, freedom from possessiveness. Practically, renunciation implies that one should not regard anything in the universe as a necessary object of possession, nor as possessed by another and not by oneself, nor as an object of greed in the heart or the senses.

This attitude comes from the perception of unity. Therefore, by transcending ego and realizing the One Self that exists in all, we come to possess the whole universe; we do not need to possess is physically.

By oneness with the Lord, we have the possibility of an infinite and free delight in all things.

– Sri Aurobindo

In verse 1, Isa, the Lord refers to *Brahman*, the Reality. The verse says that It pervades in everything – even in the movement which characterizes the universe. Is Reality also moving? If that is the case, how can Reality be everywhere at the same time?

In order to be omnipresent, Reality must be Timeless. Time implies succession in which things happen not at once, but one after the other. But in the unmanifest, all things happen together.

When one tries to comprehend the existence of Timeless through the process of time-succession, the result is a paradox. A paradox is the placing of two opposites in juxtaposition. A paradox can be resolved only when two opposites are seen as existing together at the same place and at the same time. Human mind cannot conceive of this. According to the mind's thinking, two opposites existing together would cancel each other – and the result would be nothingness. Isa Upanishad – like many other Upanishads – speaks in the language of paradox. The mind comes to its highest when it deals with a paradox.

Brahman is inevitably the non-moving center of endless mobility. To see infinite rest and infinite motion simultaneously is indeed to comprehend the nature of Reality. Rest and Motion are the Being and Becoming of Indian philosophy. If Becoming (Motion) is detached from Being (Rest) then such Becoming becomes a monstrous evil, rushing towards an unending aimlessness. Motion and Rest must exist simultaneously for the whole to exist in parts. This, indeed is the *Brahman* of Isa Upanishad - It pervades everything, whatever exists in this constantly changing universe.

'To see infinite rest and infinite motion simultaneously is, indeed, to comprehend the nature of Reality.'

How to comprehend the coexistence of Rest and Motion? How to perceive the whole in the parts? The Upanishad gives a solution in the same verse, but again in the form of a paradox. It says: 'Enjoy and renounce at the same time!' How is this possible? Do not covet the wealth of others, says the Upanishad. Do not seek enjoyment through what does not legitimately belong to you. The wealth that is assigned to one can alone be the source of one's joy.

To accept what the Lord gives is not a gospel of passivity. It is indeed the basis for joy and for right action. When intense activity is rooted in immense Acceptance, one comes close to his real Self, close to *Brahman*, Bliss.

It is to be noted that the Upanishad asks you to enjoy what is assigned to you. The word used is "enjoy", not "endure". If you do so, you will be free from many worries and anxieties; and therefore, you can expect to live happily up to a hundred years. The Upanishad says that actions can never bind a man so long as they arise from the ground of Acceptance. Such a man can live as long as he likes, because he has brought the very movement of Time itself under his control. It is not his mind, but his Self, *Atman* which moves him, and *Atman* is Timeless.

The justification for the practice of Acceptance is provided in the concluding part of verse 8. It says that the Lord has ordered objects perfectly according to their nature, for years eternal.

The crux of the problem posed by Isa Upanishad is to have clarity in the midst of intense activity.

– *Rohit Mehta*

VERSE 2

Sri Sankara and many other commentators interpret this and the previous verse to conclude that there are two paths available to man for attainment of *Brahman*: path of Renunciation and path of Action, filled with rituals as presented in the Vedas. Swami Chinmayananda writes: "He who cannot afford to live the noble life of renunciation must live a life of activity, striving his best to fulfill all his desires through sweat and toil. He must strive to live a full hundred years in the service of man and in the glorification of the Lord."

However, commentators like Dr. S. Radhakrishnan and Sri Aurobindo feel that both verses advocate only one and the same path – internal renunciation coupled with external activity. According to Dr. S. Radhakrishnan, the first verse told us that we can attain inner freedom by renunciation. Verse-2 emphasizes that renunciation should apply to the spirit and not to the mind-body. When we act by merging our self-interest with some cosmic purpose, and by dedicating all our actions to God, we will be no more entangled in selfish desires. Therefore, our action will not bind us. The way to true freedom is not abstention from action, but selfless action.

In ancient times in India, there was a general tendency to regard contemplation as superior to action. This verse says that it is not necessary to withdraw from active life in order to lead a life of contemplation. Wisdom without work is beautiful but barren. Faith without work is futile.

Justifying the path of action while commenting on this verse, Sri Aurobindo writes: "The active *Brahman* fulfills Itself in the world by work. Man also is in the body for self-fulfillment by work."

And again:

"Desire is only a mode of the emotional mind, which because of ignorance seeks its delight in the objects of desire. By destroying that ignorance, one can do action without entanglement in desires."

– *Miscellaneous Sources*

VERSE 3

Readers must not forget that soul is immortal and imperishable – it can be neither hurt nor killed. However, in the poetic language of this verse, persons who are following neither the path of renunciation nor the path of action have been called 'slayers of their souls or killers of divinity within'. After death, such persons do not disappear completely – they only pass from the material world into some other states of consciousness. These states are dark and demonic, enveloped in blind gloom.

The first word *Asurya* in the original Sanskrit text of this verse has two translations – demonic and sunless. Both the translations seem appropriate. Demons are

---

'When intense Activity is rooted in immense Acceptance, One comes close to real Self, Brahman, Bliss.'

those who follow the philosophy of 'eat, drink and be merry'. Sunless means without sun. In the Upanishads, sun and its rays are associated with the world of wisdom, and its opposite is the world of ignorance.

– *Miscellaneous sources*

4-5 It moves and It moves not

VERSE 4

It is One:

God is One, Changeless, Eternal, Absolute, Ultimate Reality. It is beyond space, time and causality.

God is One, because there is nothing else. All existences and non-existences are He.

God is Changeless because He does not increase or diminish.

God is Eternal because He possesses eternally in Himself all that is, was and will be.

God is Absolute, because He is beyond relativity. There is no change of relations in His Being.

God is Ultimate Reality because everything emanates from Him and dissolves in Him.

God is beyond space, time and causality.

God is beyond space because It contains all formations of space in Itself and It does not have to run to conceivable limits of space.

God is beyond time because It contains all formations of time – past, present and future – in Itself, and It does not have to run to conceivable limits of time.

God is beyond causality because It contains in Itself all eventualities and potentialities; and it does not have to run to conceivable limits of cause and effect.

God and the world, even when they seem to be distinct, are not really different from each other. They are One, *Brahman*. The Lord and the world are one.

It is motionless:

God is motionless because motion implies change in space and time, and He is beyond both space and time.

Everything is already present in the oneness of the Lord, even before it is accomplished by the separated personalities in the world of movement and change.

Reality cannot and need not move anywhere, because there is no spot wherein It is not already existing. This idea is indicated in the epithet 'motionless' used here by the great Rishi of this Upanishad.

– *Swami Chinmayananda*

The world is a cyclic movement of Divine Consciousness in space and time. Its law, and in a sense its objective, is progression. It exists by movement. It will dissolve if movement ceases.

What is the basis of this movement? The basis is not material; it is the energy of Divine Consciousness.

More swift than the mind...

Consciousness is 'Motionless and One'. However, It projects out of Itself the principles of motion and multiplicity. These appear different in appearance but are same in essence. Consciousness creates what to the human mind look like oppositions of unity and multiplicity, divisions of time and space, or relationships of causality.

But mental perception is not what creates the universe. That which creates the universe is something infinitely more powerful and swift than the mind. The laws of relativity, upheld by the senses (referred to as gods in Upanishadic verses), are Its 'within-limits' creations. They are valid eternally but only within the world which they govern. They are laws which regulate motion and change, not laws which bind the Lord of movement. The Lord is, therefore, more swift than the mind.

The gods (senses) are described as unable to reach It, as It is always ahead of them.

Standing still, It goes faster than those who run after It.

Even in Its material manifestations, *Brahman* exceeds movement in time, space and causality.

'Consciousness is One. However, It creates what look like oppositions of unity and multiplicity, divisions of time and space, or relationships of causality.'

Matarisva and Apah, Air and Water

What is God's intention in creating movement in the universe?

Movement is a rhythm of life created by the Lord out of Itself. It is symbolically expressive of the Unknowable. It is so arranged that each movement really represents something beyond itself. Everything in the universe seems to be moving towards a goal outside itself, or other than its immediate idea of itself. *Brahman* is the goal, though the entity which is in movement may not be aware of it. *Brahman* is the beginning and the end, the cause and the result of all movement in the universe.

Brahman, self-extended in space, time and causality, is the universe. In this extension, *Brahman* manifests Itself as Nature, the universal Mother, the Earth Principle.

In matter or in physical beings, *Brahman* expresses Itself as the universal Life Force. This is referred to as *Matarisva* in verse-4. *Matarisva* is the Lord of Air, Life Force, *Prana*. It moves in living beings as vital energy, supporting life.

Life Force is said to have seven constituents.

We are generally conscious of our three physical constituents: Body, Mind and Life. But this is not the whole of our being. Behind this, we have a super-conscious existence which also has three elements – Existence, Consciousness and Bliss, or *Sat – Chit – Ananda*.

Sat or Existence is the divine counterpart of physical body. It is the essence of our being – changeless, infinite and undivided. In contrast, our physical body is changeable, finite and divisible.

Chit or Consciousness is the divine counterpart of mind. It is free in its rest and in its action, sovereign in its will. In contrast, the energy of *Prana* is hampered and dependent for its sustenance on physical substances – generically called *anna* or food in the Upanishads.

Ananda is Bliss of existence as pure Consciousness. *Ananda* is the divine counterpart of a life of emotions and sensations.

The higher Divine is linked to the lower mortal existence by *vigyana*, translated as 'supra-mental knowledge'. It secretly guides the confused activities of the Mind, Life and Body towards the right arrangement of the universe. It leads the divided Consciousness back to the One. It also helps to see unity in multiplicity. *Vigyana* or supra-mental knowledge is the divine counterpart of human intelligence.

Thus, there are seven constituent powers in living beings: Mind, Body and Life at the perceptible individual level; Existence, Consciousness and Bliss at the imperceptible divine level and supra-mental knowledge which connects the two levels. These are spoken of by the Vedic Rishis as the waters, *Apah* in Sanskrit. They are like currents flowing into or rising out of the ocean of Consciousness –*hridaya samudra* or ocean of the heart in human beings. They are all coexistent in the universe, eternally and inseparably. They can be withdrawn into pure Infinite Being and can again be manifested out of It.

– *Sri Aurobindo*

VERSE 5

This verse teaches us how to perceive *Brahman* within our self-existence, and also outside us in the universe.

We have to perceive *Brahman* in Its Totality, both as moving and not-moving. We must see It as Eternal, Changeless, Absolute, Ultimate Reality. We must also see It in all the perishable and changing manifestations of the universe of relative and interdependent phenomena.

We have to perceive all things in space and time – the far, the near, the distant past, the immediate present and the distant future – with all their contents and happenings, as one *Brahman*.

We have to perceive *Brahman* as That which exceeds, contains and supports all individual entities, as well as the whole universe.

We have to perceive *Brahman* as That which transcends Space, Time and Causality. It is That which dwells in the universe and possesses the universe with all Its constituents.

– *Sri Aurobindo*

'Movement is a rhythm of life created by the Lord out of Itself.'

The Divine has two sides – One and many, unmoving and moving. The Upanishads do not deny the reality of either. They see 'One' in many. 'One' is the eternal truth of all things; 'many' are manifestations of that eternal truth. It is like many ornaments being made from one piece of gold.

– S. Radhakrishnan

The motionless Self is not a dull, inert entity. In fact It is beyond both activity and inactivity. This idea is conveyed by stating that Self is inactive in Its own real nature but most active in Its manifestations. For example, in a steam engine, water, which in a way is motionless, evaporates to manifest itself as steam. Steam moves the train and can therefore be explained as that which 'goes faster than those who run after it' – the bogies.

Think of the ocean with its high-tide waves. The ocean is termed as surging, seething, heaving, roaring etc. But in its own true nature, the ocean is not waves alone. It is tranquil and peaceful, motionless and majestic. So too is life and *Atman*. In its all-pervading nature, *Atman* is motionless. It neither acts nor works, while life is defined as thinking, feeling or acting. The boat moves, but never the lake.

– Swami Chinmayananda

[Sri Krishnananda Math, Hyderabad in its publication on Isa Upanishad (author not stated) also gives the example of a moving train with much greater elaboration. – Editor]

Atman is motionless by Itself, but It makes Nature, *Prakriti*, move by Its simple presence. So it is said that 'It moves'. When It is all-pervading and all-full, where can It move? Hence it is motionless. 'It moves not'.

It is very far for those who are selfish, proud, egoistic, hot-tempered and passionate. It is very near for those who are equipped with purity of mind.

It is very subtle. It fills and covers everything. Hence It is within and without. *Brahman* is the substratum and support of all beings. It is inside all and It pervades all.

– Swami Sivananda

It is near to those who have the power to understand It, for It dwells in the heart of everyone. But It seems far to those whose mind is covered by the clouds of sensuality and self-delusion. It is within, because It is the innermost soul of all creatures. And, It is without as the essence of the whole external universe, in-filling it like the all-pervading ether.

– Swami Paramananda

6-8 Signs of Self-realization

WHAT IS SELF-REALIZATION?

Brahman–Atman is the immutable existence of all that is there in the universe. Anything that changes in us – mind, life, body, action – is not our real Self, but becoming of Self. In Nature, all things that exist – animate or inanimate – are becomings of one Self. All living beings are one indivisible existence. When this unity has been realized by an individual in every part of his being, he becomes perfect and pure. He is considered liberated from ego and dualities. He is said to have attained Self-realization.

THREEFOLD *PURUSHA*

Atman, our Self, is *Brahman*. It is pure, and indivisible. Its existence is light and bliss. It is timeless, spaceless and free.

Atman, which is same as *Purusha* or Cosmic Person, presents itself in three states. These are dependent upon the relationship between *Purusha* and *Prakriti*, Soul and Nature.

Akshara : unmoving, immutable
Kshara : moving, mutable
Para or *Uttam* : Supreme, Highest

Kshara Purusha reflects the changes and the movements of Nature. It enjoys the dualities of pleasure and pain, but it also appears to be their victim.

Akshara Purusha stands back from changes and movements of Nature. It is calm and pure. It watches, but it does not participate. It is like the sky that never moves and changes, but always looks down upon the waters that are never at rest. *Akshara* is the hidden freedom of *Kshara*.

'All living beings are one indivisible existence. When this unity has been realized by an individual, he is said to have attained Self-realization.'

Para Purusha or *Purushottam* is the Self that contains and enjoys both stillness and movement, but It is not conditioned or limited by either of them. It is *Brahman*.

SELF AND MIND

The Lord pervades the universe as *Virat Purusha*, the Cosmic Soul. In living beings, he manifests as *Jivatman* or individual Self.

Atman is reflected in the mind. If the mind is pure and still, there is the right reflection. If the mind is impure and troubled, the reflection is distorted. Therefore, according to the states of the reflecting mind, we may either have purity of Self-knowledge or distortion of knowledge in the dualities of pleasure and pain. It is the mental ego-sense that creates this distortion by division and limitation of Self.

STAGES OF SELF-REALIZATION

The first sign of Self-realization is a sense of unity with other existences in the universe. Its early or crude form is on attempt to understand or sympathize with others, to show compassion for fellow-beings, and to want to work for service of others.

The next stage is the perception of oneness - one matter, one life, one mind, and one soul - in many forms.

Next, we see matter to be only a play of life, life a play of mind, mind a play of truth, truth a play of Supreme *Brahman*. We perceive the soul in all bodies to be this one *Brahman*. We also see all bodies, lives and minds to be active formations of the same *Brahman*.

A materialist view of life is that of a world of innumerable, separate creatures, each self-existent and striving for maximization of its gains. A spiritual view of life is that of a world of innumerable creatures, each supporting the other and all pervaded by one *Brahman*.

Self-realization means two things:
(i) To have knowledge of the transcendent Self, the sole unity.
(ii) With that knowledge, to extend one's conscious existence so as to embrace the whole multiplicity.

This is the dual objective of Isa Upanishad. In verses that follow (9-14), we are asked to embrace both knowledge and ignorance; One and many; freedom and peace of immortality, as also bondage and activity of mortal life.

– Sri Aurobindo

These verses explain how unity is the basis of multiplicity. The essence of the Supreme is Its Being. Multiplicity is Its 'becoming'. *Brahman* is the one Being of all; and the 'many' are the 'becomings' of One Being, *Brahman*.

When this unity is realized by an individual, he becomes liberated from sorrow; as sorrow is the product of dualities. The vision of all existences in Self and of Self in all existences is the foundation of freedom and joy.

– S. Radhakrishnan

Verse 6 explains vividly the state of perfect tranquility gained by a Self-realized sage. It has been quoted often.

To realize one's own Self is to realize Its oneness with Self of everyone else. To realize the nature of a wave is not only to realize the nature of all the waves, but the very nature of the ocean. Life is one and unbroken. To experience the life center within us is to experience at once the life centers everywhere (verse 7).

Here is a verse, typical of the Upanishadic literature, which attempts an exhaustive definition of *Brahman*. The expressions in their very groupings indicate that the *Atman* is neither the physical body, nor the subtle body, nor the causal body. It transcends them all (verse 8).

– Swami Chinmayananda

When a man sees God in all beings and all beings in God, and also God dwelling in his own soul, how can he hate any living being? Grief and delusion rest upon a belief in diversity, which leads to competition and selfishness. With the realization of oneness, the sense of diversity vanishes, and the cause of misery is removed (verse 7).

– Swami Paramananda

Hatred is born of self-interest. This, in turn, has its basis in the sense of separateness. When one

---

'A materialist view of life is that each living being strives for maximization of its gains.
A spiritual view is that each supports all others, as each is pervaded by one Brahman.'

realizes the unity of Self in all, there is no room for hatred (verse 7).

– Swami Sarvananda

9-11 Ignorance and Knowledge

Human consciousness is of two types – consciousness of unity, and consciousness of multiplicity. Unity is an eternal and fundamental fact. Consciousness of unity is therefore called *vidya* or knowledge. Consciousness of multiplicity is called *avidya*, or ignorance.

Unity and multiplicity are the two sides of *Brahman*. He is the Lord of both, *vidya* and *avidya*.

Perfection of man lies in an accord between *vidya* and *avidya*. Multiplicity must become conscious of its oneness. Oneness must embrace its multiplicity. The purpose of the Lord in the world cannot be fulfilled by following *vidya* alone, or *avidya* alone.

The highest goal of man is neither fulfillment in movement as a separate individual, nor in silence separated from movement; but in *Uttam Purusha*, the Lord.

Ego created by *avidya* is a necessary mechanism for affirming individuality in the universe. By *avidya* one attains wealth, power, and worldly knowledge in the path of self-enlargement. But this alone is not the goal of man. Even though it brings transcendence of ordinary human limits, it does not bring divine transcendence.

Real knowledge is that which perceives *Brahman* in Its Totality. It is no more attached to *vidya* than to *avidya*. *Vidya* depends upon *avidya* for the preparation and the advancement of the soul towards the great unity. Neither could exist without the other. The purpose of *vidya* is not to destroy *avidya* as something that should not have been there. The purpose of *vidya* is to continually draw *avidya* towards itself, support it, and help it deliver itself progressively. *Avidya*, fulfilled by turning more and more to *vidya*, enables the individual to become conscious of God's manifestations as well as non-manifestations; free in birth as well as in non-birth.

The first necessity for man, therefore, is to continually enlarge the limits of his ego, so that he becomes more and more powerful to deal with the dualities of Nature. This self-enlargement should then become conscious of something bigger than itself. Man has to enlarge his conception of self as to see all in himself and himself in all (verse 6). He has to see that "I" is universal, and not just his personal ego. He has to see that the universe – all its forms, actions and egos – are only becomings of one Being (verse 7). When he does so, *avidya* becomes one with *vidya*.

Immortality does not mean survival of the ego after dissolution of the body. By immortality is meant Consciousness that is beyond birth and death, beyond all bondage and limitation, free, blissful, and self-existent.

Having realized his own immortality, the individual has yet to fulfil God's works in the universe. He has to help the life, the mind and the body of all beings to evolve progressively towards immortality. This he may do by rebirth in a material body, or from some position in another world, or from the world beyond. But birth in the body is the most close, divine and effective form of help which a liberated soul can give.

– Sri Aurobindo

Verse 9 refers to the dichotomy of work and wisdom. It suggests that those who are lost in work without spiritual wisdom enter into darkness. Those who are devoted exclusively to pursuit of wisdom and neglect of work enter into still greater darkness. Selfish seekers of spiritual wisdom miss their aim. The Upanishad repudiates both the extremes. It advocates a combination of work and wisdom. Just as a bird cannot fly with one wing alone, a man can gain salvation only by combined pursuit of wisdom and work. Meditation and active life should go together.

The state of those who are lost in ignorance and who cling to materialism is pitiable indeed. But the state of those who are intellectually learned but spiritually poor is worse. The darkness of intellectual conceit is worse than that of ignorance.

Both knowledge and ignorance lead to distinct results, as both are real. Consciousness of oneness and consciousness of multiplicity are two different sides of Self-awareness. One *Brahman* is the basis of innumerable manifestations.

'Unity and multiplicity are the two sides of Brahman. He is the Lord of both, vidya and avidya.'

Work by itself does not lead to salvation, but it prepares our mind for it. If we imagine that we can attain wisdom without such previous preparation, we are mistaken. If we delight only in work and despise wisdom, then too we are mistaken. Both work and wisdom are essential. By work we start our journey; by wisdom, we reach our journey's end.

Ignorance is an essential prerequisite for spiritual life. Man cannot rise to spiritual enlightenment if he has not first become conscious of himself as a separate ego. In spiritual life we transcend this sense of separateness. To reach the higher Self, we must conquer the lower self. Ignorance has its place; without it there is no individuality. But ignorance must be transcended in knowledge.

– S. Radhakrishnan

The terms used in the verses 9-11 for outward activity and inward contemplation are *avidya* and *vidya* respectively. These two terms have been much loosely used even in ancient times. The context here suggests that we take *vidya* to be higher meditation, and *avidya* as selfless dedicated action. They are to be pursued in a happy synthesis. They must be considered as serially connected. Selfless, dedicated work prepares one for contemplation. A contemplative person undertakes *karma* as a sacred, satisfying fulfillment of his spiritual experience.

Without *vidya*, to act in the outer world of *avidya* causes stress. Without knowing the rhythm and harmony of the entire cosmos, to act in the world of multiplicity will only bring about more and more confusion in the mind.

Mortality is the fate of the matter, and not the destiny of the soul. The pot may break, but the space in the pot is neither broken, nor made. The all-pervading space is ever the same. Similarly birth and death, sorrow and joy are all experiences available only to the ego-center. Ego ends where God-experience starts.

– Swami Chinmayananda

In the normal experience of man, work and wisdom come one after the other – not simultaneously. There is always a gap between the two. It is this gap which brings darkness and desolation in life. Verse 9 says that mere activity leads a person to darkness, but mere wisdom leads him to still greater darkness. In spiritual life, there is an endeavour to bridge the gulf between belief and behavior. When a belief is to be translated into behavior, the attempt is to construct a bridge between two points – one of which is fixed and the other is constantly moving. Belief is absolute and therefore constitutes a fixed point. But behavior is relative to situations in life. It is subjected to constant flux, because life itself is in a state of flux. How can one construct a bridge between a fixed point and a constantly moving point? It is to this baffling problem that the Upanishad refers as action leading to deep darkness and wisdom leading to still greater darkness (verse 9).

In verse 11, there is obvious reference to simultaneous existence of work and wisdom, so that there is no question of bridging a gulf.

– Rohit Mehta

12-14 Manifest and Unmanifest

Self has two positions – within nature, and outside nature. These two positions of conscious existence have been called birth and non-birth, *sambhuti* and *asambhuti*. The knot of birth is ego-sense. Dissolution of ego-sense takes us to non-birth. Therefore, non-birth is also called dissolution.

Birth and non-birth are not physical conditions, but soul-states.

Neither attachment to non-birth nor attachment to birth is the perfect way. Each of these tendencies, pursued in harmony with the other, has its own fruit. Non-birth should be pursued as a goal of birth. Birth should be pursued as a means of progress and self-enlargement.

– Sri Aurobindo

To be absorbed in the world around, without understanding the principle at the base of it, is one extreme. To be absorbed in contemplation of the transcendent without regard to the events of the manifest world, is another extreme. Verses 12-14 ask us to lead a life in the manifested world with a spirit of non-attachment. We must live in this world without being choked by it. We must remember that the eternal is the soul of the temporal.

– S. Radhakrishnan

'We take vidya to be higher meditation, and avidya as selfless, dedicated action.
They are to be pursued in a happy synthesis.'

The pair of words used in these verses is unmanifest and manifest. The unmanifest can be understood as the Impersonal God, and the manifest as the Personal God. There is always a controversy regarding the relative merits of worshipping a Personal God, or meditating upon an Impersonal God. Even in the Vedic period, there were personal Gods like Vayu, Agni and Indra; just as these days we have personal Gods like Rama, Krishna, Shiva, Devi, Ganesha, etc. In modern times, the controversy expresses itself as to whether wisdom or worship, *Gyana* or *Bhakti* are supreme. Isa Upanishad says that the controversy is meaningless and baseless. Just as *vidya* and *avidya* are complementary to each other, so are *Gyana* and *Bhakti*. In fact, each in the lap of the other grows stronger and more established.

We can get over the sorrows of death because of our faith and devotion to the Lord with a form; while our evolution can be fulfilled completely as a result of our higher meditation upon the formless Reality.

Sri Ramakrishna's glory was his experience of Self, but his life was devoted to the worship of his beloved Mother Kali. Sri Sankara had a superhuman experience of Self, but he had a staunch faith in the Goddess of Learning, Mother Sharada.

– Swami Chinmayananda

15-18 The Last prayer

THE WORLDS AFTER DEATH

The Upanishad admits three states of the soul in relation to the manifested world:

(i) Terrestrial life by birth in the body
(ii) Survival of the individual soul after death
(iii) Immortal existence beyond birth and death

The Upanishad does not speak expressly of rebirth, but the belief is implied in verse-17. On the basis of this belief, a man may aim at three distinct possibilities after death:

(i) a better life on earth
(ii) eternal enjoyment of bliss in an extra-terrestrial world of light and joy
(iii) merger in the Supreme

REBIRTH

Rebirth is an important intermediate state so long as the soul is in a state of growth and self-enlargement; and has not attained liberation. After liberation, the soul is free. It may still participate in the entire movement and return to birth. But it will do so not for its own sake, but for the sake of others and according to the will of the Supreme Soul.

Rebirth is not an immediate entry after death into a new body. There is an interval in which the soul assimilates its terrestrial experiences. During this interval the soul dwells in states or worlds beyond. These may be favorable or unfavorable. The Upanishadic heavens are states of light; hells are states of darkness.

SURYA AND AGNI

Surya and *Agni*, Sun and Fire are the Upanishadic gods representing Truth and Will. Truth illuminates, Will makes action perfect.

In order to appreciate the relevance of invoking *Surya* and *Agni*, we must understand the Vedic concept of the seven worlds and the Principle of Consciousness they represent.

THE SEVEN WORLDS

Spirit is pure Existence (*Sat*), pure Self-awareness (*Chit*), and pure Self-delight (*Ananda*). *Sat*, *Chit* and *Ananda* seem three different terms, but they are really one. All pure existence is in essence pure Self-conscience; and all pure Self-conscience is in essence pure Self-delight.

Spirit is capable of infinite potential complexity and multiplicity. The working of this potential complexity and multiplicity is called 'creation' or the world of 'becoming'. The power by which spirit brings out of Itself the potential complexities is termed *Tapas*, Force or Energy. This power is also called Will, or *chit shakti*. This Will is inherent both in Being and in becoming. It becomes what it sees and knows. It is expressed as force of its own work; and it formulates itself in the result of its work.

---

*'Surya and Agni, Sun and Fire are the Upanishadic gods representing Truth and Will.
Truth illuminates, Will makes action perfect.'*

- When *tapas* or Will-power dwells upon *sat* or pure existence as its basis, the result is *satyaloka*, or the world of true existence.
- When *tapas* or Will-power dwells upon *chit* or pure awareness as its basis, the result is *tapoloka*, or the world of energy.
- When *tapas* or Will-power dwells upon the delight of being or *ananda* as its basis, the results is *gyanaloka*, or the world of creative delight.

To summarize:
Will power on *Sat* results in *Satyaloka*
Will power on *Chit* results in *Tapoloka*
Will power on *Ananda* results in *Gyanaloka*

In the lower creation also, there are three principles – Matter, Life and Mind. *Sat* or pure existence corresponds to Matter. Will or Force appears as Life. Mind evolves from matter and life. Wherever there is matter, there exists the potentiality of life and mind evolving from matter.

When *Tapas* or Will-power dwells upon Matter as its basis, the result is *Bhurloka*, the material world. When *Tapas* dwells on Life force as its basis, the results *Bhuvahloka*, the world of free vital life. When *Tapas* dwells on Mind, the result is *Suvahloka*, the world of free, luminous mentality.

Between these two creations of three worlds each and linking them together is *Maharloka*, or the world of vast Consciousness. The principle of *Maharloka* is *Vigyana*. *Vigyana* means intuition, revelation and inspiration. It is the vision at once of the essence and the image. It is the Truth. It is represented by *Surya*.

INVOCATION TO *SURYA*

The face of Truth is covered from the view of human Consciousness as with a golden lid. We can see the Truth only if *Surya* works in us to correct our concepts and precepts about ourselves and about the world. For this we must learn to see things as they are; we must see ourselves as we are. Our present action is one in which Self-knowledge and Will-power are divided. We start with a fundamental falsehood that our existence is separate from others. We try to know the relationships between separate beings in their separateness, and we act on the knowledge so formed. The law of Truth will work in us if we see the totality of our existence, containing all others. *Surya* is the Nourisher. *Surya* can transform the divided self-perception and action of Will into an integrated Will and knowledge. He is the sole seer. His unifying vision enables us to arrive at oneness. That intuitive vision of totality – of One in All and All in One – ordains in us the right law of action, the law of Truth.

Truth is revealed to us by *Surya* in two stages. First *Surya* spreads forth its rays. This brings out the truths concealed behind our concepts and precepts. Next, *Surya* gathers its radiant light. By this, we arrive at totality of intuitive knowledge (Verse 16).

Thus, by this action of *Surya*, we arrive at our pure Self-vision. The Upanishad expresses this vision in a brief word '*Soham asmi*, That I am.'

INVOCATION TO *AGNI*

Surya, as we have seen, represents divine light of Consciousness. Likewise, *Agni* represents divine force of Consciousness, or Will-power. The prayer to *Agni* completes the prayer to *Surya* (verses 17-18).

As in knowledge, so in action, unity is the true foundation. We normally act within the limits of our ego, without knowledge of the integrated working of the total universe. Our actions are therefore fragmented and full of errors. But behind all our errors there is a secret Will, which attracts us towards Love and Harmony. This Will is represented by *Agni*, the force of Consciousness.

IMMORTAL LIFE PRINCIPLE

Life is the Principle from which Light and Will emerge. It is said that *Vayu* (Life Principle) brings down *Agni* (Will-power) from *Surya* (Light of Consciousness). The Vedic gods are a parable of human life emerging from the Supreme and lifting itself to the Supreme.

Life, body, action and Will – these are our instruments. Matter supplies us with the body. But it is only a temporary knot of our movement. It dissolves into ashes as soon as it is thrown aside by life-principle. Therefore, the body is not ourselves, but only an outer tool. Immortal man must not identify himself with the body.

'Mind evolves from matter and life. Wherever there is matter, there exists the potentiality of life and mind evolving from matter.'

The Life Principle in us is immortal. It is superior to the principle of birth and death. At first it may appear that birth and death are attributes of life, but it is not really so. Birth and death are processes of Matter, of the body. The Life Principle is not formed or dissolved in the formulation or the dissolution of the body. Life forms the body, it is not formed by the body. Life is the thread upon which the continuity of our successive bodily existences is arranged. Life dissociates itself with the perishable body and carries forward the mental being upon its onward journey.

WILL POWER

The journey of life consists of a series of activities continued from one life to another. But the presiding god of these activities is not Life Principle; it is Will. Will is the effective power behind the act. It is the energy of Consciousness. This Will is present in all states – conscious, subconscious and super-conscious; physical, vital and mental. However, it becomes active only when it emerges in the mind. It uses the mind to direct human activities towards the goal of the individual.

In man, use of Will is imperfect because man's memory is limited. We remember very little of what we have done in the past. The Upanishad solemnly invokes the Will to remember all the past deeds. Instead of being carried from life to life in a crooked path, as by winds, it will then be able to proceed more and more in a straight and ordered series. Eventually, the mental Will, *kratu*, becomes what at present it only represents – the divine Will, *Agni*.

What is divine Will? In divine Will, Consciousness and Energy, Knowledge and Force are one. It knows all manifestations, all things that take birth in the worlds. It has therefore been called *Jataveda* in Kena Upanishad. It knows them in their relationship to each other, in their aim and method, in their unity with all and differences from all. It is this divine Will which conducts the universe. Its being, its knowledge, its actions are inseparable from each other. What it is, it knows. What it knows, that it does and becomes.

In contrast, human Will is an impulse, ignorant of its real aim. This is because we are not conscious of our Self, our true being. We are guided only by our ego. What we are, we do not know. What we know, we cannot do. Knowledge is real and action is in harmony with true knowledge only when our Will, knowledge and action are one movement. This change happens when human Will approximates more and more to divine Will.

The sign of right action is increasing and finally complete submission of individual Will to divine Will.

Knowledge of the Lord as the One in All and submission to the Will of the Lord in right action are the two keys of the divine gates, the gates of Immortality. This is a fitting close to Isa Upanishad.

– Sri Aurobindo

To eminent commentators like Sri Sankara and others, the verses represent a prayer of a man on his deathbed. Orthodox Hindu families repeat these stanzas in the ears of a dying person. However, the dying entity meant here is the ego-center. It is the last prayer of an active spiritual seeker in his meditation seat, when he is shaking-off his last vesture of ego, which is lingering to veil the Self in him.

The world of matter is like a brilliant and shining golden lid, which veils the Truth. The seeker is knocking at the door of Truth and demanding the Nourisher (*Pusan*, Sun) to open the door and reveal Itself in all Its spiritual glory. And what right does the seeker have to make such a demand? Because he is himself a practitioner of Truth (verse 15).

In Vedic times, *Agni* was an important God. Verse 16 is an invocation to *Agni*, the Fire God. Wealth in this verse refers to spiritual wealth.

The phrase '*Soham* or I am also That' signals the end of ego. When ego is ended, the roar is not 'I am He' but 'He am I'. 'He' refers to *Brahman* or Cosmic Consciousness (verse 16).

A Self-realized man will face death as happily as he would face life. To him, death is not a tragic culmination of mortal existence, but a joyous beginning of an immortal existence. Therefore, he says that his life should merge with the all-pervading Air (Life Principle), and that his body should go back to dust (verse 17).

'Human Will is an impulse, ignorant of its real aim. This is because we are not conscious of our Self, our true being. We are guided only by our ego.'

Namaskar (salutation) is not merely an elaborate demonstration of physical prostration. It is a sign of spiritual humility and the beginning of a new awareness (verse 18).

– Swami Chinmayananda

Here (verse 16) Sun, who is the giver of all light, is used as the symbol of Infinite, giver of all wisdom. The light of Truth helps to discriminate between the real and the unreal. The knowledge thus gained convinces the person who is praying that he is one with the Supreme; that there is no difference between himself and the supreme Truth. Or, as Jesus Christ said: "The Father and I are One".

Verse 17 is often chanted at the hour of death. It reminds one of the perishable nature of the body and the eternal nature of the soul. When a clear vision of the distinction between the two dawns in the heart, then all craving for physical pleasures drops away. One can then say: 'Let the body be burnt to ashes, and let the soul attain its freedom.'

– Swami Paramananda

Verse 15 contains a very inspiring idea. It says that the face of Reality is covered with a golden veil. Spiritual experience is a process of uncovering. The veil, being golden, so fascinates and attracts us that we are unwilling to remove the veil. But who has put this golden veil over the face of Truth? The veil is indeed cast by thought. Thought or mind has woven it out of beautiful material supplied to it by its own accumulated background. The material for the veil has been drawn from the realm of continuity. Reality, however, is Timeless and outside the stream of mind's continuity. When the veil of mind's projections is removed, then there stands the *Supreme Spirit*, in all Its majesty.

– Rohit Mehta

More commentaries appear on pages 216-217.

– Editor

'There is no difference between a man and the Supreme Truth; or, as Jesus Christ said: The Father and I are One.'

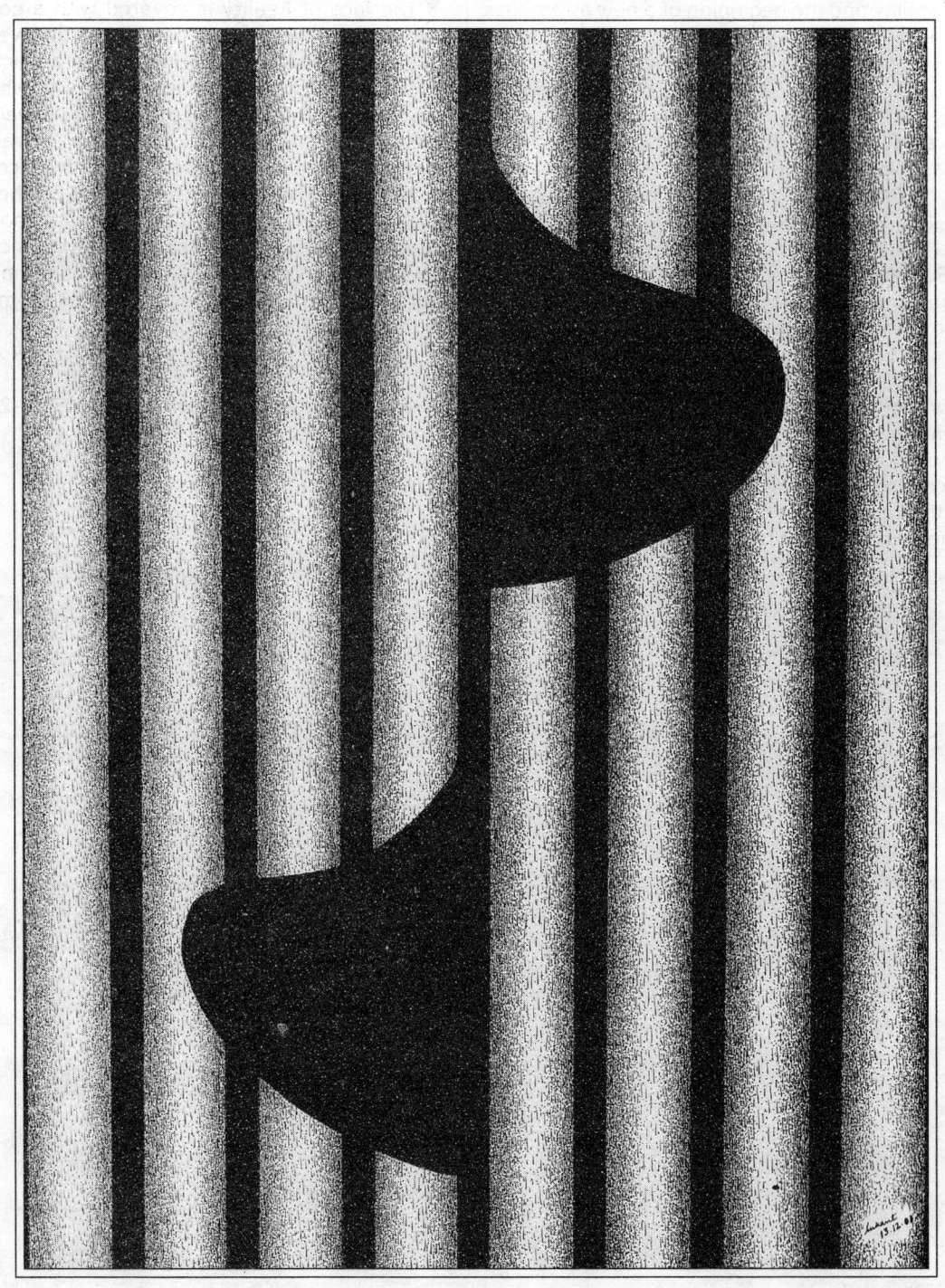

Katha Upanishad

Dialogue with Death

OVERVIEW

Katha Upanishad starts with the story of a young boy, Nachiketa, first questioning his father about a certain ritual of mistaken charity; and then persuading Lord of Death, Yama, to explain the mystery of death.

We fear death because we do not know what happens after death. Knowledge about death, however, can be gained only when our mind is interested in such knowledge. This requires a life-style of righteousness, meditation, self-discipline, self-enlargement and divine grace. Self-enlargement means to equate self-interest with universal good.

Yama explains that the word 'death' applies to human body, but not to Self. He then elaborates on the nature of Self. It is Immortal and Imperishable. It is the prime mover of both man and universe. It exists both within and without. When realized within, It is a source of happiness. When realized without, It is perceived as a great power which governs the world. It is imperceptible to the senses; It can be perceived only in meditation. Its awareness makes a person fearless. The Upanishad uses the metaphor of air, fire, sun, tree and match-sticks to illustrate various aspects of Self, or Atman.

An important theme of Katha Upanishad is that Self is both Immanent and Transcendent. It is summarized in the declaration: 'This, verily, is That'. 'This' signifies the Self which sustains man and the world, That signifies the transcendental Hereafter.

COMMENTARIES

The commentators quoted here are: Swami Chinmayananda, Swami Sivananda, Swami Sarvananda, Swami Paramananda, Dr. S. Radhakrishnan, Paul Deussen, Klaus G. Witz, Sri Aurobindo and Rohit Mehta. The chapter title is from Commentary by Swami Chinmayananda.

KATHA UPANISHAD
Dialogue with Death

Peace Invocation

CHAPTER 1
In search of secrets of Death.. 259

1.1, 1-6	A teenager knocks at the door of Death
1.1, 7-29	From relative to Absolute in three steps
1.2, 1-6	Two paths to choose from
1.2, 7-14	Preparation for knowledge of Self
1.2, 15-17	The mystic word *Aum*
1.2, 18-22	Self never dies, says Lord of Death
1.2, 23-25	Self is realized through divine grace
1.3, 1-9	Analogy of a chariot
1.3, 10-17	Progression to the Supreme

CHAPTER 2
This, verily, is That 280

2.1, 1-4	Self is realized by looking inwards
2.1, 5-15	This, verily, is That
2.2, 1-5	Power behind Life-breath and senses
2.2, 6-12	Theory of rebirth
2.2, 13-15	Light of all lights
2.3, 1	Tree of Creation
2.3, 2-3	Fear of the Supreme
2.3, 4-5	Levels of Consciousness
2.3, 6-13	Yoga, the highest state
2.3, 14-18	From mortal to Immortal

1 In search of secrets of death

SIMPLIFIED SYNOPSES

1.1, 1-6
A teenager knocks at the door of Death

'Human beings are like corn that grow, decay, die and are born again.'

We all fear death because we erroneously think that death marks the end of life. Katha Upanishad uses a very imaginative story, *Katha*, to dispel our ignorance. Nachiketa, a young boy of 13, is the hero of the story. Like teenagers of modern times, he feels confused by acts of seemingly meaningless rituals and mistaken charity performed by his father, Vajashrava. Rather than accepting these disinterestedly, he questions his father about their efficacy; but he does so very discreetly and respectfully. Unfortunately, instead of explaining the situation to his inquisitive son, Vajashrava retorts in anger, almost with words we hear so frequently from stressed people these days: 'Go to Hell (Death)'. Nachiketa takes his father's words literally, and sets out to meet Yama, Lord of Death. Instead of being upset over his father's angry outburst, Nachiketa is filled with Faith – that the incident is a blessing in disguise, that it is intended to serve some profound purpose.

Nachiketa's journey to meet the Lord of Death should not be construed as a sign of childlike ignorance. On the contrary, Nachiketa assures his repentant father that he should not feel sorry for unintentionally giving away his son to Death. Human beings, says Nachiketa, are like corn that grow, decay, die and are born again.

We all are so frightened of death that we avoid even thinking of the day when death will inevitably knock at our doors. Young Nachiketa is different. He goes to meet Death at its doorstep, and waits there patiently for three days. These, according to one commentator, symbolize the three disciplines – physical, mental and spiritual – which are essential to conquer the fear of death.

1.1, 7-29
From relative to Absolute in three steps

'Is there anything of man that remains after death?'

In Vedic culture, a guest was revered as a representative of God. Yama, Lord of Death therefore apologizes for the unintended neglect of his guest Nachiketa and offers him three boons. These represent three stages in man's ascent from the relative to the Absolute.

Nachiketa's first wish is for harmonious relationships in life on earth. As his second wish, Nachiketa wants to know the significance of an important ritual of fire-sacrifice and how it leads to heavenly pleasures. Yama readily grants both these wishes. As his third wish, Nachiketa wants to know if there is anything of man that exists after death? If yes, what is it? Yama is hesitant to reveal the secret of death. He offers many temptations of material pleasures to Nachiketa, but Nachiketa declines them all. He is determined to know the Truth. Impressed by his determination, Lord of Death accepts Nachiketa as a student and begins his discourse.

Harmonious interpersonal relationships, desire for knowledge and determination to remain on the spiritual path of righteousness are the three steps in evolution of man from the relative to the Absolute.

1.2, 1-6 Two paths to choose from	Yama begins his discourse by outlining two paths that confront a man in all challenging situations. These have been called *Shreya* and *Preya*, the Good and the Pleasant. *Shreya* is the path of righteousness, *Preya* is the path of convenience. A man of spiritual wisdom chooses the Good; a man of spiritual ignorance opts for the Pleasant, unmindful of the fact that all worldly pleasures are transient. Nachiketa had asked about the great 'Hereafter'. Yama indicates to him that it is along the path of Good that the knowledge of the great 'Hereafter' can be attained.
1.2, 7-14 Preparation for knowledge of Self	Yama then explains to Nachiketa that spiritual knowledge is not attainable by logic, rituals or ceremonies. Instead, it requires a good teacher. Self is seated in the depth of our inner being and therefore It cannot be perceived by the senses. However, it can be realized by practice of deep meditation, *Adhyatma Yoga*. It also requires *Vigyana*, power to discriminate between the material and the spiritual. Once a person has realized Self, he rises above joy and sorrow. Self is beyond vice and virtue, beyond cause and effect, beyond past and future.
1.2, 15-17 The mystic word *Aum*	Strictly speaking, Self cannot be given any name, because the Infinite cannot be bound by any finite word. However, for the sake of convenience, the Vedas use the syllable *Aum* to refer to Self. *Aum* is indeed a symbol of *Brahman*, the Absolute, the Supreme, the ultimate support of the cosmos. He who knows the significance of the syllable *Aum* has all his desires satisfied; he rises above all desires.
1.2, 18-22 Self never dies, says Lord of Death	Self is beyond birth and death. It is imperishable and eternal. It is the most subtle and the greatest of all that exists. Its glory is experienced only when one has rid oneself of all desires and sorrows, and also disciplined one's senses and mind. Self is beyond dualities. All opposites merge in Self. This fact is expressed through the language of contradictions used so frequently in the Upanishads. For example, though sitting, It travels far. Though lying, It goes every where. Being without a body, It pervades everything.
1.2, 23-25 Self realized through divine grace	Individual efforts – like study of scriptures, listening to spiritual discourses and intellectual reasoning – are not sufficient to attain knowledge of Self. Self-realization comes only through divine grace. This in turn requires righteous conduct and a disciplined life-style.
'For Self, death is like sauce.'	Self has been earlier described as the support of the whole universe and the source of all joy. Verse-25 describes Self as that into which everything dissolves. This view is expressed through the metaphor of a meal. For Self, all men – priests or warriors – are like food and death is like sauce.

'Shreya is the path of righteousness, Preya is the path of convenience.'

1.3, 1-9
Analogy of a chariot

'A man's journey of life is like a moving chariot.'

Self within and without – Self in man and Self that pervades the universe – are one and the same. They are like shadow and light. This is the belief held by all persons – those in quest of spiritual knowledge as well as those who have faith in performance of rituals – says the Upanishad.

A man's journey of life is compared to a moving chariot. Self is the Lord of the chariot, human body is like the chariot, intellect is the driver, mind is the reins, senses are the horses, and sense objects are the roads. A man's Self, intellect, mind, body and senses must act in complete harmony and mutual co-operation if the chariot of his life is to move smoothly and reach its desired destination. It is the intellect, acting through the mind as reins, which keeps the horselike senses under control and on the right track.

Intellect (*buddhi*) is influenced by spiritual awareness (*vigyana*), ability to discriminate between the material and the spiritual. Without spiritual awareness, a man's mind and senses remain very sensitive to ups and downs of life. It is deep-rooted spiritual awareness, which helps a man's intellect to discipline his mind and senses, and thereby reach the goal of life. This goal, says the Upanishad, is to transcend rebirth.

1.3, 10-17
Progression to the Supreme

'Arise, Awake, Understand what life means.'

Pursuit of spiritual knowledge is like climbing a ladder – from the most gross to the most subtle, from the relative to the Absolute, from the lowest to the highest. The senses represent the lowest rung of the ladder. Cosmic Person or Consciousness is like the highest rung. The steps in descending order – from top to bottom – are as follows:

Supreme Being (Pure Consciousness, *Purusha*)
Unmanifested (*Avyakta*)
Universal Self (*Mahan Atman*)
Individual Self (*Atman*)
Intellect (*Buddhi*)
Mind (*Manas*)
Objects of senses (Material World, *artha*)
Senses (Physical body, *Indriyas*)

A climb to the highest state requires progressively controlling the senses by the mind, mind by the intellect, intellect by individual Self, and individual Self by universal Self.

Verse 14 contains the inspirational words, which Swami Vivekananda used for the motto of Ramakrishna Mission: 'Arise. Awake'. The verse also asks us to understand what life means, and not to waste it. We are advised to remain firm in our chosen faith, despite its being sharp as a razor.

Self cannot be perceived by the senses because It does not have any sensory attributes like sound, touch, form, taste or smell. It is imperishable and eternal, without a beginning and without an end. It is unchanging. It is beyond the manifest. Knowledge of Self makes a person free from fear of death.

The concluding verses glorify the legend of Nachiketa.

'Without spiritual awareness a man's mind and senses remain very sensitive to ups and downs of life.'

Translated Text

Peace Invocation

Om.
May He protect us both (teacher and pupil).
May he nourish us together.
May we work jointly with great energy.
May our study be vigorous and fruitful.
May we not have any dispute.

Om. Shanti. Shanti. Shanti.
Let there be Peace, Let there be Peace, Let there be Peace.

CHAPTER 1

Section 1

Once, desirous of heavenly pleasures, Vajashrava performed a sacrifice and distributed gifts. He had a son, named Nachiketa. **1**

When the gifts were being distributed, reverential faith (*shraddha*) filled the heart of Nachiketa who was still a boy. He thought... **2**

'(These old cows) have drunk water (almost) for the last time, eaten grass (almost) for the last time, have yielded all their milk and are barren. The worlds attained by him who gives such presents will indeed be joyless.' **3**

Nachiketa asked his father:

"Father to whom will you give me away?"
He repeated this for a second time, and a third time... (Enraged, the father) replied "To Death shall I give you away." **4**

(Nachiketa thought):
'Among many (sons and disciples), I rank in the top few; at times I rank in the middle (meaning I am never a third-rate). What is the objective Yama (Lord of Death) is fulfilling through me?' **5**

(Seeing his father in a repentant mood, Nachiketa said): "Remember, how our forefathers acted. Likewise, remember others. (In any case), mortal beings decay and die like corn and they are born again like corn." **6**

(Between the previous and the next verse, there is a dramatic silence. This is to be supplemented from our knowledge of the same story as narrated in the *Brahmana* portion of the Veda. Nachiketa comforted his father and persuaded him to live up to his words – even though these were not intended. The young boy then entered the domain of death. There, he had to wait for three nights without any food. To atone for his neglect of hospitality, Lord of Death, Yama offered the boy three boons.

"Nachiketa asked his father: "Father to whom will you give me away?"..."

A guest is like god. A learned guest visiting a house is respected like fire. A fire should be quenched. Therefore, O Son of Sun, bring water. **7**

The foolish man in whose house a learned guest remains without food loses every thing – all his hopes, expectations, sons and cattle, as also merits gained by the company of holy men, good words and good deeds. **8**

Yama said:

O learned One, O Revered guest, Salutations to you. As you have remained in my house without food for three nights, please choose three boons, and bless me. **9**

Nachiketa said:

O Death! May Gautama, my father be free from anxious thoughts (about me). May he be kind and free from anger towards me. May he recognize me and greet me when I am sent back by you. This is the first of the three boons that I choose. **10**

Yama replied:

Through my favor, Uddalaka Aruni (your father) will recognize you and be affectionate, like before. When he sees you released from the mouth of death, he will be free from wrath, and will sleep peacefully at night. **11**

Nachiketa said:

In heaven, there is no fear. You (Death) are not there, nor is there fear of old age. Having crossed both hunger and thirst, and being above grief, one rejoices in heaven. **12**

O Death! You know the fire sacrifice which leads to heaven. Explain it to me, as I am full of faith. How the dwellers in heaven gain immortality? This I choose as my second boom. **13**

Yama said:

Knowing well as I do that fire which leads to heaven, I shall describe it to you. Listen to me, O Nachiketa. That fire is the means of attaining endless worlds, and also their support. It is seated in the cavity (of the heart). **14**

Death then explained to him the ritual of that fire sacrifice which energizes all the worlds – what bricks are required for the altar, how many, and how they are to be placed? Nachiketa repeated back all that was explained to him. Then Death, being pleased with him, again spoke. **15**

Being delighted, the magnanimous Yama said to him (Nachiketa):

I give to you another boon. This fire sacrifice will be named after you. Take also this garland of many colors. **16**

"May Gautama, my father be free from anxious thoughts (about me)."

Whosoever performs this Nachiketa fire sacrifice three times, associating himself with the "three" (father, mother, guru) and fulfilling the "three duties" (study of scriptures, sacrifice, charity); he overcomes birth and death. When he has understood this worshipful, shining, *Brahma*-born Fire, and also realized it, he attains eternal peace. **17**

He, who knows and meditates on threefold Nachiketa fire and performs the Nachiketa fire sacrifice three times, throws off the chains of death; He goes beyond sorrow and rejoices in heaven. **18**

This is your Fire, O Nachiketa, which leads to heaven, and which you have chosen as your second boon. People will call this fire after your name. O Nachiketa, now you choose your third boon. **19**

(Verses 16-19 are regarded by some as later additions.)

There is this doubt in regard to a man who is said to be 'dead'. Some say, 'he exists'; and some say, 'he does not'. I would like to be instructed by you on this subject. Of the boons, this is the third. **20**

Yama replied:

Even the gods (Devas) have doubts on this point from ancient times. So subtle is this truth that it is not easy to understand. Choose another boon, O Nachiketa. Do not press me. Release me from this. **21**

Nachiketa said:

You say that even gods have doubts about this, and that it is not easy to understand. I cannot find a better teacher than you. Therefore, no other boon can be equal to this one. **22**

Yama said:

Ask for sons and grandsons who shall live a hundred years. Ask for herds of cattle, elephants, horses and gold. Choose a vast territory on earth, and ask for as long a life as you like. **23**

If you think of any other boon as equal to this, choose that in addition to wealth and longevity. Be the ruler of this vast earth. O Nachiketa, I shall make you the enjoyer of all material desires. **24**

Whatever objects of desires are difficult to attain in this world of mortals, ask for them as you wish. Here are lovely maidens with their chariots and musical instruments. Indeed, the likes of them are not obtainable by mortals. Be served by these, as I give them to you. O Nachiketa, do not ask regarding death. **25**

Nachiketa said:

O Lord of Death, all these are fleeting and they also wear out the vigor of senses in man. Besides, life is of short duration. So, you keep the chariots, the dance and the music. **26**

"O Nachiketa, I shall make you the enjoyer of all material desires. Do not ask regarding (the secrets of) death."

Man cannot be satisfied by wealth. How can we enjoy wealth when we see you (we have fear of death)? We shall live as long as you endure. Therefore I desire only that boon (which I have chosen). **27**

Having come close to the imperishable immortality, and having reflected on (the reality behind) beauty and pleasures of senses, no mortal being in the world below will like to live a long life. **28**

O Death, tell me that about which everyone has doubts, about 'the Great Hereafter'. Nachiketa does not opt for any other boon except that which resolves the mystery (of what happens after 'death'). **29**

Section 2

(Yama said):

(There are two paths): One is Good, the other is Pleasant. These two, having different end-results, chain a man. Blessed is he who chooses the Good alone. He who chooses the Pleasant, loses his true aim. **1**

Both the Good and the Pleasant approach a man. A wise man examines them thoroughly, and discriminates between them. He prefers the Good to the Pleasant; but a foolish man chooses the Pleasant for the sake of worldly well being. **2**

O Nachiketa, after wise reflection, you have renounced all that is pleasant or seems to be pleasant. You have not taken the path of wealth on which many mortals sink to ruin. **3**

Wide apart and leading in opposite directions are these two – ignorance and wisdom. I know you, Nachiketa, to be eager for wisdom, since many objects of pleasure did not distract you. **4**

Foolish men – dwelling in ignorance, but imagining themselves to be wise and learned – go round and round in crooked ways, like the blind led by the blind. **5**

The inevitability of death is not apparent to an ignorant man, who is childish and fooled by the glamour of wealth. 'This is the only world, there is no other', he thinks, and thereby falls under my control. **6**

Many are not privileged even to hear about It (Self, *Atman*). Many are not able to comprehend It even after hearing about It. Wonderful is the teacher who is able to teach (about Self). Wonderful is the student who comprehends Self, as taught by an able teacher. **7**

When taught by a man of inferior understanding, this *Atman* (Self) cannot be known correctly, as It is thought of in many ways. There is no way (to know It) unless It is taught by a preceptor who knows It as himself. Self is more subtle than the subtlest, and beyond argument. **8**

"Both the Good and the Pleasant approach a man. A wise man prefers the Good to the Pleasant."

Knowledge about *Atman* is not attainable by logic. It is truly known only when taught by a wise teacher. O Nachiketa, you can attain that knowledge, because you are fixed in Truth. May we have an inquirer like you. **9**

Know that wealth is transitory. That which is eternal cannot be obtained by things that are transitory. Nachiketa fire has been propitiated by me, but I have attained only long-lasting (not eternal) sovereignty. **10**

The Imperishable cannot be attained by the perishable. This shows that no amount of rituals and ceremonies can lead to the Eternal. Although the Nachiketa fire sacrifice may bring results which seem eternal to mortals because of their long duration, yet they too must come to an end.

O Nachiketa, you have seen the fulfillment of all desires, the basis of the universe, the endless fruits of sacrificial rites, the other shore where there is no fear, the greatness of fame, and the wide support. Yet, being wise, you have rejected all of them, with firm resolve. **11**

The wise know God, who is beyond Time, through meditation (*Adhyatma Yoga*). Seated in the innermost recess, hidden in the cavity of the heart, dwelling in the depth of inner being, It is difficult to perceive. He who knows It, is liberated from the fetters of joy and sorrow. **12**

A mortal rejoices when he has heard and fully grasped this, and realized the subtle virtuous Self through discrimination; because he has obtained That which is the source of all joy. I think such an abode is wide open for Nachiketa. **13**

Nachiketa asked:

Tell me That which you see beyond vice and virtue, beyond cause and effect, beyond past and future. **14**

Yama replied:

That Word which all the Vedas glorify, which all the austerities (*tapas*) proclaim, desiring which people practice *Brahmacharya* (self-control in pursuit of knowledge), that word I will briefly tell you. It is *Aum*. **15**

This Word (*Aum*) is indeed *Brahman*. This Word is indeed the Supreme. He who knows this Word obtains whatever he desires. **16**

This support (*Aum*) is the best. This support is the highest. He who has realized this support becomes great in the world of *Brahma*, *Brahma-loka*. **17**

Self is never born, nor does It die. It did not spring from anything, nor did anything spring from It. It is unborn, eternal, everlasting, primeval. It is not slain even when the body is slain. **18**

If a slayer thinks that It slays, or if the slain thinks that It is slain, both of them do not know. It neither slays, nor It is slain. **19**

"Self is never born, nor does It die. It is not slain even when the body is slain."

Self is subtler than the subtle, greater than the great. It dwells in the heart of each living being. He who is free from desire and grief, whose mind and senses are tranquil, he beholds the glory of Self. **20**

Though sitting, It travels far. Though lying, It goes everywhere. Who else, besides me, is fit to know that God, who is both joyful and joyless. **21**

The wise, who knows Self as bodiless, seated in perishable bodies, great and all pervading, does not grieve. **22**

Self cannot be attained by study of scriptures, nor by intellectual power, nor by frequent hearing of It. It is attained by him alone whom It chooses. To such a person Self reveals Its true nature. **23**

He who has not turned away from evil conduct, whose senses are not controlled, who is not tranquil, whose mind is not at rest, he can never attain this Self even by knowledge. **24**

For Self, priesthood and nobility are like food, and even death is like a condiment. Who can know where is this mighty Self? **25**

Section 3

There are two who enjoy the fruits of good deeds (*Karma*) in the world - (*Paramatma* and *Jivatman*). Both dwell in the cavity of the heart, the seat of the Supreme. The knowers of *Brahman* call them shadow and light; (they are called) so also by householders, who perform five fire-sacrifices or three Nachiketa fire-sacrifices. **1**

May we master that Nachiketa fire-sacrifice which is a bridge for those who perform sacrifice. May we also know the highest Imperishable *Brahman* for those who wish to cross over to the other shore, which is beyond fear. **2**

Know *Atman* (Self) as the lord of the chariot, and the body as the chariot. Know also intellect as the driver and mind as the reins. **3**

Senses are the horses; sense-objects are the roads. *Atman*, when united with the body, senses and mind, is the enjoyer; so the wise declare. **4**

He who is without discrimination and whose mind is always undisciplined, his senses are out of control; like the wicked horses of a charioteer. **5**

But he who is full of discrimination (*Vigyana*) and whose mind is always disciplined, his senses are manageable, like the good horses of a charioteer. **6**

He who does not possess discrimination, whose mind is undisciplined and always impure, he does not reach that goal (of liberation), but falls again into realm of birth and death (*samsara*). **7**

But he who possesses right discrimination, whose mind is disciplined and always pure, he reaches that goal, from which he is not born again. **8**

"Know Atman (Self) as the lord of the chariot, and the body as the chariot.
Know also intellect as the driver and mind as the reins."

The man, who has a discriminating intellect as his driver, and a disciplined mind as the reins, he reaches the end of the journey, the Supreme abode of the All-pervading. **9**

Beyond the senses are sense objects; beyond sense objects is the mind, beyond the mind is the intellect, beyond the intellect is the great Self. **10**

Beyond the great Self (*Mahat*) is the Unmanifest (*Avyakta*). Beyond the Unmanifest is the Supreme Being (*Purusha*): Beyond Supreme Being, there is nothing. That is the end; that is the final goal. **11**

This *Atman*, hidden in all beings, does not reveal (Itself to all). It is seen only through sharp and subtle intellect. **12**

A wise man should control speech (senses) by mind, mind by intellect and intellect by the great *Atman*. He should submerge the great *Atman* in the tranquil *Paramatma*. **13**

Arise. Awake. Having attained the great (human life), understand what it means. Like the sharp edge of a razor, the path is difficult to cross and hard to travel – thus say the wise. **14**

Knowing That – which is without sound, without touch, without form, without decay, without taste, without smell, eternal, without a beginning and without an end, unchanging, beyond the unmanifested – man is freed from the mouth of death. **15**

That intelligent person, who has heard and reflected on the legend of Nachiketa, as told by Lord of Death, is glorified in *Brahma-loka*, world of *Brahma*. **16**

He, who with devotion recites this highest secret of immortality before an assembly of pious men, or at the time of rituals (*shraddha*) for the dead, gains everlasting rewards. He gains everlasting rewards. **17**

"A wise man should control speech (senses) by mind, mind by intellect and intellect by the great Atman."

Focussed Commentaries

1.1, 1-6 A teenager knocks at the door of Death

Western scholars have described Katha Upanishad as 'a perfect specimen of mystic philosophy and poetry of ancient India.' It has received great respect for its teachings on the theme of death.

Men live in constant fear of death. Prolongation of earthly existence cannot free men from the fear of death. Men must know the secret of death. In Katha Upanishad, *Yama* the Lord of Death, himself is the teacher; and Nachiketa, a young determined inquirer, is the disciple.

The Upanishad uses a story, *katha* to impart its teachings, and hence is named Katha Upanishad.

The story begins with one Vajashrava performing what is known as *vishvajit* sacrifice, with the sole purpose of getting heavenly rewards. The name Vajashrava means one who has become famous by distributing food. Now, distribution of food is a symbol! – it indicates performance of religious practices as ordained by the scriptures. So, Vajashrava represents traditional religion, which requires observance of certain rituals to get heavenly rewards.

Vajashrava had a son named Nachiketa. The word Nachiketa means, something unperceived, something beyond the normal range of perception. So, Nachiketa symbolizes that aspect of religion, which goes to the core of things, and is not concerned with external practices.

— *Rohit Mehta*

Vajashrava : One who has become famous by distributing food in charity.
Nachiketa : One who does not know, but seeks to know.

Vajashrava was a man of charity. He was engaged in performance of a great sacrifice called *vishvajit*, in which the performer has to give away in charity all that he possesses.

Reverential faith: (*Sanskrit, Shraddha*). Sri Sankara's commentary explains the term as "an unswerving faith in the words of a teacher, teachings of scriptures, or dictates of one's own Self." In the present context, the word refers to Nachiketa's concern for the welfare of his father (1.1, 2).

The worlds... joyless: We find here the expression of a revolt against mechanical performance of rituals for gaining heavenly pleasures, as reflected in the poor quality of cows given away as gifts to priests (1.1, 3).

'Father, to whom will you give me away?': Nachiketa is offering himself at the altar of his duty towards his father. Or, may be, it was an intelligent hint suggesting criticism of his father's miserliness.

To Death shall I give thee: This was a harmless but angry outburst, like: "Go to Hell!" (1.1, 4).

What objective Yama is fulfilling? Nachiketa knew that his father never meant what he said. So he started wondering what is the great mission that is to be fulfilled by the Lord of Death through him? (1.1, 5).

Mortal beings decay and die like corn: This verse is one of the earliest declarations of the theory of transmigration in Vedic thought. It says that present life is only an incident in the eternal existence of the Soul, like seasonal seeds. Generations come to earth, feed themselves, grow to maturity, breed their kind, and die away, yielding their place to the next generation (1.1, 6).

Remember how our forefathers acted: This is a very significant advice. In moments of moral and ethical challenges in our lives, it is not always possible for us to keep our cool and retain our sense of judgement. Here is a practical tip for such situations. Try to recollect what great men of past or present did under similar circumstances.

— *Swami Chinmayananda*

According to Sri Sankara, Nachiketa reminds his father that neither his ancestors nor his contemporaries broke their word. After all, human life is transitory. Like a blade of grass man dies and is born again. Death is not the end; rebirth is a law of nature. The life of vegetation, on which all other life depends, passes through the seasonal round of birth, growth, maturity, decay, death and rebirth. The unity of all life suggests the application of this process to

---

'In moments of moral and ethical challenges, try to recollect what great men of past or present did under similar circumstances.'

human beings also. So, the son persuades his father to keep his word and send him to the abode of *Yama*, the Lord of Death.

– *S. Radhakrishnan*

Seeing his father giving useless cows as gifts, Nachiketa understood that his father had no intention to comply in spirit with the rules of the sacrifice, i.e. to give away all his possessions. So he thought that it was his duty as a son to save his father from a terrible sin.

– *Swami Sarvananda*

The idea of sacrifice is to give freely for the joy of giving, without asking anything in return. Nachiketa observed that the animals his father was gifting were worthless. As a boy of tender age, Nachiketa had no right to question his father's actions. Yet he was impelled by sudden awakening of his higher nature. He reflected: "By gifting these useless cows, my father cannot gain any merit. If he has vowed to give away all his possessions, then he must also give me away." Therefore, anxious for his father's welfare, he approached him gently, and reverently. His father, conscious that he was not making a true sacrifice, first tried to ignore the boy's question. Later, irritated by his son's persistence, Vajashrava said in anger: "I shall give thee to *Yama*". The fact that anger could rise so quickly in his heart proved that Vajashrava did not have a proper attitude as a sacrificer. A sacrificer must always be tranquil, uplifted, and free from ego.

– *Swami Paramananda*

Instead of giving away things that were of any worth, Vajashrava was giving away cows that were not of any use. The Upanishad says that at that time *shraddha* entered into the heart of his son Nachiketa. I would not translate this word *shraddha* to you, it would be a mistake. It is a wonderful word to understand, and much depends on it. The boy wanted to solve the problem which was in his mind – the problem of death. The solution could be obtained only by going to the house of Death, and the boy went. There he was, brave Nachiketa, waiting at the house of Death for three days and he obtained what he desired. What we want is this *shraddha*. What makes the difference between man and man is this *shraddha*, and nothing else. What makes one man great and another weak and low is this *shraddha*.

– *Swami Vivekananda,*
(Selections from Complete Works)

1.1, 7-29 From relative to Absolute in three steps

The visible world is a conglomeration of actions and reactions. Everything is interdependent. Also, everything is relative. We live in a world of interdependence and relativity. We mistake a part for the whole; a localized experience for all-in-all. This is a sign of spiritual ignorance. By repeated births and deaths, we gain spiritual wisdom and move from the relative to the Absolute. Katha Upanishad, like other Upanishads, is an exposition of the various stages of the ascent of man from the relative to the Absolute. The teachings of *Yama*, the Lord of Death, to Nachiketa, a young lad of 12, are all descriptions of three stages in the rise of the soul to the Absolute.

The first stage is mistaking the external for the ultimate. This is represented by ritual of sacrifice by Vajashrava. Man's conception of after-death experiences, of life in the heaven, is only a magnified and modified form of the pleasures of senses that we have in this earthly world. Vajashrava aspired for a heaven of pleasures of senses; and for this he performed a mechanical act of pretended charity. He was not prepared to part with everything he had.

Nothing can be so painful to human ego as to part with its own pleasures. It wants to seek satisfaction of the senses both here and hereafter. If the scripture says that charity is a means to gain a place in the heaven, the ego makes a counterfeit charity by giving what it does not need. You have given in charity, and yet you have not lost anything. This was the kind of mistaken charity carried out by Vajashrava, when he gave away old cows as gifts to the priests.

The Upanishad wants to lift the human mind – exemplified by Vajashrava – from a state of spiritual ignorance to wisdom. For this, it creates in the form of a story, another mind – that of Nachiketa, a young boy and son of Vajashrava. Also, as death is the greatest teacher, Lord of Death is made the great guru of Katha Upanishad.

The desire of Nachiketa to search for Truth is the second stage in the ascent of the mind from the relative to the Absolute.

The third stage is the temptations offered by *Yama* to Nachiketa, his determination to remain on the spiritual

---

'Nothing can be so painful to human ego as to part with its own pleasures.'

path, and finally, the revelation of knowledge of the Absolute, by *Yama* to Nachiketa.

Nachiketa had gone knocking at the door of death – instead of death knocking at his door. And he waited at the door of death, even though no hospitality was given to him. Nachiketa had to wait without food for three days before he could meet *Yama*. This symbolizes the threefold discipline of Yoga – an essential aid in spiritual quest – the physical, the psychological and the spiritual. Nachiketa does well in the practice of these disciplines. So *Yama*, the Lord of Death awards him three boons.

FIRST WISH

Nachiketa's first wish relates to life on earth. Nachiketa thinks that the most important element for happiness in life is harmonious relationships at home. Every relationship has two components – external behavior and internal intent. In life, we tend to give more importance to external behavior of the person we are dealing with, and overlook his genuine intents. So Nachiketa was concerned about the angry behavior of his father. *Yama* assured him that a father will always love his son, despite occasional outbursts of anger. In fact, *Yama* went a step further when he said that in the presence of his son, he (father) will "sleep peacefully at night" (1.1, 10-11).

SECOND WISH

The exemplary mind of Nachiketa wants to enlarge itself from interpersonal relationships to cosmic interdependence. In many philosophies, Fire is considered very sacred, a symbol of universal Energy. The very first mantra of Rg Veda is an invocation to Fire, *Agni*; and Vedas prescribe many fire-based sacrificial rites. Also, a sacrificial rite is considered a symbol of give-and-take, a symbol of interdependence between man and cosmic powers. So, as his second wish, Nachiketa asks for knowledge about the sacrificial fire. *Yama* gladly imparts the same to Nachiketa. Pleased with his student's spirit of enquiry, *Yama* even names the sacrificial fire rite after Nachiketa.

THIRD WISH

The first two questions of Nachiketa relate to the physical and the psychological aspects of life, the third relates to the spiritual. He wants to know from *Yama*, the Lord of Death, what 'death' really means? After a person is said to be 'dead', is there or is there not anything of him that exists? (1.1, 20)

It is to be noted that the question is not about life after death. Nachiketa already knows that like corn, mortal beings decay, die and are born again (1.1, 6). The question is about *Atman* – its existence or otherwise. It is also to be noted that Nachiketa is a young boy. It is Youth, and not Old Age that is enquiring about death.

Yama was reluctant to reveal the secret of Death. He placed before Nachiketa many temptations of earthly pleasures – such as would have broken the determination of anyone. But Nachiketa was above all temptations. He was also aware that a man cannot really enjoy wealth when death is in sight. So he told *Yama*: "You keep the chariots, the dance and the music... just tell me the mystery of Death" (1.1, 26-29).

Yama had not come across any inquirer of such integrity and determination as Nachiketa. He finally relented and prepared his disciple to receive the great secret, step by step.

– *Rohit Mehta*

A GUEST IS LIKE GOD

Just as fire is appeased by water, so a guest should be welcomed with appropriate offerings. The word for fire used here is *Vaisvanara*, the universal fire, which affirms the unity of all life. The guest comes as an embodiment of the fundamental oneness of all beings.

– *S. Radhakrishnan*

According to the ancient Vedic ideal, a guest is a representative of God. He should be received with due reverence and honor, specially a learned person or an ascetic. Anyone who fails to show proper hospitality to a holy guest invites misfortune on himself and his household.

– *Swami Paramananda*

A guest is *Atithi Narayana*, or an embodiment of God. Hospitality towards guests is one of the five *yagyas* (sacrifices) which a householder ought to perform.

– *Swami Sivananda*

'We give more importance to external behavior of the person we are dealing with, and overlook his internal intents.'

Some people ask: 'How could a mortal child enter the domain of Death?' This is, after all, a story. It is meant to bring a great student to a great teacher. Nachiketa was keen to learn about the principle of life, and chain of birth and death. And there could be no better teacher, than Lord Death.

In the Vedic period, worship of fire was very popular. The term *Vaisvanara* has been used as many as sixty times in Rg Veda to indicate fire in all its aspects. The comparison of a guest with fire is therefore very appropriate. Even in modern societies, a cultured and educated guest is always respected and revered.

We see Lord Death himself apologizing for his unintentional neglect, and begging the young guest to accept his apologies in the form of three boons! If only men in power were to be so sincere in following the laws, others could not dare to break them.

– Swami Chinmayananda

NACHIKETA PREFERS WISDOM TO WEALTH

Nachiketa has no doubt about birth and death. In verse 6, he has already said that mortal beings die and are born again like corn. His doubt is about the condition of the liberated soul. Even the Buddha was repeatedly put the question: 'Does the *Tathagata* survive after death, or does he not survive?' The Buddha responded to this question only with complete silence.

The gods cannot have doubts about life on earth. It is about the state of liberation that there is uncertainty.

The temptations offered by Lord of Death to Nachiketa are similar to those offered to Gautama the Buddha, by Mara. Both rejected the promises of transient pleasures in order to obtain true wisdom. There is, however, also a difference. While *Yama* eventually reveals the liberating truth to Nachiketa, Mara is the evil one, the tempter.

In verse 26, Nachiketa portrays the human aspiration to reach the eternal. The verse also suggests the Buddhist view that everything that exists is fleeting.

Man cannot be satisfied by wealth: *Na vittena tarpaniyo manusyah*. The material guarantees of human security are fragile. What is the value of wealth or life, as both are impermanent? So long as death is in power, we cannot enjoy wealth or life; for fear of death destroys the zest for living. So Nachiketa asks for knowledge of Self, *atma-vigyana*, which is beyond the power of death.

Nachiketa says: "We shall live as long as *Yama* endures." In other words, he is certain of his continuance in this cosmic cycle presided over by *Yama*. What Nachiketa is doubtful about is in regard to the state of liberation. *Yama* says even the gods have doubts about this state (1.1, 27).

Anyone who knows the joys of immortal life cannot be attracted by an earthly life of passion and speed. One who has a foretaste of immortality will not find pleasures in earthly delights.

– S. Radhakrishnan

The third boon asked by Nachiketa concerning knowledge of Hereafter was one, which could be granted only to those who are freed from all mortal desires and limitations. Therefore *Yama* first tested Nachiketa to see whether he was ready to receive such knowledge. The boy proved his strength and worthiness by remaining firm on his resolution to know the great secret of life and death.

– Swami Paramananda

Nachiketa wants to know whether there is any immortal entity – Soul, *Atman* or *Brahman* – which exists separate from body, senses, mind and intellect? He wishes to have the knowledge of the real nature of *Atman*, the Absolute.

The story apart, death indeed holds the secret of life. Meditation on death helps us to realize that physical life is transient and different from Consciousness, which is our real Being. Moreover, from the very beginning of human history, the fear of death has been one of the strongest motive powers of religion.

The real Upanishad begins from the second section. It constitutes *Yama's* sacred discourse on the supreme principle of life.

– Swami Sarvananda

The third wish concerns not so much the knowledge of life after death, because this is already presumed as certain. On the contrary, it is directed towards the knowledge of *Atman* as the true essence of man and along with it, towards eternal release.

– Paul Deussen

'Fear of death destroys the zest for living. So Nachiketa asks for knowledge of Self, which is beyond the power of death.'

1.2, 1-6 Two paths to choose from

Yama starts his teaching by saying that at every challenge in life, a man is confronted with two paths: the path of Good (*shreyas*), and the path of Pleasant (*preyas*). The path of Pleasant is a mixture of opposites, like pleasure and pain. However, the path of Good is not a mixture of good and evil; it is a path of Absolute good, a path of righteousness. A person of spiritual wisdom always opts for the path of Good.

Nachiketa has asked about 'the Great Hereafter'. *Yama* indicates to him at the very beginning that it is along the path of Good that the secret of the 'the Great Hereafter' can be found. *Yama* also congratulates Nachiketa for discarding the path of Pleasant, and accepting the path of Good (1.2, 1-6).
— *Rohit Mehta*

Sri Sankara suggests that *avidya* or ignorance is concerned with the Pleasant, and *vidya* or wisdom with the Good.

According to Plato, there are two directing principles in each of us. We follow their guidance, wherever they may lead. One is an innate desire for pleasure, the other is an acquired judgement which aspires for excellence. At times these two principles are in harmony, and at times they are at feud within us.

He who is filled with selfish desires and attracted by worldly possessions becomes subject to the law of *karma*, which leads him from birth to birth. And so, he is under the control of *Yama*, Death.
— *S. Radhakrishnan*

There are two paths – one leading to God, the other leading to worldly pleasures. They conflict like light and darkness. One leads to the imperishable spiritual realm; the other to the perishable physical realm. Both confront a man at every step of life. The discerning man chooses the good and attains the highest. The ignorant man prefers that which brings him immediate pleasures, but he misses the true purpose of his existence.
— *Swami Paramananda*

That which is 'good' need not necessarily be always 'pleasant', although there are pursuits which are both 'good' and 'pleasant' at the same time.

To the perfect seeker of the Absolute, both the paths of Good and Pleasant are bondage indeed.
— *Swami Chinmayananda*

1.2, 7-14 Preparation of knowledge of Self

Next, *Yama* explains that knowledge about *Atman* is not attainable by logic (1.2, 9). It requires a wise teacher and a willing student. Likewise, rituals also cannot lead to knowledge of *Atman* (1.2, 10-11). *Atman* can be known only through deep-meditation, *Adhyatma Yoga* (1.2, 12-13).
— *Rohit Mehta*

Vedic scriptures declare that no one can impart spiritual knowledge unless he has himself attained Self-realization. What is meant by Self-realization? It means knowledge about Self, *Atman*, based on direct perception. Very often, many good teachers have no formal learning. But their character is so shining that one learns merely by coming in contact with them. Conveying spiritual wisdom does not depend upon words only. It is the life, the illumination of the teacher, which counts. A Self-realized teacher cannot be found easily, and even with such a teacher, knowledge of Self cannot be gained unless the heart of the disciple is open and ready for Truth. Hence, *Yama* says both the teacher and the taught must be wonderful (1.2, 7).

Knowledge regarding Self cannot be known through reasoning. It is attained only in that state of Consciousness which transcends reasoning.
— *Swami Paramananda*

Only he who has realized his oneness with *Brahman* should teach about Self. He alone can teach with serene confidence and conviction.

Self is unknowable by argument, as It is very subtle, and beyond the reach of the senses. It can be apprehended only by intuition.

It is not only the pupil who is in search of a teacher, but the teacher is also in search of pupils.

RITUALS CANNOT LEAD TO THE ETERNAL

Some translators (e.g. Max Muller and Hume) attribute verse 1.2, 10 to Nachiketa. This is unlikely, as Nachiketa has not yet performed the sacrifice known by his name.

'Knowledge regarding Self cannot be known through reasoning.
It is attained only in that state of Consciousness which transcends reasoning.'

Sri Sankara attributes these words to *Yama*, who says that he has attained the sovereignty of heaven through the sacrificial fire; but his sovereignty will endure only as long as the universe lasts. The universe, with all that it contains, will be absorbed into the Eternal at the end of the cosmic day.

Verse-11 suggests the contrast between the Vedic ideal of heaven and the Upanishadic ideal of life eternal. The fulfillment of all desires can apply only to immortal *Brahman*. It is the support of the world, the Ultimate.

Verse-12: We have to get behind the senses, the mind and the intellect to realize Self. The Buddhists look upon every creature as an embryo of the Buddha, *Tathagata-garbha*, because every creature has the potentiality to become the Buddha. When we get into the inner being of the spirit, we are in immediate relationship with the Eternal.

Adhyatma means pertaining to Self. This is distinct from *Adhibhautic*, pertaining to material elements, and *Adhidaivic*, pertaining to deities. *Adhyatma Yoga* is yoking with one's inner Self. It is a practice of meditation – a quiet, solitary, sustained, effort to apprehend the Truth.

Verse-12 contains *Yama's* answer to the question raised earlier by Nachiketa about the mysterious divine Being behind the phenomenal world (1.1, 29). It is hidden in the depth of one's own being. It is difficult to access by ordinary means, but it is open to spiritual contemplation. *Yama*, in different ways and phrases, brings out the impenetrable mystery of the inmost Reality.

Verse-14: *Beyond cause and effect*: Another translation is beyond what is done or not done. A knower of Self is not vexed with the thought: Why have I not done the good, or why have I done the evil?

Beyond past and future: The eternal is a 'now', without a duration.

Nachiketa asks for an account of that deepest Reality – rid of all extraneous externalities – which is deeper than all the happenings of time.

– *S. Radhakrishnan*

Yama praises Nachiketa (verse 11). When all earthly pleasures – as also knowledge of all realms and their enjoyments – were offered to him, he cast them aside. He remained firm in his desire for Truth alone.

ADHYATMA YOGA

The scriptures give three progressive steps in spiritual attainment. First, the aspirant must hear about Truth from an enlightened teacher. Next, he must reflect on what he has heard. Finally, by constant practice of discrimination and meditation, he must realize the Truth. With Self-realization comes the fulfillment of all desires (1.2, 13).

– *Swami Paramananda*

Verses 7-11 state that Supreme Reality is amazing and difficult to understand. The importance of a real guru is explained. *Yama* accepts Nachiketa as a disciple and compliments him. The student has excelled the Master in respect of *vairagya* or renunciation.

– *Swami Chinmayananda*

Verse-13: *Virtuous Self*... The Sanskrit word is *Dharmyam*, connected with *Dharma*, or righteousness. The world is upheld by *Dharma*. *Brahman* is the very center of *Dharma*. Why does a man lead a life of righteousness? Because he wants to attain *Brahman*, Self. Therein alone he can rejoice. The essence of *Brahman* is Bliss.

In *Brahman-Atman*, there is neither virtue nor vice; neither cause nor effect, neither past nor future. All these are mental creations. Even Time is a mental creation. Time is caused by succession of events. In *Brahman*, everything is 'present' or 'now' only. *Brahman* is Eternity. He is beyond Time. (1.2, 14)

– *Swami Sivananda*

Verse-13: *Adhyatma Yoga*, according to Sri Sankara, is withdrawal of the mind from sense objects and its concentration on Self. Its practice requires merging speech in the mind, mind in Knowledge-Self (*gyana atman*), Knowledge-Self in Great Self, (*mahan atman*) and Great Self in Tranquil Self (*shanta atman*).

– *Klaus G. Witz*

'The scriptures give three progressive steps in spiritual attainment:
Know the Truth, reflect on It and experience It.'

1.2, 15-17 The mystic word *Aum*

What name can man give to God? How can the Infinite be bound by any finite word? Yet, it is very difficult for mortals to think or speak of anything without calling it by a definite name. Knowing this, the sages gave the name *Aum* to the Supreme. The first letter 'A' is the mother sound. It is the natural sound uttered by every creature when the throat is opened; no sound can be made without opening the throat. The last letter 'M' is spoken by closing the lips. It terminates all articulation. When one carries the sound from the throat to the lips, it passes through the sound 'U'. These three sound, therefore cover the whole field of verbal articulation. Their combination is called *Akshara*, or the imperishable Word. It is the Word, which was in the beginning. It corresponds to the Logos of Christian Theology. It is used in Vedic scriptures to designate the Absolute. He who meditates on It and grasps Its full significance, realizes the glory of God. He has all his desires satisfied, because God is fulfillment of all desires.

– Swami Paramananda

The final goal and the home of man – the ultimate in evolution – is a world of true and vast existence. It is called *Brahma Loka*. It is beyond birth and death.

– Sri Aurobindo

1.2, 18-22 Self never dies, says Lord of Death

Verse 1.2, 20: Self, *Atman* is subtler than the most subtle because it is the invisible essence of everything. It is greater than the greatest because It is the sustaining power of the whole universe.

Although this *Atman* dwells in the heart of every living being, it cannot be perceived by the senses. A finer spiritual sight is required for its perception. Also, the heart must be pure and free from selfish desires and the mind must be withdrawn from all external objects. Only then it is possible to perceive that effulgent *Atman*.

– Swami Paramananda

Verses 18-19 are identical with verses 2.19-2.20 in the Bhagavad Gita, with slight alteration. The Bhagavad Gita contains the essence of the Upanishads.

– Swami Sivananda

Verse 1.2, 21: By these contradictory predicates, the impossibility of conceiving *Brahman* through empirical determinations is brought out.

Brahman has both the aspects of peaceful stability and active energizing. In the former aspect He is *Brahman*; in the later, *Ishvara* is an active manifestation of Absolute *Brahman*.

– S. Radhakrishnan

1.2, 23-25 Self-realized through divine grace

Verse 23: No one can realize the Truth without illumination, and no one can have illumination without a thorough cleansing of one's moral being. Until our mind and heart are effectively purged, we can have no clear vision of God. It follows that man's effort is essential to grasp Divine grace and profit by It. It is open to us to accept or reject Divine grace.

– Swami Sivananda

Verse 25: Life and death are both like food for Self. Just as the light of the great sun swallows all the lesser lights of the universe, all the worlds are lost in the effulgence of Self.

– Swami Paramananda

1.3, 1-9 Analogy of a chariot

'Two' in verse 1.3,1 signifies the Higher Self and the lower self, the individual soul (*Jivatman*) and the Supreme Self (*Paramatma*). The significance of verse-2 is: May we acquire the knowledge of *Brahman* in both manifested and unmanifested form. He is manifested as the Lord of sacrifice for those who follow the path of rituals. He is Unmanifested Supreme Being for those who follow the path of wisdom.

The other shore is the realm of immortality. It is said to be beyond fear, because disease, death and all that mortals fear cease to exist there.

It is believed by many that these two verses (1.3,1-2) are a later interpolation.

The driver of a chariot must possess a thorough knowledge of the road. He must also understand how to handle the reins and control the horses. Only then he will drive safely to his destination. Similarly, in our

---

'The Infinite cannot be bound by any finite words.
Yet, for convenience, the sages gave the name Aum to the Supreme.'

journey of life, our mind and our senses must be wholly under the control of our higher discriminating faculty, our inner Self. We can hope to reach our goal only when all our forces – Self, discriminating faculty, mind, senses and body – work in unison (1.3, 3-9).

— Swami Paramananda

In verse-2, two ways of crossing the river of *samsara* (world) are indicated: performance of Vedic sacrifices, which leads to the heaven of gods, and knowledge of *Brahman*. The first prepares the way for the second on the path of gradual liberation, *kramamukti*.

The chariot, with its horses, represents the psycho-physical vehicle in which Self rides. Mind holds the reins. It may either control or be dragged by the senses. The concept of Yoga – derived from the root *yug*, to yoke, to harness, to join – is connected with the symbolism of the chariot. *Yoga* is complete control of different elements of our nature – psychical and physical – and harnessing them to the highest end.

— S. Radhakrishnan

The two are *Paramatma* and *Jivatman*, Supreme Soul and individual Soul. The former is the light, the later is the shadow. The former is ever free, the later is bound. Hence the simile of light and shadow is used here.

The ego in man, the shadow, is called *Jivatman*. The light that causes the shadow – the God Principle in us – is called *Paramatma*.

Enjoyment of fruits of action is the lot of *Jivatman* alone. *Paramatma* is neither a doer, nor an enjoyer (1.3, 1).

— Swami Chinmayananda

Verses 1.3, 1-2

This beautiful analogy of shadow and light is quoted very often. Pure *Atman*, Self, is neither the enjoyer nor the doer; It is always the silent witness. It appears as the enjoyer when, out of ignorance, it is identified with the mind, senses and the body. Attributes of the soul (*Atman*) then seem to be transferred to mind-body, and those of mind-body to the soul. Through this mutual superimposition, the insentient mind-body is misunderstood as Self.

How can the Supreme Self be said to enjoy the rewards of good deeds? It is above all deeds and their fruits. This should be taken only as a metaphorical expression.

These two mantras may be later additions.

— Swami Sivananda

VIGYANA IN KATHA UPANISHAD

Verses (1.3, 3-9) compare a man to a chariot that is moving over the land. Self, *Atman*, is the Lord of the chariot, standing behind the charioteer. Body is the chariot itself. Inner intelligence (*buddhi*) is the driver, mind is the reins, senses are the horses, and sense objects are the paths over which the horses run.

The text contrasts the person that is endowed with discrimination (*vigyana*) and has his mind and senses under control, with one who is without *vigyana* and is at the mercy of the vagaries of his mind and the demands of his senses. It is *vigyana* or deep-seated inner Infinite Consciousness, which leads and enables the individual to live his life with senses, mind and passions held in control (1.3, 6). Without this, senses and mind will become a plaything of the forces to which one is subjected in life. It is such deep-seated higher awareness, which ultimately enables an individual to transcend rebirth (1.3, 8-9).

In the words of Sri Ramana Maharishi, "*Vigyana* is that tranquil state of existence-consciousness which is like the waveless ocean or motionless ether". It exists naturally in everyone – though perhaps only a little developed. More developed *Vigyana* implies increased spiritual insight.

Vigyana is a "state" or "level" of consciousness, and not consciousness "of" something.

— Klaus G. Witz

1.3, 10-17 Progression to the Supreme

Sense objects are superior to senses, because without sense objects senses are of no value. Mind is superior to sense objects, because unless the objects affect the mind, they cannot influence the senses. Intellect is superior to mind, and intellect is governed by Self. Beyond Self is the undifferentiated creative energy called *Avyakta*, and above *Avyakta* is the Supreme Self, *Purusha*. There is nothing beyond

---

'In our journey of life, our mind and our senses must be wholly under the control of our higher discriminating faculty, our inner Self.'

Purusha. That is the goal, the highest abode of Peace and Bliss.

– *Swami Paramananda*

Avyakta: It is *Prakriti*, Nature, the universal Mother, out of which all existences emerge through the influence of *Purusha*.

Mahat, *Avyakta* and *Purusha* are terms also used in Sankhya philosophy. The account in the Upanishads, however, is different from the classical Sankhya in many respects.

Purusha is the subject side of that within which are both subject and object, the light of unity and the darkness of multiplicity. We do not reach it until the end of the cosmic day. So we can say that there is nothing beyond *Purusha*.

Verses 10-11 contain a hierarchy of principles or beings. We are asked to pass from the outward nature to the one world-ground, *avyakta*; and from it to the spirit behind, *Purusha*. Between the two, *Purusha* and *Prakriti*, a certain priority is given to *Purusha*, because it is the light of *Purusha's* Consciousness that is reflected on all objects of the manifested universe – high or low, gross or subtle. From the waking world – where the senses reveal their objects – we pass to the dream world where *manas* or mind operates independent of the senses. From this we pass to the world of dreamless sleep where the unmanifest *Prakriti* becomes the divine mother. But the bliss and freedom of dreamless sleep lacks illumination. For that we must get to *Purusha*, who is the source of all.

The wise disciple discriminates between the unchanging light, *Atman*, and the changing objects of the senses and the mind – which are illumined by *Atman* Itself. The technique for attaining spiritual consciousness requires the soul (*Atman*) to stand clear of all thoughts and objects – and enter into its own depth. *Atman* is not an object of any sort; it is the eternal subject. We hear, touch, see, feel, and think by *Atman*. By withdrawing from all outward things, by retreating into the depths of our soul, we find the Infinite. There, Self is raised above all empirical concepts of sound, touch, forms, etc.

"Let it be plainly understood that we cannot return to God unless we enter first into ourselves. God is everywhere but not everywhere to us. There is only one point in the universe where God communicates with us; and that point is the center of our own soul. There He waits for us; there He meets us; there He speaks to us. To seek Him therefore we must enter into our own interior." (Bishop Cillathorne quoted by S. Radhakrishnan)

– *S. Radhakrishnan*

This seems to be the end of the Upanishad. Subsequent sections are perhaps later additions.

Verses 10-12 provide an aspirant with a line of thinking, which he could pursue during deep meditation upon *Brahman*.

In the language of the Upanishads, 'beyond' and 'within' indicate the comparative subtleties between two or more factors. Subtleties are measured by greater pervasiveness of one factor over the other.

Avyakta is the unmanifest world, something like an embryo in the mother's womb. It may be noted here that *avyakta*, *pradhana*, *mula-prakriti*, *avyakrti* and *maya* are synonymous terms.

In these two verses, the teacher shows the process of discrimination by which one attains knowledge of Self. Beginning with the senses, he leads up to the less and less gross, until he reaches that which is the subtlest of all, Supreme Being.

– *Swami Chinmayananda*

Intellect is superior to mind, because it is subtler than the mind. Mind provides inputs to the intellect, which discriminates and decides. Intellect is like the Prime Minister, mind is like a Head Clerk. Or, intellect is the judge; mind is the advocate.

The great Self is also called *Hiranyagarbha*, cosmic intelligence, sum total of all individual souls. *Hiranyagarbha* is the 'golden egg', the first-born of *Avyakta*, the unmanifested or primal matter. Beyond *Hiranyagarbha* is *Avyakta*. Beyond *Avyakta* is *Purusha*. *Purusha* is the subtlest of them all. Beyond *Purusha*, there is nothing.

– *Swami Sivananda*

'God is everywhere but there is only one point where He communicates with us; and that point is our own Self.'

② This, verily, is That

SIMPLIFIED SYNOPSES

2.1, 1-4
Self is realized by looking inwards

These verses bring out the contrast between senses and Self, as also between spiritual ignorance and wisdom. Senses are inherently outgoing. Therefore, a sensual person is preoccupied with pursuit of only external pleasures, unmindful of the fact that such pleasures are always transient. This is a sign of spiritual ignorance. To such a person, death is a frightening reality. A spiritual person, however, is aware of the real power behind the senses – the eternal Self within. It is Self that makes the mind and the senses function in various states of consciousness – waking and dream. Occasionally turning the senses away from the external and meditating on the inner Self is a sign of spiritual wisdom.

2.1, 5-15
This, verily, is That

Readers will recall Nachiketa's third question: What is That which exists after death? This question is now answered by Yama, Lord of Death.

'This Self within is That which exists even after death.'

This Self, *Atman* – which sustains life and makes the senses perform their respective functions – is also *That* which exists even after death. It is Pure Consciousness. It dwells within, without and beyond. Life Principle (Air), Energy (Fire) and Light (Sun) are its three important expressions. It lies concealed in the body like fire in fire-sticks or like embryo in a womb; and yet it is all-pervading. This is That from which the Sun arose and into which it will eventually dissolve.

This Self is both immanent and transcendent. There is no difference between this which pervades the universe and That beyond which there is nothing. It is both the Creator and His Creation. Untouched by psychic and physical processes, It is like smokeless fire.

This Self is the Lord of everything – past and future. Never-changing, It remains the same today and tomorrow.

The text uses a simile of water to urge perception of unity in multiplicity. A person who fails to see the unity behind multiplicity is like rainwater falling on a mountain-top and running down the rocks on all sides. In contrast, a person who sees oneness of divine presence in every being is like pure water being poured into pure water.

The maxim 'This, verily, is That' is analogous to 'That thou art' of Chandogya Upanishad.

2.2, 1-5 Power behind Life-breath and senses	In another simile the human body in which Self resides is compared to a city having eleven gates, or openings. This Self which resides within, is also That which resides in everything outside – as brightness in sun, as air in space, as fire in a sacrifice, and as a guest in a house. This Self is That which pervades all living beings, physical objects and natural phenomena. This Self is the power behind the life-breath and the senses. Without this Self, the body ceases to function and disintegrates.
2.2, 6-12 Theory of rebirth	Unlike the body, which is perishable, Self is Immortal and Imperishable. This Self is Pure Consciousness, which remains active even when we are in a state of deep sleep. It is the support of the whole universe. There is nothing beyond It. When a person dies, his body perishes but Self assumes another form. Present deeds determine the next form, but Self remains unchanged. This important fact is illustrated by three beautiful metaphors of fire, air and sun. Fire assumes the form of what it burns. Air assumes the form of what it fills. Likewise, it is the same One Self in all beings, though it assumes many different forms. Sun is the power behind the eyes, but it is not contaminated by any impurities seen by the eyes. Likewise, Self is the essence of all beings, but it remains untouched by their deeds or conditions.
2.2, 13-15 Light of all lights	Self is the changeless base of the ever-changing world. A Self-realized person is eternally happy. Self being Itself the light of wisdom, does not need any other light to illumine It. The section ends with a memorable verse. The brightness of the self-effulgent Self is not dependent on the sun, the moon, the stars or the lightening; on the contrary, it is Self which lights them all.
2.3, 1 Tree of Creation	The whole creation is compared to an inverted tree – the roots facing upwards for spiritual nourishment and the branches facing downward to enjoy the material world.
2.3, 2-3 Fear of the Supreme	Self, *Brahman* exists both within and without. When realized within, It is perceived as the source of all happiness. When realized without, It is perceived as the great power, which governs all the cosmic phenomena and objects.
2.3, 4-5 Levels of Consciousness	Human life, says the Upanishad, is an opportunity to realize Self, and thereby be liberated from cycle of birth and death. The Upanishad also talks about different levels of Consciousness – the physical world, the world of forefathers, the world of angels, and the highest world of Pure Consciousness, *Brahma Loka*. Perception of Self becomes clearer as we ascend to higher levels of Consciousness. Reflection in a mirror, seeing a dream, reflection in water and contrast between light and shadow are cited as examples of vision with increasing degree of clarity.
2.3, 6-13 Yoga, the highest state	Emphasizing the distinction between senses and Self, the text says that senses are the most gross expression of Consciousness. Mind, intellect, Self, and Unmanifest are increasingly more subtle expressions of Consciousness. Beyond the Unmanifest is the all-pervading, imperceptible Cosmic Being (*Purusha*). He cannot be perceived by the senses. He is revealed only through meditation.

'Human life is an opportunity to realize the Self.'

The state of Consciousness in which He is revealed, is called the highest state, the state of Yoga. It is a state which is achieved by keeping the senses under control and making the mind still. It is a state in which the physical world dissolves, and in its place arises another world of Supreme Bliss. The Upanishad cautions that practice of Yoga should not be confused with a life-style of laziness.

Self cannot be realized as an object visible to the eyes, describable by speech or thinkable by the mind. It is realized only through strong faith in Its existence.

**2.3, 14-18
From mortal to Immortal**

A mortal being becomes Immortal when the knots which tie his heart to the physical world are cut asunder. This state can be achieved even as one lives a worldly life. Self of such a person leaves the body at the time of death through the crown of the head.

Self is metaphorically described to be of the size of a thumb and residing in the heart. This metaphor is useful in concentrating the mind on Self during meditation and isolating It as the highest goal, distinctly separate from the body. Simile of pith and reed is used to describe the practice of such meditation.

'The state of Consciousness in which He is revealed is called the highest state.'

Translated Text

CHAPTER 2

Section 1

The self-existent (*Brahman*) made the senses outgoing? For this reason man sees the external, but not the inner *Atman* (Self). However, some wise men who desire immortality, see *Atman* within, with eyes turned away (from the external).
1

The childlike (ignorant) pursue external pleasures, so they fall into the snares of widespread death. The wise, however, seek life eternal; and in their search for it, they are not tempted by fleeting things.
2

One perceives form, taste, smell, sound and sensual enjoyments by That (Self). To That, nothing is unknown. This, indeed, is That (which you wanted to know).
3

That, by which one perceives in dream state as well as in waking state, after knowing that great all-pervading *Atman*, the wise do not grieve any longer. **4**

He who knows this *Atman* – the cause of all enjoyments, the sustainer of life, the lord of the past and the future, always very near – he fears no more. This, verily, is That (about which you had put a question).
5

It (Self) was born through *Tapas* even before the primordial waters. It dwells in the cavity of the heart and looks forth through beings. This, verily, is That. **6**

It (Self, *Aditi*) expresses Itself as life-breath.(*Prana*). Having entered into the cavity of the heart, it exists in the body of five elements as the power behind the senses (called gods). It appears as if 'born'. This, verily, is That.
7

It is the omniscient *Agni* (Fire) hidden in fire-sticks, like the embryo well preserved by a pregnant woman. It is worshipped daily by seekers of wisdom, as also by performers of sacrificial rites. This, verily, is That.
8

That from which the sun rises, and That into which it merges, on That all the gods depend. No one ever goes beyond That. This, verily, is That.
9

That which is here (in the visible world), the same is there (in the invisible). What is there, the same is here. He goes from death to death who sees the two (*Brahman* and the world) as different.
10

By mind alone can That (*Brahman*) be attained. There is no difference between the two (*Brahman* and the world). He, who sees them as different, goes from death to death.
11

Purusha (Self), of the size of a thumb, resides in the middle of the body as the lord of the past and the future. He who knows It fears no more. This, verily, is That.
12

"There is no difference between the two (Brahman and the world).
He, who sees them as different, goes from death to death."

That *Purusha*, of the size of a thumb, lord of the past and the future is like a flame without smoke. It is the same today, and the same tomorrow. This, verily, is That. **13**

Rain water falling on top of a mountain runs down the rocks on all sides. Similarly, he who views things as different (overlooking their underlying unity), runs after them in all directions. **14**

O Gautama (Nachiketa), as pure water poured into pure water becomes one, so also the Self of an illumined knower (becomes one with the Supreme). **15**

Section 2

This unborn, even-minded (Self) resides in the city (body) of eleven gates. A man who meditates on It grieves no more. Freed from ignorance, he attains liberation. This, verily, is That. **1**

It dwells in the bright heaven as sun. It dwells in space as air. It is the fire in the sacrificial altar. It dwells in a house as a guest (*atithi*). It dwells in men, in gods, in sacrifice, in sky. It is all that which is born in water, in earth, in sacrifice, in mountains. It is true and great. **2**

It is that which sends the in-breath (*Prana*) upward, and throws the out-breath downward. All the senses (gods) worship It, the adorable *Atman*, seated in the heart. **3**

When this *Atman* that dwells in the body, goes out from the body, what remains then? (Nothing remains). This, verily is That. **4**

No mortal being lives by the incoming breath (*Prana*) or by the outgoing breath (*Apana*). He lives by something else on which these two depend. **5**

O Gautama, I shall now explain to you the secret of the eternal *Brahman*, and what happens to Self (*Atman*) after death. **6**

Depending upon their deeds and knowledge, some enter a womb to have a body, and some go into immovable forms (like plants). **7**

Purusha, who is awake while we are asleep, shapes our objects of desires (into dreams). That is Pure Consciousness. That is *Brahman*. That is also said to be Immortal. On That rests all the worlds. None can go beyond That. This, verily, is That. **8**

Just as fire, after it has entered the world, though one, assumes different forms according to what it burns; so also *Atman*, though one within all living beings takes different forms according to what It enters. It also exists outside them. **9**

Just as air, after it has entered the world, though one, assumes different forms according to what it fills; so also *Atman*, though one within all living beings, takes different forms according to what It enters. It also exists outside them. **10**

"As pure water poured into pure water becomes one, so also the Self of an illumined knower."

Just as sun – the eye of the whole world – is not contaminated by external impurities seen by the eye; so also *Atman* – the innermost essence of all beings – is not contaminated by external sorrows of the world. It is beyond them. **11**

That one Ruler, the soul of all beings, makes Its one form manifold. The wise who perceive It as seated within, to them belongs eternal happiness; and to none else. **12**

It (Self) is that which is Eternal among the ephemeral, Consciousness among the conscious. Though One, It fulfils the desires of many. The wise who perceive It as seated within, to them belongs eternal happiness; and to none else. **13**

The wise perceive It as indescribable and as highest Bliss. They wonder: 'How shall I know It? Does It shine (by Its own light), or does It shine by another (reflected) light?' **14**

There, the sun does not shine, nor the moon, nor the stars, nor the lightening, much less this fire. When It shines, everything shines after It. By Its light, all is lighted. **15**

Section 3

This ancient Ashwattha (*Pipal*) tree has its roots above, and branches (spread) below. That (root) is, verily, Pure. That is *Brahman*. That alone is called the Immortal. All the worlds rest in That. None can transcend That. This, verily, is That. **1**

This whole universe evolved from *Brahman* (Consciousness) and it vibrates as *Prana* (energy). *Brahman* is a great terror, like an uplifted thunderbolt. Those who know That become immortal. **2**

From fear of It Fire burns, from fear of It Sun shines; from fear of It *Indra*, *Vayu* and Death, the fifth, perform their respective functions. **3**

If one is not able to know It here in this life, before the death of the body, then he has to take birth again in the created worlds. **4**

(*Brahman*) is seen within one's intellect as (one sees oneself) in a mirror. It is seen in the world of forefathers, as (one perceives oneself) in dreams; in the world of *gandharvas* (divine nymphs) as one's reflection is seen in water; and in the world of *Brahma* as light and shade. **5**

Knowing that nature of the senses is distinct (from Self), that they originate separately (from various subtle elements); and that their rising and setting is also separate; a wise man does not grieve. **6**

Beyond the senses, is the mind; beyond the mind, is the intellect; beyond the intellect, is the great *Atman*; beyond the great *Atman*, is the Unmanifest. **7**

Beyond the Unmanifest is the All-pervading and imperceptible (*alingah*) Being (*Purusha*). By knowing Him the mortal is liberated and attains immortality. **8**

"There, the sun does not shine, nor the moon, nor the stars, nor the lightening, much less this fire. When It shines, everything shines after It. By Its light, all is lighted."

His form is not within the field of vision. No one can see Him with the eyes. He is revealed by the heart, the mind and the intellect (through meditation). Those who know Him become immortal. **9**

When the five organs of perception, together with the mind become still, and when the intellect becomes calm, they call that state the highest. **10**

Firm control of the senses is called Yoga. During its practice, one should not become lazy. Yoga is creation and dissolution. **11**

Self cannot be reached by speech, by mind or by sight. It is realized by him who says, "It exists"; and not by any other way. **12**

Self is to be realized in two ways – first as 'It exists', and then in Its real nature. When It is realized as existence, Its real nature becomes clear. **13**

When all desires dwelling in the heart are cast away, then the mortal becomes Immortal, and he attains *Brahman*, even here. **14**

When all the knots of the heart are cut asunder, then the mortal becomes Immortal, even here. This alone is the instruction. **15**

There are a hundred and one nerves of the heart. Of these, one leads to the centre of the head. Going upwards through that nerve, one attains Immortality. The others lead the departed to different worlds. **16**

The Supreme Being (*Purusha*), the inner Self, of the size of a thumb, is ever seated in the heart of all living beings. One should draw Him out from the body with perseverance; as one draws pith from reed. Know Him as Pure and Immortal. Yes, know Him as Pure and Immortal. **17**

Nachiketa, having been so instructed by the Lord of Death in this knowledge, and in the whole process of Yoga, became free from all impurities and from death. He attained *Brahman*, and so will any other, who knows the Inner Self. **18**

Peace Invocation

Om.
May He protect us both (teacher and pupil).
May he nourish us together.
May we work jointly with great energy.
May our study be vigorous and fruitful.
May we not have any dispute.

Om. Shanti. Shanti. Shanti.
Let there be Peace, Let there be Peace, Let there be Peace.

"The Supreme Being (Purusha), is ever seated in the heart of all living beings."

Focussed Commentaries

2.1, 1-4 Self is realized by looking inwards

Spiritual search has an inward movement, leading to the revelation of the Divine in the inner most soul. It is this aspect which is emphasized in verse 2.1,1.

The soul is like an eye. When the eye is absorbed in the perishable things of the world, it does not know the truth of things. When it turns inward, it perceives the truth.

Coleridge wrote.

> "It were a vain endeavour
> Though I should gaze forever
> On that green light which lingers in the west;
> I may not hope from outward forms to win
> The passion and the life whose fountains are within."

In his famous simile of the cave, Plato compares the ignorant to prisoners in a cave. They have a fire behind them and a wall in front. They see shadows of themselves – and of objects behind them – cast on the wall by the light of the fire. They are so bound that they cannot turn their neck to look back. They regard the shadows as real, and they have no notion of the objects that cause them. At last, some wise man succeeds in escaping from the cave to the light of the sun. He sees real things and becomes aware that he had hitherto been deceived by the shadows.

Descartes also points to the necessity of turning away from external appearances, and rising to the spiritual realities which Self-knowledge reveals. However, Descartes asks us to know the truth through reason, while the Upanishad says that truth is beyond reason – it can be realized only through meditation.

A Christian hymn reads:

> "Swift to its close ebbs out life's little day,
> Earth's joys grow dim, its glories pass away,
> Change and decay in all around I see,
> O Thou who changest not, abide with me."

– *S. Radhakrishnan*

Those who are devoid of discrimination fail to discriminate between the real and the unreal, the permanent and the fleeting. They set their hearts on the changeable things of this world. To them, death seems a reality, because they identify themselves with that which is born and which dies. But wise men see deeper into the nature of things. They are not deluded by the charm of the phenomenal world. They do not seek permanent happiness among its passing enjoyments.

All knowledge, and all perception by the senses in every state of consciousness – sleeping, dreaming or waking – is possible only because of Self. There can be no knowledge or perception independent of Self.

– *Swami Paramananda*

Ignorance or *avidya* is the forgetfulness of our divine nature. It manifests itself in the mental plane as desires. Desires are expressed as "actions" in the outer world. Ignorance, desires and actions – these three are called "knots of the heart" (*hridaya granthis*) in the Upanishads. With the end of ignorance, knowledge comes to shine forth and *Avidya* is changed in *Gyana*. To quote Blake:

> "To see a world in a grain of sand,
> And heaven in a wild flower
> Hold infinity in the palm of your hand
> And eternity in an hour."

Vedanta calls upon man to rediscover himself, and be nothing short of God. When a man has fully realized God-consciousness, no sorrow can approach him.

– *Swami Chinmayananda*

2.1, 5-15 This, verily, is That

Verse 6: According to Vedas, the first manifestation of Consciousness or *Brahman* was *Brahma*, the creator, born from the fire of wisdom (*Tapas*). *Brahma* existed even before the five elements.

Verse 7 is somewhat obscure.

'Ignorance or avidya is the forgetfulness of our divine nature.'

Verse 8: Fire is called all-knowing (*Jataveda*) because its light makes everything visible. In Vedic sacrifices, fire was kindled by rubbing together two sticks made from a special wood. Fire was regarded as one of the perfect symbols of divine wisdom. It was to be worshipped by all seekers after Truth – whether they followed the path of meditation or the path of rituals.

Verse 10: There is no difference between the creator and the created. Even physical science has come to recognize that cause and effect are but two aspects of one manifestation of energy.

– *Swami Paramananda*

Verse 7: *Aditi* means not bound, boundless. Aditi is said to be the mother of gods. The term is used here in the sense of Mother Nature. A verse in *Rg Veda* reads: Aditi is the sky, Aditi is the air. Aditi is mother, father and son, Aditi is all the gods (senses) and the five elements. Aditi is whatever has been born (past) and will be born (future).

Verse 8: This verse is quoted from *Sama Veda*, and also from *Rg Veda*.

The ancient Vedic gods are recognized by the Upanishads but they are all said to derive their being from the one Supreme Reality. In verses 5-7, the living soul, the soul of the universe, and the infinite nature, all are identified with *Brahman*. In verses 8-9, Fire and Sun are said to have their Reality in *Brahman*.

Verses 10-11: In these two verses, the Supreme is declared to be devoid of any differentiation. The multiplicity of the world does not touch the unity of the Supreme.

Verse 12: In the mythological legend of Savitri, it is said that *Yama* extracted from the body of her husband Satyavan a soul of the size of a thumb. Ramanuja and Nimbarka hold that Self is called thumb-sized since it dwells in the thumb-sized heart of the worshipper.

– *S. Radhakrishnan*

Jiva (individual soul) and *Hiranyagarbha* (cosmic-soul) are two aspects of *Brahman*. *Brahman* appears as *Jiva* through the limiting adjuncts of ignorance, *Avidya*. The sum total of all *Jivas* is *Hiranyagarbha*. Micro-cosmic aspect of *Brahman* is *Jiva*; macro-cosmic aspect of *Brahman* is *Hiranyagarbha*. When the limiting adjuncts drop, *Hiranyagarbha* and *Jiva* become identical with transcendental *Brahman*.

Hiranyagarbha is the first manifestation of *Brahman* through Its *tapas*, or Will. *Brahman* willed, and *Hiranyagarbha* came into being.

He who thinks 'I am different from *Brahman*' goes through the cycle of birth and death. He who thinks and feels 'I am the all-pervading *Brahman*' attains immortality.

– *Swami Sivananda*

The cause of all enjoyments (verse 5): The Sanskrit word is *madhavadam*, which literally means 'enjoyer of honey'. However, this statement goes against the philosophy of Vedanta, as *Atman* is neither an enjoyer nor a doer. *Atman* – as conditioned by the mind, intellect and body – is actually what is meant here.

Verse 6: The theory of creation is a knotty problem in the Upanishads. No two Upanishads concur among themselves as regards the details of the process of creation. Whatever be the explanations given and the processes elaborated, each master was concerned only with leading the student ultimately to a state of Pure Consciousness.

Verse 9: The Rishi of the Upanishad here declares that the vital truth from which the Sun had arisen at the time of its manifestation and into which it will withdraw at the time of its dissolution, is Pure Consciousness. Here, the word Sun is representative of all cosmic objects and phenomena.

Verse 10: All different waves are nothing but the ocean. What looks like a serpent is nothing but the rope. A mirage is nothing but the desert. There is no difference between the Supreme Reality, *Brahman* and the reality behind the world of names and forms. Where there is no *Brahman*, there cannot be a manifested world of objects.

Verse 11: Meditation is the process by which the mind attains *Brahman*.

'The ancient Vedic gods are recognized by the Upanishads, but they are all said to derive their being from one Supreme Reality.'

Verse 12: The description of *Atman* as thumb sized, smokeless flame is intended to provide the meditator with a prop to develop his concentration in the early stages of meditational practices.

Verse 15 reasserts the oneness of the Divine in man and the Divine that pervades everywhere. Man minus his ego is God. God plus ego is man. Annihilation of ego-sense in us is the becoming of God.

— *Swami Chinmayananda*

2.2, 1-5 Power behind Life-breath and senses

This human body is called a city with eleven gates. In it dwells the unborn, eternal Self. The eleven gates are the two eyes, two ears, two nostrils, the mouth, the two lower apertures, the navel and the imperceptible opening at the top of the head (*Brahmarandhra*).

In the Bhagavad Gita, the body is conceived as the city of nine gates (excluding the navel and the imperceptible opening in the head.)

The real source of life is *Atman*, not the in-breath or the out-breath. Verse 2 reveals the omnipresent nature of *Atman*.

— *Swami Sivananda*

The liberated soul is said to leave the body at death through *Brahmarandhra*.

The verses repudiate the materialistic doctrine that the soul is just an assemblage of parts. The house and the dweller are separate, and destruction of the house does not mean destruction of the dweller. Loss of the body does not mean dissolution of the soul. Desertion of the body by the soul, however, would mean disintegration of the body.

Verse 4: What remains then? With this question, the Upanishad confronts us with the sacred truth that there remains practically nothing upon which we may glorify that empty shell, the dead body!

— *S. Radhakrishnan*

2.2, 6-12 Theory of rebirth

Verse 7: While the Upanishads insist on the independent reality of Supreme Self, they also affirm the reality of the individual soul. Verse 7 implies the law of *karma*, that we are born according to our deeds.

Verse 11: The verse admits the reality of the pain of the world, but denies that it touches the Supreme Self, which is our inner Being. We confuse between Self and ego. Self does not suffer, because It is not subjected to ignorance. It does not identify Itself with any of the events to which Its various psycho-physical vehicles are subject.

— *S. Radhakrishnan*

Verse 6: In the Upanishads, the word *Atman* is used in many contexts to indicate the body, or the mind, or the intellect, or the *Jiva* (Consciousness conditioned by the mind). In verse 2.2, 6 the word *Atman* is used to indicate the ego-center, and not Self or Pure Consciousness. Nothing ever happens to Pure Consciousness. When Pure Consciousness presides over the functions of the body, with reference to the body it is said to be the 'individual soul' – just as the all-pervading space is called 'room-space' with reference to the four walls of a rooms. In fact, the infinite space can never be conditioned or limited by the walls.

Verse 9: The electric current, which passes through a fan, a bulb, a refrigerator and a heater, is certainly the same. However, because of the differences in the instruments through which the electric current passes, it manifests itself differently as air, light, cold, and heat. Similarly, the *Atman-tatva* (essence of *Atman*), remains the same, despite the differences in forms into which it enters. You and I are different because our minds and bodies are constituted differently; but our *Atman* is the same.

Verse 12: The mind-intellect equipment has a prism effect when the undivided beam of Self's light passes through it – it disperses Self into innumerable names and forms which constitute the world, *Jagat*. The *yogi*, in his discriminating wisdom, withdraws the mind from the impressions of plurality.

— *Swami Chinmayananda*

'You and I are different because our minds and bodies are constituted differently; but our Atman is the same.'

The text shows the application of the law of cause and effect to all forms of life. The thoughts and actions of present life determine future birth and environment.

Verse 10: By using the analogies of fire and air, the teacher tries to show the subtle qualities of Self. Although formless, It assumes different shapes according to the form in which It dwells. But being all-pervading and infinite, It cannot be confined to these forms. Therefore, it is said that It also exists outside.

Verse 11: Sun is called the eye of the world because it reveals all objects. Even when the sun shines on the most impure object, it remains uncontaminated by it. Likewise, divine Self is not touched by the impurity or suffering of the physical forms in which It dwells.

— *Swami Paramananda*

Verse 8: *Brahman* is the silent witness of the three states viz. waking, dream and deep sleep. In deep sleep you actually come in contact with *Brahman*, but there is a veil of ignorance. Therefore, you are not actually conscious of *Brahman*.

A snake is superimposed on a rope when seen in dark or dim light. Likewise, the world and the body are superimposed upon *Atman-Brahman* on account of ignorance, *Avidya*.

The rope is not affected by the snake which is imagined in its place. Likewise, *Atman* is not affected by the superimposition of the world on It. This is called the doctrine of superimposition, *Vivarta-vada*, propounded by Sri Sankara.

— *Swami Sivananda*

2.2, 13-15 Light of all lights

Verse 13: The world is like a fleeting shadow. Body, mind, senses and life are included in the term 'world'. The very idea of change implies that there must be something like a base, which is permanent. Constant change can take place only around something, which is changeless. The screen in a cinema hall never changes, but the pictures come and go on the screen. *Brahman* represents the screen, and this universe of fleeting forms represents the pictures.

— *Swami Sivananda*

Verse 13: Waves, ripples, bubbles, froth and foam can exist in an ocean only when there is a constant, unchanging depth of the ocean beneath them. No river can flow without a bed. Similarly, no world of flux would be possible without a base that is changeless.

Verse 14: '*Tad etad iti*, This, verily, is That.' Self cannot be perceived, or felt, or determined. Perception, feeling and determination are functions of the sense organs, the mind and the intellect, respectively; and these can function only in the plane of plurality. When in meditation, a person has successfully hushed the senses, the mind and the intellect in the silence within, he becomes conscious of Self. This is a state of intuitive experience, and not physical cognition. It is to show this intimate 'awareness of Self' that we have in the inimitable language and style of the Upanishads, the expression 'This, verily, is That!'

Self, being Itself the light of wisdom, needs no other light to illumine It. When the clouds have moved away, the ever-shining sun becomes visible in all its brightness. When the veiling disturbances of the mind and the intellect caused by our ignorance of Self are stopped, *Atman*, in Its own effulgence comes out to shine forth in glory.

Verse 15: No ritual is concluded without chanting this verse soon after '*aarti*'. Lord Death is reaffirming that in the realm of *Brahman-Atman*, there is no need for any other agent of light to illumine It. There is no need for a torch to illumine the sun!

When It shines, everything shines after It: everything shines by Its illumination.

The importance of this verse is reflected in the fact that it has been repeated in Mundaka 2.2,10. The same idea is reflected in slightly different words in the Bhagavad Gita (15.6).

— *Swami Chinmayananda*

The symbol of light is most natural and universal. Plato compares the sudden inspiration of the mystic to a leaping spark. Also in his mythical account of the cave, the real world is a realm of light outside the cave. The Old Testament and the Zoroastrian religion speak of the antagonism between darkness and light. In the First Epistle of John, we read, 'God is light, and in Him is no darkness at all.'

— *S. Radhakrishnan*

'Even when sun shines on impure objects, it remains uncontaminated.
Likewise, divine Self is not touched by evil forms in which It dwells.'

2.3, 1 Tree of Creation

The description here has its analogue in the tree Igdrasil in Scandinavian mythology.

The tree of life has its unseen roots in *Brahman*. The tree and the branches represent *Brahman* in Its manifested forms. The tree grows upside down. It has its roots above (in the spiritual realm) and branches below (in the material realm). This illustration is also used in the Bhagavad Gita (15.1-15.4).

– *S. Radhakrishnan*

This verse describes the tree of creation which is rooted in *Brahman*, and which sends its branches downward into the phenomenal world.

– *Swami Paramananda*

The Upanishad is here bringing out a beautiful comparison of the universe, projected out from Reality, like a fig (Pipal) tree. Even the great philosopher Sri Sankara was carried away by the beauty of deep suggestions contained in this verse.

The Upanishad could not have thought of any other tree, more appropriate than Pipal. This tree is extensive in growth, sturdy in build and long in its duration of life. The word *Ashwattha*, when broken into its components is also translated as 'that which will not be tomorrow'. Thus, it represents the world of perishable objects. The words 'roots above' suggest that the roots derive their sap from the all-pervading *Brahman*.

In a way, the comparison also reminds one of a family tree, which starts from a great grandsire, and branches out into children, grandchildren, grand grandchildren, and so on. The family tree also looks like an inverted tree.

– *Swami Chinmayananda*

2.3, 2-3 Fear of the Supreme

The source and the sustaining power of the universe is *Brahman*. Evolution is not a mechanical process. It is controlled by *Brahman*. *Brahman* is represented here as *Prana*, the life giving power.

– *S. Radhakrishnan*

Just as mind-body cannot live or act without the soul, nothing in the created world can exist independent of *Brahman*. *Brahman* is the basis of all existences. Its position is like that of a king whom all must obey. It is like an upraised thunderbolt, which all powers obey.

– *Swami Paramananda*

All existences – sun, moon, planets, and stars – obey cosmic laws, which are unrelenting and inexorable. No one can transgress *Brahman*. Everything is under Its strict control. Creation, preservation and dissolution are governed by an unalterable divine law, which no one can violate or break. Therefore, *Brahman* is called a great terror, like an uplifted thunderbolt.

The verse is repeated in Taittiriya Upanishad (2.8, 1) with slight changes.

– *Swami Sivananda*

The whole universe arose from *Brahman* and moves in *Prana*, or the whole universe comes out of Him, and vibrates in Him.

Modern science has come to the conclusion that matter is constituted of energy units moving at high speeds. Atom consists of electrons and protons, moving with high velocity around a central motionless neutron. Scientists have also discovered that if by some method they change the frequency of vibration of energy particles, they could transform one element into another. Subatomic particles are now believed to be vibrating strings. Physics seems to be converging on Upanishadic philosophy that creation is caused by vibrations in Consciousness. And, it is possible for a vibration to maintain itself only if there is a motionless and non-vibrating medium, the Absolute Reality.

'Subatomic particles are now believed to be vibrating strings. Physics seems to be converging on Upanishadic philosophy that creation is caused by vibrations in Consciousness.'

Changes need a substratum, a constant axis upon which they can play.

Verse 2.3, 2 indicates that the source of the universe is not something inert or non-existent, but an active and dynamic existence. It is Cosmic Consciousness Itself.

The systematic and scientific consistency in the laws of nature is due to *Brahman*. But for the eternal fear of this Supreme authority, collisions between stars and planets would have been as frequent as motor accidents, train collisions and plane crashes! But we see that the universe is running smoothly, in a perfect and harmonious manner. Sun, Fire, *Indra*, *Vayu* and Death are all working with a beautiful team spirit, due to the fear of the Supreme.

– Swami Chinmayananda

2.3, 4-5 Levels of Consciousness

Verse 4: Having woken from a dream, a man need not get a gun to shoot down the tiger that chased him in the dream. Having woken from the dream state of egocentric pursuits into the waking state of the knowledge of Self, one need not repeat the to-and-fro swings between birth and death.

The mission of life is to evolve into a state of Godlike perfection. Man is the only living being who has been endowed with necessary faculties to hasten his evolution.

Verse 5: As men, we are living in certain planes of Consciousness. Our experiences in waking state are not the same as our experiences in dream state. Likewise, there can be other planes of Consciousness where experiences can be of a different kind. Thus we have the world of forefathers (*pitraloka*), where one has only mind-intellect, and not a physical body. Naturally, the experiences gained by such a subtle body must be different from our own experiences. Here, the Upanishad is trying to compare the clarity with which the Absolute is perceived by seekers in different planes of existence.

– Swami Chinmayananda

Verse 5: Just as one perceives one's image in a mirror very distinctly, so also one can perceive *Brahman* in one's intellect. There are degrees of perception. Perception becomes less and less distinct in the worlds of forefathers and *gandharvas*; like a dream, and like a reflection in water. But in *Brahma-loka*, *Brahman* is realized very distinctly – like light and sound.

– Swami Sivananda

The goal of evolution is to attain the world of true and vast existence. It is called the world of Truth in the Vedas and *Brahma-Loka* or *Swarga-Loka* in the Upanishads. It is beyond the symbols of birth and death. It is a state belonging to knowledge, not ignorance. It is the infinite existence and beatitude of the soul. It is the light of Mind beyond mind, the joy and eternal mastery of Life beyond life, the power of the senses beyond the senses. The soul finds in it not only its own largeness, but also the infinity of the One. It is a state of supreme Silence, eternal Peace, absolute Joy.

– Sri Aurobindo

2.3, 6-13 Yoga, the highest state

Verse 6: The senses are separate from *Atman*, Self. The rising of the senses refers to their functioning during the waking state. The setting of the senses refers to their dormancy during the state of deep sleep. Unlike the senses, *Atman* does not rise or set. It is always the same.

Verses 10-11: Yoga literally means to join or to unite the lower self with the higher Self, the object with the subject, the worshipper with God. In order to gain this union, however, one must first disunite oneself from all that scatters the physical, mental and intellectual forces. So the outgoing perceptions must be detached from the external world and in-drawn. When this is accomplished through constant practice, union takes place on its own accord. But it may be lost again unless one is watchful.

– Swami Sivananda

'The mission of life is to evolve into a state of God-like perfection.'

Verses 7-8: These verses contain only a repetition of what has been stated earlier (1.3, 10-11) regarding the ascending spiral that takes us from the most gross to the most subtle principle in us.

The word *lingah* has a particular connotation. When there is a smoke seen rising from a distant point on a hill, we infer that there is a fire on the hill. The sign or distinctive mark viz. smoke which led to our inference is called *lingah*. *Purusha*, the all-pervading Being is *alingah*, without a distinctive mark, imperceptible.

Verses 10-11: The highest state is that when individual Self (*Atman*) meets universal Self (*Brahman*). It is called the state of *samadhi*, or deep meditation. The five senses, the mind and the intellect are perfectly quiet in this state. Skeptics may ask: 'What is the difference between deep meditation and deep sleep?' In both the states, the sense organs, the mind and the intellect are at rest. But the comparison is only so far as it explains this common similarity.

During deep meditation, the individual transcends his senses, mind and intellect to reach the realm of eternal Consciousness. In deep sleep, the individual only folds up his sense organs, mind and intellect to reach a state of unconsciousness! The one in sleep is drowned in the darkness of ignorance, the one in meditation rises in the sunshine of knowledge.

– Swami Chinmayananda

Verse 12: According to Sri Sankara, this verse warns against meditation on Truth as manifested with attributes (*Saguna Brahman*); it advocates vigorously meditation on the Absolute Truth, Unmanifest and Attributeless.

In earlier verses, *Yama* has already pointed out to Nachiketa that a meditator meditating upon *Aum*, the symbol of lower *Brahman*, shall attain the joys of *Hiranyagarbha*. However, when one meditates on *Aum* as a symbol of Attributeless, Pure Consciousness, the meditator realizes the Absolute Reality.

Verse 17: The metaphor of thumb-sized Self is intended to provide the seeker with a prop to concentrate upon during meditation.

During meditation, one should not strain oneself in the least. This is brought out vividly by the analogy of drawing out pith from a reed – a very delicate operation. The reed itself is a very delicate plant, and its stalk is more so.

Verse 9: Even though we cannot form a visual image of the Supreme Being, we can still apprehend Him by devotion and meditation.

As the concept of God is formed by our mind, it cannot be identical for all.

Verse 12: The primary assertion that can be made about Self is the declaration of It's existence, pure and simple. Faith in the existence of *Brahman* leads to spiritual experience in which Its true nature is revealed and understood.

– S. Radhakrishnan

2.3, 14-18 From mortal to Immortal

Verses 14-15: These emphasize that man can attain Godlike perfection in this life itself. Such a state is called *jivan-mukti* (liberation during life-time), and such a man is like God living on earth.

Some thinkers hold that liberation can come only after the body falls off. This state is called *videha-mukti* (liberation after death).

A knower of *Brahman* becomes *Brahman*. Such a complete and total liberation is called *kaivalya-mukti*.

A *Jivan-mukta* also attains *kaivalya-mukti*.

Verse 16: The subtle spiritual body is said to contain some 101 subtle nerves. Of these, the most important is *susumna*. It runs parallel to the backbone and extends up to the center of the human crown. The ego-center of a spiritually advanced person escapes through *susumna* at the time of his death. Such a person attains liberation in progressive stages, *kramamukti*.

The subtle nervous system of the body provides the channel through which the mind travels. Its desires and tendencies determine the direction of its travel.

'As the concept of God is formed by our mind, it cannot be identical for all.'

When the mind becomes pure and desireless, it takes the upward route, and at the time of death passes out through the imperceptible opening at the crown of the head. But as long as it remains full of desires, its course is downward, through the openings in the head or lower parts of the body – to the realms where those desires can be satisfied.

Verse 17: Just as you draw pith or stalk from a reed, so also you have to draw out *Atman* from the five sheaths – patiently and with discrimination.

– *Swami Sivananda*

Verse 16: This is identical to verse 8.6 in Chandogya Upanishad. The soul of a liberated person exits by an artery called *susumna,* to an aperture in the crown of the skull – known as *Brahmarandhra or Vidriti* – from where it first entered at the beginning of life. Exit by any other point implies rebirth.

– *S. Radhakrishnan*

'When the mind becomes pure and desireless, it takes the upward route at the time of death. But as long as it remains full of desires, its course is downward.'

Taittiriya Upanishad

Five layers of human personality

OVERVIEW

Taittiriya Upanishad deals with self-discovery of Self within. It tells us how to practice the famous precept which the Greek philosopher Thales (625-545 BC) taught around the same time as the Upanishads: "Know Thyself".

Self can be known only when the seeker lives a virtuous and disciplined life. So the Upanishad first summarizes the essentials of good-living. It then states: 'Brahman is Truth-Knowledge-Infinitude.'

Brahman is declared to be same as Atman or Self. It is the inmost Essence of both human beings and the universe. In humans, it illumines five concentric layers of human personality - physical, vital, mental, spiritual and blissful. Its presence can be experienced only through meditation. This is explained through the story Bhrigu's step-by-step meditation leading to Self-realization. It is to be noted that Bhrigu discovered 'himself' by his own efforts and some helpful hints from his father.

COMMENTARIES

The translated text has been supplemented with commentaries by Sri Aurobindo, Sri Sankara (translation by Swami Gambhirananda), Swami Sarvananda, Dr. S. Radhakrishnan, N. A. Nikam, Klaus G. Witz and Paul Deussen.

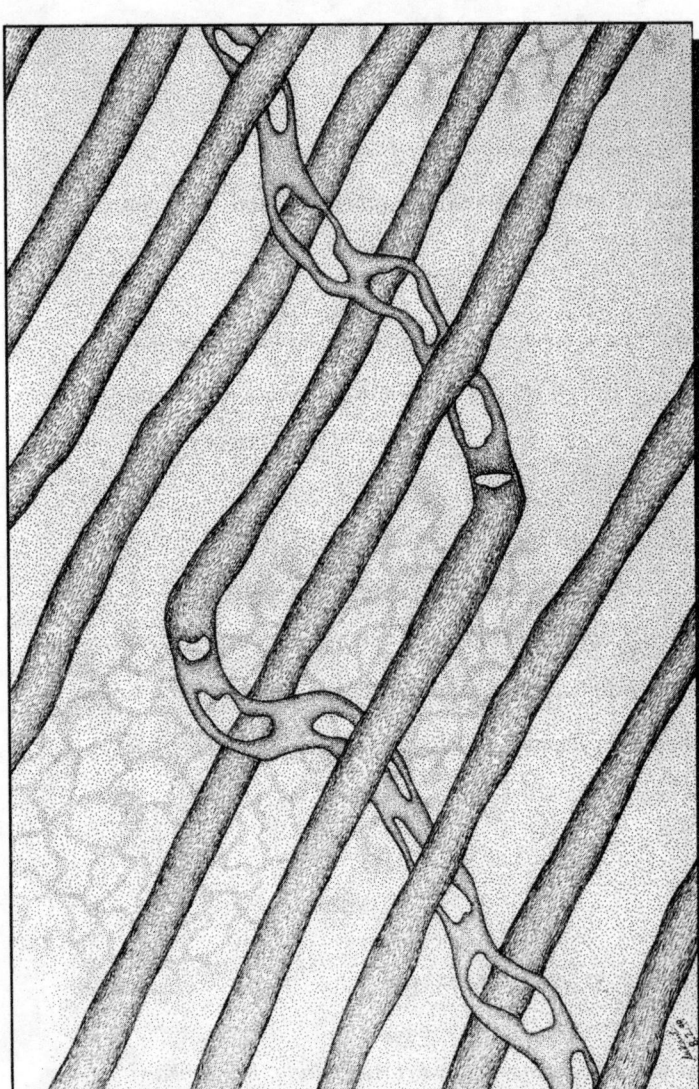

TAITTIRIYA UPANISHAD
Five layers of human personality

CHAPTER 1
Know your Self: Preparatory steps
.... 295

1.1 Peace Invocation
1.2 Science of phonetics
1.3 Meditation on cosmic conjunctions
1.4 Prayer for intelligence, health and wealth
1.5 Meditation on four mystic words
1.6 Inner space in the heart
1.7 Significance of number five
1.8 Importance of *Om*
1.9 Scriptures: Study, reflect, then act
1.10 Ecstacy of Self-realization
1.11 Essentials of good living
1.12 Thanksgiving

CHAPTER 2
Know the Cosmic Self 308

Peace Invocation

2.1   *Brahman* is Truth – Knowledge – Infinitude
2.2-2.5   Human personality has five layers
2.6-2.7   Relative is inseparable from Absolute
2.8-2.9   As Bliss of *Brahman* increases, fear of world decreases

CHAPTER 3
Bhrigu's self-discovery of Self 325

Peace Invocation

3.1-3.6   Self realized through step-by-step reflection
3.7-3.10, 1 Show respect for food
3.10, 2-5   A mystical chant

1 Know your Self: Preparatory steps

SIMPLIFIED SYNOPSES

The first chapter covers a dozen diverse preparatory subjects considered essential for knowledge of inner Self.

1.1 Peace Invocation

The Upanishad starts with an invocation addressed to Cosmic Powers, to ward-off all possible obstacles – internal, external and providential.

1.2 Science of phonetics

A brief account of the principles of phonetics is then given to emphasize the importance of correct pronunciation of sacred texts.

1.3 Meditation on cosmic conjunctions

Reflection and enquiry can be conducted fruitfully only if the mind is made pure by meditation. Section 3 starts with a prayer for glory to both the teacher and the disciples. It then identifies five objects and phenomena for meditation – universe, light, knowledge, progeny and self – and the relationships subsisting among their components, four in each case. The section concludes with enumeration of rewards that accrue from such meditation – a happy family, material possessions and splendor of spiritual wisdom.

1.4 Prayer for intelligence, health and wealth

The prayer addressed to *Om*, the symbol of *Brahman*, is for intelligence, wisdom, energetic body, soft speech, clear hearing, and good memory. The last item prayed for is abundant and uninterrupted supply of material objects. The ultimate objective of all these is stated to be Immortality.

The first half of the prayer seems to be by disciples. In the second half, the teacher expresses his eagerness to transmit wisdom to an increasing number of worthy disciples. He concludes with two beautiful similes: 'As water flows downwards, as months pass to make up a year, so may numerous disciplined students come to me from all directions.'

The sincerity of the teacher is reflected in his prayer: 'O Lord, may I enter into Thee... may Thou enter into me... may I purify myself'.

1.5 Meditation on four mystic words

The Upanishads frequently refer to three worlds representing three states of Consciousness – the earth, the heavens and the intervening space. These are denoted by three mystic syllables – *bhur*, *bhuvah* and *suvah*. The fourth syllable, *maha* is identified here to denote *Brahman*. The main injunction here is about meditation on *Brahman* as embodied in these four *Vyahrtis*. Then follow four other subsidiary meditations on individual *Vyahrtis*.

1.6 Inner space in the heart	*Brahman* pervades everything that exists. Yet, as in chapter 8 of Chandogya Upanishad on Dahara Vidya, this section suggests meditation on *Brahman* as if It resides in the innermost space of the heart. It also makes a reference to the ascent of *jiva*, conditioned Self, from this space to the crown of the head for ultimate merger in the Absolute. *Brahman* is described here as one whose body is Infinite Space, whose essence is Truth, whose delight is Life Force, whose mind is Bliss, and who abounds in Tranquility.
1.7 Significance of number five	The Upanishads bring out the similarities between macrocosm and microcosm in many different ways. In this section, the number five is identified to be common to many important groups of objects and phenomena – both in universe and in man. The section ends with an important conclusion – the sets of five in man and in the universe are supportive of each other.
1.8 Importance of *Om*	The importance of syllable *Om* has been emphasized in almost all the Upanishads. This section also suggests meditation on *Om* as a symbol of both the Absolute *Brahman* and the relative universe. The glory of the symbol *Om* is evident from the fact that some important prayers and sacrificial rituals are commenced with its chant.
1.9 Scriptures: Study, reflect, then act:	Reading of scriptures should not be ritualistic. Reflect on what you study and use them as guide in performance of your multifarious duties. Some of these duties are enumerated in this section. Virtues prescribed in the scriptures are relative in their importance. This is illustrated with the viewpoint of three sages regarding the superiority of three irrefutable virtues – truthfulness, austerity and study of scriptures.
1.10 Ecstasy of Self-realization	Knowledge of *Brahman* is only a step in Self-realization. Self-realization means to rise above the subject-object duality; it means to be *Brahman*. This section expresses the ecstasy of a Self-realized sage, Trishanku. He declares himself to be the stimulator of the universe, which is symbolized by a tree. He compares his fame to a mountain peak. He is endowed with wealth of both wisdom and intelligence. Like *Brahman*, he is immortal, imperishable and immutable. A similar idea is expressed by sage Vamadeva in Aitareya Upanishad. Some commentators regard that frequent recitation of this verse with faith and devotion is a substitute for study of Vedic scriptures.
1.11 Essentials of good living	This section is like a convocation address to graduating students. It advocates a universally valid value system: Speak the truth, practice righteousness, do not be negligent, etc. It also preaches respect for father, mother, teacher and guest. Finally, it provides guidelines for dealing with special situations. Sermonizing passages like these are very rare in the Upanishads.
1.12 Thanks-giving	The last section repeats the opening peace invocation with a slight variation. It offers grateful reverence to the same Cosmic Powers who have helped in grasping the knowledge contained in this chapter.

'Brahman is described here as One, whose body is Infinite Space, whose essence is Truth, whose delight is Life Force, whose mind is Bliss, and who abounds in Tranquility.'

Translated Text

Peace Invocation

Om.
May He protect us both (teacher and pupil).
May he nourish us together.
May we work jointly with great energy.
May our study be vigorous and fruitful.
May we not have any dispute.

Om. Shanti. Shanti. Shanti.
Let there be Peace, Let there be Peace, Let there be Peace.

CHAPTER 1

Section 1

Peace Invocation

Om.
May Mitra, Varuna, Aryaman, Indra, Brhaspati
  and Vishnu of wide strides be favorable to us.
I bow to *Brahman*.
O *Vayu*, I bow to thee.
Indeed, you are the visible *Brahman*.
I shall call you Righteousness.
I shall call you Truth.
May that *Brahman* known as *Vayu* protect me.
May that *Brahman* protect my teacher. **1**

Om. Shanti. Shanti. Shanti.
Let there be Peace, Let there be Peace, Let there be Peace.

Section 2

We shall now explain the science of phonetics. The things to be learned are: *Varna* or pronunciation of letters, *Svara* or pitch of sound, *Bala* or emphasis in the utterance of letters, *Sama* or modulation, and *Sanatana* or continuity. **1**

Section 3

The disciples say: 'May there be glory to us both. May the splendor of knowledge of *Brahman* be with us both.'

The teacher says: 'Now we shall expound the sacred doctrine of conjunction or *samhita* under five headings. These are: universe, light, knowledge, progeny and self. These are called the great conjunctions, *maha samhita*. **1**

"I bow to Brahman. I shall call you Righteousness. I shall call you Truth."

Now with regard to the universe: Earth is the first form, heaven is the last form, space is their meeting place, and air is the link. One should meditate on the universe, bearing these relationships in mind. **2**

Now with regard to light: Fire is the first form, sun is the last form, lightening is the meeting place, and water is the link. Thus, one should meditate upon light. **3**

Now with regard to knowledge: Teacher is the first form, student is the last form, knowledge is the meeting place, and instruction is the link. Thus one should meditate upon knowledge. **4**

Now with regard to progeny: Mother is the first form, father is the last form, progeny is the meeting place, and procreation is the link. Thus one should meditate upon progeny. **5**

Now with regard to self: Lower jaw is the first form, upper jaw is the last form, speech is the meeting place, and tongue is the link. Thus one should meditate upon self. **6**

These are great conjunctions: *maha samhita*. He who contemplates on these obtains progeny, cattle, food, heavenly pleasures and the splendor of *Brahma Vidya*, knowledge of *Brahman*. He will prosper here and hereafter. **7**

Section 4

May that *Om*, who is the most excellent in all Vedic hymns, who has many forms, who has sprung from the immortal hymns, may He cheer me with intelligence. May I be the possessor of wisdom, which leads to immortality.

May my body be very vigorous. May my tongue be extremely sweet. May I hear clearly with my ears. You (*Om*) are the symbol of *Brahman*. Pray, preserve my learning. **1**

O Lord, after having endowed me with intelligence and good health, confer on me prosperity – consisting of food, drink, clothes, furry animals and cows – without any delay and for all times, in increasing quantities. *Svaha*.

May students come to me from far off places and from different directions. *Svaha*.
May they come in large numbers. *Svaha*.
May they be self-disciplined and calm. *Svaha*. **2**

May I become renowned among men. *Svaha*.
May I become the best among the wealthy. *Svaha*.

O Lord, may I enter into Thee. May Thou, O gracious Lord, enter into me (Let there be complete union between Thee and me).

O Lord, may I purify myself in your vast diversity. *Svaha*.

As water flows downwards, as months mingle with the year, similarly, O Creator, may disciplined students come to me from all directions. *Svaha*.

"O Lord, after having endowed me with intelligence and good health, confer on me prosperity."

You are my ultimate support. May You enlighten me. May I attain You. **3**

Section 5

Bhur, *Bhuvah* and *Suvah* – indeed, these are three celebrated mystic utterances. Sage Mahachamasya proclaimed a fourth *Vyahrti* by divine intuition. That is *Mahan*. That is *Brahman*. That is *Atman*. Other deities are its limbs.

Bhur indeed is this world. *Bhuvah* is the sky. *Suvah* is the next world. *Mahan* is the sun. It is by sun that all the worlds are nourished. **1**

Bhur is fire. *Bhuvah* is air. *Suvah* is sun. *Mahan* is moon. It is by moon that all the luminaries flourish. **2**

Bhur is *Rg Veda*. *Bhuvah* is *Sama Veda*. *Suvah* is *Yajur Veda*. *Mahan* is *Brahman*. By *Brahman*, indeed, all Vedas become great. **3**

Bhur is *Prana*, in-breath; *Bhuvah* is *Apana*, out-breath, *Suvah* is *Vyana*, diffused-breath. *Mahan* is food. By food, indeed, all vital breaths are sustained. **4**

These, indeed, are the four *Vyahrtis*. Each is again fourfold. He, who knows them, knows *Brahman*. All deities pay homage to Him. **5**

Section 6

There is within the heart, a bright space called *antar hridaya akash*. Let the aspirant mediate upon the discriminating, immortal and radiant Self (*Purusha*, Cosmic Person) residing in this space. A narrow cavity called *susumna* lies between two arteries of the upper palate, like a nipple, and passes through the roots of the hair and the centre of the skull. This is the passage leading to the Supreme Lord. At the time of final departure, when a wise person contemplates on four *Vyahrtis* – *Bhur*, *Bhuvah*, *Suvah* and *Maha*, or Earth, Sky, Heaven and *Brahman* Itself – his soul passes through this passage. He then obtains sovereignty and lordship of the powers of sight, hearing, speech and mind. After that he becomes immortal and divine *Brahman* – whose body is Infinite Space, whose essence is Truth, whose delight is Life Force, whose mind is Bliss, and who abounds in Tranquillity. You, O Prachinayogya, meditate in the manner prescribed above. **1-2**

Section 7

Earth, space, heaven, main quarters and intermediate quarters;
Fire, air, sun, moon and stars;
Water, plants, trees and body;
These are the components of cosmic existence.
Now with regard to human beings, the components are:
Exhaling, diffusing, inhaling, ascending and equalizing breaths;
Sight, hearing, mind, speech and touch;
Skin, flesh, muscle, bone and marrow.

Having grouped various objects in sets of five, the sage declared that both man and universe are based on a fivefold principle. One set of five preserves the other set of five. **1**

"Brahman: His body is Infinite Space, His essence is Truth,
His delight is Life Force, His mind is Bliss, and He abounds in tranquility."

Section 8

Om is *Brahman*. *Om* is all this universe. *Om* is uttered to indicate consent. (During the performance of sacrifice), instruction for recitation of prayers begin with the word *Om*. With *Om* (Udgatr priests) commence singing *Samana* (songs of *Sama* Veda). With '*Om Som*' (Hotr priests) recite the prayers. With *Om*, Adhavaryu priests utter eulogy. With *Om* one gives assent for offering oblations to fire. With *Om* a Brahmin begins to recite, 'May I obtain *Brahman*.' Thus wishing, verily, he attains *Brahman*. One should therefore meditate on Om. **1**

Section 9

Practice study and teaching of scriptures, righteous deeds, reflection, truthfulness and sincerity in action, penance or self-denial, self-restraint, tranquillity, daily offering of oblations to fire (*agnihotra*), hospitality to guests, benevolence, bringing up of family and marriage of children.

Satyavacha, son of sage Rathitara believed that *satya* or truth alone is supreme. Taponitya, son of Purushisti held that *tapas* or austerity is supreme. Naka, son of Mudgala stressed the study and teaching of Vedas. Indeed, that is *tapas*; that is *tapas*. **1**

Section 10

"I am the stimulator of the tree of the universe. My fame is high like a mountain top. Like the sun, I am supremely pure. I am the immortal one. I am endowed with the power of wealth of both wisdom and intelligence. I am imperishable and immutable." This is the sacred recitation of Vedic knowledge by Trishanku, a Self-realized sage. **1**

Section 11

(After completing the teaching of Vedas, the teacher advises as follows:)

Speak the truth.
Practice righteousness.
Do not ignore solemn study of scriptures.
Offer appropriate gifts to your teacher.
Do not cut-off the line of descendants.
Let there be no neglect of truth.
Let there be no neglect of duty.
Let there be no neglect of welfare of others.
Let there be no neglect of learning and teaching.
Let there be no neglect of offerings to gods and to ancestors.

Treat your mother like a god.
Treat your father like a god.
Treat your spiritual teacher like a god.
Treat your guest like a god.
Perform those deeds which are blameless, not others.
Adopt only good qualities of your elders, not others.

"Speak the truth. Practice righteousness. Let there be no neglect of duty."

Offer a seat to your superiors and elders.
Give gifts with faith and modesty, willingly and in plenty, without any fear.
Gifts must be appropriate for the recipient.

If you have any doubt regarding any of your deed or conduct, act like a person who is wise, impartial, experienced, gentle and law-abiding.

With regard to those who are accused of wrong-doing, deal with them like a wise person who is impartial, experienced, law-abiding, not harsh, and not influenced by others.

This is the advice. This is the teaching. This is the important instruction of the Upanishads. Live your life in the manner stated. Understand it. Meditate on it. Follow it till the last.

1

Section 12

Om.
May Mitra, Varuna, Aryaman, Indra, Brhaspati
   and Vishnu of wide strides be favorable to us.
I bow to *Brahman*.

O *Vayu*, I bow to thee.
Indeed, you are the visible *Brahman*.
I shall call you Righteousness.
I shall call you Truth.
May that *Brahman* known as *Vayu* protect me.
May that *Brahman* protect my teacher.

1

Om. Shanti. Shanti. Shanti.
Let there be Peace, Let there be Peace, Let there be Peace.

"Give gifts with faith and modesty, willingly and in plenty, without any fear.
Gifts must be appropriate for the recipient."

FOCUSSED COMMENTARIES

CHAPTER 1

1.1 Peace Invocation

The deities invoked here are manifestations of One Absolute, *Brahman*.

Mitra	: the deity of in-breathing and also day-time.
Varuna	: the deity of out-breathing, and also night.
Aryaman	: the deity identified with the sun and the eyes.
Indra	: chief of all deities, identified with the strength of hands.
Brhaspati	: the deity of wisdom and eloquence (speech).
Vishnu	: the deity identified with feet. His 'wide strides' is a reference to his incarnation as Vamana, the dwarf. He transformed himself in a gigantic form and covered the entire earth in just one step.

The Upanishads regard man as an epitome of the cosmos. Deities symbolizing different aspects of the cosmos are invoked with the objective of strengthening the corresponding aspects in man.

Vayu symbolizes cosmic *Prana* or life-force. He is described as a visible manifestation of *Brahman* because he can be perceived by the mind and the senses.

Om is the symbol of *Brahman*. The word *Shanti*, meaning peace, is uttered three times to ward-off three types of trouble:

- internal or *adhyatmic*: trouble from within one's self
- external or *adhibhautic*: trouble from outside
- supernatural or *adhidaivic*: trouble of providential origin.

– Swami Sarvananda

The first chapter is appropriately titled *Siksa Valli*, chapter on education. It contains miscellaneous teachings, such as: phonetics, prayers to be uttered during instructions, exhortations of teacher to the departing students, allegorical interpretations of *Samhitas* (joining of letters) and *Vyahrtis* (mystic words), and significance of *pranav* (holy syllable Om). However, a closer connection of the individual parts is not discernible.

Here are some golden rules, which the teacher imparts to departing students with regard to the way of life. Moralizing sections like this are rarely to be found in the Upanishads, as they are contrary to the spirit of the Upanishads. Therefore, Sri Sankara also finds it necessary to justify the occurrence of this moralizing section by pointing out its mere preparatory and purifying effect.

The rules organize themselves as follows:

- Three basic regulations
  a) Speak the truth
  b) Practice Righteousness
  c) Do not be negligent
- Relationships with father, mother, teacher and guests.
- Guidelines for dealing with special and doubtful situations.

– Paul Deussen

1.2 Science of phonetics

The efficacy of a *mantra* lies in its proper pronunciation. Vedic scholars give considerable importance to correct recitation of Vedic verses.

– Swami Sarvananda

1.3 Meditation on cosmic conjunctions

True glory is that which is a result of noble living, high thinking and righteous works.

The term *Samhita* means combination of letters. The philosophical observations presented here are based on linguistic phenomena.

All the five objects of meditation enumerated in the text are symbolic. In initial stages an aspirant meditates on a visible or visualized object outside his innermost Self, and exalts it as a great deity or *Brahman* Itself. The central point of all symbolic meditation is that the

---

'The word Shanti, meaning peace, is uttered three times to ward-off three types of trouble: internal, external and providential.'

symbol should be regarded as superior to its visible form.

Meditation on the universe helps to contemplate on cosmic existences as an interrelated whole. By doing so, the mind goes beyond trifling preoccupations and attunes itself to the Infinite.

Light appears on earth as fire; in the intermediate region as lightening; and in heaven as sun. Such meditation helps to steady the mind by dwelling on a unifying principle of cosmic magnitude, such as light.

The Upanishadic seer must have chosen the process of learning as a theme for meditation because of the close relationship existing between the teacher and the disciples.

As regards progeny, sexual union with the motive of procreation is a divine attribute. Sages have therefore deemed it worthy of holy reflection.

By 'self', all physical and psychic aspects of personality are meant here.

– *Swami Sarvananda*

1.4 Prayer for intelligence, health and wealth

These verses are uttered when oblations are poured into sacrificial fire with periodic recitation of the word *Svaha*. It is to be noted that the prayer is for wisdom, health and wealth in that order.

The prayer is addressed to the sacred symbol of *Brahman*, Om. Another word for *Om* is *Pranav*.

– *Swami Sarvananda*

1.5 Meditation on four mystic words

Vyahrtis are used in connection with various vedic rituals. They form a theme for internal meditation here.

The four *Vyahrtis*, mystic utterances, represent an attempt to describe *Brahman*, the *Mahan*, the great. *Bhur*, *Bhuvah* and *Suvah* – earth, ether and the worlds beyond – are the limbs of *Mahan*, *Brahman*.

In the next verse, the *Vyahrtis* are again identified as follows:

Bhur : with fire
Bhuvah : with air
Suvah : with sun
Mahan : with *Brahman*

Worlds in the Upanishads represent planes or levels of Being, of Consciousness. The number varies between 3 to 6. It is at least three, and generally five.

– *Swami Sarvananda*

1.6 Inner space in the heart

Brahman pervades everything. Yet to make it easier for beginners to concentrate on *Brahman*, the Upanishad prescribes that He should be meditated upon, as if residing in an inner space within the heart, *antar hridaya akash*. (This type of meditation is discussed under *Dahara Vidya* and *Sandilya Vidya* in Chandogya Upanishad).

This verse also describes how a yogi's soul leaves his body at the time of death. It passes through an important artery above the heart (called *susumna*) and exits through the centre of the head. This is called the path of *Devayana*.

According to Swami Vivekananda, *susumna* lies in the spinal cord and is ordinarily closed. Meditation releases the vast energy and infinite potentialities stored within it. Reaching the brain, this results in a blaze of illumination and perception of Self.

This difficult passage in the text perhaps testifies to the advanced physiological knowledge of the seer in as much as it refers to the intellectual and sense centres of the brain.

– *Swami Sarvananda*

The inner space in the heart is not physical. It has no parts and it is not divisible. Hence, it is both infinitesimal and infinite. Also, it is not a "void", the space within the heart is "full". It is the highest place wherein resides *Brahman*. A mystic meditates on Him who is seated in this inner space, in the "secret" place of his heart.

– *N. A. Nikam*

'Worlds in Upanishads represent planes or levels of Consciousness. The number varies between 3 to 6.'

1.7 Significance of number five

There is a technique of meditation called *Sampat*, in which a lower thing is thought of as some other higher thing because of some point of similarity. The number five is used as a point of similarity here between a human being and the universe. Five factors constituting human personality are identified with the factors making up Cosmic Person, *Virat*. Thereby, everything becomes identified with *Pankti*, the number Five. Meditation on fivefold factors relating to human beings strengthens the relationship with corresponding factors in the cosmos.

– Sri Sankara, Translation
by Swami Gambhirananda

1.8 Importance of *Om*

All prayers to gods, all oblations, and all recitation of scriptures begin with the word *Om*. Any activity begun with chanting of the word *Om* is more likely to be successful.

Om is a symbol in which there is no rigid distinction between sound and silence. The sound of *Om* originates from silence, and becomes silence out of which it originated. It is a symbol in which silence becomes sound, and sound becomes silence.

Om symbolizes both being and becoming. *Om* is *Brahman*, *Om* is also all this universe.

– N. A. Nikam

1.9 Scriptures: Study, reflect, then act

This lesson emphasizes that study or teaching of scriptures must be combined with practice of prescribed duties. The last portion of the verse presents three different views of three sages regarding the superiority of truthfulness, austerity and study of Vedas. The first sage had partiality for truthfulness, the second insisted on devout austerity, and the third exalted learning and teaching of scriptures.

– Swami Sarvananda

1.10 Ecstasy of Self-realization

The statement here by a Self-realized sage Trishanku, is considered a substitute for Vedic study. Daily recitation of this with faith and devotion leads to realization of Self as *Brahman* Itself. It is to be noted that in the verse both wealth and wisdom are sought after. While wealth alleviates worldly suffering, wisdom dispels sorrow.

In Vedic tradition, a tree is often taken as a symbol of the universe. It grows from the potentialities hidden in a small seed and rises high up in the sky. At times it stands still and firm in calm air, and at times it trembles with the wind. Vedic scriptures refer to this symbol of the universe, *Brahmavrksa,* both in upright and inverted positions.

– Miscellaneous Sources

1.11 Essentials of good living

Good conduct is a prerequisite for spiritual life. This lesson enumerates the essentials of good conduct. Some commentators consider this lesson as a parting advice by the teacher to his outgoing students.

The lesson is self-explanatory. However, some points need to be emphasized.

Let there be no neglect of learning and teaching: Learning should never stop in life time. Knowledge gained today will turn into wisdom tomorrow.

Adopt only good qualities of your elders: The transgressions of great men are like the eclipse of the sun or the moon. We should look up to them only when the eclipse has passed.

Some of the commandments of this lesson which have permeated deep in Indian culture, are worth repeating.

> Speak the truth
> Practice righteousness
> Treat your mother, father, spiritual teacher
>   and guest like a god.

This passage corresponds to the convocation address of modern times delivered at the universities to graduating students. It was reported to have been read out by the vice chancellor at Banaras Hindu University on the convocation day even in modern times.

– S. Radhakrishnan

'Wealth alleviates worldly suffering, wisdom dispels sorrow.'

The convocation or commencement address lays down four types of commandments.

(i) In the first commandment the pupil is asked to pay his 'debts' to his father, mother, teacher and superiors. The commandment implies that there are no rights if there are no obligations.

(ii) The second commandment is against negligence of any kind.

(iii) The third commandment enjoins the pupil to "give" – give out of faith, give with modesty, give in plenty, give what suits the recipient.

(iv) The fourth commandment is 'behave yourself'. Conduct yourself in a manner in which the wise and the virtuous conduct themselves. The commandment is not merely 'do' but 'be'. Be Yourself.

These commandments have passed into the currency of Hindu life.

– N. A. Nikam

1.12 Thanksgiving

It will be recalled that the deities mentioned here were invoked at the beginning of the lesson to ward-off all the obstacles. It is assumed that they have brought about the necessary results. So it is only proper that the student should offer grateful thanks to the deities who have helped in the study.

– Swami Sarvananda

2 Know the Cosmic Self

SIMPLIFIED SYNOPSES

2.1
Brahman is Truth - Knowledge - Infinitude

'A knower of Brahman sees the relative in the light of the Absolute.'

'Absolute is defined as Truth-Knowledge-Infinitude, all three in their inseparable unity. Existence-Consciousness-Bliss is a later adaptation.'

Chapter 2 begins with an invocation for all-round harmonious progress of both the teacher and his disciples.

Next, the Upanishad repeats one of its famous themes: Knower of *Brahman* attains the highest. This is because One Absolute *Brahman* is the only Constant that underlies the whole relative universe of ever-changing objects and events. A knower of *Brahman* sees all these lower things in the light of the Highest; he sees the relative in the light of the Absolute.

But what is this Absolute? It is defined as Truth – Knowledge – Infinitude; not three separate principles, but all three in their inseparable unity. *Brahman* is infinite existences, the truth (ultimate reality) behind infinite existences, and the self-knowledge of infinite existences. Infinity includes all infinities of time, space and causality. This *Brahman*, Truth-Knowledge-Infinitude, pervades the whole universe, but the place to realize It is the inmost space in the heart.

A later definition of *Brahman* as Existence – Consciousness – Bliss or *Sat-Chit-Ananda* is an adaptation of the definition presented here.

But what does one get by knowing *Brahman*, and thereby becoming the Highest? The text says that when one identifies oneself with the Highest, one rises high above the lower desires of the senses and the mind.

But how can a man identify himself with *Brahman*? Is there anything common between the two, to facilitate such an identification? 'Yes, there is', says the Upanishad. It is the Self within. This Self, *Atman* is the same as *Brahman*. Also, the Upanishad traces even the origin of man to *Brahman* Itself. It says that the five elements constituting the inorganic world – Space, Air, Fire, Water and Earth – have emanated from *Brahman* in that order. The organic world of vegetation and food evolved from the inorganic world. This was followed by emergence of life. Man is the highest form of life.

Usually a man is not aware of the existence of *Brahman* within him. Why? This is because normally a man limits his attention to his physical body alone – food for its nourishment and material possessions for satisfaction of its sense organs. This is important, but not an end in itself. There is much more to a person than his or her body.

2.2-2.5
Human personality has five layers

'After whatever you do, you want to be at peace with yourself.'

'The correspondence between the macrocosm and the microcosm is emphasized repeatedly in the Upanishads.'

Who am I?

Ask this question to yourself when you are in a reflective mood, and see what answers emerge from within.

The first answer is likely to be that you are what you see when you look in a mirror – your physical body.

With a little introspection, you will realize that there is more to you than just your body. Your life-style – what you do and how you live – is also a part of your personality.

Upon deeper introspection you are also likely to identify your mental make-up – ego, emotions, attitudes, ability to analyze and to reason, etc. – as an important component of your personality.

Upon still deeper introspection you will find yourself asking some philosophical questions, like: 'Who sent me here? Why am I doing all this? For whom? Is this the purpose of my life? How will it help me in my next life, if there is one?' These or similar questions are indicators of a deep spiritual awareness within you. This again, is a very important component of your personality.

Continue the introspection. You will find that answers to all the questions that you have been asking yourself have one common goal: After whatever you do, you want to be at peace with yourself.

Thus, human personality has five layers – physical, vital, mental, spiritual and blissful. The Sanskrit words for these are *Annamaya*, *Pranamaya*, *Manomaya*, *Vigyanamaya* and *Anandamaya*. In Taittiriya Upanishad, each of these five layers has been called *Atman* or Self. In post-upanishadic period, the theory of five selves has been named *Panchakosha Vidya*, or knowledge of five sheaths.

Salient points emerging from the text of Chapter 2 and commentaries thereupon are as follows:

(i) Each layer of personality is different from and surrounded by the preceding layers. Thus, the physical self is the outermost layer and blissful self is the innermost layer.
(ii) Each layer is more subtle or formless than the preceding layer and is like its soul. Thus, blissful self is most subtle and the 'soul' of all the other selves.
(iii) The five selves are manifested alike in mankind and in nature as a whole. Stripping off these layers one by one and gradually penetrating deeper, we finally reach the Absolute – both in man and in nature. This is an important point. The correspondence between the macrocosm and the microcosm is emphasized repeatedly in the Upanishads.
(iv) Following from the above, the Upanishad metaphorically compares each self with the body of a physical person, or a bird. In the case of physical self, it identifies five important body-parts: head, right side, left side, trunk and base. The vital self is described to have as its body the five

---

'Human personality has five layers – physical, vital, mental, spiritual and blissful. These are manifested alike in mankind and in nature.'

'Spiritual self comprises of Faith, Righteousness, Truth, Yoga and Cosmic Mind.'

forms of like-breath: *Prana*, *Apana*, *Vyana*, *Samana* and *Udana*. The body of the mental self is imagined to be comprising of the four Vedas – Rg, Yajur, Sama and Atharva – and the essence of their teaching, the Upanishads. The spiritual self is thought of as comprising of Faith, Righteousness, Truth, Yoga and Cosmic Mind (*Mahat*). Finally, the five parts of blissful self are: Love, Joy, Delight, Bliss and Absolute *Brahman*, as the base.

(v) The phrase *Vigyanamaya Atman* has been translated as spiritual awareness by one commentator. Intellect, understanding, intuition, wisdom and knowledge are some other translations.

(vi) A recognition of these five selves helps one to develop a broader, more universal outlook and become less self-centered.

For a person who is caught up in the relative world, the Absolute *Brahman* is non-existent; but in reality It does exist. He who refuses to accept this Reality becomes a nonentity, because he drifts without any aim of existence. He who accepts *Brahman*'s existence as Truth strives for self-perfection through spiritual and blissful layers of his personality (2.6, 1).

2.6-2.7 Relative is inseparable from Absolute

Previous sections have explained the Absolute and the relative – both in man and in nature. The relative is perceptible to the senses, but the Absolute is not. So doubts may arise about the existence of the Absolute. Also, even if the Absolute is assumed to exist, it has been stated that Its existence is identical in all – believers and non-believers. So the second doubt which arises is this: After death, will non-believers be differentiated from believers? Sections 2.6 and 2.7 attempt to clarify these doubts.

Brahman is not realized by mere knowledge of *Brahman*. Only he attains the blissful state of *Brahman* who has become one with *Brahman*, and not he who thinks that *Brahman* is an object of knowledge.

'This elegant universe is a self-manifestation of One Absolute. All creatures partake Its bliss.'

What is the relationship between *Brahman* and the world, the Absolute and the relative? The answer is contained in a very famous cosmological passage (2.6,3). It says that the One Absolute first willed to become many. It then became many by power of concentration (*tapas*) and then It entered into Its own creation as Its Soul. By Its act of creation, *Brahman* is the First Cause of the Universe. By Its entry into creation, *Brahman* is the First Principle of the universe.

Verse 2.6,3 emphasizes that Absolute *Brahman* is the totality of all opposites – being and not-being, defined and undefined, knowledge and ignorance, everything that exists in the relative world. It is therefore called Truth.

This elegant universe of innumerable relative manifestations has emerged from One Unmanifested Absolute. Rightly, the universe is called self-created and well-made.

The universe is only a self-manifestation of *Brahman*, which is essentially Bliss. As a consequence of the omnipresence of *Brahman*, all creatures partake Its Bliss (2.7, 2).

---

*'By Its act of creation, Brahman is the First Cause of the universe.
By Its entry into creation, Brahman is the First Principle of the universe.'*

2.8-2.9 As Bliss of *Brahman* increases, fear of world decreases

The universe is inseparable from *Brahman*. The relative is inseparable from the Absolute. A human being is inseparable from Self, *Atman*. When a man realizes this oneness, there is nothing, which can frighten him. Fear exists only when there is a thought of duality.

Brahman is the abode of everything, including opposites like fear and bliss. Not just human beings but even cosmic powers have a fear of God, so to say. Powers like Air, Sun, Fire, Lightening (Indra) and Death follow their laws without any error because they fear God, says the Upanishad.

Then follows an analysis of bliss. It is stated that there are many levels of Consciousness, each representing a distinct type of existence: men, fairies, angles, deities, teachers of deities, kings of deities, creative aspects of *Brahman* and *Brahman* Itself. Each level represents progressively lower 'worldly' element and progressively higher 'blissful' element. In other words, as we go up in the hierarchy, the relative decreases but the Absolute increases. At the level of Absolute Consciousness or *Brahman*, the diversity of the world is completely replaced by the oneness of Bliss. Thus, *Brahman* and Bliss are one and the same.

'Brahman and Bliss are one and the same.'

By frequent repetition, the Upanishad emphasizes that Supreme Bliss is realized by him alone, who is fully enlightened and free from desires.

Verse 2.8 ends with a reaffirmation that the innermost Self (Absolute Consciousness) in man and in a far-off cosmic object like the sun are one and the same. A person who comprehends this, transcends all the five selves of his personality, to eventually become one with Absolute *Brahman*.

The state of *Brahman* is beyond description, beyond conceptualization, beyond the thought of good or bad. It is a state in which there is no fear of any kind. It is a state of supreme bliss.

Man fears God only when he regards God as an external Power. All fear vanishes when he realizes that God is also the Power within.

---

*'Man fears God only when he regards God as an external Power.
All fear vanishes when he realizes that God is also the Power within.'*

Translated Text

Peace Invocation

Om.
May He protect us both (teacher and pupil).
May he nourish us together.
May we work jointly with great energy.
May our study be vigorous and fruitful.
May we not have any dispute.

Om. Shanti. Shanti. Shanti.
Let there be Peace, Let there be Peace, Let there be Peace.

CHAPTER 2

Section 1

Om! The knower of *Brahman* attains the highest.

With reference to this fact, it has been declared: *Brahman* is Truth – Knowledge – Infinitude. He who knows It as existing in the cavity of the heart and in the farthest space, he fulfils all his desires, like the Omniscient *Brahman* Itself.

From *Brahman* that is also *Atman*, was produced space, from space was born air, from air came fire, from five emerged water, from water arose earth, from earth herbs, from herbs food; from food man came into existence.

Thus man is made from the essence of food. His body has five parts – this is his head (teacher demonstrates); this right side, this left side, this trunk, and this hind part is its lower part as a support and foundation. There is also this verse about it. **1**

Section 2

From food, verily, are produced whatever creatures dwell on earth. Moreover, by food alone they remain alive, and they return to it in the end. Surely, food is the first and foremost among all that is created; hence it is regarded as medicament for all. Those who regard food as *Brahman* obtain all foods; hence food is regarded as medicament for all. Living beings are born from food; having been born, they grow on food. Food is called *Anna* because creatures consume it and are consumed by it.

Different from *Annamaya* or physical self but within it, there is another self, consisting of *Prana* or vital energy, *Pranamaya*. *Annamaya* self is filled with *Pranamaya* self. Truly, this one also is exactly of the form of a person. *Prana* is its head, *Vyana* is its right side, *Apana* is its left side, *Samana* is its trunk, and *Udana* is its support and foundation. There is also this verse about it: **1**

"May we work jointly with great energy. May our study be vigorous and fruitful. May we not have any dispute."

Section 3

Whatever gods or men or animals exist, all of them depend on *Prana* or life-breath to remain alive. Truly, *Prana* is the life of the animate world. So it is regarded as universal Life Principle. Those who meditate on *Prana* as *Brahman* attain a full life. *Prana* is the life of the animate world, so it is regarded as Universal Life Principle. (Repetition is for emphasis).

Pranamaya self is the inner self of *Annamaya* self.

Different from *Pranamaya* self but within it, there is another self, consisting of mind, *Manomaya*. *Pranamaya* self is filled with *Manomaya* self. Like the other two, *Manomaya* self is also like a person (of five parts). *Yajur Veda* is its head, *Rg Veda* is the right side, *Sama Veda* is the left side, their teachings are the trunk; the hymns of the *Atharva Veda* are the support and foundation. There is also this verse about it: **1**

Section 4

That from which speech and mind recoil, without being unable to attain It, he who knows the bliss of that *Brahman,* does not fear anything at any time.

Manomaya self is the inner self of *Pranamaya* self.

Different from Manomaya self but within it, there is another self which consists of wisdom, *Vigyanamaya*. Like the other three, this self is also in the form of a person of five parts: Faith is its head, Righteousness is its right side, Truth is its left side, Yoga is its trunk and *Mahat* or Cosmic Mind is its support and foundation. There is this verse about it: **1**

Section 5

Vigyana or wisdom directs sacrifice. It also directs deeds. All gods worship *Brahman* as the foremost wisdom. If one knows *Brahman* as wisdom, he leaves his sins behind in the body and fulfils all his desires.

Vigyanamaya self is, indeed, the embodied self of *Manomaya* self.

Different from *Vigyanamaya* self but within it, there is another self, consisting of Bliss, *Anandamaya*. Like the other four, this too is in the form of a person of five parts. Love is its head, Joy is its right side, Delight is its left side, Bliss is its trunk, and *Brahman* is its support and foundation. **1**

There is also this verse about it:

Section 6

If a person regards *Brahman* as non-existent, he becomes non-existent, as it were. If he understands that *Brahman* is real, others respect him as a wise sage.

Anandamaya self is, indeed, the inner self of *Vigyanamaya* self. **1**

"Physical self is dependent on vital self, vital on mental, mental on spiritual, and spiritual on blissful self." ..... (Adapted)

Now, the following question arises in respect of what has been taught so far:

Does he, who does not know *Brahman,* attain It after departing from this world? Alternatively, does he who knows *Brahman,* attain It after departing? **2**

Brahman desired, 'Let me become many, let me be manifested'. He performed meditation (*tapas*). Having performed *tapas*, He brought forth all this universe, whatever there is. Having brought forth this universe, He entered it. Having entered it, He became *Sat* (existence, what is manifested) and *Tyat* (that which is not manifested), defined and undefined, abode and non-abode, knowledge and ignorance, truth and falsehood. He is the ultimate Reality of all that exists. Therefore, *Brahman* is called Truth.

Regarding this also, there is the following verse. **3**

Section 7

In the beginning all this was unmanifested *Brahman*. From It emerged the manifested. Brahman created Itself (the universe) by Itself. Therefore, the universe is called self-created (also translated as well-made). **1**

That which is known as self-created, verily, is a source of joy; one becomes happy by coming in contact with that source of joy. Who will inhale and who will exhale if this sky-like vast bliss was not there within and without? Indeed, this bliss cheers (people). **2**

A person becomes fearless only when he is firmly established in the imperceptible, formless, inexpressible, all-pervading *Brahman*. Whenever he entertains even a little difference between himself and *Brahman*, he is overcome by fear. Even a wise man has fear when he is not reflective. **3**

Section 8

Air blows out of His fear. Sun rises out of His fear. Fire, Indra and Death as the fifth, all do their task out of His fear.

Now this is an analysis of Bliss. Imagine an enviable young person in the prime of his life, well read, prompt in action, steady in mind and strong in body. Imagine further that the whole wealth of this earth belongs to him. (Thus he is fully satisfied in every respect). That is *one unit* of human bliss.

One hundred times the human bliss is the bliss of human *gandharvas* (fairies). A sage full of enlightenment and without any desire also possesses the same bliss (100 units).

One hundred times the bliss of human *gandharvas* is the bliss of celestial *gandharvas*; and also that of a sage full of enlightenment and without any desire (10,000 units).

One hundred times the bliss of a celestial *gandharvas* is the bliss of *pitras* (souls of ancestors) inhabiting their long-enduring world; and also of a sage full of enlightenment and without any desire (one million units).

"Brahman created the universe out of Itself. Therefore, the universe is called self-created, well-made."

One hundred times the bliss of *pitras* is the bliss of deities-by-birth; and also of a sage full of enlightenment and without any desire (100 million units).

One hundred times the bliss of deities-by-birth is the bliss of those who become god by their deeds (*Karma Deva*); and also of a sage full of enlightenment and without any desire (10 billion units).

One hundred times the bliss of *Karma Devas* is the bliss of the highest deities; and also of a sage full of enlightenment and without any desire (1 trillion units).

One hundred times the bliss of the highest deities is the bliss of Indra (chief of all deities); and also of a sage full of enlightenment and without any desire (100 trillion units).

One hundred times the bliss of Indra is the bliss of Brhaspati (guru of Indra and god of wisdom); and also of a sage full of enlightenment and without any desire (10,000 trillion or 10^{13} units).

One hundred times the bliss of Brhaspati is the bliss of *Prajapati* (Lord of living beings), and also of a sage full of enlightenment and without any desire (10^{15} units).

One hundred times the bliss of *Prajapati*, is the bliss of *Brahma* (creative aspect of *Brahman*); and also of a sage full of enlightenment and without any desire (10^{17} units).

He (*Brahman*), who is there in human beings and in the sun, is one and the same. A person who comprehends this fully, after departing from this world transcends all five selves – physical (*Annamaya*), vital (*Pranamaya*), mental (*Manomaya*), spiritual (*Vigyanamaya*) and blissful (*Anandamaya*). With regard to this, there is this verse.

1

Section 9

After knowing the Bliss of That (*Brahman*), which words are unable to describe and mind is unable to conceive, a man fears nothing. He is not distressed by thoughts like, 'Why have I not done what is good? Why have I committed sin?' A knower of *Brahman* regards both (good and bad) as manifestations of Self. He redeems himself from both. This is the secret teaching.

1

Peace Invocation

Om.
May He protect us both (teacher and pupil).
May he nourish us together.
May we work jointly with great energy.
May our study be vigorous and fruitful.
May we not have any dispute.

Om. Shanti. Shanti. Shanti.
Let there be Peace, Let there be Peace, Let there be Peace.

"He (Brahman), who is there in human beings and in the sun, is one and the same."

FOCUSSED COMMENTARIES

CHAPTER 2

Peace Invocation

In the given context the prayer is for mutual goodwill between the student and the teacher. However, it can be used for goodwill between any two persons or groups working together.

– *Editor*

2.1 *Brahman* is Truth – Knowledge – Infinitude

WHAT IS *BRAHMAN*?

Brahman is That by which all existences subsist. It is the Eternal behind all instabilities, the Truth hidden in all appearances, the Constant that supports all mutations, without being increased, decreased or abrogated.

If we were only what we seem to be to our normal self-awareness, there would be no mystery. If the world was only what the senses perceive and the mind analyses, there would be no riddle. If the present state of our life and the universe was the limit of our knowledge and action, there would be no problem. But there is more. That more is the hidden head of the Infinite and the secret heart of the Eternal. It is the Highest. To know the Highest is to know all. It is the beginning and the source of all things, so everything else is its consequence. It is the support and constituent of all things, so the secret of everything is explained by its secret. It is the sum and end of all things, so everything else amounts to it. By throwing itself into it, everything achieves the sense of its own achievement.

HOW KNOWER OF *BRAHMAN* ATTAINS THE HIGHEST?

To live in our present state of knowledge is to live in ignorance. We are ignorant of ourselves because as of now we know only that in us which is always changing – from moment to moment, from hour to hour, from period to period, from life to life. We do not know that in us which is eternal. True knowledge is knowledge of the highest, the inmost, the infinite. A knower of *Brahman* sees all these lower things in the light of the Highest. He sees the external and the superficial as a translation of the internal and the essential.

Knowledge does not end with knowing, it has its full value only when it leads to being. Knowledge, action, creation, enjoyment are only a fulfillment of being. Since we are incomplete in being, our aim is to grow.

Mere existence is not fullness of being. Being knows itself as power, consciousness and delight; greater being means greater power, consciousness and delight.

A knower of *Brahman* gains that which is supreme. He gains the highest being – highest power of being, highest consciousness and highest delight.

The Supreme is not something aloof and shut up in Itself. The Highest is the Infinite and Infinite contains All. Whoever attains the highest consciousness becomes infinite in being and embraces All.

To make this clear, the Upanishad has defined *Brahman* as Truth, Knowledge, Infinitude – *satyam, gyanam, anantam*. It has defined the result of knowledge of Him – in the secret cave of the heart and also in the supreme ether – as the enjoyment of all desires in the attainment of self-existence.

Our highest state of being is indeed becoming one with *Brahman* in His eternity and infinity. It is also an association with Him in the delight of self-fulfillment. And that principle by which this association is possible is the principle of His knowledge.

TRUTH – KNOWLEDGE – INFINITUDE

Brahman is Truth – Knowledge – Infinitude not as three separate things but in their inseparable unity. It is an Infinite being, an infinite Truth of being, an infinite Knowledge of being. Take one of these away, and the idea of the Eternal fails us.

Infinity of the Eternal is timeless, spaceless and causeless. It contains all the infinities of time, space and endless succession of cause-and-effect, or what we call causality.

Truth is the truth of the Infinite and Eternal; it is the truth of being. All things are *Brahman*.

'We are ignorant of ourselves because we know only that in us which is always changing – from moment to moment, from life to life. We do not know that in us which is eternal.'

Knowledge means direct experience of Eternal's infinite self-existence; and of Its truth and reality. Mind in its ordinary state is incapable of this knowledge. However, it can reflect on this knowledge – though inadequately – when it is touched by a ray from the secret luminous cavern of our superconscient being.

To know the eternal Truth-Knowledge-Infinitude is to know *Brahman*.

– Sri Aurobindo

The sentence 'knower of *Brahman* attains the highest' is a statement in brief of the purport of the second chapter. It refers to *Brahman* as a knowable entity, and it also implies that *Brahman* is not different from one's own in-dwelling Self.

Brahman is defined as Truth-Knowledge-Infinitude, *satyam gyanam anantam Brahman*. Truth, *satyam* distinguishes *Brahman* from mutable things. *Gyanam* is translated as Knowledge or Consciousness. It affirms that *Brahman* is not insentient like earth. Use of the word knowledge may convey the impression that *Brahman* is limited, for human knowledge is seen to be finite. In order to obviate this, the text says that *Brahman* is *anantam*, Infinitude.

Etymologically, *Brahman* is derived from the root *brh*, which conveys a sense of growth and vastness, without any limit. *Brahman* is that which is not limited by time, space or causation. Thus the word has its own positive import and cannot refer to void.

The word *satya* indicates an existing entity that cannot be sublimated. The word *gyana* means the self-revealing cognition of things. The word *anantam* is used with regard to something pervasive, like the sky.

That *Brahman*, which has been defined as Truth-Knowledge-Infinitude, is said to exist in the supreme space in the heart. The text wants to present space here as a part of knowledge.

One who has known *Brahman*, what does he do? The answer is – he enjoys all enjoyable things. Does he enjoy sons, heavens etc. as we do? The text says: 'No, a man of knowledge, having become *Brahman*, enjoys as *Brahman*, all the desirable things simultaneously. The things enjoyed by him are not dependent on causes such as merit, or on sense organs as the eyes. The idea is that he enjoys his identity with the all-knowing *Brahman*.'

– Sri Sankara, translation by Swami Gambhirananda

The reality, which we experience through the senses and the mind, is a display of multiplicity and variety. There must be a unity behind all this multiplicity – a unity, which includes all, which is complete in itself, which is determined by itself, and which is capable of being explained entirely from itself. This metaphysical Reality which is the substance of physical reality, or this spiritual Reality which is the substance of material reality, is called *Brahman*.

The Reality that forms the background of the external phenomena, is identical to that which is the substratum of human beings. The universal Self and the individual Self are essentially the same.

Brahman is Supreme. Its knowledge through identity with It is the attainment of perfection. The purpose of *Brahman*-realization is self-perfection, it is the final goal of evolution.

Brahman can never be made an object of knowledge, or defined strictly. The three predicates given here – Being or Existence, Intelligence or Consciousness and Infinitude or Transcendence of spatial, temporal and causal limits – merely state what *Brahman* is in essence.

Existence is the most universal concept which leaves nothing whatsoever outside it. It is a value which is always judged by a conscious being. The experience of Reality as various phenomena is made possible because of the Intelligence underlying the apparatus of Consciousness. It is the nature of Intelligence to generate consciousness of things. Thus Existence and Consciousness are the two sides of the same coin. They constitute the essence of Reality.

Existence is dimensional, Consciousness is non-dimensional. Matter is cognized only in space-time relationships. In fact, matter is self-limitation of Spirit or Consciousness. Whatever is material is thus limited. Intelligence is non-material and therefore unlimited – it is Infinite. Thus, *Brahman*, the Ultimate Reality, is in essence, Existence, Intelligence and Infinitude.

'Brahman is derived from the root brh, which conveys a sense of growth and vastness, without any limit. Brahman is that which is not limited by time, space or causation.'

The phrase *Sat-Chit-Ananda*, or Existence-Consciousness-Bliss of Vedantic thought may be traced to Taittiriya Upanishad. The term *Sat* has two translations – Existence and Truth. *Chit* and *Gyana* are equivalents. Also, there is no difficulty in equating *Anantam*, (Infinitude) with *Ananda* (Bliss). One need not believe that it is an ancient error as Paul Deussen cautiously suggests. It is stated in Chandogya Upanishad that Infinite alone is Bliss; and there is no Bliss in the finite.

Guha or cavity in the text can stand for the heart or the intellect. *Paramavyoma*, supreme space, may be construed either independently or as a term qualifying 'cave'. Sri Sankara contends that in the text under consideration, realization of *Brahman* in the farthest space is out of tune with the rest of the passage; hence the text should be read as 'He who knows It (*Brahman*) as existing in the intellect which is lodged in the supreme space in the heart'.

The felicity that accrues to one who has realized his identity with all-knowing *Brahman*, is not an experience of a succession of sensual pleasures; it is a simultaneous experience of the entire bliss in an eternal 'now'. That unsurpassed beatitude is only imperfectly grasped by the intellect, and is totally beyond the senses.

The terms *Brahman* and *Atman* refer to the First Principle from which the whole universe has emanated. Both terms are sometimes interchanged, sometimes they appear side by side. From this principle of Pure Consciousness, which is also Existence and Infinitude, first emanates space. This then evolves into progressively more gross forms to constitute the whole relative universe. The five elements constitute the inorganic creation. This in turn gives rise to the organic creation through vegetation and food. Life is described as emerging from the essence of food. Man is cited specially because he alone is competent to realize *Brahman*.

— Swami Sarvananda

The second chapter, *Brahmananda Valli*, is one of the most beautiful evidences of ancient India's deep absorption in the mystery of nature, as also of the inner depths of human beings.

The basic idea of this chapter is that *Atman* – the innermost kernel of man, as also of the whole universe – is not attainable through cult worship burdened with egoistic thoughts (*manomaya*). It is also not attainable through knowledge or *Vigyanamaya* alone. It is attainable only through communion with It and becoming one with It, after stripping off all outer layers that cover It, like shells.

The theme of the whole chapter is stated in the opening verse 2.1, which says, 'He who knows *Brahman* – psychically within the heart and physically outside, in the world around – he attains all peace and satisfaction which *Brahman* Itself possesses'.

Brahman is defined as *satyam, gyanam, anantam*

Satyam : True reality, not the empirical
Gyanam : Knowledge, which is not split into subject and object.
Anantam : Boundless or Infinite.

The word *anantam* seems to have crept in by mistake. It should have been *anandam* or Bliss.

Then follows the oft-quoted passage of creation – starting from the elements, through earth, plant, food and semen down to the creation of man. This is the material man. Through it the essential nature of *Atman* is obtained.

— Paul Deussen

2.2-2.5 Human personality has five layers

Our personality consists of five layers:

Physical : *Annamaya*
Vital : *Pranamaya*
Mental : *Manomaya*
Spiritual : *Vigyanamaya*
Blissful : *Anandamaya*

Each layer of personality is permeated by all the other succeeding layers. Also, each succeeding layer is more subtle than the previous one. Thus, the physical body is the most gross form of personality; vital, mental, spiritual and blissful are increasingly more subtle forms.

Bliss is not a local sensation, the whole personality is pervaded by it. So, *Anandamaya* self is taken to pervade all the other selves.

Pain is believed to be the property of *Manomaya* self, whereas joy alone is the property of *Anandamaya* self.

'From Pure Consciousness, which is also Existence and Infinitude, first emanates Space. This then evolves into progressively more gross forms, to constitute the whole universe of relativity.'

Chandogya Upanishad states that infinitude, without any limitation whatsoever, is true bliss. This verse states that *Brahman*, which is Infinitude, is the foundation of *Anandamaya* self.

Anandamaya self-expresses itself in various degrees in different beings. It is experienced as love, joy and delight. A person experiences more and more bliss as he reduces his attachment to external sense objects, and directs his mind deeper and deeper on the innermost *Anandamaya* self.

Vigyanamaya and *Anandamaya* together form the individual soul as the agent and the enjoyer, while the three other selves are its instruments.

Knowledge of *Brahman* is not acquired at once. There are different stages by which an aspirant approaches to a clearer and clearer idea of *Brahman*. In *Arundhati Nyaya*, one big star is shown first to a man, then a small star close to it, then a smaller star and finally the smallest star in the sky. Likewise, verses 2.2-2.5 take the mind from the gross to the subtle, from the subtle to the subtler, and eventually to the subtlest of all - the *Atman* encased within the five sheaths.

– Swami Sarvananda

There are five planes of Being and Consciousness – Matter, Life, Mind, Understanding and Delight. These have an order of a hierarchy, the highest is the most inward. There is in each plane, another plane which is different from it and yet within it. Thus, within Matter is Life, within Life is Mind, within Mind is Understanding, and within Understanding is Delight – delight of being *ananda,* which is the true nature of Self.

Katha Upanishad also deals with this subject, but there is a slight difference. The inmost plane in Taittiriya is *ananda*; in Katha it is *shanta atman*, silence, peace, tranquillity.

The five planes of Being and Consciousness represent an ingression of forms – Matter to Life, Life to Mind, Mind to Understanding, and Understanding to Bliss. This is an ingression towards That which is the basis of all forms, viz. the Formless. Experience of the Formless is a failure of speech, as also a failure of mind. Speech cannot describe the Formless, mind cannot comprehend It. But this failure coexists with an unfathomable joy of liberation from fear. Mystical experience is that delight which is freedom from fear (2.5, 1).

– N. A. Nikam

FIVE SHEATHS (*PANCHA KOSHA*) VIDYA

There are five selves (*atman*) which exist in oneself and which one can feel oneself to be. Spiritual path consists of discriminating these selves, and ultimately going beyond them and merging in *Brahman*.

The first self is the physical person. Each succeeding self lies within the preceding one. Thus;
(i) within the physical person (*Annamaya*) that one is, there is
(ii) the emotional, subtle or psychic energy (*Pranamaya*). Within this is
(iii) mind (*Manomaya*). Within the mind is
(iv) the self that is inner spiritual awareness or knowledge (*Vigyanamaya*). Within that is
(v) the self which is bliss (*Anandamaya*).

In later texts, the five selves are called five sheaths (*koshas*, vessels) in which the One Self is encased. The whole teaching is more commonly known as *Pancha Kosha* or Five Sheaths *Vidya*.

1. First level self (the physical person)

The physical person consists of the essence of food (*anna*). It is described schematically as having the form of a person or a bird, and the same schema is used for the other more interior selves later. Its head is simply the head that one has ("this head here"), its left side is simply the left side or left wing of one's body ("this left here"), and so on. Thus the *annamaya* person is clearly the physical individual which one thinks oneself to be. But there is more to him than just that. Later, in Chapter 3, Bhrigu realizes that food is not only eaten by living beings, it also eats them. Living beings are slaves to food because they constantly have to procure it and are dependent on it. So Food is a higher force. By regarding food as a higher force – as *Brahman* according to a later verse 3.2,1 – one is lifted to a level where one has a more universal outlook and less self-interest.

2. Second level self (*Prana*)

Within the person that is made of the essence of food, and different from him, is the person consisting of energy (*Prana*). This is the self that one

---

'Experience of the Formless is a failure of speech and mind.
Speech cannot describe the Formless, mind cannot comprehend It.'

thinks one is when one feels one's vital power, one's various mental and emotional dynamics and one's subtle energy in psychic, yogic and spiritual experiences. Instead of energy, we can also say 'breath', because experience of energy is intimately connected with breath. One's vital energies and emotional states are closely mirrored in one's breathing. In yoga, regulating the breath leads to stilling the mind. So the *Pranamaya* self is the individual feeling that he/she is energy or breath.

According to the Upanishads, *Prana* or life-breath distributes itself inside the body into five specific ways, in five specific areas. It therefore has five forms – *Prana*, *Vyana*, *Apana*, *Samana* and *Udana*. These are again compared to the head, the right and left sides, the trunk and the support of vital self.

Pranamaya self is usually assumed to refer to subtle body, or *suksham sarira*. Gradually deepening awareness of the subtle body signals spiritual progress. To quote Sri Satya Sai Baba:

'You can say that *Pranamaya* is the soul of *Annamaya*, for it makes the physical body function from head to foot. By contemplating that *Pranamaya* is the *Atman* of *Annamaya*, the notion that the body is Self will disappear. You rise from the gross to the subtle. *Prana* is like the molten metal in the crucible'.

It is a fact that in ordinary life – as also in yogic, psychic and spiritual fields – experiences of a subtle nature are felt to be more powerful than ordinary experiences based on the senses, and one attributes greater significance to them.

3. Third level self (Mind)

Manomaya self or self consisting of the mind is the inner agency that perceives, feels and directs attention. Its movements are movements of the mind. It is the self that one believes oneself to be when one is identified with one's mental impulses and decision-making. It is the self within *Pranamaya* self in the sense that it is behind all the *Pranamaya* level phenomena.

Like the other selves, *Manomaya* self also has a structure on the model of the physical person or bird. Somewhat surprisingly, this structure is specified in terms of the different types of Vedic *Mantras* – 'Yajur Veda is its head' etc. (2.3,1). The implication is that *Manomaya* self is that aspect of one's self by which one is capable of knowing the Vedas and putting their teachings into practice. However, notes the Upanishad, even *Manomaya* self is unable to reach *Brahman*.

4. Fourth level self: *Vigyana*

Vigyana, as stated earlier, is inner spiritual awareness or knowledge. It is described as having Faith, Righteousness, Truth and Yoga as its aspects. It is different from *Manomaya*-level knowledge, where scriptures provide the injunctions to which one subordinates oneself. *Vigyana* has qualities associated with true wisdom. Sri Satya Sai Baba calls *Vigyana*, 'the super knowledge that confers perfect equanimity and purity'.

When there is *Vigyana*, impressions from *karma* and desires are not operating. For that reason, *Vigyana* will grow naturally into *Atma gyana*, knowledge of Self.

It may take many years of religious or spiritual life before one is able to identify *Vigyana* unmistakably in one's experience. Or *Vigyana* may already be in one's inner experience from childhood. In any case, it is the first really deep stage on the road to becoming *Brahman*. It is also a prerequisite for still further stages. Realization of Truth comes only after there is *Vigyana*, and involves entering and passing through the *Anandamaya kosha*, which is deeper than *Vigyanamaya kosha*.

Vigyana is the door to the glimpse of Truth. But majority of mankind is caught in the pulls of perceptions, desires and activities at the first three levels.

According to Sri Sankara, *Vigyana* is the inner self that discriminates between good and bad deeds.

Gaudapada, the teacher of Sri Sankara's teacher, writes in his Karika: 'Consciousness (*Vigyana*) which appears to be born or to move or to take the form of matter, is really ever unborn, immovable and free from the character of materiality; it is all peace and non-dual'

Sri Ramana Maharishi says, '*Vigyana* is that tranquil state of existence-consciousness which is experienced

---

*'One's vital energies and emotional states are closely mirrored in one's breathing.
In yoga, regulating the breath leads to stilling the mind.'*

by the aspirant like the waveless ocean or motionless ether'.

We find, therefore, that *Vigyana* covers a wide range of Consciousness – from the beginning level 'deep-seated inner awareness' to 'near-highest *Atman-Brahman* Consciousness.' Such a broad yet unitary understanding of *Vigyana* is deeply impressive.

In a fundamental sense, *Vigyana* is almost always treated as a form of Consciousness, or as a state of Knowledge; not as consciousness or knowledge of something. It cannot be analyzed as content of Consciousness or object of Knowledge. It is Reality itself.

5. Fifth level self: *Ananda*

The first and the most important point about *Ananda* or Bliss that is being made is that it arises only when there is *Vigyana*, inner spiritual awareness (2.5,1). The *Ananda* or Bliss, which emerges from *Vigyana* or *Atman*-Consciousness, is something like "higher bliss". At this point even the author becomes visibly inspired: "Who will inhale and who will exhale if this sky-like vast bliss was not there within and without?" (2.7,2).

According to Sri Satya Sai Baba:

'The Supreme Being is the source of contentment. He is the embodiment of the purest *rasa*, the purest emotion. Attaining Him, the *jiva* (= living being) can be immersed in joy: If He is not shinning in the firmament of the heart, who is to taste, who is to live? He feeds all with *Ananda*.'

This blissful self is again visualized in the from of a person having love, joy, delight and bliss as its head, two sides and trunk respectively; while *Brahman* itself is its support. The implication is that awareness of this blissful self need not be confined to times when one is in meditation. It may be felt in all states in life.

Love, delight and joy, *priyam*, *moda* and *pramoda* are the stages through which we pass in the fulfillment of our desires. Sri Satya Sai Baba gives an example of buying mangoes at the market. *Priyam* is the joy of seeing the fruit on sale, *moda* is the joy of buying it and *pramoda* is the joy of eating it. 'But even this joy is not a lasting experience so long as the object desired is a worldly object. Man gets real and everlasting happiness only if he desires for God and treads the Godward path. When the mind is steadfastly centered on the Lord, Love, Joy and Delight acquire a divine character and confer the Bliss of Immortality on man.'

From the lowest joy to the highest bliss of *Brahman*, all are stages of *ananda*. In fact, all types of *ananda* are derived from one basic source, *Brahmananda*, Bliss of *Brahman*.

– *Klaus G. Witz*

2.6-2.7 Relative is inseparable from Absolute

The five selves constitute the personality and the individuality of humans. Is there anything beyond or interior to these five selves? The Upanishad now establishes that *Brahman* is a positive Reality. He who refuses to accept this reality becomes as good as a nonentity, he drifts without any aim of existence. He who understands *Brahman* as Real, strives to realize the infinitude of Bliss and Intelligence that *Brahman* is. He treads the moral and the spiritual path with the motive of self-perfection.

In the preceding verses the five sheaths or *koshas* (selves) have been introduced for the purpose of setting forth the knowledge of *Brahman*. *Brahman* has descended into human personality through the five elements and the five sheaths. But *Brahman* is the true Self of every person – irrespective of whether he is wise or ignorant about Its existence. Hence the questions raised in verse 2.6, 2. Their answers are contained in verse 2.7, 3.

He (*Brahman*) desired: 'Let me become many. Let me procreate Myself.' He then brooded (did *tapas*). He projected all that exists. Having created it, verily, He entered into it. Having entered into it, He became both Being (manifest, form) and Beyond, (unmanifest formless), defined and undefined, the sustained and the sustaining, the conscious and the unconscious, the real and the unreal. Whatever else there is, He became the entire Reality. For this reason the sages say that *Brahman* is Existence (*sat*).

Verse 2.7, 3 is quoted very often as a cosmological passage. It gives a sublime statement of creation. It says that Will of Divine Being is what is behind this projected universe. Divine Will, however, is different from human desire. It is a manifestation of multiplicity,

---

*'Awareness of blissful Self need not be confined to times when one is in meditation.
It may be felt in all states in life.'*

diversity and variety in the universe. The passage establishes that *Brahman* is both the efficient cause and the material cause of the universe. Metaphysically, however, the universe does not have any separate existence outside of *Brahman*.

The passage also associates austerity (*tapas*) with *Brahman*. The word *tapas* literally means heat, or heat of meditation. In the present context, the word *tapas* means knowledge, concentrated thinking or creative power.

It should not be supposed that the Divine enters into created objects as a person enters a house built by him. This is impossible. He is the whole, and the whole can never be contained by a part. The allegory is meant only to point out that evolution of Nature is only a manifestation of the Spirit. Unless Spirit is somehow involved in Nature, its evolution is unintelligible for us. The allegory of God's entrance into creation stresses the fact that Nature is the living garment of God, for He in-dwells, inspires and controls the whole universe.

It is not possible to correct the erroneous perception of a snake in a rope without knowledge of the identity between the superimposed snake and the actual rope. Likewise, it is not possible to realize that there is only one Reality, *Brahman* without the knowledge of the identity between the world and *Brahman* (2.7, 3).

In the beginning: This does not denote the start of any era, but only an order. Creation is an eternal flow.

A person becomes fearless: This verse presents an analysis of fear and its remedy. The basis of fear is a feeling of separation. Fear departs when a person identifies his own Self with *Brahman*, the Supreme. Love tends to union, separation tends to fear. As long as one considers *Brahman* as an object of knowledge and not one's own Self, one is exposed to fear. One gets afraid of something outside oneself. It is not possible that individual Self would be afraid of universal Self, if a person considers them as one and the same.

Recall the question: 'Who will attain *Brahman*, the ignorant or the wise?' The ignorant will certainly not attain It. Even a knower of *Brahman* will not attain It if he does not identify his individual Self with universal Self.

– Swami Sarvananda

Verse 2.6, 3 suggests an analogy between the macrocosm nature and the microcosm man. It brings out the ascent of Reality from matter to God. While man has all these five selves in his being, he may stress on one or the other – the physical or the vital or the mental or the spiritual or the blissful. He who harmonizes all these is a complete man.

This analysis is accepted by the Buddha who speaks of five kinds of food – physical vital, psychological, logical and spiritual. The enjoyment of *Nirvana* is food for the spirit.

Behind all our growth is the desire for perfection. We are constantly 'becoming' until we possess our 'being'. Consciousness goes on changing until it is able to transcend change. The Beyond is the absolute fulfillment of our self-existence. It is *ananda*, the truth behind matter, life, mind and intellect. It controls them all by exceeding them.

– S. Radhakrishnan

For him who is caught up in the phenomenal world, there is mere non-existence; but in reality, there is existence. The two questions that follow, serve to clear up this contradiction. Is it an ignorant one, or the knowing one who attains *Brahman*? The answer to this is: Neither. Only he attains the blissful (*anandamaya*) state of *Brahman* who has become one with *Brahman*; and not he who thinks that *Brahman* is an object of knowledge.

As long as a person regards *Brahman* as an object of knowledge, there is duality, and duality leads to fear. Verse 2.8,1 signifies that even gods are fearful of *Brahman* as they perceive Him as different from themselves.

– Paul Deussen

2.8-2.9 As bliss of Brahman increases, fear of world decreases.

It is generally observed that one works incessantly under pressure of fear. Great cosmic forces follow their laws ceaselessly, without any error. On the analogy of human activity, it is illustrated that these forces work under fear of the Almighty. In fact, the Will of *Brahman* is expressed in the laws of Nature, and hence they cannot act differently at any time. The verse does not imply a wrathful God. As explained

---

'Love tends to union, separation tends to fear.'

earlier, *Brahman* is the cause of both fear and fearlessness. One becomes fearless when one finds support in the Divine. Fear comes when one perceives a distinction between one's self and the Divine Reality.

HIERARCHY OF BLISS

Joy, happiness or bliss can arise from two sources – material and spiritual. Material happiness arises from contact between subject and object. Spiritual happiness arises from within, as a natural flow. It is comprehended by the intellect, independent of any external occurrence or entity.

Enlightenment eliminates the distinction between the subject and the object of material happiness. It vanquishes all desires and leads to an intrinsic, all pervading bliss.

Spiritual bliss is qualitatively different from material bliss. A direct comparison is therefore not possible. But how to make the concept of spiritual bliss comprehensible to an ordinary man? The Upanishad does this through an imaginary scale of measurement. It gives a value of one unit to material happiness of the highest order. Progressively higher values are then given to the bliss enjoyed by mythological gods and demi-gods, *gandharvas*, *pitras*, deities, Indra, Brhaspati, *Prajapati* and *Brahma*. Indra is the chief of all deities. Brhaspati, Indra's teacher is considered to enjoy higher bliss than Indra himself. *Prajapati*, the Cosmic Person is ranked still higher. The whole universe – earth, heavens and space in-between – is thought to be His body. All beings exist in Him alone. He is the sum total of all lives.

Brahma is the Cosmic Mind. The bliss enjoyed by him is a zillion times the material happiness enjoyed by the most enviable human being.

Even the bliss of *Brahma* is only a fraction of Supreme Bliss. The bliss of various entities enumerated in the passage are like drops of water. They merge into an ocean of Bliss, which is *Brahman*. According to another Upanishad, *Brahman* and Bliss are one and the same.

By frequent repetition, the passage emphasizes that Supreme Bliss is realized by him alone who is fully enlightened and free from desires.

And what is enlightenment? The passage that follows explains this.

BRAHMAN IS ONE IN MANY

The Sanskrit word *Aditya* in verse 2.8,1 is translated as Sun. It literally means the Being that exists eternally. The passage states that a person can be considered enlightened when he realizes that his innermost Self and *Brahman* – who gives light and energy even to Sun – are one and the same.

An enlightened person transcends all the five layers of his self and establishes himself in the Supreme Bliss of *Brahman*. In fact, that Supreme Bliss is *Brahman* Itself.

KNOWER OF *BRAHMAN* BECOME FEARLESS

Brahman cannot be determined by thought or described in words. Nonetheless, he who understands It transcends all fear. *Brahman* is the source of heavenly bliss for those who know It or feel It within. It is also the cause of constant fear for those who deny It, or feel separate from It.

One who has realized *Brahman* requires no conscious effort to be virtuous, just as a trained dancer does not require any special effort to avoid wrong steps. His conduct becomes compatible with divine perfection. It is no longer impelled by any external standards of good and bad.

– *Swami Sarvananda*

Deep meditation draws off from man one sheath after another – *annamaya, pranamaya, manomaya* and *vigyanamaya* – until finally it arrives at *anandamaya* as the innermost core of man, and the ultimate nature of *Brahman*.

This peeling off of the sheaths of *Atman* holds good in the case of whole Nature as well. There are many passages pointing out that these five *Purushas* or *Atmans* or sheaths, are to be sought as much in the whole nature as in an individual man.

Annamaya Atman, is the material man and material nature. If we peel it off, we attain *Pranamaya Atman*. This is the vital principle in man as well as in nature. If we peel it off, we get *Manomaya Atman*. This is the man consisting of thought, will and wish. It is also the

---

*'One who has realized Brahman requires no conscious effort to be virtuous,
just as a trained dancer does not require any special effort to avoid wrong steps.'*

nature personified in Vedic gods – *Agni, Vayu, Indra* etc. The four Vedas together with *Brahman* form the physical part of this *Manomaya Purusha*. When we peel off the *Manomaya Atman* we are again raised one step higher to *Vigyanamaya Atman*. He who knows *Brahman* as *Vigyanamaya Atman* fulfils all his desires, but he has still not reached the highest.

Penetrating further, we find *Anandamaya Atman*, which consists entirely of Bliss.

The concluding part of verse 2.8,1 says that Bliss of *Brahman* is infinitely superior to all kinds of human or divine bliss. He who knows that everything is *Brahman* – that *Atman* in man and in sun are one – he transcends all the five selves and attains the highest of them all, that which can not be described by words or conceived by the mind. With this attainment, all sense of fear vanishes, as also sorrow about perishable things, good or bad.

– *Paul Deussen*

THE WORLD BORN IS OUT OF BLISS

Why are these five selves described in the first place? Their recognition helps to transcend the narrow identification of oneself merely as a physical individual; to develop a more broader, more universal outlook; and to become less self-centered. Their recognition also brings out various inner potentialities that exist in all human beings.

There is another aspect which is perhaps the most important of all. This is the fact that all levels of beings and experiences - from *annamaya* self to *vigyanamaya* self - are phenomena arising from and then dissolving into *anandamaya* self. They are mere plays on the surface of *anandamaya* self. This point is illustrated in section 2.8. States like man, human *gandharva*, divine *gandharva* etc. represent specific, quantitatively and qualitatively different existences. As we climb up each level, "Bliss" increases, while "World" decreases. At the level of *Brahman*, "World" is virtually gone, and diversity is replaced by Oneness of Bliss. Thus Bliss is associated more with *Brahman* than the World. When Bliss goes up World goes down. Because the context is clearly cosmic and objective, the implication is that Bliss is in some sense the foundation of the World and all experiences.

Later in chapter 3, Bhrigu realized that *Brahman* was Food, *Prana,* Mind, *Vigyana*; and that these were aspects from which all being are born, by which they are sustained and into which they merge. In all the four cases Bhrigu always returned to his father for further instructions. He was not completely satisfied, as he was still subject to suffering, or to human condition. But on realization of *Brahman* as *Ananda,* he did not return. There was complete satisfaction; suffering or human condition had been transcended. This suggests that in some metaphysical sense the world is born out of and ever merges into Bliss, *Ananda*.

Sri Satya Sai Baba uses the example of a doll made from sea-salt and then immersed into the sea. The four selves are born out of blissful self; they merge into it and become identical with it.

The primary objective of *anandamaya* self is *sankalpa*, the deepest will or determination in oneself. This *sankalpa* loses all its manifestations when it merges with inner Self, *Atman*. We might say that this *sankalpa* is a sacred aspect of *Atman*. It represents the reason for individual's existence. It has to do with the meaning of individual's life, and with his/her contribution (perhaps over many life-times) to creation, to world-total. An individual's *sankalpa* can be said to be contained in a universal *sankalpa* of *Brahman*. Blissful self has to do with this universal desire becoming realized. When this happens, the individual desire dissolves in Bliss. The salt-doll dissolves again in the ocean from whence it came. The merger of individual Self into *Brahman* is the final fulfillment of individual Self. It is becoming one with the Universal and the Total, and with the source of that Universal and Total, *Atman/Brahman*.

In Indian philosophy the question whether the *anandamaya* stage represents "being *Brahman*" or whether *Brahman* is beyond this stage, has a long history. Sri Sankara, in his commentary and elsewhere, argues that *Brahman* is not the sheath of Bliss, but lies within that sheath. With Ramanuja the pendulum swings the other way. *Anandamaya* Self is *Brahman*.

– *Klaus G. Witz*

'Having a universal outlook and not being self-centered brings out various inner potentialities that exist in all human beings.'

3. Bhrigu's self-discovery of Self

SIMPLIFIED SYNOPSES

3.1-3.6
Self realized through step-by-step reflection

Knowledge of the Highest cannot be attained through a high jump, it requires a step-by-step climb. Also, none can spoon-feed an aspirant with such knowledge; one has to persevere on one's own. Of course, a good guide can be a great help.

The Highest is also the inmost, encased in five selves. Its knowledge requires step-by-step reflection. This is illustrated with the story of a young aspirant Bhrigu and his learned father Varuna.

When Bhrigu approaches his father with a desire for knowledge of *Brahman*, he is given two tips:

- Reflect on the first three layers of human personality – physical, vital and mental – as doorways to knowledge of *Brahman*.
- Reflect on *Brahman* as the First Cause of all creation, preservation and dissolution.

Bhrigu begins his quest by reflecting on the physical self (*Annamaya Atman*). Human body is born from food (through the medium of procreative fluid, which the Upanishads regard as the essence of food). It is sustained by food and eventually it dissolves into primeval elements to become food for them. Therefore Bhrigu infers that food is *Brahman* and he goes to his father for confirmation. Varuna knows that Bhrigu's inference is only a fraction of the truth. So he sends him back with a third tip:

Think again, even focussed thinking (meditation) is *Brahman*.

Bhrigu reflects on a succession of inadequate conceptions of *Brahman* – the vital self (*Pranamaya Atman*) the mental self (*Manomaya Atman*) and the spiritual self (*Vigyanamaya Atman*). Every time he is asked by his father to reflect more on the subject. Finally, Bhrigu realizes that *Brahman* is bliss (*Ananda*). In some way, everything is born out of bliss and merges into bliss. When this realization dawns on Bhrigu, he does not go back to his father for confirmation. Correct understanding of *Brahman* makes one free from all doubts.

Does knowledge of *Brahman* lead to any fruitful results? Yes, the benefits are both material and spiritual, says the Upanishad.

> *'In some way, everything is born out of bliss and merges into bliss.'*

> *'Correct understanding of Brahman makes one free from all doubts.'*

3.7-3.10, 1
Show respect for food

Food sustains life. According to the Upanishads, food creates life by transforming itself into procreative fluid; and it also influences the mind. Therefore, the Upanishads glorify food in quite a few passages. Sections 3.7-3.10 contain injunctions to show respect for food: Do not criticize food, do not waste food, grow plenty of food, cook food with good feelings, and gift food to whosoever is in need of food. Gifts return back to the giver with the same sentiments as they are given, either in this life itself or in the next life.

Respect for food is a prerequisite for knowledge of *Brahman*.

3.10, 2-5
A mystical chant

Brahman or Cosmic Consciousness is present in everything – all organs of body and all objects of nature. Verses 3.10, 2-3 say that we become whatever is the object of our meditation. What we think with intensity and concentration, that we become.

Verse-4 repeats that it is the same *Brahman*, Absolute Consciousness, which pervades both man and cosmic objects like the sun.

Verse-5 is a song of joy which proclaims that the singer has become one with *Brahman*. The liberated soul sees itself in all existences, without any differentiation between the subject and the object. A rapturous embrace of the universe is the result. The Buddha is reported to have experienced a similar state of bliss at the time of his enlightenment.

'What we think with intensity and concentration, that we become.'

Translated Text

CHAPTER 3

Peace Invocation

Om.
May He protect us both (teacher and pupil).
May he nourish us together.
May we work jointly with great energy.
May our study be vigorous and fruitful.
May we not have any dispute.

Om. Shanti. Shanti. Shanti.
Let there be Peace, Let there be Peace, Let there be Peace.

Section 1

Bhrigu, the well-known son of Varuna, approached his father with a request: Revered Sir, please teach me about *Brahman*?

Varuna replied: "Food, life-breath, mind, sight, hearing and speech – these are the doors (aids) to the knowledge of *Brahman*."

Then he added: "Seek to know That from which all beings are born; having been born, by which they remain alive; and into which they enter on departing . That is *Brahman*."

Bhrigu practised austerity (of thought, *tapas*). He meditated.   **1**

Section 2

(After some meditation) Bhrigu thought that food (*Anna*) is *Brahman*. Certainly, all beings are born from food; having been born they remain alive by food, and on departing they enter into food. Having thus reflected (but not convinced) he again approached his father, saying: "Revered Sir, please teach me about *Brahman*"

Then Varuna replied: "Seek to know *Brahman* through meditation, *tapas*. Meditation is *Brahman*".

Bhrigu again practised meditation, after practising meditation...   **1**

Section 3

He (Bhrigu) thought that life-breath (*Prana*) is *Brahman*. Certainly, all beings are born from life-breath, having been born they remain alive by life-breath; and on departing they enter into life-breath. Having thus reflected (but not convinced), he again approached his father, saying: "Revered Sir, please teach me about *Brahman*."

Then Varuna repeated: "Seek to know *Brahman* through meditation (*tapas*). Meditation is *Brahman*."

"Seek to know Brahman through meditation (tapas). Meditation is Brahman."

Bhrigu again practised meditation. After practising meditation...   **1**

Section 4

He (Bhrigu) thought that mind (*manas*) is *Brahman*. Certainly, all beings are born from mind, having been born they remain alive by mind; and on departing they enter into mind. Having thus reflected (but not convinced), he again approached his father, saying: "Revered Sir, please teach me about *Brahman*."

Then Varuna again gave the same reply: "Seek to know *Brahman* through meditation (*tapas*). Meditation is *Brahman*."

Bhrigu again practised meditation. After practising meditation...   **1**

Section 5

He (Bhrigu) understood that intellect (*Vigyana*) is *Brahman*. Certainly, all beings are born from intellect, having been born they remain alive by intellect, and on departing they enter into intellect. Having thus reflected (but not convinced), he again approached his father, saying: "Revered Sir, please teach me about *Brahman*."

Again, Varuna replied: "Seek to know *Brahman* through meditation (*tapas*). Meditation is *Brahman*."

Bhrigu again practised meditation. After practising meditation...   **1**

Section 6

He (Bhrigu) realized that Bliss (*Ananda*) is *Brahman*. Certainly, all beings are born from Bliss, having been born they remain alive by Bliss, and on departing they enter into Bliss.

This is the knowledge learned by Bhrigu under guidance of Varuna. Supreme Bliss, *Brahman* is established in the highest heaven (within and without).

He who understands this becomes firmly established in Bliss. He (also) becomes possessor of food and cattle (wealth), eater of food (good health), great in progeny, fame and spiritual lustre. He gains fame from righteous conduct.   **1**

Section 7

Do not find fault with food. Let this be your pious rule.

Prana (vital energy) depends on food. Body is also nourished by food and kept alive by *Prana*. So both *Prana* and body are mutually dependent, and both depend on food.

He who understands this becomes firmly established. He also becomes possessor of food and cattle (wealth), eater of food (good health), great in progeny, fame and spiritual lustre.   **1**

"Bliss (Ananda) is Brahman. Certainly, all beings are born from Bliss.
Having been born, they remain alive by Bliss; and on departing they enter into Bliss."

Section 8

Do not waste food. Let this be your pious rule.

Water is food (as it is needed to grow food). Fire (energy latent in the digestive system) consumes (digests) food. Both water and fire are mutually dependent (as rain clouds are formed by heat of sun) and food needs both of them.

He who understands this becomes firmly established. He also becomes possessor of food and cattle (wealth), eater of food (good health), great in progeny, fame and spiritual lustre. **1**

Section 9

Produce plenty of food. Let this be your pious rule.

Earth is food, space is the consumer of food. Space surrounds earth. Earth is placed in space. Thus, one food is lodged in another.

He who understands this becomes firmly established. He also becomes possessor of food and cattle (wealth), eater of food (good health), great in progeny, fame and spiritual lustre. **1**

Section 10

Do not decline shelter to anyone. Let this be your pious rule. Also, store and offer sufficient food (to the person who seeks shelter).

Food prepared and offered (to a guest) with good feelings (*sattvic*) comes back to the host (in due course) with good feelings. Food prepared and offered with indifference comes back with indifference. Food prepared and offered grudgingly comes back likewise.

He who knows this (importance of offering shelter and food), to him benefits accrue as per his merits. **1**

It (*Brahman*) resides as preservation in speech, as acquisition and preservation in in-breath and out-breath, as activity in hands, as movement in feet, as evacuation in anus – these are the powers pertaining to human beings.

Next, with reference to cosmic powers, It (*Brahman*) resides as satisfaction in rain, as energy in lightening, as fame in ownership of cattle, as light in stars, as procreation, immortality and joy in the generative organs, as everything in space.

When one meditates upon It as the support of all, one becomes well-supported.
When one meditates upon It as greatness, one becomes great.
When one meditates upon It as mind, one becomes of good-mind.
When one meditates upon It as salutations, all desires bow down before one.
When one meditates upon It as the supreme, one acquires supreme wisdom.
When one meditates upon It as a destructive aspect of *Brahman*, one's rivals and enemies perish. **2-3**

"Food prepared and offered (to a guest) with good feelings comes back to the host (in due course) with good feelings."

He who is here in the person, and He who is there in the sun is one.

He who knows thus, on departing from this world, transcends successively the self consisting of *Anna*, *Prana*, *Manas*, *Vigyana* and *Ananda*. He lives in the world, enjoying food and form, at will. He sings this *Sama* song: **4**

"Oh, wonderful! Oh wonderful!
I am food; I am food.
I am the eater, I am the eater, I am the eater.
I am the unifier, I am the unifier, I am the unifier.
I am the first-born of this cosmic order.
I existed even prior to gods.
I am the centre of immortality.
He who gives to me alone saves.
I, food as I am, eat the eater of food.
I have overcome the whole world.
I am brilliant like the sun."

He who knows this (gets the results mentioned earlier). This is the Upanishad. **5**

Peace Invocation

Om.
May He protect us both (teacher and pupil).
May he nourish us together.
May we work jointly with great energy.
May our study be vigorous and fruitful.
May we not have any dispute.

Om. Shanti. Shanti. Shanti.
Let there be Peace, Let there be Peace, Let there be Peace.

Om.
May Mitra, Varuna, Aryaman, Indra, Brhaspati
    and Vishnu of wide strides be favorable to us.
I bow to *Brahman*.

O *Vayu*, I bow to Thee.
Indeed, you are the visible *Brahman*.
I shall call you Righteousness.
I shall call you Truth.
May that *Brahman* known as *Vayu* protect me.
May that *Brahman* protect my teacher.

Om. Shanti. Shanti. Shanti.
Let there be Peace, Let there be Peace, Let there be Peace.

"I am the centre of immortality."

FOCUSSED COMMENTARIES

CHAPTER 3

3.1-3.6 Self-realized through step-by-step reflection

It is remarkable and splendid that Varuna does not himself impart the doctrine of *Brahman*. He only speaks a few oft quoted words in which *Brahman* is recognizable (3.1,1). Whereupon, Bhrigu himself, by way of continued austerities, comprehends *Brahman* in an increasing introspection – as Food, as Vital Breath, as Mind, as Knowledge and finally as Bliss.

– *Paul Deussen*

A good teacher gives hints to students and encourages them to work out the problem by themselves. He never extinguishes a disciple's spirit of enquiry by supplying him with instant, ready-made answers. Likewise, Varuna gave only a suggestive answer to Bhrigu. By enumerating various aids to knowledge of *Brahman*, Varuna was alluding to four of the five layers of human personality: physical (food or *Annamaya*), life-breath (*Pranamaya*), mind (*Manomaya*), and Intellect (*Vigyanamaya*), Varuna also described the three well-known aspects of *Brahman* – creation, sustenance and dissolution.

'Bhrigu practised meditation (austerity of thought, *tapas*).' This sentence is repeated five times at the end of the first and the four subsequent lessons. The repetition is meant to emphasize that concentration is the most effective means of knowing *Brahman*.

The value of *tapas* or meditation is emphasized repeatedly in various Upanishads. The literal meaning of the word *tapas* is 'to give heat' or 'to suffer pain'. In the initial stages *tapas* consists of physical austerities like fasting. In advanced stages *tapas* means mastery of will and thoughts. Getting rid of desires and focussing the mind on the Divine Reality is the purest and the highest form of *tapas*.

Bhrigu was not satisfied with his first inference that food or, more appropriately, matter is *Brahman*. So, he approached his father again for knowledge about *Brahman*. Noticing Bhrigu's inference that food is *Brahman*, his father realized the need for further *tapas* by Bhrigu. So he instructed his son to seek *Brahman* again through *tapas*.

Through contemplation and reasoning, Bhrigu found that body (referred to as food or *Anna*) is perishables, breath (*Prana*) is unconscious, mind (*Manas*) is changeable and intellect (*Vigyana*) is limited and exposed to pleasure and pain. Therefore, none of these satisfied the definition of *Brahman* given by his father. Eventually, he contemplated on the highest layer of human personality – Bliss or *Ananda* – and concluded that Bliss itself is *Brahman*.

Varuna took his son step by step from the gross to the subtler and subtler aspects of existence – from the gross physical self to the innermost Bliss – and made him recognize Bliss to be *Brahman* Itself.

Does knowledge of *Brahman* lead to any fruitful results? Yes, says the Upanishad. The benefits are both spiritual and material. At the spiritual level, the knower of *Brahman* attains the blissful state. At the physical level, he gains plenty of wealth, good health, fame and a good family.

– *Swami Sarvananda*

Varuna defines *Brahman* as That from which all beings are born, by which they remain alive, and into which they eventually dissolve. This definition applies to all planes or levels of beings – Matter, Life, Mind, Understanding and Bliss. Now, if in his enquiry, Bhrigu knew that Matter is *Brahman*, why did he not stop at Matter? The implication in Taittiriya is that materialism is a phase and a first step in the enquiry into *Brahman*. In the teaching of Self by Prajapati to Indra among the gods and Virochana among the demons in Chandogya Upanishad, Virochana *stopped* at the first stage of teaching viz. Self is the body, but Indra did not. Bhrigu did not stop at Matter, or Life, or Mind, or Understanding, because he was not convinced that these satisfied the definition of *Brahman* as given by his father.

– *N. A. Nikam*

'A good teacher never extinguishes a disciple's spirit of enquiry by supplying him with instant, ready-made answers.'

3.7-3.10, 1 Show respect for food

It is astonishing that falling down from the high standpoint attained by equating Bliss with *Brahman*, this teaching glorifies *Brahman* as food (3.7-3.9). Section 3.10 extols *Brahman* as the essence of food and as the eater of food; that is, as the object and the subject, as *bhogyam* and *bhokta*.

— Paul Deussen

Sections 3.7 to 3.9 glorify food and ask us to treat food with respect. We should make it a spiritual rule not to find fault with food and not to waste food. We should also produce plenty of food.

Food is essential for a healthy body, and for life itself. Food also has strong relationships with the five elements of nature – air, water, fire, earth and space.

The suggestion is that the body, which is the first and the fundamental instrument for knowing *Brahman*, should not be neglected even when one has progressed far in the spiritual path. We can keep our body healthy only when we respect food and thank *Brahman* for the food that He gives us to eat.

Respect for food is a prerequisite for knowledge of *Brahman*.

— Swami Sarvananda

3.10, 2-5 A mystical chant

Verse 3.10,5 is a song of joy. The manifold diversity of life is attuned to a single harmony. A lyrical and rapturous embrace of the universe is the result. The liberated soul, filled with delight, recognizes its oneness with the subject and the object – food, eater of food, and the principle which unites them. He feels that he is one with *Brahman*, with *Ishvar* (Lord of manifested universe) and with *Hiranyagarbha* (Cosmic Mind).

The chant proclaims that the Enlightened One has become one with all. The liberated soul passes beyond all limitations and attains to the dignity of God Himself. It feels as one with God in all His fullness and unity. It has overcome the whole world.

Compare this with the Buddha's declaration after attaining enlightenment:

'Subdued have I all, all-knowing am I now.
Unattached to all things, and abandoning all,
Finally freed on the destruction of all craving,
Knowing it myself, whom else should I credit?
There is no teacher of mine, nor is one like me;
There is none to rival me in the world of men and gods;
Truly entitled to honor am I, a teacher unexcelled.
Alone am I a Supreme Buddha, placid and tranquil,
To found the kingdom of righteousness, I proceed to Kasi's capital,
Beating the drum of immortality in the world enveloped by darkness.'

— *Ariyaparyesana Sutta. Majjhima Nikaya*

— S. Radhakrishnan

---

*'The liberated soul, filled with delight, recognizes its oneness
with the subject and the object – and the principle which unites them.'*

Chandogya Upanishad

That thou art

OVERVIEW

Chandogya Upanishad declares the oneness of man and God in the great aphorism, 'That thou art.'

The main theme of the Upanishad is meditation. Its eight long chapters describe various principles and techniques of meditation. These are called Vidya or Upasana; and they have been presented in the form of dialogues. Important Vidyas and dialogues are tabulated on the next page for ease of reference.

Chapter 1-2 and some sections of chapter 3 may not interest many readers and can therefore be skipped.

COMMENTARIES

The translated text has been supplemented with commentaries by Sri Sankara (translation by Swami Gambhirananda), Swami Swahananda, Swami Krishnananda, Paul Deussen, Klaus G. Witz, Dr. S. Radhakrishnan and Sri Aurobindo (Incomplete writings). There is also a very insightful commentary by Swami Gambhirananda on Meditation (page 349).

Some important dialogues have been presented as renditions, to avoid back and forth reference between translated text and commentaries. This is in addition to the normal commentaries.

PRINCIPAL VIDYAS OF CHANDOGYA UPANISHAD

Sr. No.	Name of Vidya	Chapter/Section	Description
1	Om	1.1	Meditation on Om as a symbol of Brahman.
2	Udgitha and Saman	1.2-2.24	Meditation on songs of Sama Veda.
3	Madhu Vidya	3.1-3.11	Meditation on Sun.
4	Gayatri Vidya	3.12	Meditation on Gayatri Mantra.
5	Parajyotir Vidya	3.13	Meditation on Light of Brahman in man.
6	Sandilya Vidya	3.14	Meditation Self within and without.
7	Samvarga Vidya	4.1-4.3	Meditation on Cosmic Life Principle as Life-breath.
8	Panchagni Vidya	5.3-5.10	Five Cosmic Fires, two paths.
9	Vaisvanara Vidya	5.11-5.18	Meditation on Brahman as Totality.
10	Prana Agnihotra	5.19-5.24	Five symbolic offerings of food to Life-breath.
10	Bhuma Vidya	7.1-7.15	Infinite alone is Happiness.
11	Dahara Vidya	8.1-8.15	Meditation on Self within.

PRINCIPAL DIALOGUES OF CHANDOGYA UPANISHAD

Sr. No.	Participants in the Dialogue	Chapter/Sections	Subject
1	Raikva and Janashruti, (Cart-driver and King)	4.4-4.3	Samvarga Vidya (A special technique of meditation).
2	Satyakama and Nature	4.4-4.9	'Four feet' of Brahman, Absolute Consciousness.
3	Shvetaketu and his father Uddalaka	6	'That thou art' (one of the four great aphorisms).
4	Narada and Sanatkumar (Sage and Warrior)	7	Bhuma Vidya or 'Infinite alone is Happiness'.
5	Seeker and Preceptor	8.1-8.6	Dahara Vidya, or Meditation on Self within.
6	Prajapati, Indra and Virochana (Creator, Chief of gods and Chief of demons)	8.7-8.12	Self (Atman) and its three states.

CHANDOGYA UPANISHAD
That thou art

Peace Invocation

CHAPTER 1
Meditation on Om 333

1.1	Greatness of the symbol *Om*
1.2-1.3	*Om* identified with Life Principle
1.4	*Om* protects from fear of death
1.5	Sun, *Prana*, *Om* and *Udgitha* are same
1.6-1.7	Sun and Self illumined by same Cosmic Person
1.8-1.9	Space is the ultimate support
1.10-1.11	Deities of *Saman* songs
1.12	A satire on priestly rituals
1.13	Mystical meaning of *Saman*

CHAPTER 2
Meditation on Vedic Chants 352

2.1-2.7	Meditation on fivefold *Saman*
2.8-2.10	Meditation on sevenfold *Saman*
2.11-2.21	Meditation on all-inclusive *Saman*
2.22	Recitation of *Saman*
2.23	*Om*: Origin and importance
2.24	*Soma* sacrifice: Its symbolic significance

CHAPTER 3
Vidya: Art of Meditation 362

3.1-3.11	*Madhu Vidya*: Meditation on Sun
3.12	*Gayatri Vidya*: *Brahman* is space outside and within man
3.13	*Parajyotir Vidya*: Light of *Brahman* in man

3.14	*Sandilya Vidya*: Meditation on Self within and without	
3.15	Prayer for son's longevity	
3.16	Prayer for a life of 116 years	
3.17	Man's life is like a sacrifice	
3.18	Meditation on Mind and Sky as *Brahman*	
3.19	Meditation on Sun as *Brahman*	

CHAPTER 4	SPIRITUAL LESSONS FROM NATURE AND FIRES	380
4.1-4.3	*Samvarga Vidya*: Meditation on Life-breath	
4.4-4.9	Satyakama learns about *Brahman* from Nature	
4.10-4.15	Upakosala learns about *Brahman* from three Fires.	
4.16	Silence and speech in sacrificial rituals	

CHAPTER 5	MAN'S CONNECTION WITH COSMOS	398
5.1- 5.2, 3	*Prana*: Parable on its superiority	
5.2, 4-8	*Mantha rite* for harmony with cosmos	
5.3-5.9	*Panchagni Vidya*: Five cosmic fires	
5.10	Two paths after death: Liberation and rebirth	
5.11-5.18	*Vaisvanara Vidya*: *Brahman* is Totality	
5.19-5.24	*Prana Agnihotra*: Five symbolic offerings of food	

CHAPTER 6	THAT THOU ART	413
6.1	A famous question	
6.2-6.4	From Absolute to elements, then their multiplication	
6.5-6.7	From elements to mind, speech and life-breath	
6.8-6.16	That thou art	

CHAPTER 7	*BHUMA VIDYA*: IT IS ALL ABOUT HAPPINESS	433
7.1-7.7	Wisdom gives greater happiness than learning	
7.8-7.12	Physical strength and primal elements	
7.13-7.15	Memory, Aspiration and Life-breath	
7.16-7.22	A happy man is an active man	
7.23-7.26	Happiness = Infinitude = Self = I	

CHAPTER 8	*DAHARA VIDYA*: MEDITATION ON SELF WITHIN	450
8.1	Vast universe in a small space in the heart	
8.2-8.5	True desires are always fulfilled	
8.6	Infinitization of Self	
8.7-8.12	One teaching, two interpretations	
8.13-8.15	Ecstasy of Self-realization	

1 Meditation on *Om*

SIMPLIFIED SYNOPSES

1.1
Greatness of the symbol *Om*

The Upanishad begins with an instruction to concentrate on the holy syllable *Om* during meditation; and then describes the greatness of this syllable.

- *Udgitha* is an important song of *Sama Veda*. It is sung during *Soma* sacrifice. As it begins with the syllable *Om*, it is given the same importance as *Om*, a sacred symbol of *Brahman*. (1)
- *Om* is the quintessence of all essences. (2-3)
- *Om* has the quality of fulfilling all desires. (4-7)
- *Om* is a sign of consent and prosperity. (8)
- All Vedic rites begin with *Om* and are performed for worship of *Om* itself. (9)

In conclusion, it is stated that a ritual is more effective when it is performed with faith, concentration and knowledge of its significance.

1.2-1.3
***Om* identified with Life Principle**

Section-2 uses a parable to explain meditation on *Udgitha* or *Om* as a symbol of Life Principle, *Prana*, with reference to the self. When gods meditated on *Udgitha* as sense organs – smell, speech, sight, and hearing – demons afflicted them with evil. However, when gods meditated on *Udgitha* as *Prana* or Life Principle, demons could not inflict any harm. The section ends with examples of three sages to indicate the benefits that accrue from meditation on *Prana* as *Udgitha*, or *Om*.

Section-3 describes meditation on *Prana* as *Udgitha* (*Om*) with reference to cosmic powers. Here, *Prana*, Life Principle is compared to the Sun. Also, in the Upanishads, life-breath is considered to have five forms. The identity of one of these – *Vyana* or diffused breath – is traced to *Udgitha* (1-5). This is followed by an etymological significance of the word *Udgitha* (6-7), and instructions regarding what the mind should concentrate upon during the singing of *Udgitha*.

Passages in Sections 2-3 suggest that *Prana* is not merely a psychical but also a Cosmic Principle. It is not only the breath of life in man, but also the universal breath of life, which prevails throughout the whole of nature.

1.4
***Om* protects from fear of death**

Chanting of *Om* is more effective than even Vedic rituals for alleviating fear of death. This is brought out by a short parable. Once, gods took shelter in Vedic hymns to hide themselves from Death, but they got noticed, like fish in water. However, when they hid themselves in the syllable *Om*, Death could not see them.

1.5
Sun, *Prana*, *Om* and *Udgitha* are same

In earlier sections it has been stated that *Udgitha* is a symbol of Sun and also *Prana*. The same holds good in the case of syllable *Om*, which is identical with *Udgitha*. Sun represents the vitalizing force in nature, *Prana* represents the vitalizing force in man. Kausitaki is stated to have only one son because he meditated on the unity underlying Sun and *Prana*. But this unity is not without multiplicity. Meditation on not just Sun but on its many rays, and not just *Prana* but on its many aspects, would yield multiple benefits like many sons, says the Upanishad.

1.6-1.7
Sun and Self illumined by same Cosmic Person

Verses of *Rg Veda* are called *Rk* and songs of *Sama Veda* are called *Saman*. *Saman* is supported by *Rk*, just as fire is supported by earth, air by sky, sun by heavens, moon by stars and darkness by light. Just as *Udgitha* governs both *Rk* and *Saman*, the Cosmic Person (*Purusha*) governs the above-mentioned cosmic powers. (1.6, 1-4) This Cosmic Person is described as having golden hair and beard. (1.6, 5-8). As sun is illumined by this Cosmic Person, He is said to reside in sun.

At the psychical level also, life-breath and speech, physical form and eye, mind and ear are interrelated. The Being who rules them resides in the eye. (1.7,1-4).

Next, the Upanishad makes an important declaration. The Being in the eye who illumines man and the Being in the sun who illumines the universe, is One and the same. When a person sings *Saman*, he is in fact singing to this Being (*Purusha*) in both His forms – the Cosmos and man.

1.8-1.9
Space is the ultimate support

These two sections narrate a conversation on *Udgitha* between two learned scholars of priestly class, Silaka Salavatya and Chaikitayana Dalbhya, and a learned warrior–king, Pravahana Jaivali. Dalbhya's view is that the heavenly worlds are the ultimate support of all, represented by *Saman* and *Udgitha*. Silaka's view is that heavenly worlds are dependent on earthly world, which therefore must be the ultimate support of *Saman* and *Udgitha*. Finally, king Pravahana proves that it is space (*Akash)*, on which both heavenly worlds and earthly world are dependent. Therefore, *Akash* is to be adored as the highest and the best symbol of *Udgitha*.

Interestingly, elsewhere the same king has also propounded the doctrine of transmigration of the soul (Brhadaranyaka 6.2, Chandogya 5.3-5.10).

1.10-1.11
Deities of *Saman* songs

A *Saman* has three important parts – *Prastava*, *Udgitha* and *Pratihara*. Their corresponding deities are *Prana*, Sun and Food respectively. One must know the deity to whom a hymn is devoted, before one starts singing a hymn. This is the essence of these two sections. It has been narrated in the form of a story for easy comprehension. A poor but learned *Brahmin*, Usasti, warns the priests that they should not sing these hymns without knowing their presiding deities.

1.12
A satire on priestly rituals

In this brief section, a few dogs imitate some priests in singing hymns and asking gods to bring food for them. Some commentators interpret this section allegorically, while others consider it to be a satire on priests.

1.13
Mystical meaning of *Saman*

This section provides a mystical meaning (Upanishad) of certain sounds, which occur during the singing of *Samans*. Thirteen sounds in the chant called *stobha* are interpreted as thirteen world phenomena, but without any proof or explanation.

'The Being in the eye who illumines man and the Being in the sun who illumines the universe, is One and the same.'

Translated Text

Peace Invocation

Om.
May my limbs, speech, life-breath, eyes, ears, and senses grow in strength.
All existence is *Brahman* of the Upanishads.
May I never be unaware of *Brahman*.
May *Brahman* never spurn me.
May there be no ignorance of *Brahman*.
May the Truths stated in the Upanishads repose in me.
Delighting in *Atman*, may they repose in me.

Om. Shanti. Shanti. Shanti.
Let there be Peace, Let there be Peace, Let there be Peace.

CHAPTER 1

Section 1

Om, One should meditate on this syllable. It is identified with Udgitha (a high song of Sama Veda sung at the time of Soma sacrifice), as the singing of Udgitha begins with *Om*. The explanation (of meditation) is as follows: **1**

The essence of all beings is earth. The essence of earth is water. The essence of water is vegetation. The essence of vegetation is man. The essence of man is speech. The essence of speech is Rk. The essence of Rk is Saman. The essence of Saman is Udgitha.   **2**

The syllable *Om*, which is identified with Udgitha, is the quintessence of all the essences, the Supreme. It deserves the highest rank in (the aforesaid) eight essences.   **3**

What is Rk? What is Saman? What is Udgitha? This is considered now.   **4**

Speech alone is Rk; *Prana* is Saman. The syllable *Om* is Udgitha. That is why they form a pair - Speech and *Prana*, Rk and Saman.   **5**

These pairs are joined together in the syllable *Om*. Whenever a pair (couple) are together, they fulfil each other's desire.   **6**

He who meditates on this syllable as Udgitha, knowing it thus, he truly fulfils all desirable ends.   **7**

Om is a sign of concurrence. Whenever one concurs with anything, one says *Om*. Concurrence leads to prosperity. He who, with this knowledge, meditates on *Om* as Udgitha, prospers (in the fulfillment of his desires).   **8**

Vedic rites are begun with *Om*. These are meant for worship of *Om* itself. Hymns,

---

"May I never be unaware of Brahman."

songs in praise of God and prayers also begin with *Om*. With its greatness and essence (Vedic rites are performed). **9**

With *Om*, both perform rites: he who knows it and he who does not know it. Knowledge and ignorance lead to different results. Whatever is performed with knowledge, faith and concentration is more effective. Indeed, this is an approximate explanation of the syllable *Om*. **10**

Section 2

Once, when gods and demons (Devas and Asuras) – both descendants of *Prajapati* – were fighting with each other, gods took Udgitha. They thought they will vanquish demons with it. **1**

Then they (the gods) meditated on Udgitha as sense of smell in the nose; but the demons afflicted it with evil. That is why through the nose one smells both sweet-smelling and bad-smelling objects. It is afflicted with evil. **2**

Then they meditated on Udgitha as speech; but the demons afflicted it with evil. That is why through speech one speaks both truth and untruth. It is afflicted with evil. **3**

Then they meditated on Udgitha as sight in the eyes; but the demons afflicted it with evil. That is why through eyes one sees both, what is worth seeing and what is not worth seeing. It is afflicted with evil. **4**

Then they meditated on Udgitha as hearing in the ears; but the demons afflicted it with evil. That is why through ears one hears both, what should be heard and what should not be heard. It is afflicted with evil. **5**

Then they meditated on Udgitha as the mind; but the demons afflicted it with evil. That is why with mind one thinks both good and bad thoughts. It is afflicted with evil. **6**

Then they meditated on Udgitha at life-breath (*Prana*) in the mouth. The demons hit against it; but they were destroyed, like one who hits against a hard rock. **7**

A lump of clay is destroyed when it strikes against a hard rock; so also he who wishes evil or tries to injure one who knows (the purity of *Prana*); because such a knower is like a hard rock. **8**

Through this (life-breath) in the mouth one smells neither sweet smell nor bad-smell. Whatever a person eats or drinks through it, that nourishes life-breaths. When one departs finally, the mouth is left open for want of life-breath. **9**

Angirasa meditated upon *Prana* as Udgitha. People think it (*Prana*) is Angirasa, because it is the essence of all limbs. **10**

"Whatever is performed with knowledge, faith and concentration is more effective."

Brhaspati meditated upon *Prana* as Udgitha. People think it (*Prana*) is Brhaspati, because speech is great and *Prana* is its Lord. **11**

Ayasya meditated on *Prana* as Udgitha. People think that it (*Prana*) is Ayasya, because it goes out from the mouth. **12**

Baka the son of Dalbhya knew *Prana* well, so he became the Udgatr priest of the people of Naimisa. He sang (Udgitha) to fulfil their desires. **13**

He who knows thus and meditates on Udgitha as the syllable *Om*, fulfils his wishes by singing (Udgitha). **14**

These verses refer to meditation with reference to Self, Atman.

Section 3

Now, meditation on Udgitha with reference to gods is described.

One should meditate on him who shines like Udgitha. As the sun rises, it sings the song of Udgitha for all creatures; it dispels darkness and fear. He who has this knowledge, surely becomes destroyer of darkness and fear. **1**

Surely, Life-breath (*Prana*) and Sun are similar. This is warm (life-breath keeps the body warm) and that too is warm. They identity *Prana* with vibrations, and Sun with moving on and coming back. Therefore, one should meditate on this *Prana* and that Sun as Udgitha. **2**

One should also meditate on *Vyana* (diffused-breath) as Udgitha. When one breathes in, it is *Apana*; when one breathes out, it is *Prana*. The connecting factor between *Prana* and *Apana* is *Vyana*. *Vyana*, however, is same as speech. One utters speech without breathing-in or breathing-out. **3**

That, which is speech, that is Rk. One pronounces Rk without breathing-in or breathing-out.

That, which is Rk, that is Saman. One sings Saman without breathing-in or breathing-out. **4**

Whatever actions there are that require strength – such as the kindling of fire by friction, running a race, bending a strong bow – these are performed without in-breathing and without out-breathing. Therefore, one should meditate on diffused-breath, *Vyana,* as Udgitha. **5**

Now, one should meditate on the syllables of Udgitha - *ut, gi, tha*. *Prana* is *ut,* because of *Prana* one is able to stand up; speech is *gi*, because speech is called *girah*; food is *tha* because all this is rooted (*stitham*) in food. **6**

> Heaven is *ut*, sky is *gi*, earth is *tha*,
> Sun is *ut*, air is *gi*, fire is *tha*.
> *Sama Veda* is *ut*, *Yajur Veda* is *gi*, *Rg Veda* is *tha*.

"Surely, Life-breath (Prana) and Sun are similar.
This is warm (Life-breath keeps the body warm), and that too is warm."

Speech yields milk (capacity to recite) to him who knowing thus, meditates on the syllables of Udgitha (viz. *ut, gi, tha*). He becomes rich with nutrition by consuming food. **7**

Now (the method for) fulfillment of desires. One should meditate on desired objects. One should reflect on the appropriate Saman through which one sings the *stotra* (verse in praise of a deity). **8**

One should reflect upon the Rk on which the Saman occurs, upon the sage to whom it was revealed, and upon the deity, which is to be worshiped in the *stotra*. **9**

One should reflect upon the meter in which one proceeds to sing a *stotra*. He should also reflect upon the hymn with which one proceeds to sing it. **10**

One should reflect on the quarters (of heaven) towards which he is about to sing a *stotra*. **11**

Finally, one should turn inward into one's own Self and sing the *stotra*, meditating faultlessly on one's desires Very quickly, there will be fulfillment of the desire for which he sings the *stotra*; yes, the desire for which he sings the *stotra*. **12**

Section 4

Om, one should meditate on this symbol. It is identified with Udgitha, as the singing of Udgitha begins with *Om*. Its explanation is follows: **1**

The gods, being afraid of death, took refuge in the three Vedas (Vedic-rites). They covered themselves with metrical hymns, which came to be known as *chandas* (lit. 'to cover'). **2**

Death saw them in (in the rites connected with *Rg, Sama* and *Yajur Veda*), just as one might see fish in water. When the gods found this out, they got out from *Rg, Sama* and *Yajur*, and entered into the syllable *Om*. **3**

Verily, when one learns Rk, he loudly pronounces *Om*. It is the same with Saman, and with Yajus. The sound syllable *Om* is immortality and fearlessness. Meditating upon this sound, the gods became immortal and fearless. **4**

He, who worships this syllable, knowing it thus, enters this syllable, the sound, which is immortality and fearlessness. And having entered it, he becomes immortal by that nectar which made the gods became immortal. **5**

Section 5

Now, that which is Udgitha is, verily, Pranav. *Om* and Pranav are both Udgitha. The yonder Sun is Udgitha and also Pranav. It moves along as if pronouncing 'Om'. **1**

"The sound syllable Om is immortality and fearlessness.
Meditating upon this sound, the gods became immortal and fearless."

'I meditated on Sun alone, therefore I got you as my only son' so said Kausitaki to his son. When you reflect upon the rays of the sun, you will have many sons. This is the meditation with reference to the gods (*adhidaiva*).   **2**

Now with reference to the self (*adhyatman*), one should meditate on *Prana* as Udgitha; because it moves along in the mouth as if pronouncing *Om*.   **3**

'I sang to *Prana*, therefore I got you as my only son', so said Kausitaki to his son. 'I shall get many sons', thinking thus, sing praise of Udgitha as the manifold *Prana*.   **4**

Now, Udgitha is Pranav; and Pranav is Udgitha. Therefore, mistakes in singing of Udgitha can be corrected by the Hotr Priest; yes, corrected.   **5**

Section 6

Earth is surely Rk, fire is Saman. This Saman rests upon that Rk. Therefore, Saman is sung as resting upon Rk. Earth is *sa*, fire is *ama*; and that adds up to *Sama*.   **1**

Sky is surely Rk, air is Saman. This Saman rests upon that Rk. Therefore, Saman is sung as resting upon Rk. Sky is *sa*, air is *ama*; and that adds upto *Sama*.   **2**

Heaven is surely Rk, Sun is Saman. This Saman rests upon that Rk. Therefore, Saman is sung as resting upon Rk. Heaven is *sa*, sun is *ama*; and that adds up to *Sama*.   **3**

Stars are Rk, moon is Saman. This Saman rests upon that Rk. Therefore, Saman is sung as resting upon Rk. Stars are *sa*, moon is *ama*, and that adds up to *Sama*.   **4**

Now, the white light of the sun is Rk, the blue (light) that is extremely dark is Saman. This Saman rests upon that Rk. Therefore, Saman is sung as resting upon Rk.   **5**

Again, the white light of the sun is *sa*, the blue (light) that is extremely dark is *ama*, and that makes *Sama*. Now, that Person, effulgent as gold, who is seen in the sun, who is with a golden beard and golden hair, is exceedingly effulgent to the very tip of His nails.   **6**

His eyes are bright like a red lotus. His name is *ut*. He has risen above all evils. Verily, he who knows thus rises above all evils.   **7**

Rk and Saman are his two joints. Therefore He is Udgatha. Because the priest is the singer of this *ut*, he is Udgatha. Moreover, He (this Person called *ut*) controls the worlds, which are above that sun, as also the desires of gods. This is with reference to the gods.   **8**

"Now, that Person, effulgent as gold, who is seen in the sun, who is with a golden beard and golden hair, is exceedingly effulgent to the very tip of His nails."

Section 7

Now (meditation) with reference to Self: Speech is Rk, *Prana* is Saman. This Saman rests upon that Rk. Therefore Saman is sung as resting upon Rk. Speech is sa, *Prana* is *ama*, and that makes *Sama*. **1**

Eye is Rk, Self (reflected in that eye) is Saman. This Saman rests upon that Rk. Therefore Saman is sung as resting upon Rk. The eye is *sa*, the Self is *ama* and that makes *Sama*. **2**

Ear is Rk, mind is Saman. This Saman rests upon that Rk. Therefore Saman is sung as resting upon Rk. Ear is *sa*, mind is *ama*, and that makes *Sama*. **3**

Now, white light of the eye is Rk, blue (light) that is extremely dark is Saman. This Saman rests upon that Rk. Therefore Saman is sung as resting upon Rk. White light of the eye is *sa*, blue (light) that is extremely dark is *ama*, and that makes Saman. **4**

Now, this Person who is seen the eye – he indeed is Rk, he is Saman, he is *Uktha*, he is Yajus, he is the *Vedas*. The form of this (Person seen in the eye) is the same as the form of that (Person seen in the sun). His joints are the same as those of the other; his name is the same as that of the other. **5**

That (Person in the eye) is the lord of all the worlds, as also of the desired objects of men. So those who sing on the lute, *veena*, sing of him alone and thereby become endowed with wealth. **6**

Now he who sings Saman after knowing the deity Udgitha thus, sings to both. Through that (Person in the sun), he (that singer) gets the worlds above him and also the desired objects of gods. **7**

Similarly, through this Person in the eye, one gets the world that are below him, and also the desired objects of men. For this reason, the Udgatr priest who knows thus should ask (the sacrificer):

'What desire shall I obtain for you by singing the Saman?'

For he alone becomes capable of obtaining desires by singing; who knowing thus sings Saman. Yes, he sings Saman. **8-9**

Section 8

In ancient times there were three persons well versed in Udgitha: Silaka, son of Salavatya, Chaikitayana of Dalbhya family, and Pravahana, son of Jaivali. They said, 'We are proficient in Udgitha. Let us have a discussion on Udgitha.' **1**

'Let it be so', saying this they sat down. Then Pravahana Jaivali said, 'You two, revered sirs, speak first; and I shall listen to the words of two *Brahmins*.' **2**

"The form of this (Person seen in the eye) is the same as the form of That (Person seen in the sun)."

Then Silaka Salavatya said to Chaikitayana Dalbhya, 'If you permit, I shall question you.' 'Question', said he. **3**

Silaka	:	What is the essence of Saman?
Dalbhya	:	Sound.
Silaka	:	What is the essence of sound?
Dalbhya	:	*Prana*.
Silaka	:	What is the essence of *Prana*?
Dalbhya	:	Food.
Silaka	:	What is the essence of food?
Dalbhya	:	Water.

4

Silaka	:	What is the essence of water?
Dalbhya	:	That (heavenly) world.
Silaka	:	What is the essence of that world?
Dalbhya	:	One cannot carry (Saman) beyond the heavenly world. We regard heavenly worlds as the support of Saman, for Saman is praised as heaven.

5

Silaka : O Dalbhya, your Saman has no support. (Your error is so serious that) at this time, if someone were to say, 'Your head shall fall off', your head will fall. **6**

Dalbhya	:	Will you permit me, sir, to learn this from you?
Silaka	:	What?
Dalbhya	:	What is the essence of that (heavenly) world?
Silaka	:	This earth.
Dalbhya	:	What is the essence of this earth?
Silaka	:	One cannot carry Saman beyond this world as its support.
Dalbhya	:	We regard this earth as the support of Saman, for Saman is extolled as the earth.

7

Pravahana	:	O Silaka, your Saman, really, has a further end. If someone now were to say, 'Your head shall fall off, surely your head would fall.'
Silaka	:	Will you permit me, sir, to learn this from you?
Pravahana	:	What?

Section 9

Silaka	:	What is the essence of this world?
Pravahana	:	Space, *Akash*. All these beings arise in *Akash* alone and are finally dissolved into *Akash*; because *Akash* alone is greater than all these and *Akash* is the support at all times.

1

This is Udgitha, the highest and the best. It is endless. He who, knowing it thus, meditates upon the highest and the best Udgitha, obtains the highest and the best life and wins the highest and the best worlds. **2**

When Atidhanvan, son of Saunaka, taught this to Udara Sandilya, he also said, 'As long as this knowledge of Udgitha continues among your descendants, their

---

"All these beings arise in Akash (Space) alone and are finally dissolved into Akash."

life in this world will be the highest and the best. And in the other world also their state will be similar.'

He who knows and meditates thus, his life in this world surely becomes the highest and the best, and so also his state in the other world. Yes, in the other world.

3-4

Section 10

When the crops in Kurus country had been destroyed by hailstorms, there lived Usasti, son of Chakra, with his young wife Atiki. They lived in a deplorable condition in the village of elephant-drivers. **1**

He begged food from an elephant-driver, who himself was eating beans of poor quality.

The driver said to him, 'There is no other food than what is set before me'. **2**

'Give me some of it', said Usasti.

The driver gave some to him and said, 'Here is also some water to drink, if you please.'

'Then I shall be drinking what is defiled', said Usasti. **3**

'Are not these beans also defiled?'

'Unless I ate them, surely, I would have not survived; but for drinking water, I have other options'; said Usasti. **4**

Usasti, after he had eaten, brought the left over beans to his wife. As she had already obtained her food by alms; she kept the beans safely. **5**

Next morning Usasti arose and said, 'Alas, if I could get a little of food, I could earn a little money. A king is going to perform a sacrifice over there; he might appoint me to all the priestly offices'. **6**

His wife said to him, 'Well, lord, here are the beans (you gave me)'. Having eaten them, he went over to that place where the sacrifice was being performed. **7**

He sat down near the singer priests in the place earmarked for singing *Stotras*. And then he addressed Prastotr priest. **8**

'O Prastotr, if you sing Prastava (introductory praise) without knowing the deity that belongs to it, your head will fall off'. **9**

In the same manner he addressed Udgatr priest, 'O Udgatr, if you sing Udgitha without knowing the deity that belongs to it, your head will fall off.' **10**

"He who practices meditation, his life in this world becomes the best, and so also his state in the next world." ..... (Adapted)

In the same manner he addressed Pratihartr priest, 'O Pratihartr, if you sing Pratihara without knowing the deity that belongs to it, your head will fall off.' Then they all sat down silently, suspending their duties. **11**

Section 11

Then the king who was organizing the sacrifice said to Usasti, 'I would like to know you, revered Sir'.

'I am Chakrayan Usasti', said he. **1**

The king said, 'I searched for you, revered Sir, for all these priestly offices; but not finding you, I have chosen others'. **2**

'Revered Sir, now you please take up all the priestly offices'.

'Be it so, but let these same priests sing the hymns under my direction. Also you should give to me as much wealth as you give to them'.

'Very well', said the organizer.' **3**

Then Prastotr priest approached him and said, "Revered Sir, you said to me. 'O Prastotr, if you sing Prastava without knowing the deity that belongs to Prastava, your head will fall off.' Which is that deity?" **4**

'*Prana*', said Usasti. 'All these movable and immovable being merge in *Prana* (during dissolution) and rise out of *Prana* (during creation). This is the deity that belongs to Prastava. If you had sung Prastava without knowing him, after your having been warned by me, your head would have fallen off.' **5**

Then Udgatr priest approached him and said, "Revered Sir, you said to me: 'O Udgatr, if you sing Udgitha without knowing the deity that belongs to Udgitha, your head will fall off.' Which is that deity?" **6**

'Sun', said Usasti. 'All these movable and immovable beings sing praise of sun when he is up. This is the deity that belongs to Udgitha. If you had sung Udgitha without knowing him, after your having been warned by me, your head would have fallen off'. **7**

Then Pratihartr priest approached him and said, "Revered Sir, 'you said to me: O Pratihartr, if you sing Pratihara without knowing the deity that belongs to Pratihara, your head will fall off.' Which is that deity?" **8**

'Food', said Usasti. 'All these movable and immovable beings live by partaking of food only. This is the deity that belongs to Pratihara. If you had sung Pratihara without knowing him, after your having been warned by me, your head would have fallen off.' **9**

"All these movable and immovable being merge in Prana (during dissolution) and rise out of Prana (during creation)."

Section 12

Next begins the Udgitha seen by the dogs. Once Dalbhya Baka, known as also Maitreya Glava, went out (of the village) for study of Vedas. **1**

Before him, there appeared a white dog. Other dogs gathered around it and said, 'Revered Sir, please obtain food for us by singing; we are hungry'. **2**

The white dog said to them, 'Come to me over here tomorrow morning'. (Overhearing this), Dalbhya Baka or Maitreya Glava kept watch. **3**

(Next day) just as those (priests) who were to recite the *Bahispavamana* hymn joined one another, even so did the dogs. They (the dogs) sat down and began to sing. **4**

(The dogs sang) '*Om*, let us eat! *Om*, let us drink! *Om*, may the Sun god – who is called also Varuna and *Prajapati* – bring us food here. O lord of food, bring food here, yes, bring it here. *Om*!' **5**

Section 13

Verily, this world is the syllable *hau* (which is a Stobha), air is the syllable *hai*, moon is the syllable *atha*, self is the syllable *iha* and fire is the syllable *i*. **1**

Sun is the syllable *u* (which is a *Stobha*), invocation is the syllable *e*, *Vishvedeva* is the syllable *auhoyi*, *Prajapati* is the syllable *him*, *Prana* is the *Stobha* sound, food is the Stobha *ya* and *Virat* is the *Stobha* speech. **2**

The undefinable and variable thirteenth *Stobha* is the syllable *hum*. **3**

For him, speech yields the milk which is the milk of speech itself. He becomes rich in food and an eater of food, who thus knows this mystical meaning of Saman. Yes, who knows the mystical meaning of Saman. **4**

GENERAL COMMENTARY BY SWAMI GAMBHIRANANDA

MEDITATION AND KNOWLEDGE

A major portion of Chandogya Upanishad consists of *Upasanas*, the import of which is a little difficult to understand. It is roughly translated as Upanishadic meditation.

To our forefathers, philosophical teachings were recognized only when they had some bearing on daily life. For example, chanting of Vedas was the daily duty of students of those days. But lest it should degenerate into a mechanical process, the students were encouraged to add a little reflection in the form of *upasana* to their routine work (1.3, 8-9).

Thus, *upasana* means both a life of action and an actionless life of meditation. A literal meaning of the word *upasana* is to sit near an ideal and approach it mentally. First, it is a secret thing, to be diligently protected as one's own, and not to be talked or argued about. Second, it is a mental attitude in which things are not to be looked upon as detached entities, but as interrelated parts of a cosmic whole. And that attitude again has to change into an experience. Thereupon, the whole personality gets transformed and elevated. It is both an objective outlook and a subjective realization.

Meditation or *upasana* is a mental process. It is different from knowledge or *Vidya*, which is not a process. Knowledge is determined by the object, but meditation is dependent on the subject. Besides, meditation implies a meditator, an object of meditation, and an uninterrupted thought. It also requires an element of faith in the object and the process of meditation. Knowledge does not presuppose any such faith. Again, meditation is a process of building up from the bottom upward, extending the ego at every step; whereas knowledge achieves its object by removing ignorance. Thus knowledge and meditation are entirely different.

TYPES OF MEDITATION

Meditation is broadly of three types. The first type consists of *upasana* which are joined with sacrifice to lead to greater results. Chapters 1-2 of this Upanishad are devoted to this type of *upasana*. A second type of *upasana* looks upon death and suffering etc. as penances (Brhadaranyaka 5.11). A third type of *upasana* leads to *Brahman* in stages (*Kramamukti*).

From another perspective, meditation on *Brahman* may be direct or indirect. Meditation on *Brahman* by attributing to It qualities like Bliss, Fearlessness and Immortality is direct meditation. These qualities in no way point to the real nature of *Brahman*; they are mentioned by scriptures only to facilitate meditation. Meditation on a symbol like Om or an image of a deity is indirect meditation. Here again, there are two possibilities. First, the object of meditation may be of a lower order and qualities of a higher thing are superimposed on it. Verse 4.3,1 'Air, indeed is the absorber' is an example of this type of meditation. Second, the object of meditation itself predominates. For example, 'Mind is *Brahman*, thus one should meditate' (3.18, 1); or 'Sun is *Brahman* – this is the teaching' (3.19, 1).

It is to be noted that there can be no direct meditation on God so long as the mind hovers in the plane of symbols.

Meditation may be undertaken either with a desire to secure some result; or without any desire, only to adore God. Such adoration purifies the mind and eventually leads to realization of the Supreme. As stated earlier, results of rites performed without meditation are inferior to results of rites enjoined with meditation. Now a question may arise: Why are meditations motivated by desires included in the Upanishads? This is done with the purpose of urging people to cultivate dispassion towards results of rites, of duties or even of meditation. Even *Brahma loka*, which is the highest attainment through any means – is impermanent. At the end of a cosmic cycle, those who had attained *Brahma loka* must suffer rebirth in a new cycle of creation.

Nevertheless, rites, duties and meditation are not to be totally overlooked. Rites and duties bring the mind under control; meditation turns the mind inward.

MEDITATION AND DEVOTION

There is no significant difference between ancient practice of Vedic meditation and later development of

---

'Knowledge is determined by the object, but meditation is dependent on the subject.'

devotional worship. In fact, one may state that *Bhakti* or devotion is a form of meditation or *upasana*. Meditation has in it many elements of devotional worship. For example:

- In Brhadaranyaka Upanishad, the state of Self-realization is illustrated through the imagery of a couple lost to everything in an all-absorbing embrace (4.3, 2,1).

- About *Brahman*, it is said that 'He is a source of joy; for one becomes happy by coming in contact with that source of joy (Taittiriya 2.7, 2).'

- Verses 1.6, 6-8 of Chandogya Upanishad offer an example of meditation on a personal God. Here, the mind is directed towards divine presence in the sun. His beard is golden, His hair is golden, everything is golden upto the tips of His nails. His eyes are bright, like a red lotus.

- Mundaka Upanishad (2.1,4) speaks of Cosmic Person as having fire as His head, sun and moon as His eyes, Vedas as His voice, earth as His legs and so on.

- Mundaka Upanishad also teaches meditation on Om through a beautiful metaphor of bow and arrow (2.2, 3-4).

- The Upanishads contain many references to *japa* (repetition) of hymn or mantra. For example, Brhadaranyaka Upanishad suggests *japa* of *Gayatri Mantra* (6.3, 6) and also a Yajus hymn, '*Asato ma sad gamaya*' (1.3, 28).

- The Upanishads also contain references to Divine Grace (Katha 1.2, 23).

The presence of these elements in the Upanishads demolishes the theory of Puranic origin of *bhakti*.

PROGRESSIVE STAGES IN MEDITATION

Sections 1.8-1.9 of Chandogya Upanishad describe a meditation in which imagination is guided to ascending order of things, till it loses itself in the Highest, *Brahman*.

In sections 1.13 and 2.21, 2.1 meditational ascent is combined with gradual expansion. First we are asked to meditate on some meaningless words which are added in Sama songs to make a complete tune. These are equated with gross objects of the universe. Then we come to Sama song as a whole, divided into five parts; these are equated with both gross and subtle objects of the universe. Next stage leads us to a higher synthesis, where a bigger Sama song having seven parts is taken up as a symbol for all conceivable things. In the fourth stage, Sama songs bearing different names are used as symbols. The climax is reached in the last stage when the whole universe is superimposed on all the Samans conceived as a unified entity. The Upanishad concludes: 'He who meditates thus becomes identified with all.'

The Upanishads prescribe meditation of different degrees and subtlety for people in various stages of life. As a rule, they start with meditation on some most familiar thing. Then step-by-step, they lead to meditation on a grand synthesis in which everything loses its separate existence – the gross and the subtle, the microcosm and the macrocosm.

At every stage of our ascent to the Supreme through meditation, the Upanishads remind us of the interconnectedness of personal, natural and supernatural elements – *adhyatmic, adhibhautic* and *adhidaivic*. On the personal level, the series runs thus: gross body, vital force, thought, intellect and bliss. On the natural level, the ascent is from smaller to larger and from grosser to subtler. On the supernatural level, the advance is from individual presiding deities to their cosmic counter parts. On the cosmic level, the ascent is as follows: First comes the gross, *Virat*; then the subtle, *Hiranyagarbha*; then the causal, *Ishvar*, or Saguna *Brahman*; and finally, the transcendental Reality, Nirguna *Brahman*.

Meditation thus consists in 'covering all this with God' – as verse 1 in Isa Upanishad puts it – through progressive stages.

Meditation is not something which should be practiced for a few minutes everyday. Chandogya Upanishad says that we must be constantly aware of Reality in the midst of daily duties. It says, '*Atman* is in the heart'; he who meditates thus goes to heaven every day' Heart is the temple of God from which He is directing and watching all our activities.

– Swami Gambhirananda

'The Upanishads remind us of the interconnectedness of personal, natural and supernatural elements.'

FOCUSSED COMMENTARIES

1.10-1.11 Deities of *Saman* song

According to Vedic code of propriety; food and drink consumed by someone else from the same container are considered defiled. These are normally not accepted, except when life is at stake. Usasti accepted defiled food, but declined to accept defiled water because there was no shortage of it. (1.10, 4)

— *Swami Swahananda*

In addition to personal religion, the Vedas advocated public worship by means of sacrifices. In the period of the Vedas, there were no temples. Also, Gods and Goddesses like Ram, Krishna, Shiva, Ganesh, Laxmi, Durga, Saraswati were not known or worshipped. Instead public worship in the form of *yagyas* or sacrifices was very common. *Yagyas* were regarded as solemn and stately social acts. (1.10, 7)

— *Miscellaneous Sources*

1.12 A satire on priestly rituals

Sri Sankara has provided an allegorical interpretation. Pleased at the study of Vedas by a sage called by two names — Baka and Glava — the gods appeared before him in the form of dogs. Their aim was to make Baka understand that food is essential for nourishment of vital breath.

Bahispavamana is the hymn sung at the time of extracting soma juice on the last day of soma sacrifice. (1.12, 4)

The sun is referred to as *Savitra, Varuna* and *Prajapati* because it illumines the world, causes rainfall, produces food through rains and thereby nourishes the creatures.

— *Swami Gambhirananda*

This passage ridicules exceedingly well — through what the dogs do and say — the beggar-like behavior of the priests.

— *Paul Deussen*

This section is a satirical protest against the externalism of sacrificial creed without an inward spiritual life. Madhava attributes the hymn to Vayu who assumed the form of a dog.

— *S. Radhakrishnan*

'In the period of the Vedas, there were no temples. Instead public worship in the form of yagyas or sacrifices was very common.'

2 Meditation on Vedic Chants

SIMPLIFIED SYNOPSES

2.1-2.7
Meditation on fivefold *Saman*

The Sama Veda consists of stanzas chanted melodiously. Each of these is called a *Saman*. For the purpose of singing, *Saman* is divided into many parts in different ways. Each part is called a *bhakti*.

In a fivefold division, the five divisions of *Saman* are: (i) *Himkara* (ii) *Prastava*, (iii) *Udgitha* (iv) *Pratihara* and (v) *Nidhana*. Sections 1-7 prescribe meditation on *Saman* as a whole with all its aforesaid five divisions. The universe, rain, water, seasons and senses of perception are specified as objects of meditation. These are symbolic of fivefold *Saman*. Within each of these, there is further enumeration of various other objects representing five divisions of the corresponding *Saman*.

2.8-2.10
Meditation on sevenfold *Saman*

Likewise, sections 8-10, prescribe meditation on sevenfold *Saman*. The two additional divisions of *Saman* in this case (besides the five mentioned earlier) are *Adi* and *Upadrava*.

Section 8 suggests meditation on speech.

In section 9, the passages enumerate seven phases of sun from pre-sunrise to post sunset – and various types of living beings (animals, birds, men, deities, fetuses, wild animals, and forefathers) which are dependent on these phases.

Section 10 describes how the syllables of sevenfold *Saman* add up to 22. By meditation on the 21 syllables, one reaches the yonder Sun (beyond the physical sun). By meditation on the 22 syllables of *Saman*, one attains a state, which is beyond the yonder Sun, beyond death. This state is free from sorrow. It is the state of Bliss.

2.11-2.21
Meditation on all-inclusive *Saman*

The different *Samans*, which are sung during Soma sacrifice, are described here as interwoven into ten psychical and cosmic phenomena. The eleventh *Saman* is interwoven into all. Each of these eleven phenomena are neatly divided into five parts, which are equated with five divisions of *Saman*. The thrust of these sections is that the universe is an embodiment of *Brahman*, and that *Saman* is interwoven into the whole world.

The summary position is as tabulated hereunder:

Saman chants and their cosmic interconnectedness

Sec.	Chant	Himkara	Prastava	Udgitha	Pratihara	Nidhana	Interwoven into
11	Gayatra	Mind	Speech	Eye	Ear	Breath	Life-breath
12	Rathantara	Friction	Smoke	Blaze	Embers	Extinction	Fire
13	Vamadeva	Summon	Make request	lie alongside	lie over	make love	Sex
14	Brhat	Rising Sun	Early-day sun	Midday sun	Afternoon sun	Setting sun	Sun
15	Vairupya	White clouds	Rain-bearing cloud	Rain	Flash and Thunder	Rain	Rain-cloud
16	Vairaja	Spring	Summer	Monsoon	Autumn	Winter	Seasons
17	Sakvari	Earth	Sky	Heaven	Directions	Ocean	Cosmos
18	Revati	Goats	Sheep	Cows	Horses	Men	Animals
19	Yajnavajniya	Hair	Skin	Flesh	Bone	Marrow	Body
20	Rajana	Fire	Air	Sun	Stars	Moon	Deities
21	All-inclusive Saman	Three Vedas	Three Worlds	Fire, Air and Sun	Stars, birds and light	Serpents, celestial singers, ancestors	All

At the conclusion of every section there follows the promise of a reward and a vow — that the respective phenomena into which the *Saman* is interwoven should not be scorned.

2.22
Recitation of *Saman*

This section deals with the ways of singing *Saman* and what one has to contemplate during singing in order to achieve definite results. *Saman* texts are placed under the protection of specific gods.

2.23
***Om*: Origin and Importance**

Verse-1 is a forerunner of later theory of four *Ashrams*, or stages of life: *Brahmacharya, Grahastya, Vanaprastha* and *Sanyas*.

Verses 2-3 describe the origin and the importance of the syllable Om, a symbol of *Brahman*.

2.24
***Soma* sacrifice: Its symbolic significance**

This liturgical section teaches how the performer of a Soma sacrifice (*yajamana*) can secure for himself after his death a place in the three realms of the universe – earth, aerial space and heaven. The earth is said to belong to the *Vasus*, with *Agni* as their head, and the morning libation of Soma sacrifice is dedicated to them. The aerial space belongs to the *Rudras* with *Vayu* as their head, and the midday libation is dedicated to them. The heavens belong to the *Adityas* and *Vishvedevas*, and the evening libation is dedicated to them. A request is granted when these deities are appeased through a special ceremony.

'The universe is an embodiment of Brahman and Vedic chants like Saman are interwoven into the whole world.'

Translated Text

CHAPTER 2

Section 1

Om. Surely, meditation on the whole Saman is good. Anything that is good, people know it as Saman; anything that is not good, as *Asaman*. **1**

Thus, when people say, 'He approached him with Saman', they mean, 'He approached him with a good motive.' And when they say, 'He approached him with *Asaman*', they mean, 'He approached him with an evil motive'. **2**

Again, people say, 'Oh, this is Saman for us', when it is something good. They say, 'Oh, this is *Asaman* for us', when it is not good. **3**

He who knowing this meditates on Saman as good, all good qualities hasten towards him and serve him. **4**

Section 2

Among the worlds one should meditate upon Saman as fivefold: earth as the syllable *Him*, fire as Prastava, sky as Udgitha, sun as Pratihara, and heaven as Nidhana. This meditation pertains to the higher worlds. **1**

Now in the reverse order: heaven is the syllable *Him*, sun is Prastava, sky is Udgitha, fire is Pratihara, and earth is Nidhana. **2**

The worlds, in ascending or descending orders, belong to him who knowing it thus meditates on the fivefold Saman. **3**

Section 3

One should meditate on the fivefold Saman as rain. The wind that precedes is the syllable Him, the cloud that is formed is Prastava, the shower is Udgitha, lightning and thunder are Pratihara, and their cessation is Nidhana. It rains for him – indeed, he causes rain – who knowing it thus, meditates on the fivefold Saman as rain. **1-2**

Section 4

One should meditate on the fivefold Saman as waters: When a cloud gathers, it is syllable Him; when it rains, it is Prastava; those (waters) that flow to the east are Udgitha; those that flow to the west are Pratihara. The ocean is Nidhana. **1**

He who, knowing it thus, meditates on the fivefold Saman as waters, does not drown in water and he becomes rich in water. **2**

"He who meditates on Saman, as good, all good qualities hasten towards him."

Section 5

One should meditate on the fivefold Saman as the seasons: Spring is syllable Him, summer is Prastava, rainy season is Udgitha, autumn is Pratihara, and winter is Nidhana. **1**

He, who knowing it thus, meditates on the fivefold Saman as seasons, him the seasons serve, and he becomes rich (in the objects typical of respective) seasons. **2**

Section 6

One should meditate on the fivefold Saman as the animals. Goats are syllable Him, sheep are Prastava, cows are Udgitha, horses are Pratihara, and man is Nidhana. **1**

He, who knowing it thus, meditates on the fivefold Saman as the animals, to him belong the animals, and he becomes rich in animals. **2**

Section 7

One should meditate on the highest fivefold Saman as the senses. Organ of smell is syllable Him, organ of speech is Prastava, eye is Udgitha, ear is Pratihara, and mind is Nidhana. Indeed, these are the highest. **1**

He, who knowing it thus, meditates on the fivefold highest Saman as the senses, to him belong the highest worlds. So much for (meditation on) the fivefold Saman. **2**

Section 8

Next is the meditation on the sevenfold Saman. One should meditate on the sevenfold Saman as speech. Whatsoever is in speech is 'hum', that is the syllable Him; whatever is 'pra', that is Prastava; whatever is 'a', that is Adi (the first); whatever is 'ut', that is Udgitha; whatever is 'prati', that is Pratihara; whatever, is upa', that is Upadrava; and whatever is 'ni', that is Nidhana. **1**

He who knowing it thus, meditates on the sevenfold (whole) Saman as speech, for him speech yields milk, i.e. its appropriate benefit, and he becomes rich in food and an eater of food. **2**

Section 9

Next, one should meditate on the sevenfold Saman as the yonder sun. He is Saman because he is always the same, he is the same to everyone, since everyone thinks, 'He faces me, he faces me'. **1**

One should know that all beings depended on him. What he is before rising is Himkara. On this, animals are dependent. As they participate in Himkara part of this Saman, they utter *hummim* (before sunrise). **2**

"The sun is always the same to everyone. Everyone thinks, 'He faces me, he faces me'..."

Then, the form of the sun when it has just risen, that is Prastava. On this, men are dependent. As they participate in Prastava part of this Saman, they are desirous of praise, direct and indirect. **3**

And the form of the sun as it appears in early part of the day, that is Adi. On this, birds are dependent. As they participate in Adi part of this Saman, they hold themselves unsupported in the sky and fly about. **4**

Next, the form of the sun that appears, just at midday, that is Udgitha. On this, gods are dependent. As they participate in Udgitha part of this Saman, they are the best among the offspring of *Prajapati*. **5**

Next, the form of the sun past midday and before afternoon, that is Pratihara. On this, foetuses are dependent. As they participate in Pratihara part of this Saman, they are held up (in the womb) and they do not fall down. **6**

Next, the form of the sun past afternoon and before sunset, that is Upadrava. On this, wild animals are dependent. As they participate in Upadrava part of this Saman, they run away to some hiding place when they see a man. **7**

Now, the form of the sun that appears, just after sunset, that is Nidhana. On this, manes are dependent. As they participate in Nidhana part of this Saman, people place them aside (during ceremonies for ancestors).

Thus, verily, does one meditate on the sevenfold Saman in the yonder sun. **8**

Section 10

Now, verily, one should meditate on sevenfold Saman, which has all its parts similar, and which leads beyond death. Himkara has three syllables; Prastava has three syllables. So they are equal to each other. **1**

Adi has two syllables; Pratihara has four syllables. We take one syllable from Pratihara to Adi. So they are equal to each other. **2**

Udgitha has three syllables; Upadrava has four syllables. Three and three become equal with one syllable left over. So it also becomes equal. **3**

Nidhana has three syllables, and this too is equal (to the others). These, indeed, are the twenty-two syllables (of the sevenfold Saman). **4**

One reaches the sun through 21 syllables. The yonder sun is, verily, twenty-first from here. By the twenty-second, one conquers that which is higher than the sun. That is bliss. That is free of sorrow. **5**

He obtains victory over the sun, and then a still higher victory becomes his, who knowing thus, meditates on sevenfold Saman as identified with the Self and transcending death. Yes, he who mediates on Saman. **6**

"Now, verily, one should meditate on sevenfold Saman, which leads beyond death."

Section 11

Mind is Himkara, speech is Prastava, eye is Udgitha, ear is Pratihara, and *Prana* is Nidhana. This is the Gayatra Saman woven in life-breath and the senses. **1**

He who thus knows this Gayatra Saman as woven in *Prana* and the senses, he becomes the possessor of perfect senses, reaches full length of life, lives gloriously, becomes great with offspring and cattle, and great also with fame. His holy vow is that he should be high-minded. **2**

Section 12

One rubs. The fire-sticks are Himkara. The smoke that is produced is Prastava. It blazes, that is Udgitha. The embers are formed, that is Pratihara. It goes down, that is Nidhana. It is completely extinguished, that is (also) Nidhana. This is the Rathantara Saman woven in fire. **1**

He who thus knows this Rathantara Saman as woven in fire, he becomes radiant with the holy effulgence born of sacred wisdom. He is endowed with good appetite, reaches full length of life, lives gloriously, becomes great with offspring and cattle, and great also with fame. His holy vow is that he should neither sip water nor spit facing the fire. **2**

Section 13

One summons, that is Himkara. He makes request that is Prastava. He lies down along with his woman, that is Udgitha. He lies on the woman, that is Pratihara. He makes love, that is Nidhana. He reaches climax, that is (also) Nidhana. This is the Vamadeva Saman woven in sex. **1**

He who thus knows this Vamadeva chant as woven in sex, he has sex and he procreates. He reaches full length of life, lives gloriously, and becomes great with offspring and cattle, and great also with fame. His holy vow is that he should not despise any woman. **2**

Section 14

The rising sun is Himkara; the risen sun is Prastava; the midday sun is Udgitha; the sun in the afternoon is Pratihara, and the setting sun is Nidhana. This is the Brhat Saman woven in the sun. **1**

He who thus knows this Brhat Saman as woven in the sun, he becomes effulgent and endowed with good appetite; reaches full length of life, lives gloriously, becomes great with offspring and cattle, and great also with fame. His holy vow is that he should not find fault with the burning sun. **2**

Section 15

The white clouds gather, that is Himkara. The (rain-bearing) cloud is formed, that is Prastava. It rains, that is Udgitha. It flashes and thunders, that is Pratihara. It

---

"He who knows Rathantara Saman as woven in fire,
becomes radiant with the holy effulgence born of sacred wisdom."

ceases, that is Nidhana. This is the Vairupya Saman woven in the rain-cloud. **1**

He who thus knows this Vairupya Saman as woven in the rain-cloud, he acquires cattle of handsome and manifold forms, reaches full length of life, lives gloriously, becomes great with offspring and cattle and great also with fame. His holy vow is that he should not find fault with the rain-cloud when it rains. **2**

Section 16

The spring is Himkara, the summer is Prastava, the monsoon is Udgitha, the autumn is Pratihara, and the winter is Nidhana. This is the Vairaja Saman woven in the seasons. **1**

He who thus knows this Vairaja Saman as woven in the seasons, he shines with offspring, cattle and the holy effulgence born of sacred wisdom, reaches full length of life, lives gloriously, becomes great with offspring and cattle and great also with fame. His holy vow is that he should not find fault with the seasons. **2**

Section 17

The earth is Himkara, the sky is Prastava, heaven is Udgitha, the quarters are Pratihara, and the ocean is Nidhana. This is the Sakvari Saman woven in the cosmos. **1**

He who thus knows this Sakvari Saman woven in the cosmos, he becomes the possessor of the cosmos, reaches full length of life, lives gloriously, becomes great with offspring and cattle and great also with fame. His holy vow is that he should not find fault with the cosmos. **2**

Section 18

The goats are Himkara, the sheep are Prastava, the cows are Udgitha, the horses are Pratihara, and man is Nidhana. This is the Revati Saman woven in the animals. **1**

He who thus knows this Revati Saman woven in the animals, he becomes possessor of animals, reaches the length of life, lives gloriously, becomes great with offspring and cattle and great also with fame. His holy vow is that he should not find fault with animals. **2**

Section 19

The hair is Himkara, the skin is Prastava, the flesh is Udgitha, the bone is Pratihara, and the marrow is Nidhana. This is the Yagyayagniya Saman woven in the limbs of the body. **1**

He who thus knows this Yagyayagniya Saman woven in the limbs of the body, he is endowed with all the limbs, and is not crippled in any limb; he reaches full length of life, lives gloriously, becomes great with offspring and cattle and great

"He who knows Revati Saman, his holy vow is that he should not find fault with animals."

also with fame. His holy vow is that he should not eat fish and meat for a year, or rather, he should not eat fish and meat at all. **2**

Section 20

Fire is Himkara, air is Prastava, sun is Udgitha, stars are Pratihara, and moon is Nidhana. This is Rajana Saman woven in the deities. **1**

He who thus knows this Rajana Saman woven in the deities, he abides in the same world or gets the same prosperity as these very deities or attains union with them. He reaches the full length of life, lives gloriously, becomes great with offspring and cattle and great also with fame. His holy vow is that he should not find fault with the *Brahmins*. **2**

Section 21

The three Vedas are Himkara; the three worlds are Prastava; Fire, Air and Sun are Udgitha; stars, birds and light are Pratihara; serpents, celestial singers and ancestors are Nidhana. This is the collection of Saman woven in all things. **1**

Verily, he who thus knows this collection of Saman as woven in all things, he becomes the lord of all things. **2**

There is this verse about it: That which is fivefold in groups of three, there is nothing else greater than these (fifteen). **3**

He who meditates thus becomes identified with all. All the quarters of space bring offerings to him. His holy vow is that he should meditate 'I am all'. Yes, that is his vow. **4**

Section 22

Of the Saman, I choose the high-sounding one as good for cattle. This is the song sacred to *Agni*, the undefined one to *Prajapati*, the defined one to Soma, the soft and smooth to *Vayu*, the smooth and strong to Indra, the heron-like to Brhaspati, and the ill sounding to Varuna. Verily, one may practise all these, but one should avoid that which is sacred to Varuna. **1**

'May I obtain immorality for the gods by singing', (thinking) thus one should sing. 'May I obtain by singing, oblation for ancestors, hope for men, grass and water for animals, heavenly world for the sacrificer, and food for myself,' thus reflecting in his mind on all these, he should sing the *Stotra* attentively. **2**

All vowels are the embodiments of Indra; all sibilants are the embodiments of *Prajapati*; all *Sparsha* consonants are the embodiments of Death. If anyone should reproach him for pronunciation of his vowels, he should tell him, 'I have taken refuge in Indra, he will answer you.' **3**

"He should meditate. 'I am all'..."

And if some one should reproach him for his sibilants he should tell him, 'I have taken refuge in *Prajapati*; he will crush you'. And if some one should reproach him for his *Sparsha* consonants, he should tell him, 'I have taken refuge in Death; he will burn you up'. **4**

All vowels should be pronounced resonant and strong (with the thought), 'May I impart strength to Indra *(Prana)*'. All sibilants should be pronounced, neither inarticulately, nor leaving out the elements of sound, but distinctly, (with the thought), 'May I give myself to *Prajapati* (*Virat*)'. All *Sparsha* consonants should be pronounced slowly, without mixing them with any other letter, (with the thought), 'May I withdraw myself from Death'. **5**

Section 23

These are three divisions of religious duty. Sacrifice, study and charity are the first. Austerity is the second. Celibacy, study of sacred knowledge, living with dedication in a teacher's house, is the third. All these become possessors of meritorious worlds; but he who is established firmly in *Brahman*, attains immortality. **1**

Prajapati meditated on the worlds. From them, thus meditated upon, issued forth the knowledge of three Vedas. He meditated on this. From this, thus meditated upon, issued forth the syllables *Bhur*, *Bhuvah* and *Suvah*. **2**

He meditated on them. From them, thus meditated upon, issued forth the syllable *Om* (*Brahman*). Just as all leaves are held together by a stalk, so is all speech held together by the syllable *Om*. Verily, the syllable *Om* is all this. Yes, syllable *Om* is all this. **3**

Section 24

The expounders of *Brahman* say, 'The morning libation is of the Vasus, the midday libation is of the Rudras and the third libation is of the Adityas and of the Vishvedevas. Where, then, is the world of the sacrificer?' Why should he who does not know the answer, perform (sacrifices)? It is only after knowing this that he should perform (sacrifices). **1-2**

Morning Libation

Before the commencement of the morning chant, the sacrificer sits down behind the Garhapatya fire, facing north, and sings the Saman sacred to the Vasus:
'(O Fire), open the door of this world, that we may see you for obtaining its sovereignty.' **3-4**

Then he offers the oblation (with the mantra)
'Salutation to Fire, who dwells on earth in this world. Please obtain this world for me, the sacrificer. This world indeed, is for me. I shall come to this world after death. *Svaha*. Unlock the door of this world.'
Saying this he gets up. The Vasus then grant him (the world connected with) the morning libation. **5-6**

"Just as all leaves are held together by a stalk, so is all speech held together by the syllable Om."

Midday libation

Before the commencement of the midday libation, the sacrificer sits down behind the Agnidhriya fire, facing north, and sings the Saman sacred to the Rudras:
'(O Fire), open the door of the region of the sky that we may see you for obtaining the sovereignty of the sky'. **7-8**

Then he offers the oblation (with the mantra):
'Salutation to *Vayu*, who dwells in the region of the sky. Obtain this region for me, the sacrificer. This region, indeed, is for me. I shall come to this region after death. *Svaha*. Unlock the door of this region',
Saying this he gets up. The Rudras then grant him (the region of the sky connected with) the midday libation. **9-10**

Evening libation

Before beginning the third libation, the sacrificer sits down behind the Ahavaniya fire, facing north, and sings the Saman sacred to the Adityas and the Vishvedevas:

'(O Fire), open the door of the region of heaven so that we may see you for obtaining the sovereignty of heaven'.

This is the Saman sacred to the Adityas. Next is the one sacred to the Vishvedevas:

'(O Fire), open the door of the region of heaven so that we may see you for obtaining the supreme sovereignty.' **11-13**

Then the sacrificer offers the oblation (with the mantra):

'Salutation to the Adityas and to the Vishvedevas, the inhabitants of the region of heaven. Obtain the region of heaven for me, the sacrificer. This region, indeed, is for me. I shall come to this region after death. *Svaha*. Unlock the door of the region.'
Saying this, he gets up. **14-15**

The Adityas and the Vishvedevas grant him (the region appropriate to) the third libation.

He alone knows the true nature of sacrifice, who knows thus. **16**

"(O Fire), open the door of heaven so that we may see you for obtaining the sovereignty of heaven."

3 Vidya: Art of Meditation

Simplified Synopses

3.1-3.11
Madhu Vidya: Meditation on Sun

'The Upanishadic seers compare the Sun to honey.'

Brahman is the 'Sun' of the cosmos. The physical sun that we see is only a phenomenal form of *Brahman*. This is the basic idea of *Madhu Vidya*, as presented here. It is also presented in Brhadaranyaka Upanishad (2.5) from a different perspective.

In a very remarkable feat of imagination, the Upanishadic seers compare the sun to honey which nourishes the gods. In this image, the heavens are the support of the sun, and the intermediate sky between earth and heavens is the honeycomb. The rays lodged in the intermediate space are like offsprings born from the eggs of the bees.

The solar rays spreading towards east, south, west, north and above are the tubular honey cells of this honeycomb. Honey streams through these rays towards the center and forms the body of the sun.

What are the flowers from which this honey in the form of the sun is obtained? These are the four Vedas – *Rg, Yajur, Sama* and *Atharva* – and *Brahman*. According to Sri Sankara, *Brahman* here signifies *Pranav*, the syllable *Aum*.

Who are the bees, which extract honey out of the aforesaid flowers? It is the *Rks* of *Rg Veda*, Yajus *mantras* of *Yajur Veda*, Saman songs of *Sama Veda*, verses of *Atharva Veda* (also Epics and *Puranas*), and the secret teachings of the Upanishads (named here as *Brahman*).

When the bees – Vedic Rks, mantras, songs, verses and Upanishadic teachers – press upon the Vedas as flowers (*abhitapanti*, implying *tapas*), through that is obtained an immortal sap or fluid of nectar. This nectar streams out of the Vedas and *Pranav* (*Aum*) in the form of fame, splendor, alertness of senses, virility or strength, and food. It collects itself in the sun in the form of red, white, black, deep black and bubbling forms at its center. Among them, the Upanishadic teachings stand top-most. They are the essence of essences, the nectar of nectars (3.1-3.5).

The food and drink of gods is not like that of human being. Gods are satisfied merely by seeing the aforesaid nectars.

- Vasus with *Agni* as their leader are satisfied with red nectar from *Rg Veda*.
- Rudras with Indra as their leader are satisfied with white nectar from *Yajur Veda*.
- Adityas with Varuna as their leader are satisfied with black nectar from *Sama Veda*.
- Maruts with Soma as their leader are satisfied with deep black nectar from *Atharva Veda*.
- Sadhyas with *Pranav* as their leader are satisfied with bubbling nectar from the Upanishads.

> *'For a knower of Upanishads, the sun of knowledge never sets.'*

He who knows the nectar of the respective Vedas partakes in its drinking, like the Vasus, the Rudras, etc. Besides, he even exercises supremacy over the respective class of deities (Vasus, Rudras etc.) and retains sovereignty over their kingdom.

How long does the knower enjoy the nectar of the Vedas? For unimaginably long periods. The passages express this by imagining an impossible situation to occur – like the sun rising in the West and setting in the East! The time available to a knower of Vedas for enjoyment of the nectar is said to be a multiple of the time required for such an impossibility to occur! (3.6-3.10)

What about the knower of the Upanishads? For him the sun never sets – it is eternal daylight. For him has dawned the day of perfect knowledge – the day which knows no night.

3.12 Gayatri Vidya: Brahman is space outside and within man

> *'Gayatri protects us from fear.'*

This section explains the etymological significance of the famous *Gayatri mantra*. The word *Gayatri* derives its name from *gana*, which means singing, and *trana*, which means protecting. So *Gayatri* is identified with speech, and it is said to protect all living beings from fear.

Gayatri mantra has four meters, each of six letters. The six letters are equated with speech, living beings, earth, body, heart and life-breath by linking each entity with the previous one. The four meters are said to be the four feet of *Brahman* (1-5).

In a beautiful verse (Rk) reproduced from *Rg Veda*, it is stated that the relative universe represents only one foot of *Brahman*, the other three feet are symbolic of the realm of the Absolute, the Immortal self-effulgent *Brahman* (6).

Verses 7-9 contain another beautiful description of *Brahman* from a different perspective. *Brahman* is identical with the space outside a man, the space within a man and the space in the heart of man. One commentator regards these as representing waking, dream and deep sleep states respectively. According to another interpretation, the vast space pervaded by *Brahman* has been narrowed down to a small subtle space within the heart. This is an aid for concentration on *Brahman* during meditation.

3.13 Parajyotir Vidya: Light of Brahman in man

The previous section identifies *Brahman* with the space outside and within a man, as also with the subtle space in the heart. In this section, *Brahman* is identified as the Light beyond and within man.

The Upanishad describes the heart as having five doors. It also personifies *Brahman* as the five forms of life-breath, which guard these doors. Further, each of these forms of life-breath are identified with a sense organ, like eye or speech, and with its corresponding presiding deity (cosmic power) like Sun or Fire. Thus, the senses, the cosmic powers – which energize the senses – and *Brahman*, the great power behind all of them, are imagined to meet in man. This explains how the Light of *Brahman* – which shines in this elegant universe and beyond – is also the Light which shines in man. But can this Supreme Light, *Parajyotir,* be felt within? It can be felt as the warmth in the body. It can also be felt as the sound of silence in solitude.

'Light of Brahman – which shines in this elegant universe and beyond – is also the Light which shines in man.'

3.14 Sandilya Vidya: Meditation on Self within and without

This section provides a practically useful summary of the entire philosophy of the Upanishads in just four verses. It is recommended for repeated study and reflection.

Sandilya Vidya is about meditation: What to mediate upon? Why? How? It says, 'Meditate on *Brahman*, which is the same as *Atman*. Meditate on the universal Self, which is the same as the Self within us.'

First, what is *Brahman*? It is That from which everything originates, by which everything is sustained and into which everything dissolves. In fact, everything – this whole universe – is *Brahman* Itself. It is both the Cause and the Effect. Cause becomes Effect, and Effect again becomes Cause.

But why meditate at all? Because a person becomes what he does, with concentration. The Sanskrit word used is *kratu*. This has been translated differently by commentators as faith, exercise of intelligence and will-power. The Upanishad says that how we live in this life also influences our next life (Verse-1).

'How we live in this life also influences our next life.'

Verse-2 describes *Brahman* in greater detail. The Absolute manifests Itself as Mind and Life in us. It is Effulgence, Truth and Infinitude personified in us. Accordingly, It performs all actions, possesses all desires and experiences all objects of senses, but It does so without any agitation or anxiety.

Verses 3-4 describe the Self or *Atman* that resides in our heart. It is infinitesimally small and infinitely large. The contradiction is resolved by stating that the Self in us is not a spark of the Universal Self, but Universal Self Itself. *Atman* and *Brahman* are One. Accordingly, like *Brahman*, *Atman* also performs all actions, possesses all desires and experiences all objects of senses, but without any agitation or anxiety.

Next, how to meditate? Meditate with faith. Meditate in tranquility. Meditate on the whole universe first. Then imagine that this whole universe comes from That *Brahman*. Next think that 'this' and 'That' are the same, One.

Finally, the result – One who understands all this and meditates thus will not have any doubt whatsoever in life, or about life.

3.15 Prayer for son's longevity

The essence of this section is the underlying unity of man and the physical world. The universe is imagined as a chest rich with treasures. Its four-corners are equated with four directions, upper lid with heavens, lower lid with earth and contents with *karma*, results of actions. Air is symbolized as the son of directions. In his prayer, the father seeks for his son the protection of this treasure chest and *Prana*. He also seeks – under a very arbitrary interpretation of the syllables *bhur*, *bhuvah* and *suvah* – the protection of the three divisions of the universe, the three regents, and the three Vedas.

In section 3.13, there was a promise of birth of a hero in the family. This section describes a ritual-prayer for the longevity of a son.

'The Absolute manifests Itself as Mind and Life in us. It is Effulgence, Truth and Infinitude personified in us.'

3.16
Prayer for a life of 116 years

In this section man's life is equated with the ritual of a sacrifice, *yagya*, and prayers are prescribed for a life of 116 years. Youth, middle age and old age are equated with morning, midday and evening libations *(savana)* respectively, and each is associated with an important Vedic meter. The morning libation is associated with *Gayatri* meter. It has 24 letters representing 24 years of youth. Middle age corresponds to midday libation and *Tristubh* meter, which has 44 letters. Old age corresponds to evening libation and to *Jagati* meter, which has 48 letters. Simple additions show that up to the age of 68 a person is middle-aged and ideal span of life is 116 years.

If a person faces any health problem in youth, he is advised to invoke the deity known by the name Vasu. Rudra should be invoked in middle age, and Aditya in old age. All these three classes of deities are identified as symbols of *Prana*, life-force. The thrust of the prayer is that if there is any deficiency (health problem) in the morning libation, let it be united with the midday libation; likewise let the midday libation be united with the evening libation. He who knows this and practices this is assured a healthy life of 116 years, as exemplified by a sage, Mahidasa Aitareya.

3.17
Man's life is like a sacrifice

Here again, human life is compared with the ritual of a sacrifice. Hardships of life are equated to hardships of initiatory rites, and pleasures are equated to uplifting ceremonies like chanting of hymns. Virtues of life like charity and truthfulness are like gifts, *dakshina* given to priests performing a sacrifice. The ceremony of extracting *Soma* juice is compared to a man's birth and the bath taken at the completion of a sacrifice is compared to death.

It is stated that Ghora Angirasa expounded this doctrine to none other than Lord Krishna. He concluded his teaching by quoting three mantras from *Yajur Veda*, which should be recited at the time of death.

The section ends with two beautiful citations from *Rg Veda* about the Highest Light, *Brahman*.

3.18
Meditation on Mind and Sky as *Brahman*

This section recommends meditation on *Brahman* in Its Totality. Mind is treated as a symbol of *Brahman* at the individual level, and Sky at the cosmic level. Each of these symbols has four feet, so to say. Speech, smell, sight and hearing are the feet of the Mind; Fire, Air, Sun and Directions are the feet of the Sky. Organ of speech 'shines' with Fire; of smell with Air, of sight with Sun and of hearing with Directions (Space). He who knows thus shines with fame, renown and effulgence born of sacred wisdom.

3.19
Meditation on Sun as *Brahman*

The text again elaborates a recurring theme of the Upanishads – man is a mini-cosmos.

Sun is *Brahman*. This is explained with the metaphor of an egg. The two parts of the cosmic egg are compared to heaven and earth. Its other contents are equated with mountains, clouds, rivers and ocean. Sun is that which was born from the egg. Cosmic sounds, which emanated at the time of its birth, are equated with the sounds made by creatures at the time of sunrise. The text enjoins meditation on Sun as a symbol of *Brahman*.

'Up to the age of 68 a person is middle-aged, and ideal span of life is 116 years.'

Translated Text

CHAPTER 3

Section 1

Om. The yonder sun indeed is the honey of the gods (sense-powers and life-breath). Of this honey, heaven is the crossbeam, sky is the honeycomb, and sun's rays are the eggs. **1**

The eastern rays of that sun are its eastern honey-cells. The Rk mantras are the bees, the *Rg Veda* is the flower and water is the nectar. Those very Rk (the bees) pressed this *Rg Veda*. From it, thus pressed, issued forth as juice, fame, splendor (of limbs), (alertness of) the senses, virility, and food for eating. **2-3**

That juice flowed forth; it settled by the side of the sun. Verily, this is what appears as the red hue of the sun. **4**

Section 2

And its southern rays are its southern honey-cells. The Yajus *mantras* are the bees. The *Yajur Veda* is the flower; and water is the nectar. **1**

Those very Yajus *mantras* pressed this *Yajur Veda*. From it, thus pressed, issued forth as juice, fame, splendor of limbs, alertness of the senses, virility, and food for eating. **2**

It flowed forth, it settled by the side of the sun. Verily, this is what appears as the white hue of the sun. **3**

Section 3

And its western rays are its western honey-cells. The Saman are the bees. The *Sama Veda* is the flower; and water is the nectar. **1**

Those very Saman pressed this *Sama Veda*. From it, thus pressed, issued forth as juice, fame, splendor of limbs, alertness of the senses, virility, and food for eating. **2**

It flowed forth; it settled by the side of the sun. Verily, this it is what appears as the black hue of the sun. **3**

Section 4

And its northern rays are its northern honey-cells. The verses of the *Atharva* Veda are the bees. Itihasa and Purana are the flowers; and water is the nectar. **1**

Those mantras of the *Atharva* Veda pressed this Itihasa. From it, thus pressed, issued forth as juice, fame, splendor of limbs, alertness of the senses, virility, and food for eating. **2**

"The yonder sun indeed is the honey of the gods (sense-powers and life-breath)."

It flowed forth; it settled by the side of the sun. Verily, this is what appears as the deep black hue of the sun. **3**

Section 5

And its upper rays are its upper honey-cells. The secret teachings (Upanishads) are the bees. *Brahman* (Pranav) is the flower. Those waters (the results of the meditations on Pranav) are the nectar. **1**

Those secret teachings pressed this Pranav. From it, thus pressed, issued forth as juice, fame, splendor of limbs, alertness of the senses, virility, and food for eating. **2**

It flowed forth; it settled by the side of the sun. Verily, this is what appears as the bubbling form in the middle of the sun. **3**

Verily, these hues (Upanishads teachings) are the juice of juices; for the Vedas are the essences and these are their essence. These hues indeed are the nectar of nectars, for the Vedas are the nectar and these are their nectar. **4**

Section 6

That which is the first nectar (i.e. the red form), that verily the Vasus enjoy with *Agni* as their leader. The gods, indeed, neither eat nor drink; they are satisfied only by seeing this nectar. **1**

They enter into this very form (color) and out of this form they emerge. **2**

He who knows this nectar thus, he becomes one of the Vasus, with *Agni* as the leader. He is satisfied only with seeing this nectar. He enters into this very form and out of this form he emerges. **3**

As long as the sun rises in the east and sets in the west, that long he (the knower) retains the sovereignty and the heavenly kingdom of (or similar to that of) the Vasus. **4**

Section 7

And that which is the second nectar (i.e. the white form), that verily the Rudras enjoy with Indra as their leader. The gods, indeed, neither eat nor drink; they are satisfied only by seeing this nectar. **1**

They enter into this very form and out of this form they emerge. **2**

He who knows this nectar thus, he becomes one of the Rudras, with Indra as the leader. He is satisfied only with seeing this nectar. He enters into this very form and out of this form he emerges. **3**

As long as the sun rises in the east and sets in the west, twice so long it rises in the south and set in the north, and that long he (the knower) retains the sovereignty and the heavenly kingdom of the Rudras. **4**

"Brahman is the flower, Vedas are the nectars and Upanishads are the Nectar of nectars." ..... (Adapted)

Section 8

And that which is the third nectar (i.e. the black form), that verily the Adityas enjoy with Varuna as their leader. The gods, indeed, neither eat nor drink; they are satisfied only by seeing this nectar. **1**

They enter into this very form and out of this form they emerge. **2**

He who knows this nectar thus, he becomes one of the Adityas, with Varuna as the leader. He is satisfied only with seeing this nectar. He enters into this very form and out of this form he emerges. **3**

As long as the sun rises in the south and sets in the north, twice so long it rises in the west and sets in the east, and that long he (the knower) retains the sovereignty and heavenly kingdom of the Adityas. **4**

Section 9

And that which is the fourth nectar (i.e. the deep black color), that verily the Maruts enjoy with Soma as their leader. The gods, indeed, neither eat nor drink; they are satisfied only by seeing this nectar. **1**

They enter into this very form and out of this form they emerge. **2**

He who knows thus this nectar, thus he becomes one of the Maruts, with Soma as the leader. He is satisfied only with seeing this nectar. **3**

As long as the sun rises in the west and sets in the east, twice so long it rises in the north and sets in the south; and that long he (the knower) retains the sovereignty and the heavenly kingdom of the Maruts. **4**

Section 10

And that which is the fifth nectar (i.e. the bubbling form within the sun), that verily the Sadhyas enjoy with *Pranav* as their leader. The gods, indeed, neither eat nor drink; they are satisfied only by seeing this nectar. **1**

They enter into this very form and out of this form they emerge. **2**

He who thus knows nectar thus, he becomes one of the Sadhyas, and with *Pranav* as the leader. He is satisfied only with seeing this nectar. **3**

As long as the sun rises in the north and sets in the south, twice so long does it rise overhead and set below; and that long he (the knower) retains the sovereignty and the heavenly kingdom of the Sadhyas. **4**

Section 11

Then rising from there upward, it will neither rise nor set. It will remain alone in the middle. There is this verse about it: **1**

"There is perpetual daylight (of wisdom) for one who knows the secret teachings of the Upanishads."
...... (Adapted from next page)

Never will this happen there. Never did the sun set there nor did it rise. O gods, by this assertion of truth, may I not fall from *Brahman*. **2**

Verily, the sun neither rises nor sets for one who knows this secret teaching of the Vedas; for him there is perpetual daylight. **3**

Hiranyagarbha imparted this Doctrine of Honey to *Prajapati*, *Prajapati* to Manu, and Manu to his progeny. Uddalaka Aruni obtained this knowledge of *Brahman* from his father. **4**

A father may declare this Honey Doctrine to his eldest son or to any other worthy disciple. **5**

And not to any one else, even if one should offer him this whole earth surrounded by water and filled with wealth. This (doctrine) is certainly greater than that. It is certainly greater than that. **6**

Section 12

Gayatri indeed is all this that exits. Speech indeed is *Gayatri*; for speech sings (*Gayatri*) to all these creatures and protects them from fear. **1**

That which is this *Gayatri* is surely this earth too; for on this earth are all living beings established and they do not exist outside it. **2**

That which is this earth (as *Gayatri*) is surely this body which a man has; for these senses are indeed established in this body and they do not exist outside it. **3**

That which is a man's body is surely (identical with) the heart within the body; for these life-breaths are indeed established in it and they do not exist outside it. **4**

This sixfold *Gayatri* has four feet. About this a Vedic verse (*Rg Veda* 10.90.3) says: Great is the mystery of Nature. **5**

Even greater is the mystery of the Spirit high above (*Purusha*).
All this world represents only His one foot.
The other three feet of the Immortal are established in His own effulgence. **6**

What is called *Brahman* is the same as the space outside man.
That space which is outside man is the same, which is inside man.
And that space which is inside man is the same, which is inside the heart.
And that is *Brahman*, the all-pervading and unchanging.
He, who knows (*Brahman*) thus, attains glory, which is full and indestructible. **7**

Section 13

The said heart has five doors for the gods. The eastern door is for *Prana*. He is the eye, he is the sun. He should be meditated upon as brightness and as health. He who meditates thus becomes resplendent and healthy. **1**

"All this world represents only His one foot.
The other three feet of the Immortal are established in His own effulgence."

The southern door of this (heart) is for *Vyana*. He is the ear, he is the moon. He should be meditated upon as prosperity and fame. He who meditates thus becomes prosperous and famous. **2**

The western door of this (heart) is for *Apana*. He is speech, he is fire. He should be meditated upon as holy effulgence born of sacred wisdom and good health. He who meditates thus becomes radiant with holy effulgence born of sacred wisdom and good health. **3**

The northern door of this (heart) is for *Samana*. He is mind, he is *Parjanya* (the rain-god). He should be meditated upon as fame and grace. He who meditates thus becomes famous and graceful. **4**

The upper door of this (heart) is for *Udana*. He is air; he is *Akash*. He should be meditated upon as strength and nobility. He who meditates thus becomes strong and noble. **5**

Indeed, these, verily, are the five Persons of *Brahman*, and sentinels of His heavenly world (in the heart). He who adores these five Persons of *Brahman* and sentinels of the heavenly world, he reaches the heavenly world. In his family a hero is born. **6**

The Light which shines beyond this heaven, beyond the whole creation, beyond everything, in the incomparably good and highest worlds; surely that Light is also the Light in man. **7**

This is the perception of That Light. It can be felt as warmth when one touches the body. It can be heard as a humming sound on closing the ears, when one hears something like the sound of a chariot or a bellowing bull, or a blazing fire. One should meditate on this Light as seen and heard. One who meditates on this, becomes beautiful to see and renowned to hear about. Yes, one who meditates thus. **8**

Section 14

Verily, all this universe is *Brahman*. From Him do all things originate, into Him they dissolve and by Him they are sustained. On Him should one meditate in tranquillity. For as is one's faith, so indeed one is; and as is one's faith in this world, so one becomes on departing from here. Let one, therefore, cultivate faith. **1**

He (*Brahman*) permeates the mind (*manomaya*). He has Life Principle (*Prana*) for His body. His form is effulgence, His resolve is truth. His essence is the all-pervasive space. He is the performer of all actions. He is possessed of all pure desires, all agreeable odors and all pleasant tastes which pervade all this, He is without speech (and other senses). He is free from agitation and eagerness. **2**

This Self (*Atman*) of mine, residing in (the lotus of) the heart, is smaller than a grain of paddy, a barley corn, a mustard seed, a grain of millet or even the kernel of a grain of millet. This Self (*Atman*) of mine residing in (the lotus of) the heart is also greater than the earth, greater than the sky, greater than heavens, greater than all these worlds. **3**

"Verily, all this universe is Brahman.
From Him do all things originate, into Him they dissolve and by Him they are sustained."

This Self of mine is the performer of all actions. It is possessed of all pure desires, all agreeable odors and all pleasant tastes. It pervades all this. It is without speech (and other senses). It is free from agitation and eagerness. It is my *Atman*, residing in the (the lotus of) my heart. It is also *Brahman*. On departing from here, I shall attain to Its Being.

One who possesses this true faith has no further doubt. Thus declared Sandilya. Yes, Sandilya. **4**

Section 15

The chest (i.e. the universe), having the sky as its inside and the earth as its (curved) bottom, is infinitely long lasting. The quarters are indeed its corners and heaven its upper lid. This chest is the vault for results of actions. All things rest in it. **1**

Of this chest, the eastern quarter is named Juhu, the southern is named Sahamana, the western is named Rajani and the northern is named Subhuta. The Air is their son. He who knows this Air as the son of the quarters, he never suffers loss of a son.

"I know, this Air as the son of the quarters. May I never suffer the loss of my son. **2**

I take refuge in the imperishable chest for such and such and such. I take refuge in *Prana* for such and such and such. I take refuge in *Bhur* for such and such and such. I take refuge in *Bhuvah* for such and such and such. I take refuge in *Suvah* for such and such and such. **3**

When I said, 'I take refuge in *Prana*', (it was because) all these beings, whatsoever exist, are indeed *Prana*, therefore I take refuge in that itself.' **4**

Then when I said, 'I take refuge in *Bhur*', I meant: 'I take refuge in the earth, I take refuge in the sky, I take refuge in heaven.' **5**

Then when I said, 'I take refuge in *Bhuvah*', I meant: 'I take refuge in Fire, I take refuge in Air, I take refuge in the Sun'. **6**

Then when I said, 'I take refuge in *Suvah*', I meant: 'I take refuge in *Rg Veda*, I take refuge in *Yajur Veda*, I take refuge in *Sama* Veda.'

Yes, that was what I said." **7**

Section 16

Man's life is a (symbolic) sacrifice. His (first) twenty-four years are the morning libation. The meter *Gayatri* has twenty-four letters, and the morning libation is related to *Gayatri* meter. With this the *Vasus* are connected. The *Pranas*, indeed, are the *Vasus*, for they make all this stable. **1**

"This Self of mine is the performer of all actions. It is possessed all pure desires. It is Atman, residing in my heart. It is also Brahman."

During this period of life if anything (e.g. illness) causes him pain, he should pray: "O *Pranas*, *Vasus*, unite this morning libation of mine with the midday libation. May I, who am a sacrifice, not be lost in the midst of the Vasus who are the *Pranas*". He surely recovers (from illness) and becomes healthy. **2**

Now, (his next) forty-four years are the midday libation, (for) the meter *Tristup* is made up of forty-four letter, and the midday libation is related to the *Tristup* meter. With this, the *Rudras* are connected. The *Pranas* indeed are the *Rudras*, for they cause all this (universe) to weep. **3**

During this period of life if anything (e.g. illness) causes him pain, he should pray: 'O *Pranas*, *Rudras*, unite this midday libation of mine with the third libation. May I, who am a sacrifice, not be lost in the midst of the *Rudras* who are the *Pranas*.' He surely recovers from that and becomes healthy. **4**

Then (his next) forty-eight years are the third libation. The meter *Jagati* is made up of forty-eight syllables and the third libation is related to the *Jagati* meter. With this, the *Adityas* are connected. The *Pranas* indeed are the *Adityas*, for they accept all this. **5**

During this period of life if anything (e.g. illness) causes him pain, he should pray: 'O *Pranas*, *Adityas*, extend this third libation of mine to a full length of life. May I, who am a sacrifice, not be lost in the midst of the *Aditya* who are the *Pranas*.' He surely recovers from that and becomes healthy. **6**

Knowing this well-known (doctrine of sacrifice), Aitareya Mahidasa said, 'Why do you (illness) afflict me thus? I cannot be so killed.' He lived for one hundred and sixteen years. He who knows thus lives with vigor for one hundred and sixteen years. **7**

Section 17

When one feels hungry, thirsty and refrains from pleasure – these are like the initiatory rites (of a sacrifice). **1**

And when one eats, drinks and enjoys pleasures – these are like the Upasad ceremonies. **2**

And when one laughs and eats and makes love – these are like sacrificial chants and recitations. **3**

And his austerity, charity, sincerity, non-violence and truthfulness – these are like gifts to the priests. **4**

When they say *sosyati* (He will procreate), and *asosta* (He has procreated), That is his new birth. Death is the final bath (after the ceremony). **5**

"He who knows thus lives with vigor for one hundred and sixteen years."

Ghora Angirasa expounded this doctrine to Devaki's son Krishna and said, Such a knower should, at the time of death, repeat this triad, without any desires in his mind: 6

"Thou art the imperishable.
Thou art the unchangeable.
Thou art the subtle essence of *Prana*."

The following two Rk stanzas deal with the same theme.

"They (knowers of *Brahman*) see everywhere
that Supreme Light of the Primeval One
who is the seed of the universe,
which shines like the all-pervading daylight." (*Rg Veda*, 8.6,30) 7

"We have realized That Light which removes ignorance.
It is not different from the Light within our hearts.
It is higher than all other lights.
We have attained the sun.
We have attained the Highest Light.
Yes, the Highest Light.   (*Rg Veda* 1.15,10) 8

Section 18

'Mind is *Brahman*' thus one should meditate. This (meditation) is with regard to self. Next is meditation with regard to gods. 'Sky is *Brahman*', thus (one should meditate). Both meditations, with regard to self and with regard to gods, become enjoined. 1

This *Brahman* has four feet. Organ of speech is one foot, organ of smell is one foot, eye is one foot and ear is one foot. This is with reference to self. Next, with reference to gods. Fire is one foot, Air is one foot, Sun is one foot and the Directions are one foot. Thus both the meditations, with reference to self (*adhyatmic*) and with reference to gods (*adhidaivic*), are enjoined. 2

Organ of speech is one of the four feet of *Brahman* (symbolized by Mind). With the light of fire it shines and glows. He who knows thus shines and glows with fame and renown, and with holy effulgence born of sacred wisdom. 3

Organ of smell is one of the four feet of *Brahman*. With the light of air it shines and glows. He who knows thus shines and glows with fame and renown, and with holy effulgence born of sacred wisdom. 4

Eye is one of the four feet of *Brahman*. With the light of the sun it shines and glows. He who knows thus shines and glows with fame and renown, and with holy effulgence born of sacred wisdom.

Ear is one of the four feet of *Brahman*. With the light of the directions it shines and glows. He who knows thus shines and glows with fame and renown, and with holy effulgence born of sacred wisdom. Yes, he who knows thus. 5

"Thou art the Imperishable. Thou art the Unchangeable. Thou art the subtle essence of Prana."

Section 19

Sun is *Brahman* – this is the teaching. Further explanation of this (is given here. In the beginning, this (universe) was non-existent. Then it became existent. It grew; it turned into an egg; it lay for a period of one year; (and then) it burst open. Of the two halves of that eggshell, one was of silver and the other of gold. **1**

Of these, that which was of silver is this earth. That which was of gold is heaven. That which was the outer membrane is the mountain. That which was the inner membrane is the mist together with the clouds. Those, which were the veins, are the rivers. That which was the water in the lower belly is the ocean. **2**

And that which was born (from the egg) is the yonder sun. When he was born, there arose sounds spreading far away, as also all beings and all desired objects. Therefore, according to the rising and setting of the sun, there arise sounds spreading far away, as also beings and desires for objects in them. **3**

He who knows the sun thus and meditates on it as *Brahman*, auspicious sounds will hasten to him and continue to delight him. Yes, they will continue to delight him. **4**

"In the beginning, this (universe) was non-existent. Then it became existent. It grew; it turned into an egg; (and then) it burst open."

FOCUSSED COMMENTARIES

3.1-3.11 *Madhu Vidya*: Meditation on Sun

This passage on honey-doctrine is concluded with a warning that it should not be communicated to an unworthy person; and a tribute that its position is higher than that of the whole earth with all its riches (3.11, 6).

— *Sri Sankara's translation by Swami Gambhirananda*

The movements of the sun are intended to help the creatures to experience the results of their actions. When these experiences have ended, the sun takes the creatures unto itself (3.11).

In the region of *Brahman*, the sun never rises, nor sets. The author calls the gods to bear witness to the truth of this statement (3.11, 2).

The knower *Brahman* becomes eternal *Brahman*, unconditioned by time, as marked by rising and setting of the sun.

— *S. Radhakrishnan*

3.12 *Gayatri Vidya*: *Brahman* is space outside and within man

Brahman is devoid of all qualifications and therefore difficult to comprehend. *Gayatri* is accepted as the door to knowledge of *Brahman*. It is through *Gayatri* that *Brahman* is spoken of. *Gayatri* is like one's own mother.

Gayatri as a meter has four feet of six letters each. There is a legend on how *Gayatri* became the most eminent of all meters. Once, the gods engaged three meters — *Tristup*, *Jagati* and *Gayatri* for getting Soma juice for them. *Tristup* and *Jagati* returned without any success; on the contrary, they left behind some of their letters. *Tristup* left behind one letter and *Jagati*, three. Then, *Gayatri* alone was able to defeat the protectors of Soma juice and obtain it for the gods. She also picked up the four letters left behind by the other meters, and added them to herself. This is how *Gayatri* pervades other meters.

The totality of all living beings — moving and non-moving — is *Gayatri* itself.

Since *Gayatri* is just a meter, how can it be identified with all living beings? This is because *Gayatri* is identified with speech; and speech with living beings. It is through speech that we talk about all living beings, like: 'That one is a cow, this one is a horse etc.' Speech also provides protection from fear, for example, when we assure someone, 'Do not be afraid, there is nothing to fear'. In fact, *Gayatri* derives its name from *gana*, singing and *trana*, protecting.

Just as speech connects all living beings to *Gayatri*, living beings connect *Gayatri* to earth. As all beings live on earth, *Gayatri* is also the earth.

Likewise, the human body is made of earthly elements. Therefore, *Gayatri* is also the human body.

The five senses of the human body are established in the heart. Therefore, *Gayatri* is also the heart. Also, from other Upanishadic texts, we know that the heart is established in life-breath, *Prana*.

Thus, *Gayatri* has six identities — speech, living beings, earth, body, heart and life-breath. These correspond to the six letters of each of the four feet of *Gayatri* (3.12, 2-5).

Brahman is *Gayatri*, *Brahman* inheres in *Gayatri*, and *Brahman* is expressed through *Gayatri*. This idea is also contained in a verse (Rk) from *Rg Veda* (10.90.3).

He who knows that the All-pervading, Unchanging *Brahman* is expressed through *Gayatri*, he gains glory which, like *Brahman*, is full and indestructible (3.12, 7).

— *Based on Commentary by Sri Sankara, translated by Swami Gambhirananda*

3.13 *Parajyotir Vidya*: Light of *Brahman* in man

The first six verses of this section use the analogy of human heart having five gates and gate-keepers to illustrate the interrelatedness of five forms of life-breaths, five senses and their deities. These are summarized in the table on next page. An understanding of this interrelatedness is essential for meditating on *Brahman* within.

'The knower of Brahman becomes eternal Brahman, unconditioned by time.'

Interrelatedness of Man and Cosmos

Heart's Gate	Gate-keeper (life-breath)	Inter-related Sense	Presiding Deity	Aspect to be meditated upon
East	*Prana*, In-breath	Eye	Sun	Brightness and Health
South	*Vyana*, Out-breath	Ear	Moon	Prosperity and Fame
West	*Apana*, Diffusing-breath	Speech	Fire	Wisdom and Health
North	*Samana*, Equalizing-breath	Mind	Rain	Fame and Grace
Zenith	*Udana*, Ascending-breath	Air	Space	Strength and Nobility

Brahman is not just in the space within, it is also in the space outside. Last two verses of this section describe how the Light of *Brahman* can be 'seen' and 'heard' in this body.

– Editor

This section is connected with the foregoing one (3.12, on *Gayatri*), but it also has an independent significance.

There are two ways to attain *Brahman* – the mysterious *Devayana* (path of gods) and the esoteric *Brahma Vidya* (knowledge of *Brahman*). Both these ways seem to be implied in this section.

Verses 1-6 describe five openings for gods analogous to *Devayana*. The way to *Brahman* through vital breaths, sense organs and Nature-gods points outwards.

Verses 7-8 state that the light beyond the heavens is the same as the light within the heart. It makes itself perceptible as warmth in the body and as whizzing in the ears. The verses establish identity of *Brahman* with the Soul in the esoteric sense.

– Paul Deussen

By controlling the eyes, ears, speech, mind and breath through meditation – by checking their outward activities – we are enabled to reach *Brahman* in the heart (3.13, 6). In verse-8, the Upanishad seems to refer to visions and voices of which some mystic seers speak.

– S. Radhakrishnan

The five persons described in verses 1-5 in connection with the five gates, are the gate keepers of *Brahman* in the heart, similar to the gate keepers of a king. As long as the sense organs – the gate keepers – are not controlled, the mind refuses to concentrate on *Brahman*. When the sense organs are controlled and identified through meditation with their presiding deities and supporting life-breaths, then they help in attaining the knowledge of *Brahman*.

A heroic son is born to one who adores *Brahman* and its five gate keepers. How? The Vedic law is that a person is inclined towards worship of *Brahman* only when his debts are discharged by his descendents. Thus, a son becomes a cause for attainment of heavenly regions (3.13, 6).

The warmth of the body signifies the presence of the Light of *Brahman* in it.

– Swami Swahananda

3.14 *Sandilya Vidya*: Meditation on Self within and without

Vidya is a meditation, an art of thinking on the supreme goal. Meditation on the all-inclusive *Brahman* is known by the name *Sandilya Vidya*, as it was the great Rishi Sandilya who had its revelation.

Verse 3.14, 1 says that we should to meditate on *Brahman* – calmly, quietly, and peacefully. We should meditate that everything comes from Him, is sustained by Him, and returns to Him.

As *Brahman* is the cause of everything and every effect, this whole creation is contained in *Brahman*, all of us included. No effect can be separated from the cause. There is an undifferentiated relationship between the effect and the cause. We are therefore not isolated from the cause, *Brahman*. We are always connected to the Absolute, on whom we should meditate. This is not easy. We can think of something

---

'Vidya is a meditation, an art of thinking on the supreme goal.
Meditation on the all-inclusive Brahman is known by the name Sandilya Vidya.'

outside us – like the whole universe – but we cannot think of something in which we ourselves are involved. (Mind cannot think 'thinking', like we cannot directly see our own eyes). So, *Brahman* cannot be thought by the mind; yet this is the injunction of the Upanishad.

To meditate '*Sarvam khalvidam Brahma*, all this is *Brahman*' is the highest kind of meditation. How to practice such meditation? First imagine the whole universe. Then imagine that this whole universe comes from That *Brahman*. Next imagine that there is no disconnection between this and That; this is always connected with That; and eventually this will go to That.

The word *kratu* (translated as faith in verse-1) has several meaning: an effort of Will Power, an action of the mind, a determination of understanding, and a meditation that you practice. Any individual is an embodiment of action performed through Will. Whatever we will, that we become, depending on the intensity and the continuity of our Will. So, what should we think – what should be our Will throughout our life – if we want to become *Brahman*? The answer is obvious. Meditate on *Brahman* (3.14, 1).

The whole mental world is permeated by *Brahman*. It appears to be embodied through the Life Principle (*Prana*), and the body. They are vehicles to particularize this Infinite Consciousness. Consciousness is the cause, life and body are the effects. As the effect is not different from the cause, the life-body complex is not different from the Absolute. Quantitatively, the particular is limited in comparison with the universal; but qualitatively, the two are the same. Just as from a drop you can know the ocean, from the particular you can reach the universal.

Some Sanskrit words used in the text (3.14, 1-4) need an explanation.

Satyakama : Whatever is willed through Pure Consciousness is materialized at once.

Akash-atman : *Brahman* is as vast as space. It is therefore all-comprehensive.

Sarva-karma : All actions are His actions. It performs everything – whatever you, I, or anyone else does; or whatever happens anywhere.

Sarva-kamah : All our desires are nothing but a movement of Consciousness towards universality in some way or the other.

Sarva-gandha : Everything we smell is an activity of That Being.

Sarva-rasah : All tastes are nothing but His activity.

Sarvam-idam Abhiyattah : Everything is enveloped by Him. It pervades everything – inside and outside.

Avaki : It does not speak, but It can convey Its message.

Anadarah : It is free from agitation and eagerness.

Sandilya Vidya is not a teaching giving some information, it is an instruction on meditation. It describes how the mind should be organized in daily meditation so that it does not wander from place to place or from object to object. The mind will not think of multiplicity when it knows the Totality (3.14,2).

This great Being, Supreme *Brahman*, is in one's own heart – as fine and subtle as one can think of – subtler than a grain of rice etc. At the same time, It is vaster than the whole creation. This symbology is given only for the purpose of meditation. We must know that the infinite expanse outside us is identical with our own Being. The Upanishads are never tired of hammering this idea into us that the Supreme Being is both the infinite universe as an object, and the Self within us as the subject. This is the principal meditation (3.14,3).

The reason why *Atman* is called *Brahman* is because It is the Self of all. As the Self of an individual, It is called *Atman*; as the all-comprehensive Self, It is called *Brahman*.

"This *Brahman* is what I am," thus we should meditate. When we get up in the morning, this is the first thought that should come to our mind. Our progress in the spiritual path can be judged from our first thought when we get up.

Sandilya Vidya contains the art of adjusting the mind inwardly as well as outwardly. In the beginning this is

---

'Our progress in the spiritual path can be judged from our first thought when we get up.'

done by alternate processes; and then finally by grasping the Totality of *Brahman* in Its dual aspect of universality and individuality. Though very short, *Sandilya Vidya* contains everything. It is like clinching the whole subject of the Upanishad inside a fist (3.14,4).

– Swami Krishnananda

The word *tajjalan* in Verse-1 is explained by Sri Sankara as, *ja*: beginning, *la*: ending and *an*: continuing in it.

Sandilya Vidya affirms the oneness of the individual soul and the Supreme *Brahman*. According to Sandilya:

(i) *Brahman* is that from which things are born, to which they repair, and by which they live.
(ii) Our next life depends on what we do in this life.
(iii) *Atman* is both transcendent and immanent.
(iv) The end of man is union with Self.

– S. Radhakrishnan

The doctrine of Sandilya is perhaps the oldest passage in which the identity of *Brahman* with *Atman* – of God with the Soul – is expressed with full consciousness. The soul which appears to be the equivalent of a drop of ocean or a spark of the great world fire, is in reality not so. It is not a part, an emanation of the divine essence, but fully and entirely this divine essence itself. It appears infinitely small in us and infinitely great outside us; but in both cases it is one and the same. For elucidation, as also for confirmation of this truth, the following beautiful words of Plotinus deserve to be quoted.

"First then let every Soul consider that it is the universal Soul which created all things, breathing into them the breath of life – into all living things which are on earth, in the air, and in the sea, and the Divine stars in heaven, the sun, and the great firmament itself. The Soul sets them in their order and directs their motions, keeping itself the thing-in-itself apart from the things which are appearances, which it orders and moves and causes to live." (Enneades 5, 1, 2).

– Paul Deussen

Sandilya Vidya appeals to a basic fact of life: 'As is a man's *kratu* or "will", so is the deed he does; as is the deed he does, so is that which he attains to – in this life and after death'. Will is something that comes from my heart, my inmost Self. All scripture teach that one be fully devoted to the Infinite, to God, to *Atman/Brahman*. They presume that one will never question why one should be so devoted. So an initial step is to resolve this question. This is what the Upanishad suggests in verse-1.

– Klaus G. Witz

In this meditation, *Brahman* is identified with everything that is good, noble and beautiful. The meditator then thinks himself to be none other than *Brahman* (3.14,4).

– Swami Gambhirananda

3.15 Prayer for son's longevity

In section 3.13, there was a promise of the birth of a hero in the family. This section describes a ritual-prayer for the longevity of a son. (A similar prayer appears in Brhadaranyaka 1.5, 17).

The text compares the universe to a vast treasure-chest. The four directions are imagined as the four corners of the treasure-chest. Their assigned names are not without significance.

- Eastern corner is named *Juhu*, a sacrificial ladle in which oblations are offered facing east.
- Southern corner is named *Sahamana*, region of *Yama*. One should not sleep with his feet facing south.
- Western corner is named *Rajani*, which is presided over by *Varuna* and also connected with the evening glow.
- Northern corner is named *Subhuta*, which is presided over by *Kubera*, the deity of wealth. Facing north is considered auspicious for creation of wealth.

The chest... is infinitely long-lasting: This is not an absolute negation of the material resources of the world getting exhausted. It only implies their continuation for an incalculably long period (3.15, 1).

– Swami Swahananda

3.16 Prayer for a life of 116 years

Prana here stands for both the senses and the vital breaths. The Upanishads make use of various devices to emphasize an important idea. One of these

'Sandilya Vidya affirms the oneness of individual soul and Supreme Brahman.'

is to create an etymological connection, sometimes fancied, between two terms or relations, which occur in the same context. In this section, mention is made of the *Vasus, Rudras and Adityas* as resident deities of three libations and also three divisions of life. *Prana* is identified with all of them.

– Swami Swahananda

Here is one of the grandest concept of Life as a sacrifice. The Upanishad says, 'Man himself is a sacrifice' and shows in detail how it can be so. Man's life is divided into three stages and compared to the three periods in a sacrifice, called Savanas. Each period is given to its proper deity. The first stage is presided over by Vasus. They symbolize stability, which is the biggest need of childhood. They are succeeded by Rudras, who symbolize energy as well as ruthlessness. Therefore, a person must be extremely judicious in what he does in his youth. Old age is presided over by Adityas. They attract everything towards them. Elderly persons are therefore attracted more towards spirituality.

– Swami Gambhirananda

3.17 Man's life is like a sacrifice

The meaning of verse-7 is that knowers of *Brahman*, who have become pure in heart through spiritual disciplines, see the Supreme Light everywhere. It is the Light of the self-effulgent, transcendental *Brahman*. It is the Light by which the sun spreads its rays, the moon shines, the planet and the stars twinkle.

In verse-8 another seer, while visualizing the Light described above says that we have attained the Light, which is the Supreme Light in the sun. It is beyond the darkness of ignorance. An alternate reading is that It dispels ignorance. That Light is our own. The Light established in our hearts and the Light in the sun is the same. While seeing that Light, which is supreme, we have attained the sun-god, who activates the vital forces of the world. We have attained the Highest Light, *jyotir uttam*. The repetition of *jyotir uttam* is for showing the conclusion of meditation imagining man's life as a sacrifice.

– Sri Sankara, translated by Swami Gambhirananda

3.18 Meditation on Mind and Sky as *Brahman*

The four feet of *Brahman*, as mentioned first in *Rg Veda* (10.90.3) have repeatedly influenced the thought of the succeeding periods. According to the original viewpoint, one foot is the manifested world, and the other three are transcendental. This is not so in these passages.

– Swami Swahananda

3.19 Meditation on Sun as *Brahman*

Vedic scriptures contain two views regarding the origin of the universe:

(i) A cosmic egg, *Hiranyagarbha* originating in primeval waters (*Rg Veda*, 10.129.3 and 10.121.1).
(ii) *Brahman* as the Sun.

Both these views are presented here to form a myth of creation.

– Paul Deussen

Non-existence or *asat* does not mean absolute non-being. It is a state in which name and form were not manifested (Taittiriya, 2.7,1). This view is questioned later (in Chandogya 6.2, 1).

In the Orphic Cosmogony, Chronos and Adrastea produce a gigantic egg, which is divided into two – the upper half forming the sky and the lower the earth.

– S. Radhakrishnan

'Knowers of Brahman see the Supreme Light everywhere.'

4. Spiritual lessons from Nature and Fire

SIMPLIFIED SYNOPSES

4.1-4.3
Samvarga Vidya: Meditation on Life-breath

'Everything in the universe is food for (merges into) some bigger, more powerful entity.'

'By refusing food to me, you have withheld food from the Supreme Being.'

Identification of important body functions with certain cosmic objects is a recurring theme in the Upanishads. In *Samvarga Vidya*, Air and Life-breath, *Vayu* and *Prana* are identified as one Life Principle: Air operates at the universal level and Life-breath at the individual level. Further, it is stated that everything in the universe is food for something else, or everything merges into a bigger, more powerful entity. For examples, Fire, Sun, Moon and Water merge in Air at the universal level; Speech, Sight, Hearing and Mind merge in Life-breath during deep sleep at the individual level. As a side line, it may be noted that the enumerated entities add up to ten. To make the narration interesting, this number ten is identified as a common factor in *Samvarga Vidya*, a dice with four numbered faces adding to ten, and a Vedic meter *Virat* which has 10 letters.

The teaching of *Samvarga Vidya* is imparted through an anecdote. There lived a cart-driver named Raikva. He was materially poor and physically unclean, but endowed with immense wisdom. It is said that the intense radiance of his wisdom could even scorch birds flying near him. A conversation to this effect between two birds was overheard by a king, Janashruti. He wanted to know what deity did Raikva worship? After locating Raikva, the king offered him expensive gifts for this information, which Raikva refused to divulge. It was only when the king offered his daughter in marriage to Raikva that he revealed the deity worshipped by him – Life Principle as *Vayu* and as *Prana*.

The teaching ends with another story within the anecdote. A student of *Samvarga Vidya* begged food from two scholars who were in the middle of a feast. However, they ignored him. Surprised at their behavior, he lectured them on *Samvarga Vidya*: 'By refusing food to me, you have withheld food from that Supreme Being which is both the Provider and the Devourer – He provides food to all and He devours even cosmic entities'. This embarrassed the two scholars. One of them elaborated on what the student had said: 'Yes, we know that there is a Supreme Power which resides in all beings. He not only creates and protects but also destroys everything. So figuratively, everything is food for Him and He eats with 'golden teeth' of knowledge.'

The two humbled scholars also provided food to the needy boy.

The Supreme Being is without any differentiation. In Him, one cannot say which is 'food' and which is 'eater of food'; there is no subject-object difference. Food flows to Him from all directions and from Him into all directions.

4.4-4.9
Satyakama learns about *Brahman* from Nature

The text in Sections 4.4-4.9 is also known as *Sodasha Kala Vidya* or knowledge of sixteen 'parts' of *Brahman*. It must be remembered that there is only One Partless *Brahman*, but He can be seen and known only through His innumerable manifestations, or 'parts'.

> *'Satyakama overcame the obstacle of his illegitimate birth by courageously speaking the truth up front.'*

> *'Space, Matter, Energy and Life Principle are all aspects of One Absolute.'*

The student in these sections is Satyakama, an illegitimate and fatherless son of a serving girl, Jabala. He wanted to pursue spiritual studies but his mean birth was an obstacle. Satyakama overcame this obstacle by courageously speaking the truth about his birth – up front.

Besides being a seeker of Truth, Satyakama was also a hard working boy, determined to achieve super-success in whatever work was assigned to him. As a starter, his teacher Gautama sorted out 400 old and weak cows and asked Satyakama to look after them. Anyone could have seen that they would not live long, let alone breed and multiply. But Satyakama promised his teacher that he would return only when their number increased to a thousand.

Time passed by as Satyakama attended to the cows with great care. Then, on four different days, he had four supernatural revelations through the medium of a bull, fire, a swan and a diver bird. These are said to represent the three chief deities of ancient times – Air, Fire and Sun – and Life Principle as the fourth.

What did nature reveal to Satyakama about *Brahman* through its four representatives? *Brahman*, the Absolute Ultimate Reality, is imperceptible. However, It reveals Itself in Nature through many perceptible manifestations. Figuratively, *Brahman* is said to have four feet (as also in 3.18,2). In the text, the first three feet are said to represent the directions, the physical world and the universal light. With our present state of knowledge, these could be interpreted to represent Space, Matter and Energy. The text also says that each of *Brahman*'s four 'feet' again has four parts, for example, space has four directions. In short, all things around us are images of *Brahman* and we should think of Him whenever we are involved with these images in any way. When we do so, we will acquire qualities of *Brahman*, like Radiance, Infinitude, Effulgence and Support.

The fourth 'foot of *Brahman*, Life Principle, is of special significance. Life-breath, mind and sense organs (represented by eye and ear) are said to be its parts. This foot has been called 'support'. Recall that in Aitareya Upanishad it was stated that human body is the abode of Cosmic Powers – they entered man through his various sense organs and became individual powers. Here it is stated that these powers are like one 'foot' of *Brahman*. When we look at our life, mind and sense organs as a part of *Brahman*, we feel well supported.

The passages do not imply that the four meditations described here are to be practiced independently. Space, Matter, Energy and Life Principle are all aspects of One Absolute. When this realization dawns on us, we become Radiant, Infinite and Effulgent. We also become a Support, not only of ourselves but also of others; not only in this world but also in the other world.

4.10-4.15
Upakosala learns about *Brahman* from three fires

Satyakama who was a student of *Brahma Vidya* in previous sections is the teacher in these sections. His student Upakosala is sad and depressed because his education is not complete even after twelve years of study. Again, in a figurative language, the three sacrificial fire whom Upakosala had worshipped all these years try to cheer him up with a profound statement: Life Principle is *Brahman*, Joy is *Brahman*, Space in the heart is *Brahman* (4.10, 4).

'Life Principle is Brahman, Joy is Brahman, Space in the heart is Brahman.'

Next, each of the three Fires identifies itself with Sun, Moon and Lightening respectively. Each fire says: 'The person who is seen in the Sun, that I am', and similarly for Moon and Lightening. The five elements and food etc. are stated to be other forms of Fires. What the Fires emphasize is that the same *Brahman* is seen manifested in all the illustrative examples enumerated in the text.

Knowledge of *Brahman* imparts a lustrous glow to the face. Satyakama noticed this on the face of Upakosala, just as Gautama had noticed it on his face. Satyakama had acquired *Brahma Vidya* through revelations coming from Nature, Upakosala through revelations coming from Fires. However, realizing that Upakosala's knowledge was not complete, Satyakama added to what the Fires had taught him.

Brahman is the Seer in the eye. He is the Power that makes the mind and various sense organs do their respective functions. He is Self, *Atman*. He is Immortal and Fearless. He is the goal as well as the source of all things that anyone prays for. He is the Giver of merit and luster.

The passages also contain the famous simile of lotus leaf and water. Just as water does not cling to a lotus leaf, so also a sinful act does not get attached to one who knows *Brahman*. A knower of *Brahman* would never commit a sin.

In conclusion it is stated that for a knower of *Brahman,* all rituals – even the last rites – are of no consequence.

4.16-4.17
Silence and speech in sacrificial rituals

This supplement to the fourth chapter describes the functions of Brahma priest (not to be confused with *Brahman*), the chief priest supervising a sacrifice. It also specifies when he has to remain silent (Sec.16) and when he has to speak (Sec. 17). In contrast to other priests (Hotr, Udgatr, Adhavaryu), Brahma has to remain silent, as a rule. His silent reflection and speech of other priests are like two paths in a sacrifice. When a Brahma priest breaks his silence without any necessity, he makes the sacrifice defective and causes harm to the sacrificer.

Section 17 prescribes the procedure for atonement in the event a sacrifice is rendered defective through an unwarranted speech of Brahma priest. Depending upon the nature of the defect, the priest has to offer oblations in an appropriate fire with a recitation of *bhur svaha*, *bhuvah svaha*, or *suvah svaha*.

The sounds *bhur*, *bhuvah* and *suvah* are quintessence of creation. These are said to have been extracted by the Creator, *Prajapati* through *tapas*, as follows:

- from earth, fire; from fire, *Rg Veda*; from *Rg Veda*, *bhur*.
- from sky, air; from air, *Yajur Veda*; from *Yajur Veda*, *bhuvah*.
- from heaven, sun; from sun, *Sama Veda*; from *Sama Veda*, *suvah* (4.17, 1-6).

The last four verses describe the importance of a Brahma priest in rituals of sacrifice (4.17, 7-10).

'Brahman is the Seer in the eye. He is the Power that makes the mind and sense organs do their respective functions.'

Translated Text

CHAPTER 4

Section 1

Om. There lived Janashruti Pautrayana. He gave gifts with respect, and liberally. He had much food cooked (for others). He built rest houses all over, thinking, 'Everywhere people will eat food provided by me'. **1**

Once at night, two swans flew along. Then the swans addressed each other thus,

'Ho, Ho, O Bhallaksa, Bhallaksa, the radiance of Janashruti Pautrayana has spread in the sky. Do not come near it, lest it should scorch you.' **2**

'What? How can you so describe him as if he were Raikva, the cart driver?'

'What sort man is this Raikva, the cart driver?' **3**

'Just as all the lower throws of a dice go to the winner with the highest throw, so goes to Raikva whatsoever good men do; so also to him who knows what Raikva knows. Such is he, who has thus been spoken of by me'. **4**

Janashruti Pautrayana overheard those words. As soon as he got up next morning, he said to his attendant: 'Listen, do not praise me like Raikva, the cart driver. Instead, find him out.' (Janashruti then repeated the words of the swan):

'Just as all the lower throws of a dice go to the winner with the highest throw, so goes to Raikva whatsoever good men do; so also to him who knows what Raikva knows. Such is he who has thus been spoken of by me'. **5-6**

The attendant, having searched for him, came back and said, 'I could not find him'. Janashruti said to him, 'Well, where the knower of *Brahman* should be searched for, search for him there.' **7**

(After searching) he came to a man sitting under a cart and scratching eruptions on his skin. Sitting near him, he asked, 'Revered sir, are you Raikva the cart driver?' 'Yes friend, I am', he admitted. Glad to have found him, the attendant returned. **8**

Section 2

On hearing this, Janashruti Pautrayana took with him six hundred cows, a gold necklace, and a chariot drawn by mules and went to Raikva. He addressed him thus: 'O Raikva, (here are for you) these six hundred cows, this gold necklace, and this chariot drawn by mules. Now, revered sir, teach me about the deity whom you worship.' **1-2**

"Do not praise me like Raikva, the cart driver. Instead, find him out."

The other man answered him thus: 'Ah, O Sudra, let this gold necklace together with the chariot and the cows remain with you'. Thereupon Janashruti Pautrayana again took with him one thousand cows, a gold necklace, a chariot drawn by mules and his daughter and went back to Raikva. **3**

Janashruti said to him: 'O Raikva, (here are for you) these one thousand cows, this gold necklace, this chariot drawn by mules, this wife, and this village in which you reside. Now, revered sir, please instruct me.' **4**

Looking at the face of the princess, Raikva said, 'O Sudra, you have brought all these! Even by this means alone (i.e. the princess) you could have me talk'. The king gave away to him all those villages in the Mahavrsa country known as Raikvaparna where Raikva lived. Raikva began his teachings. **5**

Section 3

Air indeed is the absorber. For when a fire goes out, it is in air that it merges; when the sun sets, it is in air that it merges; when the moon sets, it is in air that it merges. **1**

When water dries up, it is in air that it merges. Air absorbs all these. This is (the doctrine of *Samvarga*) with reference to the gods. **2**

Next is (the doctrine of *Samvarga*) with reference to the self. Life-breath, *Prana* indeed is the absorber. When one sleeps, speech merges in *Prana*, the eye merges in *Prana*, the ear merges in *Prana*, the mind merges in *Prana*; for *Prana*, indeed, absorbs all these. **3**

These, indeed, are the two absorbers: Air among the gods and *Prana* among the sense organs. **4**

Once upon a time, while Kapeya Saunaka and Kaksaseni Abhipratarin were being served with food, a celibate student of sacred knowledge begged food from them. They did not give him anything. **5**

The *Brahmachari* said, 'One god – the protector of the worlds – swallowed up the might of four great ones. O Kapeya, O Abhipratarin, mortals do not see him though he abides in many forms. Indeed, you have withheld this food from him for whom it is meant.' **6**

Kapeya Saunaka, reflecting on these words, approached him (and said); 'He is the Self of all gods, the creator of all beings, with golden teeth, the truly wise one. Himself remaining unconsumed, he consumes even what is not consumable. Therefore, (the knowers) describe his magnificence as unmeasurable. Such indeed is *Brahman*, O *Brahmachari*, whom we worship'. (Then he said to the servants): 'Give him food'. **7**

They gave him food. Now, these five (cosmic entities) and the other five (senses), together make ten; they signify the highest throw in dice. Therefore, these ten are the food in all ten quarters. This is Virat, the eater of food; through him all this

---

"These, indeed, are the two absorbers; Air among the gods and Prana among the sense organs."

is perceived. He who knows this, sees all this and becomes an eater of food. Yes, one who knows this. **8**

Section 4

Once Satyakama addressed his mother Jabala, 'Mother, I desire to live the life of a celibate student of sacred knowledge in a teacher's house. Of what lineage am I?' **1**

She said to him, 'My child, I do not know of what lineage you are. I was engaged in many works, and while attending on others, I got you in my youth. So, I do not know of what lineage you are. However, I am Jabala by name and you are named Satyakama. So you may speak of yourself as Satyakama Jabala.' **2**

He went to Haridrumata Gautama and said, 'I desire to live under you, revered sir, as a *Brahmachari*; may I approach your venerable self (for the same)?' **3**

Gautama asked him, 'Dear boy, of what lineage are you?' He replied, 'Sir, I do not know of what lineage I am. I asked my mother; she replied, "I was engaged in many works and while attending on others, I got you in my youth. So I do not know of what lineage you are. However, I am Jabala by name and you are named Satyakama". So, sir, I am Satyakama Jabala.' **4**

The teacher said to him, 'No one who is not a *Brahmin* can speak thus. Dear boy, bring the sacrificial fuel, I shall initiate you as a *Brahmachari*, for you have not deviated from truth'. Having initiated him: he sorted out four hundred lean and weak cows and said, 'Dear boy, attend to them'. While he was driving them towards the forest Satyakama said, 'I shall not return till they become one thousand'. He lived away for a long time, till they had increased to one thousand. **5**

Section 5

Then a bull addressed him, 'Satyakama!' 'Yes, revered sir', thus he responded. 'Dear boy, we have become a thousand, take us to the house of the teacher. **1**

(For this favor) I will instruct you about one foot of *Brahman*'. 'Please instruct me, revered sir'. (The bull) said to him, 'The eastern quarter is one part, the western quarter is one part, the southern quarter is one part, the northern quarter is one part. This indeed, dear boy, is one foot of *Brahman*, consisting of four parts, named the Radiant. **2**

He who knows this one foot of *Brahman* consisting of four parts thus, and meditates on it as the Radiant, becomes radiant in this world. He who knows this one foot of *Brahman* consisting of four parts thus, and meditates on it as the Radiant, wins the radiant regions (in the next world). **3**

"Then a bull addressed him, 'Satyakama! I will instruct you about one foot of Brahman'..."

Section 6

Fire will tell you of another foot of *Brahman*'. At dawn the next, Satyakama drove the cows towards the teacher's house. Towards evening, at the place where those cows came together, he kindled the fire, penned the cows, collected fuel and sat down near them, behind the fire, facing east. **1**

The fire addressed him, 'Satyakama!' 'Yes, revered sir', he responded. **2**

'Dear boy, let me instruct you about one foot of *Brahman*'. 'Please instruct me, revered sir'. (The fire) said to him: 'The earth is one part, the sky is one part, heaven is one part, and the ocean is one part. This indeed, dear boy, is one foot of *Brahman*, consisting of four parts, named the Endless. **3**

He who knows this one foot of *Brahman* consisting of four parts thus, and meditates on it as the Endless, becomes endless in this world. He who knows this one foot of *Brahman* consisting of four parts thus, and meditates on it as the Endless, wins endless regions. **4**

Section 7

The swan will tell you of another foot of *Brahman*'. At dawn of the next day, Satyakama drove the cows towards the teacher's house. Towards evening, at the place where the cows came together, he kindled the fire, penned the cows, collected fuel and sat down near them, behind the fire, facing east. **1**

The swan flew to him and addressed him, 'Satyakama!' 'Yes, revered sir', he responded. **2**

'Dear boy, let me instruct you about one foot of *Brahman*'. 'Please instruct me revered sir'. (The swan) said to him: 'Fire is one part, the sun is one part, the moon is one part, and lightning is one part. This indeed, dear boy, is one foot of *Brahman*, consisting of four parts, named the Effulgent'. **3**

He who knows this one foot of *Brahman* consisting of four parts thus, and meditates on it as the Effulgent, becomes effulgent in this world. He who knows this one foot of *Brahman* consisting of four parts thus, and meditates on it as the Effulgent, wins the effulgent regions. **4**

Section 8

Madgu bird will tell you of another foot of *Brahman*'. At dawn of the next day, Satyakama drove the cows towards the teacher's house. Towards evening at the place where the cows came together, he kindled the fire, penned the cows, collected fuel and sat down near them behind the fire facing east. **1**

The Madgu bird flew to him and addressed him, 'Satyakama!' 'Yes, revered sir', he responded. **2**

"The earth is one part, the sky is one part, heaven is one part, and the ocean is one part."

'Dear boy, let me instruct you about one foot of *Brahman*'. 'Please instruct me, revered sir'. (The Madgu bird) said to him: '*Prana* is one part, the eye is one part, the ear is one part, and the mind is one part. This indeed, dear boy, is one foot of *Brahman*, consisting of four parts, named the Support'. **3**

He who knows this one foot of *Brahman* consisting of four parts thus, and meditates on it as the Support, he has solid support in this world. He who knows this one foot of *Brahman* consisting of four parts thus, and meditates on it as the support, wins support in all regions (of the next world)'. **4**

Section 9

Satyakama reached the house of the teacher. The teacher addressed him, 'Satyakama!' 'Yes, revered sir,' he responded. **1**

'Dear boy, you shine like a knower of *Brahman*; who has instructed you'? Satyakama assured him, 'People other than men. But I wish, revered sir, that you also teach me. **2**

I have definitely heard from persons like your venerable self, that knowledge learnt directly from one's teacher is most beneficial'. The teacher taught him the same thing, and nothing was omitted from this. Yes, nothing was omitted. **3**

Section 10

Once upon a time, Upakosala Kamalayana lived with Satyakama Jabala the life of a *Brahmachari*. He tended his fires for twelve years. Satyakama performed for other disciples the ceremony of completing studies and returning home, but he did not do so for Upakosala. **1**

Satyakama's wife said to him: 'This *Brahmachari* has undergone severe austerities and has tended the fires properly; you should teach him so that the fires may not blame you'. But the teacher went away on a journey without instructing him. **2**

Because of mental suffering Upakosala stopped eating. His teacher's wife said to him, 'O *Brahmachari*, do eat; why are you not eating?' He replied, 'In this man (i.e. myself) there are many desires running in various directions; I am full of mental suffering; so I am unable to eat'. **3**

Thereupon the fires said among themselves, 'This *Brahmachari* has undergone severe austerities and has tended us properly; come let us instruct him'. They then said to him, '*Prana* (life) is *Brahman*, *Ka* (joy) is *Brahman*, *Kha* (space) is *Brahman*'. **4**

He said, 'I understand that *Prana* is *Brahman*; but I do not understand *Ka* and *Kha*'. They said, 'What is *Ka*, even that is *Kha*; and what is *Kha*, even that is *Ka*'. Then the fires instructed him about *Prana* (*Brahman*) and the *Akash* (space associated with it) within the heart. **5**

"He who knows this one foot of Brahman consisting of four parts and meditates on it as the Support, he has solid support in this world."

Section 11

Then the Garhapatya fire instructed him: 'Earth, fire, food and the sun (are my forms). The Person who is seen in the sun, that I am, that I am, indeed.   **1**

He, who knows it thus and meditates on it, destroys sinful acts, wins the region (of fire), reaches the full length of life, lives gloriously, and his descendants never perish. We protect him in this world and in the next, who knows it thus and meditates on it'.   **2**

Section 12

Then the Anvaharyapacana fire instructed him: 'Water, the quarters, the stars and the moon (are my forms). The Person who is seen in moon, that I am, that I am, indeed.   **1**

He who knows it thus and meditates on it, destroys sinful acts, wins the region (of fire), reaches the full length of life, lives gloriously, and his descendants never perish. We protect him in this world and in the next, who knows it thus and meditates on it'.   **2**

Section 13

Then the Ahavaniya fire instructed him, '*Prana*, *Akash*, heaven, and lightning (are my forms). The Person who is seen in lightning, that I am, that I am, indeed.   **1**

He, who knows it thus and meditates on it, destroys sinful acts, wins the region (of fire), reaches the full length of life, lives gloriously, and his descendants never perish. We protect him in this world and in the next, who knows it thus and meditates on it'.   **2**

Section 14

The fires said, 'O Upakosala, dear boy, to you (are revealed) this knowledge of the fires and the knowledge of the *Atman*; but the teacher will tell you the way'. Then the teacher came back and addressed him, 'Upakosala!'   **1**

'Yes, revered sir,' he responded. 'Dear boy, your face shines like that of a knower of *Brahman*; who is it that has instructed you?' 'Who should instruct me sir?' said he. (Pointing to the fires), he said, 'They are like this now, but earlier they were different.' 'What did they tell you, dear boy?'   **2**

'Such and such' Upakosala acknowledged.
'Dear boy, they have told you about these regions only; but I shall tell you about That (*Brahman*). Just as water does not cling to a lotus-leaf, so also sin does not cling to him who knows *Brahman* thus'.
'Revered sir, please instruct me further'. (The teacher) said to him: **3**

"The Person who is seen in the sun, that I am, that I am, Indeed."

Section 15

'This Person who sees through the eye, He is Self, *Atman*. He is immortal and fearless. He is *Brahman*. Hence, even if one sprinkles clarified butter or water into the eye, it goes away to the edges. **1**

The knowers of *Brahman* call Him the goal of all attractive things, because all things that are sought after proceed from Him, as also towards him who knows thus. **2**

He is also Giver of merits; for He bestows all merits. He who knows it thus bestows all merits. **3**

He is also Giver of lustre; for He shines in all the regions. He who knows it thus shines in all the regions. **4**

Now, for such persons, whether the cremation rites are performed or not, they go to light. From light they go to day; from day to bright fortnight; from bright fortnight to those six months during which (the sun) rises towards the north; from months to the year; from the year to the sun; from the sun to the moon; from the moon to the lightning. Then, there is a Person, not human. He leads them to *Brahman*. This is the path of the gods and the path to *Brahman*. Those who go by this path do not return to this human whirlpool. Yes, they do not return. **5**

Section 16

This one that blows (i.e. air) is indeed a sacrifice; when moving, it purifies all this. And because it purifies all this, it is a sacrifice. Mind and speech are the two paths of this sacrifice. **1**

Of these two paths, Brahma priest performs (sacrifice rituals) with his mind (silent reflection). Hotr, Adhavaryu and Udgatr priests perform with their speech. After Prataranuvaka (the morning recitation) is commenced, and before Paridhaniya Rk (concluding recitation) is begun, if Brahma priest speaks out (breaking silence), then he purifies only one path (viz. speech) and the other is injured.

Just as a man walking with one leg, or a chariot moving with one wheel, suffers injury, so also the sacrifice of this one suffers injury. And when the sacrifice suffers injury, the sacrificer also suffers injury. For having performed a (defective) sacrifice, he becomes a sinner. **2-3**

But, after Prataranuvaka is commenced and before Paridhaniya Rk is begun, if Brahma priest does not break his silence then both the paths are purified; neither one is injured. **4**

And just as a man walking with both the legs and a chariot moving with both the wheels remain intact, so also the sacrifice of this one remains intact. If the sacrifice remains intact, the sacrificer also remains intact. He becomes great by performing the sacrifice. **5**

"This Person who sees through the eyes, He is Self, Atman. He is immortal and fearless."

Section 17

Prajapati brooded on the worlds. Brooding thus, he extracted their essences: fire from the earth, air from sky, and the sun from heaven. **1**

He brooded on these three deities. Brooding thus, he extracted their essences – Rk verses from fire, Yajus *mantras* from air, and Saman chants from the sun. **2**

He brooded on the three Vedas. Thus brooding, he extracted their essences: *Bhur* from Rk verses, *Bhuvah* from the Yajus *mantras* and *Suvah* from Saman chants. **3**

Therefore, if a sacrifice is rendered defective on account of Rk verses, then with the mantra '*Bhur Svaha*', (the Brahma priest) should offer an oblation in Garhapatya fire. Thus verily, through the essence of Rk verses, through the virility of Rk verses, he makes good the injury of sacrifice in respect of Rk verses. **4**

And if a sacrifice is rendered defective on account of Yajus *mantras*, then with the mantra '*Bhuvah Svaha*', (the Brahma priest) should offer an oblation in Dakshinagni fire. Thus verily, through the essence of Yajus *mantras*, through the virility of Yajus mantras, he makes good the injury of sacrifice in respect of Yajus *mantras*. **5**

And if a sacrifice is rendered defective on account of Saman chants, then with the mantra '*Suvah Svaha*', (the Brahma priest) should offer an oblation in Ahavaniya fire. Thus verily, through the essence of Saman chants, through the virility of Saman chants, he makes good the injury of sacrifice in respect of Saman chants. **6**

One joins gold with (borax) salt, silver with gold, tin with silver, lead with tin, iron with lead, wood with iron, or wood with leather. Likewise, (the Brahma priest) rectifies the defect of sacrifice through the virility of these regions, of these deities, and of the three Vedas. That sacrifice, indeed, is healed where there is a Brahma priest knowing thus. **7-8**

That sacrifice, indeed, becomes inclined to north, where there is a Brahma priest knowing thus. It is with reference to Brahma priest knowing thus that there is this song: 'He goes to all those places, wherever sacrifice is rendered defective.' **9**

Just as a horse protects (the soldier), even so a Brahma priest is the only priest who protects people engaged in rituals. The Brahma priest who knows thus verily protects the sacrifice, the sacrificer, and all the priests. Hence one should appoint as a Brahma priest only him who knows thus; not one, who does not know thus. Yes, not one, who does not know thus. **10**

RENDITION

4.1-4.3 *Samvarga Vidya*: Meditation on Life-breath

There lived a very generous king, Janashruti Pautrayana. He practiced charity liberally. So his fame spread widely, like a radiant fire. Once, two swans were flying close to where the king was relaxing outdoors in the evening. He overheard this conversation between the two swans.

First swan (cautioning his companion flying ahead of him):

Hey, are you short-sighted? Be careful. Don't fly over the king, or his radiance will burn your wings.

Second swan: Who are you talking about? You are speaking of his radiance as if he was Raikva, the cart-driver.

First swan: Who is this Raikva?

Second swan: He is a very wise person. He is so wise that it appears that whatever good deed men do, their results accrue to Raikva in the form of wisdom. Not only this, whosoever knows Raikva well, becomes like him.

The king becomes curious to meet Raikva, so next morning he sends his attendant to search for him. After some time...

Attendant: I am sorry, your majesty, I could not find Raikva.

King: Did you look for him in the right places? Look for him in places of solitude. That is where men of spiritual wisdom are normally found.

The attendant goes out again in search of Raikva. He notices a man in rags, sitting with a cart.

Attendant: Revered Sir, are you Raikva, the cart-driver.

Raikva: Yes, I am.

The attendant goes and informs the king, who then comes to meet Raikva personally with gifts considered expensive in those times.

King: O Raikva, Revered Sir, I would like to present to you these six hundred cows, this necklace, and this chariot, complete with mules to draw it. Please accept these. In reciprocation, please teach me about the deity you worship.

Raikva (speaking derogatively): Keep them all for yourself.

The king goes back disappointed, but returns with some more gifts, and also his daughter to offer her as Raikva's wife.

King: Revered Sir, Here are for you a thousand cows, a gold necklace, a chariot, this beautiful lady as your wife and this village for your residence. Pray, teach me now.

This time Raikva accepts the gifts and begins his teachings, known by the name *Samvarga Vidya*.

Raikva: There are two fundamental entities into which everything merges – Cosmic Life Energy symbolized by Air or *Vayu* at the universal level; and Life-breath or *Prana* at the level of an individual. A dying fire, setting sun, moon and water are examples that illustrate merger at the universal level. At the level of self, in deep sleep, all the senses like speech, sight and hearing and the mind merge into Life-breath.

Let me illustrate *Samvarga Vidya* with a story. Once, two learned men – Kapeya Saunaka and Kaksaseni Abhipratarin were being served with food. A student of scriptures begged some food from them, but they ignored him. The student was surprised at this behavior and said:

"The food you have refused to me, you have really refused to the Mighty Creator".

Thereupon, one of them, Saunaka, approached the student and said:

"You think we are ignorant of this great God to whom all food belongs. Then what is that we are meditating on? I will tell you. There is a great Soul, the Self of all beings. He eats through the mouth of knowledge itself. It is not an ordinary mouth with physical teeth and tongue. Symbolically, one may say that He has golden

---

'Look for him in places of solitude. That is where men of spiritual wisdom are normally found.'

teeth, which are shining with luster of knowledge. He swallows all things. Everything is food for Him, and He consumes it through His own being, not through any external instrument. He cannot be eaten or swallowed by anybody. For Him, everything is food. He eats non-food also. Even the eaters are eaten up by Him. This is what we are meditating upon".

He also gave him food.

The King: Revered Raikva, I do not understand the connection between this story and your teaching about Air and Life-breath being the absorbent of everything at the macro and micro levels.

Raikva: Recall the four cosmic entities that merge in Air – fire, sun, moon and water. Also recall the four senses – speech, sight, hearing and mind – which merge in Life-breath. All these, together with the two absorbents, *Samvarga,* add up to ten. They represent the highest throw in a four-faced dice (4+3+2+1). They also represent food in all ten directions. The absorbents and the absorbed total ten. The absorbents (Air and Life-breath) are like eaters of food, and the absorbed are like food.

Now, the number ten also features in Vedic texts as a symbol of *Virat*, and Vedas says that *Virat* is food. In short, the universe is not different from the deity *Virat*. He, who equates his own identity with the universe, perceives everything.

– *Editor*

Focussed Commentaries

In this meditation, *Virat*, the gross Cosmic Person is first thought of as food, which is raised by stages from the ordinary to the cosmic plane. Also everything is seen to merge in its cause, which is called 'the eater of food'. The final eater is none other than *Virat*, and eating too is *Virat*. When everything is reduced to *Virat*, cause and effect lose their duality. The meditator identifies himself with non-dual *Virat*. Thus, *Samvarga Vidya* is meditation on the merger of everything in the Cosmic Person and self-identification with Him.

– *Swami Gambhirananda*

It is strange that this knowledge, so dearly purchased or acquired by Janashruti – the knowledge on account of which Raikva is considered very wise – is in no way quite new.

– *Paul Deussen*

Sri Sankara quotes a verse to the effect that there are six ways to attain knowledge; these include gift of wealth and gift of love.

– *S. Radhakrishnan*

Raikva, who was desirous of getting married, welcomed the offer of Janashruti and imparted the knowledge.

– *Swami Swahananda*

It appears Saunaka and Abhipratarin ignored the *Brahmachari's* request for food because they wanted to test his knowledge of *Samvarga Vidya*, in which he was supposed to be proficient.

Samvarga Vidya is meditation on Air as *Vayu* at the cosmic level and as *Prana*, Life-breath at the individual level. The four great ones, which are figuratively swallowed by this god, are the other lesser deities – fire, sun, moon and water. These are comprehended in the being of *Vayu*, *Hiranyagarbha*, the Supreme Reality. At the individual level also, *Prana* is the devourer of eye, ear, mind and speech. It is possible for one to have a mistaken notion that the cosmic Vayu is different from the individual *Prana*; but the two represent a single Reality.

In Vedic texts, *Virat* is a meter with ten letters. So, there is a comparison introduced here between the meter *Virat* having ten letters, the ten merged entities enumerated in the text and also the total of numbers in a dice (*krita*), which is ten. In a more general way, *Virat* is the Cosmic Person, the All-Being, the most comprehensive Reality to which everything is food. In *Virat*, you cannot say which is the eater and which is the eaten. There is no subject-object difference. Food flows from all directions to *Virat*, and to all directions as *Virat*.

– *Swami Krishnananda*

'Samvarga Vidya is meditation on the merger of everything in the Cosmic Person and self-identification with Him.'

Do pairings like Speech-Fire and Life breath-Air have any scientific or objective basis? In the Upanishads, these have been conceived as micro-macro equivalents, or identifications of the body and the cosmic deities (powers). The role of these equivalents – and the inner truth behind them – has been evaluated very differently by various authors.

Some pairings like Sight-Sun, Life breath-Air and Hearing-Space can be traced back to *Purusha* Hymn in *Rg Veda*. While they may not play a cosmic role, they still give a cosmic dimension to human actions.

Vayu operating in the body as *Prana* is a major element of Ayurvedic medicine. So part of the objective basis for *Prana-Vayu* equivalence is found in Ayurvedic medical theory and practice.

– *Klaus G. Witz*

RENDITION

4.4-4.9 Satyakama learns about *Brahman* from Nature

Once there lived a young boy. His mother had named him Satyakama, which means seeker of truth. True to his name, the boy wanted to study at the feet of a renowned teacher. According to the custom of those days, to be accepted as a student he had to know his father's name. So he approached his mother, Jabala.

Satyakama: Mother, I want to enroll myself as a student of spiritual knowledge. What is my family name?

Jabala: I do not know who your father was, my child. However, as I am Jabala and you are Satyakama, you may call yourself Satyakama Jabala.

Thereafter, Satyakama left his home and reached the *gurukul* of a famous teacher, Haridrumata Gautama.

Satyakama: Revered Master, I want to become your student.

Gautama: Dear boy, to what family do you belong?

Satyakama: I asked my mother and she did not know the name of my father. However, she said that as her name is Jabala and my name is Satyakama, I may call myself Satyakama Jabala.

Gautama: Only one from a good family can speak the truth like you. So, I am accepting you as my student. Bring the normal symbolic sacrificial fuel, so that I may initiate you as my student.

Satyakama did as asked. After the initiation ceremony, Gautama sorted out 400 lean and weak cows from his dairy farm and said:

Gautama: Go, look after these for some time.

Satyakama: I will be delighted to do so, and I shall return only when these cows are rendered healthy and they multiply to become one thousand (4.4, 1-5).

Satyakama looked after the cows with great care. After sometime, all the cows became healthy and increased to one thousand. During this time, Satyakama also practiced meditation and contemplated on the wonders of nature. His desire for Truth was so intense that he experienced four supernatural revelations through the medium of a bull, fire, swan and diver-bird. These are considered to be the representatives of four Vedic deities – *Vayu* (Air, represented by a bull), *Agni* (Fire), *Aditya* (Sun, represented by swan) and *Prana* (Life force, represented by a diver-bird).

Bull: Satyakama, do you remember saying that you will return to the teacher's hermitage with us only when our number has increased from 400 to 1000? We are now one thousand, so please take us back. On my part, I will teach you about *Brahman*, the Absolute, Ultimate Reality.

Satyakama: Thank you, dear Bull. Please go ahead with your teaching.

Bull: Well, *Brahman* has four phenomenal aspects. Let me tell you about one of these – directions. This aspect again has four parts – East, West, North and South –

'Only one from a good family can speak the truth.'

and it is named Radiant, *Prakashvan*. He who knows this and meditates on *Brahman* as the Radiant, becomes radiant like Him (4.5, 1-3).

Fire will tell you about another aspect of *Brahman*.

Next day, at dawn, Satyakama drove the cows towards the teacher's hermitage. In the evening, he gathered the cows for rest, lighted the fire, fed the cows, and set down near the fire, facing east. Then he heard a voice, as if it was coming from fire.

Fire: Satyakama, Let me tell you about another aspect of *Brahman* – the physical world. It has four parts – Earth, Sky, Heaven and Ocean – and it is named Endless, *Anantavan*. He who knows this and meditates on *Brahman* as the Endless, becomes endless in this world and wins endless regions (4.6, 1-4).

The swan will tell you about the third aspect of *Brahman*.

Next day, Satyakama resumed his journey towards the teacher's house. Again, in the evening, a swan – symbolizing the sun – flew to him and spoke thus:

Swan: Satyakama, Let me teach you about still another aspect of *Brahman* – universal light. It has four parts – Fire, Sun, Moon and Lightening – and it is named Effulgent, *Jyotishvan*. He who knows this and meditates on *Brahman* as the Effulgent, become effulgent (4.7, 1-4).

The diver-bird will tell you of about another aspect of *Brahman*.

Again, next evening as before, when Satyakama was resting near the fire facing east, a diver-bird flew to him and said:

Diver bird: Satyakama, Let me instruct you about the fourth aspect of *Brahman* – vital breaths. It has four parts – Life-breath, Eye, Ear and Mind – and it is named Support, *Ayatanvan*. He who knows this and meditates on *Brahman* as the Support becomes well supported (4.8, 1-4).

Satyakama reflected what had been revealed to him about *Brahman*, the Absolute. It has four primary phenomenal forms, each consisting of four parts, and thus making a total of 16.

Knowledge revealed by	Aspect	Four Parts	Name
Bull (symbol of Air)	Directions	East, West, North, South	Radiant
Fire	Physical world	Earth, Sky, Heaven, Ocean	Endless
Swan (symbol of Sun)	Universal Light	Fire, Sun, Moon, Lightening	Effulgent
Diver-bird (symbol of Water)	*Prana*, Life-Breath	Life-breath, Eye, Ear, Mind	Support

But Satyakama could not see the connection between these 16 aspects and sub-aspects of *Brahman*. In the meantime, he along with the herd of a thousand cows, had reached the hermitage of his teacher, Gautama. The teacher noticed how Satyakama's face was serene and shining.

Gautama: I notice you have acquired knowledge of *Brahman*. Your face is shining, and only a knower of *Brahman* can have such a shine on his face. Who has instructed you?

Satyakama: Yes, I have learned something about *Brahman*, but not from any man. I have heard that knowledge gained directly from a teacher is most beneficial. So, revered master, please teach me about the nature of *Brahman*.

Gautama: You have heard that east and west are *Brahman*, earth and sky are *Brahman*, sun and moon are *Brahman*, eye and ear are *Brahman*. All these are parts of *Brahman*; as *Brahman* is everywhere. *Brahman* is everything. *Brahman* is Radiance, *Brahman* is Effulgence, *Brahman* is Endless, *Brahman* is the Support of all. Everything finds its rest in *Brahman*.

And *Brahman* is realized by knowing the Self, your true nature. When you truly know *Brahman*, you become *Brahman* – Radiant, Effulgent, Endless and Support of all (4.9, 1-5).

– Editor

'When you truly know Brahman, you become Brahman – Radiant, Effulgent, Endless and Support of all.'

FOCUSSED COMMENTARIES

The story of Satyakama is one of the most typical in the Upanishads. It is full of sidelights on early Vedantic teaching of yogic *sadhana* and deep psychical knowledge. The story contains several points of capital importance in understanding the ideas of the times. Satyakama, as we gather from other passages, was a great Vedantic teacher of his times, but his birth is the meanest possible. His mother is a serving-girl, not a maidservant. She is therefore unable to name her son's father. Satyakama has neither a caste, nor a family name, nor any position in life. It appears from stories like this that although the system of four castes was firmly established, it was not an obstacle in the pursuit of knowledge and spiritual advancement. A *Kshatriya* could teach a *Brahmin*, an illegitimate and fatherless son of a serving girl could be a *guru* to even the purest and the highest blood in the land.

Satyakama must have known perfectly well that he was the illegitimate son of a sex-worker, but he wished to hear the truth first-hand from his mother. Also, he persisted in speaking the truth without mincing words. His prospective *guru* Gautama therefore concluded that whatever may be Satyakama's physical birth, spiritually he was of the highest order.

– Sri Aurobindo

*S*odasha Kala Vidya teaches meditation on immortal Self, as manifested in the universe. It says that *Brahman* has four feet, each of which in turn has four parts; hence its name, viz. *Brahman* of sixteen parts. As in section 3.18, the student is asked to contemplate on a series of major features and experiences of the external world as *Brahman*. Four successive inner revelations are given to Satyakama by Nature itself; a bull, night fire, a swan and a diver bird. The four feet of *Brahman* evoke a sense of completeness and fullness.

When one becomes serious about Reality, the first and the most natural thing to do is to bow down before It, and worship It is as the cause of everything that one sees around. This is the essential motivation in the first three feet of *Brahman* in this *vidya*. All the things around us are manifestations of God and by contemplating upon them correctly, the soul gets appropriate ideals and images.

But the *vidya* does not stop here, it goes on to the fourth foot or aspect of *Brahman*. This consists of Life-breath, Sight, Hearing and Mind. These are four of the five "powers" that were mentioned earlier in section 3.18 for meditation on *Brahman*. Also, in section 3.18, there was 'pairing', which is missing here.

In Aitareya Upanishad 1.2, the deities asked *Atman* to find an abode, and *Atman* gave them man. So the cosmic powers entered into man through his various sense organs and became individual powers. In other words, cosmic powers like Sun and Air have their abode in man's eyes and life-breath etc. As a result, man's body is a place in which a metaphysical entity, *Purusha*, reveals or manifests Itself; and it is experienced directly by man.

Ordinarily, one looks at one's breath, sight, hearing and mind as different from oneself. But when one knows them all as *Brahman*, then they become one's home and abode. Then they are not separate from one's Self. Thus, when there is knowledge that the powers of life and mind etc. are *Brahman*, then one becomes *ayatanvan*, one with an abode, namely *Brahman*. So the *vidya* enjoins meditation on the powers of life and mind as *Brahman*.

The four feet of *Brahman* were revealed to Satyakama separately on four different nights by four different deities. They also have four different fruits, which are connected with the nature of each foot. The student becomes radiant, infinite, effulgent and with a proper abode. Thus, at least in the initial stages, four separate *upasanas* must be carried out. But the *vidya* clearly teaches a single *Brahman*, and implies that it is one and the same *Brahman* that is seen and known in these four feet. This implies that there are more phases to this *vidya*. The fruit of the *vidya* as a whole is deeper than the fruits of the four individual *upasanas*.

– Klaus G. Witz

*S*atyakama, after being accepted as a student, is entrusted with the task of keeping of the cows. While doing so, he becomes a partaker of supernatural revelations through the medium of a bull, fire, swan and diver bird – like Moses through the burning bush. These according to Sri Sankara represent the three chief Vedic deities – *Vayu*, *Agni* and *Aditya* – and

---

'Satyakama had supernatural revelations through the medium of a bull, fire, swan and diver bird – like Moses though the burning bush.'

fourthly, *Prana*. The four feet of *Brahman* symbolize his four phenomenal forms – directions, world-parts, world-lights and vital-breaths. Each of these is again divided into four parts, just as in section 3.18.

The nature of *Brahman* appearing in these fourfold forms has not been revealed by the bull, fire, goose or diver bird. It remains for the teacher to impart the same. What the teacher imparts to Satyakama is not stated explicitly.

– Paul Deussen

Verse 4.9, 2. 'What I know of the divine sciences and the holy scriptures, I learnt in woods and fields. I have had no other masters than the beaches and the oaks (St. Bernard).'

– S. Radhakrishnan

Verse 4.9,2. A knower of *Brahman* is recognized by the clarity of his perception, cheerful countenance, and freedom from anxiety. Satyakama's response suggests Gautama's suspicion that he might have been weaned away by another teacher.

– Swami Swahananda

Rendition

4.10-4.15 Upakosala learns about *Brahman* from three fires

In due course, Satyakama Jabala married and himself became a teacher. He had a student, Upakosala Kamalayana, who studied under him for twelve years; but still his education was not considered complete. Satyakama's wife pleaded the case of the student, but Satyakama did not pay any attention and went on a journey. This caused much mental anguish to Upakosala, and he stopped even eating food. At this, the three sacrificial fires, whom he had tended for many years, took pity and instructed him on the nature of *Brahman* – just as Satyakama had been instructed by Nature's representatives.

First, all the three fires address Upakosala jointly:

Dear Upakosala, *Brahman* cannot be attained by living in anguish and refraining from food. Know that Life (*Prana*) is *Brahman*; Joy (*ka*) is *Brahman*; Space (*kha*) is *Brahman*.

Upakosala: I understand that *Prana*, Life force is *Brahman*, but I do not understand how *ka* and *kha*, Joy and Space can be *Brahman*? Joy is momentary, and Space has no consciousness. How can an entity which is momentary and without any consciousness be *Brahman*? (4.10, 1-5)

Then each Fire spoke separately:

First Fire: *Brahman* has many forms, like: Earth, Fire, Food and Sun. The Person who is seen in Sun is *Brahman*, indeed.

Second Fire: Water, Directions, Stars and Moon are also forms of *Brahman*. The Person seen in Moon is also *Brahman*, indeed.

Third Fire: Life force, Space, Heaven and Lightening are again forms of *Brahman*. The Person seen in Lightening is *Brahman*, indeed.

What the Fires emphasized was that the same Being, *Brahman* is seen in all the aforesaid twelve illustrative manifestations (4.11-4.13).

After various promises, the three Fires conclude their instructions by saying that whereas they have revealed the knowledge of Fires, and of *Brahman*, the teacher will explain the way to attain *Brahman*.

When the teacher Satyakama returned, he noticed a shine on the face of Upakosala – indicating that he had acquired the knowledge of *Brahman* – just as in earlier years his own teacher Gautama had noticed a similar shine on his (Satyakama's) face. He asked Upakosala who had instructed him on *Brahman*? Upakosala pointed to the three fires, and narrated all that he was taught by them. Then, the following dialogue pursued.

Satyakama: Dear boy, they have told you about the manifestations of *Brahman*. I shall tell you about *Brahman* Itself.

'Knowers of Brahman describe Him as the goal of all attractive things, Bestower of merit, Bestower of lustre.'

The seer in the eye is Atman. He is *Brahman*. He is Immortal and Fearless. Should anyone put water or butter on It in the eye, it will not cling there, just as water does not cling to a lotus leaf. It will flow to the edges. So also sin does not cling to a person who knows *Brahman* (4.15, 1).

Upakosala: Revered Teacher, Can you please describe *Brahman*?

Satyakama: It is not easy, but knowers of *Brahman* use three words to describe Him

- *Samyadvama*: Goal of all attractive things
- *Vamani*: Giver of merit
- *Bhamani*: Giver of lustre

He who knows *Brahman* becomes *Brahman*, and therefore such a person can also be described as above (4.15, 2-4).

Also, a knower of *Brahman* attains *Brahman* through the path of gods, *Devayana*. There is no rebirth for him (4.15, 5).

– Editor

FOCUSSED COMMENTARY

Verse 4.10, 4 implies that the space within the heart is the abode of Prana, vital force. This vital force has the quality of Bliss. It follows that the space possessed of the quality of Bliss is *Brahman*; and the vital force existing there is also *Brahman*. In this way, the fires spoke of vital force and space as *Brahman*, by associating them together.

The identity between Sun and Fire is absolute, as they both have the common qualities of being eaters, ripeners and illuminators. Earth and food become related to these two by way of becoming things of enjoyment. Likewise, the identity between water and stars, as also between space and heavens, is relative (4.11-4.13).

In verse 4.15,5 knowledge is being praised by showing disregard for last rites. However, it does not mean that last rites are not to be performed for a knower of *Brahman*. In case of those who are not knowers of *Brahman*, some obstacles are inferred if last rites are not performed. But those who meditate on the Cosmic Person, *Purusha*, as the goal of all attractive things, and giver of merit, they verily reach the deity identified with light – irrespective of the performance or non-performance of any other (e.g. funeral) rites for them.

– Sri Sankara, translation by
Swami Gambhirananda

5 Man's connection with Cosmos

SIMPLIFIED SYNOPSES

5.1-5.2, 3
Prana: Parable on its superiority

'The departure of life-breath is compared to a powerful horse shaking itself and uprooting the pegs to which it is tied.'

The opening verses ascribe certain adjectives to various sense organs. *Prana*, Life Principle is called the eldest because it appears in the foetus before any other sense organ. It is the best because all other sense organs can function only if there is life in the body, but life can continue even in the absence of one or more sense organs. This is illustrated with a parable, which has been repeated in other Upanishads also, but with minor variations.

Once the senses disputed among themselves about their individual superiority. Unable to resolve the dispute, they went to *Prajapati*, the Creator, for arbitration. He gave a thumb rule: 'One whose absence makes the body worst off is the most superior'. So the sense organs left the body one after another for one year. When each of them returned, it found the body was able to survive in its absence, though somewhat handicapped without it. When life-breath proposed to depart, the sense organs became conscious that none of them could exist without it. So they accepted its supremacy. They also realized that the senses are not separate from life-breath. In fact, very often the Upanishads refer to the senses as *Prana*.

The departure of life-breath is compared to a powerful horse shaking itself and uprooting the pegs to which it is tied.

Continuing the parable, the text says that life-breath, *Prana* enquired what would be its food and dress? The senses replied that whatever a man eats is really food for *Prana*, and water is like its dress.

Meditation on *Prana* is relatively simple. Select a place of solitude, sit in a meditative pose and concentrate on your in-breaths and out-breaths. All the time, keep in mind the importance of Life Principle, both at cosmic and at personal level. The benefits derived from such meditation are immense. Satyakama Jabala, the sage to whom the previous Chapter 4 is devoted, says that mere narration of the doctrine of *Prana* can make even a dry stump grow branches on it! What to say of the benefits if a living being was to practice meditation on life-breath?

5.2, 4-8
Mantha rite for harmony with cosmos

The ritual described here has also been covered in Brhadaranyaka 6.3. *Mantha* is a paste prepared specially by mixing the powder of ten specific varieties of grains with curd, honey and melted butter. The rite is performed on an auspicious day after 12 days of fasting, living on just milk. *Mantha* paste is offered as an oblation in fire with recitation of prescribed invocatory hymns. The left-over *Mantha* is eaten by the performer of the rite in four installments along with recitation of *Gayatri mantra*. In the night the performer sleeps near the sacrificial fire.

The significance of the ceremony is that by it a man creates harmony between his own life-breath and its cosmic counterpart, the Eternal Life Principle.

Mantha rite is also performed for fame and prosperity. The text says that if the performer sees a woman in dream, it is an indicator of success.

The concluding text in Brhadaranyaka Upanishad 6.3 is slightly different.

5.3-5.9
Panchagni Vidya: Five cosmic fires

'The five fires are: Heaven, Rain, Earth, Man and Woman.'

Sections 5.3-5.10 are repetition of section 6.2 in Brhadaranyaka Upanishad. The passage starts with King Jaivali asking young Shvetaketu five questions about soul's journey after death and its rebirth in a new body. Neither Shvetaketu nor his father know the answers. Jaivali accepts Shvetaketu's father, Gautama Aruni as a student. He then answers his own questions, using the simile of a ritualistic fire-sacrifice.

Sacrificial rites are symbolic of profound spiritual truths. Typically, the performance of a ritualistic sacrifice requires a fire, a fuel for lightening it, and an oblation which is offered into the fire. Smoke, flame, embers and sparks are the phenomena observed during the performance of sacrifice. Different types of sacrifices yield different end-results.

The section describes five types of sacrifices, and hence the title *Panchagni Vidya*, meaning knowledge relating to five fires. The section is full of very imaginative and interconnected similes. These, when taken together, describe beautifully the interconnectedness of human birth and the cosmos.

The essence of this section is that the whole creation is like a great sacrificial rite. Every action is like an oblation. It produces a subtle vibration, which in due course assumes a gross form, like the outcome of a sacrifice. Besides, everything in the universe is interrelated; just as in a sacrifice, fire, fuel, smoke, etc. are all interrelated. Also, the outcome of one sacrifice is an oblation for another sacrifice. For example, cosmic phenomena are like oblations in the first fire, the cosmic fire. They produce a subtle body called *King Soma* in allegorical terms. This acts as an oblation into the second fire, whose outcome is rain. This is offered as an oblation in the third fire, and the outcome is food. The fourth fire is symbolic of man himself. It receives food as an oblation and the outcome is procreative fluid in man. This is poured as an oblation in a woman – symbolic of the fifth fire – and the outcome is a newborn child. This is how a man's subtle body – comprising of his deeds and impressions – travels through the five symbolic fires and eventually acquires the gross body of a newborn child.

It is to be noted that even a sexual act acquires spiritual significance if it is performed as a sacrifice for obtaining progeny.

Thus, the five fires, *panchagni* are: Heaven, Rain, Earth, Man and Woman. Fire is symbolic of sacrifice performed through contemplation. For each fire, the Upanishad provides imaginative similes for fuel, smoke, flame, embers, spark, oblation and end-results. These are summarized on the next page.

'The whole creation is like a great sacrificial rite. Every action is like an oblation. It produces a subtle vibration which assumes a gross form.'

Fire	Fuel	Smoke	Flame	Embers	Sparks	Oblations	Outcome
1. Heaven	Sun	Rays	Day	Directions	Intermediate quarters	Faith	King Soma
2. Rain	Year	Clouds	Lightening	Thunderbolt	Rumbling sound of clouds	Soma (Moon)	Rain
3. Earth	Earth	Fire	Night	Moon	Stars	Rain	Food
4. Man	Open Mouth	Life-force	Speech	Eye	Ears	Food	Semen
5. Woman	Sexual organ	Hair	Womb	Sexual act	Pleasurable feelings	Semen	Newborn child

When a man dies, offering of the dead body to the cremation fire is the final sacrifice.

5.10
Two paths after death: Liberation and rebirth, *Devayana* and *Pitrayana*

Depending upon his deeds in this world, the subtle body of a person follows one of the two paths after death – *devayana* or *pitrayana*. *Devayana* is the path of light, leading to the Sun, and then to the world of *Brahma*. This is symbolic of knowledge leading to the state of liberation. *Pitrayana* is the path of smoke and darkness. It symbolizes ignorance. One who is obliged to travel on this path goes only as far as the moon, and then he returns back, to be born again on earth.

5.11-5.18
***Vaisvanara Vidya*: Brahman is Totality**

There were five learned scholars. They were perfect in their techniques of meditation, but they had a doubt – that the technique itself was not perfect. They had no clear understanding of what is *Atman*, and what is *Brahman*? To clarify their doubt, they all went together to another sage, Uddalaka Aruni. Not confident about his knowledge, he accompanied them to a king, Ashvapati. After the usual formalities and initial hesitancy, the king began his teachings of what is called *Vaisvanara Vidya* (5.11, 1-7).

'The learned men had obviously mistaken a part for the whole.'

Before giving his own views, the king asked each of the six learned men what was is it that they concentrated upon during meditation? Each gave a different answer: Heavens, Sun, Air, Space, Water, and Earth. The king pointed out that all these are only a part of the whole Reality, and not the Reality in totality. The learned men had obviously mistaken a part for the whole, as in the proverbial story of the elephant and the five blind men. In effect, this is what the king said:

You have mistaken the finite for the Infinite. Another mistake made by you is that you have thought of *Atman* as an object, something outside yourself – like Heavens, Sun, Air, Space, Water or Earth. You have really committed a blunder in conceiving your own Self as something external to you. All these parts which you have mentioned are like various limbs of a Cosmic Person, each with a unique characteristics. Thus:

- Heaven, which is highly luminous, is like the head. (5.12)
- Sun, the universal energizer, is like the eyes. (5.13)
- Air, which has diverse paths, is like the life-breath. (5.14)
- Space, a symbol of vastness, is like the trunk. (5.15)

'Another mistake made by you is that you have thought of Atman as an object, something outside yourself.'

- Water, a symbol of wealth, is like the lower belly. (5.16)
- Earth, a symbol of foundation, is like the feet. (5.17)

Continuing the analogy of Cosmic Person (*Vaisvanara*) with a human being, the text says that the sacrificial alter is like the chest; *Kusa* grass is hair on the chest; and the three household fires are the heart, the mind and the mouth.

Meditation on any of the aforesaid has its benefits; but consequences of regarding the part as a whole – the relative manifestations as the Absolute *Atman* – can also be disastrous. Therefore, you have to bring the parts together and conceive the whole in your Consciousness. *Vaisvanara Atman* is the whole, Totality.

5.19-5.24
***Prana Agnihotra*: Five symbolic offerings of food**

> *When one meditates constantly on Self (Atman) as Totality, one's personality undergoes a transformation.*

When one meditates constantly on Self (*Atman*) as Totality or *Vaisvanara*, one's personality undergoes a transformation. He then regards all his activities like sacred oblations in the cosmic sacrificial fire.

The text implies that all our activities should be performed with some thought of their corresponding cosmic aspects. Food, for example, is interrelated with Life-breath at the individual level and Life Principle at the cosmic level. So the first five morsels that we eat should be symbolically offered as oblations to five forms of life-breaths, with recitation of the following *mantras*:

- *Pranaya Svaha* – for satisfaction of eyes, sun and heavens.
- *Vyanaya Svaha* – for satisfaction of ears, moon and quarters.
- *Apanaya Svaha* – for satisfaction of speech, fire and earth.
- *Samanaya Svaha* – for satisfaction of mind, rain-god and lightening.
- *Udanaya Svaha* – for satisfaction of skin, air and sky.

Prana Agnihotra is a part of *Vaisvanara Vidya*, meditation on Cosmic Person.

A sacrificial ritual (like *Prana Agnihotra*) can produce results only if it is performed with knowledge of its implied meaning and significance. The text illustrates this fact with two analogies. Just as pouring oblations (of melted butter) on burnt-out ash is a waste, so is a sacrifice or ritual performed without knowledge of its significance.

Lighting a sacrificial fire with a burning cotton wick is like performing a sacrificial ritual with full knowledge of its meaning. Thus, when a person performs *Prana Agnihotra* knowing what it means, he may offer anything to anyone – however little – but it will reach *Vaisvanara*, the Cosmic Person. There are many stories in Indian mythology to illustrate this viewpoint.

'Our activities should be performed with some thought of their corresponding cosmic aspects.'

Translated Text

CHAPTER 5

Section 1

Om. Verily, he who knows the eldest and the best, surely, becomes the eldest and the best. Life-breath, *Prana* is indeed the eldest and the best (of all the organs). **1**

Verily, he who knows the richest, becomes the richest among his people. Speech is indeed the richest. **2**

Verily, he who knows stability becomes stabilized in this world and in the next. The eye is indeed stability. **3**

Verily, he who knows prosperity fulfils all desires, both divine and human. The ear is indeed prosperity. **4**

Verily, he who knows the abode, becomes the abode of his people. The mind is indeed the abode. **5**

Now, once the five senses disputed among themselves about their individual superiority. Each said: 'I am superior,' 'I am superior'. **6**

These senses approached their father *Prajapati* and said to him, 'Revered sir, who is the best amongst us?' He replied, 'He amongst you is the best on whose departure the body would appear the worst, as it were'. **7**

Speech departed. Staying out for a year, it came back and asked, 'How have you been able to live without me?' (The others replied) 'Just like the dumb, not speaking, yet breathing with the breath, seeing with the eye, hearing with the ear, and thinking with the mind'. At this speech entered the body. **8**

The eye departed. Staying out for a year, it came back and asked, 'How have you been able to live without me?' 'Just like the blind, not seeing, yet breathing with the breath, speaking with the organ of speech, hearing with the ear, and thinking with the mind'. At this the eye entered the body. **9**

The ear departed. Staying out for a year, it came back and asked, 'How have you been able to live without me?' 'Just like the deaf, not hearing, yet breathing with the breath, speaking with the organ of speech, seeing with the eye, and thinking with the mind'. At this the ear entered the body. **10**

The mind departed. Staying out for a year, it came back and asked, 'How have you been able to live without me?' 'Just like infants without developed minds, yet breathing with the breath, speaking with the organ of speech, seeing with the eye, and hearing with the ear'. At this the mind entered the body. **11**

"Once the five senses disputed among themselves about their individual superiority."

Then, as *Prana* was about to depart, it uprooted the other senses just as a spirited horse would uproot the pegs to which it is tied. They all then came to it and said, 'Revered sir, be our lord, you are the best amongst us; do not depart from the body'. **12**

Then speech said to that one (*Prana*), 'Just as I am the richest, in the same manner you are also the richest'. Then the eye said to that one, 'Just as I am stability, in the same manner you are also stability'. **13**

Then the ear said to that one, 'Just as I am prosperity, in the same manner you are also prosperity'. Then the mind said to that one, 'Just as I am the abode, in the same manner you are also the abode'. **14**

Verily, people do not call them as organs of speech, nor as eyes, nor as ears, nor as minds. But they call them only as *Prana*; for *Prana* indeed is all these. **15**

Section 2

He (*Prana*) asked, 'What will be my food?' 'Whatever there is here, up to dogs and birds,' replied the senses. Whatever is eaten, all that is food, *Ana*. The word '*Ana*' indeed is self-evident. For him who knows thus there is nothing that is not food. **1**

He asked, 'What will be my garments?' 'Water', replied the senses. Therefore, indeed, those who are about to eat, cover it with water, both before and after. (He who knows thus) becomes receiver of garments. **2**

Satyakama Jabala imparted this (doctrine of *Prana*) to Govsruti, the son of Vyaghrapada, and said, 'If anyone should impart this even to a dry stump then branches would certainly grow on it, and leaves will sprout from it.' **3**

Next, if a knower of *Prana* desires to attain greatness, then he should perform initiatory rites on the new moon day. On the full moon night he should add curd and honey to a mash of all herbs; then offer it as an oblation in fire on the spot prescribed for offerings, with the Mantra '*Svaha* to the eldest and the best'. What remains attached to the ladle should be thrown into a mash-pot. **4**

With the Mantra '*Svaha* to the richest', he should offer an oblation into the fire on the spot prescribed for offerings, and throw what remains attached to the ladle into the mash-pot.
With the Mantra '*Svaha* to what is stable', he should offer an oblation into the fire on the spot prescribed for offerings, and throw what remains attached to the ladle into the mash-pot.
With the Mantra '*Svaha* to prosperity', he should offer an oblation into the fire on the spot prescribed for offering, and throw what remains attached to the ladle into the mash-pot.
With the Mantra '*Svaha* to the abode', he should offer an oblation into the fire on the spot prescribed for offerings, and throw what remains attached to the ladle into the mash-pot. **5**

"Revered sir, be our lord, you are the best amongst us; do not depart from the body."

Then, moving a little away and taking the mash-pot in his hands, he should recite (the Mantra):

'You (*Prana*) are *Ana*' by name, for all this (universe) coexists with you. You are the eldest, the best, the effulgent and sovereign. May you lead me to long-life, to best position, to effulgence, and to sovereignty. Verily, I wish to become all this'.
6

Then, he should take a sip at each foot of this Rk-mantra.

'We pray for the food pertaining to the Progenitor,' saying this (line) he should sip.
'It is the food of the effulgent one', saying this he should sip.
'The best and the all-sustaining', saying this he should sip.
'We readily meditate upon the deity',
Saying this and emptying the bowl, he should drink the whole preparation. Then he should lie down behind the fire on a deer skin or on the ground, controlling speech and mind. If he should see a woman (in a dream), he should know that the rite has been successful.
7

There is this verse about it: 'During the performance of rites for desired results if the performer sees a woman in a dream, then he should recognize success in the seeing of that dream. Yes, in the seeing of that dream.'
8

Section 3

Once Shvetaketu, the grandson of Aruni, came to the assembly of Panchala. Pravahana, the son of Jaivali, enquired of him, 'My boy, has your father instructed you?' 'He has indeed, revered sir'.
1

'Do you know where created beings go from here (after death)?' 'No, revered sir'. 'Do you know how they return again?' 'No, revered sir'. 'Do you know the place of parting of two paths – the path of gods and the path of fathers?' 'No, revered sir'.
2

'Do you know why the other world is not filled up?' 'No, revered sir'. 'Do you know how, at the fifth oblation, water comes to be designated as a person?' 'No, indeed, revered sir'.
3

'Then why did you say, "I have been instructed"? For, how can he who does not know these things say, "I have been instructed"?' Feeling distressed, Shvetaketu came to his father's place and said to him, 'Revered sir, without having instructed me properly, why did you say that you have instructed me?
4

That fellow, a *Kshatriya* asked me five questions and I was not able to answer even one of them'. The father said, 'As you have narrated (these questions) to me, I do not know even one of them. If I had known, why would I have not told you?'
5

Then Gautama (father) went to the king's place. When he arrived, the king made reverential offerings to him. In the morning he presented himself to the king when he was in the assembly. The king said to him, 'O revered Gautama, please

---

"Lead me to long life, to best position, to effulgence, and to sovereignty. Verily, I wish to become all this."

ask for a boon of human wealth. He replied, 'O king, let the human wealth remain with you, answer those questions, which you asked my boy'. The king was perturbed. **6**

The king commanded him, 'Stay here for a long time'. At the end of the period he said to him, 'O Gautama, prior to you, this knowledge never went to *Brahmins*, it remained only with *Kshatriyas*'. Then he instructed him. **7**

Section 4

The world yonder, is indeed fire, O Gautama. Of that, sun is fuel, rays are smokes, day is flame, moon is ember, and stars are sparks. **1**

Into this fire the deities offer oblation of faith. Out of that oblation King Soma arises. **2**

Section 5

Parjanya (god of rain) is indeed fire, O Gautama. Of that, air is fuel, cloud is smoke, lightning is flame, thunderbolt is ember, and rumblings of thunder are sparks. **1**

Into this fire the deities offer the oblation of King Soma. Out of that oblation rain arises. **2**

Section 6

The earth indeed is fire, O Gautama Of that, year is fuel, *Akash* is smoke, night is flame, directions are embers, and intermediate directions are sparks. **1**

Into this fire the deities offer the oblation of rain. Out of that oblation food (in the shape of vegetation) arises. **2**

Section 7

Man indeed is fire, O Gautama. Of that, speech is fuel, *Prana* is smoke, tongue is flame, eyes are embers, and ears are sparks. **1**

Into this fire the deities offer the oblation of food. Out of that oblation procreative fluid arises. **2**

Section 8

Woman indeed is fire, O Gautama. Of that, sexual organ is fuel, hair is smoke, womb is flame, sexual act is ember, and pleasurable feelings are sparks.

Into this fire the deities offer the oblation of procreative fluid. Out of that oblation foetus arises. **3**

Section 9

Thus after the fifth oblation, water (procreative fluid) comes to be designated as man. That foetus, covered with membrane, sleeps (in mother's womb) for nine to ten months, and then takes birth. **1**

"Thus, after the fifth oblation, water comes to be designated as man."

After birth, he lives as long as he is destined to live. When he dies to attain his merited world; they carry him (for cremation) to fire itself, from which he arose (through succession of oblations). **2**

Section 10

Those who know thus (significance of *Panchagni Vidya*) and who are devoted to faith and austerity in the forest, they go to light. From light they go to day, from day to bright fortnight, from bright fortnight to those six months during which the sun travels northward; from these months to the year, from year to sun, from sun to moon and from moon to lightning. There (in the region of Brahma) a Person, who is non-human, leads them to *Brahman*. This is the path of gods. **1-2**

Those living (as householders) in villages and practising sacrifice, social service and charity, they go to smoke, from smoke to night, from night to dark fortnight, from dark fortnight to those months during which the sun travels southward. From there they do not reach the year (like those going along the path of the gods). **3**

From the months, (they go) to the region of ancestors, from the region of ancestors to *Akash*, from *Akash* to moon. This (moon) is King Soma. This is food for the deities. This, the deities eat. **4**

Residing in that (region of the moon) till they have exhausted (the results of their actions), they return again the same way as they went. They come to *Akash* and from *Akash* to air. Having become air, they become smoke. Having become smoke they become white cloud.

Having become white cloud, they become (rain-bearing) cloud. Having become this cloud they fall as rain. Then they are born in this world as rice and barley, herbs and trees, sesame plants and beans. But release from these is more difficult. Whoever eats the food and sows his seed, they become like him only. **5-6**

Among them, those who perform good deeds, they quickly reach a good womb – the womb of a *Brahmin*, a *Kshatriya*, or a Vaisya. But those who perform bad deeds, they reach an evil womb, the womb of a dog, a hog, or a Chandala. **7**

Those small creatures who are continually revolving, do not go by either of these two paths. They are subject to the saying, 'Be born and die'. This is the third state. Therefore that region (of the moon) is never filled up. Hence one should despise (this state). There is this verse about it. **8**

One who steals gold, one who is addicted to liquor, one who dishonors the teacher's bed, and one who kills a *Brahmin* – all these four fall, as also the fifth, one who associates with them. **9**

Moreover, he who knows these five fires thus, even if he associates with these sinners, he is not tainted by sin. He who knows these becomes clean and pure, and obtains a meritorious world. Yes, he who knows thus. **10**

"Those who perform good deeds, they quickly reach a good womb.
But those who perform bad deeds, they reach an evil womb."

Section 11

Prachinasala Aupamanyava, Satyayagya Paulusi, Indradyumna Bhallaveya, Jana Sarkaraksya and Budila Asvatarasvi – these five great householders and great Vedic scholars, having come together, held a discussion on, 'What is Self, *Atman*? What is *Brahman*?' **1**

They discussed among themselves. 'Uddalaka Aruni is at present studying this *Vaisvanara Atman*. Well, let us go to him'. And they went over to him. **2**

Uddalaka reflected, 'These great householders and great Vedic scholars are going to question me. I may not be able to answer them satisfactorily. So let me direct them to another teacher'. **3**

Uddalaka said to them, 'Revered sirs, at present Ashvapati, the son of Kekaya, is studying this *Vaisvanara Atman*. Well, let us go over to him'. Then they all went over to him. **4**

When they arrived, the king welcomed them individually. After rising, he said: 'In my kingdom there is no thief, no miser, no drunkard, no man without a sacrificial fire, no illiterate person, no adulterer, much less any adulteress. Revered sirs, I am going to perform a sacrifice. As much wealth as I give to any other priest, I shall give to each of you also. Revered sir, please stay on'. **5**

They said, 'The purpose for which a man comes, about that alone he should speak. You are at present studying the *Vaisvanara Atman*. Please tell us about that'. **6**

The king said to them, 'I shall answer you in the morning'. The next morning, they approached him with sacrificial fuel in their hands. The king, without the formality of initiating them as pupils, spoke thus: **7**

Section 12

'O Aupamanyava, what is that *Atman* on which you meditate?'
He replied, 'Heaven only, O venerable king'.
The king said: 'This, that you meditate upon as *Atman*, is the *Vaisvanara Atman* known as "the highly luminous". Therefore, in your family are seen the *Suta, Prasuta* and *Asuta* libations of Soma-juice.

You eat good food and you see what is pleasing. One who meditates on this *Vaisvanara Atman,* eats good food and sees what is pleasing. In his family, there arises the holy effulgence born of sacred wisdom. But this is only the head of the *Atman*. If you had not come to me, your head would have fallen down'. **1-2**

Section 13

Then the king said to Satyayagya Paulusi, 'O Prachinasala, what is that *Atman* on which you meditate?'
He replied, 'The Sun only, O venerable king.'
The king said: 'This, that you meditate upon as *Atman*, is the *Vaisvanara Atman*

"The purpose for which a man comes, about that alone he should speak."

known as "the universal energizer". Therefore, in your family are seen all kinds of enjoyable things. (For example) You have a chariot drawn by mules, maidservants and gold necklaces.

You eat good food and you see what is pleasing. One who thus meditates upon this *Vaisvanara Atman* eats good food and sees what is pleasing. In his family, there arises the holy effulgence born of sacred wisdom. But this is only the eye of the *Atman*. If you had not come to me, you would have become blind.' **1-2**

Section 14

Then the king said to Indradyumna Bhallaveya, 'O descendant of Vyaghrapada, what is the *Atman* on which you meditate?'
He replied, 'Air only, O venerable king.' The king said: 'This, that you meditate upon as *Atman*, is the *Vaisvanara Atman* known as "of diverse paths". Therefore, from diverse directions offerings come to you, and various rows of chariots follow you.

You eat good food and see what is pleasing. One who thus meditates upon this *Vaisvanara Atman,* eats good food and sees what is pleasing. In his family, there arises the holy effulgence born of sacred wisdom. But this is only the *Prana* of the *Atman*. If you had not come to me, your *Prana* would have departed.' **1-2**

Section 15

Then the king said to Jana, 'O Sarkaraksya, what is the *Atman* on which you meditate?
He replied, '*Akash* only, O venerable king.'
The king said: 'This, that you meditate upon as *Atman*, is the *Vaisvanara Atman*, known as "vastness". Therefore, you are full offspring and wealth.

You eat good food and see what is pleasing. One who thus meditates upon this *Vaisvanara Atman*, eats good food and sees what is pleasing, In his family, there arises the holy effulgence born of sacred wisdom. But this is only the trunk of the *Atman*. If you had not come to me, your trunk would have been shattered.' **1-2**

Section 16

Then the king said to Budila Asvatarasvi: 'O Vaiyaghrapadya, what is the *Atman* on which you meditate?'
He replied, 'Water only, O Venerable king.'
The king said: 'This, that you meditate upon as *Atman*, is the *Vaisvanara Atman* known as "wealth". Therefore, are you endowed with wealth and bodily strength.

You eat good food and see what is pleasing. One who thus meditates upon this *Vaisvanara Atman*, eats good food and sees what is pleasing. In his family, there arises the holy effulgence born of sacred wisdom. But this is only the lower belly of the *Atman*. If you had not come to me, your lower belly would have burst. **1-2**

"This, that you meditate upon as Atman, is the Vaisvanara Atman, known as "wealth". Therefore are you endowed with wealth."

Section 17

Then the king said to Uddalaka Aruni, 'O Gautama, what is the Atman on which you meditate?'

He replied, 'The earth only, O venerable king.'

The king said: 'This, that you meditate upon as *Atman,* is the *Vaisvanara Atman* known as "foundation". Therefore, are you well founded in offspring and cattle.

You eat good food and see what is pleasing. One who thus meditates upon this *Vaisvanara Atman*, eats good food and sees what is pleasing. In his family, there arises the holy effulgence born of sacred wisdom. But this is only the feet of the *Atman*. If you had not come to me, your feet would have withered away.' **1-2**

Section 18

The king said to them, 'All of you eat food (live) knowing only parts of *Vaisvanara Atman*. One who meditates upon this *Vaisvanara Atman* as a whole and identical with Self, he eats food in all worlds, through all beings, through all constituents of a person. **1**

Of the aforesaid *Vaisvanara Atman*, the head is 'the highly luminous', the eye is 'the energizer, the breath is 'of diverse paths', the trunk is 'vastness', the lower belly is 'wealth', the feet are 'the foundation'. (Of this *Vaisvanara Atman*), the chest is the altar, the hair on the chest are the Kusa grass, the heart is Garhapatya fire, the mind is Anvaharyapachana fire, and the mouth is Ahavaniya fire. **2**

Section 19

Therefore, food should be first offered as an oblation. The first oblation should be offered with the mantra, '*Svaha* to *Prana*'; thereby *Prana* is satisfied. **1**

Prana being satisfied, eye is satisfied; eye being satisfied, sun is satisfied; sun being satisfied, heaven is satisfied; heaven being satisfied, whatever is under heaven and sun is satisfied. Through it, the eater himself is satisfied. (He is also satisfied) with offspring, cattle, food, lustre and holy effulgence born of sacred wisdom. **2**

Section 20

Then, when he offers the second oblation, he should offer it with the mantra, '*Svaha* to *Vyana*'; thereby *Vyana* is satisfied.

Vyana being satisfied, ear is satisfied; ear being satisfied, moon is satisfied; moon being satisfied, quarters are satisfied; quarters being satisfied, whatever is under the moon and the quarters is satisfied. Through it, the eater himself is satisfied. (He is also satisfied) with offspring, cattle, food, lustre and holy effulgence born of sacred wisdom. **1-2**

"All of you live knowing only parts of Vaisvanara Atman (Universal Self)."

Section 21

Then, when he offers the third oblation, he should offer it with the mantra, 'Svaha to *Apana*'; thereby *Apana* is satisfied.

Apana being satisfied, speech is satisfied; speech being satisfied, fire is satisfied; fire being satisfied, earth is satisfied; earth being satisfied, whatever is under earth and fire is satisfied. Through it, the eater himself is satisfied. (He is also satisfied) with offspring, cattle, food, lustre and holy effulgence born of sacred wisdom. **1-2**

Section 22

Then, when he offers the fourth oblation, he should offer it with the mantra, '*Svaha* to *Saman*'; thereby *Saman* is satisfied.

Saman being satisfied, mind is satisfied; mind being satisfied, *Parjanya* (rain-god) is satisfied; *Parjanya* being satisfied, lightning is satisfied; lightning being satisfied, whatever is under lightning and *Parjanya* is satisfied. Through it, the eater himself is satisfied. (He is also satisfied) with offspring, cattle, food, lustre and holly effulgence born of sacred wisdom. **1-2**

Section 23

Then, when he offers the fifth oblation, he should offer it with the mantra, '*Svaha*' to *Udana*'; thereby *Udana* is satisfied.

Udana being satisfied, skin is satisfied; skin being satisfied, air is satisfied; air being satisfied, *Akash* is satisfied; *Akash* being satisfied, whatever is under air and *Akash* is satisfied. Through it, the eater himself is satisfied. (He is also satisfied) with offspring, cattle, food, lustre and holy effulgence born of sacred wisdom. **1-2**

Section 24

If one performs *Agnihotra* (sacrifice) without knowing thus, it would be like removing live embers and pouring oblation (of melted butter) on the ashes. **1**

If knowing thus, one performs *Agnihotra*, his oblation is poured into all worlds, all beings, and all selves. **2**

Just as cotton wick when laid on fire is burnt up, so also the sins of one, who knowing thus, performs the *Agnihotra*. **3**

Knowing thus, when one offers remnant of food even to a Chandala or undeserving person, that food becomes his offering to *Vaisvanara Atman* only. There is this verse about it. **4**

'As, in this world, hungry children gather round their mother (expectantly); likewise all creatures gather around the performer of *Agnihotra*. Yes, they gather around the performer of *Agnihotra*.' **5**

"If knowing thus, one performs Agnihotra, his oblation is poured into all worlds, all beings, and all selves."

Focussed Commentaries

CHAPTER 5

5.1-5.2, 3 *Prana*: Parable on its superiority

The verses are identical to those in section 6.1 of Brhadaranyaka Upanishad. For commentaries, please turn to page 233.

5.2, 4-8 *Mantha* rite for harmony with cosmos

The verses are identical to those in section 6.3 of Brhadaranyaka Upanishad. For commentaries, please turn to page 238.

5.3-5.9 *Panchagni Vidya*: Five cosmic fires

The verses are identical to those in section 6.2 of Brhadaranyaka Upanishad. For commentaries, please turn to page 233.

5.10 Two paths after death: Liberation and rebirth, *Devayana* and *Pitrayana*

The verses are identical to those in section 6.2, 15-16 of Brhadaranyaka Upanishad. For commentaries, please turn to page 235.

5.11-5.18 *Vaisvanara Vidya*: *Brahman* is Totality

Comparing Cosmic Person, *Vaisvanara*, with a human being, the text says that the sacrificial altar, is like the chest. *Kusa* grass is hair on the chest; and the three household fires are the heart, the mind, and the mouth.

Meditation on any of the aforesaid has its benefits; but consequences of regarding the part as a whole – the relative manifestations as the Absolute *Atman* – can also be disastrous. Therefore, you have to bring the parts together, and conceive the whole in your consciousness. *Vaisvanara Atman* is the whole, Totality.

Vaisvanara Self is the whole, the all comprehending Infinite. It is wrong to identify a particular deity – one perceived as presiding over a limited part of the world – with universal Self.

– S. Radhakrishnan

5.19-5.24 *Prana Agnihotra*: Five symbolic offerings of food

When one meditates on *Atman* as the Totality of All, or *Vaisvanara*, his personality undergoes a transformation. Whatever he does then becomes an action of *Vaisvanara Atman*. His daily activity is then like a cosmic sacrifice. This is called *Prana Agnihotra*, the sacred oblation to the universal fire of the Absolute. It signifies the interrelatedness of the individual and the universal. In this state, even simple acts like eating and working become universally significant.

Ritualistically conceived, *Prana Agnihotra* means daily performance of *Yagya* by a householder. The three fires which householders esoterically worship in their houses are called Garhapatya, Anvaharyapachana and Ahavaniya. However, the Upanishad tells us that we have to perform a contemplative sacrifice. We must regard the external ritual as an activity, which is going on within ourselves. These fires are within the body of *Vaisvanara*; and as we are inseparable from *Vaisvanara*, these fires are inside our own Self. As an example, hunger is not just a function of the stomach; it has universal significance. *Vaisvanara* is the word used to describe both the Ultimate Reality, and also the fire that digests food in our body.

The food that we eat is digested by the action of *Prana*, life breath. Life-breath has five components. These are like the five tongues of a flaming fire. It is one single force, which is working as five different vital energies.

"*Pranaya Svaha*" is an invocation, which means 'May *Prana* be satisfied.' This is to be recited inwardly, while eating the first morsel. The inward feeling is as important as the silent utterance. Through this act we touch the cosmic border and invoke the universal Being. As every river is connected to the ocean, every *Prana* is connected to the Cosmic Force. The Upanishad says that when *Prana* is satisfied, the eye is satisfied; when eye is satisfied; its deity, the sun is satisfied; when sun is satisfied, heavens are satisfied. This results in

---

'When one meditates on Atman as the Totality of All, or Vaisvanara, even simple acts like eating and working become universally significant.'

vibrations of happiness from different quarters of heavens. So if heavens are happy, we are also happy with wealth, luster, glory and wisdom; because *Vaisvanara* is satisfied.

And so is the case with every morsel we eat. In summary, the first five morsels that we eat should be symbolically offered as oblations to five life-breaths, with following mantras:

- *Pranaya Svaha* — for satisfaction of eye, sun and heavens.
- *Vyanaya Svaha* — for satisfaction of ear, moon and quarters.
- *Apanaya Svaha* — for satisfaction of speech, fire and earth.
- *Samanaya Svaha* — for satisfaction of mind, rain-god and lightening.
- *Udanaya Svaha* — for satisfaction of skin, air and sky.

This is not a ritual but a meditation. *Prana Agnihotra* is an act of introducing a universal significance into what are apparently individual functions.

Thus, the message of *Prana Agnihotra* is that even a simple activity like intake of food should be performed with meditation on universal implications of one's existence.

Prana Agnihotra is a part of *Vaisvanara Vidya* – meditation on Cosmic Being.

A ritual cannot produce expected results if it is performed without knowledge of its significance. However, when a person performs a ritual like *Prana Agnihotra* with full knowledge of its meaning and significance, he is transformed from an individual to a cosmic being. His feelings, his thoughts, his consciousness are tuned up to a transcendental Reality. His actions become universal performances. Whatever he does is offered simultaneously to all the worlds, all persons, and all beings. No merit or demerit accrues from the actions of such a person. He may give a little remnant of his food even to the lowest of beings, but it shall be offered into the Universal Reality, forthwith. He may offer anything to anyone, it will reach *Vaisvanara*, because of his self-identification with That Cosmic Being. Just as hungry children sit round their mother craving for food, so do all beings eagerly gather around the performer of *Prana Agnihotra*. Thus, this highly mystical discourse makes out that the highest meditation is communion with *Vaisvanara*, the Cosmic Being, the Totality of All.

– Swami Krishnananda

'The highest meditation is communion with Vaisvanara, the Cosmic Being, the Totality of All.'

6 That thou art

SIMPLIFIED SYNOPSES

'The world has 'That' as its Self.'

We know very little about that, which we refer to as Truth, Reality, Sacred, Divine, Creator, Self, or Lord in faith-neutral words; and which is also addressed in faith-specific words like God, Allah and Ishvara. Very often, the Upanishads denote It simply as 'That' – spelled with a capital 'T' – or as 'That Being'.

'That Being which is the subtle essence of all, this world has That for its Self. That is the Truth. That is *Atman*. That thou art.'

This famous passage contains the essence of all the Upanishads. It is also the main theme of this chapter. The concluding sentence – That thou art – is one of the four great sayings of the Upanishads. It has been explained with as many as nine illustrations. The chapter starts with a prelude to explain how the Absolute is the essence of the whole phenomenal world as well as all living beings.

The Upanishad imparts its teaching through a long but profound dialogue between a young man, Shvetaketu and his father Uddalaka. Because of its importance, the dialogue has been also presented as a rendition in easily comprehensible and conversational style.

6.1 A famous question

Knowledge imparts humility. The father-son conversation starts with Uddalaka noticing Shvetaketu's arrogance even after 12 years of study of scriptures. His learning seems to be superficial. This is confirmed by his inability to respond to a famous question, which also appears in Mundaka Upanishad: 'What is That by knowing which even the unknown becomes known?' The implication is that study of 'substance' must have priority over study of its 'forms'. Clay, gold and iron are used as illustrative examples.

6.2-6.4 From Absolute to elements, then their multiplication

Uddalaka begins his discourse with a brief account of creation. He alludes to the controversy as to whether the universe emerged from Being or Non-Being; and then assumes that it all started from Being alone (*Sat*), one only, without a second. This Being willed and created the primal elements; simultaneously It entered into them. It then transposed the elements into each other. Multiplicity is a consequence of this principle of transposition.

Elsewhere, the primal elements are supposed to be five in number. Here the text confines itself to just three – Fire, Water and Earth (symbolized by food).

6.5-6.7 From elements to mind, speech and life-breath

The text states that in human body each of the primal elements divides itself into three parts – gross, middle and subtle. The subtle parts, which emanate from food, fire and water – are said to constitute mind, speech and life-breath respectively. Emergence of butter from churning of curd is cited as an illustrative example.

Food influences the mind significantly. To emphasize this point, Shvetaketu is made to fast for fifteen days, each day corresponding to one of the sixteen parts of man. Fasting is found to effect his memory of Vedic verses. However, he is able to recall and recite these after breaking his fast. Revival of memory

6.8-6.16
That thou art

'There is a natural tendency for the effect to move towards the cause, its root.'

'That Being cannot be perceived by any of the five senses which man possesses.'

'That Being which is the subtle essence of all, this world has That for its Self. That is the Truth. That is Atman. That thou art.'

is compared to revival of a large fire by a single left-over ember. It is also stated that one cannot live for long without water because water is the subtle essence of life-breath.

Uddalaka analyzes the phenomena of sleep, hunger and thirst to reaffirm the presence of the Absolute, That Being, *Sat* in man. Next, he explains that the body has food as its root, food has water as its root, water has fire as its root and fire has That Being as its root.

There is a natural tendency for the effect to move towards the cause, its root. For example, mind flies around in various directions during waking and dream states, but it comes back and rests in That Being during sleep. Likewise, at the time of death, speech merges in mind, mind in life-breath (*Prana*), life-breath in fire (body-heat), and fire in That Being.

The Upanishad uses nine illustrative examples to facilitate comprehension of the great saying, 'That thou art'.

1. A bird tied with a string. After flying around in various directions, it comes back to where it is tied. Likewise, mind comes back to That Being during deep sleep.
2. Bees extracting honey from flowers. Once the honey is made, essence of one flower cannot be distinguished from that of another. At death, *Jivatman* merges into That Being – and thereby loses its individual identity – before its re-emergence in another body.
3. Rivers and ocean. Rivers rise from ocean – as evaporated water forming rain-clouds – and eventually merge into ocean. Likewise living beings arise from That and merge into That.
4. A large tree. It exudes sap only as long as it lives, and not after it dries (dies). Human body is like a tree. The body perishes but not the Self in it.
5. Seed of a fruit. The essence of a seed, which has the potentiality to give rise to a tree, in not perceptible to the eyes. Similarly, That cannot be seen by the eyes.
6. Salt dissolved in water. Dissolved salt cannot be perceived by the senses except the sense of taste. Likewise, That Being cannot be perceived by any of the five senses which man possesses.
7. A blindfolded man left in an unknown place. The man cannot reach home even after the blindfold is removed, unless someone shows him the right direction. Likewise, That can be realized only with guidance from a teacher who has himself experienced Self-realization.
8. A dying person. He cannot speak after his speech has merged in mind; he cannot recognize people after his mind has merged in *Prana*; he is dead when *Prana* has merged in Fire and Fire has merged into That.
9. Trial by ordeal. The presumption behind this ancient (deplorable) practice was that fire would burn only a false and not a true person. Likewise, a person who is ignorant of That is in bondage of his actions, and not one who knows That.

This profound and profusely illustrated discourse between Shvetaketu and his loving father Uddalaka is very famous. Its essence should be committed to memory:
'That Being which is the subtle essence of all, this world has That for its Self. That is the Truth. That is *Atman*. That thou art.'

'Mind flies around in various directions during waking and dream states, but it comes back and rests in That Being during sleep.'

Translated Text

CHAPTER 6

Section 1

Om. Once there lived Shvetaketu, grandson of Aruni. His father said to him, 'O Shvetaketu, go and study as a celibate student. O dear son, there has never been anyone in our family who did not study and was a *Brahmin* only in name.' **1**

Having gone (to teacher's house) when only twelve years old, he came back when he was twenty-four. After studying all the Vedas, he became conceited and arrogant, and regarded himself as very learned. His father said to him, '*Shvetaketu*, dear son, I see you are conceited, and arrogant. You regard yourself as very learned. Did you ask for that teaching by which what is unheard becomes heard, what is unthought becomes thought of, what is unknown become known?' 'Of what nature, revered sir, is that teaching?' **2-3**

Dear son, through a single clod of clay all that is made of clay becomes known; for all modification is but name based upon words, and clay alone is real.
Dear son, through a single nugget of gold, all that is made of gold becomes known; for all modification is but name based upon words, and gold alone is real.
Dear son, through a single pair of iron tongs all that is made of iron becomes known; for all modification is but name based upon words, and iron alone is real. This, dear son, is that teaching.' **4-6**

'Surely, my revered teachers did not know it, for if they had known, why would they have not told it to me? However, revered father, teach it to me.'
'Be it so, dear son,' said (the father). **7**

Section 2

'In the beginning, dear son, this was Being alone, one only, without a second. Some say that in the beginning, this was Non-being alone, one only, without a second. From that Non-being arose Being.' **1**

Aruni continued: 'But how, dear son, could it be so? How could Being arise from Non-being? In truth, dear son, in the beginning (before creation), there was Being alone, one only, without a second. **2**

That Being willed, "May I become many, may I grow forth." It created fire. That fire willed, "May I became many, may I grow forth." It created water. Therefore, whenever a man grieves or perspires, then it is from fire (heat) that water issues. **3**

That water willed, "May I became many, may I grow forth." It created food. Therefore, wherever it rains, abundant food grows there; it is from water that food for eating is produced. **4**

---

*"Through a single clod of clay all that is made of clay becomes known;
for all modification is but name, and clay alone is real."*

Section 3

Of the living beings, there are three origins: those born from eggs, born from wombs, and born from sprouts. **1**

That Being willed, "Well, let Me enter into these three deities through this living Self (*Jivatman*), and disseminate many names and forms. **2**

Of these, let Me make each one threefold." Willing thus, that Being entered into these three deities through this living Self and differentiated names and forms. **3**

It made each one of them threefold. But, dear son, how each of these three deities becomes threefold (outside the body), know this from me. **4**

Section 4

In fire, red color is color of fire; that which is white belongs to water and that which is black belongs to food (earth). Thus vanishes (the idea of) quality of fire from fire; for all modification is but name based upon words, only the three forms are real. **1**

In sun, red color is the color of fire, that which is white belongs to water and that which is black belongs to earth. Thus vanishes (the idea of) quality of sun from sun; for all modification is but name based upon words, only the three forms are real. **2**

In moon, red color is the color of fire; that which is white belongs to water and that which is black belongs to earth. Thus vanishes (the idea of) quality of moon from moon; for all modification is but name based upon words, only the three forms are real. **3**

In lightning, red color is color of fire; that which is white belongs to water and that which is black belongs to earth. Thus vanishes (the idea of) quality of lightning from lightning; for all modification is but name based upon words, only the three forms are real. **4**

It was indeed on knowing this (triplication) that the ancient great householders and great Vedic scholars said, "There is, at present, nothing that anyone would point out to us as unheard, unthought or unknown"; for from these they understood everything. **5**

Whatever else appeared red, that they knew to be the color of (untriplicated) fire; whatever appeared white, that also they knew to be the color of water; whatever appeared black, that also they knew to be the color of earth. **6**

Whatever appeared to be unknown, that also they knew to be a combination of these very deities. But, dear son, know from me how, on reaching man, each of these three deities becomes threefold. **7**

---

*"That Being willed, "Well, let Me enter into these deities
(primeval elements) and disseminate many names and forms."..."*

Section 5

Food, when eaten, becomes divided into three parts. What is its grossest ingredient, that is faeces; what is the middle ingredient, that is flesh; and what is the subtlest ingredient, that is mind. **1**

Water, when drunk, becomes divided into three parts. What is its grossest ingredient, that is urine; what is the middle ingredient, that is blood; and what is the subtlest ingredient, that is *Prana*. **2**

Fire (fat), when eaten, becomes divided into three parts. What is its grossest ingredient, that is bone; what is the middle ingredient, that is marrow; and what is the subtlest ingredient, that is speech. **3**

Hence, dear son, mind is made up of food, *Prana* is made up of water, and speech is made up of fire.'
'Explain it further to me, revered sir,' said Shvetaketu.
'Be it so, dear son', said the father. **4**

Section 6

'Dear son, when curd is being churned, that which is the subtlest part rises upwards and becomes clarified butter. **1**

So also, dear son, of food which is eaten, that which is the subtlest part rises upwards and becomes the mind. **2**

Dear son, of water which is drunk, that which is the subtlest part rises upwards and becomes *Prana* (Life-breath). **3**

Dear son, of fire (fat) which is eaten, that which is the subtlest part rises upwards and becomes speech. **4**

Hence, dear son, mind is made up of food, *Prana* is made up of water, and speech is made up of fire.'
'Explain it further to me revered sir', said Shvetaketu.
'Be it so, dear son', said the father. **5**

Section 7

'Dear son, man consists of sixteen parts. Do not eat for fifteen days; drink as much water as you like. *Prana* is made of water, and *Prana* of one who drinks water is not cut off.' **1**

Shvetaketu did not eat for fifteen days. Then he approached him saying, 'What shall I speak of?' The father said, 'The Rk, the Yajus, and the Saman, dear son.' 'They do not come to my mind, sir.' **2**

The father said to him, 'Dear son, a single ember of the size of a firefly, left over from a large burning fire, cannot burn any more than itself. Likewise, dear son, out of your sixteen parts only one part is left over; by means of that you cannot

---

"Hence, dear son, mind is made up of food, Prana is made up of water, and speech is made up of fire."

perceive the Vedas. Eat, then you will understand me.' **3**

He ate and then approached his father. Whatever he was asked, he could answer everything. **4**

The father said, 'Dear son, when a single ember of the size of a firefly, left over from a large burning fire, is made to blaze by adding straw, it burns much more than before. Likewise out of your sixteen parts, the one part which remained and was nourished by food, has been made to blaze up. By that you perceive the Vedas now. Hence, dear son, mind is made of food, *Prana* is made of water, and speech is made of fire.' From his words, (Shvetaketu) understood it. Yes, he understood it. **5**

Section 8

Then Uddalaka Aruni said to his son Shvetaketu, 'Dear son, know from me the true nature of sleep. When a man is in deep sleep, then, dear son, he is united with his Being, his Self. **1**

A bird tied to a string, after flying in various directions and finding no resting-place elsewhere, takes refuge at the very place whereto it is tied. Even so, dear son, that mind, after flying in various directions and finding no resting place elsewhere, takes refuge in *Prana* alone. Mind, dear son, is tied to *Prana*. **2**

Dear son, know from me (the true nature of) hunger and thirst. When a man is said to be hungry, then (it is to be understood that) water is leading away what has been eaten. Just as people speak of the leader of cows, the leader of horses, and the leader of men, even so they speak of water as the leader of food. Hence, dear son, know (this body) to be a shoot that has sprung up; it cannot be without a root. **3**

Where could its root be apart from food? Even so, dear son, with food as the shoot, look for water as the root; with water as the shoot, look for fire as the root; with fire as the shoot, look for Being as the root. All these creatures have Being as their root, have Being as their abode, and have Being as their support. **4**

Again, when a man is said to be thirsty, then (it is to be understood that), fire is leading away what has been drunk; (therefore fire may be designated as thirst). Just as people speak of the leader of cows, the leader of horses, and the leader of men, even so they speak of fire as the leader of water. Hence, dear son, know this (body) to be the shoot that has sprung up; it cannot be without a root. **5**

Where could its root be, apart from water? Dear son, with water as the shoot, look for fire as the root; with fire as the shoot, look for Being as the root. All these creatures have Being as their root, have Being as their abode, and have Being as their support.

How each of these three deities, on reaching man, becomes threefold has been explained to you earlier. When this man is about to depart, his speech merges in mind, mind in *Prana*, *Prana* in fire, and fire in the Supreme Deity. **6**

"When a man is in deep sleep, he is united with his Being, his Self."

That Being which is the subtle essence of all, this world has That for its Self. That is the Truth. That is *Atman*. **That thou art,** O Shvetaketu.'

'Revered sir, please explain it further to me.'
'So be it, dear son', said (the father). **7**

Section 9

'Bees make honey by collecting juices from different plants and reduce them into one essence. These juices have no discrimination like, "I am the juice of this plant, I am the juice of that plant". Even so, all these creatures, having merged into Being, do not know, "We have merged into Being." **1-2**

Whatever these creatures are here, tiger or lion or wolf or boar or worm or flying insect or gadfly or mosquito, that they become again. **3**

That Being which is the subtle essence of all, this world has That for its Self. That is the Truth. That is *Atman*. **That thou art**, Shvetaketu'.

'Revered sir, please explain it further to me.' 'So be it, dear son', said (the father). **4**

Section 10

'These eastern rivers, dear son, flow along to the east and the western ones to the west. They rise from the ocean and merge in the ocean, and become that ocean itself. And there as these rivers do not know themselves as, "I am this river, I am that river", even so, all these creatures, having come from Being, do not know, "We have come from Being". And whatever these creatures were here, tiger or lion or wolf or boar or worm or fly or gadfly or mosquito, that they become again. **1-2**

That Being which is the subtle essence of all, this world has That for its Self. That is the Truth. That is *Atman*. **That thou art**, O Shvetaketu.'

'Revered sir, please explain it further to me.' 'So be it, dear son', said (the father). **3**

Section 11

'Dear son, if anyone were to strike at the root of this large tree, it would exude sap, though still living. If anyone were to strike in the middle, it would exude sap, though still living. If anyone were to strike at the top, it would exude sap, though still living. As this tree is pervaded by living Self, it stands firm, drinking constantly and rejoicing. **1**

If life leaves one branch of this tree, then that branch dries up; if it leaves the second one, then that dries up; if it leaves the third, then that dries up; if it leaves the whole tree, the whole tree dries up. **2**

"All these creatures, having come from Being, do not know, "We have come from Being"..."

Dear son, know that even so, when the living Self leaves this body, the body surely dies, but the living Self does not die.

That Being which is the subtle essence of all, this world has That for its Self. That is the Truth. That is *Atman*. **That thou art**, O Shvetaketu.'

'Revered sir, please explain it further to me.' 'So be it, dear son', said (the father)

3

Section 12

'Bring a fruit from this banyan tree.'
'Here it is, revered sir.' 'Break it.'
'It is broken, revered sir.'
'What do you see in this?'
'These seeds, like small atomic particles, revered sir.'
'Break one of these, my child'.
'It is broken, revered sir.' 'What do you see in it?'
'Nothing, revered sir.'

1

The father said to him, 'Dear son, this subtle essence which you do not perceive, growing from this subtle essence, the large banyan tree thus stands. Have faith in what I say, dear son.

2

That Being which is the subtle essence of all, this world has That for its Self. That is the Truth. That is *Atman*. **That thou art**, O Shvetaketu.'

'Revered sir, please explain it further to me.' 'So be, it, dear son', said (the father).

3

Section 13

'Put this salt into water and then come to me in the morning.' He did so. The father said to him, 'Dear son, take out the salt that you put into water last night.' Having searched for it, he did not find it, as it had completely dissolved. 'Dear son, take a sip from the top of this water. How does it taste?' 'It is salty.' 'Take a sip from the middle. How does it taste?' 'It is salty.' 'Take a sip from the bottom. How does it taste?' 'It is salty.' 'Throw this water away and then come to me.' He did so (and returned saying), 'That salt was always there in the water.' The father said to him, 'Dear son, likewise you cannot perceive That Being, though It surely exists in this body.

1-2

That Being which is the subtle essence of all, this world has That for its Self. That is the Truth. That is *Atman*. **That thou art**, O Shvetaketu.'

'Revered sir, please explain it further to me,'
'So be it, dear son', said (the father).

3

Section 14

'Dear son, (some robber) having brought a man from Gandhara region with his

---

"That salt was always there in the water. Likewise, you cannot perceive That Being, though It surely exists in this body."

eyes blindfolded, might leave him in a very desolate place. Just as that man would shout towards the east, or towards the north, or towards the south, or towards the west, (saying), "I have been brought here with my eyes blind folded, I have been left here with my eyes blind folded." **1**

And as some one might remove his blind fold and tell him, "Gandhara region is in this direction, proceed in this direction". He, enquiring his way from village to village, and being instructed and capable of judging himself, would reach Gandhara region. Even so, in this world, that person knows who has a preceptor. And for him, only so long is the delay as he is not liberated from ignorance and then he realizes That Being. **2**

That Being which is the subtle essence of all, this world has That for its Self. That is the Truth. That is *Atman*. **That thou art**, O Shvetaketu.'

'Revered sir, please explain it further to me,'
'So be it, dear son', said (the father). **3**

Section 15

'Dear son, the relatives of a man who is ill assemble round him and ask, "Do you know me? Do you know me?" As long as his speech is not merged in the mind, the mind in *Prana*, *Prana* in fire, and fire in the Supreme Deity, that long he knows them. **1**

But when his speech is merged in mind, mind in *Prana*, *Prana* in fire, and fire in the Supreme Deity, then he does not recognize them. **2**

That Being which is the subtle essence of all, this world has That for its Self. That is the Truth. That is *Atman*. **That thou art**, O Shvetaketu.'

'Revered sir, please explain it further to me.' 'So be it, dear son', said (the father). **3**

Section 16

'Dear son, (the officers of a king) bring a man, holding him by the hand (while saying), "He has stolen something, he has committed a theft, heat the axe for him." If he is the doer of that, then he makes himself false. And being addicted to falsehood, he covers himself with falsehood. When he grasps the heated axe, he gets burnt, and then he is punished. **1**

If, however, he is not the doer of that, then he makes himself true. And being attached to truth, he covers himself with truth. When he grasps the heated axe, he is not burnt, and then he is released. **2**

And as in this case he (man attached to truth) is not burnt, (similarly a man of knowledge is not born again).

That Being which is the subtle essence of all, this world has That for its Self. That is the Truth. That is *Atman*. **That thou art**, O Shvetaketu.'

From his words Shvetaketu understood That. Yes, he understood. **3**

"But when his speech is merged in mind, mind in Prana, Prana in fire, and fire in the Supreme Deity, then he does not recognize them."

RENDITION

CHAPTER 6

That thou art

Shvetaketu was a twelve years old son of a very wise man, Uddalaka Aruni. As per the custom prevalent in ancient times, he was sent to a *gurukul* for study of scriptures. When he returned back home after 12 years, he was very proud of his learning. Uddalaka realized that his son's arrogance reflected ignorance of Truth – the root cause of the universe – and man's relationship with that Truth. So one day, he called Shvetaketu and had the following dialogue.

Uddalaka : Shvetaketu, have you learned about that by which even the unheard becomes heard, the unthought becomes thought, the unknown becomes known? (compare Mundaka 1.1,3).

Shvetaketu : Revered Father, what is that teaching? How can the unknown be known? (6.1, 1-3).

Uddalaka : When you examine a piece of clay, gold or iron and know all about it, you automatically know about all the objects made from that substance. When you know the substance or the root cause, its numerous modifications (*Vikara*) which are called by different names are easily known. Do you know the root cause of the universe?

Shvetaketu : (Afraid of being sent back for study): Surely, my revered teachers did not know about that; for if they did, they would have certainly taught that to me. Revered Father, please teach that to me (6.1, 4-7).

Uddalaka : Okay, let us start from the very beginning. Before creation, all this universe was Being alone; only one and without a second, *sat eva ekam eva advaitiyam*. Some say that in the beginning all this was Non-being alone, only one and without a second; and that Being arose from that Non-being. But how can Being arise from Non-being? So the truth is that in the beginning, there was Being alone, only one and without a second (6.2,1-2). (Also compare Taittiriya 2.7,1 and Chandogya 3.19,1).

Shvetaketu : What happened next?

Uddalaka : That Being willed: 'I am One, may I become many'; and It became three things – fire, water and food. You will notice all these are interrelated. When a man cries or perspires, the heat (fire) in the body is converted into water in the form of tears or perspiration. Likewise, good agricultural crop resulting from good rains is conversion of water into food (6.2, 3-4).

Shvetaketu : And what happened to fire, water and food created by the One Being, *Sat*?

Uddalaka : Let us call these three – fire, water and earth (of which food is an aspect) - as deities, *devata*. That Being entered into these three deities through what is called *Jivatman*. His objective was to create many differentiated names and forms.

Jivatman, often called simply as *Jiva*, is nothing but *Atman* conditioned by adjuncts; and *Atman* is nothing but *Brahman*. So *Jiva* is an effect of *Brahman*, the Ultimate Cause (6.3,2-3).

Shvetaketu : But how did the material world evolve?

Uddalaka : That Being transposed each of the three elements in the remaining two elements. This yielded innumerable permutations and combinations of material objects and phenomena, with varying ratios of the three elements and their attributes (6.3, 4).

Let me explain. Consider objects like fire, sun and moon, or phenomenon like lightening. In all these we see, among other thing, three colors – red, white and

'When you know the substance or the root cause, its numerous modifications are easily known.'

black. These really represent the threefold presence of three primal elements - fire, water and earth, respectively. Without these, there can be no sun, no moon, in fact nothing. All objects and phenomena that we observe in the world – by whatever name we call them – are in reality manifestations of just three primal elements. These may not be perceptible to us directly. However, their presence can be inferred from their primary colors – red for fire, white for water and black for earth or food (6.4, 1-4).

This is what the ancient masters found out. They considered these three primal elements as the secret of the whole universe. They knew how one became three, and three became many. Thus, in reality, the many are One (6.4, 5-7).

Shvetaketu : I have understood the Reality of the universe, but what about human beings?

Uddalaka : Well, these three elements are also the essence of human beings, but in a slightly different way. Each of these undergoes a further threefold division into gross, middle and subtle forms; instead of intermixing, as in the creation of the universe. The scheme of division is as follows:

Primal Element	Gross Form	Middle Form	Subtle Form
Food	Excreta	Flesh	Mind (*Manas*)
Water	Urine	Blood	Life-breath (*Prana*)
Fire	Bone	Marrow	Speech (*Vac*)

Accordingly, my dear son, our mind is influenced significantly by the food we eat. Also, our life-breath is strengthened by frequent consumption of water; and our speech improves when we consume foods like oil and butter, which generate heat.

Shvetaketu : I don't understand all this. How can the food that we eat influence the mind? (6.5, 1-4)

Uddalaka : Have you seen curd being churned? You must have noticed that the subtle part contained in the curd rises upward during churning, and becomes butter. Likewise, the subtlest part of food becomes mind; that of water becomes life-breath; and that of fire becomes speech (6.6, 1-5).

Shvetaketu : I still cannot accept this proposition. Please give me some more solid proof.

Uddalaka : Okay, I suggest an experiment. As you may know, human beings are said to have sixteen important parts – five each of senses of perception, organs of action, forms of life-breath and mind as the sixteenth. A man can live without food for fifteen days, but the sixteenth day can be dangerous. Now, Shvetaketu, experiment fasting for fifteen days. Do not take any solid diet during your fasting, but you can drink as much water as you like.

(Shvetaketu did as suggested and came back to his father after fifteen days of fasting to continue the dialogue).

Uddalaka : Well done my dear boy. It is commendable that you managed without food for fifteen days. Now recite some verses from the Vedas.

Shvetaketu : I can't remember them! It is surprising. I knew them so well. But now my mind does not seem to be functioning.

Uddalaka : There is no mystery in it. You cannot remember because your mind has not received any nourishment for fifteen days. It is like a large fire being reduced to a small ember without fuel. Go and eat, then you will understand.

(Shvetaketu ate some food and came back. He could then recall and recite verses from the Vedas.)

'Our mind is influenced significantly by the food we eat.
Also, our life-breath is strengthened by frequent consumption of water.'

Uddalaka	: Dear Shvetaketu, now do you understand? Fifteen of your sixteen parts had become almost inactive without food. The one that was active reactivated the others after it received nourishment for itself. It is like one ember making a fire blaze again when provided with fuel.
Shvetaketu	: Yes father, now I know that in the ultimate analysis, a man has just three elements as his essence (6.7, 1-6).
Uddalaka	: No, my son. There is something more in us than just these elements. That is the Being about which I spoke to you in the beginning of our conversation. That Being is not perceptible through our five senses of perception, but we come close to It when we are in a state of deep sleep (6.8, 1).
Shvetaketu	: I don't follow, Father. Please elaborate.
Uddalaka	: Let me again give you an illustration. Imagine a bird tied to a string. After flying in various directions and finding no resting-place, it comes back to where it is tied and takes rest there. Likewise, mind is tied to *Prana,* life force. During waking and dream states, mind flies around in various directions; but during deep sleep it comes back to *Prana* and rests there. Of course, *Prana* is symbolic of That Being, the One, without a second, the ultimate cause of all.
Shvetaketu	: This is a very insightful explanation of deep sleep. What about hunger and thirst?
Uddalaka	: Hunger and thirst again represent an interplay of these three elements. Why does one feel hungry just a few hours after a meal? It is because water dissolves the solid food into itself, and so one feels the need for it again. It is as if water is a leader of food, just as there is a leader of a herd of cows or horses, or a group of men. Similarly, thirst is absorption of water in the fire principle; as if fire is a leader of water. Thus, this body has food as its root, food has water as its root; water has fire as its root, and fire has That Being, as its root. In fact, all living beings have That Being as their root.
	There is a natural tendency for the effect to move towards the cause – its roots – and become absorbed into it. The whole process of absorption of effect into cause leads us to conclude that all living beings have the Supreme Being, *sat* as their ultimate cause, as their ultimate abode and as their ultimate support. Everything is pulled by the Supreme Being towards Itself (6.8, 3-5).
Shvetaketu	: What happens when a person dies?
Uddalaka	: I have already explained to you how the three primal elements subdivide themselves to form Life-breath, Mind and Speech. At the time of death, Speech ceases to function first and gets absorbed in Mind. Then Mind stops functioning and is absorbed in Life-breath. Then Life-breath, *Prana* merges into Fire. At this stage, while the dying person cannot speak and is devoid of any awareness, his body is still warm. Finally, Fire, as indicated by the warmth of the body, withdraws and merges into That Being.
	That Being, which is the subtle essence of everything, is the Ultimate Truth. That is the Self, *Atman* of all living beings, including yourself. Therefore, Shvetaketu, That thou art, *tat tvam asi*.
Shvetaketu	: You have startled me by your statement that I am That Being, *Brahman*! Please explain.
Uddalaka	: You know how bees make honey by collecting essence of flowers from various plants. Once the honey is made, one cannot distinguish the essence of one flower from that of another flower. There is a total consciousness of the honey, but there is no individual consciousness of flowers. This is what

'All living beings have the Supreme Being as their ultimate cause, and are therefore pulled towards It.'

happens to a person when his *jivatman* goes to That – either in deep sleep or after death. Its individual identity ceases to exist, as it becomes one with That.

That Being, which is the subtle essence of everything, is the ultimate Truth. That is the Self, *Atman* of all living beings, including yourself. Therefore, Shvetaketu, That thou art, *tat tvam asi*.

Incidentally, when living beings return back from That – waking up after sleep, or rebirth after death – they become what they were earlier. In other words, tendencies of the transmigrating *jivatman* do not get eliminated as long as *jiva* is not liberated from the bondage of birth and death (6.9, 1-4).

Shvetaketu : Why are we not normally aware that we came from That, and we will eventually merge into That?

Uddalaka : Shvetaketu, you know there are many rivers. They rise from an ocean – in the form of evaporated water forming clouds that rain - and they eventually merge into an ocean to become one with it. No river thinks, 'I am Ganga', 'I am Jamuna', before its origin from an ocean or after its merger into an ocean. Likewise, individual beings do not remember that they have come from That.

That Being, which is the subtle essence of everything, is the ultimate Truth. That is the Self, *Atman* of all living beings, including yourself. Therefore, Shvetaketu, That thou art, *tat tvam asi*.

Shvetaketu : Father, what is *jiva*? Earlier you said that *jiva* is conditioned Self, or conditioned *Atman*. Please explain.

Uddalaka : Son, imagine a large tree. The exuberant growth of the tree is due to the life that is in the tree. This Life Principle is called *jiva*. It pervades the whole tree. If it departs from a particular branch of a tree, that branch dries up. If life departs from the whole tree, the whole tree dries up. The same applies to human beings as well. What we call death is the departing of Life Principle, *jiva* from a particular body. *Jiva* does not die, it merely transmigrates from one body to another. This *Jiva* is the same in all beings. Though there are innumerable living forms, the Life Principle, *jiva* in them is one, and same as That.

That Being, which is the subtle essence of everything, is the ultimate Truth. That is the Self, *Atman* of all living beings, including yourself. Therefore, Shvetaketu, That thou art, *tat tvam asi*.

Shvetaketu : Self, *Jivatman* is extremely subtle. How can this extremely gross universe be produced from something, which is extremely subtle?

Uddalaka : A good question. I cannot answer it directly, but I will explain it with an illustration. You see that banyan tree? Bring a fruit from it.

Shvetaketu : Here it is, revered Father.

Uddalaka : Now, break it.

Shvetaketu : It is broken.

Uddalaka : What do you see inside the fruit?

Shvetaketu : These seeds, very small in size.

Uddalaka : Break one of these seeds, my son.

Shvetaketu : It is broken, Father.

Uddalaka : What do you see?

Shvetaketu : I cannot see anything.

Uddalaka : Dear boy, there is a subtle essence inside that seed. It is invisible to the eye, but it has the potentiality to become a large tree. As this may sound unbelievable, have faith in what I say. Just as a large tree arises from that which is the subtle

---

'What we call death is the departing of Life Principle, jiva from a particular body. Jiva, does not die; it merely transmigrates from one body to another.'

essence of a small seed, even so this vast universe has arisen from That Being.

That Being, which is the subtle essence of everything, is the ultimate Truth. That is the Self, *Atman* of all living beings, including yourself. Therefore, Shvetaketu, That thou art, *tat tvam asi*.

Shvetaketu : Father, why can't That Being be perceived?

Uddalaka : Again, I will have to answer your question with an illustration. Bring some salt and water, mix the two, and let the mixture stand overnight. We will resume our discussion next morning.

(Next morning)

Uddalaka : Shvetaketu, take out the salt which you put in the water last night.

Shvetaketu : I cannot separate it, it is completely dissolved.

Uddalaka : OK. Now, taste the water from different parts of the glass. Take a spoonful from the top, the middle and the bottom. How does it taste?

Shvetaketu : All the samples taste salty.

Uddalaka : Now think. The salt was always present in the water. You could not perceive it through the sense of sight, though you could perceive it through the sense of taste. Likewise, That Being is always there, but It cannot be perceived by any of the five senses that we posses. However, It may be known by other means.

That Being, which is the subtle essence of everything, is the ultimate Truth. That is the Self, *Atman* of all living beings, including yourself. Therefore, Shvetaketu, That thou art, *tat tvam asi*.

Shvetaketu : What are the other means by which That Being can be known?

Uddalaka : One of the means is to have a spiritual master to show the direction. Let me again give an illustration. Consider a man is brought to a desert blind folded, and then left there with blindfolds removed. The man cannot reach his home unless some informed person shows him the correct direction. Likewise, only a preceptor who himself has realized That Being, can provide guidance for knowing It (compare Katha, 1.2,8).

That Being, which is the subtle essence of everything, is the ultimate Truth. That is the Self, *Atman* of all living beings, including yourself. Therefore, Shvetaketu, That thou art, *tat tvam asi*.

Shvetaketu : Father, you had earlier explained that in deep sleep, the soul, *jiva* comes very close to That; and after death, *jiva* merges with That. What is the difference between deep sleep and death?

Uddalaka : As I explained earlier, a person is said to be dead only after his speech has merged in Mind, Mind in *Prana*, *Prana* in Fire; and Fire has departed from the body to merge with the Ultimate Reality. In deep sleep, *Prana* and Fire do not depart from the body, as they do at the time of death.

When a person dies he enters the Being of all beings, He enters That Being.

That Being, which is the subtle essence of everything, is the ultimate Truth. That is the Self, *Atman* of all living beings, including yourself. Therefore, Shvetaketu, That thou art, *tat tvam asi*.

Shvetaketu : Father, just one more question. What is the difference between an ignorant man and a man of Self-realization, between one who does not know That, and one who knows That?

'Only a preceptor who himself has realized That, can provide guidance for knowing That.'

Uddalaka : A Self-realized person is not affected by pains and sorrows of worldly existence; whereas an ignorant person is caught-up in these. Ignorance brings bondage, whereas knowledge of That brings deliverance. As an illustration, think of the ancient tradition of trial by ordeal (deplorable as it was), in which a suspect was required to touch a red-hot iron. The presumed logic was that a false person's hand would be burnt by it, while a true person would not be affected by it. Likewise, a person who is ignorant of That Being is in bondage of the fruits of his actions, while one who knows That Being acts freely, without any feeling of bondage.

That Being, which is the subtle essence of everything, is the ultimate Truth. That is the Self, *Atman* of all living beings, including yourself. Therefore, Shvetaketu, That thou art, *tat tvam asi*.

And then Shvetaketu understood the answer to his father's first question which started the dialogue: Have you learned about That by which even the unknown becomes known, or That by knowing which everything is known.

– Editor

FOCUSSED COMMENTARIES

6.1, 3

All learning is useless unless one knows the truth with regard to Self (Sri Sankara).

6.1, 4

Vikara: Modification, manifestation, development, change. The Upanishad suggests that all modifications are based on the reality of its substance, like clay.

6.2, 1

This verse brings out the logical priority of *Brahman* to the world.

Eva: without any limitation or *upadhi*.

Idam: This, the universe of name and form, the world of manifestations. Prior to its manifestation, this world was Pure Being alone. There is no second to Being. It does not have a 'being', as other things have a 'being'; It is Its own Being. Being is God. Being is above all conceptions and conceptual differentiations. It is prior to all things. All other things arise from Being, live in It and end in It. Anything other than Being is nothing, non-existence.

According to Indian logic, there are four kinds of non-existences, or *abhava*:

(i) *Atyantabhava*: Absolute non-existence.

(ii) *Vandhyaputra-abhava*: Self-contradictory non-existence, like a barren woman's son. Barrenness and motherhood contradict each other. Such existence is inconceivable and impossible.

(iii) *Prag-abhava*: Potential existence. The world was non-existent before its creation. It was existent potentially, or as a possibility, though not as an actuality. Creation is not out of absolute non-existence but out of the world of possibility. This type of non-existence has no beginning, but it has an end, when the possibility is actualized.

When, according to some, Non-being or *asat* is said to be the root of existence, *asat* does not mean absolute non-existence but only prior or antecedent non-existence, or potential existence, *prag-abhava*.

(iv) *Pradhvanisabhava*: Posterior non-existence. It is the opposite of prior non-existence. It has a beginning, but no end. When a jar is destroyed, its non-existence begins at the time it is destroyed, but it has no end.

6.3-6.4

Devata: Literally, divinity.

All the varied manifestations of the world are produced by the union of *sat* or Being with the three elements of fire, water and earth. In relation to the three elements which are called *devatas*, *sat* is called *paradevata*,

---

'The world was non-existent before its creation. It was existent potentially, though not as an actuality.'

the Highest Being. *Tejas* or Fire is its first product. Out of *tejas*, water is produced; and out of water, food. *Sat* penetrates into these three as their inner soul, and by mixing them up makes each of them threefold. The red color is the color of *tejas* or fire, the white of *apah or* water, and the black of *anna* or earth.

These three colors are taken over by the Sankhya system to correspond to the three *gunas* – *sattva, rajas* and *tamas*.

6.8, 3

In the condition of deep sleep, personal consciousness subsides and individual Self is said to be absorbed in universal Self. Speech, mind and the senses are in a state of rest; only the breath is active. *Jiva*, the living soul, returns for a while to the Highest Self in order to recover from the fatigue.

6.8, 7

Tat tvam asi: That thou art. This famous text emphasizes the divine nature of human soul. It brings out the need to discriminate between the essential Self and the accidents with which it is confused, or the fetters by which it is bound. He who knows his body or mind knows the things that may be his, but he does not know himself.

This text applies to the inward person, *antah purusha*, and not to the physical person with a unique name and body.

This text appears in other Vedic scriptures also, but in slightly different versions. For example:

- 'What I am, that is He; what He is, that I am"
  (Aitareya Aranyaka II 2.4.6)
- 'I am thou, O Great God, and thou art I'
  (Jabala Upanishad)

Ramanuja interprets 'That thou art' as affirming that the principle of God is common to both the universe and the individual. *That* means God having the entire universe as His body; *thou* means God having the individual being as His body. The principle of God is common to both.

In another Vedic scripture, when the deceased reaches heaven, he is asked: 'Who art thou?' The person who answers by his personal and family name is subjected to the law of *karma*. Another person answers differently, and the following dialogue follows:

Prajapati: 'Who are you?'

Person: 'I am the light thou art. As such, I have come to thee, heavenly light.'

Prajapati: 'Who thou art, that same am I; who I am that same art thou. Enter in.'
(Jaiminiya Upanishad Brahman III.14.1-5)

Rumi speaks to us of a man who knocked at his friend's door and was asked:
'Who art thou?'
'I.'
'Go away.'

After years of suffering and separation, the man came and knocked again. This time, the conversation went like this:

'Who art thou?'
'It is Thou at the door.'
'Since thou art I, come in, O Myself.'
(Mathnavi I.3056-3065)

6.14, 2

Sri Sankara makes out that our real home is *sat,* or Being. Our eyes are in bondage of desires for worldly possessions, which blind us. Some day, we meet a person who knows the Self, whose own bonds have been broken. When he points the way, we feel that we are not mere creatures of the world, but we belong to the Ultimate Reality. We are released when the body, reared by our past deeds, falls off. While the deeds performed after the attainment of saving knowledge do not bind us, prior acts have to exhaust their consequences.

Alexander, the great warrior, used to show greater respect to his teacher Aristotle than he did to his father. Once asked why, he replied: 'From my father I derived the blessings of life; from my teacher, the blessing of a good life.'

– S. Radhakrishnan

'... 'That thou art'. "That" means God having the entire universe as His body; "thou" means God having the individual being as His body.'

6.2, 1-3

There was only a single Reality existing in the beginning. The so-called variety was not there. It was one. It was without a second. There was nothing outside It, nothing external to It, to compete with It, to equal It, or to be different from It. There was absolutely no differentiation whatsoever – neither external nor internal.

In Indian philosophy, differences are of three types:

(i) *Sajatiya Bheda*: Differences within a category, like no two human beings are the same.
(ii) *Vijatiya Bheda*: Differences between categories, like trees and animals.
(iii) *Svagata Bheda*: Differences within one's own self, like one finger is different from another finger.

The Absolute Reality was completely free from all these three possible differences. It was a tremendous unity, inconceivable to the human mind.

The relationship between cause and effect is the crux of many philosophical arguments. Has the effect come from the cause? Is effect something different from the cause, or is it the same as the cause? Is there a process linking the effect to the cause? There is no unanimity on these issues. After alluding to the controversial nature of the subject, Uddalaka states that let us take it for granted that there was creation. Therefore, there must be a creator. That creator was the Absolute Being. This is what I posit as ultimate Reality. The intention, the will, the meditation, the *tapas* of the creator is the cause of creation. It willed.

What the Upanishad speaks of here as fire, water and earth are not the physical fire, water and earth that we see. They are super-physical elements called *Tanmatras*. Their intermixing in varying proportions leads to the variety that we see in this world. This threefold mixing of the original elements is called *Trivitkarana*.

6.3, 4

Vibration of Consciousness in a particular manner becomes cognizable as an object. Therefore, what we call creation is nothing but Consciousness appearing in a particular manner due to a certain vibration.

Whenever we perceive an object, we perceive only those aspects of it, which our five senses of perception can cognize. There are other aspects in the object, which our senses are not capable of contacting. It does not mean that our five senses are everything. If we had more senses, we would have perceived many other things in the world.

6.3, 5-7

The whole world of objects is made of these three primal elements – fire, water and earth. Now, says Uddalaka to Shvetaketu, I am going to show you that your personality itself is of that nature. You yourself do not exist apart from these elements. Whatever is in you is the mixture in some form or the other of these three elements.

6.8, 1-2

You have no support anywhere in this world except your own Self, as the peg is the resting place of the bird in the illustration. You seek support outside, and you work hard in search of it; but it is not there. You become exhausted and fatigued. Then you go to the Being that you are and for that you enter in deep sleep. This, you do every day.

6.8, 6

What is the meaning of ultimate cause? Ultimate cause is that which is not absorbed into a higher cause. The absorption process ceases when the ultimate cause is reached. Grosser forms get absorbed into subtler forms, and the subtler ones eventually get absorbed into the ultimate cause. This ultimate cause dissolves in the Absolute. That Absolute is the Ultimate Reality, which is called *Sat*, Pure Being.

6.8, 7

All this variety of creation is rooted in that Pure Being, which is incapable of further absorption into any higher cause; because nothing can be greater than Being. Everything is an effect of It. Everything is an expression of It; but It is Itself not an expression of anything else.

There is a tendency in every effect to return to its cause. This is what we call the evolutionary process. It is impossible for the effect to rest in itself, because

---

*'Vibration of Consciousness in a particular manner becomes cognizable as an object.
Therefore, creation is nothing but Consciousness.'*

of the pull exerted by the cause. This pull is invisibly felt and inexorably exercised universally everywhere, in all creation. So, everything is restless, everything moves. That is why there is such endless activity in the world. This itself is a pointer to the existence of a cause beyond an effect. Everything tries to move towards higher objectives, until it reaches the Ultimate Cause, the Pure Being.

O Shvetaketu, you cannot be separated from That; you cannot stand outside That. As everything has come from That, you too have come from That. That is the Self of all beings, and therefore, naturally, you too are That. The great conclusion to which you come by the analysis of the three elements is: 'That thou art'.

6.9, 1-4

The essences of flowers do exist in the honey made from flowers, but there is no thought like: 'I am this flower, I am that flower', and so on. Similarly, when one reaches That Being, one does not cease to exist; though one does not have such thoughts as, 'I am so and so'. All distinctions vanish.

The entry of individual Consciousness into Cosmic Consciousness can be of two types – a conscious entry and an unconscious entry. Deep sleep represents an unconscious entry. One just stumbles upon it, as it were. One does contact That in some mysterious manner, but one does not really get absorbed into That. One's individual Consciousness is no doubt abolished, but it does not become universal Consciousness. It becomes like unconsciousness. There is something common between unconsciousness and Absolute Consciousness. The common principle is that in both these states there is no particularized Consciousness. But there is also a very important difference. Because individual Consciousness is not absorbed into universal Consciousness, it comes back from that state.

Even at death, one does not get conscious entry into That Being, Cosmic Consciousness. One is not able to continue in the state of either deep sleep or death for a long time on account of unfulfilled desires. These prompt individual Consciousness to revert to waking state – in the same body after deep sleep, and in another body after death.

Self-realization represents conscious entry and absorption into universal Consciousness, That Being.

In the process of Self-realization, there is transcendence, there is no coming back. When you have outgrown a particular level of experience, you do not come back to it. But when you have been forced to exist from a particular experience, the desire for that experience still lingers, and you will have to come back to complete your experience.

The desires of mind are not destroyed in sleep, and therefore, there is a return to waking or dreaming state after sleep. The desires of mind are not destroyed even in death; and therefore, there is rebirth after death. But the desires of the mind are destroyed in Self-realization; and therefore, there is no return.

That Being cannot be perceived by the senses. The senses are capable of contacting only the externals; whatever is not external cannot become an object of their perception. That Being is not outside, and therefore It cannot be the object of the senses. Nor can the mind conceive That Being, because the function of the mind is principally to synthesize the functions of the senses. Fortunately, the mind has one additional capability – it can reflect and infer. It is this special power which has to be employed for the purpose of gaining an insight into That Being.

– Swami Krishnananda

6.2, 1

The term 'Being' denotes a positive entity. The other two terms 'one' and 'without a second' qualify the term 'Being'; so also the terms 'this' and 'was' in the sentence 'this was Non-Being'. The sentence does not connote negation of Being. It has been used to deny any possible wrong notions.

6.2, 3

In another Upanishad it is said that from *Atman*, five elements were successively produced: Space, Air, Fire, Water and Earth. (Taittiriya 2.1,1) In this passage, only three elements are mentioned. The purpose of the passage is not the enumeration all the elements, but merely to assert that everything is a product of That Being.

---

*'The entry of individual Consciousness into Cosmic Consciousness can be of two types –
a conscious entry and an unconscious entry.'*

It may be questioned how fire etc. can will? This doubt is answered by stating that the Supreme Lord Himself exists as fire. He wills and creates water, etc.

6.3, 2

It is to be remembered that although in a sense *Jiva* is an effect of *Brahman*, it is not different from *Brahman*. It is none other than *Brahman,* conditioned by adjuncts.

Jiva is a mere reflection of *Brahman*, like reflection of a man standing before a mirror.

The mind is like a mirror. When the mirror is removed, the reflection is supposed to revert to its original source. Similarly in deep sleep, when the mind removes itself to rest in *Prana*, *Jiva* reverts to its original nature, Pure Being.

Brahman is not affected by pain and other experiences of the body, as only Its reflection enters the body to become *Jiva*.

6.8, 7

THAT THOU ART. The core of the Upanishads is contained in four great sayings, called *Mahavakya*. The supreme place among these is accorded to the great saying: That thou art. By a series of illustrations, the phenomenal universe is traced to the subtle principle of Being, *Sat*. This principle, which underlies the whole universe, is also the true Self of man. Man, stripped of his external adjuncts, is identical with the Reality that supports the entire universe.

6.14, 2

Karma is of two types:
  (i) *Prarabdha*: that which has already become operative in the form of its results.
  (ii) *Sanchita*: that which has not yet become operative.

As a result of Self-realization, the second variety of *karma* is destroyed. The first, which has already become operative, has to be exhausted completely by bodily experience. In the case of a Self-realized person or *Jivan-mukta*, *prarabdha* gets exhausted before the fall of the body, and the person does not have any rebirth. There is no time interval between the fall of his body and his attainment of *Brahman*. It takes place immediately.

– *Swami Swahananda*

6.1, 4-6

That Being is one and all. He who knows That Being knows everything, even the unknown. The Upanishad illustrates this doctrine by three examples: as through a lump of clay, copper or iron, everything made of clay, copper or iron is known; so also through the knowledge of That Being, everything that exists is known.

This is the oldest passage in which the unreality of the manifold world is expressed. Not long after this, Parmenides in Greece said almost the same thing, "That is why everything which trustful men have accepted as truth is all what arises and disappears, a mere name." Spinoza also expresses the same thought when he explains all individuals as modes (*modi*) of a divine substance (*substantia*).

6.2, 1-4

The primeval Being was already characterized in Rg Veda as neither non-existent nor existent (10:129.1). In Taittiriya Upanishad (2.7, 1) and Chandogya Upanishad itself (3.19, 1), the primal Being is characterized as non-existent, *asat*. Against this, the author of the present passage raises the question as to how Being could arise out of Non-Being? He asserts that in the beginning, there was only Being.

Our author knows only three elements of which everything consists. Elsewhere, there is a mention of two additional elements – Air and Space – to make a total of five elements (Taittiriya 2.1, 1).

6.3, 1-4

This passage interrupts the contents and appears to have been interpolated later.

6.8-6.10

In death, first speech enters into mind (leading to speechlessness); then mind into *Prana* (leading to

---

'... 'That Thou art.' Man, stripped of his external adjuncts, is identical with the Reality that supports the entire universe.'

unconsciousness); then *Prana* enters into Being (signifying death). This description corresponds to the factual process. However, it is contrary to section 6.5, according to which speech does not originate out of mind, but out of fire; mind does not originate out of *Prana*, but out of food; and *Prana* does not directly originate out of fire, but out of water.

THAT THOU ART. Really striking is the directness with which the whole essence of the mysterious Highest Being has been recognized in this discourse. The words *tat tvam asi* are rightly regarded as the sum total of all Upanishadic teachings.

Individual beings, when they enter into Absolute Being (in deep sleep and in death) have no awareness of entering into Being. Likewise, when they rise forth again out of Being (in waking and rebirth), they have no awareness of rising again out of Being. Both these processes have been elucidated through two similes – juices of flowers becoming one with honey, and rivers becoming one with ocean. However, these similes do not elucidate the contrast between 'entering into' and 'arising out of' something. Further, these similes elucidate unawareness of the particular individuality; and not the unawareness of entry or re-emergence.

– Paul Deussen

'That thou art. The words "tat tvam asi" are rightly regarded as the sum total of all Upanishadic teachings.'

7 *Bhuma Vidya*: It is all about happiness

SIMPLIFIED SYNOPSES

What is Happiness? Where to look for it? How to attain it? This chapter on *Bhuma Vidya* contains thought-provoking answers to these questions. The presentation is in the form of a dialogue between a senior sage and a young warlord – Narada and Sanatkumar – as disciple and teacher respectively.

Just as a wealthy person is unhappy despite his vast wealth, Narada is unhappy despite his vast learning; and he wants to know, Why? Through a series of questions and answers, Sanatkumar implies that there is a no single possession, which can make a person happy. Happiness comes from a totality of experiences at many levels – mental, physical, emotional and spiritual.

7.1-7.7
Wisdom gives greater happiness than learning

At mental level: Education or learning is the starting point. Ability to express what you know (Speech), Mind, Will-power, Intelligence, Contemplation (Concentration) and Wisdom are progressively higher sources of happiness.

7.8-7.12
Physical strength and primal elements

At physical level: Strength is the most basic requirement. Food, Water, Fire and Space are said to be the other requirements in ascending order. The reference seems to be to primal elements which constitute the body and make it strong.

7.13-7.15
Memory, Aspirations and Life-breath

At emotional level: Memory and Aspiration are identified as two fundamental factors.

All the aforesaid factors are dependant on Life, *Prana*. This is explained with the frequently cited examples of spokes in a wheel being fastened to a hub.

7.16-7.22
A happy man is an active man

Next, there is a discussion of the spiritual aspects of life, starting from Truth. One speaks Truth only when one has spiritual awareness (*Vigyana*). This in turn requires Reflection. Reflection comes from Faith, Faith from Steadfastness, Steadfastness from Action, and Action from Happiness. A person is instinctively active when he is happy. An unhappy person is habitually brooding, blaming destiny, and delaying action.

7.23-7.26
Happiness = Infinitude = Self = I

Then follows a magnificent account of what is happiness?

'Infinite alone gives happiness. There is no happiness in anything finite', says the Upanishad. How? This has been explained convincingly by some commentators. Human mind is not happy with anything that is smaller than what is within its knowledge. As soon as a person achieves his object of happiness, his mind realizes that there is something even greater than what has been achieved. So it starts its search for that object of happiness. As a result, every experience of happiness from finite objects is only momentary. Only that which is Infinite, *Bhuma*, gives happiness. *Bhuma* is a novel word, which cannot be translated easily. It implies Infinitude, Completeness, Totality and Absolute.

> *'Every experience of happiness from finite objects is only momentary.'*

But what is Infinite? Infinite is that in which one does not see, hear or understand anything, as one does in a finite space. Infinite is self-supported in its own greatness. Infinite exists everywhere – East, West, North, South, above and below. Support is needed only in a relative world, where everything depends upon something else. No such dependence is needed in the Absolute, *Bhuma*. It is Omnipresent.

Sanatkumar also emphasizes that Infinite is not something different from our Self. Infinite is the same as what we call 'I' or our ego-sense. It is also the same, as our Self, *Atman*. That which is present in the cosmos as the 'total object' is also the 'total subject' in our Self. The text says that Infinite is onefold, threefold, 110-fold, 1020-fold, or whatever you can think of. The implied meaning is that all things and all experiences are contained in the Infinite.

> *'Infinite alone gives Happiness.'*

This realization – Infinite alone gives Happiness – comes with great effort, pure nourishment leading to purity of thought, reflection, spiritual awareness and a strong memory. But when it does come, it unties the knots of the heart, viz. spiritual ignorance, undisciplined desires and activity motivated by such desires.

Thus, concludes the Upanishad, revered Sanatkumar showed to Narada, the shore beyond darkness.

---

*'Bhuma is a novel word which cannot be translated easily.
It implies Infinitude, Completeness, Totality and Absolute.'*

TRANSLATED TEXT

CHAPTER 7

Section 1

Om. 'Revered sir, teach me', thus saying Narada approached Sanatkumar.

Sanatkumar said to him, 'Be my disciple by declaring what you already know. What is beyond that, I shall teach you.'

Narada said: **1**

'Revered sir, I know *Rg Veda*, *Yajur Veda*, *Sama Veda*, and *Atharva Veda* as the fourth. I also know Itihasa-Purana as the fifth; grammar, rules for worship of ancestors, mathematics, subject of natural disturbances, mineralogy, logic, ethics, etymology, ancillary knowledge of Vedas, physical science, science of war, science of stars, science related to serpents, and fine arts. All this I know, revered sir.   **2**

Revered sir, however, I am only a knower of empirical texts, not a knower of *Atman*. Indeed, I have heard from persons like your revered self that a knower of *Atman* goes beyond grief. I am in such a state of grief. May your revered self take me across it.' Sanatkumar replied to him, 'Whatsoever you have studied is merely names.   **3**

Name indeed is *Rg Veda*, (so also) *Yajur Veda*, *Sama Veda*, and *Atharva Veda* as the fourth. Name is also Itihasa-Purana as the fifth, grammar, rules for worship of ancestors, mathematics, subject of natural disturbances, mineralogy, logic, ethics, etymology, ancillary knowledge of Vedas, physical science, science of war, science of stars, science related to serpents, and fine arts – names alone are all these. You worship names.   **4**

He who worships a name as *Brahman*, he becomes free to act as he wishes in the sphere within the reach of that name, he who worships name as *Brahman*.'

(Narada) 'Revered sir, is there anything greater than name?'
(Sanatkumar) 'Surely there is something greater than name.'
(Narada) 'Revered sir, please communicate it to me.'   **5**

Section 2

'Speech surely is greater than name. Speech indeed makes us understand *Rg Veda*, *Yajur Veda*, *Sama Veda*, and *Atharva Veda* as the fourth. Speech also makes us understand Itihasa-Purana as the fifth, grammar, rules for worship of ancestors, mathematics, subject of natural disturbances, mineralogy, logic, ethics, etymology, ancillary knowledge of Vedas, physical science, science of war, science of stars, science related to serpents, and fine arts. This also applies to heaven and earth, air and sky, water and fire, gods and men, cattle and birds, grasses and trees,

---

"I have heard that a knower of Atman goes beyond grief."

beasts down to worms, flying insects and ants, merit and demerit, true and false, good and bad, pleasant and unpleasant. Verily, if speech did not exist, neither merit nor demerit would be understood, neither true nor false, neither good nor bad, neither pleasant nor unpleasant. Speech alone makes us understand all this. (Hence) worship speech. **1**

He who worships speech as *Brahman* becomes free to act as he wishes in the sphere within the reach of speech, he who worships speech as *Brahman*.'

'Revered sir, is there anything greater than speech?'
'Surely there is something greater than speech.'
'Revered sir, please communicate it to me.' **2**

Section 3

'Mind surely is greater than speech. Just as closed hands grasp two Amalaka, or two Kola, or two *Akash* fruits, so does mind grasp speech and name. When by mind one decides, "Let me learn the Mantras", then he learns; "Let me do sacrificial acts", then he does; "Let me desire offspring and cattle", then he desires; "Let me desire this world and the next", then he desires. Mind indeed is *Atman*. Mind indeed is the world. Mind indeed is *Brahman*. Worship mind. **1**

He who worships mind as *Brahman* becomes free to act as he wishes in the sphere within the reach of mind, he who worships mind as *Brahman*.'

'Revered sir, is there anything greater than mind?'
'Surely, there is something greater than mind.'
'Revered sir, please communicate it to me.' **2**

Section 4

'Will surely is greater than mind. Verily, when one wills, then he decides in his mind, then he sends forth speech, and he speaks of a name. In name, sacred formulae, and in sacred formulae, sacrifices become one. **1**

All these, indeed, merge in will, are made up of will, and abide in will. Heaven and earth willed, air and sky willed, water and fire willed. Through the willing of these, rain wills. Through the willing of rain, food wills. Through the willing of food, *Pranas* will. Through the willing of *Pranas*, sacred formulae will. Through the willing of sacred formulae, (sacrificial) acts will. Through the willing of (sacrificial) acts, the world wills. Through the willing of the world, all things will. This is will. Worship will. **2**

He who worships will as *Brahman*, he indeed, attains the worlds willed by him – himself being permanent, the permanent worlds; himself being well-founded, the well-founded worlds; himself being happy, the happy worlds. He becomes free to act as he wishes in the sphere within the reach of will, he who worships will as *Brahman*.'

"Speech (ability to communicate) is greater than learning..... Mind is greater than speech." ..... (Adapted)

'Revered sir, is there anything greater than will?'
'Surely, there is something greater than will.'
'Revered sir, please communicate it to me.' **3**

Section 5

'Intelligence surely is greater than will. Verily, when one understands, then he wills, then he decides in mind, then he sends forth speech, and he speaks of a name. In name, sacred formulae, and in sacred formulae, sacrifices become one. **1**

All these, indeed, merge in intelligence, are made up of intelligence and abide in intelligence. Therefore, when a man who knows much is without intelligence, people speak of him thus, "He does not exist; If he was knowledgeable or if he were really learned, he would not have been so foolish." On the other hand, if a man knowing little is endowed with intelligence, people desire to listen to him. Intelligence, indeed, is the centre where all these merge, intelligence is their soul, intelligence is their support. Worship intelligence. **2**

He who worships intelligence as *Brahman*, he indeed, attains the worlds of intelligence – himself being permanent, the permanent worlds; himself being well established, the well-established worlds; and himself being happy, the happy worlds. He becomes free to act as he wishes in the sphere within the reach of intelligence, he who worships intelligence as *Brahman*.'

'Revered sir, is there anything greater than intelligence?'
'Surely, there is something greater than intelligence.'
'Revered sir, please communicate it to me.' **3**

Section 6

'Contemplation surely is greater than intelligence. The earth contemplates, as it were. The sky contemplates, as it were. Heaven contemplates, as it were. Water contemplates, as it were. Mountains contemplate, as it were. Gods and men contemplate, as it were. Therefore, verily, those who attain greatness among men, they seem to have obtained a share of the result of contemplation. And those who are small people, they are quarrelsome, abusive and slanderous; but those who are great men, they appear to have obtained a share of the result of contemplation. Worship contemplation. **1**

He who worships contemplation as *Brahman* becomes free to act as he wishes in the sphere within the reach of contemplation, he who worships contemplation as *Brahman*.'

'Revered sir, is there anything greater than contemplation?'
'Surely, there is something greater than contemplation?'
'Revered sir, please communicate it to me.' **2**

"Will-power is greater than mind..... Intelligence is greater than will-power..... Contemplation is greater than intelligence." ..... (Adapted)

Section 7

'Wisdom surely is greater than contemplation. By wisdom alone one understands *Rg Veda*, *Yajur Veda*, *Sama Veda*, *Atharva Veda* as the fourth. He also understands Itihasa-Purana as the fifth, grammar, rules for worship of the ancestors, mathematics, subject of natural disturbances, mineralogy, logic, ethics, etymology, ancillary knowledge of Vedas, physical science, science of war, science of stars, science related to serpents and fine arts. This also applies to heaven and earth, air and sky, water and fire, gods and men, cattle and birds, grasses and trees, beasts down to worms, flying insects and ants, merit and demerit, true and false, good and bad, pleasant and unpleasant, food and drink, this world and the next. One understands (all this) by wisdom alone. Worship wisdom. **1**

He who worships wisdom as *Brahman* attains the worlds of those who understand the Vedas, and of those who have knowledge of other subjects. He becomes free to act as he wishes in the sphere within the reach of wisdom, he who worships wisdom as *Brahman*.'

'Revered sir, is there anything greater than wisdom?'
'Surely, there is something greater than wisdom.'
'Revered sir, please communicate it to me.' **2**

Section 8

'Strength surely is greater than wisdom. A single man with strength causes even a hundred men with wisdom to tremble. When a man becomes strong, then he progresses; progressing, he serves; serving, he approaches nearer; approaching nearer, he sees, hears, reflects, understands, acts and realizes. By strength, indeed, the earth stands; by strength, the sky; by strength, heaven; by strength, the mountains; by strength, gods and men; by strength, cattle and birds, grasses and trees, beasts down to worms, flying insects and ants; by strength the world stands. Worship strength. **1**

He who worships strength as *Brahman* becomes free to act as he wishes in the sphere within the reach of strength, he who worships strength as *Brahman*'.

'Revered sir, is there anything greater than strength?'
'Surely, there is something greater than strength'.
'Revered sir, please communicate it to me.' **2**

Section 9

'Food surely is greater than strength. Therefore, if one does not eat for ten days, even though he might live, yet, verily, he does not see, does not hear, does not reflect, does not understand, does not act, and does not realize. But with intake of food, he sees, hears, reflects, understands, acts, and realizes. Worship food. **1**

He who worships food as *Brahman*, verily, he attains the worlds supplied with food and drink. He is free to act as he wishes in the sphere within the reach of food, he who worships, food as *Brahman*.'

"Wisdom is greater than contemplation..... Strength surely is greater than wisdom." ..... (Adapted)

'Revered sir, is there anything greater than food?'
'Surely, there is something greater food.'
'Revered sir, please communicate it to me.'   **2**

Section 10

'Water surely is greater than food. Therefore, where there is not good rain, living creatures are in agony (thinking), "Food will be scarce". But when there is good rain, living creatures become joyous (thinking), "Food will abound". Water, indeed, has assumed all these forms – this earth, this sky, this heaven, these mountains, these gods and men, cattle and birds, grasses and trees, beasts down to worms, flying insects and ants. Water, indeed, has assumed all these forms. Worship water.   **1**

He who worships water as *Brahman* obtains all desires and becomes satisfied. He becomes free to act as he wishes in the sphere within the reach of water, he who worships water as *Brahman*.'
'Revered sir, is there anything greater than water?'
'Surely, there is 'something greater than water.'
'Revered sir, please communicate it to me.'   **2**

Section 11

'Fire surely is greater than water. It is this fire that having seized air warms up the sky. Then people say, "It is hot, it is burning hot, it will surely rain." There, it is fire that shows itself first, and then creates water. It is (because of) this fire that thunders roll along with lightning flashing upwards and across; and so people say, "Lightning is flashing, it is thundering, it will surely rain." There, it is fire that shows itself first and then creates water. Worship fire.   **1**

He who worships fire as *Brahman*, he, being resplendent himself, attains resplendent worlds, full of light and free from darkness. He becomes free to act as he wishes in the sphere within the reach of fire, he who worships fire as *Brahman*.'

'Revered sir, is there anything greater than fire?'
'Surely there is something greater than fire.'
'Revered sir, please communicate it to me.'   **2**

Section 12

'Space surely is greater than fire. In space, indeed, exist both the sun and the moon, lightning, stars and fires. Through space one calls, through space one hears, through space one answers. In space one rejoices, in space one feels sad. In space a thing is born, and towards space it grows. Worship space.   **1**

He who worships space as *Brahman*, he indeed, attains vast worlds, full of light, unconfined and spacious. He is free to act as he wishes in the sphere within the reach of space, he who worships space as *Brahman*.'

"Food is greater than strength..... Water is greater than food.....
Fire is greater than water..... Space is greater than fire." ..... (Adapted)

'Revered sir, is there anything greater than space?'
'Surely, there is something greater than space.'
'Revered sir, please communicate it to me.' 2

Section 13

'Memory surely is greater than space. Therefore, if many persons assemble and if they have no memory, they surely would not hear any sound, they would not think, they would not know. But surely, if they have memory, then they would hear, then they would think, then they would know. Through memory, indeed, one discerns one's sons, one's cattle. Worship memory. 1

He who worships memory as *Brahman* becomes free to act as he wishes in the sphere within the reach of memory, he who worships memory as *Brahman*.'

'Revered sir, is there anything greater than memory?'
'Surely, there is something greater than memory.'
'Revered sir, please communicate it to me.' 2

Section 14

'Aspiration surely is greater than memory. Kindled by aspiration (one's) memory recites the hymns, performs rites, and desires sons, cattle, this world and the next world. Worship aspiration. 1

He who worships aspiration as *Brahman*, by aspiration all his wishes fulfil; his prayers become infallible. He is free to act as he wishes in the sphere within the reach of aspiration, he who worships aspiration as *Brahman*.'

'Revered sir, is there anything greater than aspiration?'
'Surely, there is something greater than aspiration.'
'Revered sir, please communicate it to me.' 2

Section 15

'*Prana*, Life-breath surely is greater than aspiration. Just as the spokes of a wheel are fastened to its hub, so is all this fastened to this *Prana*. *Prana* moves by *Prana*, *Prana* gives *Prana* to *Prana*. *Prana* is the father, *Prana* is the mother, *Prana* is the brother, *Prana* is the sister, *Prana* is the preceptor, and *Prana* is *Brahman*. 1

If one answers something harsh to his father, mother, brother, sister, preceptor or a *Brahmin*, people say thus to him, "Shame on you! You are indeed a slayer of your father, you are indeed a slayer of your mother, you are indeed a slayer of your brother, you are indeed a slayer of your sister, you are indeed a slayer of your preceptor, you are indeed a slayer of a *Brahmin*". 2

On the other hand, when *Prana* (Life) has departed from them, even if one piles them together, dismembers them or burns them up, surely people would not say to him; "You are a slayer of your father", nor "You are a slayer of your mother", nor

---

"Memory is greater than space..... Aspiration is greater than memory.....
Prana, Life-breath is greater than aspiration." ..... (Adapted)

"You are a slayer of your brother", nor "You are a slayer of your sister", nor "You are a slayer of your preceptor", nor "You are a slayer of a *Brahmin*." 3

'*Prana* indeed becomes all these. He, who sees thus, thinks thus and knows thus, transcends all in speech. If someone were to say to him, "You are transcending the limits in your speech", he should say, "Yes, I am transcending". He should not deny it. 4

Section 16

'But he really speaks well whose speech is based on Truth.'
'Revered sir, being such, I would like to base my speech on Truth.'
'But one must desire to understand Truth.'
'Revered sir, I desire to understand Truth.' 1

Section 17

'When one has spiritual awareness, then alone does one speak the Truth. Without spiritual awareness, one does not speak the Truth. It is only by spiritual awareness that one speaks the Truth. But one must desire to have spiritual awareness.'
'Revered sir, I desire to have spiritual awareness.' 1

Section 18

'When one reflects, then alone does one have spiritual awareness. Without reflecting one does not have spiritual awareness. Only he who reflects has spiritual awareness. But one must desire to understand reflection.'
'Revered sir, I desire to understand reflection.' 1

Section 19

'When one has faith, then alone does one reflect. Without faith, one does not reflect. Only he who has faith reflects. But one must desire to understand faith.'
'Revered sir, I desire to understand faith.' 1

Section 20

'When one has steadfastness, then alone does one have faith. Without steadfastness, one does not have faith. Only he who has steadfastness has faith. But one must desire to understand steadfastness.'
'Revered sir, I desire to understand steadfastness.' 1

Section 21

'When one acts, then alone does one become steadfast. Without being active, one does not become steadfast. Only on being active does one become steadfast. But one must desire to understand activity.'
'Revered sir, I desire to understand activity.' 1

"When one reflects, then alone does one have spiritual awareness.
Without reflecting one does not have spiritual awareness."

Section 22

'When one attains happiness, then only one is active. Without attaining happiness, one is not active. Only on attaining happiness one is active. But one must desire to understand happiness.'
'Revered sir, I desire to understand happiness.' **1**

Section 23

'That alone gives happiness, which is infinite, *Bhuma*. There is no happiness in anything finite. Infinite alone gives happiness. But one must desire to understand the infinite.'
'Revered sir, I desire to understand the infinite.' **1**

Section 24

'In which one sees nothing else, hears nothing else, understands nothing else, that is infinite. But that in which one sees something else, hears something else understands something else, is finite. That which is infinite, that alone is immortal; that which is finite is mortal.'
'Revered sir, in what is that infinite established?'
'In its own greatness, or not even in its own greatness. **1**

Here on earth people call (possession of) cows and horses, elephants and gold, servants and wives, fields and houses, as "greatness." I do not speak thus (of greatness), for in that case one thing would be dependent on another. What I do say is this: **2**

Section 25

'That infinite alone is below. That is above. That is behind. That is in front. That is in the south. That is in the north. That alone is all this.'
Next is the same instruction with regard to ego. 'I alone am below I am above. I am behind. I am in front. I am to the south. I am to the north. I alone am all this.' **1**

Now is the teaching in regard to the Self, *Atman*. '*Atman* alone is below. *Atman* is above. *Atman* is behind. *Atman* is in front. *Atman* is in south. *Atman* is in north. *Atman* alone is all this.'

Verily, he who sees thus, reflects thus and understands thus, has pleasure in *Atman*, delight in *Atman*, union in *Atman*, joy in *Atman*. He becomes self-sovereign; he becomes free to act as he wishes in all the worlds. But those who know otherwise than this, they are ruled by others and they live in perishable worlds; they are not free to act as they wish in all the worlds. **2**

Section 26

'Verily, for him alone, who sees thus, reflects thus and understands thus, *Prana* springs form *Atman*, aspiration from *Atman*, memory from *Atman*, space from *Atman*,

---

"Atman alone is below. Atman is above. Atman is behind. Atman is in front. Atman is in south. Atman is in north. Atman alone is all this."

fire from *Atman*, water from *Atman*, creation and dissolution from *Atman*, food from *Atman*, strength from *Atman*, understanding from *Atman*, contemplation from *Atman*, intelligence from *Atman*, will from *Atman*, mind from *Atman*, speech from *Atman*, name from *Atman*, hymns from *Atman*, rites from *Atman*. All these (spring) from *Atman* alone. **1**

There is this verse about it:
He who sees thus, does not see death, neither illness, nor any sorrow. He who sees thus sees all things and obtains all things in all ways'.

'Being one, he becomes threefold, fivefold, sevenfold and also ninefold. Then again, he is called elevenfold, also a hundred tenfold and also a thousand-and-twenty-fold.

'When nourishment is pure, nature becomes pure. When nature is pure, memory becomes strong. When memory becomes strong, there is release from all the knots of the heart.'

The revered Sanatkumar showed to Narada, after his impurities had been washed off, the farther shore beyond darkness. People call Sanatkumar as Skanda, Yes, they call him Skanda. **2**

"When nourishment is pure... memory becomes strong."

Rendition

CHAPTER 7

7.1-7.7 Wisdom gives greater happiness than learning

Narada was a very learned and highly respected sage. However, he was not a happy person, as he thought there was something missing from his vast learning. But there was no one who could be a teacher to a learned sage like Narada. So, Narada approached a teacher with a very different profile – a young warlord, Sanatkumar.

Both Narada and Sanatkumar excelled in their respective fields. In the Bhagavad Gita, Lord Krishna says: 'I am Narada among the divine sages and among the generals, I am Skanda.' Skanda is another name for Sanatkumar.

Narada approaches Sanatkumar for what he thinks is missing in his life – knowledge of *Atman-Brahman*. One after another, Sanatkumar sets forth nearly two dozen attributes – each greater than the preceding one – leading to *Bhuma*, *Brahman* itself, the Greatest, Infinite, Unlimited.

Narada : Revered Master, please be my Teacher.

Sanatkumar : OK, but first tell me what you already know. Then I will teach you what you do not know.

Narada : Revered Master, I have studied all the scriptures, all the sciences, music, art and dancing. There is hardly anything, which I have not studied. But I do not know the real substance, the common thread of these arts and sciences. Therefore, I am not very happy with my learning. There is something, which seems to be missing in my life. Could it be the knowledge of *Atman*? I have heard that one who knows *Atman* goes beyond grief. O great Master, please teach me that which will take me beyond grief.

Sanatkumar : Whatever you have studied is only empirical learning, what you might call 'names'. You know the nature of things, but not their ultimate Reality. No learning can make you happy unless it becomes a part of your Being, your Self, your *Atman*. Knowledge begins with gathering information, and to that extent you have done well. But this is only the first step.

Narada, do you know the two important principles of meditation? The first is that whatever your object of meditation be, you should regard that as the Highest, the Absolute. There should not be anything external to it, anything bigger than it. If your mind conceives something greater than that, that should become the object of your meditation. The object of meditation should be the last reach of your mind beyond which it cannot go. The second principle of meditation is that whatever you meditate upon, that you become. If you meditate on a personal God, *Ishta Devata*, you become Him. If you meditate on a spiritual master, a guru, you become him. If you meditate on the formless, attribute-less Absolute, *Brahman*, you become Him.

You have been worshipping (meditating on) learning. The result of this worship is limited freedom, but not complete freedom.

Narada : Is there any thing greater than learning? If so, please tell me about it.

Sanatkumar : Speech is greater than learning, because it is through speech alone that we can understand and express our learning, by whatever name we call it.

Narada : Is there any thing greater than speech?

Sanatkumar : Mind is great than speech, because it is the basis of both learning and speech. He who meditates on Mind acquires

---

'Speech is greater than learning, because it is through speech that we can express our learning.' ..... (Adapted)

[7.1-7.26] BHUMA VIDYA: IT IS ALL ABOUT HAPPINESS

freedom to act within the realm of the mind.

Narada : Revered Sir, is there something greater than the Mind? Please tell me about it.

Sanatkumar : Will, *Sankalpa*, is greater than Mind. Will or determination is a composite of learning (name), thoughts (mind) and words (speech). Action results only when there is a Will to act.

Narada : Revered Sir, What is greater than Will?

Sanatkumar : *Chitta* is greater then Will. The word *chitta* can be translated as 'thought', 'memory' and 'intelligence'. Let us call it Intelligence. Intelligence is a composite of all that we have discussed so far – Name, Speech, Mind and Will.

Narada : Is there anything greater than Intelligence?

Sanatkumar : Contemplation, *dhyana* is greater than intelligence. Contemplation requires on ability to concentrate on whatever you want to do. It requires tranquility, like that of sky, heavens and mountains. It is by concentration – and not by distracted thinking or action – that people have achieved greatness in this world.

Narada : Is there anything greater than contemplation?

Sanatkumar : *Vigyana* or wisdom is greater than contemplation. One must have the wisdom to make the best use of one's learning.

Narada : Revered Sir, is there anything greater than wisdom?

7.8-7.12 Physical strength and primal elements

Sanatkumar : Yes, there is. But we must now change gears from the mental to the physical. Unless one has the physical strength to be active, mental capabilities from learning to wisdom cannot be utilized to their fullest potential. In that sense, Strength, *balam* is greater than wisdom.

Strength is derived from food; in that sense food is greater than strength.

Food in the form of fruits, vegetables and grains requires water for its plantation. In that sense, water is greater than food.

Water comes from rains, and rain requires heat, which causes water to evaporate and form clouds. This heat is symbolized by fire. So, fire is said to be superior to water.

Thunder, lightening, sun, moon, stars – all these contain fire in the form of heat – but all these are contained in space. Even sound travels through space, and thereby imparts to us our ability to hear. So, space is greater than even fire.

Narada: Revered Sir, is there anything greater than space?

7.13-7.15 Memory, Aspiration and Life-breath

Sanatkumar : Yes, there is, but we must again go back to the subtle, so to say. Memory, *Smaran* is greater than space. Without memory all our possessions and relationships will be devoid of any meaning. All our activity in life is an offshoot of memory.

Narada : Revered Sir, is there anything greater than memory?

Sanatkumar : Aspiration, *asha* is greater than memory. All our prayers and rituals reflect our aspirations for something or the other—in this world or in the next world.

Narada : Revered Sir, is there anything greater than aspiration?

'Will or determination is a composite of learning, thoughts and words.
Action results only when there is a Will to act.' ..... (Adapted)

Sanatkumar : Yes, there is. *Prana* or life-breath is greater than aspiration. Just as spokes of a wheel are fastened to the hub, so are all sense organs of perception and action, the mind, the body, in fact everything, is dependent on *Prana*. A person is recognized and respected only as long as there is life-breath in him. As long as a person is alive, even to address him with harsh words is viewed negatively. Once he is devoid of life-breath, his dead body is burnt by his relatives. If they did so while there was life in him, they would have been called murderers!

A person who can speak on the subject of *Prana*, life-breath, is a profound speaker, *ativadi*. If ordinary people do not understand what he says, he should not be surprised or disappointed. Instead, he should emphasize that he is speaking about a profound subject, which can be understood only with effort and concentration.

At this point, Narada is unable to speak. He does not know what to ask next. Obviously, he thinks it foolish to ask: 'Is there anything greater than life?' Seeing his predicament, the teacher himself continues his teachings.

7.16-7.22 A happy man is an active man

Sanatkumar : He speaks well whose speech is based on truth, *satya*. But to do so, one must have a desire to understand truth.

Narada : I would like to understand truth.

Sanatkumar : Truth is known only when one has spiritual awareness, *vigyana*. So, before understanding truth, one must first have spiritual awareness.

Narada : I would like to have spiritual awareness.

Sanatkumar : Spiritual awareness comes from reflection, *manan*. So, before having spiritual awareness one must first understand reflection.

Narada : I would like to understand reflection.

Sanatkumar : Reflection comes from faith, *shraddha*.

Narada : I would like to understand faith.

Sanatkumar : Faith comes from steadfastness, *nishtha*.

Narada : I would like to understand steadfastness.

Sanatkumar : Steadfastness comes from activity, *krati*.

Narada : I would like to understand activity.

Sanatkumar : Activity comes from happiness, *sukham*. Happy persons are generally very active; while unhappy persons are brooding or blaming their stars.

Narada : I would like to understand happiness.

Sanatkumar : Infinite, *Bhuma* alone gives happiness. There cannot be any happiness in the small.

Narada : I would like to understand Infinite.

Sanatkumar : Infinite is that in which one does not see, hear or understand anything except the Infinite. That in which one sees, hears or understands is finite. Infinite alone is Immortal, finite is mortal.

Narada : Revered Sir, on what is Infinite supported?

Sanatkumar : Infinite is supported by Its own greatness, or perhaps It has no support at all. We are used to considering our material possessions and our near and dear ones as our support. The Infinite or the Absolute does not exist in this relative sense – It is self-supported. Also, it is difficult to say where It is,

---

'Spiritual awareness comes from reflection. Reflection comes from faith.
Faith comes from steadfastness. Steadfastness comes from activity.' ..... (Adapted)

because Infinite is every where. The whole cosmos is filled by Infinite alone.

Dear Narada, note another important point. Do not think of Infinite as another person or being, different from yourself. Infinite is the same as what we call 'I', your ego-sense. So, you can rightly say: "I am everywhere – below, above, in the front, at the back, in the north, in the south. I alone am all this universe." And what is I? It is nothing but *Atman*. So, what I said about the Infinite and 'I', also applies to *Atman*. *Atman* is everywhere, and *Atman* is all this.

(7.23-7.26) Happiness = Infinitude = Self = I

Sanatkumar : He who understands this reality of the Infinite – which is the same as Self, *Atman* – is not subservient to anybody else, because there is nothing other than him. He becomes a self-ruler. He acquires complete freedom of action in this world as also hereafter. He feels immensely happy. But people who do not have knowledge of Infinite, are controlled by others; They are devoid of freedom of action.

Narada, let me tell you more about Self, *Atman*. As *Atman* is the same as Infinite, *Bhuma*, everything emanates from *Atman* – life-breath (*Prana*), aspiration, memory space, heat (fire), water, creation and dissolution, food strength, understanding, reflection intelligence, will, mind, speech, names, hymns and rituals, for example. Many of these have been already covered in this discourse (7.26, 1).

Narada, let me now conclude. I have expounded *Bhuma Vidya*, knowledge of the Infinite, *Atman*. He who realizes this is free from every kind of affliction. He becomes all. Everyone and everything is comprehended within this single, ultimate Reality.

It is knowledge of the Infinite which leads to real Happiness.

Thus Sanatkumar – the revered god who is also called Skanda – showed the shore beyond darkness to Narada.

– Editor

FOCUSSED COMMENTARIES

It is common experience that human mind is not happy with anything which is smaller than what is within its knowledge. Man is not happy with the small. He wants something more than what he already possesses; and when he acquires that, he wants something still greater – until the extreme limit, the infinite, is reached. Hence, Infinity or *Bhuma* alone is declared to be unequalled, unlimited and unsurpassed bliss. This is the summit of Vedanta. This is the goal of all religious and philosophical search.

The words *Bhuma*, *Mahat* and *Brahman* denote the same Reality. Each of these words includes all finite existences. Outside this Reality, one cannot conceive anything greater in magnitude or value. The Upanishads refers to this principle by other terms also – such as *Om*, *Sat* and *Atman* – in different contexts.

Ordinarily, knowledge involves a triad – the knower, the object of knowledge and the instrument of knowing. In *Bhuma*, these merge into one. So, one who realizes the Infinite does not see, hear or understand anything else as an object of cognition. Thus, Infinite is beyond all attributes and characteristics of worldly existences. The dualistic experiences of an unenlightened man are trivial (*alpa*) in contrast with the realization of *Bhuma*, which is Immortal (*amrita*).

A clean mirror alone can reflect the face perfectly. *Sattva shuddhi*, or purity of internal organs is an essential condition for realization of the Infinite, which is the same as *Atman* within. This is achieved by

'Knowledge involves a triad – the knower, the object of knowledge and the instrument of knowing. In Bhuma, these merge into one.'

purification of the mind. Mind is like a cloth dyed in desires, hatred and other evils. Purification of the mind is a process like bleaching a stained cloth. Narada became pure through the instructions of his divine preceptor.

The name Skanda means a learned person, or Kartikeya, the son of Shiva.

— *Swami Swahananda*

That which is infinite, incalculable, unexcelled, unlimited – that is *sukham*, happiness. Anything lower is finite. There is no happiness in the finite, because finite is a cause of thirst for more; and thirst is the seed of sorrow. Hence, infinite alone gives happiness, *bhuma eva sukham*. Infinite cannot be the cause of thirst.

The meaning of the whole text is that the idea of finite exists only during the period of ignorance. For that very reason, finite is mortal, Infinite is immortal.

— *Sri Sankara, translated by Swami Gambhirananda*

Bhuma is a novel word, which cannot be translated easily. It implies completeness, totality, absolute – both in quantity and quality. *Bhuma* alone gives happiness. 'Small things do not contain happiness, *na alpe sukham asti*,' says Sanatkumar.

If finite objects do not contain happiness, how does one explain the universal quest for happiness in finite objects? The reason is that to a man in search of happiness, finite objects sought by him give an impression of being complete. When that object is achieved, a sensation of completeness – a feeling that something sought after has been achieved – is introduced in the mind. This completeness is apparent, not real, as it lasts only for a fraction of a moment. Soon the mind realizes that there is something even greater than what has been achieved. So it starts its search for another object of happiness. Thus, every experience of happiness in this world is only apparent and momentary. Even this apparent and momentary happiness is due to an awareness of the presence of *Bhuma* – the Infinite – in finite objects.

The relativity of things is the support of things in this world. Everything depends upon something else. But no such dependence is possible in *Bhuma*, the Infinite. It is self-existent, self-supported, self-complete, and self-sufficient. It is not a relative being. It is the Absolute Being.

Infinite is everywhere. It is everything. All these configurations that we see with our eyes are nothing but configurations of Its own Being.

Now, a doubt may arise that 'I' in me is different from Infinite. This is not so. The thinking subject in me is included in the Infinite, *Bhuma*. Just as we can say, 'Infinite is all things, It is everywhere,' we can also say, 'I am all things, I am every where?'

Here again, a doubt may arise, 'What is this I? Is it the individual I, the ego?' No, it is the *Atman* in the individual that is identical with *Bhuma*, the universal – just as space within a vessel is identical with the space in the outside universe.

The universal *Bhuma* is also the *Atman* in all beings. That which is present in the cosmos as the total object is also the total subject in man. *Bhuma* is both the subject and the object. In *Bhuma* alone, there is happiness, nowhere else. One who has this realization is the happiest person conceivable. He is delighted within his own Self; he enjoys his own Self; and he is rooted in the bliss of his own Self.

Now what is this 'own Self'? It is not myself, yourself, or any individual self. It is the Universal Being, the All-Being, the Omnipresent *Bhuma*. A person who acquires this realization becomes a master of himself; which means, a master of all things. Self-mastery is the mastery of the universe. To rule over Self is to rule over everything that has Self within itself, and this Self is everywhere. To such a blessed one, everything comes from his own Self. He does not have to go to things; things come to him. The ocean does not go to the rivers, the rivers go to the ocean. All things come to that person who ceases to be an individual person. Instead, he becomes a universal being. He is called *Jivan-mukta*.

The Upanishad reiterates this concept by saying that he becomes all – one, two three, four, thousand or million-folds, whatever you can think of. The meaning of this Upanishadic exclamation is that all things are contained in this single experience. Interpreters have

---

'There is no happiness in the finite, because finite is a cause of thirst for more; and thirst is the seed of sorrow.'

tried to find specific intentions behind these numbers. They say:

> Onefold is One non-dual Being, *Brahman*.
> Threefold is *Adhyatmic*, *Adhibhautic* and *Adhidaivic*.
> Fivefold is five senses.
> Sevenfold is the seven worlds.
> Ninefold is five sense organs and four faculties of the mind.
> Elevenfold is five sense organs of perception, five of action, and mind.

Bhuma is 110-fold and 1020-fold when it includes many other categories. Everything is comprehended within this single Being, the Ultimate Reality, the Absolute. It has no distinction of subject and object. It is the seer as well as the seen.

This knowledge, this realization comes with great effort, which should be directed properly. Purity of thought is a consequence of purity of diet. According to Sri Sankara, this is an exhortation to receive only pure inputs through every sense organ, including the mind. And what is purity? Purity is that which is compatible with the nature of the Absolute. When that purity arises in the mind, it brings with it the capacity of concentration on *Bhuma*, the Infinite. It also enables retention of the consciousness of *Bhuma* in mind's memory. Then all knots of the heart get broken.

The knots of the heart, *granthis*, are *Avidya*, *Kama* and *Karma* - ignorance, selfish desires, and activity for fulfillment of such desires. Sometimes these three are called *brahma-granthi*, *vishnu-granthi* and *rudra-granthi*.

Narada is free from impurities of every kind, and therefore a fit disciple. He is instructed by Sanatkumar, who is addressed as *Bhagvan*, the Lord, the great master. He is also called Skanda. One interpretation of the word Skanda is that he has crossed over the phenomenal existence. There is also a mythological legend that Sanatkumar, the second son of Lord Shiva, was known as Skanda and also as Kartikeya. To that divine person is our obeisance. He has reached the Absolute, and he takes Narada to the Absolute.

– *Swami Krishnananda*

The Infinite is rooted in its own greatness, while things which are in the realm of finite are rooted not in themselves, but in others.

Sanatkumar points out that spiritual freedom is the basis of all action, all happiness. We reach it by stages. Self, *Atman* is the source of all things - hope, memory, space, light, water, for example. It is the source of all power, all knowledge, all happiness.

Empirical dualities are absent in the experience of the Infinite.

– *S. Radhakrishnan*

The description of *Bhuma*, Infinite, is magnificent. Infinite does not see, hear or know anything outside Itself. Being Immortal, It rests alone in Its supra-mundane majesty. The soul is identical with It. It is present directly in all places. He who leads his life with this viewpoint has his joy only in *Atman*. He knows that everything is rooted in *Atman*. He finds his 'I' in all the thousands of appearances of *Atman*. He is free. He is raised above death, pain and sorrow.

– *Paul Deussen*

'The Infinite is rooted in its own greatness, while things which are in the realm of finite are rooted not in themselves, but in others.'

8. *Dahara Vidya*: Meditation on Self within

SIMPLIFIED SYNOPSES

8.1
Vast universe in a small space in the heart

Mind in its normal state traverses a vast space. Meditation requires concentrating the mind on a very small point-like space. This has been called *Dahara Akash* (small subtle space) and also *Antar hridaya Akash* (space within the heart) in the Upanishads.

So during meditation, think of the body as city of *Brahman*, think of the heart as a small lotus-like mansion, and think that within the heart there is a very small space which is point-like in size, but it contains the whole universe. Also think that this subtle space is *Atman* Itself. And how is this *Atman* to be thought of? Think of it as that which is free from evil, old age, death, sorrow, hunger and thirst. Also think of it as *Satyakama* and *Satya sankalpa*, one with true desires and true resolves.

The word *Dahara Akash*, has been translated by one commentator as, 'Sky of the heart.' Also, according to another commentator, the passage relating to the presence of the whole universe in a small subtle space within, is an indicator of the potentiality of omniscience in human beings. Omniscience has been already manifested by a few great spiritual personalities in history.

8.2-8.5
True desires are always fulfilled

The word *Satyakama* is translated as desire for Truth, and also as true desires. Normally, our desires are tainted with selfish motives – like sense longing, dependence or self-importance. However, underlying such desires are our true desires, the silent voice of our conscience.

The text explains with illustrations how 'true desires' are covered by 'untruth':

- Desires covered by untruth restrict our freedom of action, like a soldier has to act within the limits defined by his commander (8.1, 5).
- Sincere love for someone is an example of a true desire. Wanting a deceased loved one back is 'untruth', which covers a true desire. True love is not affected whether the object of love is present or not present (8.3, 1).
- A treasure hidden underneath will not be visible to a person who is ignorant of it, even though he may be walking over it again and again. Likewise, a person comes very close to *Atman* (in deep sleep) everyday, but he is carried away by 'untruth', which acts as cover over his true desires (8.3, 2).

'True love is not affected whether the object of love is present or not present.'

The text says that one who knows *Atman* gets all his true desires fulfilled and he enjoys full freedom, both in this world and in the next world. A true desire is that which serves a universal purpose and which is also in harmony with the inner voice of Self, *Atman*.

The text also provides etymological explanations of the two most important words of these passages: *Atman* and *Satyam*. It says, 'Self, *Atman* is Immortal and Fearless. It is *Brahman*. It is Truth'. A Self-realized person is said to attain the highest light, *param jyoti*, which is said to be his true nature. (8.3, 3-5)

In another analogy, Self, *Atman* is compared to a bridge between the relative and the Absolute. It leads to a state beyond the relative existence of day or night, merit or demerit etc. This state (*Brahma-loka*) is always illumined.

The text says that one of the paths for attaining *Brahma-loka* is *Brahmacharya*. Sacrificial rituals, worship, practice of silence, fasting and life of a hermit are said to be parts of *Brahmacharya*.

8.4-8.6 Infinitization of Self

This section describes what one commentator has called 'Infinitization of Self.' In a metaphor of poetic beauty, sun's rays are compared to a highway connecting the subtle (imperceptible) arteries in the heart and the sun (8.6, 2). Self, *Atman* travels on this highway right up to *Brahman* (symbolized by the sun) during deep sleep; and also after death, if its exit from the body is through the crown of the head.

Meditation on Self within is thus a method for fulfillment of all 'true' desires during this life of relative existence here on earth; and infinitization of Self into Absolute *Brahman*, hereafter.

8.7-8.12 One teaching, two interpretations

In verse 8.1, 5 at the beginning of this chapter, *Atman* is described as one which is free from evil, old age, death, sorrow, hunger and thirst. It projects true desires and true resolve (*Satyakama* and *satya sankalpa*). It is this *Atman* which should be sought and understood. He who does so, attains all the worlds, he finds all his desires fulfilled.

In verse 8.7, the aforesaid teaching is repeated by *Prajapati* to a joint assembly of gods and demons. Both are so fascinated by the teaching that they independently go to *Prajapati* to seek and understand that *Atman*, which can help them attain all worlds and fulfill all desires. But this requires a suitable conditioning of the mind; so they live a disciplined life as students for 32 years. Even after this, *Prajapati* wants his two disciples to acquire the sought-after knowledge step-by-step, and on their own. Therefore, he tells them to look at themselves in a pond of water and he asks: 'What do you see?' The two reply that they see their images. *Prajapati* says, 'This is *Atman*', but adds with a purpose, 'It is immortal and fearless'. The implied message is that the body – as perceived in waking state – is certainly one aspect of *Atman*. However, *Atman* has other aspects too, like Immortality and Fearlessness. To understand these other aspects, learning alone is not sufficient; the student must reflect on what he has learnt.

Virochana, the leader of demons, accepts what he is told by *Prajapati* as sacrosanct and final. He does not reflect on the teaching. So, to the demons, the body with its mind and senses is *Atman*. They regard satisfaction of desires of the mind and pleasures of the senses through material possessions, as the goal of life.

'Atman is free from evil, old age, death, sorrow, hunger and thirst. It projects true desires and true resolve.'

In sections 8.9-8.11, Indra, the leader of gods, reflects on what he has learnt and sees some flaws in it. So he returns back to *Prajapati* for clarification of his doubts. His perseverance is evident from the fact that he comes back to *Prajapati* a third time, and again a fourth time, to spend a total of 101 years. Learning can be instantaneous, but wisdom comes from regular reflection and gradual experiencing.

What does *Prajapati* do? He leads his enquiring student from the question, 'What do you see?' to 'Who is it that sees?' He also ensures that Indra's answer to this question is based not just on 'seeing' as experienced in waking state, but on 'total experience of seeing' in all three states – waking, dream and deep sleep. So in his instructions to Indra, *Prajapati* adds that *Atman* 'moves about adored in dreams' and is 'fully composed, serene and without dreams in deep sleep'; It is also Immortal and Fearless.

Prajapati explains the relevance of these two words, – Immortal and Fearless – when Indra questions how can something (Consciousness), which seems to have gone into annihilation during deep sleep, be *Atman*? He says that mortal body is merely a seat of *Atman*, which Itself is Immortal. It is unaffected by pleasures and pains of the body.

> *'Mortal body is merely a seat of Atman, which Itself is immortal.'*

Prajapati illustrates his teachings with examples from Nature. Phenomena like cloud, lightening and thunder emanate from sky and vanish into sky; but the sky remains unaffected and formless. Likewise, human bodies appear from *Atman* and disappear into It. Outside the body, *Atman* is the Highest Person, *Uttam Purusha*, and Light of lights, *Param Jyoti*. In the body, in its conditioned state (called *jivatman*) it experiences all worldly pleasures, unmindful of the mortality of the body in which it is born. (8.12, 2-3)

Prajapati also uses the analogy of a chariot yoked to an animal and driven by it. Likewise, *Atman* is 'yoked' to the body in the form of *Prana*, Life Principle.

Sense organs like eyes, nose, tongue and ears are only instruments of sight, smell, speech, and hearing. The One who sees, smells, speaks and hears is *Atman*. Likewise, it is *Atman* that thinks through the mind. Mind is like *Atman*'s 'divine eye'.

8.13-8.15
Ecstasy of Self-realization

The first two verses express the ecstasy of *Atman*'s merger with *Brahman*, Infinitization of the Self.

The concluding verse here suggests that *Atman*, Self can be realized even when living a worldly life.

'It is Atman that thinks through the mind. Mind is like Atman's 'divine eye'.'

Translated Text

CHAPTER 8

Section 1

Om. Now, in this city of *Brahman*, there is a mansion in the shape of a small lotus. In it there is a small inner space, *Akash*. What is within that space should be sought. That indeed one should desire to understand.   **1**

If they ask him, 'In this city of *Brahman* – in which there is a small mansion in the shape of a lotus and a small inner space within – what is it that lies there, which should be sought, which one should desire to understand?', he should say in reply: 'As large as is all this space, so large is that space in the heart. Within it, indeed, are contained heaven and earth, fire and air, sun and moon, lightning and stars. Whatever there is in this world and whatever is not, all that is contained within it'.   **2-3**

If they ask him, 'If in this city of *Brahman* is contained all this, all beings and all desires, then what is left of it when old age overtakes it or when it perishes?'   **4**

He should say: 'It (*Brahman* in inner space) does not age with the ageing of the body, it is not killed by the killing of body. This (space) is the real city of *Brahman*. In it are contained desires. This is *Atman*, free from evil, free from old age, free from death, free from sorrow, free from hunger, free from thirst. Its desire is truth, its resolve is truth. In this world, people live as they are commanded (by their desires). Whatever they desire - be it a country or a small field - they live dependent on that.   **5**

Just as this world earned by work is short-lived, even so the other world earned by righteous deeds is short-lived. So those who depart from here without having understood *Atman* and their true desires, for them there is no freedom to act as they wish, in any world. But those who depart from here, having understood *Atman* and their true desires, for them there is freedom to act as they wish in all the worlds'.   **6**

Section 2

If he becomes desirous of the world of father, by his mere will, father arises. Possessed of that world of father he feels happy and exalted.   **1**

And if he becomes desirous of the world of mother, by his mere will, mother arises. Possessed of that world of mother, he feels happy and exalted.   **2**

And if he becomes desirous of the world of brothers, by his mere will, brothers arise. Possessed of that world of brothers, he feels happy and exalted.   **3**

And if he becomes desirous of the world of sisters, by his mere will, sisters arise. Possessed of that world of sisters, he feels happy and exalted.   **4**

"As large as is all this space, so large is that space in the heart.

And if he becomes desirous of the world of friends, by his mere will, friends arise. Possessed of that world of friends, he feels happy and exalted. **5**

And if he becomes desirous of the world of perfumes and garlands, by his mere will, perfumes and garlands arise. Possessed of that world of perfumes and garlands, he feels happy and exalted. **6**

And if he becomes desirous of the world of food and drink, by his mere will, food and drink arise. Possessed of that world of food and drink, he feels happy and exalted. **7**

And if he becomes desirous of the world of song and music, by his mere will, song and music arise. Possessed of that world of song and music, he feels happy and exalted. **8**

And if he becomes desirous of the world of women, by his mere will, women arise. Possessed of that world of women he feels happy and exalted. **9**

Whatever world he is attached to and whatever desirable objects he desires, by his mere will, they arise. Possessed of them, he feels happy and exalted. **10**

Section 3

True desires are covered by untruth. Although the desires are true, they are covered by untruth. For whosoever of one's people departs from this world, one does not get him back to see. **1**

But those of his people, whether they are alive or dead, and whatever else one desires but does not get, all that one finds by going there (into *Atman*, the space in the heart); for here, indeed, are those true desires. Just as people who do not know the field walk again and again over the treasure of gold hidden underground, but do not find it; even so all these creatures here go daily into *Brahma-loka*, (during deep sleep), yet they do not find It. They are carried away by untruth. **2**

This *Atman* verily is in the heart. Its etymological explanation is this. This (*Atman*) is in the heart, hence it is the heart. He who knows thus, indeed goes daily into the heavenly world. **3**

'Now this serene and happy Being, rising out of this body and reaching the highest light, appears in His own true nature. This is *Atman*. This is the immortal, the fearless. This is *Brahman*. Verily, the name of this *Brahman* is Truth.' This is what the teacher said. **4**

These are indeed the three syllables: *sa, ti, yam*. What is *sa*, that is the immortal; and what is *ti*, that is the mortal; and what is *yam*, with it one holds the two together. Because with it one holds the two together, therefore it is *yam*. Verily, he who knows thus goes to the heavenly world. **5**

"True desires are covered by untruth."

Section 4

Now, this *Atman* is a bridge between these worlds. Neither day nor night reach this bridge; nor old age, nor death, nor sorrow, nor merit, nor demerit. All evils turn back from it, for this *Brahma-loka* is free from evil. **1**

Therefore, verily, on reaching this bridge, if one was blind, he ceases to be blind; if wounded, he ceases to be wounded; if afflicted, he ceases to be afflicted. Therefore, verily, on reaching this bridge, even night becomes day, for this *Brahma-loka* is ever illumined. **2**

But only those attain this *Brahma-loka* who live a disciplined life of *Brahmacharya*, according to their teachers' instructions. To them belongs this *Brahma-loka*. For them there is freedom to act as they wish in all the worlds. **3**

Section 5

Now, what people call sacrificial rite is really *Brahmacharya*, for only by means of *Brahmacharya* does the knower attain that world. And what people call sacrifice is really *Brahmacharya*, for only by disciplined life of *Brahmacharya* does one attain *Atman*. **1**

Now, what people call Sattraya sacrifice is really *Brahmacharya*, for only by means of *Brahmacharya* does one get protection for oneself with the help of Existence (*sat*). And what people call vow of silence is really *Brahmacharya* for only through *Brahmacharya* does one understand *Atman*, and then meditate. **2**

Now, what people call fasting is really *Brahmacharya*, for this *Atman* which one attains by means of *Brahmacharya*, never perishes. And what people call life of a hermit is really *Brahmacharya*.

Ara and Nya are two oceans in *Brahma-loka*, the third heaven from here. Therein is a lake Airammadiya; there is a tree showering Soma; there is Aparajita, the (unconquered) city of *Brahma*; and there is a golden hall specially built by the Lord. **3**

Those who reach the two oceans, Ara and Nya, in *Brahma-loka* by means of *Brahmacharya*, only to them belongs this *Brahma-loka*. For them there is freedom to act as they wish in all the worlds. **4**

Section 6

Now, these subtle arteries of the heart are filled with a fine substance, which is reddish-brown, white, blue, yellow and red. The yonder sun indeed is reddish-brown, white, blue, yellow and red. **1**

Just as a highway runs between two villages, this and that, even so rays of sun connect both these worlds, this and that. They spread out of the yonder sun and enter into these arteries. Out of these arteries they spread out and enter into the yonder sun. **2**

"On reaching this bridge, even night becomes day, for this Brahma-loka is ever illumined."

Therefore when one is sound asleep, composed and serene, so that he knows no dreams, then he enters into (the space of the heart) through these arteries. Then no evil touches him, for then he is filled with light of the sun. **3**

Now, when one is reduced to a near-death condition, those who sit around him say, 'Do you know me? Do you know me?' As long as he has not departed from this body, he knows them. **4**

But when he departs from this body, then he proceeds upwards through these very rays; (if a knower) he surely goes up meditating on *Om*. As long as it takes for the mind to travel, in that (short) time, he goes to the sun. That indeed is the door to the world (of *Brahma*) for the knowers; it is closed for the ignorant. **5**

There is this verse about it:
A hundred and one are the arteries of the heart. One of them leads up to the crown of the head. Passing upward through that, one attains immortality, while the other arteries serve for departing in various other directions – yes, they serve for departing. **6**

Section 7

'*Atman*, which is free from evil, free from old age, free from death, free from sorrow, free from hunger and thirst, whose desire is for truth, whose resolve is for truth – that should be sought, that should be understood. He who finds and who understands that *Atman*, he attains all worlds and fulfils all desires.' Thus spoke *Prajapati*. **1**

Both gods and demons heard this and said, 'Well, let us seek that *Atman* by which one attains all worlds and fulfils all desires'. Then Indra alone was selected from the gods and Virochana from the demons. Without communicating with each other, they both came into the presence of *Prajapati*, fuel in hand. **2**

For thirty-two years they lived there the disciplined life of celibate students of sacred knowledge. Then *Prajapati* asked them, 'Desiring what have you been living thus?' They replied: 'The *Atman* which is free from evil, free from old age, free from death, free from sorrow, free from hunger and thirst, whose desire is for truth, whose resolve is for truth, that should be sought, that should be understood. He, who finds and who understands that *Atman* attains all worlds and fulfils all desires.' These are the words of your revered self. Desiring that *Atman* we have been living thus. **3**

Prajapati said to them, 'The person who is seen in the eye is *Atman*'. He added, 'He is immortal. He is fearless. He is *Brahman*'. 'But, revered sir, he who is perceived in water and he who is perceived in a mirror, which of these is He?' 'He is perceived in all these,' replied *Prajapati*. **4**

Section 8

'Look at yourself in a pan of water, and whatever you do not understand of *Atman*, tell me that'. Then they looked in a pan of water. *Prajapati* asked them, 'What do you see?' They replied. 'Revered sir, we both see the self of ours as a reflection in its fullness, from top to bottom, from hair to tip of nails (of toes).' **1**

"The person who is seen in the eye is Atman..... He is immortal. He is fearless. He is Brahman."

Then *Prajapati* said to them, 'Having become well adorned, well dressed and well groomed, look again into the pan of water.' They, having become well adorned, well dressed and well groomed, looked again into the pan of water. Then *Prajapati* asked them, 'What do you see?' **2**

They replied, 'Just as we are ourselves, revered sir, well adorned, well dressed and well groomed; even so are these, revered sir, well adorned, well dressed and well groomed'. 'This is *Atman*', said he, 'He is immortal. He is fearless. He is *Brahman*'. They both went away satisfied in their hearts. **3**

Then *Prajapati* looked at them and said, 'They are going away without having understood *Atman*. Whosoever will follow such a doctrine, be they gods or demons, they will fall'. Now, Virochana, satisfied in his heart, went to the demons and declared this doctrine to them, 'In this world, the (bodily) self alone is to be worshipped, to be attended upon. It is only by worshipping the self and attending upon the self that one obtains both worlds, this as well as that.' **4**

Therefore, even to this day, in this world people say of one who is not a giver, who has no faith, who does not perform sacrifices, 'Oh, he is a demon'; for this is the doctrine of demons. They adorn the body of even the deceased with enjoyable things, clothes and ornaments; by this, they think they will win the other world. **5**

Section 9

But Indra, even before reaching the gods, saw a difficulty. 'This (reflected self) becomes well adorned, well-dressed, well groomed when this body is well adorned, well dressed, well groomed; even so, this (reflected self) also becomes blind when the body is blind, one-eyed when the body is one-eyed, crippled when the body is crippled; it perishes when this body perishes. I see no good in this.' **1**

He came back again, fuel in hand. *Prajapati* asked him, 'Desiring what, O Indra, have you come back, since you went away satisfied in your heart, along with Virochana?' Indra replied, 'Revered sir, this (reflected self) becomes well adorned when this body is well adorned, well dressed when the body is well dressed, well groomed when the body is well groomed. Even so, this (reflected self) also becomes blind when the body is blind, one-eyed when the body is one-eyed, crippled when the body is crippled, and it perishes when this body perishes. I see no good in this.' **2**

'So it is indeed, O Indra', said *Prajapati*; 'However, I shall explain this further to you. Live here for another thirty two years'. He liv__ed__ there for another thirty two years. Then *Prajapati* said to him: **3**

Section 10

Prajapati said, 'He who moves about adored in dreams, He is *Atman*. He is immortal. He is fearless. He is *Brahman*'. Indra went away satisfied in his heart. But even before reaching the gods, he saw a difficulty. 'True, this (dream-self) is not blind when the body is blind, nor one-eyed when the body is one-eyed, nor it suffers from the defects of the body, nor it is slain when the body is slain, nor it has running nose and eyes when the body has running nose and eyes. Yet it is as if they kill it; as if they chase it; it becomes conscious of pain, as it were; and it even weeps, as it were. I see no good in this'. **1-2**

"Prajapati said, 'He who moves about adored in dreams, He is Atman.
He is immortal. He is fearless. He is Brahman.'..."

He came back again, fuel in hand. *Prajapati* asked him, 'Desiring what, O Indra, have you come back, since you went away satisfied in your heart?' He replied, 'Revered sir, this self is not blind when this body is blind, nor one-eyed when the body is one-eyed, nor suffers from the defects of the body, nor is slain when the body is slain, nor has running nose and eyes when the body has running nose and eyes; yet it is as if they kill it, as if they chase it, it becomes conscious of pain, as it were, and even weeps, as it were. I see no good in this'. 'So it is indeed, O Indra', said *Prajapati*, 'However, I shall explain this further to you. Live here for another thirty-two years'. He lived there for another thirty-two years. Then *Prajapati* said to him: **3**

Section 11

Prajapati said, 'He who is fully asleep, composed, serene and knows no dream, He is *Atman*. He is immortal. He is fearless. He is *Brahman*'. Indra went away satisfied in his heart. But even before reaching the gods he saw a difficulty: 'In condition of sleep one does not know oneself as "I am so and so", nor indeed these beings. It seems as if one has gone into annihilation. I see no good in this'. **1**

He came back again, fuel in hand. *Prajapati* asked him, 'Desiring what, O Indra, have you come back, since you went away satisfied in your heart?' He replied, 'Revered sir, in truth this one does not know himself as "I am so and so", nor indeed these beings. It seems as if one has gone into annihilation. I see no good in this'. **2**

'So it is indeed, O Indra', said *Prajapati*; 'However, I shall explain this further to you and there is nothing else besides this. Live here for another five years'. He lived there for another five years. That makes one hundred and one years. So with regard to this, people say thus: 'Verily, for one hundred and one years Indra lived with *Prajapati* the disciplined life of a celibate student of sacred knowledge'. Then *Prajapati* said to him: **3**

Section 12

'O Indra, mortal indeed is this body, held by death. But it is the seat of this deathless, bodiless *Atman*. Verily, the embodied Self is untouched by pleasure and pain. Surely, there is no cessation of pleasure and pain for one who is embodied. But pleasure and pain do not indeed touch one who is bodiless. **1**

Air is bodiless. White cloud, lightening and thunder – these also are bodiless. Now as these arise out of yonder *Akash*, reach the highest light and appear each with its own form; even so this serene one rises out of this body, reaches the highest light and appears in his own nature. He is the Highest Person. He moves about, laughing, playing, rejoicing with women, vehicles or relatives, not remembering (the mortality of) this body in which he is born. As an animal is attached to a chariot, even so *Prana* is attached to this body. **2-3**

Now, the eye is only an instrument for seeing; the Person who sees through the eye whatever exists in space, He is *Atman*. The nose is an instrument for smelling; the Person who is conscious of smell is *Atman*. Tongue is an instrument for speaking.

"He who is fully asleep, composed, serene and knows no dream, He is Atman.
He is immortal. He is fearless. He is Brahman."

The Person who is conscious of his speech is *Atman*. Ears are instruments of hearing; the Person who is conscious of hearing is *Atman*. **4**

He who says, 'Let me think this', is *Atman*. The mind is his divine eye. Through this divine eye, he sees all objects in which the mind rejoices. **5**

Verily, this is the *Atman* whom the gods worship. All worlds and all desired objects are held by It. He obtains all worlds and all desired objects, who having known this *Atman*, meditates on It'. Thus spoke *Prajapati*. Yes, thus spoke *Prajapati*. **6**

Section 13

From the dark I attain the multicolored, from the multicolored I attain the dark. Shaking off evil as a horse shakes his hairs, shaking off the body as moon frees itself from the mouth of Rahu, I shall attain the world of *Brahman,* after leaving this body and achieving my purpose. Yes, I shall attain it. **1**

Section 14

Verily, That which is formless like space, That which manifests name and form within space, That is *Brahman*. That is immortal, That is *Atman,* May I attain the assembly-hall and abode of *Prajapati*. May I become the glory of *Brahmins*, the glory of *Kshatriyas*, the glory of the *Vaisyas*. I wish to attain that glory. May I become the glory of glories. May I never go to that which is reddish-white and toothless, yet devouring and slippery. Yes, may I never go to it. (May I become free from rebirth in a womb). **1**

Section 15

Brahma expounded this to *Prajapati*, *Prajapati* to Manu and Manu to his descendants. **1(a)**

He who has read the Vedas according to prescribed rules; who after performing his duties to the teacher and returning from teacher's house, and settling in his household, continues to study the Veda in a clean place; who has virtuous sons and disciples; who withdraws all his senses into *Atman*; who practises non-injury to all beings except in places specially ordained; who behaves thus throughout his life; he reaches the world of *Brahman* and does not return again. Yes, he does not return again. **1(b)**

Peace Invocation

Om.
May my limbs, speech, life-breath, eyes, ears, and senses grow in strength.
All existence is *Brahman* of the Upanishads.
May I never be unaware of *Brahman*.
May *Brahman* never spurn me.
May there be no ignorance of *Brahman*.
May the Truths stated in the Upanishads repose in me.
Delighting in *Atman*, may they repose in me.

Om. Shanti. Shanti. Shanti.
Let there be Peace, Let there be Peace, Let there be Peace.

"He obtains all worlds and all desired objects, who having known this Atman, meditates on It."

General Commentary by Klaus G. Witz

SPIRITUAL CENTER OF MAN

Dahara Vidya deals with knowledge of Self in the heart. It complements and particularizes the 'five sheaths' *vidya*. Together, the two *vidyas* form a unified complex of high-level teachings, which represent one of the major thrusts of Upanishadic wisdom as a whole.

The importance of *Dahara Vidya* lies in part in its teaching of *Dahara Akash*, or a subtle space in the heart. Sometimes it is also called *Antar hridaya Akash*, or space within the heart. *Dahara Vidya* says that in the course of spiritual evolution, the subtle space within the heart becomes *Atman*, which contains all things and all desires. This *Atman* is free from old age, death, sorrow, hunger and thirst. It inspires true desires and true resolve. It is without any sin.

The conception of *Brahman* as transcendent but still dwelling in the center of the individual is a fundamental doctrine of the Upanishads.

At the most general level, the text says that *Atman* is in the heart. 'Heart' here means something like one's spiritual center, something in which and from which higher feelings and knowledge arise. So the basic teaching is that *Atman* is in the inner center of oneself. More specifically, there is a subtle (very small) space in oneself. By appropriate inner evolution, this can be realized to be the immortal *Atman*, which contains all things and all desires.

In many religions, philosophies and literatures all over the world, heart is considered the seat of manifestation of the Divine, or a symbol of the Divine, or Divine Itself.

The statement that *Atman* 'contains all things and all desires' implies that human soul is in some sense omniscient. It suggests the possibility that specific forms of omniscience may manifest in individuals. This has some resonance with Plato's *anamnesis* and *alayavijnana* of Buddhism. Similarly, the teaching that, *Atman* is *Satyakama*, (true desire, which is always fulfilled) suggests man's direct participation in everything at the cosmic or universal level. This is also implied in *Bhuma Vidya* and *Gayatri Vidya*.

The text says: 'As far as this space here extends, so far extends the space within the heart.' The words suggest more than a certain parallelism. They allude to both 'expansive' and 'experiential' aspects of the universe being contained in the subtle space. At the same time the space in the heart has certain timeless aspects.

Then comes a famous series of eight attributes traditionally accepted as describing *Atman*:

- with sins destroyed
- without old age
- without death
- without sorrow
- without hunger
- without thirst
- of true desires (*Satyakama*)
- of true resolve (*Satya sankalpa*)

This is the high point of the teaching (8.1).

SYMBOLIC SIGNIFICANCE OF HEART

The heart in the Upanishads is regarded as the center of spiritual qualities. It is also the center of *buddhi* or inner intelligence, higher feelings like compassion, inner perception of truth, knowledge of what is the right path to take, etc. All these come into play when one tries to make decisions on the basis of one's conscience, and when one contemplates how to lead one's life.

MEDITATION

Meditation in *Dahara Vidya* has the form of thought that the Supreme is within one's heart, or one's heart is the Supreme. Also, the Supreme should be meditated upon as possessing the aforesaid eight qualities. This has been discussed at length by Ramanuja.

In the Upanishads, *upasanas* typically include injunctions to the effect that such and such should be regarded as, worshipped (*upas -*) as *Brahman*. The aphorism means that whatever one intuitively understands as *Brahman*, in meditation that should function as a part of *Brahman*. Ultimately, it is *Atman/*

'The conception of Brahman as transcendent but still dwelling in the center of the individual is a fundamental doctrine of the Upanishads.'

Brahman that is the basis of a person's inner determination to reach the Supreme Divine. That is what one is in reality. Meditation only serves to enable that aspect to emerge more purely and clearly. Meditation uses as support attributes like 'without sin', 'controller of all', etc. because these are the semantic garb in which aspirants' intuitions of *Brahman* are already flowing. These attributes should be used together, because the basic principle is to allow the Inner Supreme Divine to flourish in Its totality.

According to Swami Nikhilananda of Ramakrishna order:

'For the beginner, heart is the physical organ shaped like a lotus bud. Inside it there is a subtle, luminous space which is often described as *Brahmapuri*, the Abode of *Brahman*. As the aspirant makes progress in meditation and becomes capable of subtle perceptions, he realizes that heart denotes not really the physical organ but *buddhi*, inner intelligence. At this stage, meditation is raised from the physical to the psychic level. The devotee casts the Absolute, as it were, in the mould of his mind and fashions out of it a mental image of *Brahman*. Finally he transcends both the heart and the mind and realizes *Brahman*, the all-pervading Consciousness, in his inmost Consciousness. The image in the heart and the reflection in intellect (*buddhi*) become one with Universal Consciousness.

Meditation may be associated with or conditioned by a sound-symbol or a form-symbol.

In meditation associated with a sound-symbol, the aspirant repeats a Vedic aphorism like, 'I am *Brahman*' (*Aham Brahmasmi*), and also reflects on its meaning. The sound ultimately leads to silence.

In meditation associated with a form-symbol, the form ultimately leads to the ineffable experience of the Formlessness.'

Swami Ananyananda gives four stages in meditation.
i) Detaching mind-space (*chitta akash*) from the external surroundings, thereby creating an inner space where we can install our chosen Deity or some other object of meditation, and be without distraction.
ii) I-consciousness moves into *Dahara Akash*, space in the heart, and shines there in its own effulgence, as *Jivatman*.
iii) Soul becomes aware of a vaster state of existence and of its real nature as a part of *Paramatma*, the Supreme Being.
iv) Effort of *Jivatman* to transcend its limitations and attain union with *Paramatma*.

FIRMAMENT OF THE HEART

Some spiritual masters translate *Dahara Akash* as 'sky of the heart' instead of 'space within the heart'. Sri Satya Sai Baba writes:

'Yogis who are turned away from the objective world can attain *Brahman* in the pure clear sky of their hearts. The worlds are fixed as spokes of a wheel in the hub of *Brahman*. Decline, decay and death do not affect *Brahman*. Since It can achieve whatever It decides to, It is called *Satyakama* and *Satya sankalpa*.

This is the Truth that all aspirants seek. Attaining it, they get the status of emperors. They can travel wherever they like. A yogi who is established in *Brahman* sees all desires that dawn in his heart as expressions of that Truth only.'

FIVE TYPES OF SPACE

In later Vedanta there is a teaching involving five types of space, *Akash*. These correspond to different levels of spiritual development.

Ghata Akash: Pot space or space inside the pot
Jala Akash: Sky reflected in water
Dahara Akash or
Hridaya Akash: Sky reflected in the heart
Chitta Akash: Sky of Pure Consciousness
Mahat Akash: The Great Sky

Sky is known by several names, such as *Akash*, *gagan* and even *shunya*, meaning nothingness.

Ghata Akash: Pot space is the state that says, 'this body is I'.

Jala Akash: This is a reflected space in which one makes some distinction between the body and the Self – like, 'there is a pain in my stomach' – but Self remains chained to subtle body.

Dahara Akash: Here, one is aware that one is looking

'As the aspirant makes progress in meditation, he realizes that heart denotes inner intelligence.'

at a reflection. When the reflection is hurt physically by anybody, the injury is not felt by the object; but when the image (like a photograph) is insulted or abused by anybody, then the object also feels hurt.

Chitta Akash: This is a state in which a man just observes without being upset or influenced by emotions, even if the body is insulted or abused. The pot may be broken, the pond may run dry, the canvas may be torn to sheds, but that *Akash* stands there. The sky contained in the pot, the sky reflected in the pond, and the sky painted on the canvas only refer to the media, but not to the sky itself.

Mahat Akash: In this state, all the activities of the senses are arrested and consciousness is devoted entirely to that higher or transcendental state.

In conclusion, *Dahara Akash* has two interpretations. In the orthodox approach it is the inner space which develops in meditation on a spot or region in the heart or the chest. In the second approach, it is like the sky of spiritual awareness. My personal feeling is that the difference between the two approaches tends to diminish, if not vanquish, as spiritual life develops. The first gets absorbed in the second.

OMNISCIENCE

At Memo 81 a ff., when dealing with theory of recollection or *anamnesis*, Socrates suggests that a man's soul can get knowledge and understanding about something by recollecting what it has been before; for "It is immortal and it has been born many times." This is explained by verses 8.1, 2-3: 'Within it (space within the heart) indeed are contained heaven and earth, fire and air... all that is contained within it.' It implies that Self is always in a state of knowledge of everything. Hence Plato's intuition of *anamnesis* can be regarded as equivalent of *Dahara Vidya*.

From the proposition that human soul is in a state of knowledge at all times, it follows that in some cases human soul can manifest omniscience while in this world. In traditional Western philosophies and religions, omniscience appears almost only as an attribute of God. But in many Indian philosophies and religions, and also in Taoism, it is regarded as a capability – latent or potential – in human beings as well. It has also been manifested by a few great spiritual personalities in history. This, however, is an under-researched subject.

SATYAKAMA, SATYA SANKALPA

The word *satyakama* means true desires. These are different from normal desires, which are covered with what is false, or which are tainted with selfish motives. And then comes an example: longing for a deceased loved one, wanting him back. This involves something untrue. One knows that one cannot get a dead person back.

A person's desires are all in his or her heart. However, normally these involve aspects, which are untruth: sense-longing, dependence, self-importance, self-interest, etc. There are in the heart 'true desires', which lie covered with tainted desires. For example, true love is like a pure reality, which is not affected whether the object of love is present or not present.

True desires, *satyakama*, take the form of a true resolve, *satya sankalpa*. These tend to ultimately get fulfilled. Sri Satya Sai Baba explains it as follows:

'In our spiritual practice, the first thing we have to do is to deepen and steady our faith. God (*Atman/Brahman*) is all-pervading and He knows everything. So when our faith is steady, the essence of the spirit that flows out of our mind will be very near to God. Because God comes out of our heart in the form of speech, we must make our speech as pure as possible. God is also a form of Truth. So, whatever we will be telling through our speech, God will say: Let it be so.'

According to Sri Sankara, *satyakama* and *satya sankalpa* are natures of *Brahman/Atman*. However, they also refer to realities of spiritual life. These realities are glimpsed only vaguely at first, but they tend to become stronger and dearer as time goes on.

In the Upanishads, *Atman* is described mostly in terms of Consciousness, Existence or Bliss. Here *Atman* and benefits of Its knowledge are described in terms of desires and actions (resolve). Each *vidya* makes its own specific and special contribution to illumining the Infinite *Atman/Brahman*.

Verse 8.3.4 represents a higher level of description of *Atman* than in 8.1.5. Phrases like 'reaching the highest

---

'In the Upanishads, Atman is described mostly in terms of Consciousness, Existence or Bliss.
In Dahara Vidya, Atman is described in terms of desires and actions (resolve).'

light' and 'appears in his true nature', go beyond the straight forward description, 'free from evil, ageless', etc. in 8.1.5. They suggest a climax, something like "merger in the Supreme Light."

MAN'S CONNECTION WITH COSMOS

In verses 8.4,1-2 I have no clear intuition about what *setu* (bridge) might mean here.

In 8.5 the term *Brahmacharya* carries the traditional connotation of Vedic study, combined with inner and outer chastity and the disciplines that accompany it. But it also involves complete and selfless dedication to *Brahman*.

The text in 8.6 describes the relationships between the channels of the heart (*hita*) with (i) sun, (ii) deep sleep and (iii) process of dying. The text draws a grand picture of how a person's life and soul are connected to the sun through its rays. Sun's rays are connected with heart's channels; they are also the conduits by which Self goes to sun after death. The message is: 'Man's inmost essence is contiguous and of one piece with the sun. Also, as sun's rays are all-pervading, the connectivity which unites man and sun pervades and encompasses the entire cosmos.'

INFINITIZATION OF SELF

Both *Panchakosha Vidya* (five sheaths) and *Dahara Vidya* lead to a point at which there is 'Infinitization' of the individual Self. This infinitization takes place (temporarily) in deep sleep. Further, two meditative paths are identified to attain this infinitization; Meditation on Self, and meditation on Its symbol Om. Both these paths are of great importance. I believe that with inner guidance, both these can still be practiced by a modern aspirant or a devotee, even today.

– *Klaus G. Witz*

RENDITIONS

8.1-8.6 Meditation on Self within

The rendition here is in the form of a dialogue between a seeker of the Divine and his Preceptor. The original text has not specified any names.

Seeker : I want to practice meditation. Can you please tell me what to meditate upon?

Preceptor : Yes, I will tell you. You know *Brahmapuri*, meaning the City of God? That is your body itself. In this City, there is a small lotus-shaped mansion located in the heart. In this mansion, there is a small inner space, *antar akash*. Within that space is *Atman*. Try to seek and understand that *Atman*. Meditate upon that *Atman* (8.1, 1).

Seeker : What is in that small inner-space that I should try to seek and understand?

Preceptor : That inner space is not small in the arithmetical sense. Whatever exists in the vast space outside, all that also exists in the small inner space inside. Heaven, earth, fire, air, sun, moon, lightening, stars – whatever you can see and whatever you cannot see in this world – all that is inside the small inner space (8.1, 2-3).

Seeker : This sounds mysterious. What happens when the body perishes? When the container is destroyed, what happens to the contents? (8.1,4)

Preceptor : Dear Friend, the heart which I am speaking of is not the physical heart. It is a symbol used for the center of Consciousness. *Atman* that you are in search of is nothing but Consciousness. Obviously, Consciousness must also be located in the body, though it is not confined to the body alone.

This *Atman* is free from evil, old age, death, sorrow hunger and thirst. It is *satyakama, satya sankalpa*, meaning Its desire is for the real, the Truth; Its resolve is also for the real, the Truth.

Seeker : I do not follow what you mean by *satyakama, satya sankalpa*.

'This Atman is free from evil, old age, death, sorrow hunger and thirst. It is satyakama, satya sankalpa, meaning Its desire is for the real, the Truth; Its resolve is also for the real, the Truth.'

Preceptor : It means that the more we go deeper and inward into our *Atman*, the greater is the purity of our desires, as also the strength of our will-power. When our desires, will-power and Consciousness are in harmony with universal Truth, greater is the possibility of eventually achieving success.

Seeker : In important decisions of life, what should be given importance: the voice of *Atman* within, or the compulsions of external circumstances?

Preceptor : Let us discuss this question with an analogy. External factors are like commanders. The more dependent we make ourselves on external factors, the less is our freedom of action. Also, very often the results of our deeds – be it for fulfillment of our desires or struggle for a righteous cause – are limited.

When faced with conflict between 'external compulsion' and 'inner voice', like the subjects of a king, we surrender ourselves to 'external compulsions'.

What happens when we begin to understand *Atman* within? The more we go into the depths of our Consciousness, the more we are in harmony with the external world as well. When we know *Atman* very well, there is no conflict between its inner voice and the external circumstances. The question of internal and external does not appear when there is harmony between the two. We realize that the law of *Atman* is also the law of the universe. Therefore, there is absolute freedom of action for those who know this secret.

When we come to know *Atman*, we also discover the interconnectedness of everything in the universe. When this is discovered, the externality of objects falls away; and the distinction between the subject and the object ceases. This is true fulfillment of all desires.

Thus, says the Upanishad, for a person who does not know *Atman* – and therefore he also does not know his true desires – there is no freedom either in this world, or in the next world. But he who knows *Atman* gets all his true desires fulfilled, and enjoys full freedom, both in this world and in the next world (8.1, 5-6).

Seeker : How can all desires be fulfilled?

Preceptor : I did not say 'desires', I said 'true desires', *satyakama*. A true desire is that which is for universal good and also in harmony with the inner voice of *Atman*. The Sanskrit word for truth is *satya*. Truth is the capacity to visualize things as they are in themselves, untruth is that which obstructs vision.

Seeker : You mentioned earlier about 'this world' and 'next world'. Why can we not see people in the next world?

Preceptor : There is really no such thing as this world and next world. There is only one vast continuum of experience. The distinction of this world and next world arises on account of the varying densities of Consciousness, which appear to cause different levels of experiences.

Recall earlier I had mentioned that whatever is outside is also inside, in the caverns of the heart. Now, I go a step further and say that all those people who have passed from this world – those who are born and those who are not yet born – they are all in our hearts. They are in our Consciousness (8.3, 1).

Seeker : But then, why we cannot see them?

Preceptor : We can experience their presence if we dive deep into our Consciousness, *Atman*. They cannot be experienced in a world of intense physical and bodily awareness. Let me explain this with an example. A person may be walking over a treasure, not knowing that there is a treasure underground. Similar is the case with us.

'Truth is the capacity to visualize things as they are in themselves, untruth is that which obstructs vision.'

We carry treasures in our hearts without being aware of them. (8.3, 2)

This *Atman* is the heart itself. Truth is inside us. One who knows that the heart is the abode of Truth attains the highest heaven, the highest state of Consciousness. (8.3, 3)

When a person rises above body consciousness, there is a serenity of experience. He feels as if something new has come into his life. When consciousness is freed from bodily attachment, it rises upwards, as it were, like a flame of brilliance. It is experienced as supreme luminosity, Light of lights, *param jyotir*. When one attains this state of supreme luminosity which is one's real nature, one is established in one's Self, *Atman*. It is Immortal. It is fearless. It is Brahman. And another name for Brahman is Truth (8.3, 4).

Seeker : What is the etymological meaning of the world *satyam,* translated as Truth?

Preceptor : The word *satyam* has three syllables *sa, ti,* and *yam.* The first syllable *sa* stands for what is immortal; the second *ti* stands for what is mortal; the third syllable *yam* holds the first two together.

The immortal *sa* is Consciousness, the mortal *ti* is Matter. Both these are held together by *yam* which is *Atman* (8.3, 5).

Seeker : How does *Atman* hold Consciousness and matter together?

Preceptor : *Atman* is like a bridge between Consciousness and Matter. It is not touched by time, old age, death, sorrow or evil (8.4, 1).

Even a blind man becomes free from the evil of blindness the moment he crosses this bridge, which is called *Atman.* Wounded ones are no more wounded there; and grieved ones have no grief there. There is no night there, but only eternal light. That is *Brahma-loka,* the highest state of Consciousness.

Seeker : How can this state of Consciousness, called *Brahma-loka,* be attained?

Preceptor : It requires living a disciplined life of a student, popularly called *brahmacharya* (8.4, 2).

Seeker : What is *brahmacharya*?

Preceptor : The word *charya* means conduct. So, *brahmacharya* is the conduct of *Brahman.* To live like *Brahman* is *brahmacharya.*

Sacrificial rituals and worship are part of *brahmacharya*. A special practice called *Sattrayana* is also *brahmacharya*; and so is the practice of silence and fasting.

There are certain mystical experiences, which are also a part of *brahmacharya*. For example, it is said that in the heavens there are two oceans filled with nectar – *Ara* and *Nya*, representing this world and that world – which come together in a fraternal embrace.

There is also a lake *Airammadiya*, filled with exhilarating nectar, and a tree that showers nectar. This is the invincible city of *Brahma,* which cannot be entered by those who have not known *Atman*. It is invincible because it is not physical. In it there is a hall specially built by the Lord. These mystical descriptions refer to different exhilarating experiences of Consciousness through which we pass when we get separated from the relative world and come nearer and nearer to the Absolute, *Brahman* (8.5, 1-4).

Seeker : How does the soul travel from this world to that world, *Brahma-loka*?

Preceptor : Well, it is like this. There exist certain psychic nerve currents inside us, known as *nadis*. These are filled with a very fine

---

'When a person rises above body consciousness, there is serenity of experience.'

fluid, so to say, of same colors as sun's rays. Just as a highway connects two villages, so the sun's rays connect the sun with living beings on earth. Thus, there is a real connection between the sun and us – through sun's rays and our *nadis* (8.6, 1-2).

It is these nerve currents, *nadis* that are responsible for the withdrawal of mind into itself in deep sleep (8.6, 3).

A person is said to be living as long as he is conscious of things around him, as long as there is Consciousness within. When Consciousness, *Atman*, leaves the body, It proceeds upwards through the rays of the sun. If a person is spiritually advanced, he recites Om, a symbol of *Brahman*, at the time of death.

The sun, according to the Upanishad, is the transit point for the soul on its way to *Brahma-loka*. Pure Consciousness proceeds ahead from the sun to the Absolute, *Brahman*. Consciousness which is not fully pure is sent back, as it is not prepared for ascent to the Absolute (8.6, 4-5).

To conclude, the heart has 101 principal psychic nerves, *nadis*. One of these, called *susumna*, leads to the crown of the head. At the time of death, if one's *Prana* exits the body through this *nadi*, one attains immortality. If the exit is through any other orifice in the body, then there is rebirth.

Seeker : Salutations to you, Revered Teacher. You have explained to me very well that *Atman* which resides in my heart is in fact the whole universe. Also, I now understand that when a person dies, this *Atman*, which is really Consciousness, can either become one with *Brahman*, the Absolute; or manifest Itself in another body.

– *Editor*

8.7-8.12 One teaching, two interpretations.

All of us have a mix of good and bad qualities. In the Upanishads, those who are predominantly good are called *Deva*, meaning the shining ones; those who are predominantly bad are called *Asura*. This rendition brings out the contrast between them.

Once, *Prajapati*, the Creator, addressed a joint assembly of both Devas and Asuras on what is *Atman*, Self.

Prajapati : *Atman* is that which is not affected by evil, old age, death, sorrow, hunger and thirst.

Atman is *satyakama*, *satya sankalpa*. This means that Its desire is for the Real, the Truth; Its resolve is for the Real, the Truth. It is this *Atman* which should be investigated into. It is this *Atman* which should be known. Why? Because he who investigates and understands this *Atman*, attains all the worlds and fulfils all his desires (8.7, 1).

(Later, both Devas and Asuras met separately.)

Devas : What *Prajapati* said looks worth pursuing. If by knowing *Atman* we can attain all the worlds and fulfil all our desires, let us find out more about it. We hereby nominate our leader Indra to go to *Prajapati* to learn more about *Atman*; and then teach the same to us.

Asuras : Let us seek that *Atman* by which we can attain all worlds and fulfils all our desires. We hereby nominate our leader Virochana to go to *Prajapati* to learn more about *Atman*; and then teach the same to us.

(Both Indra and Virochana went to *Prajapati*. As per the ancient custom they carried sacrificial fuel in their hands, signifying that they were prepared to live the disciplined life of a disciple; and they did so for thirty-two years.)

Prajapati : What is it that you want to know for which you have lived here for thirty two years?

'When a person dies, this Atman, can either become one with Brahman, the Absolute; or manifest Itself in another body.'

Indra and Virochana :	In your address to our joint assembly 32 years ago, you had told us a few things about *Atman*. We want to know more about It.
Prajapati :	It is simple. The person who sees through the eye is *Atman*. It is Immortal, It is Fearless. It is *Brahman*, the Absolute Ultimate Reality.
Indra and Virochana :	We don't understand. Take an example. When we look in water or in a mirror, we see our reflection. Is that *Atman*?
Prajapati :	Yes, *Atman* is perceived in both. Go, look yourself in a pan of water and tell me what you do not understand?
	(Indra and Virochana did as told.)
Prajapati :	What do you see?
Indra and Virochana :	We see our reflection exactly as we are – right up to our hair and nails (8.8, 1).
Prajapati :	Now dress up, groom yourself very well, and look again in the pan of water.
	(Indra and Virochana did as told.)
Prajapati :	What do you see now?
Indra and Virochana :	We see our reflection, exactly like us - well adorned, well dressed, and well groomed.
Prajapati :	This is *Atman*. It is Immortal. It is Fearless. It is *Brahman*, the Absolute, Ultimate Reality.
	(Both Indra and Virochana went away looking satisfied.)
Prajapati (to himself):	Poor fellows. They are going back without having fully understood *Atman*. They have mistaken *Atman* for the person *that is seen,* while *Atman* is the person *that sees*. They have also overlooked my statement that *Atman* is Immortal and Fearless, *Atman* is *Brahman*, the Absolute, Ultimate Reality.
	(Later, in the assembly of the Asuras)
Virochana :	I have understood what is *Atman*? It is the body itself. It is through the body alone that we can fulfil our desires and also control all the worlds. So, we must look after our body very well. We should make it strong and healthy, and as beautiful or handsome as possible. Material possessions for bodily pleasures should be the goal of our life.
	(And, on his way to the assembly of the Devas)
Indra (to himself):	Can the body be *Atman*? If that is so, *Atman* is well dressed when the body is well dressed, *Atman* is well groomed when the body is well groomed. By this logic, *Atman* will be blind when the body is blind, *Atman* will be crippled when the body is crippled. Certainly, this cannot be so. I shall go back to *Prajapati* and clarify my doubt (8.9, 1).
	(Indra goes back to *Prajapati* with fuel in hand.)
Prajapati :	What brings you back here?
Indra :	I do not understand how the body can be *Atman*? The body is perishable, and you said *Atman* is Immortal. What is the truth?
Prajapati :	It is a great mystery. To understand it, you will have to live here like a student for another thirty two years.
	(Indra did as advised. Thirty two years later)
Prajapati :	Indra, have you ever seen a dream?

'They have mistaken Atman for the person that is seen, while Atman is the Person that sees.'

Indra : Yes, I have dreamed many times during my sleep.

Prajapati : That which moves about happily in dreams is *Atman*. It is Immortal. It is Fearless. It is *Brahman*, the Absolute, Ultimate Reality.

(Indra goes back, looking satisfied. But again)

Indra
(to himself): *Prajapati* says that Self which roams about in dreams is *Atman*. True, the dream-self is not affected by the defects of the physical body; yet dreams are not free from pain, grief and unpleasant experiences. Surely, these will affect the dream-self. Let me go back to *Prajapati* and clarify the position (8.10, 1-2).

(Indra goes back to *Prajapati* with fuel in hand.)

Prajapati : What brings you back once again?

Indra : I do not follow how Self which roams about happily in dreams can be *Atman*. It is True that dream-self is not affected by the defects of the body. However, you said *Atman* is Fearless, and at times dreams can be very frightening. So, how can dream-self be *Atman*?

Prajapati : This again is a great mystery. To understand it you will have to live like a student for another thirty-two years.

(Indra did as advised. Thirty two years later)

Prajapati : Come here, Indra. Did you sleep well?

Indra : Yes, I had a sound sleep.

Prajapati : *Atman* is that which is serene, composed and does not experience any dream when a person is asleep. It is Immortal. It is Fearless. It is *Brahman*, the Absolute, Ultimate Reality.

(Indra went back, feeling satisfied. But again on his way)

Indra
(to himself): In the state of deep sleep, one does not even know that one is sleeping. Deep sleep is complete annihilation. How can that which is not conscious of anything be *Atman*? Let me go back to *Prajapati* and clarify the position.

(Indra goes back to *Prajapati*, again with fuel in hand.)

Prajapati : What brings you back, Indra, for the fourth time?

Indra : I find even your last explanation no good. How can that be *Atman,* which in state of deep sleep does not know itself or other beings? How can something – which itself seems to get annihilated in deep sleep – be *Brahman*, the Ultimate Reality?

Prajapati : This is again a great mystery. To understand it you have to again live as a student, but this time, only for five years. You would have then spent 101 years in my *ashram*. But then you will be able to understand *Atman* completely.

(Indra did as advised. Five years later)

Prajapati : Let us resume our discussion of *Atman*. This body, which is mortal, is only the dwelling place of *Atman*, which is Immortal. Only in its embodied state, *Atman* experiences pleasure and pain, and that also as a witness. Pleasure and pain do not touch *Atman* when it is not embodied. *Atman* is not in any way or at any time affected by pleasure or pain (8.12, 1).

Indra : I am a little confused about the relationship between the body and *Atman*. Please explain a little more, O, Revered Father.

Prajapati : Let me explain the relationship with some examples. As a first example, think of sky.

'Atman is not in any way or at any time affected by pleasure or pain.'

It is formless and shapeless; but at times it takes the shape of clouds, lightening and thunder. They appear from the sky and then vanish into the sky. The sky remains the same. Like clouds, lightening and thunder, our bodies also appear and then vanish. Like the sky, *Atman* is Immortal. Sky, or more appropriately, space is the ultimate reality of physical phenomena like clouds and lightening. *Atman* is the ultimate Reality of all, including space.

As a second example, consider a chariot. Notice, how a chariot is yoked to an animal and driven by it. Likewise, *Atman* is attached to the body in the form of *Prana*, Life force (Also see Katha 1.3, 3-6).

When *Atman* is not yoked to a body, It enjoys indescribable freedom and serenity. Two of the many words used to describe this state are: Light of lights, *Param Jyotir*, and Highest Person, *Uttam Purusha*.

Indra : Revered Teacher, what did you mean when in our first meeting you said that *Atman* is the person who sees through the eye? Remember Virochana and I saw the reflection of our body in water and thought that was *Atman*.

Prajapati : Yes, both of you focussed on the object and ignored the subject. The body or its reflection is the object of seeing. The eyes are the instruments of seeing. But the subject, the real seer is *Atman*. When you look at the sky, your eyes do the seeing, but *Atman* is the seer. When you smell a flower, your nose does the smelling, but that which smells through the instrument of nose is *Atman*. When you speak, your voice does the speaking, but the real speaker is *Atman*. When you listen to music, you listen through the ears, but the real listener is *Atman*. When you say, 'I see', 'I speak 'I listen' etc., that 'I' is *Atman*.

Indra : But I thought the senses owed their functioning to the mind. Where does *Atman* fit in?

Prajapati : A good question. Let me try to explain the difference between mind and *Atman*.

Atman is what you might call Consciousness. This Consciousness pervades the mind in all its states – waking, dream and deep sleep. Consciousness is the power behind the mind. Mind is an instrument of Consciousness, just as senses are instruments of mind. Mind cannot function without Consciousness. Mind is like the 'divine eye' (*devam chakshu*) of *Atman*. This divine eye perceives an object in its totality, whereas the senses perceive it in parts - the eye sees the form, the ear hears the sound, and so on. In fact, in *Brahma-loka*, there are no senses, only Pure Consciousness.

Indra : What is *Brahma-loka*? Is it a physical world like the earth?

Prajapati : No, *Brahma-loka* has nothing physical about it. Remember I told you *Atman* is Consciousness. This Consciousness can exist in many states, each state signifying a certain level of intensity. Consider the phenomena of light or sound. Light and sound are waves of different frequencies. Human eyes and ears are capable of comprehending light or sound within certain frequencies only. What is beyond human comprehension is called 'infra' or 'ultra'. The same applies to Consciousness. *Brahma-loka* represents a higher level of Consciousness than *Atma-loka*. So, you see, *Brahma-loka* is not something far away, or something which is accessible only after death. *Brahma-loka* is present right here even in this room. You can experience it only if you prepare your mind – the 'divine eyes' – to be able to comprehend the high level of Consciousness, which *Brahma-loka* represents.

Indra : Thanks very much indeed, Revered Teacher. I think I have now understood what is *Atman*. But may I ask you a question, if you do not mind? Why did you

---

'Consciousness is the power behind the mind. Mind is an instrument of Consciousness, just as senses are instruments of mind.'

make me wait here and live a life of austerity for 101 years, before imparting this knowledge about *Atman*?

Prajapati : There was a reason for it. Knowledge about *Atman* cannot be attained in one dose. It is acquired only step-by-step. The first step is a proper conditioning of the mind. Thereafter, my first instruction was about the physical body. Virochana stopped after the first instruction, because he thought that the visible part of our existence alone is *Atman*. But this is only one aspect of *Atman*. To understand *Atman* fully, one must turn one's mind inward and practice meditation. He will then realize the spiritual significance of dream and deep sleep states, and eventually understand what is *Atman*.

Indra : Yes, now I understand what you meant when you said: *Atman* is Immortal. *Atman* is Fearless. *Atman* is *Brahman*, the Absolute, Ultimate Reality. If I may add, *Atman* is Consciousness.

– Editor

Focussed Commentary

8.13-8.15 Ecstasy of Self-realization

In this verse, *Atman* speaks to Itself, as it were: I shall reach the Supreme.

The first part of verse 8.13, 1 has been interpreted differently by various commentators. None can understand what these words mean, if they are translated grammatically. Some interpretations are:

- From gross I go to the subtle and from the subtle I go to the gross.
- From *Ishvara* I go to *Brahman* and from *Brahman* to *Ishvara*.
- From the universal I go to the cause thereof, and back to the universal.

All these are exclamations of joy as the Soul is about to enter *Brahma-loka*. It first shakes-off all evil. Like a horse shaking-off dust, It frees itself from the body. This is analogous to the mythological account of moon freeing itself from the mouth of Rahu, which symbolizes the darkness of a lunar eclipse. *Atman* then attains *Brahma-loka*, the Supreme Abode of the Creator, and becomes one with Him (8.13, 1).

The space that we see is the cause of differentiation of name and form. But what is the cause of space? That is *Atman-Brahman*, the Immortal.

Then, there is the exclamation of a liberated soul: I have entered the abode of *Prajapati*, the Creator, and become the glory of everyone! (8.14, 1).

Knowledge about *Atman* has come down from one generation to the next through Teacher–Disciple tradition, *guru-shishya parampara*, and not through books. (8.15, 1a)

The concluding passage relates to the duties of a householder: study and teaching of scriptures, bringing up family, meditation and non-violence. A householder is advised to practice these throughout his life (8.15, 1b).

In Vedic scriptures, life is divided in four stages:

1. *Brahmacharya* - Study
2. *Grahasthya* - Householder
3. *Vanaprastha* - Gradual withdrawal from worldly life
4. *Sanyas* - Asceticism

There is often a misconception that spiritual life needs to be lived only during the last two stages. This is refuted here. The whole of one's life should be lived in such a way that it is a preparation for Life Eternal.

– Miscellaneous Sources

'The whole of one's life should be a preparation for Life Eternal.'

Kena Upanishad

Evolution of Matter-Life-Mind

OVERVIEW

Kena Upanishad starts with a fundamental question: What drives the sense organs, life and mind in human beings? It first calls the driving force simply as 'That', and then declares: 'Know That to be Brahman'.

The main theme of Kena Upanishad is that Brahman or universal Consciousness cannot be perceived by the senses or reasoned by the mind. It can be only experienced intuitively through meditation – like a flash of lightening. This is explained in three different ways:

- Uplifting passages. These are a beautiful blend of philosophy and poetry. For example: 'There the sight does not travel, nor speech, nor mind....'
- A paradox of spiritual knowledge. Brahman is that which is known, and also not-known. Consciousness has two aspects – Relative and Absolute. Relative is known, Absolute is not-known.
- A parable. Agni and Vayu – symbolizing Matter and Life – are asked by an Unknown spirit to burn and move a blade of grass, but they both fail. When Indra – symbolizing mind – approaches the spot, the Unknown disappears. A beautiful lady symbolizing Nature then explains that the Unknown was Brahman, or Consciousness, which sustains Matter, Life and Mind.

Kena Upanishad defines Brahman as 'That Delight' whose awareness makes one loved by all.

COMMENTARIES

Commentary by Sri Aurobindo is the most insightful of all commentaries on Kena Upanishad. Other commentators quoted in the text are: Dr. S. Radhakrishnan, Swami Chinmayananda, Swami Sivananda, N. A. Nikam, Rohit Mehta and Paul Deussen.

According to Aitareya Upanishad, Matter, Life and Mind have emanated from Consciousness. In his very far-sighted commentary on Kena Upanishad, Sri Aurobindo states that these represent stages in evolution, and that evolution is not yet complete. He foresees the evolution of a Super-mind from Mind; just as Mind has evolved from Life, and Life has evolved from Matter.

KENA UPANISHAD
Evolution of Matter-Life-Mind

Peace Invocation

1, 1-8   What drives the senses, life and mind? 487

2, 1-5   Paradox of spiritual knowledge ... 488

3, 1-4.3   Parable of three gods 489

4, 4-9   *Brahman* is 'That Delight' which spreads love 492

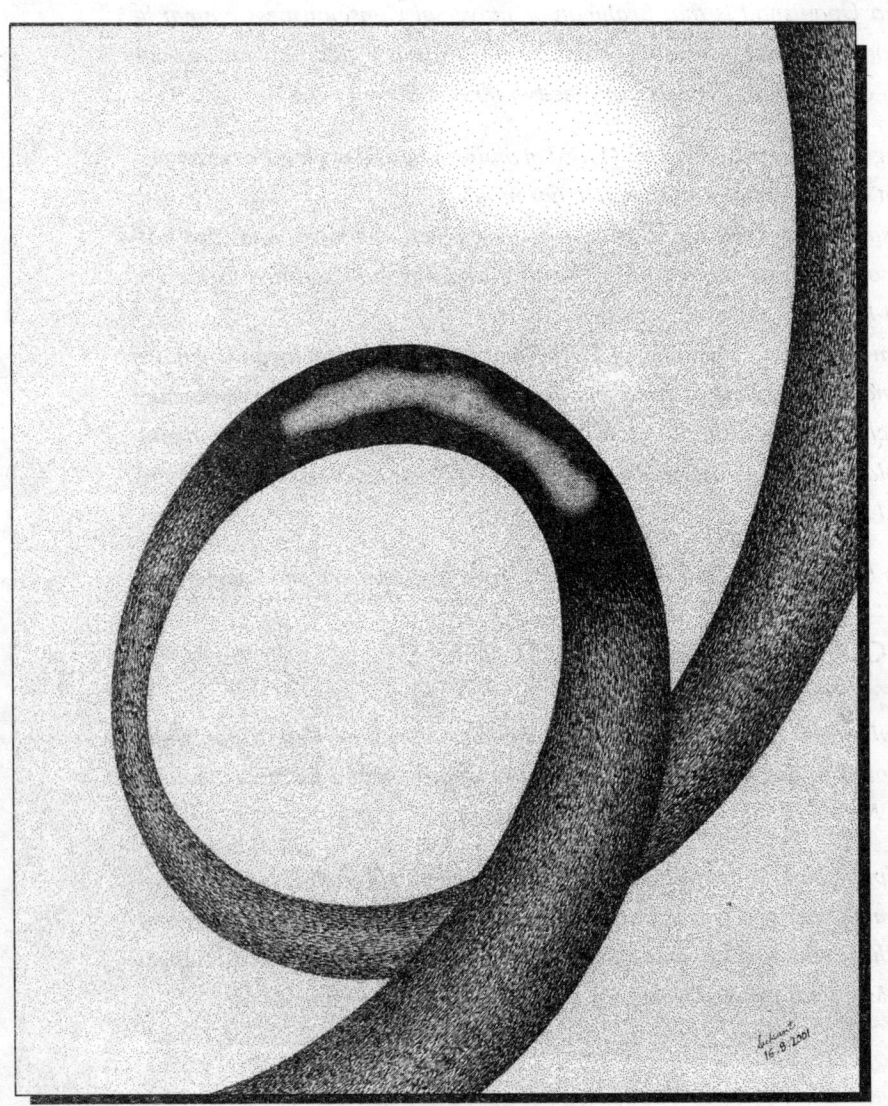

473

| **Sections 1-4** | # Evolution of Matter-Life-Mind |

SIMPLIFIED SYNOPSES

Kena Upanishad has no chapters, only four sections.

**1, 1-8
What drives the senses, life and mind?**

Kena Upanishad starts with a very fundamental question: What is it that drives the mind, the life-breaths and the sense organs like speech, sight and hearing? It then says that the power, which makes the body function, is called Mind of mind, Life of life, Speech of speech, Sight of sight and Hearing of hearing. It is something, which cannot be perceived by our organs of perception, imagined by our mind or expressed in words. It is different from what is known to us and beyond what is unknown to us. It is that by which the mind thinks but which cannot be 'thought of' by the mind; that by which the eyes see, but which cannot be seem by the eyes; that by which the ears hear, but which cannot be heard by the ears; that by which life breathes, but which cannot be breathed by life. It is that power – called *Brahman*, Cosmic Consciousness or the Absolute – which should be adored, and not this world of relativity which men normally adore.

'It is That by which the mind thinks but which cannot be 'thought of' by the mind.'

The eight brief verses of this section have attracted many lengthy commentaries on their meaning. Commentary by Sri Aurobindo is particularly noteworthy. He writes that Matter, Life and Mind represent progressively evolving states in the cosmos; but these are not our real Self. They are instruments of our becoming, and not our real being. It is *Brahman* Consciousness, which drives our senses, life and mind. *Brahman* Consciousness, according to Sri Aurobindo, is the eternal outlook of the Absolute on the relative. Mind is the cognitive aspect of *Brahman* Consciousness. Science has established interchangeability of Matter and Energy. The Upanishad, according to Sri Aurobindo, seeks the origin of Mind in Energy. Sri Aurobindo also predicts that just as Life evolved from Matter, and Mind evolved from Life, a Super-mind will evolve from Mind.

Mind communicates with the material world through the senses. Also, it reacts to material objects not directly but through Life Force, *Prana*. Therefore, all perceptions involve three steps – material images, energy images and mental images. These are not obvious to us because they take place at a lightening speed.

'A Super-mind will, evolve from Mind.'

Matter comprises of subatomic particles. These, according to string theory of modern physics, are effects of different patterns of vibration of strings. Thus, Matter contains instincts of Life. The Sanskrit word *Prana* has a much deeper spiritual meaning than physical Life Force. It is not just a variant of matter-energy of physics. It is a Cosmic Principle which supports all physical matter and physical forces – electromagnetic and gravitation, strong and weak. It also supports our mind. So by Yogic practice it is possible to control the working of the mind and to transcend its ordinary operations.

> *'Human mind is only an instrument of Cosmic Consciousness, Brahman.'*

Mind, according to the Upanishads is infinite. We know that a large part of our physical action is directed not by the surface mind, but by a larger subconscious mind. Phenomena like telepathy and ESP suggest that mind can perceive even without the use of physical eyes or ears. Human mind is only an expression – an instrument of Cosmic Consciousness, *Brahman*. The senses, in turn, are the instruments of human mind.

The Upanishad declares: 'Know That to be *Brahman*, and not this which men adore here? One commentator cautions that this should not be construed as a statement against worship of deities. Worship of an image is the starting step in the spiritual path. Slowly, we should superimpose all the attributes of the Lord in the image, and gradually widen our vision to see God in every object.

Another commentator writes that when we are preoccupied with the world outside us, we see God as a supernatural power. In meditation, however, God is revealed in the inner depths of our life.

2, 1-5
Paradox of spiritual knowledge

The first three verses of Section 2 seem very confusing but they contain profound wisdom about real knowledge and pretence of knowledge.

The Absolute is an object of intuitive realization, and not of empirical knowledge. Therefore, the belief that 'I know *Brahman*' is an erroneous notion. However, to be aware that '*Brahman* cannot be known' reflects the highest state of knowledge to which the mind can go. In the words of Socrates: 'I know that I do not know'.

> *'Unless Brahman is realized, human life will be a great waste.'*

According to another commentator, only the relative manifested aspect of *Brahman* can be known, and not Its Absolute Unmanifested aspect.

Our waking hours represent only about two-thirds of our life experiences; states of dream and deep sleep make up the remaining one-third. The Upanishads emphasize it time and again that in our attempts to know *Brahman*, we must take into account the totality of all our experiences in all the three states. *Brahman* is known rightly only when It is known as a witness in all the three states of the mind – waking, dream and deep sleep (verse 4).

Verse 5 emphasizes that unless *Brahman* is realized in this life itself, human life will be a great waste. *Brahman* is not attained by abandoning life on earth.

3, 1-4, 3
Parable of three gods

A seemingly childish story of this section hides profound wisdom.

Once, when three deities – *Agni*, *Vayu* and *Indra* – were feeling proud of their accomplishments, an unknown entity called *Yaksha* appeared before them. Aroused by curiosity, they sent *Agni* (Fire) to find out more about this unknown. Instead of revealing any thing about itself, the unknown challenged *Agni* to burn a small blade of gross. *Agni* failed to burn it and returned back without knowing who the unknown was. The same happened with *Vayu* (Air); it was not able to blow-off the small blade of grass. However, when *Indra* (Mind) approached the unknown to know more about it, the unknown simply

---

'Brahman is known rightly only when It is known as a witness in all the three states of the mind – waking, dream and deep sleep.'

> *'Agni, Vayu and Indra are equivalents of Matter, Life Principle and Mind, respectively.'*

disappeared. Instead, a beautiful lady, *Uma* appeared on that spot. She told *Indra* that the unknown was none other than the Absolute, *Brahman* Itself.

Commentators have provided some very enlightening interpretations of this story. All of them equate *Agni* (Fire), *Vayu* (Air) and *Indra* with Matter, Life and Mind respectively.

Sri Aurobindo writes that the deities are full of vanity. They see their greatness as their own and they proceed to demonstrate their power. *Agni* symbolizes the inter-convertible matter-energy of physics. *Vayu* symbolizes the Cosmic Life Principle. Without the blessings of the unknown *Brahman*, the Supreme Absolute, neither of them is able to accomplish even a very simple act like burning or moving a small blade of grass. *Indra* symbolizes the power of the Mind. Mind can grasp only that which exists in the relative Space–Time continuum. So when it approaches the Absolute for study, the Absolute simply disappears. But Mind does not turn back from the quest. It sees a beautiful lady *Uma*. *Uma* symbolizes Nature, the highest manifestation of the Absolute, *Brahman*. She alone has the knowledge of the Absolute, while the body-life-mind complex can grasp only the relative world of multiplicity.

According to Swami Chinmayananda, the failure of *Agni* and *Vayu* in their enquiry implies that Truth cannot be understood by sense organs. However, when Mind approaches the Absolute, the very vision of the Absolute disappears. At this juncture a rationalist, a logicians or a nihilist would have turned back to declare that *Brahman* is non-existent. However, Mind continues to gaze at the very spot from where the Absolute had disappeared. At such a moment of inner calmness and awakened awareness, there appears a beautiful lady, *Uma*. Born in the Himalayan caves of inner silence, she symbolizes the goddess of *Brahma Vidya*, knowledge of the Absolute. She tells Indra that the Unknown which appeared as the manifest *Yaksha* was the unmanifest Absolute Itself.

> *'Uma symbolizes the goddess of Knowledge of the Absolute.'*

The message in the character and ultimate success of Indra is that we should not be impatient in pursuit of knowledge of Absolute Truth.

Another commentator has interpreted the parable in terms of three attributes or *guna* of Nature: inertia, activity and equilibrium; or *tamas*, *rajas* and *sattva*. *Agni*, *Vayu* and *Indra* symbolize a Mind free from the limiting conditions of inertia, activity and equilibrium respectively. When Mind is free from these attributes, it comes face to face with 'nothingness'. This is a state of tranquility, free from all differentiation and symbolized by beautiful lady Uma. One meaning of Uma is Night. All differentiation vanishes in the darkness of Night. Uma is also the consort of Shiva. The trinity of Brahma, Vishnu and Shiva symbolizes the Unmanifest, the Manifest and the interval between Manifest and Unmanifest. So, this fascinating story says that vision of Absolute *Brahman* comes to an unconditioned empty mind in a state of deep silence.

4, 4-9
Brahman **is 'That Delight' which spreads love**

The vision of *Brahman*, the Absolute, is like a flash of lightening or a wink of the eye – it is momentary, natural and effortless. However, that moment has the richness of eternity.

'This fascinating story says that vision of Absolute Brahman comes to an unconditioned and empty mind, in a state of deep silence.'

> *'Our body-life-mind does not exist in isolation; it is a cosmic entity.'*

Verse-5 defines *Brahman* as 'That Delight' which spreads love. Verse-8 says that realization of *Brahman* as the Absolute Truth requires a life-style of austerity, restraint and selfless work.

What happens when one realizes the Absolute Truth? Sri Aurobindo has explained this at length. Our body-life-mind does not exist in isolation; it is a cosmic entity. When this fact is realized, we overcome our sense of separateness and begin to feel that our real body is the whole universe. We become one with the Formless, the Infinite. We see all the worlds not as external to us, but as within us. Our life becomes Superlife, our mind becomes Supermind. Eventually, our Self will ascend to the level of the Self of All. It is a state of eternal joy, transcendent Delight. One who has attained this state, sheds That Delight on all the worlds. He becomes a center of Delight.

The Upanishad says that Truth is the abode of *Brahman*. Truth refers to the ultimate state of Pure Consciousness. Truth is anything contrary to falsehood and egoism.

Kena Upanishad, according to Sri Aurobindo, suggests three progressively higher states of existence:

(i) Human Life.
(ii) Cosmic Consciousness and
(iii) Absolute, Immortal state.

Sri Aurobindo adds that in the Upanishads, the importance of individual salvation has been over-emphasized. However, just as lures of earth have to be conquered, so also lures of heaven. Practice of virtues must be without expectations of earthly or heavenly rewards. We must not seek a salvation, which deprives us of the opportunity to help others. The purpose of life should be twofold: to do good in this world and to attain the Supreme.

'The purpose of life should be twofold: to do good in this world and to attain the Supreme.'

Translated Text

Peace Invocation

Om.
May my limbs, speech, life-breath, eyes,
ears, and senses grow in strength.
All existence is *Brahman* of the Upanishads.
May I never be unaware of *Brahman*.
May *Brahman* never spurn me.
May there be no ignorance of *Brahman*.
May the Truths stated in the Upanishads repose in me.
Delighting in *Atman*, may they repose in me.

Om. Shanti. Shanti. Shanti.
Let there be Peace, Let there be Peace, Let there be Peace.

Section 1

What directs the mind to alight on its objects? What moves the life-breath forward on its path? What prompts the words that men speak? What god makes the eyes and the ears function? **1**

That, which is the Hearing of our hearing, Mind of our mind, Speech of our speech, Life of our life, and Sight of our sight. Having abandoned and rising above sense-life, the wise become immortal. **2**

There the sight does not travel, nor speech, nor mind. We do not know It, nor do we know how to explain It. It is different from what is known, and It is beyond what is unknown. Thus we have heard from ancient sages who taught us That. **3**

That which cannot be expressed by the word, but by which the word is expressed, know That to be *Brahman*; and not this which men adore here. **4**

That which cannot be thought by the mind, but by which the mind thinks, know That to be *Brahman*; and not this which men adore here. **5**

That which cannot be seen by the eyes, but by which the eyes see, know That to be *Brahman*; and not this which men adore here. **6**

That which cannot be heard by the ears, but by which the ears hear, know That to be *Brahman*; and not this which men adore here. **7**

That which is not breathed by life, but by which life breathes, know That to be *Brahman*; and not this which men adore here. **8**

"There the sight does not travel, nor speech, nor mind. We do not know It, nor do we know how to explain It."

Section 2

Preceptor: If you think that you know It (*Brahman*) well, you know It only a little. Whether It refers to you or to the gods, this also you have to enquire. **1**

Disciple: I think I know It (*Brahman*).

I do not think that I know It (*Brahman*) well, nor do I think that I do not know It. He who among us comprehends It both as 'Not-known' and 'Known', he alone comprehends It. **2**

Preceptor: To whomsoever It (*Brahman*) is not known, to him It is known. To whomsoever It is known, he does not know. It is not understood by those who understand It. It is understood by those who do not understand It. **3**

It (*Brahman*) is known rightly only when It is known through all (three) states of mind. By such knowledge one gains life eternal. By one's ego, one gains power; through wisdom, one gains immortality. **4**

If in this world one knows It (*Brahman*), then one truly is; but if he does not gain Its knowledge, there is a great loss. Seeing It in all beings, the wise pass forward from this world and become immortal. **5**

Section 3

Once *Brahman* won victory for the gods (sensory powers and mind). In the victory of *Brahman*, the gods attained glory. (However) they thought: "Ours is this victory. Ours is this glory." **1**

Knowing their conceit, *Brahman* appeared before the gods as an unknown Spirit (*Yaksha*), but the gods did not know what it was. **2**

They said to *Agni* (fire): "O Jataveda, you know all that is born. Please find out what this Spirit is?"
Agni said: "So be it." **3**

Agni rushed towards the Spirit. It said to him: " Who are you?"
"I am *Agni*", he said. "I am that who knows everything that is born". **4**

The Spirit: "If that is so, what power is there in you?"
Agni replied: "I can burn whatever there is on earth." **5**

The Spirit placed a blade of grass before him, saying, "Burn this".
Agni went towards it with all force, but could not burn it.
He then returned and said: "I have not been able to find out what this Spirit is." **6**

Then they said to *Vayu* (Air): "O *Vayu*, please find out what this Spirit is?"
"Yes", said *Vayu*. **7**

"He who comprehends It both as 'Not-known' and 'Known', he alone comprehends It."

Vayu rushed towards the Spirit.
The Spirit asked: "Who are you?"
"I am *Vayu*. I am that which moves everything on earth". **8**

The Spirit: "What power is there in you?"
Vayu replied: "I can blow-off whatever there is on earth." **9**

The Spirit placed before him a blade of grass, saying, "Blow this".
Vayu went towards it with all speed, but could not blow it off.
He then returned and said: "I have not been able to find out what this Spirit is." **10**

Then they said to *Indra*, "O Meghavan, please find out what this Spirit is".
"Yes". *Indra* said, and hastened towards the Spirit, but the Spirit disappeared from his view. **11**

At that very spot *Indra* saw a most beautiful lady, Uma, daughter of the Himalayas, and asked her: "What is this Spirit?" **12**

Section 4

She replied: "This is *Brahman*. You attained glory only through the victory of *Brahman*." From her words, *Indra* learned that It was *Brahman*. **1**

These gods – *Agni*, *Vayu* and *Indra* – surpass other gods, as they came very close to *Brahman*. **2**

Indra surpassed every one, because *Indra* came into closest contact with *Brahman*, and was the first to know that It was *Brahman*. **3**

About *Brahman*, here is an illustration. It is like a flash of lightening, like the winking of the eye. This is a description of *Brahman* relative to the gods (cosmic powers). **4**

Now a description relative to the individual. It is That towards which the mind appears to move and think, off and on. **5**

Brahman, the object of all desires, is what is called, 'That Delight'. One should adore It as 'That Delight'. He who knows It thus, is loved by all. **6**

Disciple: 'Sir, teach me the secret (Upanishad)'

Preceptor: 'The secret (of *Brahman*) has been taught to you. We have taught you the secret relating to *Brahman*.' **7**

Austerity, self-restraint and selfless work are Its support, the Vedas are Its limbs, and Truth is Its abode. **8**

He who knows this knowledge overcomes sin and is firmly established in *Swarga-loka*, the heavenly world. Yes, he is firmly established. **9**

"He who knows Brahman as 'That Delight' is loved by all."

Peace Invocation

Om.
May my limbs, speech, life-breath, eyes,
 ears, and senses grow in strength.
All existence is *Brahman* of the Upanishads.
May I never be unaware of *Brahman*.
May *Brahman* never spurn me.
May there be no ignorance of *Brahman*.
May the Truths stated in the Upanishads repose in me.
Delighting in *Atman*, may they repose in me.

Om. Shanti. Shanti. Shanti.
Let there be Peace, Let there be Peace, Let there be Peace.

General Commentary By Sri Aurobindo

ISA AND KENA

The principal Upanishads deal with just one subject – spiritual wisdom. However, they approach the subject from different angles. Each enters the great kingdom of *Brahman* or Consciousness by its own gate, follows its own path or detour, and aims at its own point of arrival.

For example, Isa and Kena Upanishads are both concerned with the same grand problem – the relationship between *Brahman*, Cosmic Consciousness and the universe; as also between Cosmic Consciousness and human Consciousness.

Isa closes with an aspiration for Supreme Happiness. Kena closes with a definition of *Brahman* as Supreme Happiness.

Oneness of all existences is the dominating theme of Isa. Kena limits itself to a narrower enquiry. It concerns itself only with the relationship of mind or human Consciousness with Cosmic Consciousness, or *Brahman*.

PURPOSE OF LIFE

The world for us is what our mind and our senses declare it to be. Life is what our mental instruments – the mind and the senses – perceive it to be. So the opening verse of Kena asks: 'What are these mental instruments? What drives them? Is body-life-mind all that there is in a living being; or is there some thing more profound behind it?'

"Yes, there is", says Kena Upanishad. Matter, Life and Mind represent progressively evolving states in the cosmos. Matter does not know life, but life emanates from matter. Life does not know mind, but mind knows life. Likewise, mind does not know That which is behind it, but That knows the mind. Stated differently, we have a more real existence than our body-life-mind; a greater life than the material life. It follows that material life – with all its forms and enjoyments, which we ordinarily pursue – cannot be the sole purpose of life for an awakened man. He must aspire beyond. He must know that he is Immortal and Eternal. This world is an inferior action, a superficial representation of something infinitely greater, more perfect, and more real.

What is that something? It is not the desires and the enjoyments of this world – which in any case men ought to seek and pursue. It is All-Bliss, *Brahman* Consciousness.

THREE COMPONENTS OF EXISTENCE

In the ancient Vedic conception of the universe, our material existence is formed from five elemental states of matter: Space (sky) Energy (fire), Gas (air), Liquid (water) and Solid (Earth). Everything that has to do with our material existence is called the elemental, *adhibhautic*.

In this elemental world, there are also non-material powers, which express themselves through the mind and through life force, *Prana*. In the Upanishads, these are called gods or *devas*. Everything that has to do with the working of the non-material in us is called *adhidaiva*, or that which pertains to the gods – Mind, Life force, five senses of perception and five organs of action. The *adhidaiva* is the subtle in us. It is represented by mind and life; as opposed to gross matter. In mind and life, we have the action of the gods.

Above the non-material powers, containing them, and bigger than them, is Self or spirit or *Atman*. Everything, which has to do with this highest existence, is called the spiritual, *adhyatma*.

To summarize, existence has three components:
adhibhautic : Material
adhidaivic : Subtle
adhyatmic : Spiritual

Kena Upanishad is not concerned with the material existence. It is concerned with the relationship between the subtle and the spiritual, *adhidaiva* and *adhyatma*.

Mind, life and the speech are governed by cosmic powers. These powers have been given proper names in the Upanishads.

Indra governs Mind.
Vayu governs Life.
Agni governs speech and other senses of perception.

'Material life – with all its forms and enjoyments – cannot be the sole purpose of life for an awakened man.'

What is it that sends forth mind on its 'errand'? Who guides it to its objects? Kena Upanishad attempts an answer to these questions.

FIVE FORMS OF *PRANA*:

Prana or life force is given much importance in the Upanishads. It is explained by using the metaphor of a horse yoked to the chariot of the gods, viz. the mind and the senses. Who has yoked this life force to the many workings of our existence? What is the secret power behind the mind, and the senses like speech?

In the body of man there are said to be five workings of life force, called the five *Prana*.

Prana (in-breath): It moves in the upper part of the body and is pre-eminently the breath of life, because it brings the cosmic life force into the physical system of man.

Apana (out-breath): It moves in the lower part of the body. It gives away the vital force out of the body and is therefore also called the breath of death.

Samana (equalizing-breath): It regulates the interchange of *Prana* and *Apana* at their meeting place and equalizes them. It is the most important agent in maintaining the equilibrium of vital forces and their functions.

Vyana (diffusing-breath): It distributes the vital energies throughout the body.

Udana (ascending-breath): It moves upward from the body to the crown of the head. It is a regular channel of communication between the physical life and the greater spiritual life.

WHAT DRIVES BODY-LIFE-MIND?

Prana, the life force in the nervous system, is indeed the main driver of life. All our five senses of knowledge and five organs of action are dependent on *Prana* for their functioning. Thus, it is because of *Prana* that the mind receives the contacts of the physical world and reacts upon its objects.

The five senses of knowledge, which act as instruments of mind to receive contacts of the physical world are: sight, hearing, smell, touch, and taste. The five organs of action, which act as instruments of the mind to react on objects of the physical world are: speech, hands, feet and organs of procreation and excretion.

The question is *Kena*? Kena means by whom or what? What drives the Mind, the Life and the Body?

We express the thought formations of our mind through speech. Speech is formed by *Vayu*, Life-breath. It is propelled by *Agni*, the fiery energy in the Mind-Body. But both *Vayu* and *Agni* are the agents. What is the secret power behind the words that we speak? The ears hear the sound. The eyes see the form. But hearing and vision are used by the Mind to communicate with the external world. Life force shapes them; Mind uses them. What is it That which sets the eyes and the ears to their working?

Kena Upanishad begins with an enquiry: What is the power that drives the Body, the Life the Mind, and the senses? This question turns our eyes away from the visible and the outward to that which is invisible and inward – a new world of realities. The Truth behind Mind, Life and senses is that which controls them by exceeding them. It is the Lord. This was the conclusion at which Isa Upanishad arrived by the synthesis of all existences. Kena Upanishad arrives at the same conclusion by a process of antithesis.

WHAT IS *BRAHMAN* CONSCIOUSNESS?

The Upanishad first affirms the existence of *Brahman* Consciousness, which drives our Mind, Life and senses.

Mind and body are not our real Self. Neither is ego our real Self. Neither is memory our real Self. Neither is moral personality our real Self. They are all instruments of our becoming, whatever we become. They are not our real being.

Behind all and dominating all that we become and experience, there is something which we cannot know unless we go behind the veil of our Mind. The Upanishad calls it: the Mind of our mind, the Sense of our senses, the Speech of our speech, the Life of our life – *Brahman* Consciousness in brief.

Obviously, *Brahman* Consciousness is not an object for our mind, senses, speech or life force. It cannot

---

'Our senses, Life and Mind are driven by Brahman Consciousness.' ..... (Adapted)

be seen, heard, expressed, sensed or thought with our existing faculties. It is not even dependent on our mind, life and senses for the exercise of Its lordship and activity.

Brahman Consciousness is the eternal outlook of the Absolute on the relative. Absolute *Brahman* in Itself is held to be unknowable, and therefore beyond description.

Brahman is unknowable because It is beyond our present instruments of knowledge and methods of learning. Its manner of being is different from that which we call existence. Its unity resists all analysis. Its multiple infinities exceed every synthesis.

POWER OF WORD

According to the Upanishads, all creation is an expression of Word – vibrations of primeval sound. *Brahman* Consciousness expresses Itself by Word – in forms which constitute the universe – just as human word expresses a mental image of these forms.

We know that vibrations of sound have power to create. The ancient Vedic literature extended this creative power of speech by chanting of *mantras*. The theory of *mantra* is that it contains a power conceived by a deeper Consciousness than the mental. After conception, it is held in the mind and then thrown out silently or vocally. A silent *mantra* is considered more potent than a spoken *mantra*.

A *mantra* can create new mental states in us, alter our psychical being, reveal our hidden knowledge or faculties. It can also produce similar results in other minds than that of the user. It can even produce vibrations, which can give rise to actions, effects or material forms on the physical plane.

In fact, man is constantly acting upon man and even upon the rest of Nature – both by silent and spoken words. The Vedic use of *mantra* is only a conscious utilization of the secret power of Word.

(Matter is the lowest plane of existence in the universe. Modern physicists have recently tried to explain the behavior of subatomic particles of matter through a string theory involving different patterns of vibrations.

Thus we see that the Upanishadic theory of cosmic creation by Word, and the theory of creation of matter by vibrations are two expressions of the same idea. – Editor)

Word has its seed sounds – A, U and M. It also has its rhythms. Life itself is a rhythm.

That which expresses speech in us and brings it out of our Consciousness is *Brahman*. *Brahman* is the Speech of our speech.

Speech is the expressive aspect of *Brahman* Consciousness.

EVOLUTION OF LIFE AND MIND FROM MATTER

Mind is the cognitive aspect of *Brahman* Consciousness. But what is the need for this theory of a cognitive principle, superior to Mind?

According to the theory of evolution upheld by science, man is only Matter that has developed a Mind by an increasing sensibility to the shocks of its environment. Thus, Matter being the basis of existence, there is nothing except the physical elements that can survive the dissolution of the body. But Matter could not develop a Mind unless there was already a principle of Mind striving towards self-expression. This principle must have been there before Mind evolved. Mind could not have possibly come into being from insentient substances.

Science has proved the interrelatedness and the interchangeability of Matter and Energy. The Upanishad seeks the origin of Mind not in Matter itself, but in the Energy which is at work in Matter. Mind is a concealed necessity, which Matter holds in itself.

SUPER-MIND: NEXT STAGE IN EVOLUTION!

As Matter contained Life in itself, as Life contained Mind in itself, so too Mind contains in itself that which is beyond itself – Super-mind.

What is the rationale for this inference?

Human psyche is composed of three principle elements – sensation, thought and will.

---

*'Science has proved the interrelatedness of Matter and Energy.
The Upanishad seeks the origin of Mind in Energy, which is at work in Matter.'*

Sensation is an attempt of Consciousness to seize upon its object and enjoy it. Thought is an attempt to seize upon the truth of the object and possess it. Will is an attempt to seize upon the potentiality of the object and use it. All the three represent an attempt, an imperfect attempt. Life is hampered by conditions of Matter. Mind is hampered by conditions of Life in matter. So, both have been compelled to call in a new principle - Matter to call Life into itself, and Life to call Mind into itself. Likewise, Mind also has to call in a new principle, which is beyond itself, more free than itself, and more powerful than itself. That principle is Super-mind.

Mind tries to arrive at Truth but succeeds in touching it only imperfectly, as there exists a veil between the mind and the truth. There is, say the Upanishads, a principle, called Truth-Consciousness, which sees the Truth directly without any veil in between. Another name for this principle is Bliss Consciousness, which corresponds to the eternal delight-giving quality of all experiences.

There is only one law, which remains valid from the lowest to the highest. Matter is found to contain instincts of Life, as is evident from the vibrations, movements, attractions, repulsion, and opposite charges of subatomic particles. So also, Life contains instincts of Mind. Mind too contains instincts of Super-mind. The Super-mind could be the final evolute out of matter. The Upanishad, however, enthrones it as an already existing creator and ruler of the Mind.

According to the Upanishads, the Super-mind has four distinguishing characteristics:
(i) It is beyond the reach of the mind and the senses.
(ii) It does not itself think with the mind.
(iii) It is that by which the mind itself thinks.
(iv) It is the nature – or description – of *Brahman* Consciousness.

Super-mind is beyond the reach of mind, speech and senses. Yet, mind, speech and senses are our only available means for acquiring and expressing knowledge. The Upanishad commands us to know this Super-mind, and by its knowledge possess it. Is there a contradiction of thoughts?

The Upanishad sets out by saying that this ruler of the mind, senses, speech and life is the Mind of our mind, Sense of our senses, Speech of our speech and Life of our life. It then explains what it means by these poetic phrases. But it also gives a warning. Neither mind, nor speech nor senses can travel to *Brahman*. Therefore by Its very nature, *Brahman* must be beyond these things. The Upanishad admits: "We neither know It nor do we know how to explain It". The reason for this inability is given next: "*Brahman* is other than the known, and It is beyond the unknown".

The means for attaining the Super-mind is to prepare the mind by admitting into it a working higher than itself. In this way, ultimately, the mind will give itself up to the Supra-mental action, which exceeds it; and which will finally replace it.

In fact, Super-mind also has to follow the law of natural progression, which has governed our evolution from matter into life, and from life into mind. Life consciousness is beyond matter. Mind consciousness is beyond the movements of life. Likewise, Supra-mental consciousness is beyond the mind. But matter is constantly prepared for the manifestation of life until life is able to move in it. Likewise, life is constantly prepared for the manifestation of mind until mind is able to use it. So it must be with Super-mind which is beyond the mind. And all this progression is possible because all these things – matter, life mind and Super-mind – are only different formations of One Being, One Consciousness, *Brahman* Consciousness.

Life reveals in matter all that is the essence of matter. Mind reveals in life all that is the essence of life. So also must Super-mind intervene to reveal mind to itself.

DIFFERENCE BETWEEN MIND AND SUPER-MIND

How does Super-mind differ from mind?

The supreme cognitive principle does not think by the mind. Mind is an inferior and secondary action, based on limitations and divisions. Super-mind is founded on an all-pervasive unity. Its action is in the universe. It is in conscious communion with a transcendent and eternal source beyond the universe.

Super-mind does not begin with an individual, or regard him a separate being. It starts from the transcendent, and sees the universe and the individual as they are in relation to the transcendent.

'Matter, Life Mind and Super-mind are only different formations of One Being, One Consciousness.'

Mind acquires knowledge and mastery by constant observation, experimentation, reasoning and willing. Super-mind already possesses knowledge and mastery. Mind gropes by divided sensation; Super-mind possesses a free and all-embracing sense. Mind arrives at a sort of oneness through sympathy; Super-mind lives in a unity of which love and sympathy are only manifestations. Mind starts from the parts and tries to extrapolate the whole. Super-mind starts from the whole, and the whole to it is only a fraction of the Infinite.

THREE SHEATHS OF CONSCIOUSNESS

As explained earlier, mind communicates with the material world through the senses. The objects sensed by us - vibrations of sound, light images of form, volley of odor containing particles, impression of *rasa* or sap that gives the sense of taste, or disturbances in our nerves which we call touch - all these represent contact of Mind with Matter. However, Mind operates upon Matter not directly, but through Life force. Life force is energy in our nerves, and not anything material. It can therefore seize Matter only through impressions. Mind takes these up and replies to them with corresponding mental values. So the objects sensed by us come to us after a process of three translations: material-images, energy-images and mind-images. This elaborate process is not obvious to us because of the lightening speed with which it is managed. In another notation of time by a differently constituted living being, each part of the operation might be distinctly perceptible.

The triple translations represent three sheaths of Consciousness in us – physical, life force and mental, or *annakosha, pranakosha*, and *manohkosha*. In the physical sheath, physical contact and images are received and formed; in the life force sheath, there is a contact with the nerves; in the mental sheath, there is mental contact and imaging. The experience of the material world has to pass through these three sheaths before it can reach us.

MIND IS INFINITE

According to modern psychologists, conscious operation of the mind is only a surface action. There is a much vaster and more potent subconscious mind. The subconscious mind loses nothing of what the senses bring to it. It keeps all its wealth in an inexhaustible store of memory. The surface mind may pay no attention, but the subconscious mind registers all that it receives with an infinite capacity. A man under anaesthesia and operated upon has felt nothing; but release his subconscious mind by hypnosis, and he will relate accurately every detail of the operation, and its appropriate suffering.

We also know that a large part of our physical action is instinctive and directed not by the surface mind, but by the subconscious mind.

The Upanishads declare that the mind in us is infinite. It knows what has been seen, and also what has not been seen; what has been heard and also what has not been heard; what has been discriminated and what has not been discriminated. While our surface mind is limited by our physical experiences, there is a larger sublime Consciousness within it, which is not thus limited. That Consciousness senses what has not been sensed by the surface mind and its organs; and knows what the surface mind has not learned by its acquisitive thought.

SENSATIONS ARISE FROM VIBRATIONS

Phenomena like telepathy and ESP provide evidence of capability in some persons to read the mind of others, or to sense things that exist only at a great distance. This suggests that senses can be employed even without the use of physical eyes or ears.

Scientific discoveries have proved that properties like color, light and sound are merely operations of force or energy of some kind. For example, color is energy in the form of light. Hearing is energy in the form of sound vibrations. Everything begins with vibrations, or movements. Without vibrations or movements in human consciousness, there can be no act of knowledge, and therefore no sensory perception. This is true of both our internal and external operations. I become angry by a vibration of some conscious force acting as nervous emotion; I feel the anger by another movement of conscious force acting as knowledge. All sensations are the same in essence – whether external or internal, physical or psychical.

'Mind acquires knowledge by observation, experimentation, reasoning and willing.
Super-mind already possesses knowledge.'

SPIRITUAL ESSENCE OF SENSORY PERCEPTION

In the highest *Brahman* Consciousness, all senses are a complex unity. *Brahman* Consciousness is not the Absolute withdrawn into Itself, but the Absolute in its outlook on the relative. It is the Lord, the Master Soul, the governing Transcendent, and All. It constitutes and controls the action of the gods (senses) on different planes of our being. Our senses are a shadow of the divine senses, our sight of the divine sight, our hearing of the divine hearing. Divine sight and divine hearing are not limited to physical things. They extend themselves to all forms and operations of conscious beings.

Brahman Consciousness does not depend upon what we call sight and sound for Its own seeing and hearing. It operates by a supreme sense – creative and comprehensive. Our physical and psychical sight and hearing are external results and partial operations of this supreme sense. In the Vedas, the supreme sense is described as the eyes of Vishnu, extended in heaven. It is that by which we see and hear. But we realize its true value when we go beyond the physical and the psychical senses to their spiritual essence. When we realize that, we will find that the whole world and everything in it is different, of a non-material value. *Brahman* Consciousness in us will still see and hear, but not for the satisfaction of desires. It will embrace the self-existent Bliss which has no cause, beginning or end; which is eternal in its own immortality.

SUPER-LIFE: LIFE OF OUR LIFE

Brahman Consciousness is more than Mind of our mind, Speech of our speech, Sense of our senses. It is also Life of our life. It is a supreme and universal energy of existence. Our own life and its sustaining energy are only a physical symbol, or a limited functioning of this universal energy. It is the superior cause and the supra-vital principle out of which our life is formed and controlled.

The Sanskrit word *Prana* has a much deeper spiritual meaning than the physical Life force. *Prana* is not a variant of the matter-energy of physics. It is a different principle, which supports matter. It acts in all material forces such as electricity. All material aspects are only fields and forms of *Prana*. *Prana* itself is pure energy. It cannot be detected by any physical analysis. It can, however be experienced through yoga. By yogic practice, we are able to distinguish the movements of *Pranic* currents not just in our physical body, but also in our subtle body. By *Pranayama* - a technique of yoga - the practitioner is able to control, suspend and transcend the ordinary operations of *Pranic* energy. He is also able to do things with his body, which seem miraculous to the ignorant. It is just as some scientific demonstrations look like magic to those who are ignorant of science.

Pranic energy supports not just our physical body, but also our mind. So by yogic practice it is also possible to control the working of the mind and transcend its ordinary operations, by activating certain nerve centres (*chakras*).

Prana is a cosmic energy present in every atom and particle of the universe. The characteristics of *Prana* as it manifests itself in us are desire, hunger, sensations and movement. Just as our mind is an inferior movement of Super-mind, our life is an inferior movement of Super-life, Life of life. *Prana* is the supreme energy, (*Tapas* or *chit-shakti*), the infinite force-in-action of *Brahman* Consciousness.

Cosmic Consciousness exists between two poles – one of stillness, and the other of infinite energy; one of pure unity, and the other of multiplicity. The stillness eternally supports movement. The unity eternally supports multiplicity. This is the Life of life, from which our life proceeds.

THE GREAT TRANSITION

The thought expressed in the first section of Kena Upanishad is that our body-life-mind are not the whole of our existence. They are an outer fringe, an inferior working of something beyond. The Upanishad does not assert the unreality, but only the incompleteness and inferiority of our present existence. It is the Lord of Isa Upanishad who inhabits all the creations and all the movements in the cosmos. Our life is a dual representation of That Lord, with two opposite elements in it – like the two poles of a magnetic field, negative and positive. The negative elements are death, suffering, strife, division and limitation. The positive elements are immortality, delight, unity, and infinitude.

'Cosmic Consciousness exists between two poles – stillness and movement, unity and multiplicity. Stillness supports movement, unity supports multiplicity.'

The passage to immortality is not attained by abandoning life on earth. It is here, in this mortal life and body that immortality must be won. The Higher *Brahman* must be known and possessed here, in the lower *Brahman*.

The Life force in us is led forward by the attraction of Super-life beyond the mortal life. Fear of death conceals something of immortality and infinity, which we have not yet achieved.

The worlds of which the Upanishad speaks are soul conditions, and not geographical divisions of the cosmos. In the material world, the soul dwells on the plane of material movement and experience. The soul that has realized immortality passes beyond all the worlds and enters into *Brahman* Consciousness. It transcends name and form by its ascent to One that is All. This victory, this immortality, it must achieve here as an embodied soul in the material world.

The way to achieve this is to open our mind to Cosmic Consciousness. We must know it through the world in which we live. For this, we must put aside what is mere form and phenomenon in the universe. Our first step must therefore be to get behind the forms of matter, forms of life and forms of mind, and go back to that which is the essences of All. When we go on analyzing and eliminating all forms into the fundamental entities of the cosmos, we shall find that the fundamental entities are really two - the gods and Self.

The gods of the Upanishad are synonymous with the senses, but they are much more than that. They represent the Divine Power in its cosmic functioning. Behind the gods is Cosmic Consciousness, or *Brahman*.

The other entity is our own Self. It is the same as *Brahman*.

So, what of *Brahman* is in the gods; and what of *Brahman* is in myself? The answer is evident. Self and the gods are one, *Brahman*.

By realization of *Brahman* as our Self, we attain the Divine Energy, which lifts us beyond the limitations and sorrows of our mortal existence. By the knowledge of One *Brahman* in all beings and in all movements of the cosmos, we attain infinitude beyond these things.

– *Sri Aurobindo (Abridged)*

Focussed Commentaries

Section 1

1, 1-8 What drives the senses, life and mind?

The eight mantras of this section are very elevating and inspiring. Their constant repetition, reflection and meditation will turn the mind inward.

Just as water in a cup draws it heat from sun, or from fire; so also the mind, the life force and the senses draw their power from *Brahman*.

Just as fire that burns other objects cannot burn itself, so also the mind which knows external objects through the avenues of the senses cannot know *Brahman*.

It is not possible to teach about *Brahman*. To define *Brahman* is to deny *Brahman*. *Sat-Chit-Ananda* or Existence-Consciousness-Bliss is only a provisional definition. That is why the sages explain *Brahman* through the doctrine of '*neti, neti*, not this, not this'.

Brahman is not what people worship on earth, such as *Ishvara* or other deities. This should not be construed as a statement against worship of deities. The Upanishad teaches an expanded form of worship.

Start your devotion with worship of an image. Superimpose all the attributes of the Lord in the image. But do not limit your devotion to that image alone. Widen your vision and see God in every object. Feel that the world is a manifestation of the Lord. The image will stimulate divine love in your heart, and ultimately lead to the realization of oneness of the world. The image is only a prop to lean upon in the beginning. Some ignorant people think that the image itself is the Lord. The Upanishads discourage this sort of worship.

– *Swami Sivananda*

Spirit cannot be objectified. The revelation of spirit is in the depths of one's life, and not in the objective world. When we are in bondage of the objective world,

---

'Start your devotion with worship of an image. Widen your vision and see God in every object. The image is only a prop to lean upon in the beginning.'

we look upon God as a great external force, a supernatural power who demands to be appeased. God is life and can be revealed only in spiritual life.

– S. Radhakrishnan

Kena Upanishad begins with the question: "Who is it that enables the mind to think, the life to function, the ears to hear, the eyes to see?" The answer is found by discriminating between the 'seer' and the 'seen', the changeless and the changing. The senses and the mind are in constant state of motion, but Self is a steady witness. Brain activity is possible only because of Consciousness, not vice-versa. All objective knowledge has its source in Self, the inmost light of Consciousness.

Supreme wisdom is to know that our conscious life is illumined at every moment by Light of all lights, the Truth of all truths – our own Self. Rightly does Kena Upanishad declare that *Brahman* is known when It is realized in every state of mind.

Brahman is the 'Life of life, Mind of mind'. This means that Consciousness is more fundamental than Life Principle. It is more important than psychic power.

– *Miscellaneous sources*

The Upanishad represents an enquiry – a deep enquiry – by the human mind into the fundamental problems of existence. A state of enquiry constitutes a healthy condition of the mind.

Enquiry is different from curiosity. Curiosity arises from a shallow and superficial mind. Enquiry emerges from the depths of human consciousness. A deep enquiry is concerned with three fundamental questions. How, Why, and What? Science is generally concerned with "How?" How things behave? Philosophy is interested to know, Why? But the Upanishads are not satisfied with 'How' and 'Why' alone. They want to find out: 'What is that which is behind all patterns and motivations of behavior?' In Kena Upanishad, the question is: 'What is that which impels and motivates particular modes and patterns of action?' The answer given by the Upanishad is: '*Brahman*.'

The Upanishad also says that to the functional faculties of bodily organs, *Brahman* remains intangible. *Brahman* is not what people adore; they adore the universe. What makes the universe alive is *Brahman*.

Kena Upanishad gets its title from the question that it asks: *Kena*, meaning 'By what?' It is a rare instance of a philosophical question becoming a name. It asks what directs the mind, the speech, the eyes and the ears to do their respective functions? The Upanishad distinguishes mind, life and senses. These do not function by themselves. So the Upanishad asks: 'What moves them?' It makes a distinction between the diversity of functions and the unitary reality that abides in diversity. That which the eye sees is the external world. As Katha Upanishad says, the senses are so pierced that they look only outwards. 'That' by which the eye sees is the power which makes the eye function. That is the Sight of our sight, the Speech of our speech, the Life of our life.

– N. A. Nikam

Section 2

2, 1-5 Paradox of spiritual knowledge

Brahman is not an object of perception. Knowledge of *Brahman* is intuitive Self-awareness. The belief that I know *Brahman* is an erroneous notion. The knower of *Brahman* knows fully well that *Brahman* is unknowable by the mind and the senses. It is realizable only through intuition, as one's own innermost Self, *Antaratman*. But he, whose conviction is that he knows *Brahman*, certainly does not know *Brahman*. He mistakes the body, mind and life as *Brahman*.

The strength gained by material wealth and power is produced by things which are themselves mortal. Such strength is external and transient. The strength gained by knowledge of *Brahman* is internal and eternal.

The hearts of the rich and the powerful are filled with fear. A knower of *Brahman* is absolutely fearless. He knows that his Self will not be affected in the least by external conditions. He can move the whole world.

– *Swami Sivananda*

The Supreme is not an object of ordinary knowledge, but of intuitive realization. If we think that we know *Brahman* and we can describe it as an object perceived in nature, or as the cause inferred from nature, we do not, in reality, know It. Those who feel that they do

---

*'Strength gained by material wealth and power is external and transient.
Strength gained by knowledge of Brahman is internal and eternal.'*

not and can not know It in this manner, do have some knowledge of It.

God is invisible from the excess of light. If anyone says he has seen God and understood what he has seen, then he has not seen God.

– S. Radhakrishnan

A man who says he knows *Brahman* well can at best have only a partial knowledge of *Brahman*. *Brahman* is the whole, and the whole is not arrived by just adding the parts. The whole is greater than the sum of its parts. That 'something' which renders the whole greater, is bound to be missed in all extrapolations.

Kena Upanishad is a conversation between the Teacher and his disciples. One of the disciples has been pondering over the answer given by the Teacher, and out of his reflections comes a very significant statement: 'I cannot say that I know *Brahman* well, nor can I say that I do not know Him'. What did the disciple know about *Brahman*? He knew the manifested aspects of *Brahman*; but manifestations are only a part of the Totality that is *Brahman*. The disciple must be complemented for this statement. To know what knowledge explains and to know also what knowledge does not explain - this is the highest state of knowledge to which the mind can go. The openness of the mind consists in simultaneous existence of knowing and not knowing.

– Rohit Mehta

Socrates said: "I know that I do not know." Kena goes a step further when it states not one but two conditions for enquiry: "I do not think that I know It well", and "I do not think that I do not know It" (2, 2). A person, who knows or thinks that he knows, will not enquire; nor he who does not know at all, and is not aware of his ignorance. He who enquires knows into what he should enquire. Kena begins with questions asked by an inquirer: 'What directs the mind? What moves the first life-breath?'

– N. A. Nikam

The preceptor here hastens to warn the disciple that if you think you know *Brahman* well, you are mistaken. The warning is probably because he could see in the face of the disciple a glow of satisfaction at his understanding of *Brahman*. What the preceptor has explained is only 'conditioned' *Brahman*, and not Absolute *Brahman*. Absolute Truth cannot be explained in words. Just as you cannot bring water without a vessel, so too, you cannot express Truth except through one of the many media of its conditionings (2, 1).

There is an entire drama packed in this single mantra (2, 2). First the disciple states that he does know *Brahman* well enough. But when he looks within, he feels that his statement is a lie. So he confesses 'nor do I think that I do not know'. He alone knows *Brahman* who understands both Its aspects – that which cannot be known, and that which can be known.

Verse-3 is a confirmation by the Teacher that what the disciple has stated in the previous verse is correct.

Absolute Truth, residing in us as Self (*Atman*), is 'known rightly' only when It is understood as the witness of the three states of Consciousness – waking, dream and deep sleep. A witness is one who is standing apart from the incident, without taking any part in it. That Absolute Truth, that witness is Consciousness.

Consciousness is separate from thought. One who realizes this becomes immortal, changeless. Change is in thought-flow, not in Consciousness (2, 4).

Pass forward from this world. It means, 'rise from sense-life.'

Built upon this line, and similar ones, we have two schools of thought among the Vedantins – one claiming that perfection cannot be achieved unless one leaves the physical body upon death (*videha-mukti*), and the other arguing that God-like perfection can be attained even while living (*jivan-mukti*). Sri Sankara advocates the latter view (*jivan-mukti*). Self-realization is possible here and now (2, 5).

– Swami Chinmayananda

Sections 3-4

3, 1-4, to 4,1-3 Parable of three gods

In the Upanishad, Matter, Life, and Mind are represented by three gods – *Agni* (Fire), *Vayu* (Air) and *Indra* (chief deity) respectively. The gods know

---

'*Consciousness is separate from thought*. Changes take place in thought-waves, not in Consciousness.'

themselves, but they do not know the Eternal. Therefore, full of vanity, they see their greatness as their own. They feel that they have conquered the world, and they proceed to demonstrate their power.

Then, *Brahman* manifests Itself before the exultant gods, but as an Unknown. The gods did not know what It was. So *Agni* got up first to find out Its identity.

Agni is the heat and the flame of energy in Matter, It is he who has made Life and Mind possible. He is called *Jataveda*, the knower of all births, all cosmic phenomena, and all laws of nature. Full of confidence, he rushes towards the object of his search and is met by the challenge:

"Who are you? What is your strength?"

Agni replied: "I am *Agni*, I can burn anything that is there on earth."

The Unknown put before *Agni* a blade of glass and said: "Burn this." But *Agni* could not burn it, and was compelled to return back without discovering who the Unknown was.

Life principle, *Vayu Matarishwan* rose next.

"Who are you? What strength do you have?" asked the Unknown.
"I am *Vayu*. I can move anything on the earth."

The Unknown put before *Vayu* a blade of grass, and said: "Move this." *Vayu* too failed and returned, without discovering the Unknown.

Indra stood up next. *Indra* is the power of the mind. But as soon as *Indra* approached the Unknown, It disappeared. The mind can envisage only that which exists within the limits of time and space; while the Unknown is beyond the limitations of time and space. So, when the mind tries to approach the Unknown for study, It vanishes from the view of the mind.

But *Indra*, unlike *Agni* and *Vayu*, did not turn back from the quest. He approached the radiant woman, Uma Hemavati who appeared there on the scene. From her, he learned that this Unknown was *Brahman*. By it alone the gods of Mind, Life force and Matter conquer and affirm themselves. By It alone they are great.

Uma is the supreme Nature from whom the whole cosmic action takes birth. She is the highest power of *Brahman*. She manifests herself in many forms. She has the knowledge and the consciousness of the 'One', while the lower nature of mind-life-body can only envisage 'the many'. No doubt, *Indra*, *Vayu* and *Agni* are great gods. However, we can know and possess Cosmic Consciousness only by coming into contact with *Brahman*, reflecting on Its nature, and eliminating the egoism of the vital-mental-physical. When we do so, Cosmic Consciousness reflects Itself in the gods. Its light takes possession of the thinking mind; Its delight takes possession of the struggling life; and Its power takes possessions of the material body. Something of Cosmic Consciousness falls upon worldly nature and changes it into divine nature.

All this is not done by sudden miracles. It comes by flashes and revelations. It is like lifting of the eyelid of an inner vision and its falling again. Repetition of these flashes and revelations fixes the gods in their upward gaze and expectation.

– *Sri Aurobindo*

Why did the teacher of Kena Upanishad relate this story? It seems to be a digression, but it is not. The story itself carries further the main topic under discussion.

What do *Agni*, *Vayu*, *Indra* and *Uma* represent?

Agni is the Lord of Fire. It is Fire, which releases the energy that is latent in all beings. This latent energy represents a condition of inertia, called *tamas*. In other words, fire releases the mind from the influence of inertia, *tamas* – one of the conditioning factors of the mind.

Vayu is the Lord of Air. It sweeps the sky with its power. It represents movement without conflict – freed from the influences of *rajas*. A mind freed from *rajas* is active; but its activity is devoid of conflict.

Tamas is a condition where mind is too lazy to differentiate between the right and the wrong. In *rajas*, there is a struggle between the right and the wrong. *Sattva* represents a temporary resolution of the conflict – and this results in self-righteousness. It gives the mind a sense of power – a feeling that it can keep the two opposites under control. A mind, which is ridden

---

'They do not know the Eternal. Therefore, full of vanity, they see their greatness as their own.'

by *sattva*, is afraid of soiling its so-called spiritual roles. While it gives, it does so with reservation. Indra represents that condition of the mind when it is freed from *sattva*. The name of Indra used in the Upanishad is Meghavan. This very name shows generosity. So, Indra represents the mind freed from the limiting factor of *sattva*.

Is the mind, freed from all its three attributes – *tamas, rajas and sattva* or inertia, activity and balance – able to comprehend the nature of the Supreme Spirit? Our story says that when Indra approached the Supreme Being, It disappeared from his gaze! There was nothing on the spot where the Supreme Being was seated a while ago. But into that 'nothing' came an exquisitely beautiful woman, Uma; and it was she who communicated to Indra the nature of Supreme Being. What does this signify?

The mind that is freed from all its attributes comes face to face with 'nothingness' – it faces emptiness. If at this stage, the mind gives 'emptiness' a name, then in a subtle manner it gets entangled once again in 'attributes'. Indra saw 'nothing', and then appeared Uma. If the mind had projected something in that emptiness then surely Uma would have not appeared.

But who is Uma and why does she appear? One of the meanings of the word Uma is Night. It also means tranquillity. Night also represents a state that is free from all differentiation. It is during the day that differentiation is seen. In the darkness of night, all differentiation vanishes.

Was Indra afraid of this silent emptiness? He was not, for he asked Uma about the nature of the Supreme Being.

The word Uma has another interpretation. In the Hindu trinity of Brahma, Vishnu and Shiva, Uma is the consort of Shiva. Brahma represents the discontinuity of the Unmanifest, Vishnu symbolizes the continuity of the Manifest. Shiva represents the interval between the Manifest and the Unmanifest. He is known as the Destroyer. He is the interval where the Manifest ends and the Unmanifest begins.

Kena Upanishad says that *Brahman* cannot be attained by thought, It comes to the thought. But when does It come? It comes only when the continuity of thought ceases – then It comes from the realm of discontinuity.

It comes only in that interval over which Shiva presides.

So, this fascinating story says that *Brahman* cannot be attained by thought. It comes to the thought of those whose minds have been freed from its three attributes of *tamas, rajas and sattva*. Vision of *Brahman* comes to an unconditioned empty mind, in a state of deep silence.

The Upanishad further says that the vision of *Brahman* comes like a flash of lightening – suddenly, instantaneously, out of the dark clouds. The flash of lightening vanishes as suddenly as it comes. It cannot be put in the framework of time. It cannot be continuous. Its appearance is so sudden that man is wonder struck. And It comes like a flash which shows very clearly the path that lies before man. The vision of *Brahman* pervades the entire being of man. He who has had a vision of *Brahman* cannot be the same person again.

– Rohit Mehta

Analogies, illustrations, comparisons and stories are often used in the Upanishads to explain to us the inexplicable. However, none of them can explain the Truth in its entirety. Each story needs a deep enquiry if the readers are to profit fully by it.

The seemingly childish story, when read as such, is but a skeleton. We must make an effort to grasp the inner essence of this narration in the Upanishad.

In order to understand the full depth of the story, let us recall how the manifest world was projected out of the Unmanifest *Brahman* – starting from the least gross to the most gross elemental matter. We should also recall that each element has its own special quality, besides the qualities of the proceeding elements.

The elements in ascending order of their emergence from the Unmanifest are shown hereunder.

Sanskrit	English	Quality
Akash	Ether	Sound
Vayu	Air	Sound + Touch
Agni	Fire	Sound + Touch + Sight
Jala	Water	Sound + Touch + Sight + Taste
Prithvi	Earth	Sound + Touch + Sight + Taste + Smell

'Vision of Brahman comes to an unconditioned empty mind in a state of deep silence; like a flash of lightening.'

In the Upanishads, the elemental powers and their qualities are called presiding deities, or gods.

The gods once won a victory over the demons with the blessings of the Supreme. Blinded by their success, they started gloating over their achievements. The Supreme, *Brahman* appeared before the gods in the form of an enchanting *Yaksha*, with a view to bless the gods again, by getting them rid of their vanity. The gods, in their immaturity, tried to meet the Supreme as an object, different from them. Both *Agni* and *Vayu* failed in their enquiry and returned back. The implied meaning is that Absolute Truth cannot be experienced as an "object" by the organs of perception and action. *Agni*'s miserable failure at burning even a thin blade of grass without the blessings of Eternal Self proves that the eye is blind without the Eye of eye. Similarly, *Vayu*'s failure proves that speech is dumb without the divine Speaker of speech.

In short, the despicable failure of *Agni* and *Vayu* is a restatement of the Upanishadic Truth described in verse 1.1, 3: 'It is different from what is known, and It is beyond what is unknown.'

Finally, the gods (senses) en mass approach their Lord, Indra. Indra is interpreted as *indriyanam raja,* the lord of sense organs, meaning the mind. And on mind's approach, the very vision of the Supreme disappears. At this juncture many aspirants would return back in haste to declare that *Brahman* is non-existent; the Rationalist, the Logicians and the Nihilists, for example. But Indra was not cowed down at the sudden and unexpected disappearance of the object of his enquiry. Full of hope, faith and a desire to know, Indra gazed at the very spot from where the vision had disappeared. At such a moment of inner calmness and fully awakened awareness, there appeared on that spot the wondrous lady of Himvana – the Goddess of *Brahma Vidya*, born in the very caves of the Himalayan inner silence. She told Indra that the *Yaksha* was none other than the manifest *Brahman*.

The message in the character of Indra and his ultimate success is that we should not be impatient in pursuit of *Brahma Vidya*, knowledge of the Absolute Truth.

– Swami Chinmayananda

4, 4-9 *Brahman* is 'That Delight' which spreads love

THE INDIVIDUAL AND THE UNIVERSAL

Is the goal of life a complete oblivion of the external? Must the mind and the senses recede inward into a trance? It is possible, but not inevitable or indispensable. The mind is cosmic, one in all the universe. So are life and senses. So too is matter of the body. When they exist in Cosmic Consciousness alone, they will know and sense universal unity. The external will cease to exist for them. The wall of individuality will break. The individual mind will cease to know itself as the individual; it will be conscious only of the universal Mind, in which the individual minds are only knots. The individual life will lose its sense of separateness and live as universal Life, in which the individuals are only whirls of activity. The senses will no longer be conscious of a separated existence; instead the individual will feel that his real body is the whole universe. Becoming one with the formless and the infinite, the individual will exceed the universe itself. He will see all the worlds not as external, but as if within him.

In still higher realization of Cosmic Consciousness, the lower life, mind and senses will be aware of not just the higher mind, life and senses but also of that which empowers them. The whole sense-view of the universe itself will be altered. The mental will become Supra-mental. Life will become Super-life, a conscious movement of infinite cosmic force. It will be impersonal, unlimited by any particular acts or enjoyments, unbound by their results, untroubled by dualities. The material world itself will become Super-senses.

This will be the transfiguration of the gods, but what of the Self? As we have seen, there are two fundamental entities – the gods (senses) and the Self. The Self in us is greater than the cosmic powers. Its march towards Cosmic Consciousness is more vital to our perfection and self-fulfillment than any transfiguration of the senses, called gods. Eventually, our Self will ascend to the level of the Self of All. This is the spiritual existence, which the Upanishads declare to be the goal of man. It is a state of eternal bliss, infinite knowledge.

'Eventually, our Self will ascend to the level of Self of All. The Upanishads declare this to be the goal of life. It is a state of eternal bliss, infinite knowledge.'

In verse 4, 6 we have the culmination of the teaching of the Upanishad. It declares that *Brahman*, in Its nature is 'That Delight', the all-blissful *Ananda*. Taittiriya Upanishad speaks of *Ananda* as the highest *Brahman*, from which all existences are born, by which all existences live and grow, and into which all existence dissolve. Kena Upanishad says it is this transcendent Delight which must be worshipped and sought. Why? The seeker will then become a centre of divine Delight, shedding it on the whole world. That Delight will be a fountain of ecstasies for all the creatures in the universe.

In the last two verses (4, 7-8), the Vedas are described as the limbs of *Brahman*. Truth is Its home. Truth does not refer to intellectual enquiry, but the ultimate state of Pure Consciousness – right knowledge, right works, right joy of existence. Truth is that, which is contrary to falsehood of egoism and ignorance. The goal of ascent is described as *Swarga-loka*, heavenly world. This *Swarga-loka* is higher than the *Brahma-loka* of Mundaka Upanishad. In *Brahma-loka*, the soul arrives by works of virtue and piety, but falls from there after exhaustion of their merit. The *Swarga-loka* of Kena Upanishad, like the *Brahma-loka* of Katha Upanishad is beyond the symbols of birth and death. It is a state belonging to knowledge, not ignorance. It is infinite, eternal, all-blissful existence.

Thus, Kena Upanishad suggests three states of existence:
(i) Human, mortal state
(ii) Cosmic Consciousness
(iii) Absolute, Immortal state

The human mortal state is a state of opposites and balances. It is this state in which we now live; and through it we have to move to the Beyond. The attainment of Cosmic Consciousness is our route from the mortal to the Immortal. Immortality is not survival of death. Immortality means the Absolute life of the soul, as opposed to the transient and mutable life in the body. It means to rise out of the world of limitations to the world of infinitude. It means to ascend out of earthly joys and sorrows into transcendent Bliss.

In the Upanishads, the importance of individual salvation has been certainly glorified, even over-emphasized. The rejection of material life frequently occurs as a dominant theme. Notwithstanding this bias, the Upanishads alone of the extant scriptures give us the truth about Cosmic Consciousness. Their value to scientific knowledge, therefore, is indispensable.

Just as the lures of earth have to be conquered; so also the lures of heaven. The lure of release from birth and death and withdrawal from cosmic labor must also be rejected, as it was by Mahayanist Buddhism. It held compassion greater than *Nirvana*. As the virtues we practice must be done without demand of earthly or heavenly reward, so also the salvation we seek must be purely internal and impersonal. Certainly, we must seek release from egoism, communion with the Divine, realization of our universality, and transcendence. However, we must not seek a salvation that takes us away from the love of His manifestations and the help we can give to the world. This hell with other suffering selves, is better than a solitary salvation.

A high-reaching soul will thus have two objectives – to do good deeds in this world and to attain the Supreme.

– *Sri Aurobindo*

Verse 4, 2 extols *Brahma Vidya* to such an extent that even the arrogant and unsuccessful *Agni* and *Vayu* are recognized as surpassing other gods, because these gods chanced to come nearest to Supreme Truth in Its manifestation as Yaksha.

Verse 4, 4: Here is an example, which beautifully explains not only the vividness of the experience, but also the flashy quickness of the vision of Truth. The illustration of the winking of the eye shows how natural and effortless is the final flight to the Beyond, in meditation.

The vision of *Brahman* has been compared to the wink of the eye. The experience of *Brahman* is momentary, but that moment has the richness of Eternity. Any desire to extend the moment would mean bringing the perception of *Brahman* in the time process. But the Transcendent cannot be perceived in the region of time. It is only in a timeless moment that *Brahman* can be known.

Verse 4, 5: Just as the sea is never without waves, the mind can never exist without thought. However, there is always an interval between two successive waves or thoughts, infinitesimal as it may be. This is the

---

'Brahman is 'That Delight' which is a fountain of ecstasies for all the creatures in the universe.'

interval when the mind is empty of thoughts, and it is in this interval that Truth can be experienced.

Verse 4, 6: The word *upasate* also appears in earlier verses, 1, 4-8. It has been translated as 'to adore' 'to worship' and 'to meditate'.

The word *tadvanam,* translated as 'That Delight' by most commentators, has also been translated as 'The Beloved of all' by some. 'That' means transcendental.

The present mantra may appear as a contradiction of earlier verses (1, 4-8) which seem to object to worship of deities. What was objected to in the earlier part is not idol worship as such, but the sad practice of misunderstanding the means as the end. Worship or meditation are not in themselves an end; they are the means for purifying and perfecting the inner instruments of the aspirants, like the mind and the intellect.

Verse 4, 7: This verse can have two implications (i) the disciple wants a clear declaration that the Upanishad has ended, or (ii) the disciple wants some more information regarding the technique of self-perfection.

Verse 4, 8: To our forefathers, philosophy was not merely a *view of life,* but a *way of life.* Realization of Absolute Truth, according to this verse, rests on austerity, restraint and selfless work.

This mantra is the only mantra in the entire Upanishad to prescribe the Upanishadic teachings as a *way of life.*

Lastly, volumes can be written about the expression *Satyamayatanam,* meaning: 'Truth's abode is Truth.'

Verse 4, 9: The concluding mantra contains a vehement assertion from its seer that he who has known the theme so far discussed shall have reached the supreme state of perfection. A similar assertion repeated frequently in other Upanishads is: To know *Brahman* is to become *Brahman*.

– Swami Chinmayananda

The first two sections of Kena Upanishad describe the doctrine of unattainability of *Brahman* through knowledge.

The third section presents through a transparent allegory, the relationship of Vedic gods with *Brahman*. All gods, meaning forces of nature, derive their power from *Brahman*. Here *Brahman* appears as a thing of wonder.

The fourth section symbolizes the timelessness of *Brahman*. The two illustrations – flash of lightening and winking of the eye – suggests sudden glimpse of Reality (4, 4).

Like lightening, *Brahman* showed Itself to the gods once, and disappeared. When such a phenomenon takes place, there is a sudden enlarging of the mind and enlightening of the intellect, causing ineffable fervor and joy.

Lives of spiritual masters tell us that the hidden word comes to them all of a sudden, in a brief moment of deep stillness.

– Paul Deussen

'Worship or meditation are not in themselves an end;
they are the means for purifying and perfecting the mind and the intellect.'

Mandukya Upanishad

Three states of Consciousness

OVERVIEW

Mandukya Upanishad, like Isa, is very short but very profound. In just a dozen verses, it deals with three interrelated subjects – Mind, Meditation and Consciousness – and establishes the Oneness of psychology, philosophy and physics.

Referring to the material world as 'All this', the Upanishad first declares that 'All this is Brahman' and then states a great aphorism: 'This Atman is Brahman'. As elsewhere, Atman and Brahman denote individual Consciousness and universal Consciousness.

The Upanishad then says that Consciousness uses the mind and the senses as its instruments for human experience of Its creation – the world. This experiences has a daily rhythm of three states – waking, dream and deep sleep. There are very significant differences in the behavior of the mind and the senses in these states. However, the three states have an eternal and unchanging substratum – Pure and Blissful Consciousness. In deep sleep, the mind comes closest to the Bliss of Brahman.

Brahman or universal Consciousness is an abstract principle which cannot be comprehended by the mind. So the Upanishad denotes it with a sound symbol – Aum. It then explains how Aum symbolizes not just Pure Consciousness, but also its three states.

COMMENTARIES

The brevity of Mandukya Upanishad has attracted many commentaries. Their study in itself generates very enlightening thoughts. Commentaries reviewed here are those by: Sri Sankara (translated by Swami Nikhilananda), Dr. S. Radhakrishnan, Swami Sivananda, Swami Krishnananda, Sri Madhava (translated by Nagesh D. Sonde), Rohit Mehta, and N. A Nikam.

The earliest commentary on Mandukya Upanishad is by Sri Gaudapada, the grand preceptor of Sri Sankara. Out of 251 verses of Gaudapada Karika, 29 verses are reproduced here. There is also a brief review of Sri Sankara's commentary on these verses, as translated by Swami Nikhilananda.

MANDUKYA UPANISHAD
Three states of Consciousness

Peace Invocation
    Simplified Synopses 497
    Translated Text 499

1	*Aum*, a symbol of Totality
2-6	Three states of Consciousness
7	The Fourth: Consciousness, Pure and Absolute
8-12	Meditation on Aum
—	Gaudapada's *Karika*: Text and Commentary.... 514

General Commentaries
1. Sri Sankara 501
2. Dr. S. Radhakrishnan ... 503
3. Swami Sivananda 506
4. Swami Krishnananda ... 507
5. Sri Madhava 511
6. Rohit Mehta 511
7. N. A. Nikam 512

Verses 1-12: Three states of Consciousness

SIMPLIFIED SYNOPSES

Mandukya Upanishad has no chapters or sections, only a dozen verses.

1
Aum, a symbol of Totality

The Absolute, *Brahman* is beyond any form of Time, Space and Causation. It can be neither perceived by the senses nor conceptualized by the mind. Truth, Ultimate Reality and Cosmic Consciousness are some of the words used to denote *Brahman*. However, ordinary mind cannot contemplate on these words, except by means of a symbol. The symbol selected by Mandukya and other Upanishads is *Aum*.

The opening verse states that the symbol *Aum* is representative of everything that exists in any form of Time and Space, or beyond. Being a symbol of the Absolute, it is eternal and imperishable.

2-6
Three states of Consciousness

The second verse contains a great saying: This *Atman* is *Brahman*. The Self in man and the Universal Self are one and the same. Mathematically,

$$Atman = Brahman = Aum$$

'This Atman is Brahman.'

This *Atman* – which is the same as Consciousness – is present in all human beings at all times. Verses 3-5 are devoted to study of Consciousness in its three relative states – waking, dream and deep sleep. The Sanskrit names for Consciousness in these states are *Vaisvanara* (or simply Visva), *Taijasa* and *Pragyan* respectively.

In waking state, Consciousness is directed outward to experience gross objects, with the mind and the sense organs as its instruments. In dream state, Consciousness is directed inward to experience subtle objects, with the mind alone as its instrument. Senses remain dormant in this state. The mind creates its own world out of impressions gained in waking states at various times.

It is to be noted that while in waking state the mind differentiates between the subject and the object, in dream state it is both the subject and the object.

All gross and subtle objects, which are experienced in waking and dream states, are poetically described as having seven limbs and nineteen mouths. These have been enumerated by some commentators.

The third state, deep sleep, is one in which both mind and senses become dormant. In this state, there are neither desires (as in waking) nor dreams. Instead, the sleeper enjoys bliss in an undifferentiated mass of Pure Consciousness. This Pure Consciousness is the same as the all-knowing Creator, the Lord of the universe, the inner guide of all beings.

7 The Fourth: Consciousness, Pure and Absolute

The fourth, which is not really a state, is Pure and Absolute Consciousness, or *Turiya*. It is different from the conditioned Consciousness of the three states. It is imperceptible to sense organs, unrelated to anything, incomprehensible, indefinable, unthinkable and indescribable. In other words it is nothing but *Atman*, which is same as *Brahman*.

8-12 Meditation on *Aum*

Aum consists of three elements or sound symbols, viz. 'A', 'U' and 'M'. These denote – from the relative standpoint – the gross, subtle and causal aspects of both *Atman* and *Brahman*. They have been equated with waking, dream and deep sleep states, respectively. The summary position is as follows:

Letters/ Sounds of *Aum*	States of Consciousness	Aspects of *Atman* or individual Self	Aspects of *Brahman* or universal Self	Distinctive Characteristics
A	Waking	*Vaisvanara*, Gross	Desirelessness, *Virat*	Outward, Perception
U	Dream	*Taijasa*, Subtle	Knowledge (*Hiranyagarbha*)	Inward, Imagination
M	Deep Sleep	*Pragyan*, Causal	Potentiality (*Ishvara*)	No desires
Inaudible Sound	Super-Conscious (*Turiya*)	Pure Consciousness (*Atman*)	Pure Consciousness (*Brahman*)	Eternal Bliss

When one meditates on *Aum* as the symbol of the Absolute, *Brahman*, there arises in one's mind the Consciousness of *Brahman*. One then begins to feel that the gross universe (A) is absorbed in the subtle (U) and the subtle in the causal (M). The causal (M) eventually merges in the Transcendental, symbolized by the silence which follows the chanting of *Aum*.

Gaudapada's *Karika*

Sri Gaudapada, the grand preceptor of Sri Sankara, has written a commentary of 251 verses (called *Karika*) to elaborate on the brief philosophical statements contained in Mandukya Upanishad. Of these, 29 verses are of direct relevance and are therefore reproduced here, with extracts or adaptations from commentary by Sri Sankara, as translated by Swami Nikhilananda.

Study of Mandukya Upanishad can be considered complete only when it is read together with the relevant verses of Gaudapada's *Karika*.

'The fourth, which is not really a state, is Absolute Consciousness. It is Atman, which is same as Brahman.'

Translated Text

Peace Invocation

Om.
O gods, may we hear auspicious words with our ears.
O Worshipful One, may we see auspicious things with our eyes.
May we live our entire life cheerfully and in good health,
   offering our praises unto Thee.

May *Indra*, the ancient and the famous, bless us.
May *Pusan* (Sun), the all-knowing bless us.
May *Vayu* (Life Principle), the Lord of swift motion,
   who protects us from all harms, bless us.
May *Brhaspati*, the Lord of wisdom, bless us.

Om. Shanti. Shanti. Shanti.
Let there be Peace, Let there be Peace, Let there be Peace.

Aum. This eternal Word is ALL that there is. What was, what is, what shall be, and whatever else there is beyond the three periods of Time, is also *Aum*, the imperishable syllable *Aum*. **1**

All this is, verily, *Brahman*. **This *Atman* is *Brahman***. This *Atman* has four states. **2**

The first state (of *Atman*) is *Vaisvanara*. Its sphere of activity is waking state, and its cognition is outward. It has seven limbs and nineteen mouths, and it experiences gross (material) objects. **3**

The second state (of *Atman*) is *Taijasa*. Its sphere of activity is dream state, and its cognition is inward. It has seven limbs and nineteen mouths, and it experiences subtle objects. **4**

The third state (of *Atman*) is *Pragyan*. Its sphere of activity is deep sleep. Deep sleep is a state in which the sleeper does not have any desires; he does not see any dreams; he has become an undivided and undifferentiated mass of Consciousness, enjoying bliss and full of bliss. It (deep sleep) is the doorway to other experiences (of dream and waking states). **5**

This (sleep Consciousness) is the Lord (*Ishvara*) of all. It is the knower of all. It is the inner controller. It is the source of all. Verily, It is the beginning and the end of all beings. **6**

The fourth is *Turiya*. It is not that which cognizes internal subject, nor that which cognizes external objects, nor that which is conscious of both, nor that which is a compact mass of consciousness, nor cognition, nor not-cognition. It is unperceived (by sense organs), unrelated to anything, incomprehensible (by the mind), uninferable, unthinkable, and indescribable. It is essentially of the nature of Pure

---

"This Atman is Brahman."... This great aphorism reveals the Oneness of individual Self and universal Self.

Consciousness, Self, with no trace of the conditional or relative world. It is peaceful, all-bliss, non-dual. It is *Atman*. It is the Self that should be realized.　　**7**

This *Atman* is the Word *Aum*. The letters of *Aum* are states of *Atman*. The states of *Atman* are the letters of *Aum* viz. 'A', 'U', and 'M'.　　**8**

The first letter 'A' is *Vaisvanara*. Its domain is the state of waking. It is all-pervasive, and the first. Whosoever knows *Vaisvanara* obtains what he desires. He becomes the first among men.　　**9**

Taijasa, whose domain is dream state, corresponds to 'U', the second letter of *Aum*. It exalts on account of being in the middle. Whosoever knows *Taijasa* becomes great in knowledge. No one ignorant of *Brahman* is born in his family.　　**10**

Pragyan, whose domain is deep sleep, corresponds to 'M', the third letter of *Aum*. It is a measure and also that in which everything merges. He who knows *Pragyan* is able to measure all and comprehend all within himself.　　**11**

That which has no letter (*amatra*) is the Fourth. It is transcendental, devoid of phenomenal existence, all bliss and non-dual.

Thus symbol *Aum* is *Atman*, Self. He who knows this merges his Self (*Atman*) with universal Self, *Brahman*.　　**12**

Peace Invocation

Om.
O gods, may we hear auspicious words with our ears.
O Worshipful One, may we see auspicious things with our eyes.
May we live our entire life cheerfully and in good health,
　offering our praises unto Thee.

May *Indra*, the ancient and the famous, bless us.
May *Pusan* (sun), the all-knowing bless us.
May *Vayu*, the Lord of swift motion,
　who protects us from all harms, bless us.
May *Brhaspati*, the Lord of wisdom, bless us.

Om. Shanti. Shanti. Shanti.
Let there be Peace, Let there be Peace, Let there be Peace.

"This Atman is the Word Aum. The letters of Aum are states of Atman. The states of Atman are the letters of Aum."

General Commentaries

Peace Invocation

The prayer is addressed to *Indra, Sun, Vayu* and *Brhaspati*. This suggests that Rama, Krishna, Shiva and Ganesha began to be worshipped as deities in a much later age. In the Upanishadic period, the sages recognized only the great elements of Nature as expressions of the Supreme, *Brahman*. The Indian culture has preached reverence for Nature since its inception so many thousands of years ago. This is particularly noteworthy in today's age of environmental awareness and ecological conservation.

– *Swami Chinmayananda*

1. Commentary by Sri Sankara (translated by Swami Nikhilananda)

IMPORTANCE OF AUM

Verse 1

Many passages in the Upanishads emphasize the value of the symbol *Aum* for realizing the essential nature of *Atman*. For example:
- *Aum* is the best support (Katha 1.2, 17)
- *Aum* is both higher and lower *Brahman*. (Prasna 5.2)
- *Aum* is *Brahman* (Taittiriya 1.8)

Aum is, verily, of the same essential character as *Atman*; it is another name for *Atman* and *Brahman*.

The relationship between *Aum* and *Brahman* is explained thus. The phenomena of the world consist of ideas or mental states. These depend upon words for their expression. *Aum* is the matrix of all sounds that give rise to words used in any language. The substratum of all sounds is *Aum*; the substratum of all phenomena is *Brahman*. Hence, *Brahman* is *Aum*.

When *Aum* is uttered with concentration, Consciousness of *Brahman* arises in the mind. Therefore *Aum* is the nearest symbol of *Brahman*. It helps to concentrate the mind and leads to realization of *Brahman*. Through meditation on *Aum,* one can realize both *para* or *Nirguna Brahman* (attributeless) and *Apara* or *Saguna Brahman* (associated with names and forms).

One who seeks to realize Self through one-pointed concentration on *Aum*, feels that the gross universe (symbolized by 'A') is absorbed into the subtle ('U'), and the subtle into causal ('M'). Finally, the universe dependent upon causal relationship is withdrawn into the transcendental. This is known as *amatra*, as it cannot be designated by any letter or sound.

THREE STATES OF CONSCIOUSNESS

Verse 2

The objective here is to emphasize the oneness of names and things signified by *Aum*. Therefore, the Upanishad says that the quarters (*padas*, translated as states in the text) are the letters of *Aum* (*matras*), and its letters are quarters.

The names given to Consciousness in the four quarters are:

- *Visva* in waking state
- *Taijasa* in dream state
- *Pragyan* in state of dreamless sleep
- *Turiya* is the fourth. It is the same as *Brahman* or *Atman*. It is not a state of Consciousness, but Pure Consciousness Itself.

The four quarters correspond to the three *matras* of *Aum* and one *amatra*. A, U and M are the three *matras*. The fourth, which is known as *amatra* or without a letter, has no corresponding letter or sound. This is the silence of *Atman* corresponding to *Turiya*. The idea of sound also suggests silence, from which sound may be said to proceed.

The waking state is merged into dreams, dream state into state of dreamless sleep, and finally, the state of dreamless sleep is merged into the transcendental *Turiya*.

Verse 3

In waking state, Consciousness appears, as it were, related to outward objects. This Consciousness, *Vaisvanara*, is visualized as a Cosmic Person having seven limbs and nineteen mouths. The seven limbs are: the effulgent region (heaven, as if it were the

---

'The idea of sound also suggests silence, from which sound may be said to proceed.'

head), the sun and the moon (taken as one, as the eyes) and the five elements (that constitute the human body). The nineteen mouths are: the five organs of perception, five organs of action, five forms of vital breath and four mental faculties. These are the instruments by which Consciousness experiences external objects. Waking state is called the first quarter because subsequent quarters are realized through it.

Verse 4

Consciousness leaves various impressions on the mind during waking state, like a piece of canvass with pictures painted on it. Possessed of these impressions, the mind creates its own subtle world during dream state. However, it acts independent of sense organs. Consciousness in dream state is called *Taijasa*. It appears as the subject, without any gross object. Its orientation is internal and its experience is that of the subtle.

Verse 5

In the third state of deep sleep, there does not exist, as in the other two states, any desire or dream experience. In this state all experiences become unified. All objects of duality reach a state of non-discrimination or non-differentiation. As at night, owing to non-discrimination produced by darkness, all objects become a mass of darkness; so also in the state of deep sleep, all objects of Consciousness become a mass of Consciousness. At the time of deep sleep, the mind is free from miseries that arise from subject - object relationships. Therefore it is called *Anandamaya*. It is endowed with an abundance of bliss, but it is not Bliss Infinite.

Whereas in the other two states of waking and dream, Consciousness experiences variety, in deep sleep it is undifferentiated. Absence of the knowledge of Reality is a common feature of all the three states.

Verse 6

Consciousness in deep sleep, called *Pragyan*, is Consciousness in its natural state; because all diversities of waking and dream states merge in deep sleep. This state, being free from the conditions of waking and dream states, manifests Pure Consciousness in a marked degree. This Consciousness has been called 'the knower of all' because it has knowledge of past, present and future, as well as the three states.

THE FOURTH: CONSCIOUSNESS, PURE AND ABSOLUTE

Verse 7

Turiya is designated here as the Fourth, and not the fourth state or condition in which *Atman* is to be viewed. *Atman* does not admit of any condition or state. *Turiya* is present in all the three states of waking, dream and deep sleep; but It is Itself not a state.

In the first half of verse 7, it is affirmed that *Turiya* is different from Consciousness that exists in the three states of waking, dream and deep sleep. The statement that It is not-cognition implies that *Turiya* is not insentient, or of the nature of matter.

Turiya cannot be perceived by the senses, and therefore It cannot be comprehended by the mind. It cannot be inferred because there is no characteristics for Its inference. It is unthinkable, and therefore indescribable. It is that Consciousness which never changes in the three states. Its nature is that of *Atman*. It is ever peaceful – without any manifestation of change – and all Bliss. Stated differently: *Turiya = Atman*.

Turiya is non-dual. There is no subject-object relationship in It. No instrument of knowledge can establish *Turiya* on account of Its non-dual and non-relational nature.

The rope did not cease to be rope when it appeared as a snake. The rope, again, is seen in its true nature when the idea of snake is removed. Similarly *Atman*, which appears as *Visva*, *Taijasa* and *Pragyan* in the three states, is realized as *Turiya* when the states are negated.

From the relative standpoint, *Atman* associated with any of the three states is, no doubt, different from *Turiya*. But from the standpoint of *Turiya*, there is no difference whatsoever between It and *Atman* associated with the three states. As a matter of fact, it is *Turiya* as the witness that is revealed in the three states.

'In deep sleep, all objects become one mass of Consciousness. The mind is free from miseries that arise from subject-object relationships. It is endowed with abundance of bliss.'

Turiya is not a state that is antecedent or subsequent to any other state. It is the substratum of all the states.

What is Ultimate Reality? From the examination of the three states it becomes clear that though the states are changing, Consciousness which is present in them is constant. Change from one state to another cannot affect the unchanging nature of Consciousness. Therefore, Pure Consciousness is the Ultimate Reality.

THIS *ATMAN* IS *AUM*

Verse 8

The three states of Consciousness are analogous to the three letters of *Aum*.

Verse 9

The first point of resemblance is pervasiveness. All sounds are pervaded by 'A'. Similarly, the entire universe is pervaded by *Vaisvanara*, the Cosmic Person. The knower of this identity gets the following results: he has all his desires fulfilled and he becomes the first of the great.

Verse 10

Consciousness of dream state, *Taijasa*, is the second letter 'U' of *Aum*. They both appear in the middle. The knower of this identity gets the following results: his knowledge is always on the increase. Further, no one ignorant of *Brahman* is born in his family.

Verse 11

Consciousness of deep sleep, *Pragyan*, is the third letter of *Aum*. There are two points of resemblance.

First, both waking and dream states appear from and disappear into deep sleep. Therefore, *Pragyan* is like a container in which *Visva* and *Taijasa* are contained. Accordingly, *Pragyan* is described here as the measure of two other states.

Second, when the word *Aum* is uttered quickly several times, the sound actually heard is *Mmmm* and not *Aum*. It can therefore be said that the sound 'A' and 'U' emerge out of 'M', and merge into 'M'.

What is the benefit of this knowledge? One who knows this comprehends the real nature of the universe. Further, he realizes himself as *Atman*, the cause of the universe. The enumeration of these merits is for the purpose of extolling the principal means of knowledge.

Verse 12

The soundless or *amatra Aum* has been called the Fourth. It is nothing but Pure *Atman*. It cannot be expressed by any sound. It is relation-less and therefore It cannot be described as the substratum of the three other sounds. Sounds point to the soundless *Aum*. All sounds must, at some time or other, merge in soundlessness. This *amatra Aum* is identical with *Turiya, Atman*.

It (Pure *Atman*) is incomprehensible because both speech and mind disappear or cease in the partless *Aum*. As the rope is realized when the illusion of snake disappears, so partless (soundless) *Aum* is realized when the illusion of duality disappears. This is a state of infinite and eternal bliss. Bliss is identical with non-duality. One can speak of duality only in a relative world.

One who knows this merges his Self in universal Self, which is the Highest Reality. This is because in his case the notion of cause, which corresponds to the third state, is destroyed. He is not born again because *Turiya* is not a cause. The illusionary snake – which has merged in the rope upon discrimination of the snake from the rope – does not reappear as before, to those who know the distinction between them.

– *Sri Sankara, translated by Swami Nikhilananda*

2. Commentary by S. Radhakrishnan

Verse 1

The syllable *Aum*, which is the symbol of *Brahman*, stands for the manifested world – the past, the present and the future – as well as the unmanifested Absolute.

Verse 2

The four quarters are: *visva*, the waking state, *taijasa*, the dream state, *pragyan*, the state of dreamless sleep

---

'Change from one state to another cannot affect the unchanging nature of Pure Consciousness.'

and *Turiya* which is spiritual Consciousness. Knowledge of the Fourth is attained by progressively merging the previous state in the succeeding one: *Visva* in *taijasa*, *taijasa* in *pragyan*, and *pragyan* in *Turiya* (Sri Sankara).

Verse 3

Waking state is the natural condition of man, who without reflection accepts the universe as he finds it. The same physical universe, bound by uniform laws, presents itself to all such men.

Verse 4

Taijasa is conscious of the internal, i.e. mental states; while *visva*, which is the subject of the waking state, cognizes material objects in external experience of the senses. *Taijasa* experiences mental states, which are dependent on predisposition left by the waking experiences. In this state the soul fashions its own world in the imagining of dreams. Here also, the basis of duality operates – the subject that knows and the object that is known. Though dream objects are experienced as external, they are said to be subtle because they are different from the objects of waking state.

Verse 5

The state of waking is a life of outward-moving Consciousness; the state of dream is a life of inward-moving Consciousness. In the state of deep sleep, Consciousness enjoys peace and has no perception of either external or internal objects.

In waking state we are bound by the fetters of sense perception and desires. In dream state we have greater freedom; our mind makes a world of its own out of inputs received during waking state. We produce our dreams out of ourselves. In deep sleep, we are liberated both from the material and the mental world.

Self in state of sleep is conceptual, while the two previous selves are imaginative and perceptual.

Undivided and undifferentiated mass of Consciousness: As at night, owing to the indiscrimination produced by darkness, all objects become a mass of darkness, as it were; so also in the state of deep sleep, all objects of Consciousness become a mass of Consciousness (Sri Sankara).

The apparent absence of duality in deep sleep has led to the view that it is the final state of union with *Brahman*. (Chandogya 8.11, 1 and Brhadaranyaka 4.3, 32).

Verse 6

This verse makes a distinction between the Absolute and God, between *Brahman* and *Ishvara*. It is like making a distinction between the invisible God and the visible Son of God.

Pragyan is in all beings and all conditions. Hence It is called all-knowing. It has entered into all beings and It directs them from within. All beings originate from It.

Pragyan is called *Ishvara* at the cosmic level. *Ishvara* does not create the universe like a potter making pots. He is the material cause as well as the instrumental or efficient cause. He wills. Everything comes into being. He projects this world and withdraws it within Himself – just as a serpent lengthens its body and coils it up; just as a lotus opens and shuts itself, just as the tortoise projects its limbs and withdraws them.

Verse 7

Turiya is beyond the distinction of subject and object. It is super theism and not atheism or anti-theism. We cannot use here terms like all-knowing, all-powerful. *Brahman* cannot be treated as having objects of knowledge or powers. It is pure Being.

In many passages, the Upanishads make out that *Brahman* is pure Being, beyond all words and thoughts. He becomes *Ishvara* or personal God with the quality of *Pragyan* or pure wisdom. He is the unmanifested, the inner guide of all souls. From Him proceeds *Hiranyagarbha*, who fashions the world. From *Hiranyagarbha* proceeds *Virat*, the totality of all existences. The last two are sometimes mixed up.

God is the logical Being, the defined Reality. We cannot define *Brahman*; *Brahman* defines itself. *Brahman* is Reality in Itself. God or *Ishvara* is Reality as defined by us.

'Brahman and Ishvara – Absolute Being and Personal God – are the equivalents of the invisible God and the visible Son of God.' ..... (Adapted)

God exists in *Brahman*. *Brahman* does not cease to become *Brahman* by becoming *Ishvara*, a personal God.

Gaudapada says that this *Brahman* is birthless, free from sleep and dream, without name and form, ever effulgent, all thought; no form is necessary for It.

Though objective Consciousness is absent in both *Pragyan* and *Turiya* Consciousness, the seed of it is present in the state of deep sleep. However, the seed is absent in transcendental Consciousness.

Verse 8

Visva and *Taijasa* are conditioned by cause and effect, but *Pragyan* is conditioned by cause alone. These two (cause and effect) do not exist in *Turiya*.

Verse 9

Vaisvanara is He who has the universe as His body.

Verse 11

In deep sleep, all waking and dream experiences disappear. This verse affirms what Parmenides, Plato and Hegel assumed that the opposition of being and not-being is the original duality from the ontological standpoint. Being is *priori* to non-being. The negation presupposes what it negates. But there is something which is *prior* to the opposition of being and non-being, and that is the Unity which transcends both.

Verse 12

In *Turiya*, the mind is not simply withdrawn from objects, but becomes one with *Brahman*.

In both deep sleep and transcendental Consciousness (*Turiya*), there is no consciousness of objects. However, objective consciousness is present in an unmanifested 'seed' form in deep sleep; while it is completely transcended in *Turiya*. Gaudapada says: 'The non-cognition of duality is common to both *Pragyan* and *Turiya*; but *Pragyan* is associated with the 'seed' in sleep, while this does not exist in *Turiya*.'

Lao Tze looks upon Tao as the ultimate Reality, which can be defined only in negative terms, as 'colorless,' 'soundless,' 'non-material.' His conception of creation was that the great monad or the material cause of the universe came out of Tao, the eternal Ultimate Principle, the One. This 'One' produced the two primary essences – Yang and Yin, positive and negative, male and female, light and shade. These gave birth to the three powers of nature – heaven, earth and man – which in their combination produced all creatures.

This soundless, partless, supreme Reality is the very Self. In deep sleep, it becomes the subject confronting the object, which is yet unmanifested. In dreams, the object is manifested in the form of mental states; in waking, the object is manifested in the form of material states. The subject-object duality is present in different forms in the states of waking, dream and dreamless sleep. It is transcended altogether in state of *Turiya*. In *Turiya*, we have Pure Consciousness of Self, Absolute.

In the experience of *Turiya* (Super Consciousness), there is neither subject nor object; neither perception nor the idea of God. It does not reflect or explain any Reality other than Itself. Those who know the Truth become the Truth. It is not a state in which objects are extrinsically opposed to one another. It is the immersion of Self in Reality, Its participation in Primary Being. It is illumined life. It is Pure Consciousness, without any trace of duality.

Aum thus represents both the unmanifested Absolute and the personal God. Gaudapada writes: 'The sacred syllable *Aum* is, verily, the lower *Brahman* and it is also said to be the higher *Brahman*. *Aum* is without beginning, unique, without anything external to it, unrelated to any effect and imperishable' (verse 26, page 515).

Aum is devoid of all elements. All dualities are resolved in It.

In this Upanishad, we find the fundamental approach to the attainment of Reality. This requires introversion. It requires progression from the sensible and changing; through the mind that dreams; through the soul that thinks; to the Divine within. The truth of our intellectual knowledge presupposes a light, Light of the Real above logic. This light shines not by itself, but by That which has created it.

– S. Radhakrishnan

'Material cause of the universe came out of Tao. This 'One' produced two primary essences - Yang and Yin. These gave birth to three powers of Nature - heaven, earth and man - which produced all the creatures.'

3. Commentary by Swami Sivananda

Mandukya Upanishad is the briefest and yet the most profound of all the Upanishads. Sri Gaudapada, the grand-preceptor of Sri Sankara has written a commentary of 251 verses (called *Karika*) to explain and elaborate on the philosophical statements contained in Mandukya Upanishad. Sri Sankara wrote a commentary on the *Karika*, as well as on the Upanishad itself. Later, many learned scholars have contributed to the vast literature that now exists on Mandukya Upanishad.

The famous mantra of Sri Guru Nanak, founder of Sikkhism, begins with "*Sat Nam Eka Omkar*, Real Name is One, *Aum*. *Aum* is everything". It means that *Brahman*, the Supreme Self denoted by the syllable *Aum*, is all this.

Brahman, the Absolute is nameless, but in the relative plane, a name is necessary to denote It. That name is *Aum*.

This Upanishad provides an explanation of the Word, *Aum*. It is of the same nature as higher *Brahman* without attributes, and also the lower *Brahman* with attributes.

Verses 1-2

It is stated elsewhere in the Upanishad that creation began with *Brahman* reflecting, "May I become many". This caused a vibration, *spanda*, and the vibration caused a sound. The first sound was *Aum*.

Aum is the basis of all sounds, words and names. Just as an object is known by its name, so also *Brahman*, the universal Self, is known through its symbol *Aum*.

There are four *mahavakyas*, or great sentences in Upanishads, one each from the four Vedas. Mandukya Upanishad of the *Atharva Veda* contains one of the four *mahavakyas* in verse 2: *Ayam Atma Brahma* or this *Atman* is *Brahman*. This great sentence reveals the oneness of individual Self, *Atman* with the universal soul, *Brahman*.

Verses 3-4

Atman has four aspects. Sanskrit word for aspects is *pada*, which literally means feet.

All gross and subtle objects, which are perceived in waking and dream states, are poetically described as having seven limbs and nineteen mouths. There is one-to-one correspondence between the limbs and mouths of macrocosm and microcosm.

The seven limbs are:

1. Heaven is the head of *Vaisvanara*, or *Visva*, the Cosmic Person.
2. The Sun and the Moon are Its eyes.
3. Air is Its breath.
4. Fire is Its mouth.
5. Sky is Its middle body.
6. Water is Its body fluid.
7. Earth is Its feet.

The nineteen mouths are:

1-5 Five *Gyana Indriyas* or organs of knowledge. These are: ears, skin, eyes, tongue and nose. Sound, touch, form, taste, and smell – these are experienced through these organs of knowledge.

6-10 Five *Karma Indriyas* or organs of action. These are: mouth, hands, feet, generative organ and excretory organ.

11-15 Five *Pranas* or vital breath. These are *Prana*, *Apana*, *Samana*, *Vyana* and *Udana* or in-breath, out-breath, equalizing-breath, diffusing-breath and ascending – breath.

16-19 Four inner facilities (*antahkarana*). These are mind, intellect, memory, and ego. The corresponding Sanskrit words are: *manas, buddhi, chitta* and *ahamkara*, respectively.

These 19 are called mouths because through these, *Jivatman* experiences the gross objects of the material world in waking state.

Virat: The sum total of all physical bodies (*Vaisvanara* or *Visva*). The whole universe is as if it is the body of *Virat Purusha* (Cosmic Person). The totality of the gross universe is called *Virat*. Gross body of a person is called *sthula sarira*.

Hiranyagarbha: The sum total of all the subtle bodies (or *Taijasa*) is *Hiranyagarbha*. The subtle body of a

---

'This Atman is Brahman. This great sentence reveals the oneness of individual Self (Atman) with the universal Soul (Brahman).'

person is called astral body, *sukshma sarira* or *lingah deha*.

Ishvara: The sum total of all causal bodies (*Pragyan*). The causal body of a person is called *karana sarira*.

Waking state is called the first because other states can be known only through waking state. In waking state, both the mind and the senses are functioning. In dream state, the senses stop functioning, but the mind is still functioning.

Verses 5-6

In deep sleep, there is a veil of ignorance, *Avidya*, between the individual soul, (*Jivatman*) and Universal Consciousness (*Brahman*). The bliss enjoyed in deep sleep is not pure bliss; it is bliss enveloped by ignorance.

When you wake up from deep sleep, you remember the bliss of deep sleep and say, "I slept happily". The remembrance of the bliss of deep sleep is an evidence of the existence of a witness of the three states of waking, dream and deep sleep. That witness is *Atman*, the inner Self.

In deep sleep, one does not attain *Brahma Vidya*, Knowledge of Self, because when a person returns from sleep to waking state, he is still ignorant about *Brahman*. He perceives multiple objects as manifold. He does not see the underlying unity of all objects, *Brahman*. However, a sage who does deep meditation has some realization of *Brahman*. He perceives unity and oneness everywhere. This is the difference between sleep and meditation.

Verse 7

The word *Turiya* has no equivalent in English. *Turiya* is distinct from the states of waking, dream and deep sleep. It is a state of total awareness, or Pure Consciousness. Strictly speaking, *Turiya* is not a state. It is the substratum of the other three states – waking, dream and deep sleep. It is *Brahman*, eternal Bliss.

Turiya or *Brahman* cannot be grasped by the senses. Therefore, It is transcendental. It is unseen, unrelated, incomprehensible, indefinable, unthinkable, indescribable.

The subject - object duality is present in different forms in the states of waking, dream and deep sleep. In waking state, object is manifested in material forms. In dreams, object is manifested in mental forms. In deep sleep, object is unmanifested, like the potentialities of a seed. In *Turiya*, the duality of subject - object is transcended altogether. In this, there is neither subject nor object, neither perception nor idea of God. There is only pure consciousness of *Brahman*, the Absolute. Those who know the Truth become the Truth.

Verses 8-12

In previous verses *Atman* has been described in its four states of waking, dream, deep sleep and *Turiya*. The same *Atman* is now described as four sounds of *Aum*.

Aum has three *matras*, (letters, sounds) and one *amatra* (inaudible sound). These correspond to the four states of *Atman*.

- A corresponds to waking state
- U corresponds to dream state
- M corresponds to deep sleep state
- *amatra* or inaudible sound corresponds to Turiya. It is Atman, Self, Pure Consciousness.

When *Aum* is chanted again and again, 'A' and 'U' appear to merge in 'M' and come out of it again. Similarly, waking and dream states appear to merge in deep sleep and come out of it again.

Meditation on *Aum* helps the aspirant in attainment of Self-realization. *Brahman* is realized when illusion of duality or *avidya* disappears through meditation on *Aum*; just as under a torchlight, illusion of a snake vanishes and the rope stands revealed.

– Swami Sivananda

4. Commentary by Swami Krishnananda

The theme of Mandukya Upanishad is a direct approach to the depths of human nature. It does not give analogies, tell stories or make comparisons. It states bare facts about man in general and Reality in its essential character. Containing only 12 *mantras*, it is a very comprehensive Upanishad.

---

*'Brahman is realized when illusion of duality disappears through meditation,
just as under a torchlight, illusion of a snake vanishes and the rope stands revealed.'*

MAGNIFICENCE OF AUM

The Upanishad begins with the Word *Aum*, and says that this eternal Word is ALL that there is, was, will be, and beyond. The implication is that the Word *Aum* comprehends all things, and it also makes auspicious beginning to everything.

Aum is believed to be the first vibratory sound that emanated as the seed of creation. It is the seed mantra for all other mantras. *Aum* is both *nama* and *rupa*, name and form. *Aum* is a self-existent cosmic vibration. It exists in its own right. When we chant *Aum*, we are not creating the sound *Aum*, but only making a connection with this eternal self-existent Word.

Names create vibrations in us. Suppose you are in a gathering and someone shouts: 'Snake!' You will get up immediately. Why? This is because you have established a contact between your psychological being, and meaning of the name 'snake'. Every name in the world has a form and a meaning attached to it. The name *Aum* has attached to it the form and the meaning of the entire universe, and beyond.

Man has a dual personality: *Jiva* and *Ishvara*, the individual and the divine. No particular language can describe *Ishvara*. *Ishvara* is not a human being. It is present everywhere. That which is everywhere cannot be designated by a language that belongs to a particular region or person. There is no language that is valid for the entire cosmos. The only such conceivable language, which was revealed to the ancient Rishis, is *Aum*. *Aum* is thus a symbol of cosmic language. All the languages are contained in it.

When we chant *Aum*, we create within ourselves a vibration, which is in harmony with the entire cosmic vibrations. Instead of thinking independently as *Jiva*, we start thinking universally as *Ishvara*. We flow into *Ishvara's* Being, like a river flowing into an ocean.

When we recite *Aum* properly, we enter into a meditative mood. We create a vibration, which burns all desires, like fire burns straw. We create a vibration, which makes us calm, quiet, and satisfied within ourselves. The chant of *Aum* should go together with the thought of the universal. It is a *Japa* and a *Dhyana*, repeated recitation and meditation combined.

The word *Aum* is imperishable and eternal. How? This is because it symbolizes the Eternal. It has no past, present or future; because the Eternal has no past, present or future. Not only this, whatever is beyond time is also *Aum*.

Aum has twofold nature – the eternal and the temporal. That which is past, present and future is the temporal nature of *Aum*. That which transcends time is the eternal aspect of *Aum*. In the analogy of the river and the ocean, the river is the temporal form, the ocean is the eternal form.

WHAT TO THINK WHEN YOU CHANT AUM?

Think that you are the ocean into which all the rivers of material objects merge. In you, then, there are no objects, no desires, and no rivers. You are the ocean. Imagine this feeling when chanting *Aum*. It is a feeling which I cannot describe. Each person should feel it for himself or herself. Chant *Aum* daily with such a feeling, even for five minutes, and notice the difference it makes to your personality.

SELF IS ABSOLUTE

Verse 2 begins with 'All this is, verily, *Brahman*'. It means that, all this creation is just the Absolute alone. It continues with a great saying, *Mahavakya*: 'This *Atman* is also *Brahman*'. Here you have the quintessence of all Upanishadic teachings. This universe which appears to be proximate to our senses is that *Brahman* which seems to be distant from us. And, this personality of ours (*Atman*) which appears to be so proximate is also that *Brahman* which seems to be so distant from us. In fact, our *Atman* is included in All. In short, This is That. These three words contain vast wisdom.

WHAT IS ATMAN OR SELF?

We speak of I-myself, you-yourself and he-himself. This self is the ego-self, imaginary self, secondary self. It is not the real Self, the primary Self. The real Self is that which is *Brahman* Itself. In the analogy of space, the space contained in a vessel is the same as universal space. Likewise, *Atman* is *Brahman*.

This *Atman* has four states. These are the four states of Consciousness. Study of Consciousness is the same

---

'When we chant Aum, we create within ourselves a vibration, which is in harmony with the entire cosmic vibrations.'

as study of *Brahman*, because Consciousness is *Brahman* (Aitareya 3.1, 3).

STATES OF CONSCIOUSNESS

The four states of Consciousness are: waking, dream, deep sleep and Pure Spirit. When we transcend a lower state to attain the next higher state, we do not negate or reject the lower. It is automatically included in the higher. In a way, it is like 8th standard is included in high school. In the grand process of self-transcendence, God-realization is the end. In this state, the world is not negated or abandoned, but absorbed into Its vitality. God-realization is an integrated Consciousness where we gain everything, and lose nothing. It is a state of perfection. It is the goal of life.

WAKING CONSCIOUSNESS

Waking consciousness is the first aspect of *Atman*. It is conscious of only what is outside. The Upanishad envisages *Atman* in this waking life not merely from the standpoint of microcosm, but also from the standpoint of macrocosm. Therefore, it is not merely an analysis of Self, but it is also a synthesis of the subjective and the objective. The Upanishad brings about a harmony between us and the world, *Jiva* and *Ishvara*, *Atman* and *Brahman*. The seven limbs of *Atman* refer to the definition of Cosmic Self; the nineteen mouths refer to the functions of the Self in its capacity as an individual. The 19 mouths are five organs of senses, five organs of action, five kinds of breaths, mind, intellect, ego and subconscious mind. In waking state, our Consciousness relates with only gross, physical objects through one or more of the 19 mouths. Consciousness in this state is given the name *Vaisvanara* or *Virat* at the cosmic level; at the individual level it is called *Jiva* or *Visva*.

The difference between *Vaisvanara* and *Jiva* is that of desires. *Vaisvanara's* strength is its desirelessness. *Jiva's* weakness is its desires.

DREAM CONSCIOUSNESS

Dream is a state of subtle perception. Objects seen in dream are psychological, not physical. While there is actual pleasure or pain in the waking state, the pleasure or pain during the dream state is only imaginary. The objects of the waking world are not our creations, but objects of the dream world are our own creations.

We regard waking as real and dream as unreal. But this is not the whole truth. Waking objects appear to be of more practical value than dream objects. Now comes the interesting question. Who makes this comparison? It must be someone who passes through both the states. Who is that someone? That someone is our Consciousness, Self, *Atman*. It is a witness to both waking and dream states.

In waking state, the mind makes a distinction between the subject and the object – the seer and the seen. This distinction disappears in dream state. Dream subject and dream object coalesce into one. They come together to form an integrated Consciousness. A similar union takes place in God-realization.

Western psychologists and psychoanalysts have studied dream state very thoroughly. Freud attributed dreams to sexual desires, Alder to inferiority complex, and Jung to an urge for growth and harmony between the extrovert and the introvert nature between us. These viewpoints are true, but only partially. Psychologists have gone from the conscious to subconscious and even unconscious level; but they have overlooked the spiritual super-conscious level.

As claimed by western psychologists, dreams are due to repressed desires and complexes. According to Upanishadic philosophers, there can be other reasons also, that cause dreams - like working of past *karmas*, telepathy, and revelations. In the case of a spiritual disciple, *guru's* grace can produce a dream to pass-over lightly some catastrophic experience, which the disciple would have otherwise endured in waking state. But why does such grace not work in waking state? The reason is that its functioning in waking state is opposed by our ego. Before operating upon a patient the surgeon puts the patient to sleep under anesthesia. In hypnosis also, the patient is put to sleep. Sleeping pills also serve to soothe agitation of mind. Dreams can also be helpful for operation of higher powers.

Consciousness in dream state is called *Hiranyagarbha* at the macro-level, and *Taijasa* or *Jiva* at the micro-level. The difference between the two is that of knowledge, *Hiranyagarbha* has cosmic knowledge, *Jiva* has no such knowledge.

'Psychologists have gone from conscious to subconscious and even unconscious level;
but they have overlooked the spiritual super-conscious level.'

CONSCIOUSNESS IN DEEP SLEEP

The mind is active in both waking and dream states. Complete cessation of mind's activity due to exhaustion is called sleep.

In state of deep sleep a person does not have any desires. He does not see any dreams. He is in a state of bliss, but he is not aware of it.

What is the instrument through which you enjoy this Bliss, *Ananda*? While you had access to 19 mouths in waking state and a lesser number in dream state, you don't need them in sleep. Here the instrument is not the mind, or the senses, but Consciousness Itself. It is Consciousness that experiences bliss. This Consciousness is called *Pragyan* at the micro-level and *Ishvara* at the macro-level. This Consciousness is the source of all creations. It is the causal state both at the macro and micro levels. The distinctions that we saw earlier - between *Vaisvanara* and *Visva* in waking state, between *Hiranyagarbha* and *Taijasa* in dream state - no longer exist in deep sleep. *Jiva* and *Ishvara* become one. It is all God and God alone during deep sleep. *Ishvara* is everywhere, and *Jiva* has no place to exist, apart from being *Ishvara*.

TRANSCENDENT CONSCIOUSNESS

Waking, dream and deep sleep are gross, subtle and causal conditions of Consciousness. Transcending them, there is pure, unconditioned Consciousness. This is described in verse 7. The state in which this pure Consciousness is realized is called *Turiya*. It is neither external, nor internal, nor a combination of the two. It is also not a mass of Consciousness. It is not featureless Consciousness without any awareness. You may think that it is awareness without any object before it. It is not even that, because the object is contained in that Consciousness. It is also not absence of Consciousness. What is it then? It is Pure Consciousness, the Absolute, in its True Being.

Pure Consciousness cannot be perceived by the senses or visualized by the mind. So, It is indescribable. One cannot have any kind of relationship with It. So, It is non-relational. Then, what is It? The Upanishad uses three very important words to attempt some description of It, incomplete as this may be. These words are:

Ekatva : Oneness
Atmatva : Selfhood
Sarvatva : Essence

It is the essence of all things, and It is One, and It is the Self. It cannot be perceived, compared or described. Knowledge of *Atman* is intuition, a non-relational understanding of Reality, independent of the operation of the senses and the mind.

Atmatva or Selfhood is when the knowing subject and the object of its knowledge come together, in a single coalescence of Being.

In state of Pure Consciousness, *Turiya*, there is no trace of the universe. The universe with all its conditions – gross, subtle and causal – ceases here, because there is no creation.

Pure Consciousness is a state of absolute, eternal peace. Our concept of peace is negative and relational. We say we are peaceful when we have everything we want, and no one disturbs us. Peace of *Atman* is non-relative and also everlasting.

Earlier, the Upanishad has called *Atman* as one sole essence. Now it says that we cannot call it even 'one'; as it would mean that *Atman* can be denoted by a numerical figure. We can only say: 'It is not two, or it is non-dual, *advaita*.'

Verse 7 concludes: This is the *Atman* that should be known, realized, made the purpose of life.

AUM IS ATMAN

Atman has three relative states, corresponding to three letters of *Aum*. Waking state is the beginning of the two other states. *Aum* begins with A, so A corresponds to waking state. Meditation on the harmony between 'A' of *Aum* and waking state of *Atman* leads to fulfilment of all desires and achievement of a place of prominence. This meditational technique is called *Vaisvanara Vidya*. It is described in great detail in Chandogya Upanishad (5.11-5.18).

The letter 'U' of *Aum* corresponds to *Taijasa*, dream Consciousness. Likewise, 'M' of *Aum* corresponds with sleep Consciousness. These comparisons are made by the Upanishad to help one in meditation. All these

---

'Knowledge of Atman is intuition, a non-relational understanding of Reality, independent of the operation of the senses and the mind.'

comparisons are symbolic, and we should not take them literally.

Just as there is a transcendent state of *Atman*, there is a transcendent state of *Pranav*, or *Aum*. In this transcendent state, *Aum* is *Atman* Itself. One who knows this secret, by deep meditation, enters *Atman* by *Atman*. This is called Self-realization.

– Swami Krishnananda

5. Commentary by Sri Madhava

According to Sri Madhava, Mandukya Upanishad contains not only the 12 *mantras*, but also the 29 *shlokas*, which are attributed to Gaudapada as his explanatory verses. These were handed down by Lord Varuna himself, in the form of Manduka, or a frog. Consequently, the seer of this Upanishad is Varuna, and the presiding deity is Sriman Narayana. According to Muktika Upanishad, Mandukya Upanishad alone is sufficient to lead one to liberation.

The Lord as *Vaisvanara* activates *Jiva* in waking state, to let it see the outward gross objects. As *Taijasa*, the Lord activates *Jiva* in dream state to see internally the subtle objects. As *Pragyan* in deep sleep, the Lord keeps the senses of *Jiva* in a suspended state, as it were. When the five senses together with the mind and the intellect cease their activities, that is the highest goal, that is *Turiya*. In *Turiya*, *Jiva* gets a glimpse of the Lord.

It is to be noted that none of the four states are superior to the others.

Reality of the world – or its illusory aspect, as believed by *Advaitic* thinkers – has been a subject of much controversy. Sri Sankara, the most original and the most famous protagonist of *Advaita* philosophy is said to have made three statements:

Brahman is real.
Universe is unreal.
Brahman is the universe.

Sri Ramana pointed out that Sri Sankara did not stop with the second statement. According to Sri Ramana, the third statement explains the first two. It signifies that when the universe is perceived apart from *Brahman*, that perception is false and illusionary. Phenomena are real when experienced as *Brahman* and illusionary when seen apart from *Brahman*.

Sri Madhava improvises this statement when he says that *Jiva* and *Jagat* are real in themselves, but illusionary when seen as independent of the influence of the Lord's energizing power. *Jiva* and *Jagat* have no real existence independent of the Lord.

– Sri Madhava, edited by Nagesh D. Sonde

6. Commentary by Rohit Mehta

RELEVANCE OF UPANISHADIC PHILOSOPHY

Science... Psychology... Philosophy...

In the West, psychology regards itself more as an ally of science than philosophy. The beginnings of Indian psychology are to be seen in the philosophy of the Upanishads.

Modern psychology does not know what is mental health. It has drawn its conclusions only from mental diseases. Therefore, what it regards as mental health is the absence of mental disease. But health is not absence of disease. It is something positive.

Modern psychology recognizes three types of influences on the conscious behavior of man: subconscious, unconscious and super-conscious. But the influence of super-conscious remains almost unnoticed. Without its comprehension, the understanding of human psyche must remain incomplete. Without listening to the voice of the super-conscious, any evaluation of man based on the subconscious and unconscious alone is bound to be erroneous. It is like trying to understand the whole by speculation based on knowledge of the parts. Human personality is a whole. It cannot be understood by summation of the parts.

Psychology through its alliance with science may know about the parts. But for the comprehension of the whole, it must form an alliance with philosophy.

THE ETERNAL SOUND OF *AUM*

In Mandukya Upanishad, the sacred word *Aum* and *Brahman* have been used as synonyms. The word *Aum*

'Phenomena are real when experienced as Brahman and illusionary when seen apart from Brahman.'

indicates co-existence of both articulate and inarticulate sounds, of perishable and imperishable sounds. Articulate sound indicates *Atman* in Its manifestations; inarticulate, imperishable sound represents *Atman* in Its unmanifest condition.

Not only the Word was with God, the Word was God. The Word being with God signifies manifestation; the Word being God is the unmanifested state. Mandukya Upanishad says: 'The Word is *Brahman*', and again '*Atman* is *Brahman*.' So it follows that the Word is *Atman*.

CONDITIONED CONSCIOUSNESS

Man's instrument of knowledge is Consciousness. In course of time, this Consciousness acquires numerous modifications. These modifications are like grooves. Every movement in the groove makes the groove deeper. This is how human consciousness gets conditioned and thereby loses sight of its true nature. Man is separated from himself due to the grooves of modification. He becomes so used to moving in grooves, that this movement becomes his second nature; and the second nature completely eclipses the original nature.

Man can be free from this bondage by being aware of his original nature. The moment of awareness is the moment of freedom. The problem of man's freedom is not the problem of acquiring something. On the contrary, it is the problem of negating what he has acquired. Man's Consciousness is covered up – conditioned – with various layers. As layer after layer is negated, there is seen Consciousness in its pure and modified form.

Mandukya Upanishad is mainly concerned with arriving at that state where human Consciousness is free from all its modifications, a state of pristine purity.

STATES OF CONSCIOUSNESS

According to Mandukya Upanishad, in waking state, Consciousness is "outward moving"; and in dream state it is "inward moving". This means that in dream state, Consciousness is moved not by outer objects, but by inner factors. In deep sleep there is no movement of Consciousness.

Modern western psychologists have made an intensive study of dreams. According to Freud and others of his school, dreams contain elements drawn from the subconscious where suppressed desires are located. Carl Jung has introduced a new factor – collective unconscious. Through it, man comes into contact with the vast storehouse of racial experiences. The experiences of human race are not lost, they lie embedded in racial memory.

Memory is the measuring rod of the mind (verse 11). Both in waking and dream states, it is memory that functions and dictates its judgements. In waking state, it is personal memory, and in dream state it is racial memory. In deep sleep, Consciousness is free from all memory.

In waking state there is identification with the past – the subconscious. In dream state there is identification with the future – the unconscious. But a Consciousness moving at the behest of the past or the future is unable to find the Good, the True, and the Beautiful. Deep sleep is an interval where there is neither a past, nor a future. In deep sleep, Consciousness is free from all movement; it is free from memory, and it is free from the flow of time.

The perception of *Atman* comes in a state which the Upanishad calls *Turiya*, and which we have translated as Super-conscious.

– *Rohit Mehta*

7. Commentary by N. A. Nikam

'AWARENESS' THAT NEVER SLEEPS

In Mandukya, states of Consciousness are distinguished as waking, dream and sleep. This gives rise to the question: What is it that is awake, and what is it that is asleep in a state of sleep? If there is an 'awareness' that is aware in sleep, then this 'awareness' never sleeps. If so, that 'awareness' which goes to sleep in sleep state is distinguishable from the 'awareness' which never sleeps. Mandukya Upanishad makes us aware of this 'awareness' which never sleeps – it is Consciousness.

'In waking, Consciousness is 'outward moving'; in dream state it is 'inward moving';
in deep sleep, there is no movement of Consciousness.'

SELF-REALIZATION

In state of sleep, there are no desires, no dreams, no awareness of possessions, not even possession of the body. The problem of Self-realization is to bring about such a situation in waking state? How to create a state of waking-sleep?

The Upanishad says of sleep that it is *ekibhutah*, "becoming one"; there is in it an absence of duality. Ramana Maharishi has illustrated the experience of "becoming one" by two examples:

(i) a bucket in a well with a rope tied to it, so that it can be pulled out again, and
(ii) a river that has joined and *become* the ocean, never to be redirected.

The first is what Ramana Maharishi calls "merging" the mind, and the second is what he calls "destroying" the mind. In the state of sleep, the mind is "merged" like the bucket. It re-merges in waking state.

The yogic practice of *Sahaja Samadhi* provides a sharp contrast to the state of sleep. In *sahaja samadhi*, the yogi enters consciously into Being, and "becomes One" with It. In this state, as per the illustration of Ramana Maharishi, the mind is "destroyed".

– N. A. Nikam

Gaudapada KARIKA: Translation by Swami Nikhilananda

1. *Visva* (the first quarter) is he who is all-pervading and who experiences the external (gross) objects. *Taijasa* (the second quarter) is he who cognizes the internal (subtle) objects. *Pragyan* (the third quarter) is he who is a mass of Consciousness. That who knows all the three states, is One, without a second.

2. *Visva* is he who cognizes in the right eye, *Taijasa* is he who cognizes in the mind within, and *Pragyan* is he who constitutes the Space (*Akash*) in the heart. Thus, one *Atman* is (conceived as) threefold in the (same) body.

3. *Visva* always experiences the gross (objects); *Taijasa*, the subtle; and *Pragyan*, the blissful. Know these to be the threefold experiences.

4. Gross satisfies *Visva*, subtle satisfies *Taijasa*, and blissful satisfies *Pragyan*. Know these to be the threefold satisfactions.

5. He who knows both the experiencer and the objects of experience that have been described (associated) with the three states, is not affected by the experience of the objects.

6. It is fully established that the coming into effect can be predicated of all positive entities that exist. *Prana* manifests all (inanimate objects); *Purusha* creates conscious beings (*Jivas*) separately, in their manifold forms.

7. Some think of creation as a manifestation of superhuman power of God; while others look upon it as dream and illusion.

8. Some attribute this manifestation to mere will of God; some look upon time as real and declare time to be the manifestor of all beings.

9. Others think that manifestation is a sport for enjoyment (of God). But creation is the very nature of the Effulgent Being (*Atman*). What desire is possible for Him whose desires are already in a state of complete fulfillment?

10. It is the changeless and the Supreme Lord. There is a cessation of all miseries in It. It is one, without a second, among all entities. It is known as *Turiya*. It is Effulgent and All-pervading.

11. *Visva* and *Taijasa* are conditioned by cause and effect. But *Pragyan* is conditioned by cause alone. These two (cause and effect) do not exist in *Turiya*.

12. *Pragyan* does not know anything of self or non-self, nor truth or untruth. But *Turiya* is ever existent and ever all-seeing.

13. Non-cognition of duality is common to both *Pragyan* and *Turiya*. (But) *Pragyan* is associated with sleep (ignorance) in the form of cause. This (ignorance of Reality) does not exist in *Turiya*.

14. The first two (*Visva* and *Taijasa*) are associated with conditions of dream and sleep; *Pragyan* is the condition of sleep without dream. Those who have known the truth know that there is neither sleep nor dream in *Turiya*.

15. *Svapna* or dream is wrong cognition of Reality. *Nidra* or sleep is a state in which one does not know what Reality is. When the erroneous knowledge of these two disappears, *Turiya* is realized.

16. When *Jiva* or individual soul, sleeping (i.e., not knowing the Reality) under the influence of *Maya*, is awakened, it then realizes the non-dual causeless Reality.

17. If the perceived universe was real then certainly non-duality would disappear. This duality (that is cognized) is mere illusion (*Maya*). Non-duality (alone) is the Supreme Reality.

18. If anyone has ever imagined the manifold ideas (for instance, the teacher, the taught, and the scripture), they might disappear. This explanation is for the purpose of teaching. Duality ceases to exist when the Highest Truth is known.

19. When the identity of *Visva* and the sound (letter) 'A' is intended to be described, the conspicuous ground is the circumstance of each being the first (in their respective positions). Another reason for this identity is the fact of all-pervasiveness of each.

'Creation is the very nature of the Effulgent Being (Atman).'

20. The reason for regarding *Taijasa* as of the same nature as 'U' is the common feature of their superiority. Another reason for such identity is that both are in the middle.

21. Of the identity of *Pragyan* and 'M', the reason is their common feature; namely, all become one in both *Pragyan* and 'M'.

22. He who knows clearly what the common features are in the three states, is worshipped and adored by all beings; he is also the greatest sage.

23. The sound (letter) 'A' helps its worshipper to attain to *Visva*, 'U' to *Taijasa* and 'M' to *Pragyan*. In the Soundless, there is no attainment.

24. Aum should be meditated upon quarter by quarter. There is no doubt that quarters are the same as sounds (letters). Having grasped the (meaning of) Aum, nothing else need be thought of.

25. The mind should also meditate on a unified *Aum*. *Aum* is *Brahman*, the ever-fearless. He who is always unified with *Aum* knows no fear whatsoever.

26. *Aum* is, verily, the lower *Brahman*; it is also the *Supreme Brahman*. *Aum* is without a cause, unique, without anything outside itself, unrelated to any effect, and changeless.

27. *Aum* is verily the beginning, middle and end of all. Knowing *Aum* as such, one, without doubt, attains immediately to That (Supreme Reality).

28. Know *Aum* to be *Ishvara*, ever present in the mind of all. A man of discrimination, realizing *Aum* as all-pervading, does not grieve.

29. One, who has known *Aum* – which is soundless and of infinite sounds, which is ever-peaceful on account of negation of duality – is the (real) sage, and none else.

'Aum is, verily, the lower Brahman; it is also the Supreme Brahman.'

Swami Nikhilananda on Sri Sankara's Commentary on Gaudapada *Karika*

Verse 1

Atman as the witness is distinct from the three states witnessed by It.

Atman is pure. Ideas of purity and impurity, pleasure and pain, are characteristics of the states. They do not in any way pertain to *Atman*, which is only a witness of the three states. *Jiva* or reflected Consciousness, which is identical with *Atman*, falsely identifies itself with the states and considers itself to be impure, miserable etc. *Atman* is ever pure.

Atman is unrelated. No relationship of any kind exists between the three states and *Atman*. It moves from one state to another without being affected in any way.

This nature of *Atman* is explained with an illustration in Brhadaranyaka Upanishad. As a powerful fish swims from one bank to another, unimpeded by the currents of the river, so also *Atman* moves in the three states, totally unaffected by them. As characteristics of the banks do not affect the fish, so also experiences of the three states do not affect the pure nature of *Atman*.

Another illustration is of a bird, which flies unobstructed in the sky and unattached to the surrounding lands.

Verse 2

The three apparent cognizers – known as *Vaisvanara*, *Taijasa* and *Pragyan* – are really one. Their apparent distinction is due to their identification with the three states.

Dream state and state of imagination in waking are nearly identical. The only difference is that dream represents a whole state whereas imagination (day dreaming) represent a part of a state.

Hiranyagarbha and *Taijasa* are what are termed as the cosmic mind and individual mind. Really speaking, macrocosm and microcosm, both being mere forms of thought, are identical.

Verses 3-5

As the heat of fire does not increase or decrease by consuming wood etc. so also nothing is added to or taken away from *Atman* by Its experiences of various objects.

He who knows that the three states are one and that their perceivers are also one, is not affected by the experiences of the states.

Verse 6

As the rays proceed from the sun, so also all different centers of Consciousness (souls, *jivas*) – which are like many reflections of the same sun in water – proceed from *Purusha*, Cosmic Person. *Purusha* projects from Itself all these entities called living beings – like fire and its sparks; like sun and its reflections in water. *Prana*, the causal Self, manifests the inanimate objects, like a spider producing a web.

It is thus indicated by the text as well as the commentary that there are two manifestors, viz. *Purusha* and *Prana*. In reality, the two are identical. *Brahman* is looked upon as the manifestor of the universe. He is said to be *Prana* when he manifests insentient objects and *Purusha* when he manifests sentient objects. (This is contrary to common understanding of *Prana* as Life force, but it conforms to *Prana* as energy).

Verses 7-9

These put forward six possible theories of creation:

Creation is manifestation of the divine power of God.
Creation is manifested as a dream, or an illusion.
Creation is a manifestation of divine Will.
Creation proceeds from Time.
Creation is for the purpose of enjoyment of God.
Creation is an act of God's sport.

Now, all these theories are refuted by the simple statement that *Brahman*, whose desires are always in a state of fulfillment, cannot create the world for any purpose whatsoever. No causal theory can relate the world to *Brahman*.

'All different centers of Consciousness (souls) are like many reflections of the same sun in water.'

Verse 10

Turiya is non-dual. It brings about cessation of miseries because misery is destroyed by knowledge of *Turiya*. *Turiya* pervades all the three states.

Verse 11

Waking and dream states are conditioned by cause and effect; deep sleep is characterized by cause only. In *Turiya*, both cause and effect are non-existent.

Verse 12

Turiya is designated as all-seeing because it subsists in all the states as their substratum.

Verse 13

Deep sleep is characterized by absence of knowledge of Reality. This is not so in case of *Turiya*.

Verse 14-18

These verses deal with the Vedanta philosophy that the duality seen in the universe is an illusion, and that non-duality (*Turiya*) alone is real and ever existent. The manifold is *Brahman*. As the wave is non-different from water, so also the world is non-different from *Brahman*, Reality.

Verses 19-22

These verses bring out the points of similarity between the three states of Consciousness and the letters of the syllable *Aum*.

Verses 23-25

These describe the results derived from meditation on individual letters of *Aum*, as also from meditation on *Aum* as One Totality.

Verses 26-29

Significance of the syllable *Aum* is described in great detail.

'As the wave is non-different from water, so also the world is non-different from Brahman.'

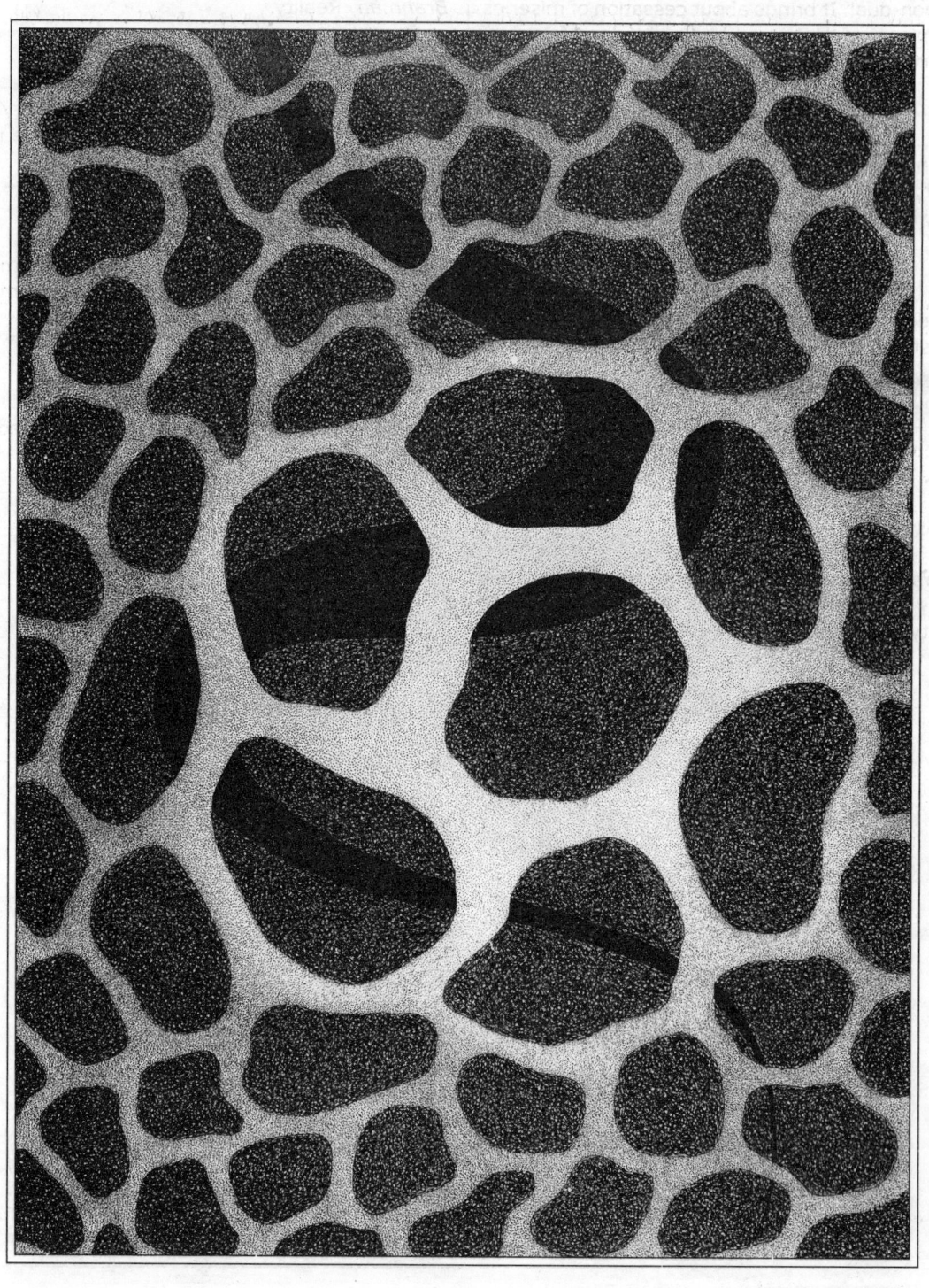

Mundaka Upanishad

One Absolute behind every Relativity

OVERVIEW

Mundaka Upanishad attempts to describe the Indescribable That, which we generally refer to as God, and which the Upanishads refer to as Atman, Brahman or Consciousness. Mundaka also uses the word Purusha or Cosmic Person for It. Various objects, phenomena and laws of Nature are said to constitute His Cosmic Body.

Another important theme of Mundaka is Self-realization, or awareness of Oneness of human Consciousness, cosmic Consciousness and the world. Self-realization is an intuitive experience, which is gained only when the mind is pure. Truthfulness, meditation, study of scriptures and self-discipline purify the mind. 'Truth alone triumphs', declares Mundaka.

The Upanishad also deals with the powers of a meditative mind and how Self-realization changes a man's perspective of life. 'Knower of Brahman becomes Brahman', says the Upanishad.

The Upanishad is full of metaphors and analogies. It also contains a very famous allegory of two birds on a tree. They represent our ego and Self. After many experiences in many lifetimes, ego realizes its Oneness with Self.

COMMENTARIES

The commentators quoted here are: Dr. Karan Singh, Dr. S. Radhakrishnan, Rohit Mehta, Swami Gambhirananda, Swami Chinmayananda, Swami Sivananda, Swami Sarvananda, Swami Paramananda and Swami Vivekananda.

MUNDAKA UPANISHAD
One Absolute behind every Relativity

Peace Invocation

CHAPTER 1
Absolute Consciousness and world of Relativity 518

1.1, 1-5	Two types of Knowledge
1.1, 6	A definition of the Indefinable
1.1, 7	Oneness of Creator and Creation
1.1, 8-9	Sequence of Creation
1.2, 1-10	Rituals: Importance and limitations
1.2, 11-13	Path of asceticism

CHAPTER 2
One Absolute, Many relative manifestations 533

2.1 Everything is rooted in One Absolute
2.2 Oneness of microcosm and macrocosm

CHAPTER 3
Merger of Relative in Absolute... 542

3.1, 1-2	Closer you get, happier you feel
3.1, 3-5	Calm mind in active body
3.1, 6-7	Truth alone triumphs, *Satyameva Jayate*
3.1, 8-10	Power of the mind
3.2, 1-8	Self-Realization is like river merging in sea
3.2, 9-11	One can become what one wants to be

1 Absolute Consciousness and world of relativity

SIMPLIFIED SYNOPSES

1.1, 1-5
Two types of Knowledge

The theme of this section is that the world around us is an emanation from the Absolute, Eternal, Infinite Consciousness called *Brahman*. *Brahman* should not be confused with *Brahma*, which refers to the creative urge latent in the Absolute.

The foundation of all knowledge is the knowledge of the Absolute, *Brahma Vidya*. This was transmitted from one generation to the next through *guru-shishya* or teacher-disciple tradition.

In Mundaka Upanishad, the teacher is Angirasa and the disciple is Saunaka, a renowned householder. Saunaka is credited with a celebrated question: 'What is that knowing which everything else is known?' That, according to Angirasa, is *Brahman*, the Absolute. In chapter 6 of Chandogya Upanishad, it is the teacher, Uddalaka Aruni who confronts his son with this question.

Angirasa makes a distinction between knowledge of Absolute Consciousness and knowledge of the relative world, *para vidya* and *apara vidya*.

1.1, 6
A definition of the Indefinable

The Absolute is beyond any definition. To define It is to limit It. Nonetheless, *Brahman*, the Absolute is said to be invisible, ungraspable, without attributes and without organs. It is also described as eternal, many-splendored, all-pervading and very subtle. It is the source of all.

1.1, 7
Oneness of Creator and Creation

It is not easy to comprehend how the universe could have come out of the Absolute, *Brahman*. Angirasa illustrates this with three analogies – a spider creating a web out of itself and then withdrawing it into itself, effortless sprouting of plants on earth, and growth of hair only on a living person.

1.1, 8-9
Sequence of Creation

Next, Angirasa explains the process of creation of the relative universe from Absolute Consciousness. The first step is *tapas*, a word that has been given many translations by commentators – like austerities, warmth of love, contemplation and will power. *Tapas* gave rise to a creative urge. From that was formed matter, five elements, life, mind, planes of Consciousness called worlds, and the phenomenon of work and its rewards, or the law of cause and effect. This ancient Upanishadic account of creation is considered to be a forerunner of the 'Big Bang' by some commentators.

'Upanishadic account of creation is a forerunner of the 'Big Bang'...'

In conclusion, Angirasa says that *Brahman* is all-knowing, that this world of names and forms has been produced out of Absolute Consciousness, or *Brahman* Itself.

1.2, 1-10
Rituals: Importance and limitations

'Heaven is a state of the mind.'

Performance of rituals and recitation of sacred hymns occupy an important place in India's culture. The Vedas prescribe specific rituals with elaborate procedures for gaining material rewards of various kind. Performance of rituals is also considered useful preparation for spiritual progress. Verses 1-2 advocate that rituals must be performed diligently and with faith. As an illustration, verse-3 enumerates certain practices which must be followed in performance of fire-sacrifice, *Agnihotra*. It also cautions that lapses can lead to adverse results.

In ancient times, Fire, *Agni* was considered a sacred object of worship and meditation. In verse-4, the various regions of a flame are described metaphorically as seven leaping tongues. These, according to one commentator, symbolize seven-colored goddess, or seven aspects of *Shakti*, the feminine power of creation. Other commentators suggest that sacrifice is an exquisite symbol of inner offering, and so we must set up sacrificial fires within us.

Those who perform sacrifices get heavenly rewards. Heaven, according to most commentators, is a state of the mind. Again, in a poetic language, verses 5-6 state that those who perform sacrificial rituals diligently are led to heaven with words of praise by the sacrificial fires – like rays of sun leading to the sun.

Despite their importance, rituals also have limitations. Their rewards are finite and once these are exhausted, one is again subjected to old age, misery and death. They are like a frail boat, which is incapable of reaching the other shore of liberation, or like a blind leading another blind.

According to one commentator, rituals serve a fundamental purpose, but it will be a tragedy to waste the entire lifetime in mere rituals. The worth of rituals is temporary and limited in comparison with the path of *Brahma Vidya*, knowledge of the Absolute.

1.2, 11-13
Path of asceticism

Asceticism and materialism are the two extremes of life-style. These verses describe the path of asceticism for gaining knowledge of the Absolute, *Brahma Vidya*. Some of the essential features of this path are: performance of austerities with faith, life of a mendicant in solitude, control over senses, and spiritual study under a teacher, who is learned and who has realized Self.

'Despite their importance, rituals also have limitations.'

Translated Text

Peace Invocation

Om.
O gods, may we hear auspicious words with our ears.
O Worshipful One, may we see auspicious things with our eyes.
May we live our entire life cheerfully and in good health,
  offering our praises unto Thee.

May *Indra*, the ancient and the famous, bless us.
May *Pusan* (sun), the all-knowing bless us.
May *Vayu* (Life Principle), the Lord of swift motion,
  who protects us from all harms, bless us.
May *Brhaspati*, the Lord of wisdom, bless us.

Om. Shanti. Shanti. Shanti.
Let there be Peace, Let there be Peace, Let there be Peace.

CHAPTER 1

Section 1

Aum. Brahma, the creator of the universe, the protector of the world, was self-born before all the gods. He taught the knowledge of *Brahman* (*Brahma Vidya*), which is the foundation of all knowledge, to his eldest son Atharvana. **1**

That knowledge Atharvana imparted in ancient times to *Agni*. He in turn taught it to Satyavaha of Bharadvaja family. Satyavaha passed it on to Angirasa. The knowledge thus descended from gurus to their disciples. **2**

Saunaka, a renowned householder, once approached Angirasa in the manner laid down by the scriptures, and asked:

'Master, what is that knowing which everything else is known?' **3**

To him, Angirasa replied: Knowers of *Brahman* declare that there are two types of knowledge to be acquired – the higher and the lower, *para* and *apara*. **4**

Lower knowledge consists of the four Vedas – *Rg Veda*, *Yajur Veda*, *Sama Veda* and *Atharva Veda* – phonetics, rituals, grammar, etymology, metrics, astronomy, and the like. Higher knowledge is that by which the Imperishable is attained. **5**

That which is invisible, ungraspable, without origin or attributes, which has neither eyes nor ears, neither hands nor feet, which is eternal and many splendored, all-pervading and exceedingly subtle; that imperishable Being is what the wise everywhere perceive as the source of all creation. **6**

As a spider spreads out and withdraws (its thread); as herbs sprout upon earth; as hair grow on the head and body of a living man; so from the Imperishable comes out the universe. **7**

"Master, what is that, knowing which everything else is known?"

From *tapas* (contemplative power, will power) springs forth *Brahma* (creative urge). From creative urge, *anna* (matter) is produced. From matter come *Prana* (life), *manas* (mind), the five elements, the worlds, work, and immortal (long-lasting) fruits of work. **8**

From *Brahman*, who is all-knowing and all-wise, whose *tapas* consists of Consciousness, are all these produced: the creator, names and forms, and food for all. **9**

Section 2

This is the truth. The rituals, which the seers beheld in the sacred hymns, are elaborated in the three Vedas. O lovers of truth! Perform them diligently, for they are your paths to the world of good deeds. **1**

When the sacrificial fire is well kindled and the flames begin to move, offer your oblations with faith, between the two portions of fire. **2**

If *Agnihotra* is not performed correctly, then it ruins one's future in the seven worlds. For example, if it is unaccompanied by rites to be performed at the new moon, the full moon, and the four months of autumn; if it is without an offering of the first-fruits of harvest; if it is unattended by guests; if it is done without worshipping the deities and feeding the birds and the animals; and if it is contrary to the procedures laid down in the Vedas. **3**

The fire has seven flickering tongues – black, fierce, swift-as-mind, crimson, smoke-colored, scintillating and many-splendored. **4**

Whoever performs the rites and makes the offerings into these shining flames at the proper time; the oblations lead him, like the rays of the sun, to the place where the Lord of gods resides. **5**

"Come with us". "Come with us", say the bright oblations as they carry the performer (of *Agnihotra*) up on the rays of the sun. They address him with pleasant words of praise: "This is the world of *Brahma* (which you have) gained by your good deeds." **6**

Verily, frail is this boat of *Yagya* (fire rituals) with its 18 supports; it represents only inferior deeds. The ignorant who acclaim it as the highest deed are repeatedly subjected to old age and death. **7**

Though they consider themselves to be wise and learned, they are fools wandering aimlessly, like the blind led by the blind. **8**

Revelling in multifarious ignorance, such people think they have achieved the goal of life. However, being bound to passions and attachment, they do not attain knowledge; and they sink down in misery when the rewards of their good deeds are exhausted. **9**

"From Brahman, whose tapas consists of Consciousness, are all these produced: the creator, names and forms, and food for all."

Such deluded fools regard fancy sacrificial and charitable acts as most important, and they do not know greater good. Having reaped in heaven their rewards of good deeds, they enter again this world, or even a lower (animal) world. **10**

Those who perform austerity (*tapas*) with faith, live in solitude, have control over their senses, are learned, and lead the life of a mendicant; they depart, freed from sin, through the path of the sun, to where the Immortal, the Imperishable Being dwells. **11**

Let an aspirant (*Brahmin*) – after he has examined the world that can be gained by work (*Karma*) – acquire freedom from all desires, reflecting that nothing that is eternal can be gained by work. To gain the knowledge of the eternal, let him take sacrificial fuel in his hands and approach that preceptor alone, who is well versed in scriptures and established in *Brahman*. **12**

To such a seeker, whose mind is tranquil and whose senses are controlled, who has approached the *guru* in proper manner, let the learned teacher impart knowledge of *Brahman*, by which alone Imperishable Being (*Purusha*) is realized. **13**

FOCUSSED COMMENTARIES

CHAPTER 1

1.1, 1-5 Two types of Knowledge

Brahma, the creator of the world, arose by exercise of his choice. His rise is unlike the birth of individuals, which is determined by their past deeds.

Lower knowledge is concerned with perishable things and beings. Higher knowledge deals with the Imperishable Being.

– S. Radhakrishnan

In the Upanishads, *Brahma* is used both in masculine and neuter genders. In masculine usage, it means that deity in the Trinity who is the creator of the world of names and forms. When the word is used in neuter gender as *Brahman*, it means the Supreme Reality out of which everything came out – including *Brahma* himself.

Brahma is not a product of sperm and ovum. He is self-born. He is the manifestation of the creative urge in Reality, *Brahman*.

In the question of verse 3, Saunaka wants to know what is that knowledge which is the very substance of all knowledge? In short, he wants to know the Light Principle in our intelligence by which we come to know of things.

Maharishi Angirasa starts his discourse with a classification of all knowledge in two distinct groups – the lower and the higher, the terrestrial and the transcendental. The question of the disciple is about the transcendental.

In verse 5, the Rishi says that even the knowledge contained in the Vedas is lower knowledge! This must have been a shock to the disciple, as the Vedas are considered to be the inspired revelations of *Brahman* Itself. The Rishi therefore hastens to add that higher knowledge is that which is beyond the word-meaning of the Vedas. It is an experience of the state of Immortality.

– Swami Chinmayananda

Vedas imply assemblage of words. Knowledge of *Brahman* is called higher knowledge, because it is not attained merely by a mastery of the assemblage of words. A realization of the Imperishable requires additional effort and practice.

– Swami Gambhirananda

In Vedic cosmology, creation is symbolized as the bursting of the cosmic egg, *Hiranyagarbha*. This is the spiritual parallel to what scientists now call the 'Big Bang' (1.1, 1).

Humility is a strong characteristic of Hindu philosophy, art and architecture. Great masters often choose to remain anonymous. If their names do appear in some way, they make it clear that they are not advocating a new doctrine, but simply expounding the perennial wisdom that has come down through the ages. They look upon themselves as inheritors and trustees of priceless treasure, which they wish to enrich and pass on to their disciples (1.1, 2).

According to the Vedas, a full human life has a span of one hundred years. Saunaka was transiting from the householder's stage – where he had made his mark in society – to the next stage in which his quest for wisdom led him to the hermitage of Angirasa. He approached the master in accord with the scriptures – that is, with humility and reverence. These are essential prerequisites for spiritual quest. Such an attitude evokes a positive response from the teacher. It also puts the seeker in a receptive frame of mind.

Saunaka's worldly success has not overshadowed his desire for enlightenment. In verse 3, he asks a very famous question, the reply to which constitutes the rest of the Upanishad. The purport of his question is to discover that knowledge which forms the basis of all other knowing (1.1, 3).

Angirasa begins his reply with the celebrated statement about two kinds of knowledge – lower and higher, *apara* and *para*. Significantly, even the Vedas – the most sacred of Hindu scriptures, believed to be the voice of the Divine Itself – are considered as lower knowledge. Clearly, what sage Angirasa is saying is that purely intellectual study of even the most sacred of all

---

'Lower knowledge is concerned with perishable things and beings.
Higher knowledge deals with the Imperishable Being.'

scriptures cannot be considered higher knowledge. Higher knowledge means spiritual realization, or to paraphrase Angirasa, attainment of the Imperishable. This is something beyond scholarly study of the scriptures. Human mind is certainly a marvellous instrument for study of lower knowledge, but when it comes to spiritual illumination, we have to transcend language and logic (1.1, 4-5).

– *Karan Singh*

In the Upanishad, knowledge about relative things has been called *apara vidya* or lower knowledge, and knowledge about the Absolute has been called *para vidya* or higher knowledge. The words lower and higher do not denote correctly what is meant by *apara* and *para vidya* respectively. *Apara* or the lower is knowledge of the immanent, while *para* or the higher is knowledge of the Transcendent. Knowledge is a means to attain an end. It is the end which determines the means. So, it is in terms of end result that knowledge is called either lower or higher.

Knowledge from sacred books does not become higher merely because of its source – what matters is its end use.

The Absolute, *Brahman*, has been called Eternal and Omnipresent, meaning It is beyond Time and Space. *Brahman* is Timeless and Spaceless. But Time and Space constitute the framework in which alone mind functions; so *Brahman* cannot be known by the normal methods of the mind – like observation, reasoning or inference. Relative knowledge belongs to the domain of the mind, Absolute knowledge lies on the edge of the mind. Relative knowledge is 'learning', as we know it. Absolute knowledge is intuition, revelation, and inspiration, about which we know very little.

– *Rohit Mehta*

1.1, 6 A definition of the Indefinable

Spiritual texts like the Upanishads deal with concepts which are beyond rationality, and therefore difficult to explain in words. The Upanishads very often use a language of paradox and contradictions, so that the disciple can see that words cannot be a substitute for experience.

In verse 6, there are two sets of description regarding *Brahman*.

The first description contains some negative attributes; it says what *Brahman* is not. This may appear to contradict the most basic doctrine of the Upanishads that *Brahman* pervades everything. The intention in enumerating the negative attributes is to make the point that *Brahman* is not something that can be restricted or limited to any form or name.

The second description of *Brahman* contains positive attributes like eternal, all-pervading, imperishable, etc. These descriptions of *Brahman* seem to contradict the earlier statement in this verse itself that *Brahman* is without attributes. Clearly, there is a profound message hidden behind these verbal descriptions of *Brahman*.

The Sanskrit word for world is *samsara*, which means 'that which constantly changes'. The ancient seers realized that behind this constant process of change, there was an unchanging Reality. The seers called it *Brahman*.

We ourselves contain in some way a direct access to the Highest, Absolute Consciousness, which has been called *Brahman* in the Upanishads. While our bodies last for only a few decades, *Atman* within us is immortal and indestructible - like *Brahman*, of which it is a part. According to the Upanishads, *Atman* and *Brahman* are one and the same.

– *Karan Singh*

Verse 6 represents the most perfect definition of the Indefinable. It has been quoted very often. A wealth of meanings lie concealed behind the words used in this verse.

Invisible : The Supreme Reality is the seer in us. With the same instrument of vision, the seer cannot see himself. For example, with a telescope an observer can observe the moon, but he cannot observe himself. However tired you may be, you cannot ride upon your own shoulders. With your eyes, you can never hope to see your own eyes. Accordingly, *Brahman* in us is described as invisible.

'Relative knowledge is 'learning', as we know it. Absolute knowledge is intuition, revelation and inspiration, about which we know very little.'

Ungraspable:	A driver at the steering wheel cannot be run-over by the same car. The moment the driver leaves his seat and rushes to the front of the car, the car will stop. The car has no motion of its own, and so cannot run-over its driver. Similarly, *Atman*, the dynamic power that vitalizes the mind and makes it possible for the mind to grasp things, cannot be grasped by the mind. To grasp *Atman* as an object, the subject (the mind) should stand apart from the object. The moment the mind divorces itself from *Atman*, it loses its power to comprehend. Hence, we say that *Brahman* cannot be comprehended.
Without origin	: Everything which is created or formed must perish or die; because that which has a beginning also has an end. The Eternal has no end, and therefore, It could not have a beginning either. To say that It has a beginning will lead to a ludicrous paradox like: There was a time when Reality was not Real.
Without attributes	: Attributes are properties perceived by the senses, felt by the mind or deduced by the intellect. In short, attributes can exist only in an object illumined by the subject. Anything that has attributes, is finite. *Brahman* is infinite, so It cannot have attributes.
Without organs	: *It has neither eyes nor ears, neither hands, nor feet:* Earlier the Upanishad explained that the Supreme is not visible to us, but can It see us? This is denied here. The Supreme has neither the organs of knowledge, nor the organs of action. The All-pervading needs no instruments for Itself. There are no objects in Him other than Himself. There is no ignorance in Him to be discovered with some knowledge. He is Knowledge itself.
	Again, action is not possible for the All-pervading. If you are already occupying the entire space in a chair, there is no additional space left in that chair for you to occupy. Similarly, Pure Consciousness, which is All-pervading, feels no necessity to act, or to move.
Eternal etc.	: The other epithets used in the verse are all logical conclusions of the above-described ideas. That which is unoriginated must be eternal. That which is eternal must be all-pervading. If It is all-pervading, then the entire world of matter must be in a sense nothing but Its own manifestation. All pervasiveness indicates a state of highest subtleness.

This exhaustive and supra-mental definition of *Brahman* must have overwhelmed Saunaka. So the Rishi assured him that in short, the Supreme is the source of all creation.

– *Swami Chinmayananda*

1.1, 7 Oneness of Creator and Creation

Certainly, analogies are the only instruments of expressing the inexpressible. Verse 7 uses the analogies of a spider, sprouts and hair to explain the concept of *Brahman*.

The moment we think of *Brahman* as the creator of the universe, we imagine the Lord as a pot-maker creating the world out of some substance, which is different from Himself. This image is denied here.

A spider creates a web out of itself, and withdraws it unto itself. The material of the web becomes the very substance of the spider. In short, the web is nothing but a modified form of the spider itself. Similarly, the material world is *Brahman* Itself.

The spider analogy may suggest a personal motivation of the spider. The second analogy is intended to deny such a motivation on the part of *Brahman*. There is no motivation for planet earth to make herbs sprout on it. Similarly, the world comes out of *Brahman* without any motivation on part of *Brahman*.

'The moment we think of Brahman as the creator of the universe,
we imagine the Lord as a pot-maker. This image is denied here.'

Could *Brahman* be insentient like earth, incapable of knowing or feeling? The third analogy denies this doubt as well. It says that the finite has come out of the Infinite, just as hair grow on the head and body of men. The growth is without any effort or suffering, and it is an indicator of vitality. No hair grows on the body or head of a dead person.

The three analogies thus give three sets of ideas:

- The world emanates from *Brahman* and dissolves into It, without any other intervention or cause than *Brahman* Itself.
- Creation is an effortless projection, a divine play, *Lila*.
- *Brahman* is a conscious Living Being, a vital Personality, an all-pervading Essence. It is Existence – Consciousness – Bliss, *Sat-Chit-Ananda*.

– *Swami Chinmayananda*

Just as seeds remain latent underground in winter and burst forth into herbs and plants in rainy season, so also *Jivas* remain latent in *Pralaya* (state of cosmic dissolution) with their different *karmas* in seed form. They come out at the time of creation as beings of different kinds, but their roots are always in *Brahman*.

– *Swami Sivananda*

There is no suggestion here that the world is an illusionary appearance of *Brahman*. The illustrations are intended to convey that *Brahman* is the sole cause. There is no second to *Brahman*, which can be used by Him.

– *S. Radhakrishnan*

Here, in three simple and homely similes, the teacher illustrates the fact that the entire universe, with all its myriad and multifaceted manifestations, is a natural and spontaneous emanation from *Brahman*. This is a clear refutation of the often–misunderstood concept of *maya*, which regards the universe as an illusion.

The illustrations also contain a hint that creation is a recurrent process, and not a one-shot event. The underlying Hindu view of time being cyclical, rather than linear, is also indicated. All the three processes of a spider weaving its web, plants growing upon earth and hair on human body are recurrent and repeated phenomena.

– *Karan Singh*

Creation is not real transformation of *Brahman*, but only a projection of Its power. In this sense, *Brahman* is both the efficient and the material cause of the universe.

– *Swami Sarvananda*

The teacher leads his pupil, step by step, to that perception of *Brahman*, which is free from interpretations of the mind. In verse 1.1, 7, he gives three illustrations from the vegetable, animal and human worlds to illustrate what the creation of the universe from *Brahman* is like. *Brahman* is both the material cause and the efficient cause of creation, like a spider creating and uncreating a web out of itself, needing no help or material from outside. Creation is without any motive, like the growth of plants from earth. And the process of creation is effortless, like growth of hair on a live body.

– *Rohit Mehta*

1.1, 8-9 Sequence of Creation

The word *tapas*, is very often misunderstood as 'austerity'. Austerity is only one of its significant aspects. Here, *tapas* seems to mean 'concentrated thinking'.

The verses explain various states in the process of creation. First, the creative urge in *Brahman* swells in an impatience of self-expression. From that emerges the whole world of matter. From matter manifests life as known to us. *Prana* here means life-breath. There is a close relationship between life-breath and mind. When the mind is agitated, the rhythm of breathing is quick; when the mind is at rest and at peace, breathing is smooth and quiet. Where there is no life, there cannot be a mind. Thus, the Upanishad concludes that mind springs forth from life.

'The worlds' in verse 1.1, 8 do not refer to physical worlds, but to 'planes of experiencing'. When there is a field of experiencing, and when matter, life, and mind are brought to play in this field, individuals indulge in action. Actions lead to reactions, or fruits of action. These are called immortal here in a relative sense. Actions may end, but their reactions do not die away till they bring their effects to bear upon the mind and

---

*'From the creative urge in Brahman, Matter is the first to emerge.
From Matter manifests Life. Mind springs forth from Life.'*

the body. In this sense, the Upanishad calls the fruits of action as immortal.

Verse 1.1, 9 summarizes the previous verses. *Brahman*, the all-knowing, is pure Consciousness. Its creative urge is the source of creation. 'Name and form' is an idiom used frequently in the Upanishads to describe the material and phenomenal world.

– *Swami Chinmayananda*

The *Tapas* of *Brahman* here is the knowledge of how to create? *Tapas* denotes reflection on the shape and character of the world which *Brahman* is about to project. Just as a father desirous of begetting a son dilates with joy, so also *Brahman* swells with joy of creation.

Brahma or *Hiranyagarbha* is the cosmic mind, the cosmic energy, the cosmic egg. He is the sprouting seed of the totality of all the creatures of this universe. He is also the common thread, the soul of this universe. He is the intelligent power that is at the back of all creation.

– *Swami Sivananda*

Tapas or contemplative power is the energy by which the world is produced.

Brahman is of the form of the indestructible Word. Creation is the dual form of Word and meaning.

– *S. Radhakrishnan*

The transmutation of infinite, formless, eternal *Brahman* into the manifested cosmos represents the mystery of creation. The notion of *Brahman* expanding into the cosmos could perhaps be linked with a 'Big Bang' at some point in time. However, there could be an infinite number of such bangs, each resulting in a cosmos. Also, regardless of how often *Brahman* manifests, It does not dilute Its transcendental dimension.

The Upanishadic world-view is positive and life-affirming. Man is not a sinner. He is not condemned to eternal suffering until redeemed by a saviour. Rather, he is a product of evolution; he can work out his salvation through outer and inner activity in this universe.

– *Karan Singh*

Here *Tapas* does not mean austerity. One of the meanings of *Tapas* is warmth. *Brahman* creates out of warmth. It means that creation of the universe is an act of love. Love is effortless and spontaneous. Effort is needed when there is a motive. If love has a motive than it is no love at all. *Brahman* creates the universe out of love, for it is motiveless. In fact, the warmth of love of *Brahman* is present in all parts of the universe. It is this warmth which sustains it. To feel this warmth in creation is to experience the presence of *Brahman*. He is Omnipresent (1.1, 8-9).

– *Rohit Mehta*

Tapas means Will to create. The creative Will of the Absolute is not like the creative will of human beings. Human beings are modified or affected by their creative will, whether it be in the sense of procreation, or making anything new. This transformation does not take place in *Brahman*, just as a desert is not affected by the appearance of a mirage in it.

– *Swami Sarvananda*

1.2, 1-10 Rituals: Importance and limitations

The Upanishad emphasizes that all sacrificial works should be practised scrupulously for attaining purity of heart. It says that fruits of sacrifices are perishable and transitory. It exhorts the thirsting aspirants to cultivate dispassion, austerity, faith, concentration and love of solitude, for the attainment of immortality and eternal bliss.

– *Swami Sivananda*

Verse 1 advocates diligent performance of rituals in the initial stages of spiritual quest. Verses 2-3 caution that rituals have their own rules of where and when they are to be performed. The path of rituals is painful, complicated and difficult; and incorrect performance can destroy the performer. In short, the Upanishad is severely emphasizing the drudgery of rules in ritualism and trying to wean the disciple away from desire-prompted rituals.

Verse 4 is a description of ritualistic fire. In Vedic times, fire was considered a sacred idol to worship and meditate upon. It is by concentrating on the different flames of fire that the sages sharpened their mind

---

'Love is effortless and spontaneous. Effort is needed when there is motive. Brahman creates the universe out of love.'

and intellect, to soar to peaks of spiritual perfection and knowledge. Verses 5-6 have an important meaning latent in them. Conscious action performed with an intense desire to gain the fruits thereof, leaves behind corresponding traits and impressions on the mind. Verses 7-10 again condemn blind ritualistic fervor of ignorant fanatics.

The Upanishads constitute the concluding part of the Vedas. The aforesaid verses generally condemn rituals motivated by desires. However, in the initial parts of the Vedas called *karma kanda*, there is a sincere advocacy of the performance of rituals. This may look like a contradiction, but it is not so. When your son is in the elementary class, you have to insist that he should recite the multiplication table daily, so that he may memorize it. However, it would be absurd if you were to do so during his postgraduate studies. Similarly, rituals have an elementary purpose, without which nothing higher is possible. But to continue wasting the entire lifetime in mere ritualism will be a terrible tragedy.

– *Swami Chinmayananda*

The opposition of the Upanishads to the observance of rites is greatly exaggerated. The performance of rites is unnecessary for those who are already liberated, but it is necessary for attaining liberation. When performing rites, we must be fully aware of what we are doing. There is a vital difference between a routine performance of rites and their performance with an understanding of their meaning and purpose.

In Vedic mythology, it is narrated that once both demons and deities set up sacrificial fires (*Agnihotra*). The demons performed the rites externally. However, the gods set up the fires in their inner Self. Having done so, the gods became immortal and invincible.

We must set up the sacrificial fires within us. We must feed the flame by truthful utterances; speaking falsehood will quench the flame.

The distinction between external conformity and inward purity is ultimately resolved when the whole life is interpreted and lived sacrificially.

– *S. Radhakrishnan*

Verse 1 advocates performance of rituals that were prescribed in scriptures in ancient times, like the holy ritual of *Agnihotra*. It involves pouring of melted butter and other offerings in sacred fire, with simultaneous chant of sacred verses in Sanskrit. Fire was looked upon as an intermediary between human beings and divine powers. Sacrifice is an exquisite symbol of inner offerings that lie at the heart of spiritual quest. In the outer sense also, sacrifice is believed to bring great rewards in present as well as future lives.

It must be remembered that the minute details built into the fire rituals (verses 2-3) were not prescribed in a casual or arbitrary manner. They emerged as a result of careful and meticulous experimentation by many generations of sages.

The Sanskrit verse for guest in verse 3 is *atithi*. It literally means one who comes without fixing a date. An unexpected visitor on an auspicious occasion is believed to carry a magical mantle. It was looked upon as a good omen if a person of wisdom and austerity arrived during a sacrifice and accepted the sacrificial meal.

The seven worlds referred to in verse 3 denote the seven states of Consciousness: *bhur, bhuvah, suvah, maha, gyana, tapa* and *satya* - starting from the material, and rising all the way to the spiritual. The drift of verse 3 seems to be that incorrect rendering of fire sacrifice can have adverse effects at many levels.

Verse 4 portrays the leaping tongues of fire in a very powerful language. These are symbolized as seven aspects of *shakti*, the feminine power of creation. The all-pervasive *Brahman* is beyond gender. However, Its power is believed to be feminine. In the present context, fire is looked upon as the seven-colored goddess, who is worshipped in many rituals. The goddess is protective of her devotees, but she is also the destroyer of the wicked.

After praising the performance of *Agnihotra*, the sage makes a dramatic turn-around and starts emphasizing its limitations. He decries sacrificial rituals performed merely for fulfillment of selfish desires. The seer does not condemn sacrificial or charitable deeds as bad. He simply points out vehemently that their worth is temporary and limited in comparison with the path of *Brahma Vidya*; which he proceeds to expound in the verses that follow.

– *Karan Singh*

'Conscious action, performed with an intense desire to gain the fruits thereof, leaves behind corresponding traits and impressions on the mind.'

1.2, 11-13 Path of asceticism

Verses 11-13 glorify asceticism and advocate it as the correct route for gaining *Brahma Vidya*.

Spiritual life in India has solitary meditation as one of its essential stages. It has been the cherished ambition and pursuit of spiritual seekers. After a prolonged practice of solitary meditation in the forests, or in the mountains, an ascetic travels like a mendicant. He has no fixed residence. Monasteries in ancient times were considered temporary rest house, or centres of learning.

The Hindu system of four *ashrams* required a person to renounce the world and become an ascetic (*sanyasi*) during last quarter of his life, which was presumed to be a hundred years. This system had a great influence on the Indian mind. Later, the Jain and the Buddhist orders became more centralized and co-ordinated. *Ashrams* and *Mutts* became more popular even among the Hindu monks. To erect an *ashram* for a wandering ascetic is now considered an act of religious piety. (This explains the mushroom growth of lavish ashrams in India and abroad, set up with finances from rich devotees.)

– S. Radhakrishnan

The word *Brahmin* (verse 12) means a fully evolved human being, who has a spiritual urge for greater existence than the world of desires and work.

In order to gain *Brahma Vidya*, a *Brahmin* must approach a guru. The Upanishad says that the guru should have two essential qualifications:
* a mastery of scriptures
* personal experience of *Brahman*.

In olden days, the student approached the teacher carrying a bundle of wood clipping or twigs in his hands. This was a symbol of the student's readiness to surrender completely to the discipline of the teacher. The teacher would reciprocate by teaching *Brahma Vidya* in all its aspects.

– Swami Chinmayananda

The Rishi now goes on to state that immortality can be gained only by renouncing worldly possessions. Curiously, the teaching is being imparted to Saunaka, who has been earlier described as a great householder. It is not recorded whether Saunaka actually renounced the world after receiving this teaching.

The basic argument of these verses is that as along as we remain caught in the net of the senses, our desires will inexorably pull us back from the spiritual path. We can attain the state of *Brahman* only if we alter our course drastically, renounce worldly attractions, and turn all our energies to the inner path.

The first chapter of the Upanishad closes with an important statement. *Brahma Vidya,* higher knowledge, can be imparted only if there is a humble and devoted spiritual seeker, and a learned and Self-realized teacher. This is to be carefully noted. Though the move towards spirituality is to be generally welcomed, an 'unripe disciple - unbalanced guru' combination can cause serious damage.

– Karan Singh

'Though the move towards spirituality is to be generally welcomed, an 'unripe disciple-unbalanced guru' combination can cause serious damage.'

2 One Absolute, many relative manifestations

SIMPLIFIED SYNOPSES

**2.1
Everything is rooted in One Absolute**

'The whole universe is like a body of the Absolute, Cosmic Person.'

All living beings emerge from the Absolute and eventually dissolve in the Absolute – like sparks leaping from a blazing fire and falling back into it. Each one of us embodies in some mysterious fashion a divine spark of Consciousness. The Absolute is both the instrumental and the material cause of the universe. The Absolute has become relative. Cause has become effect. God has become the universe (2.1, 1).

The next verse is partly a repetition and partly an expansion of verse 1.1, 6, which attempts a definition of the Indefinable. The Absolute is formless, eternal, pure and omnipresent. It is without breath or mind. It transcends even the transcendent (2.1, 2).

Verse 3 is similar to verse 1.1, 8. The Absolute is the ultimate source of life, mind, senses and the five elements.

The whole universe is like a body of the Absolute. The word used for It in verse 4 is *Purusha*, or Cosmic Person, Supreme Being. The verse uses poetic similes like: sun and moon are His eyes, space His ears, etc.

Brahman, Absolute Consciousness, is the inner Self of all beings. Verse 5 visualizes a very imaginative route for the journey of the Absolute in human beings. It says that sun and moon – which are like eyes of the Absolute – cause rainfall, which makes food grow on earth. Upon consumption this food is converted into procreative fluid, which a male casts into female. In this manner many human beings are produced from the Absolute, Supreme Being. This doctrine has also been discussed under Panchagni Vidya in Brhadaranyaka Upanishad and Chandogya Upanishad.

The Absolute is the ultimate cause of all that exists – objects, life-forms, phenomena, laws, practices and values, for example. This is illustrated in verses 6-9 with many diverse examples.

'Absolute is Omnipresent but imperceptible.'

Verse 10 sums up the quintessence of the Upanishadic viewpoint of *Brahman*, the Absolute: 'Absolute alone is all this universe'. The verse also says that It is hidden in the secret caverns of the heart. Thus, It is Omnipresent but imperceptible. Finally, It is not something one will confront at the end of one's life. It can be known during one's lifetime.

2.2
Oneness of microcosm and macrocosm

Brahman, the Absolute, is the center of our personality. It is therefore said to be bright and very close to us. It is said to be moving in the cavity of the heart, because the heart is universally accepted as the seat of all emotions and inspirations. Being the ultimate cause of everything, It is also their support. It is the foundation of all life forms. It is beyond understanding because It is Itself the Principle of Understanding.

Verse 2 is again an attempt to define the Indefinable. It is self-luminous, most subtle, imperishable and the abode of all that exists. It is life, senses and mind. It is reality. It is immortality.

Immortality does not mean mere survival after death; it means realization of the Absolute. So the Absolute must be made the goal of life. This is illustrated with a very celebrated metaphor. Realizing the Absolute is like hitting a target with an arrow shot from a bow, and simultaneously becoming one with the target. The bow is the knowledge of the Absolute contained in the Upanishads and symbolized by *Aum*. The arrow is the Self (*Atman*), sharpened by meditation. The Absolute is the target to be realized. Concentrate the mind on the target and let the Self merge in the Absolute (2.2, 3-4).

'Self, Atman is the hub of our life.'

The Absolute and Self, *Brahman* and *Atman* are one and the same. The Absolute is the center of the whole universe, of life and of mind. Knowledge of the Absolute is like a bridge to reach immortality (2.2, 5).

Verse 6 contains a very powerful and oft-repeated simile of a wheel with hub and spokes. Self, *Atman* is the hub of our life. The spokes are the imaginary nerves or channels of consciousness through which all our psychic forces radiate from the hub and support the wheel of life. 'However fast the wheel may rotate and wherever it may travel, without the hub, the Self, it will collapse into a twisted metal', writes one commentator. The Upanishad suggests meditation on *Aum* as a symbol of Self for eventually crossing over from the relative to the Absolute (2.2, 6).

'Human body is like a city of Brahman, Brahmapuri.'

The use the word *Vigyana* in verse 7 is significant. It means realization, as opposed to *Gyana*, which means science. The Absolute cannot be perceived through scientific enquiry; we need realization, direct experience. Scientific enquiry is like a road-map, it cannot be a substitute for real seeing.

In verse 7, human body is described as a luminous city of the Absolute, *Brahman*, and given the name *Brahmapuri*. Though the Absolute is imagined to reside in the heart – the center of the body – It really pervades the whole body and directs its functioning.

'Immortality does not mean mere survival after death; it means realization of the Absolute. So the Absolute must be made the goal of life.'

> 'There the Sun does not shine, nor the moon, nor the stars...'

The Upanishads often describe Absolute *Brahman* as One in which even opposites co-exist. Verse 8 uses the word *paravare* to convey this concept. This word has attracted many translations – far and near, spiritual and material, higher and lower. The important point is that when we have such a realization of *Brahman*, we are not overwhelmed by the opposites in life. Again, using a metaphor, the Upanishad says that all the knots of our heart get untied and all our doubts are dispelled.

According to the Upanishads, Self in us is enveloped by five imaginary sheaths of personality: physical, vital, mental, spiritual and blissful. The innermost blissful sheath is considered golden because of its radiance. The source of that radiance is the self-effulgent Self, the Light of lights (2.2, 9).

The Absolute, *Brahman* exists in us as Self, *Atman*. It exists in the cosmos as the Supreme Being, *Purusha*. Now the Upanishad takes our mind beyond the body-senses and beyond the cosmos to a state, which cannot be described in words. So, the teacher Angirasa describes it in negatives: 'There the sun does not shine, nor the moon, nor the stars... All these shine in the reflected glory of the Absolute, so how can the relative illumine the Absolute?' (2.2, 10)

> 'All this elegant universe is *Brahman*.'

Verse 10 is also relevant to a popular ritual, *aarti*, performed regularly by religious persons in India. In this ritual a devotee respectfully lights a small flame and circles it before his deity with worshipful chants. One commentator suggests recitation of this verse after the completion of *aarti*. Offering a small earthly fire to One who enlightens and energizes the whole universe is an apt symbol of love and humility.

Verse 11 expresses the omnipresence of the Absolute in a very poetic language: *Brahman* is everywhere – in the front, at the back, on the right and on the left. All this elegant universe is Brahman.

Verses 10 and 11 are very celebrated and frequently quoted by spiritual teachers.

'When we have a realization of Brahman, we are not overwhelmed by the opposites in life.'

Translated Text

CHAPTER 2

Section 1

This is the truth, O Dear. As from a blazing fire myriad of sparks of similar form leap out, likewise, diverse beings issue forth from the Immutable. Verily, they fall back into it again. **1**

The Divine Being (*Purusha*) is formless, eternal, pure, pervading within and without, unborn, without breath and without mind. He transcends even the transcendent. **2**

From Him are born life, mind, all the senses and the five elements - space, air, fire, water, and the all-supporting earth. **3**

Fire is His head; Sun and Moon His eyes; Space His ears; revealed Vedas His speech; Air His breath and Universe His heart. From His feet, Earth has originated. Indeed, He is the inner Self of all. **4**

From Him emerges fire; (heavens), of which sun is the fuel. (From heaven emerges moon); from moon come the rains which grow herbs upon earth. Nourished by them (energy and food), male casts his seed into female. In this manner many human beings are born from the divine. **5**

From Him are born Vedic hymns, sacred chants, sacrificial rites with all their ceremonies and gifts, time of sacrifice, sacrifice, and worlds purified by sun and moon. **6**

From Him are also born the many gods, celestial beings, mankind, animals and birds, in-breath and out-breath, rice and barley, austerity, faith, truths, self-discipline and values of life. **7**

From Him are born the seven life-breaths, the seven flames, the seven fuels, the seven oblations, the seven worlds in which life-breath moves; seven and seven, which dwell in the secret place of the heart. **8**

From Him are born all these oceans and mountains; from Him flow rivers of all description; from him grow all plants and their saps too. These together with the elements hold the inner Self. **9**

Verily, that Supreme Being (*Purusha*) alone is all this – universe, work and will-power (*karma* and *tapas*). O handsome youth, he who knows this Immortal Being as hidden in the secret caverns of the heart cuts asunder the knots of ignorance, even during this life on earth. **10**

"The Divine Being (Purusha) is formless, eternal, pure, pervading within and without, unborn, without breath and without mind. It transcends even the transcendent."

Section 2

Brahman, the bright one, exists very close to us and moves in the cavity of our heart. It is the great support of everything. In it are established all that breathe, move and wink. Know It as That which is with form and without form, the most adorable, the highest of beings, beyond all understanding. **1**

Luminous, subtler than even the subtlest, the imperishable *Brahman* is the abode of the worlds and all its inhabitants. It is life, speech, mind, reality, and immortality. It is the goal, which must be reached. Know It, O my friend. **2**

The knowledge contained in the Upanishads is like a great weapon, the bow. Fix in it the arrow, sharpened by meditation. Draw it with the mind fixed on *Brahman*. Then, O handsome youth, reach that target – the Immoral *Brahman*. **3**

The *Pranav* (*Aum*) is the bow. *Atman* is the arrow, and *Brahman* is said to be the target. It should be aimed at with full concentration. Your Self should become one with *Brahman*, like an arrow becomes one with the target. **4**

In Him are centered heaven, earth and intermediate space, together with mind and life. Know Him as *Atman*, Self, One, without a second. Dismiss other explanations. This (knowledge) is the bridge to immortality. **5**

Where all the nerves meet – like spokes of a chariot wheel meet at the hub – He moves there within the heart and becomes manifold. Meditate on that *Atman* as *Aum*. Blessings to you in crossing over to the other shore, beyond darkness. **6**

He is all-wise and all-knowing. His glory is reflected here on earth. He is seated within, as if in *Brahmapuri* – the luminous city of *Brahman*. He has become the mind, and He is seated in the heart. He lives in the whole body, and guides the body as well as the life in it. By their direct experience (*Vigyana*), the wise realize Him as a state of blissful immortality. **7**

When we see Him both as the spiritual and the material (higher and lower, or far and near), then the knots of our heart become untied; all our doubts are dispelled and all our *karmas* are consumed (we are liberated from birth and death). **8**

Brahman, Pure and Indivisible, dwells in the innermost golden sheath (of Bliss, *Ananda*). He is the Light of all lights. He is what the knowers of *Atman* realize. **9**

There the sun does not shine, nor the moon, nor the stars. If these luminous bodies do not shine there, how can this earthly fire? Indeed, everything shines as a reflection of His glory. This whole universe is illuminated by His light. **10**

Indeed, the Immortal *Brahman* is everywhere. *Brahman* is in the front, *Brahman* is at the back, *Brahman* is on the right and on the left. *Brahman* is up there and down here. All this elegant universe is *Brahman*. **11**

"Pranav (Aum) is the bow. Atman is the arrow and Brahman is said to be the target. It should be aimed at with full concentration."

FOCUSSED COMMENTARIES

CHAPTER 2

2.1 Everything is rooted in One Absolute

Brahman, the Unchangeable, has become this universe. He is not only the instrumental cause of this universe, but also its material cause. Cause has become the effect. Whenever you see an effect, you can always analyze it into a cause. It follows that if God is the cause of the universe, and the universe is the effect, then God has become the universe. This is the first step in Vedanta.

A second step in Vedanta is that every soul is a part of God, a spark of that infinite Fire. But the infinite is also indivisible, so how can It have parts? The non-dualistic Vedantins solve this problem by maintaining that there is no part. Each soul actually is the infinite *Brahman*.

Then how can there be so many *Brahman*? The sun reflected from millions of globules of water appears to be millions of suns. In the same way all these souls are but reflections of *Brahman*, and not real *Brahman*.

– Swami Vivekananda, from compilation by Advaita Ashram, Kolkatta

Every person is nothing but the Supreme Itself. He or she arises from It, exists in It, and merges back into It. This is explained with the example of sparks from a big fire.

An effect perishes only to become the cause. The seed dies to become the tree. Ornaments made of gold can change only to become a mass of gold. A body made of five elements decomposes back into five elements. Similarly, a spark of fire riding on a little matter exists only as long as it has not consumed the matter. When the consumable matter has been reduced to a speck of ash, the fire-essence in the spark rolls back into the fireplace. Similarly, an individual exists only as along as its conditioning is not eaten up. A *jiva* (living being) is born to burn-up its fruits of actions. When this is accomplished, the body falls down to perish; and the 'spark' of life rolls back to merge with the Life Principle

If all names and forms - matter and phenomena - are nothing but sparks of *Brahman*, what is *Brahman*? This question is answered next. The Sanskrit word for divine is *divya*, one which illuminates. Consciousness expresses itself in us as 'awareness'. When we say that we are aware of any object, we mean that the object is in a beam of light, which emanates from us and illuminates the object for us. Thus, the life-spark in us is described as *divya*, that which illuminates.

From what has been said above, one may conclude that Self is a limited speck within ourselves. The Upanishad explains that Self is both within and without. This all-pervading light of wisdom should naturally be unborn, as it is eternal.

Consciousness is pure in the sense that our sins have no direct contact with it. As an example, sun is not affected by the merits of a good dead, or demerits of a bad deed committed in its rays (2.1, 2).

The entire world of activity (life), feelings (mind), cognition (senses), and the five elements has as its essence the same *Brahman*. This one idea is expressed in different ways in verses 3-10.

An important concept in the Upanishads is that the microcosm and the macrocosm are the same. This idea is expressed poetically in verse 4. The entire verse is a description of the Infinite in terms of the finite. Eyes can function only in the medium of light, so sun and moon are described as the eyes of the Infinite. Sound can travel only through the medium of space, so space is described as the ears of the Infinite.

Verses 5-10 explains with many different examples that the entire world outside and within ourselves has arisen from one Eternal Principle, *Brahman*.
– Swami Chinmayananda

The ten verses of this section forcefully make the point that everything that exists owes its being to divine ground. Everything emerges from that great matrix and return back ultimately to the same ground – whether its span is a billionth of a second or a billion centuries. Birth and death, light and darkness, day and night, good and evil, joy and sorrow – all the dualities that are so striking in the manifested cosmos

---

'The entire world of activity (life), feelings (mind), cognition (senses), and the five elements has as its essence the same Brahman.'

are ultimately reconciled and united in the one Imperishable Being.

The cosmic dance of Shiva is eternal. It has no beginning and no end. It transcends space and time. In one hand of Nataraja is the drum - the creative sound from which emerge countless universes. In the other hand of Nataraja is the sacred fire into which the universes disappear after living a full life. At any moment, a billion galaxies spring into existence, and a billion disappear into the endless mystery of that great Being. Our own world - large as it may appear to us - is a grain of sand on the endless beach of eternity. We ourselves are infinitesimal sparks from the mighty fire. Yet each spark is illuminated with the fiery element. Each one of us embodies in some mysterious fashion the divine spark of Consciousness; and thereby, we all have a unique possibility of a conscious participation in the divine bliss (2.1, 1).

Long before the elements were created, long before life and mind began manifesting themselves, the Immutable Being was there, radiant with the splendor of a million suns. Without the great Being, there could be no creation, no time, no space, in fact nothing (2.1, 2-4).

There is a direct causal relationship between the divine and the earthly life. God does not sit in some seventh heaven, aloof and detached from his creation, judging human follies on doomsday. On the contrary, we are all part of His divine power. The principle that has brought us into being and that which pervades us, as also all the existences in universe, are but manifestations of His immense all-pervasive divinity (2.1, 5-6).

It is interesting that in verse 7, many diverse items are mentioned together – "gods and barely, rice and charity. The point being made is that everything – whether an abstract idea or a concrete object – derives its existence from the divine Being. The neat intellectual categorization to which we are so prone has no ultimate validity.

Breathing is the most fundamental of all activities of living beings. But it also has a deep spiritual significance. If properly regulated and accompanied by an appropriate *mantra* and psychological conditioning, the breath can open doorways into vastly enhanced states of Consciousness (2.1, 7-8).

The number seven (verse 8) has a special significance in many mystical traditions. There are seven days in a week in all civilizations of which we have any record. The seven senses are often explained as two eyes, two ear, two nostrils and one mouth. But this is unsatisfactory, as we normally talk of five senses – sight, smell, hearing, taste and touch. Perhaps there are two more extra sensory modes of perception, of which we are not aware. The seven flames have already been personified in an earlier verse as seven powers of *shakti*, the multi-splendored goddess. The seven worlds are the seven states of Consciousness. The 'secret place' referred to in verse 8 is the mystical heart, said to be located ten finger-breadths above the navel.

The Upanishads do not accept a dichotomy between matter and energy, body and soul. The elements that make up the universe are themselves manifestations of the divine. The difference is not between a divine and a non-divine, but between various gradations of evolution. Evolution begins with primordial elements, and grows into progressively higher manifestation of *Brahman*.

"Verily, that Supreme Being alone is all this universe", sums up the quintessence of the Upanishadic viewpoint of *Brahman*.

In many religious traditions, confrontation with the divine is conveniently postponed until after death; not so in the Upanishads. The Upanishads hold that given the right conditioning and aspiration, it is possible to realize *Brahman* even during lifetime (2.1, 10).

– *Karan Singh*

The ether in the pot, in the room and in the clouds is the same. We may, however, refer to it as pot-ether, room-ether and cloud-ether. So also, one *Brahman* assumes various forms as *Jivas* (souls) on account of various limiting conditions. When the pot and the walls of the room are broken, pot-ether and room-ether become one with universal-ether. Likewise, when limiting adjuncts like body and mind dissolve, *Jiva* become one with *Brahman*.

– *Swami Sivananda*

The Creator can be found at every point of creation. To indicate this, the teacher says that It is hidden in the secret caverns of heart, implying that It is imperceptible. One needs extra sensitivity to see the

---

'When the pot and the walls of the room are broken, pot-ether and room-ether become one with universal-ether. Likewise, when limiting adjuncts like body and mind dissolve, Jiva become one with Brahman.'

Creator in His creation; though manifest, It is hidden (2.1, 10).

– Rohit Mehta

2.2 Oneness of microcosm and macrocosm

There are two words – *Gyana* and *Vigyana*. *Gyana* may be translated as science and *Vigyana* as realization. God cannot be perceived through intellectual knowledge. We need realization, direct experience (2.2, 7). One who has realized God, what happens to him? Verse-8 provides the answer: 'When one becomes aware of Him, all the bonds of the heart are broken, all doubts vanish and all effects of work disappear.'

God is both near to us and far from us. He who is near can be seen, but He who is far can only be remembered. This kind of remembering is as good as seeing. This remembering, when exalted, assumes the form of seeing... this constant remembrance is denoted by the word *Bhakti*

'*There the sun does not shine, nor the moon....*' Mundaka Upanishad leads you beyond the senses, to thoughts infinitely more sublime than the suns and the stars. First, Angirasa tries to describe God through sense sublimates – that His feet are the earth His head the heaven etc. (2.1, 4). Next, he slowly takes his student Saunaka to the Beyond, until he gives him the highest idea – the negative – to describe Him (2.2, 10).

'*Brahman is in the front....*'. Every little bit, every atom inside the universe, is in a state of constant change or motion. But the universe as a whole is unchangeable, because motion or change is a relative thing. We can think of something in motion only in comparison with something, which is not moving. There must be two things in order to understand motion. The whole mass of the universe, taken as a unit, cannot move. In regard to what will it move? It cannot be said to change. In regard to what will it change? So, the Absolute is beyond any movement or change, but within It every particle is in a constant state of flux and change (2.2, 11).

(The word *paravare* in verse 8 has been translated as 'far and near' by Swami Vivekananda. 'higher and lower', and 'spiritual and material' are other translations.)

– *Swami Vivekananda, from compilation by Advaita Ashram, Kolkatta*

Atman, the divine spark in us, is considered very close to us since It is the very centre of our entire personality. Compared to Its nearness to us, even our body is a distant object.

The heart of a man is universally accepted as the seat of all emotions and inspirations.

Clay is the support of pots made of clay. Gold is the support of all gold ornaments. In this sense, *Atman* is the support of all.

Breathing, moving and winking are indicators of life, and all life has *Atman* as its base.

Atman is beyond all understanding, because It is itself the understanding principle behind all instruments of understanding (2.2, 1).

In philosophy, subtlety is measured by its pervasiveness. Solid is more gross than liquid, liquid is more gross than gas. *Atman* is all-pervading and naturally, most subtle.

Abode is that to which we go when we are tired, or when our work is over. *Brahman* is described here as the abode of the universe and the creatures living in it (2.2, 2).

The famous metaphor of bow and arrow is one of the many examples in the Upanishads where poetry and philosophy are welded together. The means for reaching *Atman* is the mind. The bow here is the chanting of AUM, with an understanding of its meaning. *Atman* is the arrow sharpened by meditation. It must be shot at the target, *Brahman*, with a steady mind (2.2, 3-4).

Hub is that part in a wheel which is in contact with every point on its circumference – through the spokes. It equalizes all the tensions working in the entire wheel. Similarly, *Atman* is the hub of our life, where all the nerves – equivalent of spokes – meet. The nerves are not physical arteries, but rays of psychic forces radiating from the centre – as channels of Consciousness - to every conceivable part of the body, controlling and directing it (2.2,6-7).

In human personality, *Atman* is believed to be enveloped by five imaginary concentric circles of matter, life, mind, intellect and bliss. The innermost

---

'*Abode is that to which we go when we are tired, or when our work is over.*
Brahman is the abode of the universe and the creatures living in It.'

bliss sheath is considered golden because of its radiance.

Atman is pure and stainless. The light from a bulb is blue not because the electricity in it is blue, but because of the blue shade of the lamp. The life force in different men is one and the same. However, personalities differ, depending upon the constitution of their mind. Even though *Atman* in two persons is the same, one can be a saint and another a sinner (2.2, 9).

Verse 10 is generally chanted soon after the offering of camphor flame in *aarti*. When in an extremely worshipful attitude, a devotee shows a tiny flame to the Lord, he is reminded that the Lord Himself is the source of all illumination.

Brahman, the cause of the world, is said to be the all-pervading homogeneous Consciousness in all the perceived things of the world (2.2, 11).

– *Swami Chinmayananda*

It should be noted that immortality does not mean mere survival after death; the Upanishads take this for granted. Immortality means realization of the divine. This enables us to transcend both birth and death, and free ourselves from the wheel of *karma*, around which all manifested beings revolve (2.2, 1-2).

These celebrated verses containing the metaphor of bow and arrow are among the best in the Upanishadic corpus (2.2, 3-4).

The simile of the spokes of a wheel meeting at the hub is a powerful one. However fast the wheel may rotate and wherever it may travel, its centre remains the hub. Without the hub, the whole structure would collapse into a jumble of twisted metal (2.2, 6).

A map is useful in giving us some idea of the typography and the routes, but it cannot be a substitute for real seeing. Likewise, intellectual knowledge alone is not sufficient for Self-realization.

The vision of *Brahman* is difficult to describe, like explaining the colors of a rainbow to a blind person.

– *Karan Singh*

When the vision of *Brahman* dawns within us, all doubts of the mind are cleared away. This does not happen by intellectual knowledge alone. The more we read and analyze, the more confused and entangled the mind becomes. But when we have a vision of *Brahman*, all the darkness of doubts disappears in the glory of His self-effulgent light – like night goes when morning comes. That brightness no one can define.

An illustration of the concentrated mind is given in the Mahabharata. Arjuna and his kinsmen were called to a contest in archery. The target was the eye of a bird on a tree. Their teacher asked each one in turn: "What do you see?". They described the tree, its branches, leaves and the bird on one of the branches. But when Arjuna was asked this question, he replied: "I see only the eye of the bird." And he alone could hit the target. If our mind is divided and scattered, we cannot meditate; and without the power of meditation, we cannot gain direct perception of the Imperishable (2.2, 4).

As long as we need someone to prove the Truth to us, we have not found It. But when His light shines in our heart, Truth becomes self-evident (2.2, 9).

– *Swami Paramananda*

'Personalities differ, depending upon the constitution of their mind.
Even though Atman in two persons is the same, one can be a saint and another a sinner.'

[3] Merger of relative in Absolute

SIMPLIFIED SYNOPSES

3.1, 1-2
Closer you get, happier you feel

The allegory of two birds on a tree is one of the most famous allegories in the Upanishads. The two birds symbolize a person's ego and Self. Tree is the body. It is the ego, which experiences joys and sorrows of life. Self – which is generally referred to as God – just looks on like a witness. A person rarely thinks of God in the midst of pleasures, but looks up to Him when faced with sorrows. Likewise, the bird eating the fruits looks up to the other bird whenever the fruit it eats tastes bitter. It is then attracted by the serenity of the other bird and moves closer to it. The closer it gets, the happier it feels. Eventually, when the bird symbolizing the ego has come close enough to the bird symbolizing Self, it realizes that it is not any different from Self. All its sorrows then pass away. Commentators have written some very interesting interpretations of this allegory of two birds on a tree.

3.1, 3-5
Calm mind in active body

An awareness of the Supreme Being – the Creator and the Sustainer of the universe – empowers us to face the ups and downs of life with equanimity. Our actions are then guided not by self-interest but by some larger interest (verse 3). When we realize that the Self in us is nothing but the Supreme Being, we are motivated to talk less and work more. The Upanishad emphasizes that Self-realization does not imply an idle life-style of mere meditation. A Self-realized person is always calm but active. He treats life like a sport and takes delight in whatever life offers to him. The highest attainment in life is to experience the bliss of Self-realization along with an active life-style.

Practice of truth, contemplation, wisdom and self-disciple are said to be the four essential requirements for Self-realization. These purify the mind of the aspirant and help him experience the Self within.

3.1, 6-7
Truth alone triumphs,
Satyameva Jayate

These celebrated words are inscribed on the seal of India, as the country's motto. According to commentators, the word Truth is not used here in the conventional sense only, it also refers to the Absolute, Consciousness, *Brahman*. The Upanishad glorifies the path of Truth as a divine path leading to fulfillment of all desires, and eventually to the abode of Truth. That abode is the Absolute, *Brahman*, Itself. It is located in the heart within us, and also in the farthest point imaginable in space, time or thought.

3.1, 8-10
Power of the mind

The Upanishad emphasizes once again that the Absolute cannot be perceived by the senses or revealed by rituals. The Absolute is realized only with a calm and pure mind in meditation.

Verse-10 states that with intense concentration one can achieve whatever one desires. This points to the power of the mind, which has been demonstrated by many practitioners of *Yoga*. Another interpretation is that when a man's mind is purified, he realizes his oneness with cosmic life. He then desires only that which is in harmony with cosmic will. Therefore, his desires fulfil themselves by natural course of law.

3.2, 1-8
Self-realization is like a river merging in sea

Self-realization requires two things – management of desires and knowledge of the Absolute.

Our unfulfilled desires carry their impressions from life to life and force us to be born again and again for their fulfillment. Management of desires is at the heart of spiritual quest. It requires looking inward to Self, rather than outward to objects of desire. A person aspiring for Self-realization should rise above desires intended to serve self-interest.

'Our unfulfilled desires carry their impressions from life to life.'

What about the second requirement of knowledge of the Absolute? Verse-1 on this subject has two interpretations: (i) meditate on the Absolute and (ii) seek knowledge from a teacher who has himself attained Self-realization. Spiritual discourses, intellectual reasoning and study of scriptures by themselves cannot lead to Self-realization. Self is realized by one who longs for It, and on whom It showers divine grace. Will-power, physical strength, sincerity and austerities are the other qualities required in spiritual aspirants.

When a man becomes aware of Self, his personality undergoes a complete transformation. He feels peaceful, unattached and completely fulfilled. Having realized the All-pervading Self, he sees Self in all beings (3.2, 5).

Self-realization leads to liberation from the law of *Karma* and bondage of birth. There are two viewpoints as to when this liberation is achieved – while living or after bodily death, *jivan-mukti* or *videha-mukti* (3.2, 6).

The spiritual entity in us has been described in Prasna Upanishad as a Supreme Being of sixteen parts. Upon physical death of a Self-realized person, the physical body merges into the five elements and the senses into their respective cosmic powers. His deeds, together with the enlightened Self become one with the Supreme Being, the Imperishable, Absolute Consciousness (verse 7). This is illustrated beautifully with a very appropriate simile of a river merging into the ocean. Origin of rivers is traceable to oceans. Evaporation causes clouds, which convert into rain, and rain water collects to form rivers. A river flows through diverse terrains and eventually merges into the sea. Once this happens, it ceases to exist there as a separate entity – it becomes one with the sea. Similarly, the *jiva*, the conditioned Self of Self-realized person becomes one with the universal Self, Absolute Consciousness, *Brahman* (verse 8).

'Management of desires is at the heart of spiritual quest. It requires looking inward to Self, rather than outward to objects of desire.'

3.2, 9-11
One becomes what one wants to be

'Knower of Brahman becomes Brahman.'

'Knower of *Brahman* becomes *Brahman*' is a maxim repeated very frequently in the Upanishads. It follows from the analogy of a river merging in an ocean. When this happens, the water which was earlier in the river, becomes ocean water. Likewise, as Self and *Brahman* are one and the same, a Self-realized person becomes *Brahman* Itself. Accordingly, he is above sorrow, sin and 'knots of the heart' viz. ignorance, work that binds and desires. He is liberated from the cycle of birth and death. He becomes immortal.

In a wider sense, the maxim also reflects the power of the mind. Acting with full determination, intense concentration and strong will-power, a man can become whatever he wants to be.

The Upanishad ends with an exhortation that knowledge of the Absolute, *Brahma Vidya* should not be imparted to one who is not prepared for it. While some of the requirements specified in verse-10 may not be relevant in modern times, it is true that spiritual texts or discourses can creates confusion in an unreceptive or doubting mind.

'As Self and Brahman are one and the same, a Self-realized person becomes Brahman Itself.'

Translated Text

CHAPTER 3

Section 1

Two birds, bound to each other in close friendship, sit on the same tree. One of them eats the fruits of the tree with relish; while the other (just) looks on, without eating. **1**

Seated on the same tree, one of them – man's ego – grieves on account of its helplessness. But when it beholds the other – the worshipful Lord, in all Its glory – then its sorrow passes away. **2**

When a seer realizes the self-effulgent Supreme Being – the ruler, the maker and the source of even the Creator – then that wise seer shakes off all good and evil. Such a person becomes free from all imperfections and attains a state of supreme equipoise. **3**

Indeed, it is the divine spirit that shines forth in all beings. Knowing this, a wise person desists from unnecessary talk. Sporting in Self, delighting in Self, yet involved in activity, such a person is the best among those who know *Brahman*. **4**

Self is attained through constant practice of truth, contemplation (*tapas*), right knowledge and self-discipline. Through these practices the impurities diminish and the practitioner beholds Him – pure and resplendent – within the body itself. **5**

Truth alone triumphs; not untruth. Truth lays down the divine path on which sages, with their desires fulfilled, ascend to the supreme abode of Truth. **6**

That Truth of *Brahman* is vast, divine, beyond all imagination, subtler than the subtlest, farther than the farthest. Yet, It is here within the body. The seers realize It as seated in the secret cavity of the heart. **7**

He (*Brahman*) cannot be described by words, nor grasped by eyes or other senses, nor revealed by rituals and austerities. Only when the mind becomes calm and purified by grace of higher knowledge; then alone, in meditation, one realizes Him, the Absolute. **8**

The subtle *Atman* within the body is pervaded by fivefold life-breath. It should be known by the intuitive faculty of the mind. Mind is normally mixed up with the senses. When mind is purified, Self shines forth. **9**

Whatever world a man of purified nature concentrates upon with his mind, and whatever objects he desires to have, he obtains those worlds and those objects. Therefore, let him who desires prosperity worship a man of Self-realization. **10**

"Satyameva Jayate. Truth alone triumphs."

Section 2

A Self-realized man knows the Supreme, *Brahman*, on whom this universe is based, and who shines radiantly. The wise who worship the Supreme Being (or, a Self-realized person) without any desire, they are freed from rebirth. **1**

Whoever in his mind longs for objects of desire is reborn here or there, for their fulfillment. But he who has realized Self feels that all his desires are fulfilled; his desires vanish even here. **2**

Self (*Atman*) is not attained by discourses, nor by logical reasoning or by much learning. It is attained only by him who longs for It. To such a person, Self (*Atman*) reveals Its true nature. **3**

Self cannot be attained by the weak (in body, mind and spirit), nor by the insincere, nor through improper austerities. But the wise – who strives with vigor, sincerity and austerities – his *Atman* attains union with *Brahman*. **4**

When sages have attained Self, they are satisfied with their knowledge. Their purpose fulfilled, they become non-attached and peaceful. Having realized the All-pervading everywhere, these wise persons of Self-realization enter into everything. **5**

Having attained knowledge of Upanishads, having purified their minds with yoga of renunciation, after death these seers attain immortality and liberation in the worlds of *Brahman*. **6**

Of the fifteen *Kalas* (parts), the physical parts enter into their elements, the senses into their corresponding gods, and the deeds together with the enlightened Self are united with the Supreme, Imperishable Being. **7**

As flowing rivers disappear into the ocean, losing their separate name and form; so also the wise, freed from all identification of name and form, become one with the Highest of the high, the Supreme Divinity. **8**

Verily, knower of *Brahman* becomes *Brahman*. In his lineage, none is born who is ignorant of *Brahman*. He passes beyond sorrow. He passes beyond sin. Liberated from the knots of the heart, he becomes immortal. **9**

Thus, it has been explained in the Vedic verse: To them alone let one teach this knowledge of *Brahman* who perform rituals, who are well-versed in scriptures, who are well-established in *Brahman*, who possess faith, who offer oblations to the sacrificial fire called Ekarsi, and who have duly performed the rite called Shirovrata. **10**

That is the truth. Rishi Angirasa imparted this to his disciples in ancient times. Let no one who has not observed the prescribed vows study this. Our salutations to the great Rishi. Our salutations to the great Rishi. **11**

"Whoever in his mind longs for objects of desire is reborn here or there, for their fulfillment."

Peace Invocation

Om.
O gods, may we hear auspicious words with our ears.
O Worshipful One, may we see auspicious things with our eyes.
May we live our entire life cheerfully and in good health,
   offering our praises unto Thee.

May *Indra*, the ancient and the famous, bless us.
May *Pusan* (sun), the all-knowing bless us.
May *Vayu* (Life Principle), the Lord of swift motion,
   who protects us from all harms, bless us.
May *Brhaspati*, the Lord of wisdom, bless us.

Om. Shanti. Shanti. Shanti.
Let there be Peace, Let there be Peace, Let there be Peace.

Focussed Commentaries

CHAPTER 3

3.1, 1-2 Closer you get, happier you feel

The whole of Vedanta philosophy is in this story. Upon the same tree there are two birds – one on the top, the other below. The bird on the top is calm and majestic, immersed in his own glory. The bird on the lower branches, eating sweet and bitter fruits by turns, hopping from branch to branch, is at times happy and at times miserable.

At times the lower bird eats an exceptionally bitter fruit. It gets disgusted and looks up and sees the other bird. That wondrous one of golden plumage eats neither sweet nor bitter fruits. He is neither agitated nor miserable. He is calm. The lower bird longs for this condition. Thinking, "I would love to be like him!" he hops a little towards the other bird. Soon, however, he forgets all about his desire to be like the upper bird, and again begins to eat the fruits.

After a little while he eats another exceptionally bitter fruit. It again makes him feel miserable. He again looks up and tries to get near to the upper bird. Once more he forgets, but after a time he looks up; and so he hops again and again, until he comes very near to the peaceful bird. He sees the reflection of light from the upper bird's plumage playing around his own body. He feels a change and seems to melt away. Still nearer he comes, and everything about him melts away. At last he understands this wonderful change.

The lower bird was, as it were, only the substantial-looking shadow, the reflection of the higher; he himself was in essence the upper bird all the time. This eating of fruits, sweet and bitter, this lower bird sad and happy by turns, was a vain chimera, a dream. All along, the real bird was there, calm and silent, glorious and majestic, beyond grief, beyond sorrow.

The upper bird is God, the Lord of this universe; the lower bird is the human soul, eating the sweet and bitter fruits of this world.

Now and then comes a heavy blow to the soul. For a time, it stops the eating and goes towards the unknown God and a flood of light comes. It thinks that this world is a vain show. But again the senses drag it down, and it begins as before to eat the sweet and bitter fruits of the world. Again an exceptionally hard blow comes. Its heart opens again to divine light. Thus gradually, it approaches God. As it gets nearer and nearer, it finds its old self melting away. It finds that its individuality—its intensely selfish individuality—is melting away.

When it has come near enough, it sees that it is not other than God, and it exclaims, "Why, it was my own glory whom I called God; and this little 'I', this misery, was all hallucination. It never existed. I was never a woman, never a man, never any of these things." Then the soul becomes free from all sorrow.

The lower bird was but a reflection of the one above. So we are in reality one with God. The reflection makes us seem as many, as when one sun reflects in a million dewdrops and seems a million tiny suns. The reflection must vanish if we are to identify ourselves with our real nature, which is divine.

The lower bird found that it was the upper bird all the time. We too, if we persevere in our efforts, will find that we are God, all the time.

– *Swami Vivekananda*

The allegory of two birds on a tree is one of the most famous allegories in the Upanishads. The two birds, living in great friendship upon the same tree are the ego and *Atman*, the divine spark of *Brahman* in us. The ego identifies itself with the mind and the body. It believes that it is the enjoyer and the sufferer, depending upon the taste of the fruits eaten by it. *Atman* does not perform any action. It merely goes on witnessing the joys and the sorrows of the ego busy with the fruits. *Atman* neither enjoys nor suffers, because it has no desire to taste the fruits.

When we identify ourselves with the changing finite, we become like the sorrowing bird; when we identify ourselves with *Brahman*, we become like the witnessing bird.

– *Swami Chinmayananda*

The two birds represent the higher Self and the lower self. The lower self is absorbed in tasting the sweet and bitter fruits of this life. It imagines that it cannot

---

'Ego identifies itself with mind and body. It believes that it is the enjoyer and the sufferer. Atman does not perform any action. It merely goes on witnessing the joys and the sorrows of the ego.'

escape from the reactions caused by them. However, when it looks towards the higher Self, it realizes its own true nature. *Jiva* or the individual soul is merely a reflection of *Paramatma*, the Supreme soul. It is the sense of ego in us which divides and separates; and as soon as we separate ourselves from our Divine nature, we feel incomplete.

– *Swami Paramananda*

The tree is the body; and the two birds are *Jivatman* and *Paramatma*. Both of them reside in the body. Or, to put it differently, below and beyond our surface personalities is the real Self, which is a spark of *Brahman* in us. The two are described as being bound to each other in close friendships. However, *Jivatman* – because of its bondage in the three knots of body, life and mind – looks upon itself as different; but in reality it is inseparably linked to *Paramatma*. The relationship is like that between the reflections of sun in a pond of water, and the sun itself.

The lower self is said to eat the fruits of the tree with relish, meaning that it experiences the unending treadmill of *karma*. Thereby, it gets caught in the cycle of opposites – joy and sorrow, birth and death. When, having tasted the material joys of life, one is suddenly brought face to face with harsh realities of life – disease, old age and death – a sense of helplessness sets in. At this stage one turns for guidance to the other bird, our higher Self, unencumbered with *karmic* burdens. The other bird has all this time been serenely sitting on the same tree, looking at us with love and compassion. As Sri Aurobindo puts it:

> "The Master of man and his infinite lover.
> He is close to our hearts had we vision to see.
> We are blind with our pride,
> and the pomp of our possessions.
> We are bound by our thoughts
> though we hold ourselves free."

Then one day, dejected and despondent, we throw down our weapons, like Arjuna did on the battlefield of Kurushetra. In despair, we look up to our inner Self, the charioteer of our life. Then a miracle occurs. Our sorrow passes away from us. We realize in a flash that the sweet and bitter fruits we have been eating birth after birth, age after age, are the real cause of our bondage. All that we have to do for release from our bondage is to surrender our false ego to our real Self, our deepest Consciousness within.

– *Karan Singh*

Some take mind, the real doer, as one bird and *Brahman* as the second bird. The two birds perch on the same tree. Tree here means body. Like a tree, the body can also be cut and destroyed.

The two birds are inseparable, just as sun's image in water cannot be separated from the sun. *Jivatman* (the individual soul) and *Paramatma* (the supreme soul) are inseparable.

Atman-Brahman is always the silent witness. He is non-doer and non-enjoyer. Enjoyment and action are superimposed on *Jivatman* by the mind. The idea of 'doer' and 'enjoyer' disappears when ignorance is destroyed. *Jivatman* then sees itself as one with *Paramatma*.

In verse 2, the first half of the verse describes the cause of bondage – delusion of "I" and "mine". The second half shows the method of release from bondage: Behold the Lord, ever content and adorable, and wish to become like Him.

– *Swami Sivananda*

3.1, 3-5 Calm mind in active body

...*that wise seer shakes off good and evil*: All *karmas*, performed with some desire, produce results. Good *karmas* produce good results, meaning happiness; bad *karmas* produce bad result, meaning pain and sorrow. No matter what the results, to experience it we need a body. No matter what the body, it comes packaged with limitations, vulnerability, disease, old age and death. That is why in the ultimate analysis, good deeds and bad deeds are both imperfections. Vedanta teaches us to do all *karmas* without any desire for results (3.1,3).

– *Notes on commentary by Swami Vivekananda*

When a person becomes aware of Self, he sports and delights in Its awareness. The Sanskrit word for sport is *krida* and for delight it is *ratih*. There is a very subtle difference in the meaning of these two words. Sport implies contact with the outside world;

'All that we have to do for release from our bondage is to surrender our false ego to our real Self.'

delight is joy gained within. Self-realization leads to joy, both within and without (3.1,4).

Inaccurate understanding of a scripture is more dangerous than not knowing it at all. It is probably the half-learned bookworms who have created the impression that a Self-realized saint does not have to do any work. There are, no doubt, statements to this effect in Vedic scriptures. However, these discourage only desire-prompted egoistic actions. In verse-4, the absurd idea of sleeping saints and idle masters has been atom-bombed by the term *kriyavan*, meaning involved in activity. Vedic scriptures denounce only selfish actions, not selfless actions.

Truth in the ordinary sense means complete agreement between the thoughts in the mind and the words expressing them. If, for example, we are thinking that a thing is bad and we say that it is good, we have committed adultery of conscience and we are said to be false or untrue.

At the spiritual level, if a person, who is convinced of the divine nature of One Self, acts contrary to his convictions, he is committing a rape of the soul. It is in this sense that the word *satyam,* truth has been used in verse-5.

Truthfulness, meditation, study of scriptures and self-discipline are not for seasonal enthusiasm. When these are practised continuously, the animalism in us slowly dies away. Our mind then becomes more and more subtle, and capable of greater awareness. Ultimately, we realize the supreme within us.

– *Swami Chinmayananda*

Play needs some external help, but delight does not require any external help. In delight, there is no attachment to an external object (3.1,4). *Tapas*, is usually translated as austerity. Concentration of mind is the highest *Tapas*. Withdrawing the mind and the senses from external objects and concentrating it on *Atman* is the most difficult form of austerity (3.1,5).

– *Swami Sivananda*

The simile of the two birds is now projected on to human conditions (verses 3-5). When we are able to realize the presence of higher Self within us, we become seers in the true sense of the term. At that point, the conventional distinctions between 'good' and 'evil' disappear – which incidentally, differ drastically from age to age, from civilization to civilization. People who argue endlessly about the superiority of their faiths or gurus rarely have the time to move forward on the road to inner quest. As Fitzgerald puts it in his superb recreation of Omar Khayyam:

'Myself when young did eagerly frequent
Scholar and saint, and heard great argument
About it and about, but evermore,
Came out by the same door wherein I went.'

The highest attainment, according to verse-4, is when a seer delights in the bliss of Self-knowledge, and yet he is involved in outer activity, *kriyavan*. This is a profound statement. Here we have a clear-cut reiteration that outer activities are not inconsistent with inner quest. This is also the central theme of Lord Krishna's discourse to Arjuna in the Bhagavad Gita. Besides, it explains the great reverence given to Raj Rishis, or royal sages in the Hindu tradition. Pre-eminent among these was King Janaka of Mithila – he attained enlightenment through actions.

Becoming aware of Self is not an easy matter. Unless we go through the fire, as it were, we cannot burn away the dross in which we are enmeshed. Four requirements are mentioned here – truth, austerity (meditation), wisdom and chastity. The fourth was generally expected only of the monks, not of householders. The powerful primeval sex drive is a force, which cannot be thwarted with impunity. It can be sublimated, not repressed without doing great psychological damage. Tantra, in fact, turns the sexual urge itself into a powerful vehicle for spiritual quest (3.1, 3-5).

– *Karan Singh*

3.1, 6-7 Truth alone triumphs, *Satyameva Jayate*

The celebrated words 'Truth alone triumphs, *Satyameva Jayate*', are inscribed on the seal of India as the country's motto. Truth is both a divine path and a supreme goal. The word 'truth' is meant here not in its conventional sense but in its totality, which is equivalent to *Brahman*.

'Truth in its totality is equivalent to Brahman. It is both a divine path and a Supreme goal.'

It must be noted that the path of Truth is an ascending one, in the sense that it requires a conscious effort to move on. Also, we can embark upon a journey on this path only when our lower desires have been fulfilled, or sublimated. If we attempt it while still overloaded with a heavy baggage of physical and emotional cravings, we will be hardly able to walk a few steps before we stumble and fall.

Yet, whatever our weakness, we have to start moving. There is a blazing Truth, far above us and deep inside us; although in the beginning it may appear just a tiny flicker within the encircling gloom. This Truth is both the path and the goal. As we move onwards and upwards, new vistas unfold. The radiant sun grows brighter until, finally at the crossing, the rainbow-bridge appears. It takes us to the other shore beyond darkness, where the great Being shines with the splendor of a million suns.

– *Karan Singh*

The truth of verses 6-7 is Pure Consciousness. It is a circle whose centre is everywhere. It is at once at every point in the heart within us, and at the farthest imaginable point in space, time, or thought.

– *Swami Chinmayananda*

I will compare truth to a corrosive substance of infinite power. It burns its way in, wherever it falls – in soft substances at once, hard granite slowly, but it must. Youth and vanity vanish, life and wealth vanish, name and fame vanish, even the mountains crumble into dust. Friendship and love vanish. Truth alone abides.

– *Swami Vivekananda*

3.1, 8-10 Power of the mind

Rituals and austerities are preparatory lessons for a seeker. To believe these to be an end by themselves is a tragic mistake. The Upanishad is indicating to us the fallacy of such a belief.

Meditation is a means; Self-realization is the goal. The relationship between meditation and Self-realization is *not* the relationship between cause and effect. Meditation only removes the veil over Self; and Self is realized in Its own light. The clouds roll away with the breeze, revealing the shining sun. Likewise, Self is realized when the mind is calm and purified. A pure mind agitates the least. In a still pool of the mind, reflection of *Brahman* is very clear (3.1, 8).

A purified mind is one, which is withdrawn from its occupation with senses and sense-objects. When the mind is purified, Self shines forth by Itself (3.1, 9).

If with a single-pointed devotion we could harness our entire mental power and wish for a thing to happen, that must come to pass. This is a certain law in life. The devotees regard this mental power as *Ishvara kripa*, God's grace. The Upanishads call it *Atma-shakti*, and the Yogis describe it as the power of *kundalini*. In fact all of them are talking of the one and the same phenomenon. Ordinarily, none of us have such a strong power of concentration. When we wish for a thing, a hundred other desires and contrary thoughts crowd the mind and loot away its powers (3.1, 10).

– *Swami Chinmayananda*

Ordinarily, the intellect of a person is tainted with passion, anger, greed, attachment and ego. It is impure and unclean. Just as you cannot see your face in a dirty mirror or muddy water; so also you cannot see *Atman* in an unclean intellect, even though It is very near. It is pure intellect that reveals *Atman*. This purification comes from the grace of higher knowledge.

A Self-realized person is certainly worthy of worship (3.1, 10).

– *Swami Sivananda*

The senses color all our mental activities. The soul can manifest its true nature only when the mind is freed from these obscuring impressions.

When a man's mind is purified, he realizes his oneness with cosmic life. He then desires only what is in harmony with the cosmic Will. Therefore, his desires fulfil themselves by the natural course of law.

Purity of mind is gained by revering and serving those who possess higher knowledge.

– *Swami Paramananda*

'There is a blazing Truth deep inside us, although it may appear just a tiny flicker in the encircling gloom. This Truth is both the path and the goal.'

Human mind is a marvellous instrument. In its subtlety and complexity, it is indeed a miracle of evolution. And yet, mind by itself is unable to behold *Brahman*, because it is *Brahman* that activates the mind.

The mind of a seer is much more powerful than that of an ordinary man, like a focussed beam of light coming through a powerful lens. Such a person can successfully apply his will-power to the attainment of any worldly or material end, if he so desires. Rishi Angirasa is advising people in search of prosperity to worship such masters and earn their blessings. This advice may appear to be slightly out of place. However, it should be recalled that Angirasa is speaking to a householder, Saunaka.

– Karan Singh

3.2, 1-8 Self-realization is like a river merging in sea

The second half of verse 1 has two readings. According to one translation, a Self realized person is liberated from rebirth. According to a second translation, even persons who worship such a Self-realized master are freed from rebirth. The implication of the second translation is that while a Self-realized soul is certainly liberated from the bondage of rebirth; even those who seek out and serve such an illumined soul gradually partake of his wisdom, and pass beyond the cycle of birth and death.

A part of verse 3 also has two readings: '*Atman* is attained by one who longs for It' and 'He *(Atman)* is attained by one whom It chooses'. In the second translation, commentators explain that Self naturally chooses one whose heart is wholly purified and ready to receive the revelation.

– Editor

Every desire is a seed from which spring birth, death and all mortal afflictions. Self-illumination alone can destroy this seed (3.2, 1).

A selfish man clings to the small and the finite. A man may wish to go to the other shore, but if he does not pull up the anchor, his boat will not move (3.2, 2).

The Upanishads lay frequent emphasis on the idea that no person of a weak will-power can attain the Truth (3.2, 4).

Self-realized persons enter into everything, meaning that they realize the universal oneness of cosmic life (3.2, 5).

When the final realization of Self comes, the various parts of man's body, life and mind - gross body, subtle body and causal body – become one with the Supreme.

As a man's Consciousness expands into universal Consciousness, the limitations of self-consciousness melt away. As soon as he attains a realization of his true Self, he transcends the realm of name and form, and enters into a union with the universal source of existence and knowledge. He becomes without parts and immortal (3.2,8).

– Swami Paramananda

Moksha, salvation is not a thing to be achieved. It is already here. *Brahman* is not a thing to be brought from some place; It is already here. One has to know *Brahman* as one's innermost Self. What one has to do is to remove the veil of ignorance (3.2, 3).

Just as ether in a pot becomes one with the universal ether when the pot is broken, so also knower of *Brahman* becomes one with *Brahman* when the body is dissolved.

Just as footprints of birds are not visible in air, and that of aquatic animals in water, so also the track of a Self-realized man is not seen.

The world of *Brahman*, though one, appears to be many, hence use of the plural 'worlds of *Brahman*' (3.2, 6).

– Swami Sivananda

Verse 3.1,10 was addressed to men who are seeking fulfillment of their desires. They were advised to worship a man of Self-realization. The same path is indicated to those who have either fulfilled or transcended all desires. They can worship *Brahman* directly, or a spiritual master who has realized *Brahman*.

'Moksha, salvation is not a thing to be achieved. It is already here.
What one has to do is to remove the veil of ignorance.'

Desires vanish even here: As a consequence, he has no further birth (3.2, 2).

Self reveals its true nature: Ignorance veils Self from the mind. True longing of the heart dispels that ignorance. Then Self, which was always there, reveals Itself.

The passage is a sanction for the doctrine of grace. Personal God, *Ishta Devata* is attained only by one whom He chooses. To such a person, He reveals His own person (3.2, 3).

Improper austerities: The Sanskrit word is *alingat tapas,* or *tapas* without *lingah*. *Lingah* refers to external signs of asceticism, like saffron robes. According to some commentators, spiritual discipline without proper external garb does not lead to the highest result. This is perhaps because the checks that the garb imposes on conduct – both consciously and unconsciously – safeguard an aspirant from going off the track (3.2,4).

After death: The Sanskrit word is *paranta kale*. This, here means 'at the time of illumination'. Just as death is the end of the body for an ignorant man, it is a moment of illumination for the knowing one. He understands henceforth that he is not the body. This interpretation gives us the extreme *Advaitic* view which denies even *Prarabdha Karma* in a *Jivan-mukta* (a Self-realized living person). *Prarabdha Karmas* are those actions whose fruits are exhausted only at the death of the body (3.2,6).

– Swami Sarvananda

Vedantic scriptures state in most unequivocal terms that service of a guru makes the aspirant more and more fit for greater exertion in the spiritual path (3.2,1).

In verse 2, we have a reference to the law of rebirth. 'As you think, so you become' is an undisputed law of life. Thought is an expression of the creative urge in us, and it is influenced by the quality of desires in us. Desires disturb a hornet's nest of thoughts, and these thoughts express themselves in our actions. The total field of all actions of all living beings is called 'world' or *loka*. Self-realization leads to a state of desirelessness, a much more glorious state of fulfillment and happiness. After a person has attained Self-realization, there is no more any cause for him to be born again in the world for fulfilling any of his unfulfilled desires (3.2, 2).

Verse-3 is open to two interpretations: '*Atman* is attained by him who longs for It' and '*Atman* is attained by one whom It chooses'. In fact, there is no contradiction between those two standpoints. Whether the river reaches the ocean, or the ocean receives the river, the effect is the same (3.2, 3).

In verse 4, the Sanskrit word for improper austerities is *alingat tapas*. It does not refer to the color of the robes, or the condition of the hair on the head. The emphasis is on the mental conditions and qualities in a seeker. Inner renunciation is more important than external symbols of renunciation (3.2, 4).

The seeker, having realized Self, becomes completely satisfied in knowledge of his rediscovered Self. If a beggar discovers that he is the inheritor of a large fortune, this discovery itself is sufficient to give him tremendous joy. Similarly, when a man with all his struggles of life discovers that he is the spiritual centre of the entire universe, this knowledge itself gives him a feeling of complete fulfillment. In such a state of complete fulfillment, there cannot be any desires. And when desires have subsided, peace follows (3.2, 5).

Yoga of Renunciation: The Upanishads attempt to explain That which cannot be explained. They define the Infinite in finite words. This is done by the method of 'suggestiveness' of words. Therefore, a seeker has to go beyond the literary meaning of the words used in the text. In this context, the yoga of renunciation is more an internal revolution of the values of life, rather than a vast advertisement board declaring externally that one is a *sanyasi*, an ascetic (3.2, 6).

Attain... the worlds of Brahman: If Supreme Reality is one, without-a-second, how can there be 'worlds of *Brahman*' which indicate plurality? According to Sri Sankara, to the seeker, the world of plurality is real. He is convinced that there is a spirit behind every material form, but he is not aware that the spirits behind various material forms are one and the same. 'Worlds of *Brahman*' is therefore addressed to such a seeker of imperfect understanding. Considered from the reality of the 'rope', no 'serpent' has ever emerged from it to frighten the deluded (3.2, 6).

'Renunciation is more an internal revolution of the values of life, rather than external signs of asceticism.'

After death: In Vedic philosophy, there are two schools of thought about liberation. Some believe that complete realization of *Brahman* is not possible so long as we exist in this physical form. Others believe that *Brahman* can be realized even here and now, and a realized soul can continue to live as a *jivan-mukta*. Sri Sankara supports the second viewpoint. He argues that if such a status was not possible, we could never have a perfect guru, defined as one who is fully established in *Brahman*. Death mentioned in this verse therefore refers to death of false vanities and delusive ego. *Brahman* starts where ego ends (3.2, 6).

The fifteen *kalas* (parts) have been described in *Prasna* Upanishad. In Hindu scriptures we have repeated references to the spiritual entity in us as the sixteen-faceted *Purusha*. This verse describes what happens to the parts when *Purusha* is realized by a *yogi* in *samadhi*. The *kalas* enter into their elements, just as the serpent enters into the rope when the rope is under the light of a torch. Likewise, the senses enter into their presiding deities, called 'gods' in the Upanishads. For example, eye is considered to be presided by the sun. This only means that eye can function only when an object is in the medium of light. In the poetic language of the Rishi, the sun is the god of vision. After death, the senses of a Self-realized person merge into their respective cosmic powers (3.2, 7).

To explain the concept of Pure Consciousness, verse-8 uses the example of rivers losing their identity upon merging into the ocean. As long as a seeker has a concept of being separate from Self, there exists an ego-centre in him. The moment he realizes that his real nature is spiritual, his ego varnishes; and he experiences Pure Consciousness (3.2, 8).

– *Swami Chinmayananda*

The Vedic seers realized that desires are like a fire. Each offering into it fans the flames further, far from appeasing its appetite. Thus, our unfulfilled desires carry their impressions or *samskaras* from life to life. They cause us to be born again and again for their fulfillment. This process will continue into infinity, unless we in our wisdom reverse the process. It is this reversal which is at the heart of spiritual quest. It requires looking inwards to the source of our Consciousness, rather than outwards to the objects of desires (3.2, 1-2).

Spiritual quest is not an easy task. It involves a total reorientation of our inner and outer perspectives. According to Sri Aurobindo, it involves a transformation in the very cellular and molecular structure of our bodies.

Improper and excessive austerities are not to be encouraged in the spiritual path. The Upanishads, the Bhagavad Gita and the Buddha – all point out that at some stage, these become counter-productive. Indeed, if Sujata had not brought Siddhartha a bowl of rice at a critical moment, he would have perished and the world would have been deprived of a great teacher, the Buddha. What is needed is a combination of strength, attention and balanced austerity (3.2, 3-4).

The simile of the rivers and the ocean is most appropriate. The rivers are themselves derived from the ocean. Water of ocean evaporates to become clouds, clouds convert into rain, and rainwater collects to become rivers. For long periods, the rivers have a separate name and location. Thus, the divine Ganga originates in the heart of the Himalayas. For thousands of kilometers it retains many names and forms. These vary from place to place and from season to season. Ultimately it merges into the ocean. Once this happens, it ceases to exist there as a separate entity. Similarly, says the Upanishad, the individual *Jiva* is born again and again, until - by its deeds (*karma*) and the grace of spiritual wisdom (*Brahma Vidya*) - it finally achieves the Absolute, *Brahman*. The dewdrop slips into the shining sea. The human journey is complete. Spiritual evolution has reached its supreme goal (3.2, 7-8).

– *Karan Singh*

3.2, 9-11 One can become what one wants to be

'He who knows *Brahman* becomes *Brahman*' is the essence of Upanishadic philosophy. A drop of water is certainly separate from the ocean, but the moment it falls into the ocean it becomes one with the entire ocean. Similarly, so long as the spirit in us chooses to identify itself with body-life-mind, it has the experience of separate existence. This is conditioned *Atman*, or the ego. The moment it becomes aware of its true all-pervading nature, It becomes one with supreme Divinity.

'Unfulfilled desires carry their impressions from one life to another.
They cause us to be born again and again for their fulfillment.'

In his lineage, none is born who is ignorant of Brahman: The implied meaning is that knowledge, like many other attributes, is passed on from one generation to the next, through the genes, as well as through nurturing.

He passes beyond sorrow and sin. All actions leave impression on the mind. These impressions come to life when in contact with ego. A Self-realized person is one who has ended his ego and discovered his true nature. He is said to be free from past encumbrances rising from sins. This is indicated here by the words: 'He passes beyond sorrow. He passes beyond sin' (3.2, 9).

The rituals mentioned in verse 10, are figurative expressions to explain that a student of Upanishads must have a burning desire to grasp their contents. Only an intellect that is on-fire can hope to understand the divine values of inner life, as advocated in the Upanishads.

The Upanishad concludes with the warning that the disciple in his turn should not give out this knowledge to one who does not have the necessary qualifications to profit from it (3.2,11).

– Swami Chinmayananda

The statement about continuation of *Brahma Vidya* from one generation to the next is rather difficult to interpret. It can hardly be taken literally. The individual *Jiva* has its own *karmas*. What is probably meant is spiritual lineage. It will be recalled that when the Buddha, after attaining enlightenment, returned as a monk to his father's kingdom, he was sternly asked by the king as to why he was setting aside his family traditions? Buddha answered that his real lineage was the line of Buddhas who labored for the welfare of mankind (3.2, 9).

The Upanishad ends with the mystic exhortation that higher knowledge about *Brahman* is not to be imparted to one who is not qualified to receive it intellectually, psychologically and spiritually. This admonition is necessary. Without the required discipline, devotion and perseverance, the teaching could be a total waste; it could even be downright dangerous. The admonition does not reflect a desire to be secretive or elitist.

The verse also enumerates the qualifications of the disciples. Interestingly, the first two qualifications – being well versed in scriptures and firmly founded in *Brahman* – are the same as those mentioned for the teacher in verse 1.2,12. Two more qualifications are added: that the students duly tend the sacred fire and perform the *shirovrata* rite.

The *shirovrata* rite can be interpreted in several ways. At one level it refers to one who has shaved his head. This is a symbol of renouncing the world and becoming an ascetic. This interpretation is justified on the ground that the whole Upanishad is called Mundaka, which could refer to the shaven heads of *sanyasis*. However, it is also mentioned in the text that the disciple Saunaka, to whom Rishi Angirasa is expounding the teaching, is not a *sanyasi*, but a householder.

Another explanation is that it refers to a special rite mentioned in *Atharva* Veda, which involves carrying a fire on the head.

Once again we have to look deeper below the surface meaning to try and find the real significance. There is a fiery serpent power, *kundalini shakti* that lies dormant at the base of the human spine. Under certain conditions, this can be aroused and led upwards along the spine. On its way, it irradiates various *chakras* or centres. Ultimately, it bursts in splendor into the cortex and illuminates the highest of these *chakras*, the thousand-petalled lotus in the head. Surely, this is the rite or the ceremony of the head to which the seer refers (3.2, 10-11).

– Karan Singh

'Knowledge about Brahman is not to be imparted to one who is not qualified to receive it intellectually, psychologically and spiritually.'

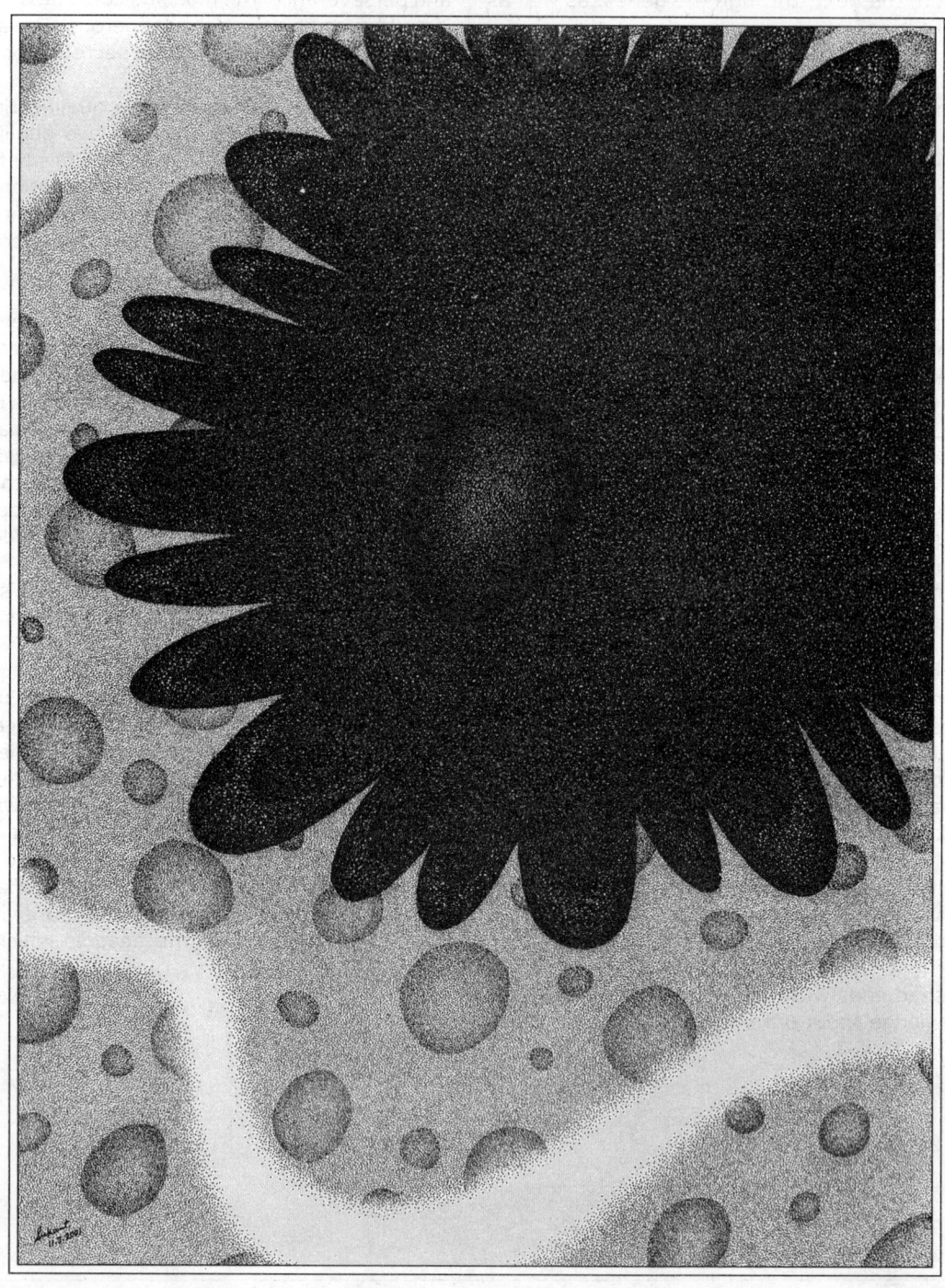

Prasna Upanishad

The Cosmic Person within us

OVERVIEW

Prasna Upanishad presents a summary of all the Upanishads. The presentation is in the form of six sets of questions and their answers by a learned teacher, Pippalada.

The first question is about creation: How One Consciousness created out of Itself the duality of Matter and Life, and how that duality was transformed into multiplicity? The second and third questions are about the Cosmic Life Principle and its existence in human beings. Answers to these three questions cover the five layers of human personality – physical, vital, mental, spiritual and blissful. The fourth question is about the three states of human experience – waking, dream and deep sleep. The fifth question is about Pure Consciousness – the substratum and the driving power behind the five layers of human personality and the three states of human experience. Its awareness is gained by practice of meditation on an appropriate symbol – like Aum.

The sixth question is about the Cosmic Person, Purusha and His sixteen facets, Sodasha Kala. It re-affirms the Upanishadic belief that man is a mini-cosmos.

The Upanishad ends with the disciples thanking the teacher in these words: 'You are indeed our father. You have ferried us to the shore across the sea of ignorance'. Gaining wisdom is like a new birth for living happily.

COMMENTARIES

The commentators quoted here are: Swami Chinmayananda, Swami Sivananda, Sri Sankara (translated by Swami Gambhirananda), N. A. Nikam, Rohit Mehta and Paul Deussen.

PRASNA UPANISHAD
The Cosmic Person within us

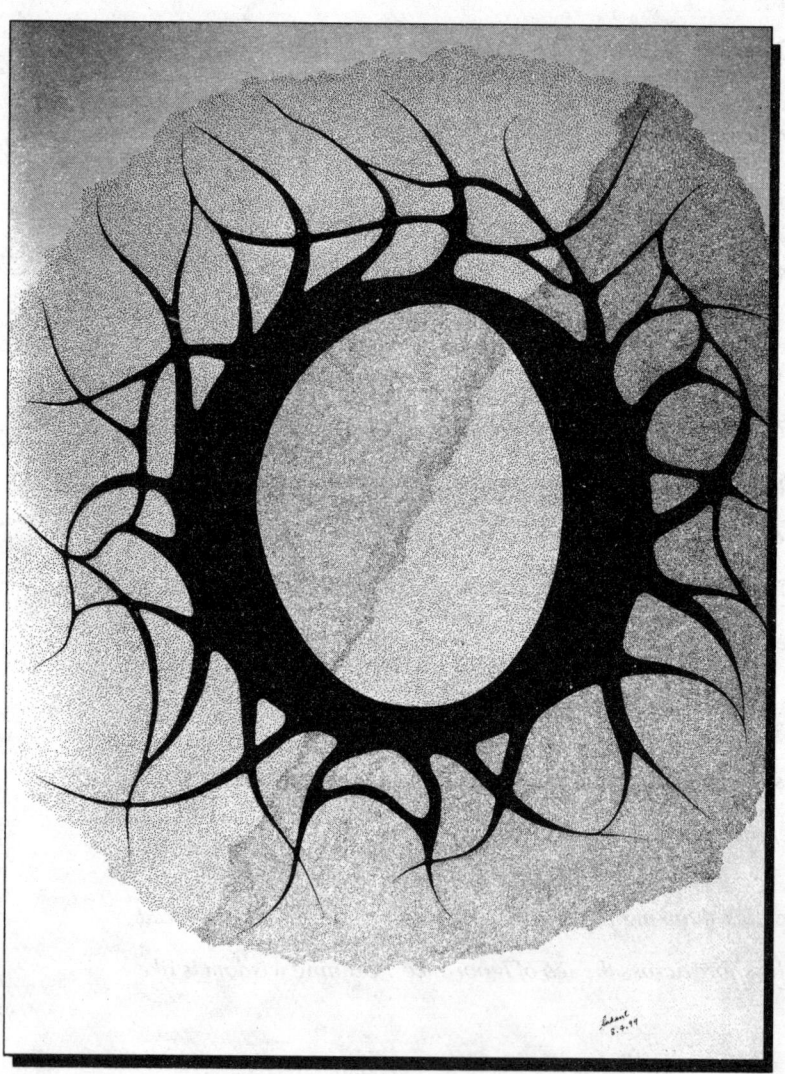

Peace Invocation

Verse 1-2	Preparation for spiritual enquiry
	559, 565, 574
Question 1:	Whence are living beings born?
	559, 565, 574
Question 2:	What powers energize living beings?
	560, 567, 577
Question 3:	How does Life-breath function?
	561, 568, 577
Question 4:	Who in man sleeps, dreams and keeps awake?
	562, 569, 578
Question 5:	Why Meditate on *Aum*?
	563, 570, 581
Question 6:	Where to look for the Cosmic Person?
	563, 571, 582

Questions 1-6 — The Cosmic Person within us

SIMPLIFIED SYNOPSES

**Verses 1-2
Preparation for spiritual enquiry**

Once there lived six young boys, all from families highly respected for their learning. They all believed in the existence of God, but they were not satisfied with His symbolic forms. They wanted to know the Ultimate Reality, the Highest One, the Formless Absolute. So they approached a very renowned teacher, Pippalada. They carried sacrificial fuel in their hands, signifying their desire to be his disciples.

Despite his fame, Pippalada was a humble man, but he was also a strict disciplinarian. He accepted the six boys as his students, but with normal conditions of those times. All of them were to live with him for one year with austerity, purity and faith; only then they could ask their questions. Practice of these disciplines is considered essential for preparing the mind to understand the Absolute.

**Question 1:
Whence are living beings born?**

After a year of disciplined life-style, the six students gathered around the teacher to begin their enquiry about the Supreme. Their questions reflect a step-by-step progression from the relative to the Absolute.

The first question by Kabandhi is about birth of living beings. Pippalada says that Consciousness is the first cause of all births. The word used here for Consciousness is *Prajapati*, literally meaning the Lord of all creatures. First, Consciousness was stirred by a desire for creation. Next, Consciousness created out of Itself the duality of Matter and Life, *Rayi* and *Prana*. All living beings are products of innumerable interactions between Matter and Life. Time is the field, so to say, in which continuity of creation is sustained. Matter, Life and Time – all three are manifestations of One Consciousness, *Brahman*.

> *'Consciousness created out of Itself the duality of Matter and Life.'*

The word *Rayi* is literally translated as Food. However, it has a much wider connotation in the text. It includes every physical object and natural phenomenon, gross and subtle. Everything is 'food' for something else; the gross is absorbed in the subtle.

In a very imaginative analogy, Pippalada equates Matter and Life with Moon and Sun. Verses 6-8 glorify the Sun as the nourisher of all life, the illuminator of all forms of matter and the provider of energy for sustenance of life as well as matter. Verses 9-13 emphasize the importance of Time by calling it Prajapati itself. They also imply that there is duality in everything that exists, even in the flow of Time. For example, a year has the duality of sun moving in northern and in southern hemispheres, a month has the duality of bright and dark fortnights, and a weekday has the duality of day and night.

The duality of year is equated with two types of life-styles – one devoted to legitimate pursuit of material pleasures and the other to spiritual pursuits. The former is said to lead to the world of ancestors (*Pitrayana*), symbolized by Moon, and then to rebirth; the latter to a state of liberation, symbolized by Sun, (*Devayana*). The former is equated with Matter, the latter with Life. (Verses 9-10).

'Food influences genes.'

Verse-11 glorifies Sun as the Father of all, the provider of life-sustaining rains, the all-knowing support of the whole universe. It also contains two beautiful metaphors to describe Sun as the Lord of Time. Sun is compared to a five-footed benevolent master moving along the roof of the world, each foot representing a season. It is also compared to a chariot drawn by seven horses – each representing a color – and moving on the wheel of Time, with six spokes symbolizing six seasons.

Continuing on the existence of duality in Time, verse-12 equates dark fortnight with Matter and bright fortnight with Life. Likewise, in verse-13, night is equated with Matter and day with Life.

Verses 13-16 touch upon some practical aspect of human birth, like when to make love and how many children to have? Verse-14 glorifies food by calling it *Prajapati* and implies that quality of food eaten by a man influences the genes in his children. Verses 15-16 commend a code of conduct for married couples.

Question 2: What powers energize living beings?

The second question follows the first. Bhargava wants to know about the powers on which living beings are dependent. Pippalada identifies these as the five elements, the mind and the senses of perception – like sight and hearing. More crucial than any of these, however, is life-breath, *Prana*. This is explained through a parable. It is said that once each of these powers thought itself as independently supporting living beings, and thereby claimed pre-eminence. *Prana* asked them not to be deluded, as it is *Prana*, which supports living beings by distributing itself in their bodies as five forms of life-breath. But the senses did not recognize the indispensability of *Prana* for their own functioning. At this, *Prana* got ready to leave the body. The senses then realized their dependence on *Prana* and accepted its supremacy.

'Prana and senses are like queen bee and bees.'

The relationship between *Prana* and the senses is like that between the queen bee and the bees that follow it (Verse 4).

Verses 5-13 are like a hymn to *Prana*. In these, *Prana* is presented not merely as life-breath in living beings, but as a Cosmic Life Principle.

In verse-5, *Prana* is identified with Vedic gods like Fire, Sun and Indra. Also, as Earth, *Prana* supports all; and as Food, it nourishes all. In verse-6, *Prana* is compared to the hub of a wheel; every thing revolves around it like spokes. In verse-7, *Prana* is described as *Prajapati*, Lord of all creatures. It moves in mother's womb as father's seed and then takes birth as a child, in the image of parents. In verse-8, *Prana* is said to be the best carrier of libations to the spirit of ancestors, as also the dynamic principle behind the senses. In verse-9, *Prana* is again identified with Vedic gods like Indra, Rudra, Vayu and Sun.

'Prana is not merely life-breath, but Cosmic Life Principle.'

Verses 9-13 are prayers addressed to the Cosmic Life Principle, *Prana*. These invoke *Prana* as Father to bless the mind and the senses; and as Mother to grant protection, prosperity and wisdom.

Question 3: How does Life-breath function?

The third question by Kausalya seeks further elaboration on *Prana* – Its origin, Its entrance, functioning and departure from the body, as also Its importance both at individual and universal levels. In response, Pippalada first compliments Kausalya for a good question. This is a way of encouragement. He then addresses each of the six parts of the question.

> *'Prana, Life Principle is born from Atman, Self.'*

Prana, Life Principle is born from Atman, Self. The two are inseparable like an object and its shadow (verse-3). The entry of *Prana* in the body is a result of thought or wish of the mind (verse-3). Later, in verses 10-12, it is explained that a person's last thoughts influence his next life.

Prana or life-breath functions in the body by dividing itself into five forms and distributing these in five regions of the body. Each form of *Prana* is said to perform a specific function. The functioning of *Prana* is explained by the analogy of a king allocating specific villages to his officers and commanding them to supervise these (verse 4).

The in-breath (*Prana*) functions in the upper region of the body, the out-breath (*Apana*) in the lower region, and the equalizing-breath (*Samana*) in the middle region. The diffused-breath (*Vyana*) moves throughout the entire body through as many as 727 million arteries and sub-arteries. These are said to originate from the heart (verses 5-6).

Prana is said to exit the body through the ascending up-breath (*Udana*) from the artery going towards the crown of the head.

Prana goes to a virtuous world, or to a sinful world, or it comes back to earth for rebirth. Virtual and sinful worlds refer to different states of Consciousness (verse-7).

> *'There is a direct relationship between the universe and the individual.'*

Life-breath in living beings is a manifestation of the Cosmic Life Principle. Each of the five forms of life-breath in human body is influenced by its cosmic counterpart. Sun corresponds to *Prana*, which is active in the eyes. Earth corresponds to *Apana*, which regulates the excretory and the regenerative system. Space corresponds to *Samana*, which regulates the digestive system. Air corresponds to *Vyana*, which energizes the entire body. Fire (*Teja*) corresponds to *Udana*, which sustains life. Thus, there is a direct relationship between the universe and the individual (verse-8).

When a person dies, his physical body disintegrates, but his senses and mind are absorbed in Life Principle for rebirth in another body (verse-9). Thus, it is not just our deeds but also our thoughts and words in this life that influence our next life.

Verses 10-12 emphasize the influence of our last thoughts on the course of our next life. It is to be noted that whatever thoughts have dominated a

---

'Prana or life-breath functions in the body by dividing itself into five forms.'

person's mind during his life, similar thoughts will emerge nearer the time of death.

Question 4:
Who in man sleeps, dreams and keeps awake?

The states of waking, dream and sleep are considered to be of great spiritual significance in all the Upanishads. In the fourth question, Gargya wants to know who is it that sleeps, who dreams and who keeps awake? When a person is happy, who is the enjoyer of that happiness? Is there any common principle on which all these states depend?

Pippalada uses the analogy of setting and rising sun to explain sleeping and waking states, respectively. The rays are like the senses and the sun is like the mind. In state of sleep, all the senses merge with the mind and lie dormant, like the rays of setting sun becoming one with the sun – invisible and indistinguishable. In waking state, the senses proceed out of the mind to do their respective functions – like the rays of a rising sun. Thus it is the senses of perception, the organs of action and the mind that sleep in the state of sleep; they keep awake in the waking state (verse-2).

'In waking state, the senses proceed out of the mind to do their respective functions, like the rays of a rising sun.'

It is the Life Principle, *Prana*, which alone keeps awake in all the three states.

Pippalada also uses the analogy of a sacrificial fire ritual, *Agnihotra*, to elaborate upon the state of sleep. He equates the five forms of life-breaths with the three sacrificial fires, the priest of sacrifice and the rewards of sacrifice. Mind is compared to the person who performs the sacrifice. The analogy seems to imply that just as sacrificial fires take the sacrificer to the desired fruit, the mind is taken daily to *Brahman* in deep sleep.

According to another learned commentator, the analogy is intended to praise knowledge and eulogize illumination (verses 3-4).

'In dreams, the mind becomes both the subject and the object.'

In dream state, the senses lie dormant and withdrawn in the mind; but the mind remains active. It fabricates its own world by its own greatness from the impressions and experiences of waking state. According to some commentators, these could relate even to previous births. In dream state, the mind experiences everything – perceived or unperceived, real or imaginary – by itself becoming both the subject and the object (verse-5).

In deep sleep, the mind is overwhelmed by its own radiance and it stops seeing dreams. Instead, it enjoys the bliss of calm, unobstructed, universal Consciousness. It is a state of total serenity.

'In sleep, the senses merge with the mind, like the rays of a setting sun.'

Pippalada explains the state of sleep with another analogy. Just as at night birds proceed towards the nest that provides them rest, in deep sleep all the faculties of man withdraw in the Self that provides them bliss (verse 7). These faculties are enumerated in verse-8: five elements, five senses of perception, five organs of action, four inner mental faculties, and life-breath, *Prana* itself.

It is Self, *Atman* which is the final substratum of everything – the discriminating Self (*Vigyana Atman*), the senses of perception, the organs of action, and all the five forms of life-breath (*Prana*). It is shadowless, bodyless, colorless,

---

'The mind is taken daily to Brahman in deep sleep.'

pure and indestructible. He who knows the Omniscient, Omnipresent Self, he sees same Self in all.

Question 5: Why meditate on *Aum*?

The responses of Pippalada to the four questions put up by his disciples so far reflect a step-by-step progression from gross to subtle aspects of life – from physical to vital to mental to spiritual. These have been called *annamaya kosha*, *pranamaya kosha*, *manomaya kosha* and *vigyanamaya kosha* respectively, elsewhere in Taittiriya Upanishad. The ultimate in life is Bliss, or *anandamaya kosha*, and this is attained through meditation. So the fifth disciple turns to the subject of meditation. Satyakama wants to know what is gained by meditation on *Aum*?

Pippalada first explains the significance of the syllable *Aum*. It is an all-inclusive sound symbol of *Brahman*, Comic Consciousness. It is a recurring theme in almost all the Upanishads. Brahman has two aspects – Relative and Absolute, Manifest and Unmanifest, Immanent and Transcendent, with attributes and without attributes, lower and higher. Both these aspects of *Brahman* are represented by Its symbol *Aum*. So by meditation on *Aum*, a wise man attains either of them (verse 2).

> *'Meditate on three syllables of Aum in their totality, as One Brahman.'*

Aum has three syllables or *matras* – A, U and M. A person can meditate on the first syllable A, the first two syllables A and U, or a blend of all three syllables. Each of these three methods of meditation leads to distinctly different end-results – rebirth on earth, lunar heaven or the world of Sun. Commentators have provided some very interesting interpretations of these three meditations. For example: they represent the paths of work, worship and wisdom; they represent the three states of waking, dream and sleep; they lead to three states of Consciousness – physical life on earth, world of ancestors (*Pitrayana*) or liberation from rebirth (*Devayana*); they are the source of the three Vedas; and so on (verses 3-7).

The correct method of meditation on *Aum* is to blend all the three syllables and meditate upon them in their totality, as One *Brahman*. The meditator should also merge himself in the imperceptible sound between two successive chants of *Aum*. Such meditation leads to results which are superior to even those obtained through ritualistic recitation of Vedic verses. It leads to That which is tranquil, imperishable, immortal, fearless and Supreme.

Question 6: Where to look for the Cosmic Person?

The personality of a complete person comprises of five layers – physical, vital, mental, spiritual and blissful. However, they are all founded on One Reality. The sixth question is: where to find that Reality? And the answer is: Right here, inside the body.

> *'He who does not know should not teach.'*

Self, Consciousness, Creator, *Atman*, *Brahman* and *Prajapati* are some of the words used to refer to this One Ultimate Reality. The word used by Sukesha Bharadvaja is *Purusha* or Cosmic Person.

Sukesha begins his question with an anecdote. This is intended to point to the difficulty involved in acquiring knowledge of the Absolute, and to emphasize that he who does not know should not teach (verse 1-2).

'Self, Consciousness, Atman, Brahman, Prajapati and Purusha are some of the terms used to refer to the Ultimate Reality.'

> *'The Cosmic Person is Formless and without any parts. He makes Himself experienced is human life through multitude of manifestations.'*

The Absolute Being, *Purusha*, is One, Infinite, homogeneous mass of Consciousness. He is Formless and without any parts. The sixteen parts referred to by Sukesha are not His limbs, but His manifestations, or what the commentators call 'His limiting adjuncts'. They are the means by which He makes Himself experienced in human life (verse 6.3).

In verse-4, Pippalada emphasizes that these sixteen 'parts' are not His 'parts' in the literal sense, but only His creations. He enumerates them as follows:

1	Life Principle, *Prana*
2	Faith, *Shraddha*
3-7	Five Elements – Space, Air, Fire, Water and Earth
8	Five senses of perception and five organs of action, considered as one.
9	Mind
10	Food
11	Vigor
12	Self-discipline, *tapas*
13	Worship or prayers, *mantra*
14	Work, *karma*
15	Wisdom or spiritual worlds, *lokas*. These represent different states of Consciousness.
16	Name, or a distinct identity.

The sixteen parts enumerated here are representative of the multitude of manifestations which constitute the cosmos. They all originate from the Unmanifest Absolute; and eventually they all dissolve into the Unmanifest Absolute. This is illustrated with a beautiful analogy of rivers merging into an ocean (verse 5).

Purusha, Cosmic Person, Absolute Being is the support of all His manifestations. This is explained with the analogy of spokes being supported by the hub of a wheel (verse 6).

> *'You have ferried us across the sea of ignorance to the shore of wisdom.'*

The concluding verse contains another imaginative analogy. The disciples thank Pippalada for ferrying them across the sea of ignorance to the shore of wisdom. They also state that his spiritual discourse has been like a second birth for them; and accordingly, they acknowledge him as their father (6.8).

'Gaining spiritual wisdom is like having a second birth.'

TRANSLATED TEXT

Peace Invocation

Om.
O gods, may we hear auspicious words with our ears.
O Worshipful One, may we see auspicious things with our eyes.
May we live our entire life cheerfully and in good health,
  offering our praises unto Thee.

May *Indra*, the ancient and the famous, bless us.
May *Pusan* (sun), the all-knowing bless us.
May *Vayu* (Life Principle), the Lord of swift motion,
  who protects us from all harms, bless us.
May *Brhaspati*, the Lord of wisdom, bless us.

> *Om. Shanti. Shanti. Shanti.*
> Let there be Peace, Let there be Peace, Let there be Peace.

Sukesha, son of Bharadvaja
Satyakama, son of Sibi
Gargya, grandson of Surya
Kausalya, son of Asvala
Bhargava of Vidarbha city,
  belonging to the Bhrigu family,
and Kabandhi, son of Katya....

All of them were deeply devoted to God, *Brahman*, and worshipped Him in some form. However, they wanted to know the Highest (Formless) *Brahman*. So, they approached the revered sage Pippalada with sacrificial fuel in hand, thinking that the Rishi will teach them everything. **1**

To them the Rishi said:

Live here for one year with austerity, purity and faith; after that, ask your questions as you please. If I know the answers, I will surely explain everything to you. **2**

Question 1

Later (after one year) Kabandhi approached Pippalada and asked him:

"Revered Master, whence are living beings born?" **3**

To him, he (Pippalada) replied:

Prajapati, the Creator, desired the joy of creation. He remained in meditation and then emerged a pair of matter (*Rayi*) and life (*Prana*). He thought that these two will produce beings of many kind. **4**

The sun, verily, is life and the moon is matter. All that has form – gross and subtle – is matter. Therefore, anything having a form is matter. **5**

"All of them worshipped Him in some form. However, they wanted to know the Highest (Formless) Brahman."

After rising, the sun goes towards east and illumines with its rays all living beings in the east. When it enters the other sides – south, west, north, below, above and in-between – it illumines with its rays all living beings in these directions. **6**

It (the sun) is *Vaisvanara*, or one who is identified with all living beings. It is *Visvarupa*, or one who assumes all forms. It rises every day as *Prana* (life) and *Agni* (fire, energy). This has been described in the following mantra of *Rg* Veda. **7**

The thousand-rayed sun exists in hundreds of forms as life of all living beings. It is resplendent, all-knowing, goal of all, sole light and giver of energy. **8**

Time (represented by the year) is indeed the Lord of creation.

It has two paths – southern and northern.

Those who engage in acts sanctioned by scriptures or considered noble, they attain the 'world of moon', and they return again to enjoy the material world. Therefore, sages desirous of (wealth and) children take the southern route. Indeed, matter corresponds to the path of ancestors. **9**

But those who seek *Atman* (Self) by penance, self-disciple, faith and knowledge are in the northern route. They attain the sun, which is immortal, fearless, and the support of all living beings. This is the highest goal. From that they do not have to return (to the material world). It is the end of rebirth. About this, there is this verse. **10**

They speak of it (the sun) as the Father, giver of rain, having five feet (five seasons) and twelve forms (twelve months), seated in the higher level of heavens. Others speak of him as the omniscient, upon whom the whole world is founded – like a chariot drawn by seven horses (seven colors of light) and running on a wheel with six spokes (seasons). **11**

The month, verily, is *Prajapati*. Of this, the dark fortnight is matter, the bright fortnight is life. Therefore, the seers perform sacrifices in the bright fortnight, others in the dark fortnight. **12**

Day and night are again *Prajapati*. Day is life and night is matter. Those who join in love during the day waste their life, while those who do so during the night are to be considered celibate (*Brahmachari*). **13**

Food indeed is *Prajapati*. From food is produced semen, and from that all these living beings are thus born. **14**

Those (married couples) who practice austerity, abstinence and truthfulness, who follow the example of *Prajapati*, and who produce (only) one pair (of children), for them alone is the heaven (*Brahma-loka*). **15**

"Those (married couples) who produce (only) one pair, for them alone is the heaven (Brahma-loka)."

The lovely heaven belongs to them alone who are free from deceit, hypocrisy and pride. **16**

Question 2

Then Bhargava of Vidarbha asked:
"O Master! What powers (gods) support living beings? What illumines the body? Which among them is the greatest?" **1**

He (Pippalada) replied:
These powers are: Space, Air, Fire, Water, and Earth (five elements of Nature); Mind, Eyes and Ear. They, exhibiting their glory, once asserted: "We hold together and support this body." **2**

Life (*Prana*), the greatest of them said: "Do not cherish this delusion. I alone, dividing myself fivefold (in five forms of breath) hold together living beings. I am their foundation." But others did not believe its words. **3**

Out of indignation, *Prana* prepared to go out of the body. When *Prana* got up to depart, all others immediately had to get up too. When *Prana* remained, all others remained. Just as bees go out when their queen goes out, and they return when she returns; so did mind, speech, eye, ear and others. Realizing *Prana*'s importance, they praised it. **4**

This (*Prana*) burns like fire, shines like sun, rains like cloud, rules like *Indra*. This bright one is wind, it is earth, it is matter. It is both – that which has form and that which is formless. It is also that which is immortal. **5**

As spokes on the hub of a wheel, everything is established in *Prana* – the mantras of Rg, Yajur and Sama Vedas, all dynamic activities, and all spiritual endeavors. **6**

As *Prajapati*, the Lord of living beings, you (*Prana*) move in the womb; you, indeed, are born afterwards as the child, you dwell in the body with other senses. To you alone, all these living beings offer oblations. **7**

You are the chief carrier of offerings to the gods. You are the first offering to *pitras* (souls of ancestors). You are the dynamic principle behind the senses. You are the essence of the body. **8**

O *Prana* (Life)! You are *Indra*, the Lord of all powers. You are *Rudra*, the protector. You move in the sky (*Vayu*). You are the Sun, the Lord of all lights. **9**

O *Prana*, when you cause rain to fall down, then these creatures become cheerful, hoping that there will be as much food as they desire. **10**

O *Prana*, you are by nature pure. You are the sacred fire, the consumer of everything, the gracious Lord of the world. We offer you oblations. O all-pervading Air, you are our father. **11**

"This Prana, Life Principle, burns like fire, shines like sun, rains like cloud, and rules like Indra. It is immortal."

Make auspicious that form of yours which exists in speech, in hearing, in seeing, and which also pervades the mind. Please do not depart from us. **12**

Whatever exists in the three worlds is all under the control of *Prana*. O *Prana*, protect us like a mother protects her sons. Give us prosperity and wisdom. **13**

Question 3

Then Kausalya, son of Asvala asked him (Pippalada):

"Venerable Master, from where is this *Prana* born? How does it enter the body? How after diffusing itself, does it abide here? In what way does it depart? How does it support the universe within and without?" **1**

To him (Kausalya), he (Pippalada) replied:

You have asked very difficult questions. But because you are deeply devoted to *Brahman*, I shall answer you. **2**

This Life (*Prana*) is born from Self (*Atman*). It is related to Self like a shadow to man. It enters the body by the activities of the mind. **3**

As a sovereign commands his officers, saying, 'You supervise these villages', so does *Prana* allot its various vital breaths to their respective functions. **4**

Out-breath (*Apana*) is in the organs of excretion and procreation. Life-breath (*Prana*) is in the eyes, the ears, the mouth and the nose. Equalizing-breath (*Samana*) is in the middle. It distributes equally whatever food is eaten. It also activates the seven flames (openings in the face). **5**

Self (*Atman*) is in the heart. It (the heart) has a hundred and one arteries. Each of these has a hundred smaller arteries. Again, each of these (smaller arteries) is divided into seventy two thousand sub-branches. Within them moves the diffused-breath (*Vyana*). **6**

Now, rising upward through one of these (arteries), the ascending-breath (*Udana*) leads to virtuous world through virtuous deeds, sinful world through sinful deeds, and human world if the deeds are a mixture of both (virtuous and sinful). **7**

The sun is, verily, the cosmic *Prana*, It blesses the in-breath (*Prana*) in the eyes. The divinity which is in earth, supports a person's out-breath (*Apana*).
The space between the sun and the earth is the equalizing-breath (*Samana*).
Air is the diffused-breath (*Vyana*). **8**

Fire (*teja*) verily is the ascending-breath (*Udana*). Therefore he, whose fire (of life) has ceased, takes a rebirth, with the senses absorbed in the mind. **9**

Whatever be one's thoughts (at the time of death), that thought remains with the outgoing *Prana*. *Prana* coupled with *Udana* and *Atman*, leads to whatever world has been conceived (in the last thoughts). **10**

"This Life (Prana) is born from Self (Atman). It is related to Self like a shadow to man."

A wise man who knows life thus, his line of progeny continues, and he becomes immortal. About this, there is the following verse. **11**

'He who knows the origin, the entry, the abode, the omnipresence, and the fivefold distribution of *Prana*, as also its internal state in the body, he attains longevity. Yes, he attains longevity.' **12**

Question 4

Then Gargya, the grandson of Surya questioned him (Pippalada).

"Revered Master, who is that which sleeps in man? Who keeps awake in him? Who sees dreams? Who is that which feels happy? On whom do all these states depend?" **1**

He (Pippalada) replied:

O Gargya, just as the rays of a setting sun become one in a circle of light, and they spread out again when the sun rises; so also all these (senses) become one in the highest god, mind. Therefore, at that time (of sleep) a person does not hear, does not see, does not smell, does not taste, does not feel, does not speak, does not grasp, does not enjoy, does not eject, does not move. They say, 'He is sleeping'. **2**

Consciousness alone remains awake in this city (body) at the time of sleep.

(The Teacher then compares the five forms of life-breath and the mind with the ritual of offering oblations to fire, *Agnihotra*)

Apana (out-breath) is the householder's fire.
Vyana (diffused-breath) is the sacrificial fire.
Prana (in-breath) is the oblation fire that is lighted from the householder's fire.
Samana (equalizing-breath) is the priest.
Udana (ascending-breath) is the reward for the ritual of sacrifice. It leads the performer of sacrifice to *Brahman*
The mind, verily, is the person performing the sacrifice (*Yajamana*). **3-4**

In dream state, the mind perceives dreams and their grandeur. It sees again what has been seen (in waking state). It hears again what has been heard. It enjoys again what has been enjoyed in different places and times. Whatever has been seen and not seen, heard and not heard, experienced and not experienced, real and unreal, it (the mind) perceives all. It perceives all by being all. **5**

When the mind is overpowered by its own radiance, then it sees no dreams. At that time it enjoys the bliss of deep sleep in the body. **6**

O dear, just as birds retire to a tree which provides rest, so indeed all these (man's faculties) rest in the Supreme *Atman*. **7**

"Consciousness alone remains awake in this city (body) at the time of sleep."

Earth and its subtle elements,
water and its subtle elements,
space and its subtle elements,
eyes and what can be seen,
ears and what can be heard,
nose and what can be smelt,
taste and its objects,
hands and whatever they can hold,
feet and whatever they can walk on,
organs of generation and the objects of enjoyment,
organs of excretion and what must be excreted,
mind (*manas*) and objects of thinking,
intellect (*buddhi*) and objects of discrimination,
ego and objects of ego,
memory (*chitta*) and objects of memory,
lustre and what is to be illumined,
Prana (life-force) and everything supported by it
all these rest in the state of sleep, like birds in their nests. **8**

That which sees, feels, hears, smells, tastes, thinks, knows and works is the spiritual Self (*vigyana Atman*), the Cosmic Person (*Purusha*). It dwells in the highest indestructible Self. **9**

My young friend, this highest Self is without shadow, without body, without color, pure and indestructible. He who knows It becomes It, omniscient and omnipresent. For this, there is the following verse. **10**

'O Beloved, he who knows the immutable Self – wherein live the mind, the senses, the life-force, the elements – he becomes all-knowing. He realizes the Self in all.' **11**

Question 5

Then Satyakama, coming near Pippalada, said:

"Venerable Master, if a man meditates with devotion upon *Aum* all his life, what world does he conquer thereby?" **1**

He (Pippalada) replied:

Satyakama, that *Brahman* which is both the higher and the lower is but *Aum*. Upon meditating upon It, a wise man attains either of the two. **2**

If a person meditates even on the first syllable of *Aum* (i.e. A), then enlightened by that, he is reborn quickly (after death) in this world. Endowed with austerity, self-discipline and faith, he achieves greatness in his new life. **3**

If he meditates on two syllables of *Aum* (A+U), upon his death he ascends to the lunar heaven; and after enjoying its pleasures, he returns again to earth. **4**

"That Brahman, which is both the higher and the lower, is (symbolized by) Aum.
By meditating upon It, a wise man attains either of the two."

If he meditates on all the three syllables of *Aum*, with full consciousness that *Aum* is the Supreme Being Itself, he becomes united with the bright Sun. He is freed from his sins just as a snake is freed from its skin. He is elevated by chants of Sama hymns to the world of *Brahma* (*Brahma-loka*). He then has an experience of the Cosmic Person, the Supreme Being, who resides in the heart of all being. There are two verses about it.   **5**

'The three syllables (A, U and M), when meditated upon separately, do not lead beyond mortality. The correct method is to blend them together as one. When they are properly employed in all their external, internal and intermediate aspects, the knower does not waver.'   **6**

'Through the Rg verses, one attains this world; through Yajur, one attains the interspace; through Sama, one attains That which the seers have attained. The wise attain That which is tranquil, imperishable, immortal, fearless, and supreme, by means of meditation on *Aum*.'   **7**

Question 6

Then Sukesha Bharadvaja asked Pippalada:

"O revered Master, the Prince of Kosala Hiranyanabha once came to me and asked, 'O Bharadvaja, do you know the *Purusha* (Cosmic Person) of sixteen parts (*kalas*)?' I said to the prince, 'I do not know him. If I knew, why should I not teach you? He who teaches what is not correct perishes completely with roots, stems, and branches. Therefore, I will not teach what I do not know.' The prince silently mounted his chariot and went away. I like to ask you that. Where is that *Purusha* located?"   **1**

He (Pippalada) replied:

My beloved son, That Being, *Purusha*, in whom originate these sixteen parts (*Kalas*), is right here, within the body.   **2**

It (*Purusha*) reflected: By what means shall I depart the body? By what means shall I stay in the body?   **3**

He created *Prana*, Life Principle.

From *Prana*, He created faith, space, air, fire, water, earth, senses, the mind and food. From food came strength, austerities (*tapas*), hymns, work and the worlds. Thereafter, in the worlds, He created names. (All these add up to 16).   **4**

Just as rivers flowing towards the sea disappear upon reaching it, their names and forms perish in the ocean, and everything is spoken of as the ocean; likewise the sixteen parts of a seeker who has *Purusha* as his goal, disappear on reaching *Purusha*. His name and form get merged with *Purusha* and thereafter he is called simply as *Purusha*, Formless and Immortal. On this point, there is the following verse: **5**

"That Being, Purusha, in whom originate these sixteen parts (Kalas), is right here, within the body."

The sixteen parts are established in *Purusha* like spokes in the hub of a wheel. It (*Purusha*) is the goal of knowledge. Know It, so that death may not afflict you.
6

Then Pippalada said (to his six disciples):
This much alone I know of Supreme *Brahman*. There is nothing higher than It.
7

The disciples worshipped the *Rishi*, and said: 'You are indeed our father. You have ferried us to the shore across the sea of ignorance. We salute all the great *Rishis*. We salute all the great *Rishis*.'
8

Peace Invocation

Om.
O gods, may we hear auspicious words with our ears.
O Worshipful One, may we see auspicious things with our eyes.
May we live our entire life cheerfully and in good health,
  offering our praises unto Thee.

May *Indra*, the ancient and the famous, bless us.
May *Pusan* (sun), the all-knowing bless us.
May *Vayu* (Life Principle), the Lord of swift motion,
  who protects us from all harms, bless us.
May *Brhaspati*, the Lord of wisdom, bless us.

Om. Shanti. Shanti. Shanti.
Let there be Peace, Let there be Peace, Let there be Peace.

GENERAL COMMENTARY BY PAUL DEUSSEN

The six questions

The Upanishad deals with six questions put by six explorers of *Brahman* to the wise Pippalada.

1. Origin of matter and living beings
2. Superiority of *Prana* over sensory organs
3. *Prana* and its ramifications in man
4. About dream, sleep and deep sleep
5. Meditation over the syllable Om
6. The sixteen parts of Man

Q.1 The first question regarding the origin of beings serves as an occasion to divide nature, a product of *Prajapati*, into two parts – *Rayi* (matter) and *Prana* (life).

Q.2 The second question concerns the number of vital organs in man and their order of precedence. The reply contains the narration of an (imaginary) quarrel among the vital organs, followed by a hymn to *Prana*, Life force.

Q.3 The answer to the third question about *Prana* and its ramifications are summarized as follows:

- The origin of *Prana*: *Prana* arises from *Atman*, and is linked to it like a shadow to an object.
- The reason for its entrance into the body: The reason lies in the word *manokrtena*, which has been interpreted by Sri Sankara, "On account of actions done through His will", Grammatically, it would be more correct to say, "without the aid of the will".
- Ramifications: There are five ramifications of *Prana*, each with a psychical as well as cosmic correspondence:

Ramification	Psychical correspondence	Cosmic correspondence
Prana	Head (seven openings)	Sun
Apana	Organs of evacuation and pro-creation	Earth
Samana	Nutritional power	Space
Vyana	Power operating in the arteries and regulating blood circulation	Air
Udana	Leads the soul through an important artery, Susumna to the head, and then the world beyond, after death	Fire

Q.4 The fourth question has four sub-sections as follows:

Q. What in man sleeps and keeps awake?
A: Five senses and five organs of senses go to sleep. They enter the mind, like rays of light entering a setting sun. The mind keeps awake in dream, but goes to sleep in deep sleep. *Prana* – with its five ramifications – always keeps awake.

Q. Who sees dreams?
A: Mind. It builds dreams out of things perceived or not perceived in waking state.

Q. Who experiences joy in deep sleep?
A: Mind, overpowered by *Tejas*, does not see dreams any more. It is not mentioned as to who experiences the joy, but it can be gathered from what follows.

Q. Which is that Unity on which all the organs depend?
A: The highest *Atman* (4.7), or the spirit consisting of knowledge (*Vigyana Atman*) and resting on the highest imperishable *Atman* (4.9).

Q.5 The fifth question is regarding meditation on the symbol of *Brahman*, *Aum*.

A symbol is required on account of utter imperceptibility of *Brahman*. The reply analyses the sound *Aum* in its three parts (a + u + m). Meditation on one letter leads to a return to a privileged human existence on earth; meditation on two letters leads to moon and back to an earthly existence, corresponding to *Pitrayana*; meditation on three letter leads to *Devayana*, from which there is no return.

Q.6 The sixth question is: Where is the man of sixteen parts located?

The answer:
Right here, in us. The answer is further elaborated as to how the sixteen parts proceed out of *Purusha*, Cosmic Being, and how they return to Him. *Purusha* creates out of Itself: (1) *Prana*, Life Force (2) Faith, the most primitive germ of man (3-7) five elements (8) ten senses and sense organs, looked upon as a unity (9) mind (10) food, (11) regenerative fluid, and

---

'There are five ramifications of Prana, each with a psychical as well as a cosmic correspondence.'

the strength which depends upon it (12) *tapas*, (will power) (13) *mantra* (hymns and prayers) (14) *Karma*, deeds (15) *loka*, the worlds whose acquisition is conditioned by *Karma* and (16) name, *nama* or individual distinctness.

The return of these organs into *Purusha* is similar to that of rivers to an ocean.

– Paul Deussen

FOCUSSED COMMENTARIES

Verses 1-2 Preparation for spiritual enquiry

Once, there were six spiritual aspirants who wanted to know the true nature of things. They were in search of a good teacher. Eventually, they found a teacher by the name Pippalada and they thought he could teach them whatever they wanted to know. So, they approached Pippalada with sacrificial fuel in hand.

The sacrificial fuel is the ancient token with which an aspiring disciple approached his prospective guru.

The Rishi's reply reflects humility, coupled with uncompromising discipline.

– Swami Chinmayananda

Pippalada was not an ordinary teacher. He asked all the six aspiring disciples to wait for one year. This waiting was not to be done in idleness, it had to be with austerity, purity and faith - *tapa*, *brahmacharya* and *shraddha*.

Answers to deep spiritual enquiry can be found in questions themselves, provided the questions are formulated properly. This requires preparation. Considering that spirituality is a serious subject, the teacher gave the students one year to formulate their questions.

But why the prerequisites of austerity (*tapa*), purity (*brahmacharya*) and faith (*shraddha*)?

For a serious enquiry, man needs much energy – particularly energy of the mind. Austerity is a process of denial of the non-essentials. It helps to free the mind from entanglement in the non-essentials. This brings about a release of mental energy. Purity helps to conserve the mental energy released through austerity.

What is the condition of the mind when the non-essentials are denied, and the essentials are not defined? It stands face to face with the unknown. And it is in the presence of the unknown that real Faith is born. A faith in the known is no faith at all – it is only loyalty. Loyalty and faith are poles apart. Faith inspires a journey into the unknown.

– Rohit Mehta

Q1. Whence are living beings born?

The first question is about the origin of creation. *Prajapati*, who is described as the Creator, is obviously the Cosmic Mind. The whole creation is described as a projection from It. According to verse 1.4, creation came into existence through meditation, or a concentrated state of the Cosmic Mind. The teacher clearly states that *Prajapati* created a duality – Matter and Life – and this duality was the very source of the continuity of creation. He says that duality is present at every level in the manifested universe, for manifestation without duality is inconceivable. He says that sun is life and moon is matter. What is the significance of this illustration? It indicates that matter is dependent upon life, just as moon is dependent upon sun for its illumination. (1, 5)

The teacher further explains that matter can be gross or subtle. From this stand point, even thought or sound is matter. Thus, matter has a diversity of forms, and a diversity of states. It is through the interaction of life and matter that continuity of manifestation is maintained.

Continuing further on the theme of duality, the teacher says that creation is synonymous with time. Time is the field in which creation continues. Time is movement in duality. Where there is no duality, there is no time. So, when the Creator created duality, he also brought time into existence.

'Time is movement in duality. Where there is no duality, there is no time.
So, when the Creator created duality, he also brought time into existence.'

The teacher takes the first measure of time as a year, the time taken by earth to go round the sun once. But the teacher is also concerned that the principle of duality – the very basis of creation – should not be lost sight of. He therefore indicates the existence of duality everywhere. Explaining this, he says that even the year, a measure of time, has two paths – northern and southern. This is commonly understood as the sun moving northwards or southwards. The characteristics of this movement are described by the teacher in terms of duality – the one leading to good results and the other leading to evil conditions (1, 9).

Even if we take month as a measure of time, the principle of duality again holds good. There is the bright fortnight and the dark fortnight – one corresponds to life, and the other to matter. (1, 12)

If the measure of time is taken as a period of 24 hours, even then there is duality – day and night. Here the teacher adds that duality has to be understood not only in terms of its physical manifestations, but also in terms of its deeper, psychological manifestations. As an illustration, the teacher says that 'to join in love during the day is a waste of life.' Why? This is because daytime is a time of many preoccupations. Love is a total action, and there cannot be love when the mind is preoccupied. So, night indeed is the appropriate time for love; night not in just physical sense, but also in psychological sense. Psychological night is a condition where the mind is free from all its occupations. The appropriate time to join in love is night in physical terms and a state of total surrender in psychological terms (1,13).

The teacher concludes his answer by stating that food is the basis of physical creation. Without food, duality at the physical level is powerless (1,14).

In summary, creation is a result of duality – Life and Matter. The principle of duality is inherent even in the flow of time – no matter in what unit we measure it. At the physical level, food is essential for sustenance of life. Thus, the teacher has explained the creation of the physical body, *annamaya kosha*.

– Rohit Mehta

All the six questions are about life. All that has life breathes, but it is only man who is conscious of his breathing. Man made the discovery that to control or regulate breath is to control or regulate life.

Life enters the body with breath, departs with breath and is sustained by breath. The Upanishads distinguish between five kinds of breath. *Pranamaya* is an exercise and a discipline involving conscious control of the breath, leading to conscious control of the mind.

But life is not merely breath. It is more. Life is desire. Life is moved by desire. *Prajapati Praja Kamah*, The Creator desired the joy of creation. (1, 4). Desire is therefore the original impulse behind creation. However, desire of the Lord is not a desire to possess anything or want anything. Desire of the Lord is to give away Its abundance.

The Upanishad says that being desirous of creation, the Lord performed austerities, *tapas*. This indicates that both desire and austerities – *kama* and *tapas* – are essential for a creative activity.

– N. A. Nikam

The term *Prajapati* (also called *Hiranyagarbha*) is symbolic of the concept of Total Consciousness. It is also representative of the creative potential in human beings. The Creator, *Prajapati*, first gets a desire to create. He then contemplates how to fulfill that desire. This requires thinking, planning, remembering. These are together indicated here as austerity, *tapas*.

Next follows execution. *Prajapati* creates a pair – life and matter, or *Prana* and *Rayi*. Life and matter interact to produce the vast, beautiful, diverse universe.

In the original Sanskrit language of the verse, matter is referred to as food, and compared to moon. Life is referred to as 'eater of the food' and compared to sun. Is there any logic behind this symbolism? Sun is the source of all energy, and hence life. Moon shines only in the reflected light of the sun. Both have a common origin – Consciousness. Modern physics is also arriving at somewhat similar conclusions.

Some commentators regard that *rayi* and *Prana* represent matter and energy, some regard them analogous to masculine and feminine principles.

The Upanishads regard the sun more than an astronomical object of light and energy. In fact, it is considered the life of all living beings.

'Desire is the original impulse behind creation. However, desire of the Lord is not a desire to possess anything or want anything; it is to give away Its abundance.'

Our eyes can see only through the medium of light, which originates from the sun. This fact is poetically expressed in the statement that the sun assumes all forms.

Vaisvanara is the essence of all living beings, while *Visvarupa* is the essence of the whole cosmos. The sun is considered to be both.

Verses 9-10 distinguishes between two types of lifestyle - one devoted to material pursuits and the other devoted to spiritual knowledge. The former leads to rebirth, while the latter leads to liberation. This is understandable. As we think, so we become.

Verse-11 glorifies the sun as lord of time. In a poetic description, time is conceived as a five-footed benevolent Master moving along the roof of the world – slowly and steadily, from season to season. In another metaphor, the sun is described as the chariot of time. It moves as though sitting in a chariot drawn by seven horses, meaning the seven colors of sunlight. The chariot moves on a wheel having six spokes, meaning the six seasons.

Sun is not just the Lord of life, but also the Lord of time.

It is useful to recapitulate how the Creative Principle transformed itself into a world of multiplicity. First, it became Life and Matter, symbolized by Sun and Moon. Then (by a combination of them) it became Time.

Year, month and day are all measures of time. They are derived from movements of Sun and Moon. As time passed - year by year, month by month and day by day – matter became food. Living beings eat food, and from its essence are generated the seeds of species. So the Master concludes: "all these living beings are thus born" (1,14). It will be recalled that Kabandhi's question was: 'Whence are living beings born?'

It is significant to note that Sun, which is nothing but *Prajapati*, produces food; so food is also *Prajapati*. Food produces the generative fluid, which also is *Prajapati*. When this causes the creation of the next generation, that too is nothing but *Prajapati*. Therefore, my father was *Prajapati*, who ate *Prajapati*, secreted *Prajapati*, impregnated *Prajapati*, and the son *Prajapati* was born as me. The tragedy is that I do not realize that I am *Prajapati*.

Verses 1,15-16 imply a code of conduct for the married couple. The phrase 'who produce one pair, *te mithunam udpadayante*' seems to suggest the advocacy of family planning, in an era which dates back to more than a millennium before Christ. The verses also say that heaven is for those who practice austerity, abstinence and truthfulness, and who are free from deceit, hypocrisy and pride.

– Swami Chinmayananda

Prasna Upanishad is a complimentary work to Mundaka Upanishad.

Prajapati, becoming desirous of creating progeny for Himself, deliberated on Vedic knowledge acquired in earlier cycle of creation. After intense austerities (*tapas*), He created a couple: *Rayi*, symbolized by moon or food; and *Prana*, symbolized by sun or eater of food. That which is the eater and that which is food are but one; they are *Prajapati,* who has become the couple. Next, *Prajapati* created the year, who is dependent on that couple. Thereby, He became identified with year. Later, He successively created and became identified with half-year, month, fortnight, day and night, rice, barley and other foodstuff, semen and creatures. *Prana* and *Rayi* convey the idea of energy and matter.

All gross and subtle things are but food and eater. When no distinction of superior or inferior is made, then everything may be called food, for everything is absorbed by something else. But when a distinction is made, as gross gets absorbed in subtle, gross is to be considered as food of subtle.

The sun comes within the vision of creatures in eastern quarters at the time of sunrise. It then pervades the eastern quarter through its light; thereby absorbing with its rays all that happens to be in that quarter. In other words, it makes them one with itself. It does so likewise in other quarters.

Verses 1, 7-8 explain how a single pair – constituted of moon, gross, *rayi*, or food (on one hand) and sun, formless, subtle, *Prana*, or eater (on the other) – could produce creatures. That pair itself is time – the year –

'Everything is absorbed in something else. As gross gets absorbed in subtle, gross is considered as "food" of subtle.'

THE COSMIC PERSON WITHIN US

which again is *Prajapati*, the Lord of creatures. This is because year is caused by sun and moon.

The question that was raised, 'From what are living beings born?' has been answered by saying that these creatures are born by passing in succession through pairs starting with sun and moon and ending with day and night, and then by proceeding through food, blood and semen.

— Sri Sankara, translated
by Swami Gambhirananda

Q 2. What powers energize living beings?

The question of the second disciple follows from Pippalada's answer to the first question about the origin of living beings. The disciple has understood that it is the principle of duality – the interactions between matter and life – which brings living beings into existence. But what keeps the body vibrant with activity?

It is the senses, which differentiate the living from the dead. The lamps of the bodily organization are kept burning by the senses. But the student has added one more question – who is supreme among these forces that keep the bodily organism united and functioning? Here, the teacher gives an imaginary episode in which all the senses are pictured as placing their claim for supremacy. *Prana* reminded them that they were under a delusion, but the senses in their pride and arrogance did not accept *Prana*s statement. Our story says that *Prana* did not utter a word, but started withdrawing. Even a sign of *Prana*'s withdrawal was enough to make the senses realize their dependence on *Prana*, the vital life-breath. Just as the whole crowd of bees keeps functioning so long as the queen bee is present, so also the senses keep functioning only as long as *Prana* is present (2, 1-4).

In a second analogy, *Prana* is described as the centre of a wheel – it is the axis around which the rim moves (2.6).

Verse 2,8 introduces a strange statement when it says that *Prana* is the first offering made to the departed. By this statement, the teacher is leading the student from the gross physical body to the vital body – from *Annamaya kosha* to *Pranamaya kosha*.

— Rohit Mehta

The implication in verse 2,2 is that the factors which support the body – instruments of knowledge and instruments of action, presided over by the Mind – are all governed by the five great elements. For example, sound cannot be created without space.

Prana is a sacred gift of God, *Prajapati*. In fact, *Prana* is *Prajapati* Itself. Verses 2, 5-13 glorify *Prana* in its various aspects. In his discourse, Pippalada calls *Prana* our 'father' and also our 'mother'. He ends his discourse with a prayer for a healthy mind in a healthy body; a prayer for longevity, prosperity and wisdom.

— Swami Chinmayananda

Q 3. How does Life-breath function?

The first question dealt with the creation of gross physical body. The second question concerned itself with *Prana*, which vitalizes the body and without which the body disintegrates. The third question is about the movement and the functioning of *Prana* in the body.

The teacher had to tell this pupil that he was asking a very difficult question. The Sanskrit word for 'difficult question' is *atiprasna*, meaning a question that transcends comprehension by man's normal consciousness (verse 3).

The teacher says: '*Prana* is born from *Atman*, *Atmana esa Prana jayate*.' He also gives a simile of substance and shadow. A shadow is projected by the substance; so also the whole universe is a projection of the spirit. A shadow has no intrinsic existence – it enjoys only a projected existence. A shadow is elusive, it can never be caught. It is intangible. This indicates that the spirit is present in the universe only in an intangible manner. Like a shadow, it remains beyond the grasp of man. It (the spirit) vitalizes the body, but remains intangible (verse 3).

The teacher also says that *Prana* enters the body through the activities of the mind. Thus, the very existence of *Prana* in the body is dependent upon the movement of the mind. The senses are vitalized by *Prana*, but *Prana* is impelled by the mind. It is an accepted principle in Yoga that *Prana* or life-breath follows thought. The movement of life-breath in the body can be controlled by the mind. And so the teacher leads his pupils from *Pranamaya kosha*, the vital body,

---

'The principle of duality – the interactions between matter and life – brings living beings into existence.'

to *Manomaya kosha*, the mental body. He has shown systematically how the physical depends upon the vital; and the vital is dependent upon the mind.

The teacher now proceeds to explain the functioning of *Prana* in the body. He describes the fivefold nature of *Prana*. Vital breath or *Prana* is but one; however, it is known by five different names in different parts of the body.

Name	English Equivalent	Location in body
Prana	in-breath	Upper regions
Apana	out-breath	Lower regions
Samana	equalizing-breath	Middle regions
Vyana	diffused-breath	Entire body
Udana	up-breath	Throat

The fivefold nature of *Prana* is only a functional division. This needs to be emphasized, lest we begin to think that there are five different vital breaths energizing the body.

Proper functioning of all five components of vital breath is essential for health and vitality of the body. Clogging of any vital breath affects the functioning of the body. As stated earlier, movement of vital breath in various parts of the body can be influenced by the mind. Thus, many chronic diseases in certain parts of the body have their root in the mind. Their cure also lies in the mind directing the vital breaths to move uniformly in the affected part (verses 4-5).

In concluding his discourse on *Prana*, the teacher says that a person who knows the relationship of *Prana* with mind discovers an elixir of long life. *Prana*, indeed, is the bridge between the body and the mind. So, the fourth question is about the operations of the mind – about human consciousness.

– Rohit Mehta

Self, *Atman* is poetically said to be residing in the most important part of the body, the heart. It is postulated that the heart has more than 727 million arteries (101x100x72000), and that *Vyana* and *Udana* move through these arteries.

Prana is the life force of not just living beings, but also the cosmos. Verses 8-9 associate the five components of life-breath with the five elements of Nature.

Prana	:	Sun
Apana	:	Earth
Samana	:	Space
Vyana	:	Air
Udana	:	Fire

When a person dies, Life Principle (*Prana*) enters another body, along with deeds (*karmas*) clinging to the mind. It is like the wind taking with it fragrances from flowers.

Importance of last thoughts

The Upanishad states that the last thoughts on deathbed determine the next life (verse 10)

It is to be noted last thoughts cannot be 'ordered' instantly at the time of death. Whatever thoughts have dominated a person's mind during his life, similar thoughts will emerge uncontrollably nearer the time of death.

– Swami Chinmayananda

Q 4. Who in man sleeps, dreams and keeps awake?

Waking, dream and deep sleep conditions refer to conscious, subconscious and unconscious layers of the mind.

Why does the mind see again in dream what it has already seen or heard? A dream is an experience of unfulfilled desires. During waking state we see and hear, but the experience remains incomplete. We would have liked to see and hear more, but could not because of various factors. Our seeing and hearing were interrupted by "censors" who asked us to behave ourselves and not indulge in activities that are considered "unrespectable". Or, our attention was distracted, and so the events of waking state moved on without our knowing them fully. Or, we had a wish to see something more than what we actually saw in the waking state – this is the element of wishful thinking. So the material for dreams is drawn from suppressed feelings, distractions, or wishful thinking. All these factors are indicated in verse 5.

A mind functioning on its own cannot experience deep sleep. Its sleep is always broken up by dreams of the subconscious state, or rendered dull by the drugging

---

'Waking, dream and deep sleep conditions refer to conscious, subconscious and unconscious layers of the mind.'

effect of the unconscious. However, according to verse 6, when the mind is overcome by its own radiance, it enjoys deep sleep. This is a condition in which the mind is illumined by Intelligence. Just as the senses must be vitalized by *Prana,* and *Prana* by the mind; similarly mind too must be illumined by Intelligence. Pippalada uses the word *vigyana Atman,* the Intelligent Being, for this condition.

– Rohit Mehta

All the Upanishads assigns considerable spiritual significance to the three states of waking, dream and deep sleep.

Waking state is a state when the sense organs are fully active. In state of deep sleep, all the sense organs retire into their very source – the mind. To illustrate the states of deep sleep and waking, the Rishi uses the metaphor of the Sun. He compares deep sleep to the setting sun and waking to the rising sun.

Thus, in response to Gargya's first enquiry, 'What is that which sleeps in man?' Pippalada's reply is that it is sense organs and mind which 'sleep' when a man goes to sleep.

Gargya's second enquiry was, "What keeps awake (during sleep)?" Pippalada replies that it is life (*Prana*) that keeps awake. He illustrates the point further by comparing life with the sacred ritual of those times, called *havana* or *agnihotra*. It involved offering oblations to sacrificial fire. In ancient times, householders always kept a small fire burning round the clock. The sacrificial fire and the oblation fire were lighted from this constantly burning fire. In verses 2-3, the five components of life-breath are compared to these three types of fire, the priest and the reward of sacrifice. The person performing the sacrificial ritual is equated with the mind.

In dream, the mind creates a world of its own out of the impressions received in waking state. The mind becomes both the perceiver (subject) and the perceived (object). Sometimes, the mind dives deep into the impressions of past lives also, and revives them. There is no coherence of time and space in dreams. In dream state, the mind is completely unconscious of the body. Dreams are a replay of subconscious thoughts and association of thoughts – experienced and not experienced, real and unreal.

In waking state, objects appear real to whosoever cares to perceive them. In dream state, objects are mental impressions, which can be perceived only by the dreamer; and they appear real only to the dreamer.

In waking state both the mind and the physical body are active; the Supreme Reality or Consciousness functions through the mind and the body. In dream state, the physical body becomes actionless and Consciousness functions through the mind alone. In state of deep sleep, even the mind becomes actionless and only Consciousness prevails. This state is described as 'when the mind is overpowered by light' in verse 4,6. Consciousness illumines for us the physical world and the mind, and is therefore referred to as light. When the mind is nearing the state of deep sleep, it is as if it comes nearer to Consciousness and gets overwhelmed by its transcendental intensity. Mind, blinded by the *Atman's* radiance, is thus the *sleeper*.

In Verse 7, all the faculties of the sleeper that retire in sleep are compared to birds that rest in their nests during the night. The faculties are enumerated in verse 8. The list looks too long, but it falls in a simple classification.

1. The five elements of the cosmos.
2. Their subtle counterparts in human body. These are called organs of knowledge or *gyana indriyas*.
3. Five organs of action or *karma indriyas*
4. The four inner faculties – mind, intellect, memory and ego. These are associated with thinking, determining, illuminating and self-asserting, respectively.

The state of deep sleep is a state of bliss, as in this state Consciousness is pure and calm, unobstructed by the mind or the body.

MEDITATION AND SLEEP

What is the difference between the state of deep meditation and deep sleep?

In deep meditation, mind becomes one with *Brahman*. In deep sleep, a thin layer of *avidya* or spiritual ignorance separates the mind from *Brahman*.

Jivatman (individual Being) is to *Paramatma* (Supreme Being) what a portion of sky enclosed by the four walls of a room is to the whole sky. Another analogy is that

---

'In waking state, Consciousness functions through mind and body; in dream state, It functions through mind alone. In sleep, only Consciousness prevails.'

just as the image of sun is reflected in water, so also image of *Paramatma* is reflected in mind-body as *Jivatman*. All perceptions and intellectualizations are due to the intelligence of *Jivatman*. The senses and the mind are the instruments through which *Jivatman* acts.

Jivatman is *Purusha* plus limiting adjuncts of cause and effect. It enters the highest Self, *Brahman*, just as the image of sun in water enters the sun when water is removed.

In verse 9, that, which arrogates to itself the feelings "I am the doer", I am the sufferer", "I am the enjoyer", refers to ego, *ahamkara*. Ego is the product of our identification with the body, mind and intellect. This ego has no vitality of its own. It is a mere superimposition on *Atman*, the indestructible Self. The waker, the dreamer and the sleeper are the personalities, which the ego assumes in respective states. These personalities function through the gross body, subtle body, and causal body, respectively.

Verse 10 provides a beautiful description of Self. Self is formless. It is therefore described as without shadow, without body and without color. Being formless, it is naturally, pure. It is without attributes and therefore, indestructible. All destructible things are noticed to have some attributes.

What happens when a man realizes that he is not a mortal ego-centre, but in his essential nature he is the supreme Self, *Atman*? He experiences the unity that underlies the seeming diversity in the world. He becomes all-knowing, and realizes Self in all.

– Swami Chinmayananda

The question asked by Gargya is: O adorable Sir, which organs in this person go to sleep, or desist from their own functions; and which keep awake, or go on performing their functions? Among those characterized as body and organs, which is the deity who experiences dreams? Is that activity performed by *Prana*, the senses, or the mind? Who experiences the happiness of sleep, which is calm, effortless, unobstructed and untouched by external objects? In the state of sleep, in whom do they all – the senses and the mind – remain completely unified? The idea is this: like the essence collected from various flowers merging in the honey of a beehive, or the rivers entering into the sea, do the senses and mind blend without the possibility of being distinguished?

There are five questions here. The first relates to the perceiver of the waking state. The entity whose cessation from activity leads to dream must be the actor in the waking state. The second question is: 'Whose function is it to maintain the body in all the three states?' The third relates to the perceiver of the dream, the fourth to the enjoyer of sleep. The fifth asks about *Turiya*, the Fourth, the Self, free from the three states of waking, dream and sleep. It is about the absolute Self that the questioner wants to know, and not the conditioned Self that supports all (4.1).

The rays of a setting sun become unified, inseparable and indistinguishable in the sun; and the rays of that very sun disperse while it is rising again. In a similar way, all the senses and their objects become unified in their high deity – the fully luminous mind. And when a man is about to wake up, they emanate – they proceed to their respective functions – from the mind itself, just like the rays radiating from a rising sun (4.2).

The sleep of an illumined man is like the performance of *Agnihotra* sacrifice. The senses of perception and the organs of action of an illumined man are as if they perform sacrifice at all times, even while he sleeps. The purpose is to praise knowledge and, to eulogize illumination (4.3-4.4).

In state of dream, senses like hearing etc. cease to function and life-breaths keep awake for the maintenance of the body. The mind, that has withdrawn all the senses into itself, experiences the greatness of assuming diverse forms – both as subject and as object. What has been seen, heard or experienced in this birth or in previous birth, whether real or imaginary, the mind is capable of perceiving all by being all (verse 5).

At the time of sleep the deity called mind becomes completely overwhelmed by Consciousness called *Brahman* and lodged in the nerves. In the state of sleep, It exists in the body like fire in wood. It pervades the body in the form of general Consciousness (as opposed to particularized Consciousness). At this time the mind does not see dreams. Instead, happiness – which is the nature of unobstructed Consciousness – pervades the whole body in a general way.

'Ego has no vitality of its own. It is a mere superimposition on Atman, the indestructible Self.'

At this time, the body and the organs – that depend on ignorance, desires and the results of past actions – become inactive. When these become quiet, the nature of Self that appears distorted due to the limiting adjuncts, becomes non-dual, one, auspicious and calm (verse-6). In order to indicate this state the text provides an illustration (verse-7). Just as birds proceed towards the tree that provides lodging, so also all the faculties of man. These are enumerated in verse-8. They are: the five organs of knowledge – sound, touch, sight, taste and smell – which are the essential attributes of space, air, fire, water and earth respectively; the five organs of action, mind, intellect, ego, memory and lustre; as also the respective objects of all these. They all are held together by *Prana*. Along with *Prana*, they rest in Supreme Self, like birds in their nests (verse 8).

Verse 9 states the reality of Supreme Self – that has entered the body like a reflection of sun in water – as the enjoyer as well as the agent of action. It is described as *Vigyanatma Purusha*. *Vigyanatma* is 'that which knows'. *Purusha* is that which fills the body which has been spoken of as a limiting adjunct. And as a reflection of sun in water enters into the sun when the water is removed, so also this Self gets wholly withdrawn in Supreme Self, the last resort of the universe.

The result achieved by one who realizes his identity with Supreme Self is stated in verses 10-11.

– *Sri Sankara, translated by Swami Gambhirananda*

Q 5. Why Meditate on *Aum*?

The teacher has led his disciples from the physical body to the vital body, then to the abode of the Mind and finally to the abode of Intelligence – *Annamaya kosha* to *Pranamaya kosha* to *Manomaya kosha* to *Vigyanamaya kosha*. The discussion has come to the point of mind's illumination by Intelligence, *Buddhi*. So the fifth disciple turns to the subject of meditation. It is in meditation that the Mind opens itself to the influence of Intelligence. The disciple wants to know what happens when one meditates on *Aum*, the sacred Word, the perfect symbol of *Brahman*. Pippalada says that it depends upon what part of *Aum* is being meditated upon.

Aum is a word of three letters. It covers a range of sounds starting from the root of the tongue to the closing of the lips. The first *matra* (letter) denotes a sound where the tongue does not even touch the palate. So meditation on the first *matra* is like the meditation of a child – an elementary stage. Verse 3 says that in such meditation, the mind does not develop enough strength to soar high. The person practicing meditation on 'A' of *Aum* attains earthly greatness, but cannot rise above the pulls of the earth. This is the path of Action, *Karma Yoga*.

Meditation on two *matras* (A+U) symbolizes the path of Devotion, *Bhakti Yoga*. Moon in verse 4 is an indicator of emotions. The teacher says that a devotee experiences heavenly joy when meditating on the two letters of *Aum*. He sees the manifested form of his deity, *saguna Brahman*. The second letter deals with articulate sound. It deals with that which is manifested.

When a person meditates on all the three letters of *Aum*, he travels into the region of the Unmanifest. He soars into the inarticulate sound. But the inarticulate sound of the meditator at this stage has innocence – innocence born not out of ignorance, but innocence that arises out of knowledge. To meditate on the three letters of *Aum* is to come to the experience of the Unmanifest, but after knowing the glories of the manifest. This is the path of knowledge, *Gyana Yoga*.

These three stages of meditation indicate a movement of the soul from the innocence of childhood through the imperfections of man to the perfection of superman. When a man learns to meditate on the three *matras* of *Aum*, then he knows both the manifest and the Unmanifest nature of Reality. The teacher says that such a meditator becomes free from his sins, as easily as a snake slips out of his old skin – without any effort (verse 5).

The word *Aum* is only a symbol. The teacher ends his discussion by saying that meditation on all the three letters of *Aum* brings an aspirant to the knowledge of that which is *Ajara* and *Amara*. These two words describe both the Immanent and the Transcendent *Brahman*. *Ajara* is in time, and yet not corrupted by time. *Brahman* is in manifestations – and yet It remains untouched by the stream of time in which the manifest exists. Why is this so? Because *Brahman* is Timeless (*Amara*), It is not affected by the flow of time, even when It manifests Itself in time (verse 7).

– *Rohit Mehta*

---

*'As a reflection of sun in water enters into the sun when the water is removed,
so also Self gets wholly withdrawn in Supreme Self.'*

Aum is the all-comprehensive sound symbol of *Brahman*. It is a recurring theme in almost all the Upanishads.

In verse-2, *Aum* is considered a symbol of both 'higher' and 'lower' *Brahman*. Higher *Brahman* is the unmanifested, unconditioned, impersonal *Brahman*. Lower *Brahman* is the manifested, conditioned, personal *Brahman*.

The sound of *Aum* is produced by the combination of three sounds: A, U and M. These are called *matras* of *Aum*. There is also a fourth *matra* of *Aum* called *amatra* – the inaudible sound, which lingers on even after the audible sound has died away. This can be detected only by fine perception and concentration.

As a sound symbol of *Brahman*, *Aum* is believed to be the first sound produced at the beginning of creation. From the three *matras* of *Aum* emerged the three meters of the most sacred *mantra*, the *Gayatri mantra*; These three meters, in turn, expanded into three Vedas. Thus —

- From A came out *tat savitur varenyam*, which expanded into Rg Veda, whose contents relate mainly to work.
- From U came out *bhargo devasya dhemahi*, which expanded itself into Yajur Veda. Its contents are mainly devotional.
- From M came out *dhiyo yo nah prachodayat*, which expanded itself into Sama Veda. Its contents relate mainly to spiritual knowledge.

So, by meditation upon the different *matras* of *Aum*, different results are obtained. In verses 3-5, the results of meditation separately on A, U and M are expressed as a hierarchy; symbolized by the earth, the moon and the sun. When all the three *matras* are blended together and chanted correctly, they truly represent the universal *Brahman*. When the mind is concentrated on *amatra*, supreme *Brahman* is realized.

According to Mandukya Upanishad, the three *matras* - A, U and M – also represent the three states of waking, dream and deep sleep. These are referred to as external, midway and internal functions in verse-6. External, midway and internal could also refer to the method of chanting - loud, muttering and mental. The Fourth, *amatra*, corresponds to the inaudible sound, and to *Turiya*. It includes and transcends the three states of waking, dream and deep sleep.

In conclusion, meditate on *Aum* as a symbol of *Brahman*, in all Its Totality. Chant *Aum* correctly in one continuous easy flow, with equal emphasis on all the three *matras*. Superimpose the idea of waking on 'A', dream on 'U' and deep sleep on 'M'. Merge yourself in the silence (*amatra*) between two successive chants of *Aum*. When you practice such meditation on *Aum* regularly and with sincerity, you will begin to experience the all-pervading Self – within yourself and all around you.

– Swami Sivananda

Visva is individual Consciousness. It is identical with Cosmic Consciousness, *Vaisvanara* or *Virat*. Its residence is in the gross body in waking state. *Taijasa* is identical with *Hiranyagarbha*. Its residence is in the subtle body and in dream. *Pragyan* is identical with *Ishvara*. It has its locus in the Unmanifested and in sleep. The yogic processes consist in meditating on them in identification with 'A', 'U' and 'M' respectively. If these are resorted to separately, and without the idea of *Brahman*, they cannot lead one beyond death (5.6).

– Sri Sankara, translation by Swami Gambhirananda

Q 6. Where to look for the Cosmic Person?

The teacher has led his disciples step by step to *Vigyanamaya kosha*, the abode of Intelligence, or *Buddhi*. *Buddhi* is the charioteer, but only the Master of the chariot can say where the chariot shall go. That Master is *Atman*. And where the Master is seated is indeed, *Anandamaya kosha*, the Abode of Eternal Bliss.

The last question is about the Master, the person of sixteen forms (6,1). The teacher says: 'My beloved son, the person of sixteen forms is here and now – it is not far from your body (6.2).' He tells his disciples that surely the Eternal Being must have thought: 'What shall constitute My manifested nature, and when will the manifest cease to be manifest?' (6,3). Having thought thus, He manifested Himself in all the forms He created, and gave a name to each form. Thus the world of name and form, *nama-rupa*, was created (6,4). A name is only a symbol, a token. Behind the name stands Reality Itself. A man clings to the name; and since the name is associated with a form, he clings to

---

'When you practice meditation on Aum correctly and regularly, you begin to experience the all-pervading Self, within yourself and all around you.'

the form too. And when the form dies and with that the name too, then the man is immersed in sorrow. But this is the man whose mind is not illumined by Intelligence, *Buddhi*. He whose mind is enlightened by Intelligence sees Many in One, and One in Many. The rivers are called rivers as long as they are in their courses; but they cease to be rivers when they merge into the ocean (6,5).

There is One, but there are also Many. Many and One do not contradict each other. He, who sees Many, but also sees One in Many, knows both the manifest and the Unmanifest. He knows the sixteen forms, but he also knows the *Purusha*, the Being who creates and uncreates these forms. This Being is *Atman* Itself. Bringing the discussion to a close, the teacher says that the forms are established in Him like spokes in the hub of a wheel (6,6).

Pippalada then informed the disciples that this was all that he knew about the great problems of life (6,7).

From question to question, the teacher has taken the pupils from the shore of ignorance to the shore of knowledge. But he has also told them that the land beyond still remains unexplored. The mind cannot go further. All communication must lead to the point of communion – beyond that it cannot go. Communion cannot be taught; it comes. But it comes when a man moves away from both the shores – the shore of ignorance as also the shore of knowledge – into the realm of Bliss. The work of the teacher is over. Now it is for the taught to practice what he has learnt. (6,7).

– *Rohit Mehta*

It has been said earlier that the entire world – consisting of cause and effect – together with Conscious soul, gets unified in the Immutable Supreme during sleep. It follows that even during cosmic dissolution, the world merges into That Immutable alone and originates from That alone; for an effect cannot get absorbed into anything other than its origin. It now remains to point out where That Immutable, That Truth called *Purusha* is to be realized. This question is begun for that purpose. And by pointing out the difficulty involved in acquiring the knowledge, the narration of an anecdote aims at inducing a special effort in those who hanker after Truth.

Purusha is another name for *Brahman*, or Consciousness. The anecdote indicates that knowledge about *Brahman* is difficult to attain. Sukesha was a sincere, truthful and humble disciple. He was not conceited. He did not give some kind of a vague answer to the prince, and project himself as a learned man. As the prince did not believe that Sukesha was ignorant, Sukesha had to explain his helplessness. In the presence of Pippalada, Sukesha sees an opportunity to remove his ignorance and acquire *Brahma Vidya*, knowledge about *Brahman*.

The Sanskrit word *kala* in verses 6,1-2 is translated as parts. It will be more appropriate to translate it as facets. The Infinite Eternal Being cannot have parts like finite objects, or limbs like the human body. It is a homogeneous whole. The analogy is only a method by which He can be explained to those who are familiar only with finite experiences.

The next verse (6,3) explains the causation chain of the finite universe. Reflection by *Purusha* is a cosmic expression of the creative urge in human beings. The Upanishads repeatedly emphasize the eternal Truth that the macrocosm functions with the same patterns and principles as the microcosm.

Verse 6.4 enumerates sixteen facets (*kalas*) of the Total Being, *Purusha*. *Kalas* are the means by which the Infinite expresses itself in the finite.

According to the Upanishads, *Brahman* has two aspects – the unconditioned and the conditioned. Unconditioned *Brahman* appears as conditioned *Brahman* on account of ignorance, *avidya*. Names and forms – *nama* and *rupa* – are characteristic of conditioned *Brahman*. In reality, *Brahman* is nameless and formless.

Most of the time we are occupied with the external world. When we turn our mind, senses and other *kalas* inward, they merge in the Total Being, just as rivers merge in the ocean. The analogy is explained in verse 6.5. This is how microcosm rises from macrocosm, and merger back into it.

The facets of human personality are connected to the whole, *Purusha*, as spokes of a wheel are connected to its hub. The wheel of life owes its strength and its movement to the spokes (*kalas*) and to the hub (*Purusha*). This is explained in verse 6,6. The analogy

---

'All communication must lead to the point of communion – beyond that it cannot go further.
Communion cannot be taught; it comes.'

of the wheel has been repeated in the Upanishads many times.

The Upanishad ends with the disciples offering salutations to Rishi Pippalada in a chorus. A teacher of *Brahma Vidya* (knowledge of *Brahman*) is considered like a father. This is because to realize one's own true nature, one has to be born again – spiritually. Thereafter, both the teacher and the disciples salute the ancient Rishis, who evolved the theory of *Brahman*, lived it in their lives, and passed down the torch of knowledge from one generation to the next.

– Swami Chinmayananda

Sukesha Bharadvaja was once asked by a prince: 'Do you know the *Purusha* – the Reality pervading the body – which is possessed of sixteen digits?' The sixteen digits or parts are superimposed on that Conscious Being, *Purusha*, through ignorance. The conclusion to be drawn from Sukesha's response is that one who knows must impart knowledge to a disciple who is competent, but one should not utter a falsehood under any condition whatsoever (6.1).

Purusha is partless. He appears through ignorance to be possessed of parts, which are only His limiting adjuncts. But this *Purusha* has to be shown as an Absolute, by eliminating – through knowledge – those parts that condition Him. That is why the parts are spoken of as originating from *Purusha*. *Purusha* or Consciousness does not increase of decrease; yet It appears diverse through attributes of limiting adjuncts. It is nothing but Self. This fact is borne out by various Upanishadic texts.

- Brahman is Truth-Knowledge-Infinitude. (Taittiriya 2.1, 1)
- Brahman is Consciousness (Aitareya 3.1, 3)
- This great infinite limitless Reality consists of nothing but Pure Consciousness (Brhadaranyaka 2.4, 12).

Consciousness is changeless. It remains unchanged even when objects change. A pot may not exist even when there is Consciousness of it; but there can be no object of knowledge without Consciousness. An object may change in relation to knowledge, but knowledge never changes in relation to objects.

Consciousness remains unchanged even in state of sleep. Consciousness is an illuminator of objects, just like light. Absence of Consciousness during sleep cannot be inferred, just as absence of light cannot be inferred from the absence of things to be lighted up.

There is but one Consciousness, which exists in all places, times or persons. It appears diversely because of the differences in the multifarious limiting adjuncts constituted by names and forms; like reflections of sun in water. Consciousness is an eternal and changeless entity, which is the basis of all appearances. The Upanishad therefore talks about the superimposition of parts or limbs on that Consciousness.

The text 'within the body' in verse 6, 2 is to be understood in the same sense as the statement that space exists within the cosmic egg. Space is the cause of the universe, but since space pervades everything, it is perceived as confined within the universe.

Purusha, who is the cause of space, is not encompassed by the body like a fruit in a vessel. As *Purusha* is experienced within the body, it is said that He is inside the body (6, 2).

Prana is energy – both mental and physical. It is called *Hiranyagarbha*, the sum total of all subtle bodies. This *Hiranyagarbha* resides inside the gross bodies, and is thought of as one's Self. Hence it is *antar* (inside) and *Atman* (Self).

Purusha created *Prana*. From this *Prana*, He created *Shraddha*, Faith, which is the source of stimulus for all beings for good action.

He also created the five great elements, the material constituents of the physical body, which is the vehicle of enjoyment of the fruits of action. These are:

Space	possessed of quality of sound
Air	possessed of the attribute of sound from its source, space; and its own attribute, touch
Fire	possessed of its own quality of color; besides sound and touch
Water	possessed of its own quality of taste; besides sound, touch and color
Earth	possessed of its own quality of smell; besides sound, touch, color and taste

'To realize one's own true nature, one has to be born again – spiritually.'

So He created ten organs for perception and action (*indriyas*); and He created mind (*manas*), the lord of these organs.

Having thus created the body and the organs of creatures, He created food (*anna*) for their sustenance. From that food, when eaten, he created ability and vigor (*Viryam*), which is at the root of engaging in all work. After that He created *tapah*, self-control. Then He created *mantras* (comprising the four Vedas), *karma* and *loka* (the worlds). In the worlds, He created *nama*, names (6, 4).

All the parts created by *Purusha* again merge in Him, like rivers merging in an ocean. The names of the rivers get eliminated as a result of that merger, and their substance – water – is merely called by the word, sea. Similarly the sixteen parts have *Purusha* as their goal; and on getting identified with *Purusha*, they disappear. He who has become thus enlightened, he becomes free from parts. The parts are creation of ignorance, desire and action. When these parts are gone, the knower becomes immortal because of his knowledge of the Partless (6,5).

The concluding verse says that the disciples worshipped the feet of their teacher by offering flowers and salutations. They said: 'Indeed, you are our father, since you have given us a new birth through knowledge. You have ferried us across the ocean of ignorance, which is infested with birth, old age, disease and sorrow. Salutations to you. Salutations to the great seers of knowledge of *Brahman*, and its transmission from one generation to the next.'

– *Sri Sankara, translated by Swami Gambhirananda*

'*Salutations to the great seers of knowledge of Brahman and its transmission from one generation to next.*'

ॐ

शान्तिः शान्तिः शान्तिः ॥

Let there be peace.

Let there be peace.

Let there be peace.

Glossary

adhibhuta, adhibhautic:
Relating to material world.

ADHAVARYU:
One of the four Vedic priests. The other three are Udgtr, Brahma and Hotr. Refer Brhadaranyaka Upanishad (Chapter 3).

adhidaiva, adhidaivic:
Divine, prudential.

adhyatma, adhyatmic:
Spirit, spiritual.

ADITI:
'One who loosens bonds'. Mother of 12 Adityas through her union with Kashyap.

ADITYA:
See Vedic deities. Twelve Adityas are: Vishnu, Indra, Vivasvat, Mitra, Varuna, Pusan, Tvastr, Bhaga, Aryaman, Dhatr, Sautr and Amsa. They signify 12 months in a year.

advaita:
Non-dual. The Upanishads declare that Ultimate Reality is One, without a second.

agni:
One of the five primal elements. Vedic deity who receives oblations and conveys them to heavenly spheres. Cosmic Power representing force of Consciousness in world and in man. Cosmic Deity of speech.

agnihotra:
Ritual of offering oblations in sacred fires. Three fires are *Ahavaniya*, *Grahapatya* and *Dakshinagni*.

Aham Brahmasmi:
'I am God'. One of the four great aphorisms, it appears in Brhadaranyaka Upanishad (1.4). 'I' here refers to inner Self, and not 'ego-I'.

aham:
'I'. The word is indicative of ego, as also of spiritual Self.

ahamkara:
Ego. Sense of I-ness, or separateness from others. It is characterized by a feeling of possessiveness and selfishness.

AJATASHATRU:
Philosopher-king who taught *Brahma Vidya* to a priest, Balaki Gargya.

akash:
Space. The most subtle of the five primal elements: Earth, Water, Air, Fire and Space. All pervasive space-time.

akshara:
Imperishable. A word used for *Brahman*.

alingah:
Without any sign of identification or existence.

alpa:
Small. Chandogya Upanishad (7.23) says that there is no happiness in anything small or finite.

amanava-purusha:
Non-human Being. In Brhadaranyaka Upanishad (6.2) and Chandogya Upanishad (5.10) it is declared that after death, if the Soul travels on the path of light, It is led from Sun to *Brahmaloka* by *amanava-purusha*.

amatra:
The inaudible sound between two successive chants of *Aum*. Refer Mandukya Upanishad.

AMBHAH:
One of the four fields that emerged at the beginning of creation. The other three were Marichi, Maram and Apah. Refer Aitareya Upanishad (1.1).

amrita:
Nectar of immortality. Legendary elixir called *Soma*.

anadi:
Without a beginning. Also see *ananta*, meaning without an end. These words are used as descriptions of *Brahman*, the Absolute.

ananda:
Bliss. Ecstasy of God-consciousness or spiritual experiences. A famous Vedic description of *Brahman* is *Sat-Chit-Ananda*, or Existence-Consciousness-Bliss. Also refer Taittiriya Upanishad (2.8-2.9).

anandamaya:
: Blissful self, innermost essence of human personality. See *Pancha Kosha*. Refer Taittiriya Upanishad.

ananta:
: Without an end. Infinitude. Taittiriya Upanishad (2.1, 1) describes *Brahman* as Truth-Knowledge-Infinitude. Also see *anandi*.

ANGIRASA:
: Teacher in Mundaka Upanishad.

anna:
: Food. The word also refers to physical matter.

annamaya:
: See *Pancha Kosha*.

antahkarana:
: Inner faculty pertaining to mind.

antah-purusha:
: Cosmic Person within man.

antar hridaya akash:
: Vast space within the heart. Refer Chandogya Upanishad (8.1).

antar jyotir:
: Inner light. Refers to God within, and light of Wisdom.

antar:
: Inner, a prefix signifying inner life.

antaratman:
: Inner Self.

antariksha:
: Interface between Heaven and Earth.

antaryami:
: Inner Guide. Refers to God within.

apah:
: Primordial Water, derived from 'ap', meaning to pervade. Also see *Ambhah*.

APAH:
: See *Ambhah*.

apana:
: See *Prana*.

apara vidya:
: Lower or empirical knowledge; as opposed to *para vidya*, or higher knowledge of Self and God.

apauruseya:
: A Divine being of non-human origin who is said to escort noble souls on the path of light, *Devayana*. Also see *amanava-purusha*.

aranyaka:
: Forest books. Sections of Vedas that preceed Upanishads and deal with inner significance of rituals and hymns.

ARTABHAGA JARATKARAVA:
: One of the scholars who questioned Yagyavalkya in Brhadaranyaka Upanishad (3.2).

ARYAMAN:
: One of the Adityas, a Vedic deity.

asat:
: Non-existence. *Brahman* is said to be both *sat* and *asat*, existence and no-existence.

ashram:
: Hermitage. Also four stages of life in ancient tradition. These were: studentship, householder, gradual withdrawal, and complete renunciation; *Brahmacharya*, *Grihastha*, *Vanaprastha* and *Sanyas*.

ASHVAMEDHA YAGYA:
: A ritual of horse sacrifice that symbolizes conquest of ego followed by sacrifices of self-interest. Refer Brhadaranyaka Upanishad (1.1-1.2).

ASHVAPATI KEKAYA:
: King who taught *Vaisvanara Vidya* to five learned priests: Prachinsala Anupamanyava, Satyayagya Paulusi, Indradyumna Bhallaveya, Java Sarkarksya and Budila Asvatarasvi. Refer Chandogya Upanishad (5.11-5.24).

ASHWATTHA:
: *Ficus religiosa*, Peepal tree, considered sacred. Used as a metaphor for creation. Refer Katha Upanishad (2.3, 1).

asura:
: Evil spirit, demon.

GLOSSARY

ASVALA HOTR PRIEST:
One of the scholars who questioned Yagyavalkya in Brhadaranyaka Upanishad (3.1).

ASVINS:
Mythological twins specializing in surgery. They transplanted the head of a horse on a sage to learn *Madhu Vidya*. Refer Brhadaranyaka Upanishad (2.5).

Atharva Veda:
See Vedas.

atithi:
Guest, one who comes without an appointment. In Vedic tradition, a guest is welcomed with respect. See Katha Upanishad (1.1).

Atman:
Self, God within, Spark of Divine in man. The Upanishads declare that *Atman* and *Brahman*, are one and same.

Aum:
Also spelled *Om*. A symbol of both manifest and unmanifest *Brahman*. Primal vibration from which all manifestations proceed. Refer Mandukya Upanishad.

avidya:
Spiritual ignorance, incorrect understanding of reality, mistaking the impermanent for the everlasting.

avyakta:
Unmanifested, word used to describe *Brahman*.

Ayam Atma Brahma:
This individual Self is also universal Self. One of the four great aphorisms appearing in Mandukya Upanishad.

balam:
Physical strength.

BARKU VARSNA:
A spiritual teacher of Janaka mentioned in Brhadaranyaka Upanishad (Chapter 4).

bhagvan:
The Lord. Also called *Ishvara*.

bhakti:
Devotion and surrender to God.

BHARGAVA VIDARBHA:
A student in Prasna Upanishad.

BHRIGU:
Sage who discovered Self with small hints from his father. Refer Taittiriya Upanishad (Chapter 3).

BHUJYU LAHYAYANI:
One of the scholars who questioned Yagyavalkya in Brhadaranyaka Upanishad (3.3).

bhuma vidya:
Knowledge about the secret of happiness. It says: Infinite alone gives Happiness. Refer Chandogya Upanishad (Chapter 7).

bhumi:
Earth, One of the five primal elements.

bhur:
Material world.

bhurloka:
Material world, physical plane.

bhuvah:
Plane of atmosphere, world between heaven and earth.

BRAHMA:
God of creation in the Trinity of Brahma-Vishnu-Shiva. The word also refers to a Vedic priest. See Adhavaryu.

brahmacharya:
See *ashram*.

Brahman:
Supreme Being, Pure and Absolute Consciousness, That which creates, sustains and annihilates the entire universe. Transcendental Reality. Also see *Atman*, *Ananda*.

brahmana:
One of the four primary sections of Vedas, dealing with use of mantras and performance of various rituals.

BRAHMANASPATI:
Master of *Yajur Veda*. Refer Brhadaranyaka Upanishad (1.3, 21).

brahmanda:
: Cosmic egg from which cosmos has proceeded.

brahmapuri:
: City of God. It refers to human body with God seated in the heart and body's openings equated with gates. Refer Chandogya Upanishad (8.1) and Mundaka Upanishad (2.2, 7).

BRHASPATI:
: Master of *Rg Veda*. Refer Brhadaranyaka Upanishad (1.3, 20).

brhat:
: Extended, big.

buddhi:
: Intellect, reason, logic. Mind is said to have four faculties: *manas* (memory), *buddhi* (intellect), *chitta* (consciousness) and *ahamkara* (ego).

CHAIKITAYANA DALBHYA:
: A participant in discussion about Ultimate Reality. Refer Chandogya Upanishad (1.8-1.9).

chitt shakti:
: Will power.

chitta:
: Consciousness, power of perception, one of the four faculties of mind. Also see *buddhi*.

DADHYACHA ATHARVANA:
: Sage who taught *Madhu Vidya* to two Asvins. Refer Brhadaranyaka Upanishad (2.5).

dahara vidya:
: Knowledge that a small space in the heart contains *Brahman*, the essence of all that exists in the world. Refer Chandogya Upanishad (Chapter 8).

DALBHYA BAKA:
: Priest who is imitated by some dogs. The passage in Chandogya Upanishad (1.12) implies mockery of rituals.

damyata:
: Self-disciple.

datta:
: Charity.

dayadhvam:
: Compassion.

deva, *devata*:
: Deities, gods, literally meaning 'shining ones'. Upanishads refer to sensory powers as *deva* or *devata*.

devayana:
: Path of light, one of the two paths on which the soul is said to travel after death. The second path is called *Pitrayana* or path of darkness. Refer Brhadaranyaka Upanishad (6.2) and Chandogya Upanishad (5.10).

dharma:
: Literally, that which upholds the universe. A complex term variously translated as Divine law, righteousness, duty and religion.

dhyana:
: Meditation.

divya:
: Divine.

gandharva:
: Celestial angels proficient in dance and music.

GARDABHIVIPITA BHARADVAJ:
: A spiritual teacher of Janaka mentioned in Brhadaranyaka Upanishad (Chapter 4).

GARGI VACHAKNAVI:
: Lady philosopher who questions Yagyavalkya in Brhadaranyaka Upanishad (3.6 and 3.8).

GARGYA BALAKI:
: Learned priest who went to King Ajatashatru to teach him *Brahma Vidya*, but ended up becoming his student. Refer Brhadaranyaka Upanishad (Chapter 2).

GARGYA SURYA:
: A student in Prasna Upanishad.

GAUDAPADA:
: Grand preceptor of Sri Sankara. He wrote a scholarly commentary on Mandukya Upanishad.

gayatri mantra:
: Famous *Mantra* of *Rg Veda* addressed to Sun, also called *Savitri Mantra*. Refer Chandogya Upanishad (3.12).

gayatri vidya:
Art of meditation on *Gayatri Mantra*. Refer Chandogya Upanishad (3.12).

guna:
Qualities of nature. These are *Sattvic, Rajsic and Tamsic*; meaning harmony, activity and inertia.

gyana indriyas:
Sensory organs of perception. These are: sight, hearing, smell, taste and touch. All information is acquired through one or more of these organs. They are called *Deva* or gods in Upanishads.

gyana shakti:
Power of Wisdom. See *shakti*.

gyana:
Wisdom about Self and God. A wise person sees one God in all beings.

HARIDRUMATA GAUTAMA:
Teacher of Satyakama Jabala. Refer Chandogya Upanishad (4.4-4.9).

hiranyagarbha:
Cosmic Mind, Cosmic egg.

HOTR:
One of four Vedic priests. See Adhavaryu.

hridaya:
Heart, spiritual center in human body.

hridyagranthi:
Knots of the hearts. These are said to be ignorance, selfish desires and work motivated by such desires.

ichha shakti:
Power of desire. See *shakti*.

idam:
This. The word is used to denote the universe.

IDANDRA:
A name for Indra, signifying respect.

INDRA:
Chief of Vedic deities, identified with thunder and strength. Also deity of Mind. For dialogue with Prajapati on *Atman*, refer Chandogya Upanishad (8.7-8.2). For parable of three gods, refer Kena Upanishad (3).

indriyas:
Sensory organs, ten in number. Also see *gyana indriyas* and *karma indriyas*. They are called *Deva* or gods in Upanishads.

ishta devata:
Cherished or chosen Deity; Deity that is the object of one's special pious attention. Also called personal God. Concept is unique to Hinduism.

Ishvara kripa:
God's Grace.

Ishvara:
Highest Lord, Supreme God.

jagat:
The world.

JANAKA:
King of Videha. Quoted as ideal king who ruled without any selfish attachment to wealth or power. He also patronized wise sages. Refer Brhadaranyaka Upanishad (Chapter 4).

JANASHRUTI PAUTRAYANA:
A very charitable king who learned *Samvarga Vidya* from a poor cart-driver, Raikva, in exchange for his daughter's hand in marriage. See Chandogya Upanishad (4.1-4.3).

japa:
Repetitive recitation of a *mantra* or God's name, silently or aloud. It is an important devotional practice in Hinduism. It purifies the mind and helps it concentrate on God.

jataveda:
All-knowing. An adjective used for *Agni* in Kena Upanishad.

JITVAN SAILINI:
A spiritual teacher of Janaka mentioned in Brhadaranyaka Upanishad (Chapter 4).

jiva, jivatman:
Individual Self in living beings. It is said to migrate after death from one body to another.

KABANDHA ATHARVANA:
A *gandharva* mentioned by Uddalaka Aruni in Brhadaranyaka Upanishad (3.7).

KABANDHI KATYA:
A student in Prasna Upanishad.

KAHOLA KAUSITAKEYA:
One of the scholars who questioned Yagyavalkya in Brhadaranyaka Upanishad (3.5).

kaivalya-mukti:
Transcendental state of oneness with *Brahman*. Also see *mukti*.

KAKSASENI ABHIPRATARIN, KAPEYA SAUNAKA:
Two scholars of *Samvarga Vidya* who did not practice what they had learnt. Refer Chandogya (4.3, 5-8).

kala:
Time in its essentiality.

kama:
Lust.

karana sarira:
See *sarira*.

karma indriyas:
Sensory organs of action. These are five: tongue, hands, feet, and organs of procreation and excretion.

karma kanda:
That part of Vedas which deals with rituals.

karma:
Thoughts, words and deeds. A very important principle of cause and effect, which says that a person will have to bear the consequences of whatever good or bad deeds are done by him.

KATYAYANI:
Second wife of famous philosopher Yagyavalkya. Refer Brhadaranyaka Upanishad (2.4).

KAUSALYA ASVALA:
A student in Prasna Upanishads.

kirya shakti:
Power of action. See *shakti*.

kramamukti:
Progressive liberation. Also see *Mukti*.

krodha:
Anger.

kshara:
Moving, mutable.

lobha:
Greed.

loka:
Planes of Consciousness. These are said to be many in number. Some examples are: *Bhuloka, Pitraloka, Swargaloka, Brahmaloka, Satyaloka, Tapoloka, Maharloka,* etc.

madhu vidya:
Honey doctrine. It says that everything in the universe constitutes a harmonious whole. Also related to art of meditation on sun. Refer Brhadaranyaka Upanishad (2.5), Chandogya Upanishad (3.12).

maha, mahan:
A prefix meaning Great.

maharloka:
Realm or level of highest Consciousness.

mahat atman:
The Great Soul, *Brahman*.

mahavakya:
Great aphorism, one in each Veda. See *Aham Brahmasmi, Ayam Atma Brahma, Pragyanam Brahma* and *Tat tvam asi.*

MAHIDASA AITAREYA:
A sage who lived for 116 years. See Chandogya Upanishad (3.16).

MAITREYA GLAVA:
Another name for Dalbhya Baka.

MAITREYI:
Learned wife of famous philosopher Yagyavalkya. Refer Brhadaranyaka Upanishad (2.4).

manas:
Mind.

manomaya:
See *Pancha Kosha*.

mantha rite:
A ritual for prosperity, see Brhadaranyaka Upanishad (6.3) and Chandogya Upanishad (5.2).

MANU:
Mythological progenitor of mankind, analogous to Adam. Refer Brhadaranyaka Upanishad (1.4, 10).

GLOSSARY

Maram:
See *Ambhah*.

Marichi:
See *Ambhah*.

Marut:
Vedic deities, Rudra's mythological children born from the laugh of lightening.

matarishwan:
That which extends itself. The word is used for Air that signifies Life Principle.

matras:
Alphabets. *Aum* is said to have three *matras*. Also see *amatra*.

maya:
Power of Lord's illusion that makes unreal look real. It is a sign of spiritual ignorance.

Meghavan:
Another name for Indra. Refer Kena Upanishad, parable of three gods.

Mitra:
One of 12 Adityas, a Vedic deity.

moksha:
Synonym for *mukti*.

mrtyu:
Death.

mukti:
A state of God-like perfection, or oneness with *Brahman*. After this, soul is free from cycle of birth and death. According to some, this state can be achieved even when a person is living (*jivan mukti*). Others hold that it can be achieved only at the point of death (*videha mukti*). Other types are: *Krama Mukti* or progressive liberation and *Kaivalya Mukti*, meaning Absolute transcendence.

Muktika Upanishad:
One of the Upanishads that provides a list of 108 Upanishads.

Nachiketa:
Young boy who perseveres with Lord of Death, Yama, in Katha Upanishad to receive knowledge about 'Hereafter'.

nama rupa:
Name-Form. Equivalent of matter and mind, or matter and phenomenon.

Narada:
Senior Sage who learnt *Bhuma Vidya* from young Sanatkumar. Refer Chandogya Upanishad (Chapter 7).

neti, neti:
'Not this, Not this'. A phrase that signifies through repeated negations the undefinable and inconceivable nature of the Absolute.

nirguna Brahman:
Without attributes and Formless. *Brahman* is said to be both *Nirguna* and *Saguna* (with form and attributes).

Om:
See *Aum*.

pancha kosha:
Five layers of human personality. These are: physical, vital, mental, spiritual and blissful; or *Annamaya, Pranamaya, Manomaya, Vigyanamaya,* and *Anandamaya*. Refer Taittiriya Upanishad (Chapters 2 and 3).

panchagni vidya:
Doctrine of five cosmic fires. Using the example of child birth, it says that every activity involves participation by the entire universe. Refer Brhadaranyaka Upanishad (6.3) and Chandogya Upanishad (5.3-5.4).

para, param:
A prefix denoting 'higher', like *para vidya* for higher knowledge, meaning knowledge of God.

parajyotir:
Highest Light, meaning *Brahman*.

parajyotir vidya:
Art of meditation on Divine Light in man. Refer Chandogya Upanishad (3.13).

Paramatma:
Great Soul, *Brahman*.

Parikshit:
A king who performed many sacrificial rituals. Refer Chandogya Upanishad (3.3).

Parjanya:
Vedic god of rain.

Patanchala Kapya:
A king about whom Uddalaka Aruni makes a reference in Brhadaranyaka Upanishad (3.7).

pindanda:
: Egg of microcosm, The Upanishads say that microcosm is a replica of macrocosm; See *brahmananda*.

PIPPALADA:
: The teacher in Prasna Upanishad.

pitraloka:
: World of ancestors. See *loka*.

pitrayana:
: See *devayana*.

Pragyanan Brahma:
: Consciousness is *Brahman*. This great aphorism appears in Aitareya Upanishad.

PRAJAPATI:
: Lord of all living beings. Creative aspect of *Brahman*. Also called Brahma, It has two aspects: Subtle form called *Hiranyagarbha* (Cosmic Mind) and gross form called *Viraj* or *Virat*. Often, these terms are used interchangeably.

prakriti:
: Primary matter. Often translated as nature. *Purusha* and *Prakriti* or Spirit and Matter are the unmanifest and manifest aspects of *Brahman*. Also see *Purusha*.

pralaya:
: Dissolution of the universe. According to Vedic philosophy, creation and dissolution are cyclic processes.

Prana:
: Life Principle. Vital energy from vibration. Life breath that divides itself into five forms in human body. These are: *prana* (incoming breath), *apana* (outgoing breath), *vyana* (retained or diffused breath), *samana* (equalizing breath) and *udana* (ascending breath).

pranamaya:
: See *Pancha Kosha*.

pranav:
: Synonym for *Aum*, a symbol of *Brahman*.

pranayama:
: Breath-control. One of the eight practices in *Patanjali's Ashtanga Yoga*.

prasad:
: A small quantity of some food offered to a deity and received back with blessings of the deity. The recipient accepts it with great respect.

PRATRDA:
: A participant in conversation about interdependence of Food and Life-breath. Refer Brhadaranyaka Upanishad (5.12).

PRAVAHANA JAIVALI:
: Philosopher-king who taught *Panchagni Vidya* to Uddalaka (Gautama) Aruni. Refer Brhadaranyaka Upanishad (6.2).

preya:
: Pleasurable. Katha Upanishad says that in decisive moments, a person has two options: path of pleasures and convenience, and path of righteousness. These are called *preya* and *shreya*.

prithvi:
: Earth, one of the primal elements.

purna:
: Whole, Full, Infinite. The Upanishads use this word for both *Brahman* and the cosmos.

Purusha:
: Cosmic Person. The Spirit that dwells in the universe, as also in human beings. Also see *Prakriti*.

Purushottam:
: Supreme Person. Synonym for *Purusha*, *Brahman*, *Ishvara*.

PUSAN:
: One who nourishes. Another name for Sun God. Refer Brhadaranyaka Upanishad (5.15) and Isa Upanishad (15-18).

RAIKVA:
: A very poor but learned cart-driver who imparted *Samvarga Vidya* to King Janashruti. Refer Chandogya Upanishad (4.1-4.3).

rajas, rajsic:
: See *guna*.

rayi:
: Movement, matter.

Rg Veda:
: See Vedas.

rishi:
Seer. A term used for an enlightened person.

rk:
Verses of *Rg Veda*.

RUDRA:
Name of Siva as God of Dissolution. Also see Vedic deities.

rupa:
See *nama-rupa*.

sadhana:
Spiritual practice like meditation. It leads to higher states of Consciousness.

saguna Brahman:
Conceptualization of a Personal God having certain attributes and some form. Also see *nirguna Brahman*.

SAKALYA VIDAGDHA:
One of the scholars who questioned Yagyavalkya in Brhadaranyaka Upanishad (3.9), also refer (4.2, 6).

Sama Veda:
See Vedas.

samadhi:
Highest state in yoga in which there is no duality between the meditator and the object of meditation.

saman:
Verses of *Sama Veda*.

samana:
See *Prana*.

SAMASRAVAS:
Disciple of Yagyavalkya. Refer Brhadaranyaka Upanishad (3.1).

samhita:
Collection of texts, verses or hymns.

samsara:
Phenomenal world. The term also denotes the cycles of birth, death and rebirth.

samskara:
Impressions of life experiences left on the unconscious mind and carried forward into next life.

samudra:
Ocean.

samvarga vidya:
A technique of meditation in which object of meditation is raised progressively from gross to more and more subtle levels. Refer Chandogya Upanishad (4.1-4.3).

sanatana:
Eternal.

SANATKUMAR:
Also called Kartikeya. He taught *Bhuma Vidya* to Narada in Chandogya Upanishad (Chapter 7).

sandilya vidya:
Art of meditation on Self within and without. Refer Chandogya Upanishad (3.14).

sankhya:
One of the six schools of Indian philosophy. It relies on logic in its enunciation of spiritual truths.

sanyasi:
Ascetic.

sarira:
Human body. A human being is said to have three bodies: gross, subtle and causal, or *sthula, sukshma* and *karana*.

sarvam:
All this. A phrase that denotes the universe.

sattva, sattvic:
See *guna*.

SATYAKAMA JABALA:
A young boy of illegitimate birth who learned *Brahma Vidya* from Nature. Later, he became a famous spiritual master. Refer Chandogya Upanishad (4.4-4.14).

SATYAKAMA SIBI:
A student in Prasna Upanishad. Also in Brhadaranyaka Upanishad (4.1, 6).

satyakama, satya sankalpa:
True desires, true resolve. Refer Chandogya Upanishad (8.1).

satyaloka:
See *loka*.

satyameva jayate:
: 'Truth alone Triumphs'. This famous sentence from Mundaka Upanishad (3.15) is inscribed on the seal of India.

satyas satyam:
: Truth of truths. One of the descriptions of *Brahmana*.

SAUNAKA:
: Student of Angirasa in Mundaka Upanishad. He was a house-holder.

SAVITRI:
: Synonymous with Gayatri, a famous Vedic prayer to Sun God. Refer Brhadaranyaka Upanishad (5.14).

shakti:
: Energy, Force, Will, self-existent Power of the Lord. This unfolds as *iccha shakti* (power of desire), *kriya shakti* (power of action) and *gyana shakti* (power of wisdom).

shanti:
: Peace.

shraddha:
: Faith.

shreya:
: See *preya*.

shrishti:
: Creation. Also see *Pralaya*.

shruti:
: 'That which is heard'. Scriptures containing truths that will remain valid for all times, like Vedas and Upanishads.

SHVETAKETU ARUNI:
: Young son of Uddalaka who taught him, 'That thou art'. Refer Chandogya Upanishad (Chapter 6).

SILAKA SALAVATYA:
: A participant in discussion about Ultimate Reality. Refer Chandogya Upanishad (1.8-1.9).

smriti:
: 'That which is remembered'. Scriptures containing teaching that are meant for specific times and cultures. They may need to be revised to suit new conditions.

sodasha kala:
: Metaphorically, Cosmic Person is said to have sixteen parts; even though in reality, He is partless, one Totality. Refer Prasna Upanishad (Q.6).

soham:
: 'That I am'. An aphorism that signifies the ecstatic state of self-realization.

soma yagya:
: Ritual of offering morning, mid-day and evening libations to three fires. Refer Chandogya Upanishad (2.24).

sthula sarira:
: See *Sarira*.

SUDHANVAN:
: A *gandarbha*. Refer Brhadaranyaka Upanishad (3.3, 1).

SUKESHA BHARADVAJA:
: A student in Prasna Upanishad.

sukham sarira:
: See *sarira*.

surya:
: Sun. Symbol of Life, Wisdom and Divinity.

susumna nadi:
: Central psychic nerve that connects the heart to the crown at the head. *Jivatman* is said to travel through it for leaving the body at the time of death.

sutra:
: Thread, signifying the Spiritual Principle that holds the world together. Also an aphorism in verse form.

svayambhu:
: Self-created and well made. Word used for the creation.

swarga loka:
: See *loka*.

taijasa, tejas:
: Universal Mind that supports our subconscious mind in dream state. Also, manifestation of *Tapas*.

tamas, tamsic:
: See *guna*.

tapa, tapas:
: Intense contemplation or severe austerity, leading to release of energy of heat. The universe is said to have arisen from *tapas* by Prajapati.

tapoloka:
: See *loka*.

Tat tvam asi:
: That thou art. One of the four great aphorisms. It appear in Chandogya Upanishad (Chapter 6).

tat:
: That. A word used to denote *Brahman*. It signifies that no name can describe the Absolute.

TRISHANKU:
: Self-realized sage. Refer Taittiriya Upanishad (1.10).

Turiya:
: Pure and Unconditioned Consciousness. It is called 'the Fourth' to emphasize that It is not a state like waking, dream and sleep.

udana:
: See *Prana*.

UDANKA SAULBAYANN:
: A spiritual teacher of Janaka mentioned in Brhadaranyaka Upanishad (Chapter 4).

UDDALAKA ARUNI:
: One of the scholars who questioned Yagyavalkya in Brhadaranyaka Upanishad (3.7). He learnt *Panchagni Vidya* from King Pravahana Jaivali in Brhadaranyaka Upanishad (6.2). He also imparted to his son Shvetaketu, the great aphorism 'That thou art'. Refer Chandogya Upanishad (Chapter 6).

UDGATR:
: One of the four Vedic Priests. See Adhavaryu.

udgitha:
: Important verses appearing in *Sama Veda*. They are chanted in melodious tones.

UMA HIMVATI:
: Daughter of Himalayas. In a parable of three gods, she appeared before Indra and revealed the mystery of the Unknown. Refer Kena Upanishad (3).

upadhi:
: Adjunct.

UPAKOSALA KAMALAYANA:
: A student of Satyakama, he learned *Brahma Vidya* from three Fires. Refer Chandogya Upanishad (4.10-4.14).

Upanishads:
: Collection of high wisdom texts that constitute the final parts of the four Vedas.

upasana, upasate:
: Worship of God, or contemplation on God.

USASTA CHAKRAYAN:
: One of the scholars who questioned Yagyavalkya in Brhadaranyaka Upanishad (3.4). Also refer Chandogya Upanishad (1.10).

uttam:
: Supreme.

vac:
: Speech.

vairagya:
: Freedom from worldly passions.

vaisvanara vidya:
: Art of meditation on *Brahman* as Totality. Refer Chandogya Upanishad (5.11-5.18).

vaisvanara:
: Universal Mind that supports our conscious mind in waking state.

VAJASRAVA GAUTAM:
: A believer in rituals. His pretence of charity was not liked by his son Nachiketa. Refer Katha Upanishad Chapter 1.

VAMADEVA:
: A sage who gained self-realization while in womb. Refer Aitareya Upanishad (2.1, 5), Brhadaranyaka Upanishad (1.4, 10).

VARNA:
: Vocational classification which later degenerated into caste system. Four traditional varnas are: Brahmin (Priests), Kshatriyas (Warriors), Vaishya (Businessmen) and Sudra (service class).

VARUNA:
See Aditya.

vasana:
Subconscious inclinations that influence one's attitude and habits; desires.

VASU:
See Vedic Deities.

vayu:
Deity of Wind and Life Principle. One of the five primal elements. Also see *akash* and *matarishwan*.

vedanta:
System of thought derived from Upanishads, which constitute concluding part of Vedas.

Vedas:
Most ancient and authoritative scriptures of Hindus. Four Vedas are: *Rg, Yajur, Sama and Atharva.*

VEDIC DEITIES:
Eleven Rudras, eight Vasus, twelve Adityas and two Asvins, making a total of 33 Vedic gods.

vedic meters:
Gayatri, Tristup and *Jagati* are three important meters on which recitation of Vedas is based. They contain 22, 44, and 48 letters respectively.

veena:
Musical instrument. See Chandogya Upanishad (2.54) for its use as an analogy.

vidya:
Spiritual knowledge, art of meditation. See *apara vidya, avidya* and *para.*

vigyana:
Spiritual Wisdom.

vigyanamaya:
See *Pancha Kosha.*

VIROCHANA:
Chief of Asuras. For dialogue with Prajapati on *Atman*, refer to Chandogya Upanishad (8.7-8.8).

VISHNU:
One of 12 Adityas. Also God of Preservation in the Trinity of Creation-Preservation-Dissolution.

VISHVEDEVA:
All-gods. Refer Brhadaranyaka Upanishad (1.4, 12).

visvarupa:
Cosmic form of Absolute, *Brahman*. The universe is said to be the body of the Supreme.

vyana:
See *Prana.*

yagya:
Sacrificial ritual or deeds.

YAGYAVALKYA:
Famous Vedic scholar. Refer Brhadaranyaka Upanishad Chapters (2-4).

Yajur Veda:
See Vedas.

YAKSHA:
Unknown spirit that symbolized *Brahman*. Refer Kena Upanishad (3).

YAMA:
Lord of Death. Refer Katha Upanishad.

Index

A

All this is, verily, *Brahman* 499
Allegories: see parables
Analogies: see metaphors
Asceticism (522 525 532)
Atman: see *Brahman*
Aum
    meaning of (84 94)
    Paramatma, Atman 86
    this and That (204 206 211)
    supreme Word (262 268 277)
    symbol of Absolute and relative (298 302 306)
    greatness of the symbol (337 339)
    identified with Life Principle (337 340)
    protects from fear of death (337 342)
    Sun, *Prana*, and *Udgitha* (337 342)
    origin and importance (353 360)
    mantra, theory of 483
    symbol of Totality (497 499)
    meditation on (498 500 563 570 581)

B

Bhagavad Gita (7 444)
Bhuma Vidya: What gives happiness?
    synopsis 433
    translation 435
    rendition 444
    commentaries 447
Birth, son's birth, rebirth (88 89 90 560 567)
Brahman
    as Life breath: see *Samvarga Vidya*
    as Totality: see *Vaisvanara Vidya*
    Light in man: see *Parajyotir Vidya*
    within and without: see *Sandilya Vidya* and *Gayatri Vidya*
    names depend on context 94
    all this Totality (101 108 117)
    incomplete definitions (121 125 135 146 161 173 175 179 196)
    neti neti, not this, not this (122 128 137)
    satyas satyam, truth of truths (122 128 137)
    breathes in you (144 152 168)
    is beyond relative attributes (144 153 169)
    is woven like warp and woof (144 153 169)
    Inner Controller (145 154 170)
    Imperishable (145 157 170)
    is one, gods many (145 159 172)
    description of (178 190 202)
    meditation on heart, truth as (204 206 213)
    language of paradox (241 243 248)
    is Existence – Consciousness – Bliss (249 254)
    is Truth – Knowledge – Infinitude (308 312 316)
    Bliss and fear of world (311 314 322)
    meditation on mind and sky as (365 373 379)
    meditation on Sun as (365 374 379)
    revealed by Nature (380 385 393)
    revealed by three Fires (381 387 396)
    'That Delight' which spreads love (475 479 492)
    defining the Indefinable (521 523 527)
    knower of (544 546 554)

C

Commentators
    Sri Aurobindo (IsaU 246 249-256; KathaU 277 292 TaitU 316-317; ChandU 394; KenaU 481-487 490-493)
    Swami Chinmayananda (AitU 84-87 90-91 94; IsaU 246 250-257; KathaU 271 274-279 287-

293; KenaU 489-494; ManU 501; MunU 526-532 538-541 548-555; PrasU 574-584)

Swami Gambhirananda/Sri Sankara (AitU 90; TaitU 306 317; ChandU 350 351 375-379 392 396-397 448; MunU 526; PrasU 576-577 580-582 584-585)

Dr. Karan Singh (MunU 527-532 539 541 549-555)

Klaus G. Witz (AitU 95; KathaU 276 278; TaitU 321 324; ChandU 378 393 395 463)

Swami Krishnananda (ChandU 392 412 449; ManU 507-511)

Swami Madhavananda/Sri Sankara (BrhadU 140-141 197 212-215 238)

Sri Madhava/Nagesh D. Sonde (ManU 511)

Mahatma Gandhi (IsaU 245-246)

N. A. Nikam (AitU 90; TaitU 305 307 319 331; KenaU 488; ManU 512-513; PrasU 575)

Swami Nikhilananda/Sri Sankara/Sri Gaudapada (ManU 501-503 514-517)

Swami Paramananda (IsaU 250-251 257; KathaU 272-279 287-291; MunU 541 549-552)

Paul Deussen (AitU 96; BrhadU 117-120 136-140 167-173 196-197 200 212-216 233 238; KathaU 274; TaitU 304 318 322 324 331-332; ChandU 351 376-379 392 395 432 449; KenaU 494; PrasU 573)

Rohit Mehta (AitU 83 90; IsaU 247 253 257; KathaU 271 273-275; KenaU 489 491; ManU 511-512; MunU 527-530 540; PrasU 574-583)

Dr. S. Radhakrishnan (AitU 86-87; BrhadU 117 136-140 167-169 172-174 198-199 202 211-213 217 233 236-238; IsaU 245 250-253; KathaU 272-279 287-294; TaitU 306 322 332; ChandU 351 375-379 392 396 411 428 449; KenaU 488-489; ManU 503-505; MunU 526 529-532)

Swami Sarvananda (AitU 84-87 90-91 94; IsaU 251-252; KathaU 272-274; TaitU 304-307 318-323 331-332; MunU 529-530)

Swami Sivananda (AitU 84-87 90 94; BrhadU 116-120 136-142 167-174 196-202 211-217 233 238; IsaU 250; KathaU 273 276-279 288-294; KenaU 487-488; ManU 506-507; MunU 529-530 539 549-552)

Swami Swahananda (ChandU 351 376-379 392 396 431 448)

Swami Vivekananda (KathaU 272; MunU 538 540 548-551)

Commentaries, general

Sri Aurobindo on KenaU and IsaU 481

Paul Deussen

on creation of world and man 95

on PrasnaU 573

Swami Gambhirananda on Meditation 349

Klaus G. Witz

on *Atman* as Sole Reality 95

meditation on *Atman* within 460

ManU 501

Complete Person 102

Conjunctions (297 299 304)

Consciousness

in man (78 80 85)

is *Brahman*, Absolute 92

and Its three states (121 127 135 176 184 197 497 499 562 569 578)

planes of (281 285 292)

evolution of matter, life and mind 483

Pure and Absolute (498 499)

Cosmic Person, *Purusha*

and Cosmic Powers (77 79 82)

illumines sun and Self (338 343)

within man (563 571 582)

One Absolute, many relative manifestations (533-538)

Cosmic Powers in sense organs (77 80 84 585)

Creation

without beginning or end 84

similarities between man and world 84

variable and constant (102 113 118)

sequence of (521 524 529)

Creator and Creation, analogies (521 523 528)

INDEX

D

Dahara Vidya: Meditation on Self within
- synopsis 450
- translation 453
- commentaries 460
- rendition, self within 463
- rendition, one teaching, two interpretations 466

Death, Nachiketa's dialogue with Lord of (261 264 271)

Deeds survive death (143 150 167)

Desires are like citadels 88

Dialogues, overview of
- Gargya and Ajatashatru 56
- Janaka and Yagyavalkya 59
- Maitreyi and Yagyavalkya 56
- Raikva and Janashruti 60
- Sanatkumar and Narada 63
- Satyakama and Nature 61
- Seeker and Preceptor 64
- Shvetaketu and Uddalaka 62
- Upakosala and Fires 62
- Yagyavalkya and others 57

E

Enlightened vision (78 81 87)

Ego and self-interest, sacrifice of (110 116)

Evil co-exists with good 100

F

Fear of Supreme (281 285 291)

Five cosmic fires, two paths (218 222 233 399 404 411)

Food
- parable of 85
- seven kinds (102 112 118)
- respect for (326 328 332)

G

Gaudapada's Karika (498 500 514)

Gayatri Mantra (205 209 215 582)

Gayatri Vidya (363 366 375)

H

Hunger, thirst, desires 82

I

Interdependence of everything 102

Origin of word 'I' 108

Ignorance and Knowledge (242 243 252)

Illness, death are austerities (204 208 214)

Inner space in heart (298 301 305)

Invocations for Peace: See Prayers

J

Journey beyond death (175 183 196)

K

Knots of heart (287 449)

Knowledge, of two types (521 523 526)

L

Last prayer (205 210 216 242 244 254)

Lead me from untruth to Truth (100 105 117)

Life
- compared to chariot (263 269 277)
- mind and senses, what drives them (473 477 487)

Life-breath
- glory of 107
- cosmic and individual (103 115 119)

    meditation on (122 128 136 205 208 215)

    food (205 208 214)

    five forms and cosmic counterparts 376

    parable on its superiority (218 221 233 398 403 411 560 567 577)

    and senses, power behind (281 284 289)

    how it functions (561 568 577)

Light of all lights (281 285 290)

Lineage of teachers (124 133 195 231)

Living beings

    whence born (559 565 574)

    powers that energize them (560 567 577)

Love, one Self in two bodies (122 129 137 178 192)

M

Male-Female duality (101 109 117)

Madhu Vidya, honey doctrine (123 131 140 362 366 375)

Mahavakya, great aphorisms

    Consciousness is *Brahman* 93

    I am *Brahman* 101

    That thou art 413

    This *Atman* is *Brahman* 499

Man's life is like a sacrifice (365 372 378)

Man's personality, five layers (309 312 318 325 327 331)

Manifest and Unmanifest (242 244 253)

Mantha rite (220 225 238 398 403 411)

Maxims on 'God and I'

    what is God 65

    one God, many names and forms 66

    who am I 66

    you and I are God 69

    cosmic person and inner Self 70

    God hidden five layers deep 70

Metaphors

    sun and moon 29

    chariot 32

    city of god 32

    rivers, ocean 34

    water, salt 35

    fire, sparks, spider 36

    tree, plants 37

    wheel, hub 38

    bow and arrow 40

    musical instruments 41

    spider, herbs, hair 41

    birds 42

    miscellaneous 43

    wealth 102

    Plato, allegory of -- 287

Mortal to Immortal (282 286 293)

Mystic words (297 301 305)

O

Om: see *Aum*

Oneness of microcosm and macrocosm (534 537 540)

P

Panchagni Vidya: see five cosmic fires

Parables

    of creation 45

    good and evil 47

    life-breath, senses 47

    cosmic fires 48

    liberation, rebirth 49

    Indra and Virochana 50

    three gods and Unknown 51

    Nachiketa and Yama 52

    two birds 52

    Bhrigu 54

Parajyotir Vidya (363 369 375)

Phonetics, science of (297 299 304)

Power of mind (543 545 551)
Prana Agnihotra (401 409 411)
Prana: see life, life-breath
Prayers
    for truth 25
    about creation 26
    for awareness of Supreme 27
    for mutual understanding 27
    for divine protection 28
    for health, happiness 28
    for intelligence, health, wealth (297 300 305)
    for son's longevity (364 371 378)
    for a life of 116 years (365 371 378)
Prenatal knowledge of Self (88 89 90)
Procreation ceremonies (220 227 238)
Progression to Supreme (263 270 278)

R

Relative inseparable from Absolute (310 313 321)
Relative to Absolute in three steps (261 265 272)
Renditions
    Samvarga Vidya 391
    That thou art 422
    infinite alone gives happiness 444
    meditation on self within 463
    one teaching, two interpretations 466
Rituals
    mockery of (338 348 351)
    silence and speech in (382 389)
    importance and limitations (522 524 530)

S

Sacrificial rituals (143 148 167)
Saman
    deities of (338 346 351)
    mystical meaning of (338 348)
    fivefold (352 354)
    sevenfold (352 355)
    all-inclusive (352 357)
    recitation of (353 359)
Samvarga Vidya (380 383 391)
Sandilya Vidya (364 370 376)
Satyameva Jayate, Truth alone triumphs (542 545 550)
Scriptures: study, reflect, then act (298 302 306)
Self
    never dies (262 268 277)
    realized through divine grace (262 269 277)
    realized by looking inwards (280 283 287)
Self-knowledge, preparation for (262 267 275)
Self-mastery and self-sacrifice (100 104 116)
Self-realization
    effect of (178 190 202)
    signs of (241 243 250)
    ecstacy of (298 302 306)
    a mystical chant (326 329 332)
    is like river (543 546 552)
Sense organs (85 167 482 506)
Sex and spirituality (186 198 550 220 227 238 566 575)
Shruti 6
Smriti 6
Soma sacrifice, symbolic significance (353 360)
Son's role in spiritual life (102 114 119)
Soul's path after death (204 208 214)
Space
    mind and Self (147 163 173)
    is ultimate support (338 344)
Spiritual enquiry, preparation for 559 574)
Spiritual knowledge, paradox of (474 478 488)
Spiritual life, fundamentals of (241 243 245)
Supermind, next stage in evolution 483

T

That is whole, this is whole
    (104 204 206 211 245)
That thou art
    synopsis 413
    translation 415
    rendition 422
    commentaries 427
This *Atman* is *Brahman* 499
This, verily, is That (280 283 287)
Three gods, parable of (474 478 489)
Time, a created factor 83
Transmigration (177 189 200 281 284 289)
Tree
    man's comparison with (147 165 174)
    of creation (281 285 291)
Triad: name, form and work (103 115 120)
Two birds, parable of (542 545 548)
Two paths
    Shreya and *Preya* (262 267 275)
    Liberation and rebirth (400 406 411)

U

Upanishads
    complete Upanishads, commentaries and synopses
        Aitareya 75
        Brhadaranyaka 97
        Chandogya 333
        Isa 239
        Katha 258
        Kena 471
        Mandukya 495
        Mundaka 578
        Prasna 557
        Taittiriya 295
    why study 3
    Vedas and 5
    eternal truths 6
    how ancient 6
    how many 7
    how different 8
    tables 8, 19, 24
    obscure texts 10
    tributes 12
    method of study 17
    road map 17
    methods of presentation 18
    translated text 21
    numbering system 21
    synopses 21
    renditions 23
    commentators 24

W

World (*Sansara*) compared to ocean 85
Wealth, metaphors for 102
Work, Wisdom power of (86 106)

V

Vaisvanara Vidya (400 407 411)
Vedas 5
Virtues: *da*, *da*, *da* (204 206 212)
Virtuous living (298 302 306)

Y

Yoga, the highest state (281 285 292)

Important Verses

All this is, verily, Brahman.
  (ManU 2) 499

Always doing selfless work... hundred years.
  (IsaU 2) 243

As large as all this space... space in heart.
  (ChandU 8.1) 453

Arise. Awake... life means.
  (KathaU 1.3, 14) 270

Asato ma Sadagmaya...
  (BrhadU 1.3, 28) 108

Atman is all pervading, bright...
  (IsaU 8) 243

Atman is free from evil, old age...
  (ChandU 8.1) 453

Atman... Its desire is Truth, Its resolve is Truth...
  (ChandU 8.1) 453

Aum is Brahman, Aum is all this universe...
  (TaitU 1.8) 302

Aum. This eternal word is all ... the Imperishable
  (ManU 1) 499

Benefits of good deeds...short-lived.
  (BrhadU 1.5, 15) 111

Beyond senses are sense objects...
  (KathaU 1.3, 10; 2.3, 7) 270, 285

Bliss is Brahman...
  (TaitU 3.6) 328

Brahman cannot be described by words...
  (MunU 3.1, 8) 545

Brahman created universe out of Itself...
  (TaitU 2.7) 314

Brahman desired. 'Let Me become many'...
  (TaitU 2.6, 3) 314

Brahman in human beings and in sun...
  (TaitU 2.9) 315

Brahman is in front...at the back...
  (MunU 2.2, 11) 537

Brahman is Truth-Knowledge-Infinitude
  (TaitU 2.1, 1) 312

Brahman... space outside ... space inside
  (ChandU 3.12, 7) 369

Brahman... moves in the cavity of our heart.
  (MunU 2.2, 1) 537

Child is father's own Self.
  (AitU 2.1, 4) 89

... comprehends It both as 'Not-known' and 'Known'...
  (KenaU 2) 478

Consciousness alone remains awake...
  (PrasU 4, 3) 569

Consciousness is Brahman
  (AitU 3.1, 3) 93

...Control speech by mind, mind by Intellect...
  (KathaU 1.3, 13) 270

Creator desired the joy of creation...
  (PrasU 1, 4) 565

... da, da, da...
  (BrhadU 5.2) 206

... death through ignorance... immortality...
  (IsaU 11) 244

... deep darkness... greater darkness...
  (IsaU 9) 243

Divine Being is Formless...
  (MunU 2.1, 2) 536

Do not covet the wealth of others.
  (IsaU 1) 243

During deep sleep...Cosmic Consciousness.
  (BrhadU 2.1, 17) 127

Dwells in earth, yet is other than earth...
  (BrhadU 3.7, 38) 155

Earth is like honey for all beings...
  (BrhadU 2.5, 1) 131

... embrace of beloved... Intelligent Self...
  (BrhadU 4.3, 21) 186

Everyone sees His sport, but none sees Him
  (BrhadU 4.3, 14) 185

Everything is impelled by Consciousness...
  (BitU 1.3, 3) 81

... Eye is instrument of seeing... Person who sees is Atman.
  (ChandU 8.12) 458

Face of Truth is covered with golden lid...
  (BrhadU 5.15; IsaU 15) 210, 244

Father, to whom will you give me away?
  (KathaU 1.1, 4) 264

Fire becoming speech, entered the mouth...
  (AitU 1.2, 4) 80

Fear arises when...
    (BrhadU 1.4, 2) 109

Flowing rivers disappear into ocean.
    (MunU 3.2, 8) 546

From blazing fire... sparks... fall back again.
    (MunU 2.1, 1) 536

From Brahman... Consciousness... produced.
    (MunU 1.1, 9) 524

From fear of It, fire burns...
    (KathaU 2.3, 3) 285

... from Imperishable comes out the universe
    (MunU 1.1, 7) 523

From unreal lead me to the Real...
    (BrhadU 1.3, 28) 108

God has created food for everyone
    (BrhadU 1.5, 2) 112

Gods ignore him who knows them...
    (BrhadU 2.4, 6) 130

... Good and Pleasant, Shreya and Preya...
    (KathaU 1.2) 267

He desired "Let a second self...
    (BrhadU 1.2, 4) 105

He is never seen, but is the seer...
    (BrhadU 3.7, 23) 157

He is your Self, inner controller, immortal.
    (BrhadU 3.7) 155, 158

He was not happy being alone...
    (BrhadU 1.4, 3) 109

He who breathes in...
    (BrhadU 3.4, 1) 152

How many gods are there?
    (BrhadU 3.9) 159

I am Brahman
    (BrhadU 1.4, 10) 110

Imperishable cannot be attained by...
    (KathaU 1.2, 10) 268

In the beginning, all this was Atman alone.
    (AitU 1.1, 1) 79

In the beginning, all this was Unmanifested...
    (TaitU 2.7, 1) 314

In the beginning, this universe was non-existent...
    (ChandU 3.19) 374

In the beginning, this was Being alone...
    (ChandU 6.2, 1) 415

In the beginning, this was Brahman...
    (BrhadU 1.4, 11) 110

Infinite alone gives happiness.
    (ChandU 7.23) 442

Into blind darkness enter those... avidya...
    (BrhadU 4.4, 10) 190

...This which is Formless like space... is Brahman.
    (ChandU 8.14) 459

It moves, It moves not...
    (IsaU 5) 243

... Know Brahman through meditation...
    (TaitU 3.1) 327

Knower of Atman goes beyond grief...
    (ChandU 7.2, 3) 435

Knower of Brahman becomes Brahman.
    (MunU 3.2, 9) 546

... knows Brahman as That Delight...is loved by all...
    (KenaU 4) 479

Life (Prana) is born from Self (Atman).
    (PrasU 3, 3) 568

Life is Brahman. Space is Brahman. Joy is Brahman.
    (ChandU 4.9, 4) 387

Life is like hub of a wheel.
    (BrhadU 1.5, 15) 114

Life of life. Eye of eye... Brahman
    (BrhadU 4.4, 18) 191

Life-breath is Brahman
    (BrhadU 4.1, 3) 180

Life Principle is imperishable
    (BrhadU 1.5, 21-23) 115

Lord pervades everything
    (IsaU 1) 243

Man cannot be satisfied by wealth...
    (KathaU 1.2, 27) 267

Man in deep sleep is united with his Being
    (ChandU 6.8, 1) 418

Man is only one half, his wife...
    (BrhadU 1.4, 3) 109

Matra devo bhava
    (TaitU 1.11) 302

IMPORTANT VERSES

May my body be vigorous...
(TaitU 1.4, 1) 300

...mighty tree... so indeed is man...
(BrhadU 3.9, 28) 166

Mind is Brahman
(BrhadU 4.1, 6) 181

Mind is made of food, Life breath of water...
(ChandU 6.5, 4) 417

Mind of mind, Life of life...
(KenaU 1) 477

Mortal beings decay and die like corn.
(KathaU 1.1, 5) 264

...Mortal body... seat of deathless Atman...
(ChandU 8.12) 458

...Motionless, yet more swift than the mind...
(IsaU 3) 243

...Moves about adored in dream...Immortal...Fearless.
(ChandU 8.10) 457

...Neti, Neti, Not this, Not this...
(BrhadU 2.3, 7; 3.9, 26; 4.2, 4; 4.4, 22) 129, 165, 183, 191

Not for the sake of husband is husband dear......
(BrhadU 2.4, 5) 129

O Gayatri... Salutations to you
(BrhadU 5.14) 210

Oh, I have seen this...
(AitU 1.3, 13) 81

Ocean is one goal of all rivers...
(BrhadU 2.4, 11) 130

Person becomes fearless only when...
(TaitU 2.7, 3) 314

Person who is seen in Sun, That I am.
(ChandU 4.11) 380

Person who is yonder in sun...
(BrhadU 2.1) 125

Person who sees through the eye, He is Atman.
(ChandU 4.15) 389

Person... in the eye... Immortal... Fearless.
(ChandU 8.7) 456

...Protect us both...
(KathaU Inv) 264

Rivers flowing toward sea disappear...
(PrasU 6, 5) 571

Satyameva Jayate, Truth alone Triumphs...
(MunU 3.1, 6) 545

Satyasa satyam. Truth of truths.
(BrhadU 2.3, 7) 123

Seeker of Brahman should live like a child...
(BrhadU 3.5, 1) 153

Sees all existences in Self, Self in all existences...
(IsaU 6) 243

...sees nothing else, hears nothing else...
(ChandU 7.24) 442

...sees thus, reflects thus... delights in Atman
(ChandU 7.25, 7.26) 442, 443

Self is never born, nor It dies...
(KathaU 1.2, 17) 268

Self is not attained by...
(MunU 3.2, 4) 546

Self is the Lord of chariot, body is the chariot...
(KathaU 1.3, 3) 269

...Self... unborn, undecaying... fearless, Brahman
(BrhadU 4.5, 25) 192

...sleeps... state of Brahman...
(BrhadU 4.3, 32) 187

Senses do not like mind to move toward Self
(BrhadU 1.4, 11) 110

Speak the Truth. Practice Righteousness...
(TaitU 1.11) 302

...Speech be rooted in mind...
(AitU Inv) 79

Spokes are held together in the hub...
(BrhadU 2.5, 15) 132

...Sun and moon stand in their respective positions...
(BrhadU 3.8, 8) 158

...sun is not contaminated... so also Atman.
(KathaU 2.2, 11) 285

...Sun rises out of His fear...
(TaitU 2.8) 314

That Being is right here, within the body...
(PrasU 6, 2) 571

That being which is the subtle essence of all...
(ChandU 6.9) 419

That Being willed. 'May I become many'.
(ChandU 6.2, 3) 416

That Infinite alone is below. That is above...
   (ChandU 7.25) 442

That is whole, this is whole...
   (BrhadU, Isa) 104, 206, 243, 244

That thou art.
   (ChandU 6.9) 419

That which cannot be thought by the mind, but...
   (KenaU 1) 477

That which is invisible...
   (MunU 1.1, 6) 523

That which sees, feels, hears...
   (PrasU 4, 9) 571

There are two forms of Brahman...
   (BrhadU 2.3, 1) 128

There is no difference Brahman and world...
   (KathaU 2.1, 11) 263

There is no happiness in anything finite.
   (ChandU 7.23) 442

There sight does not travel, ..., nor mind...
   (KenaU 1) 477

There the sun does not shine, nor the moon...
   (KathaU 2.2, 15)285; (MunU 2.2, 10) 537

There was nothing whatsoever here...
   (BrhadU 1.2, 1) 104

Thinking what is improper is evil.
   (BrhadU 1.3, 6) 106

This Atman is Brahman.
   (ManU 2) 499

This universe was undifferentiated...
   (BrhadU 1.4, 7) 109

This world is a triad of name, form and work.
   (BrhadU 1.6, 1) 115

This, verily, is the That.
   (KathaU 2.1, 2.2) 283

Those who perform good deeds... good wombs...
   (ChandU 5.10, 7) 406

Though sitting, It travels far...
   (KathaU 1.2, 21) 269

True desires (Satyakama) are covered by untruth...
   (ChandU 8.3) 454

...unheard becomes heard...
   (ChandU 6.1, 2-3) 415

Universe evolved from Brahman... vibrates as...
   (KathaU 2.3, 2) 285

...universe is Brahman...
   (ChandU 3.14, 1) 370

Universe is guided by Consciousness...
   (AitU 3.1, 3) 93

...unmanifest, ...manifest
   (IsaU 12) 244

Weak hope to defeat the strong...
   (BrhadU 1.4, 14) 111

When breathing, It is called Life Force...
   (BrhadU 1.4, 7) 110

When one attains happiness... one is active
   (ChandU 7.22) 442

When one reflects,... spiritual awareness.
   (ChandU 7.18) 441

When this man was in deep sleep...
   (BrhadU 2.1, 16) 127

When we see Him both as spiritual and material...
   (MunU 2.2, 8) 537

Where there is duality, one smells...
   (BrhadU 2.4, 13) 131

Whoever has desires, is reborn here...
   (MunU 3.2, 2) 546

Word Aum is indeed Brahman...
   (KathaU 1.2, 16) 268

World is guided by Consciousness...
   (AitU 1.3, 3) 81

World is His One foot...
   (ChandU 3.12, 6) 369

Worlds are perpetuated by progeny.
   (AitU 2.1, 3) 89

Woven like warp and woof...
   (BrhadU 3.6) 154

You cannot see the seer of seeing...
   (BrhadU 3.4, 2) 153

You have ferried us...across sea of ignorance.
   (PrasU 6, 8) 572

Bibliography

Commentaries on the Upanishads quoted in this publication

1. Sri Aurobindo, *The Upanishads: Texts, Translations and Commentaries*. Sri Aurobindo Ashram, Pondichery (1971).

2. Swami Chinmayananda, *Discourses on Upanishads*, (Aitareya, Isa, Katha, Kena, Mandukya, Mundaka and Prasna) Central Chinmaya Mission Trust, Mumbai (First Editions 1952-1954).

3. Swami Gambhirananda, translation of Commentaries of Sankaracharya on Upanishads, Advaita Ashram, Kolkatta (1957).

4. Karan Singh, *Essays on Hinduism*. Appendix on Mundaka Upanishad, Ratna Sagar (P) Ltd., Delhi (1987).

5. Klaus G. Witz, *The Supreme Wisdom of the Upanishads*. Motilal Banarsidas Publishers (1998).

6. Swami Krishnananda, *The Chandogya Upanishad*. Divine Life Society (1984).

7. Swami Krishnananda, *The Mandukya Upanishad*, An Exposition. Divine Life Society (1984).

8. *The Brhadaranyaka Upanishad with the commentary of Sankaracharya*. Translated by Swami Madhavananda, Advaita Ashram, Kolkatta (First Ed. 1934).

9. *Commentary of Sri Madhava on Mandukya Upanishad*, with Translation and Explanatory Notes. Edited by Nagesh D. Sonde, Vasantik Prakashan, Mumbai.

10. N. A. Nikam, *Ten Principal Upanishads*. Somaiya Publications (P) Ltd. (1974).

11. *The Mandukya Upanishad with Gaudapada's Karika and Sri Sankara's Commentary*. Translated by Swami Nikhilananda, Advaita Ashram, Kolkatta (First Ed. 1932).

12. Swami Paramananda, *Four Upanishads*. Ramakrishna Math, Chennai (1919).

13. Paul Deussen, *The Philosophy of the Upanishads*. Translation from German by Rev. A. S. Geden, Motilal Banarsidas Publishers (P) Ltd.; New Delhi (First Ed. German 1899, English 1906).

14. Paul Deussen, *Sixty Upanishads of the Veda*. Translation from German by V. M. Bedekar and G. B. Palsule. (Vol. I and II), Motilal Banarsidas Publishers (P) Ltd., Delhi (First German Edition 1897, Indian Edition 1980).

15. Rohit Mehta, *The Call of the Upanishads*. Motilal Banarasidas, Delhi (1970).

16. S. Radhakrishnan, *The Principal Upanishads*. Harper Collins Publishers India (First Published in Great Britain, 1953).

17. Swami Sarvananda, *Upanishad Series (Aitareya, Isa, Katha, Mundaka and Taittiriya)*. Sri Ramakrishna Math, Chennai.

18. Swami Sivananda, *The Principal Upanishads*. Divine Life Society (First Ed., 1942).

19. Swami Sivananda, *The Brhadaranyaka Upanishad*. Divine Life Society (First Ed. 1985).

20. Swami Swahananda, *The Chandogya Upanishad*. Sri Ramakrishna Math, Chennai (1956).

21. *A study of Mundaka Upanishad by Swami Vivekananda*. Advaita Ashram, Kolkatta, (2000).

Pen Art Works

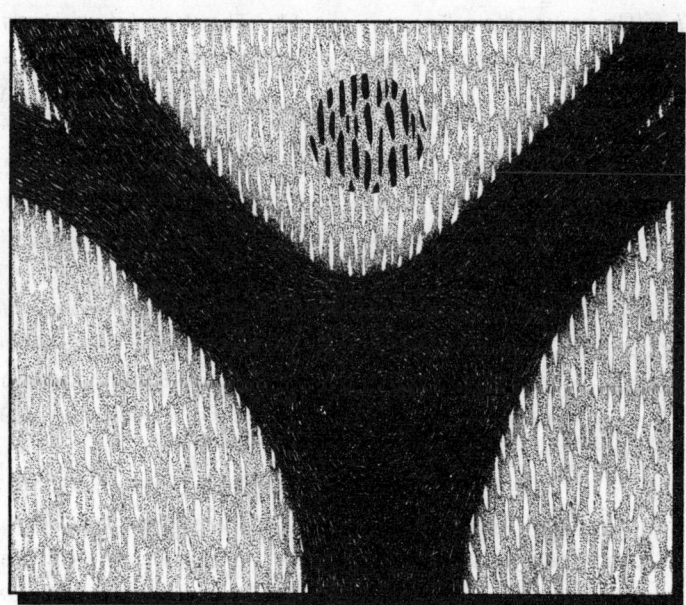

The pen art featured in this publication are by Mr. Sukant Saran. These pictures depict spiritual and mental imagery highlighting the pictorial functioning of the human mind. The processes experienced in the external world evoke images that constantly interact and change; their dynamics being shaped by our desires, fears and beliefs. Instinctively, the artist acts like a medium through whom the images flow. Invariably, after initial perception, the images undergo transformations before and during the execution.

Themes like duality, entanglement, liberation, etc. have been explored using form, tone, texture and visual illusions. The art works featuring in this book are in the size 22 x 28 inches and copyrighted by the artist. The publishers are grateful to Mr. Sukant Saran (e-mail : sukantsaran@hotmail.com) for permission to reproduce some of the exquisite works that are a source of great inspiration and visual delight.